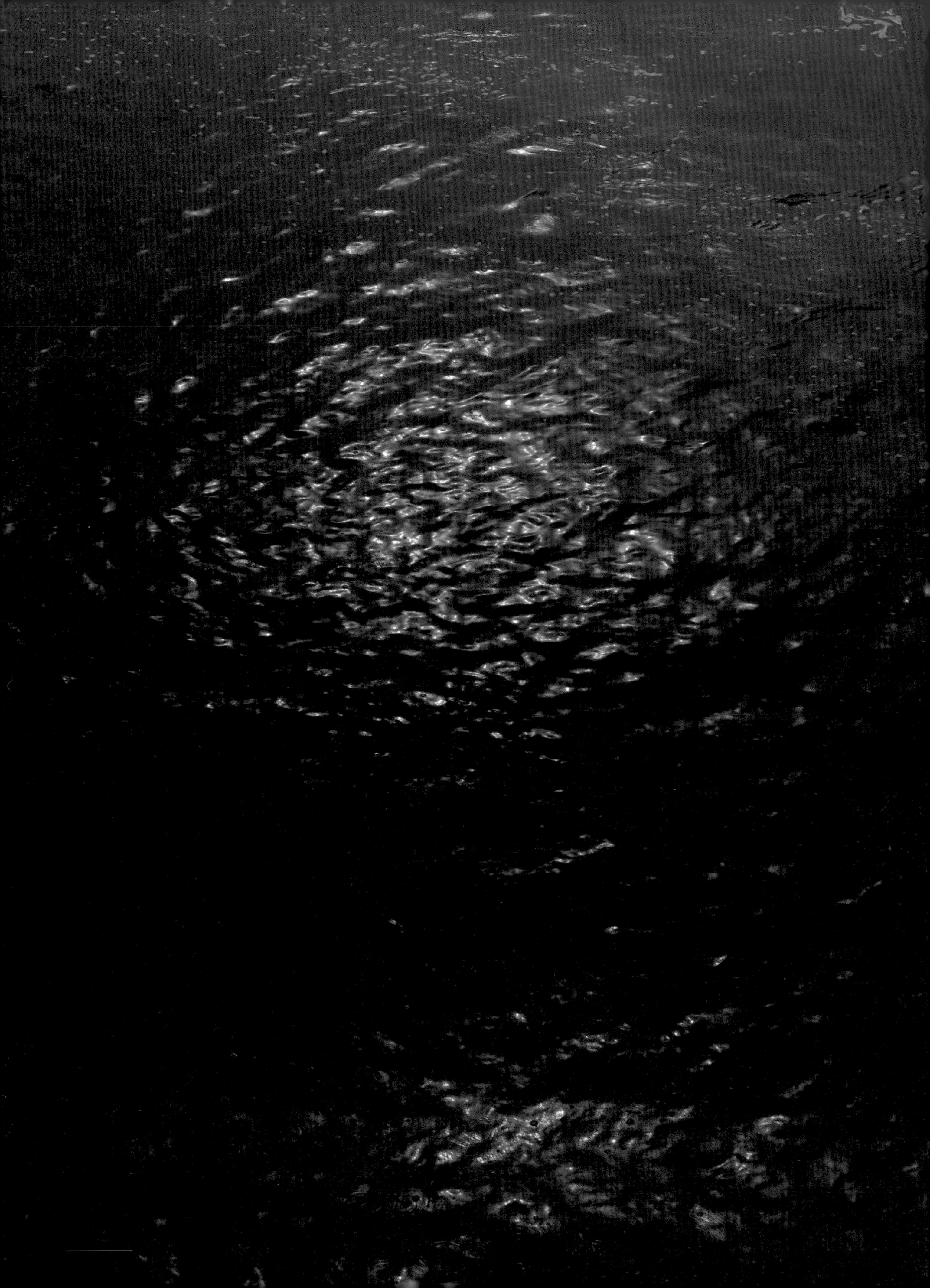

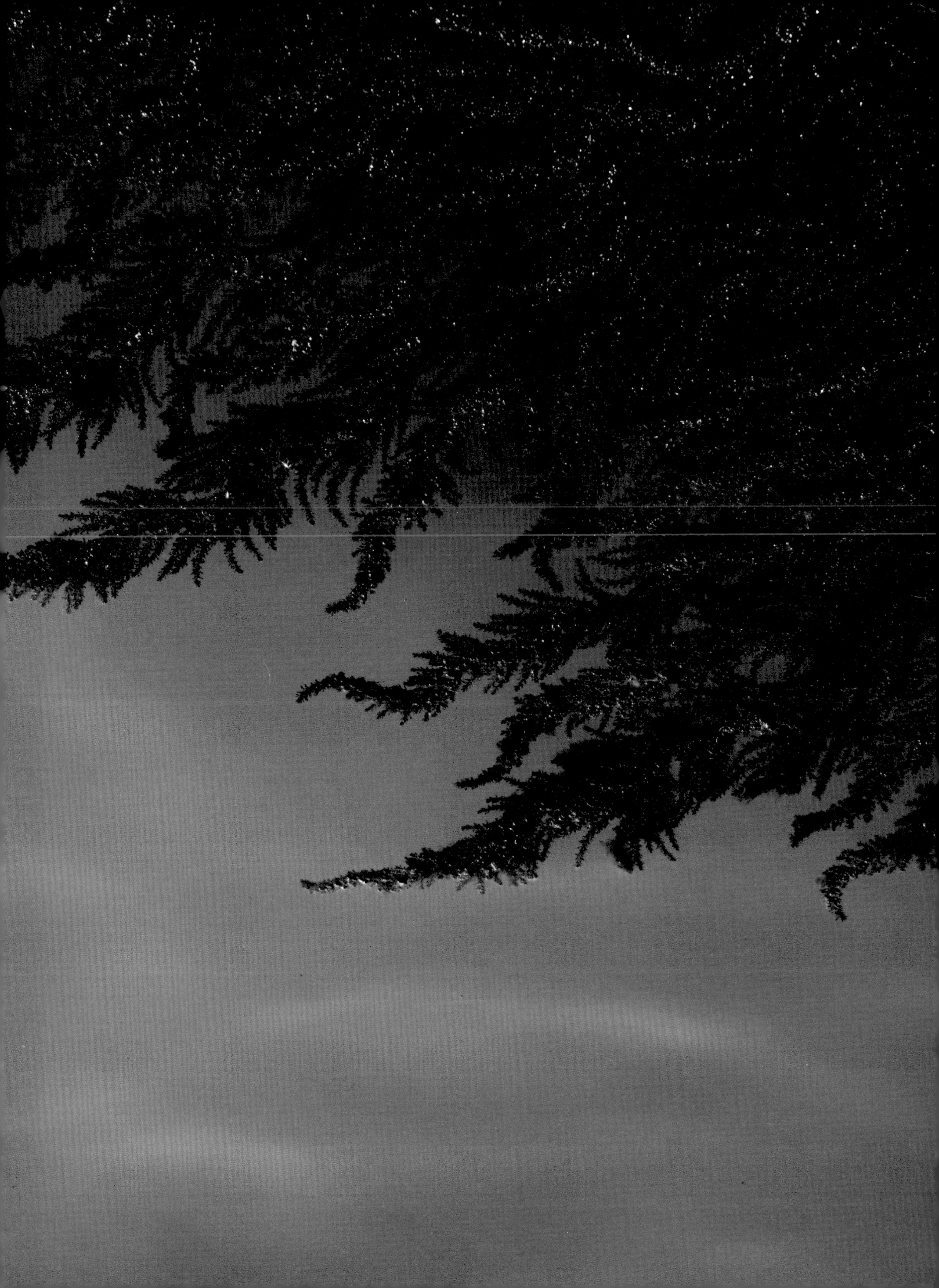

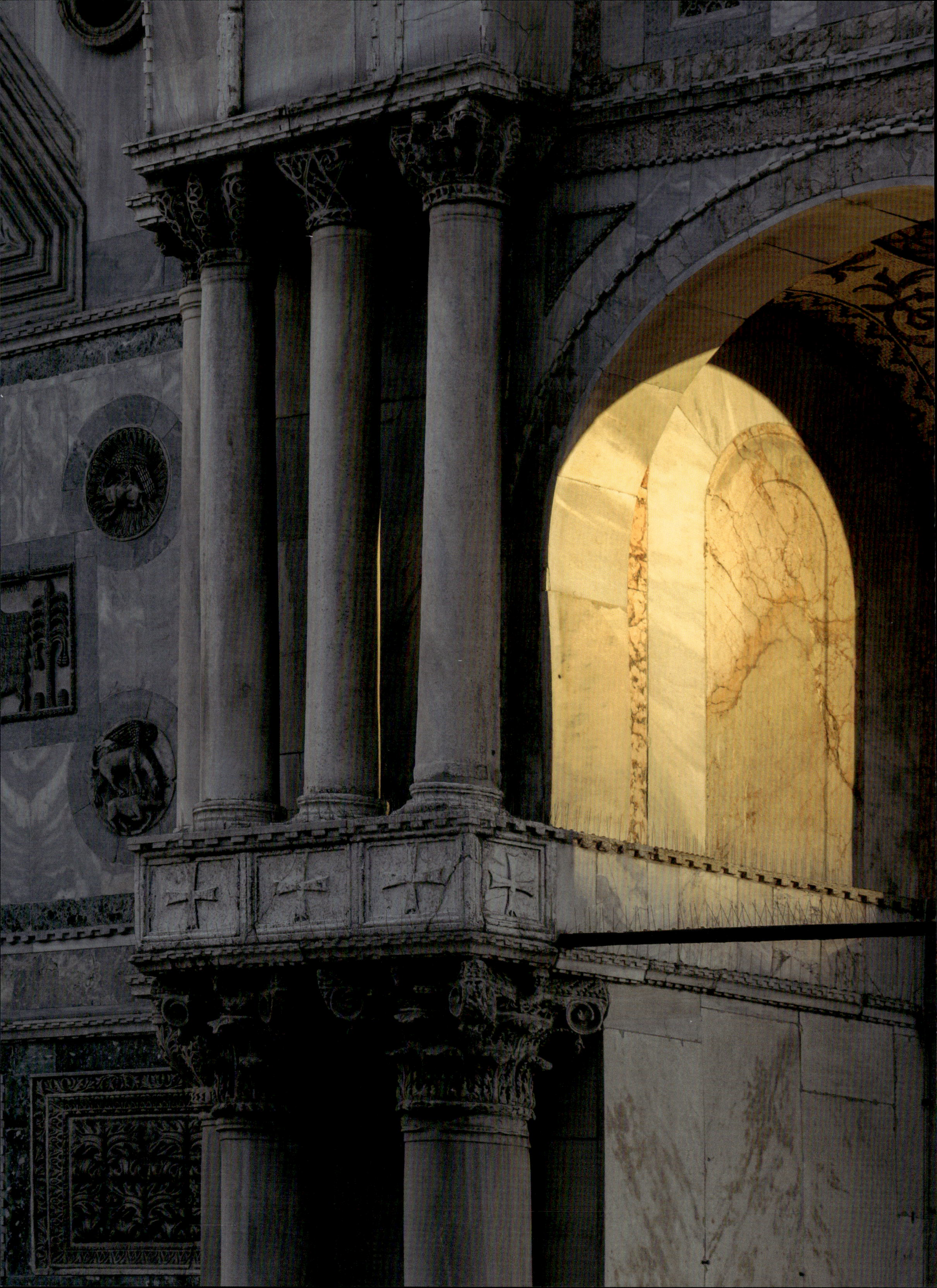

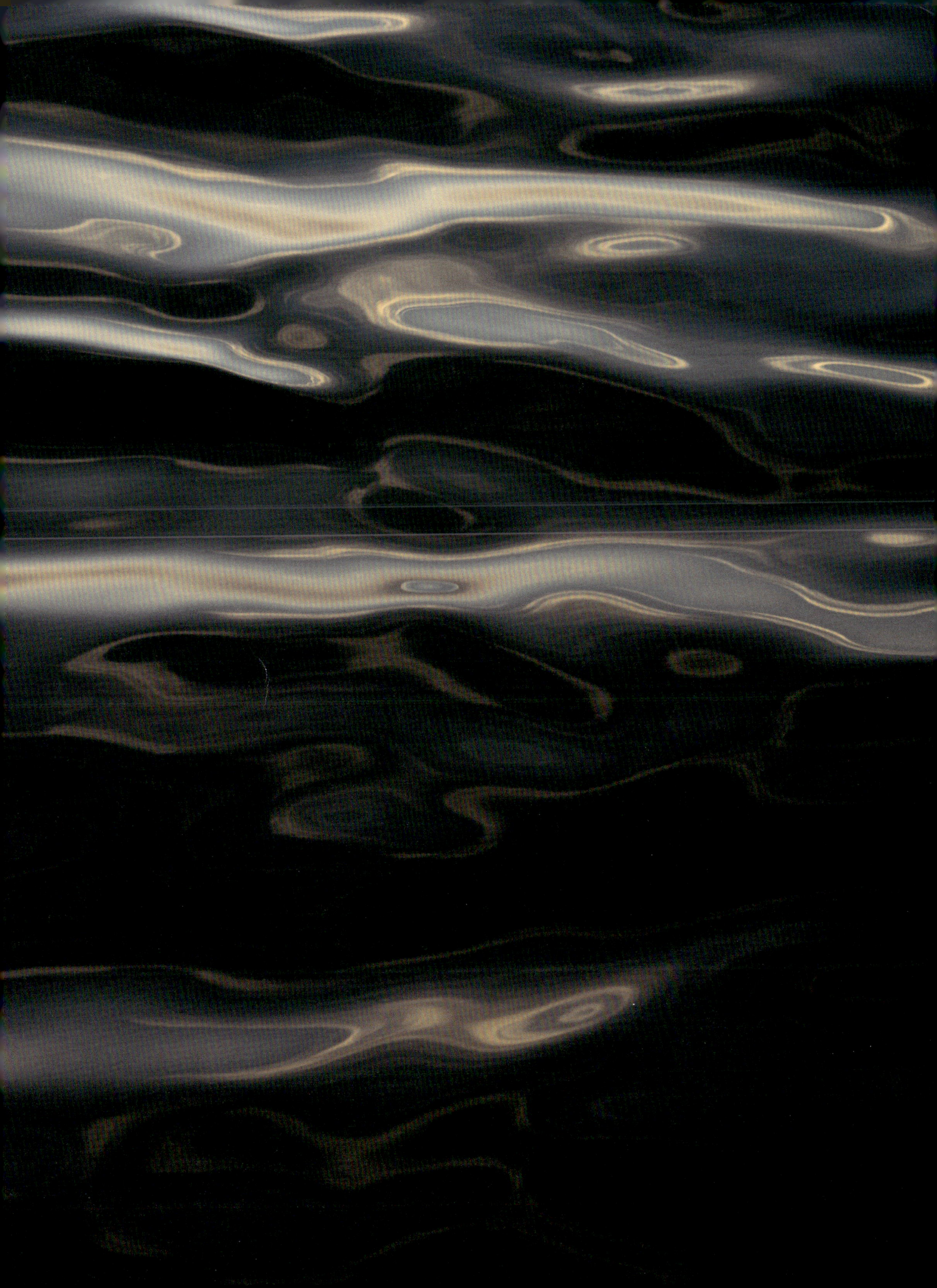

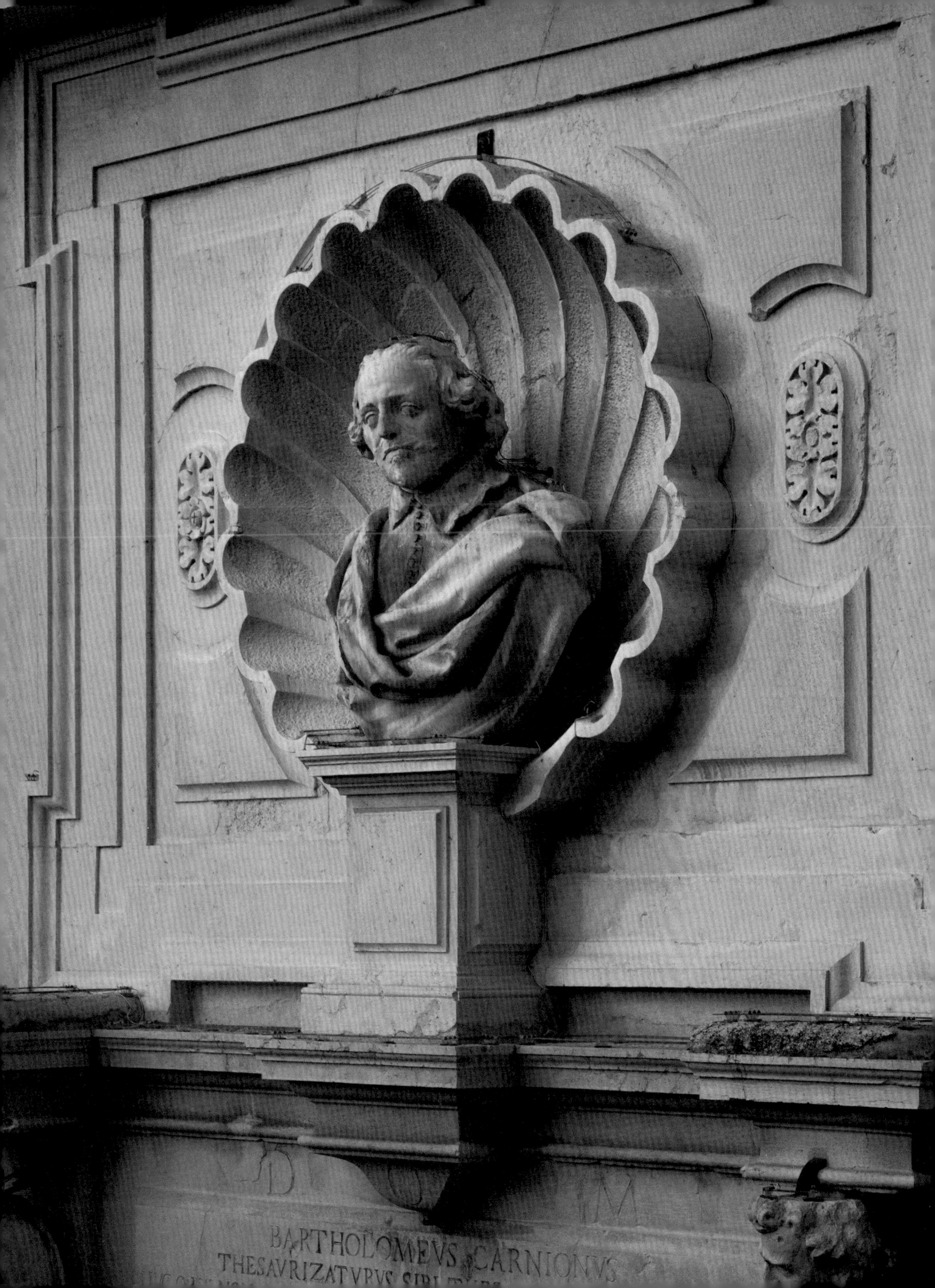
D O M
BARTHOLOMEVS CARNIONVS

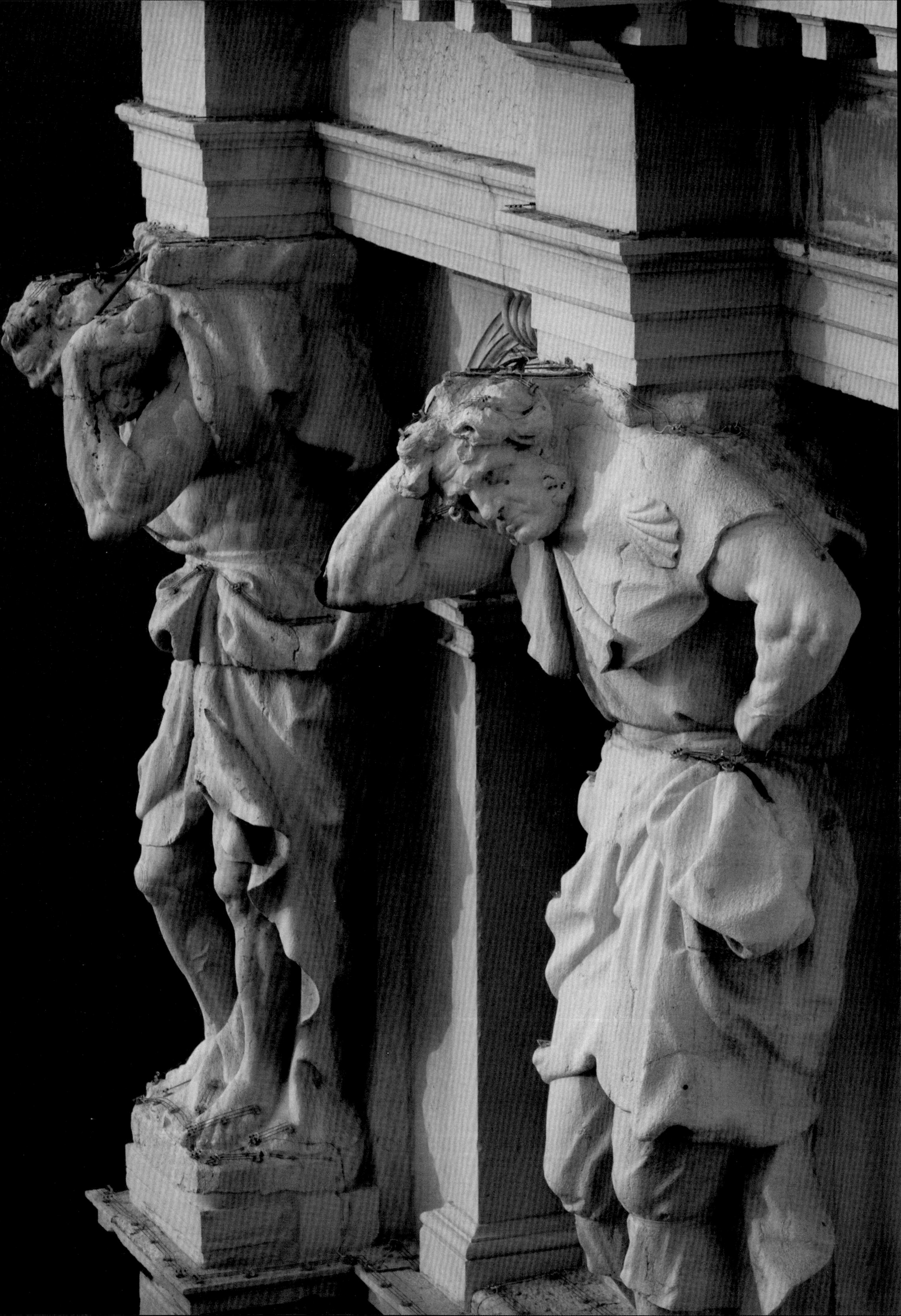

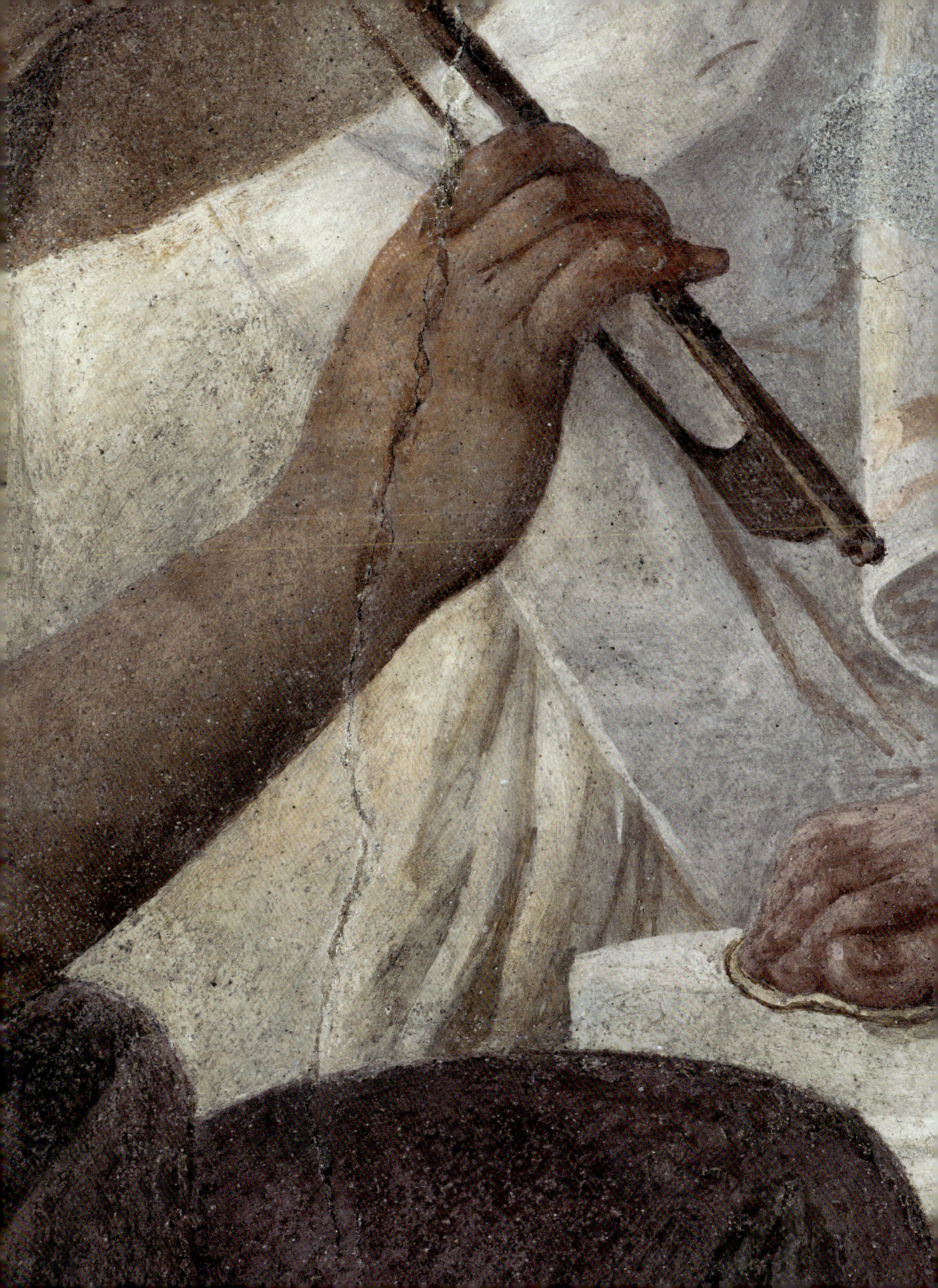

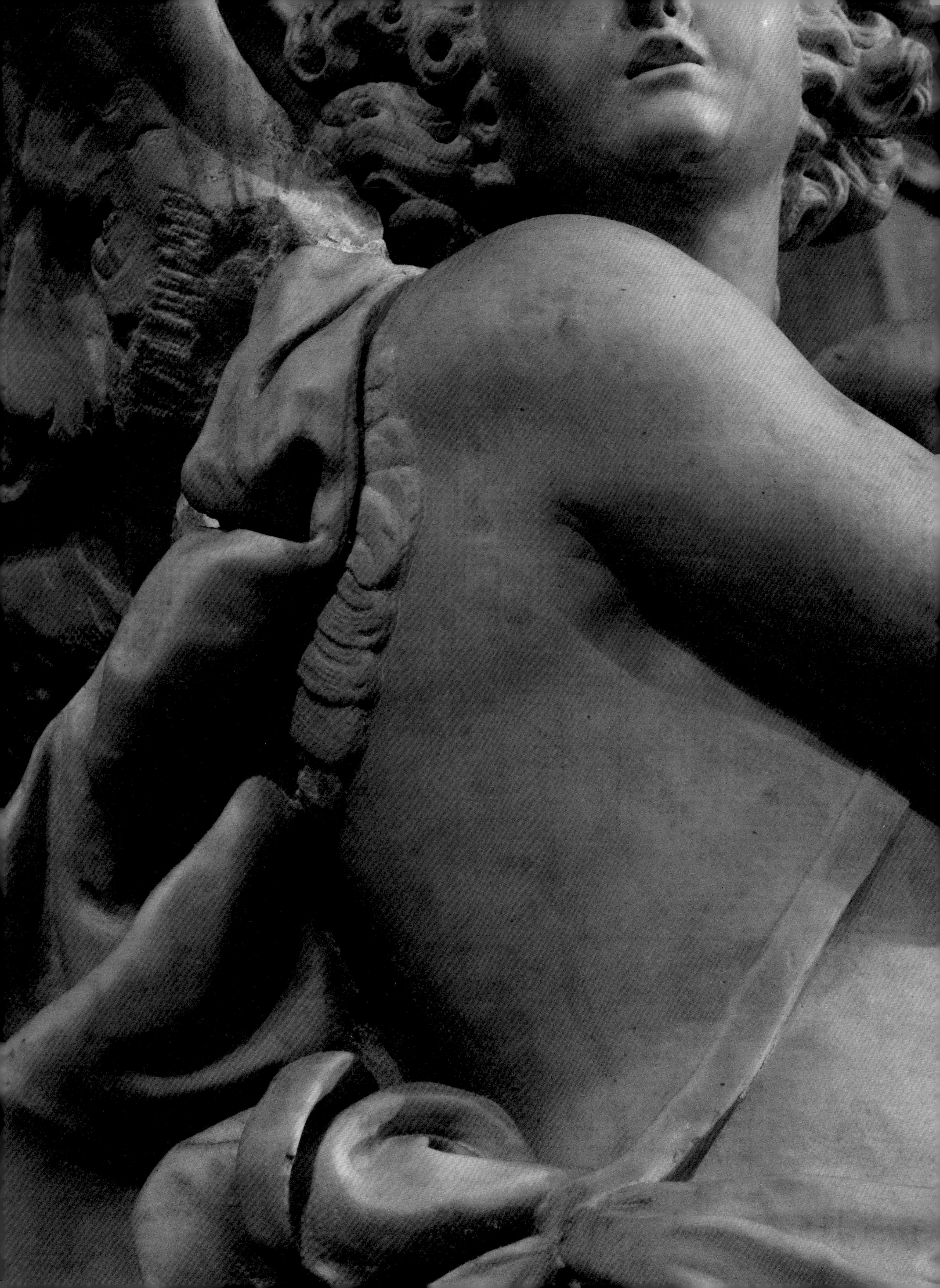

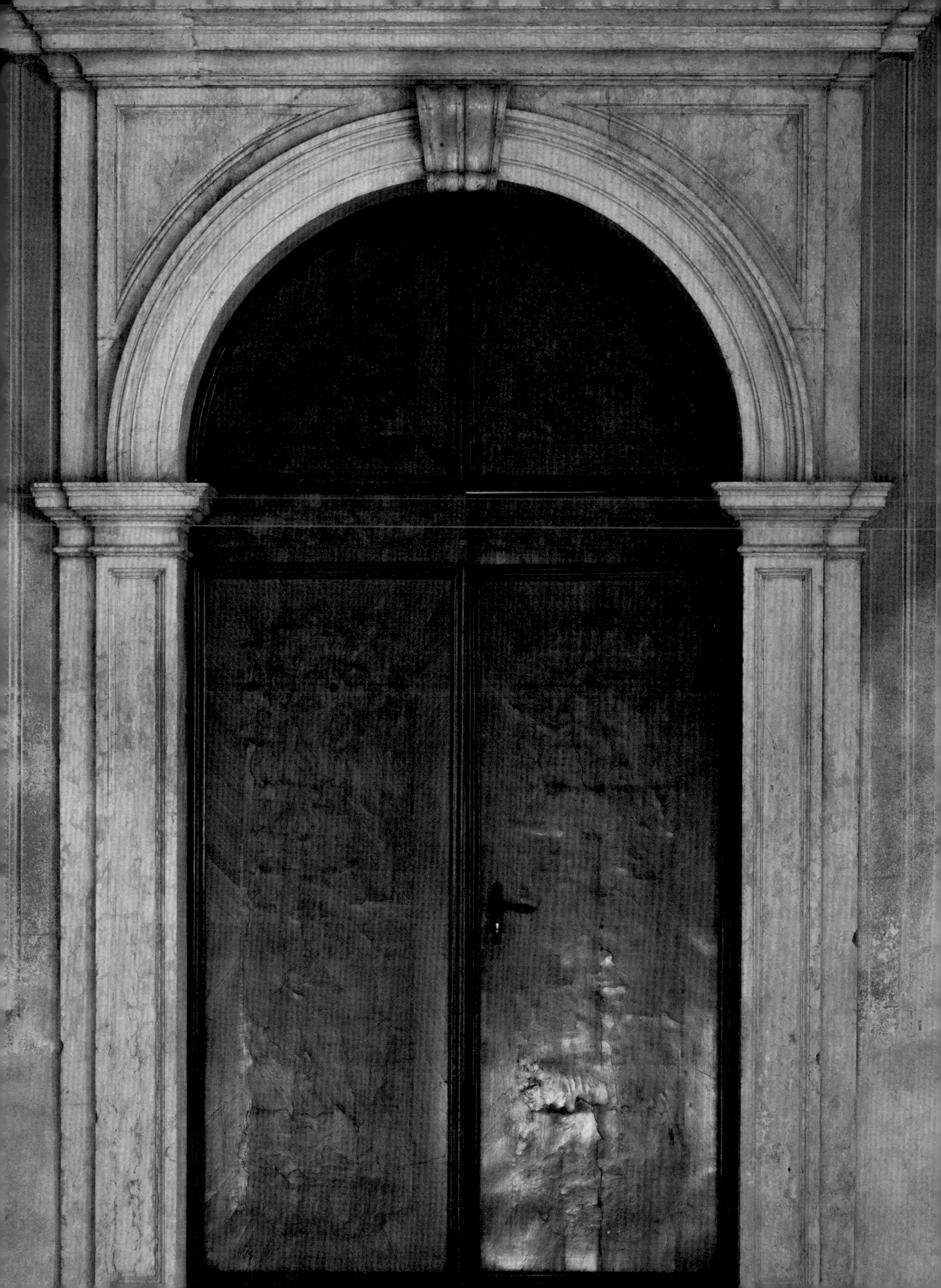

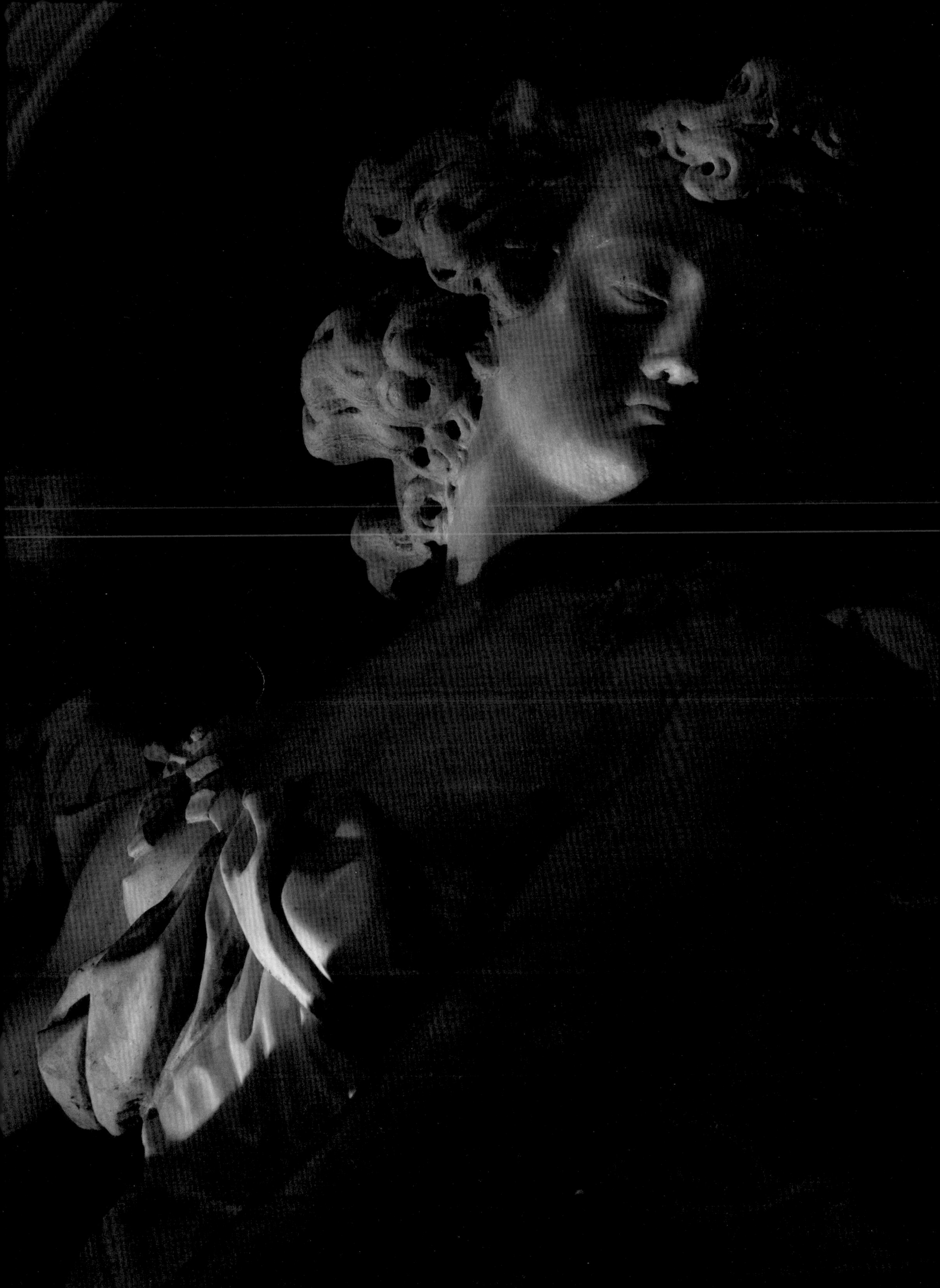

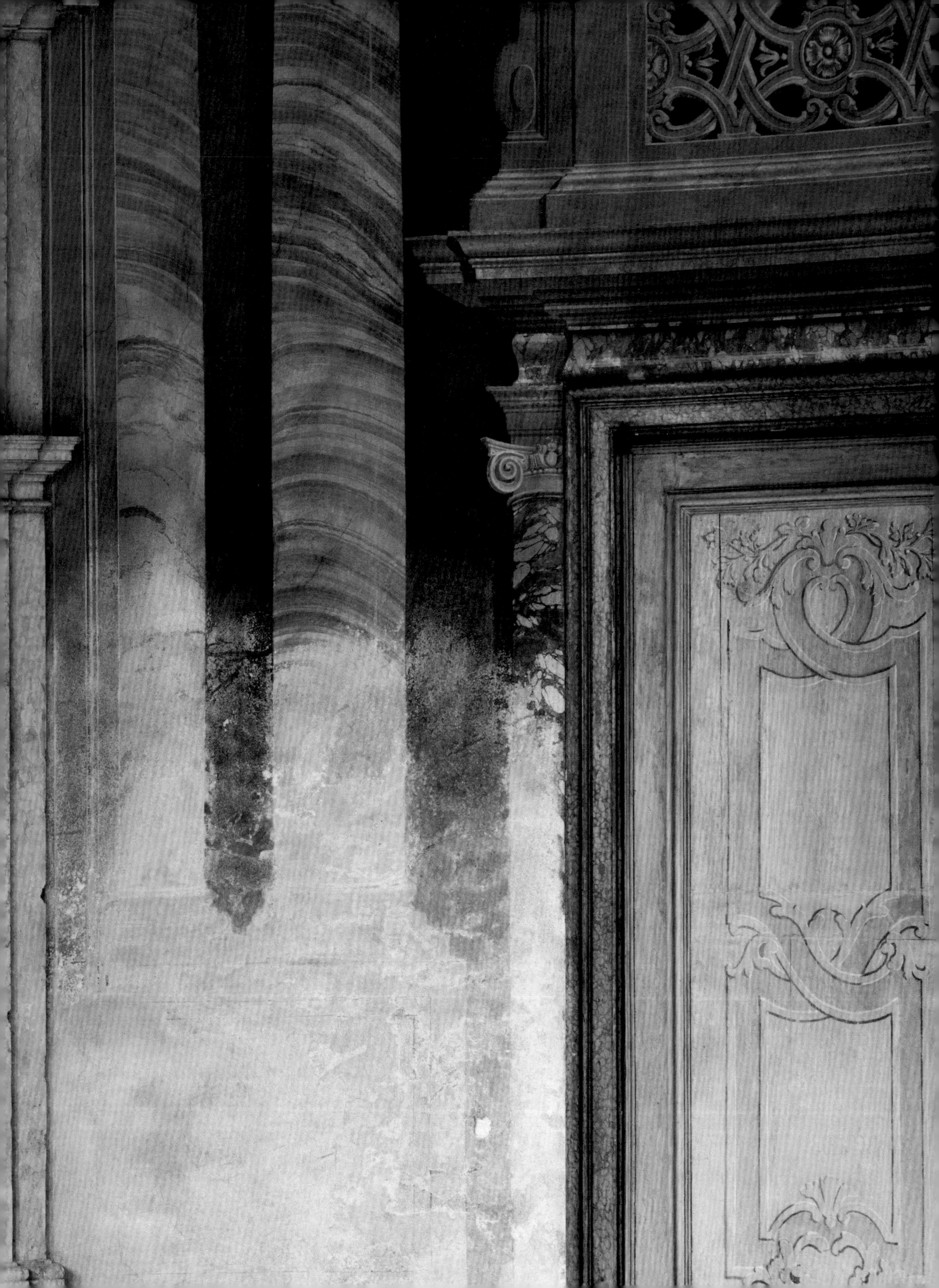

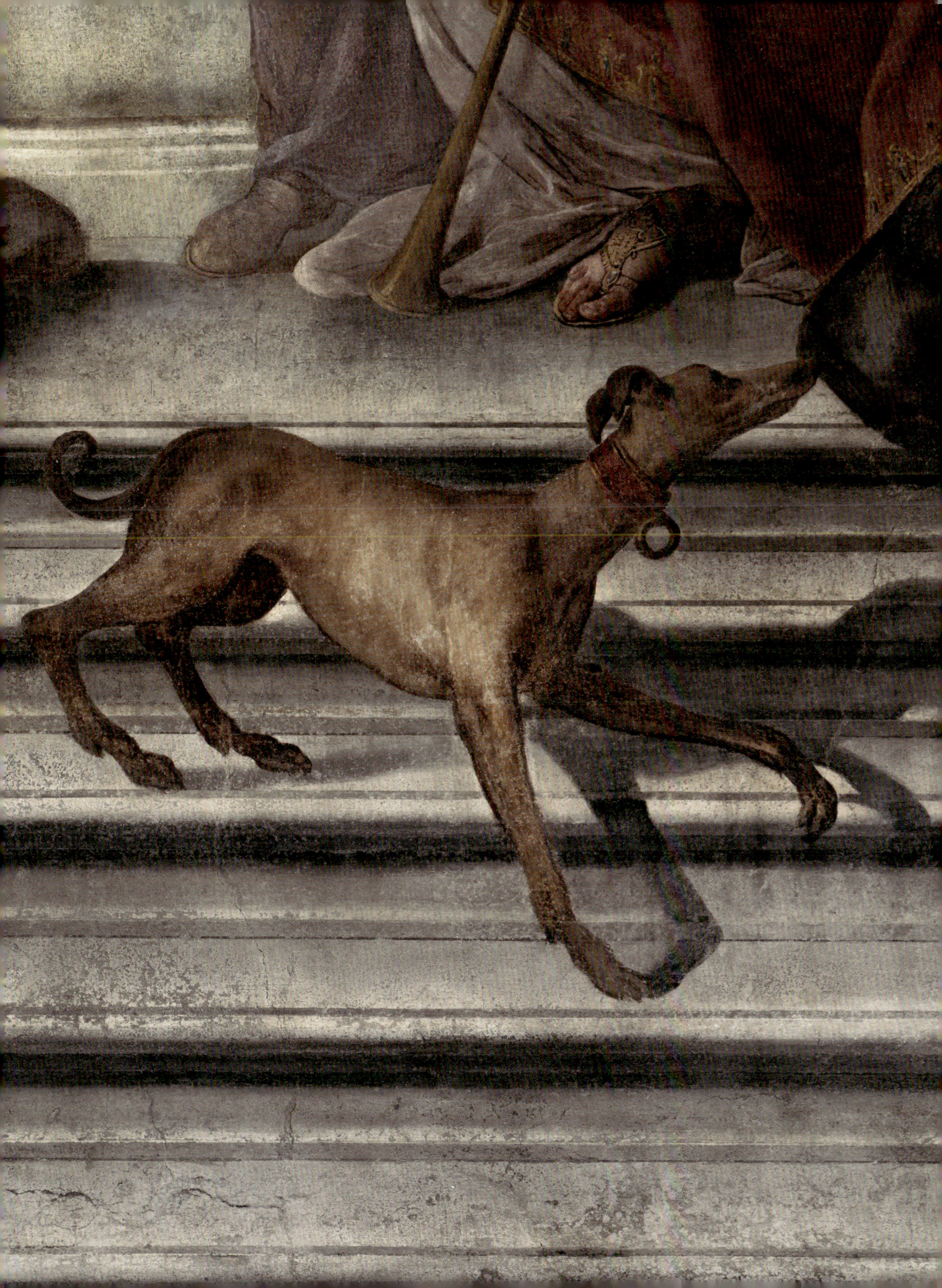

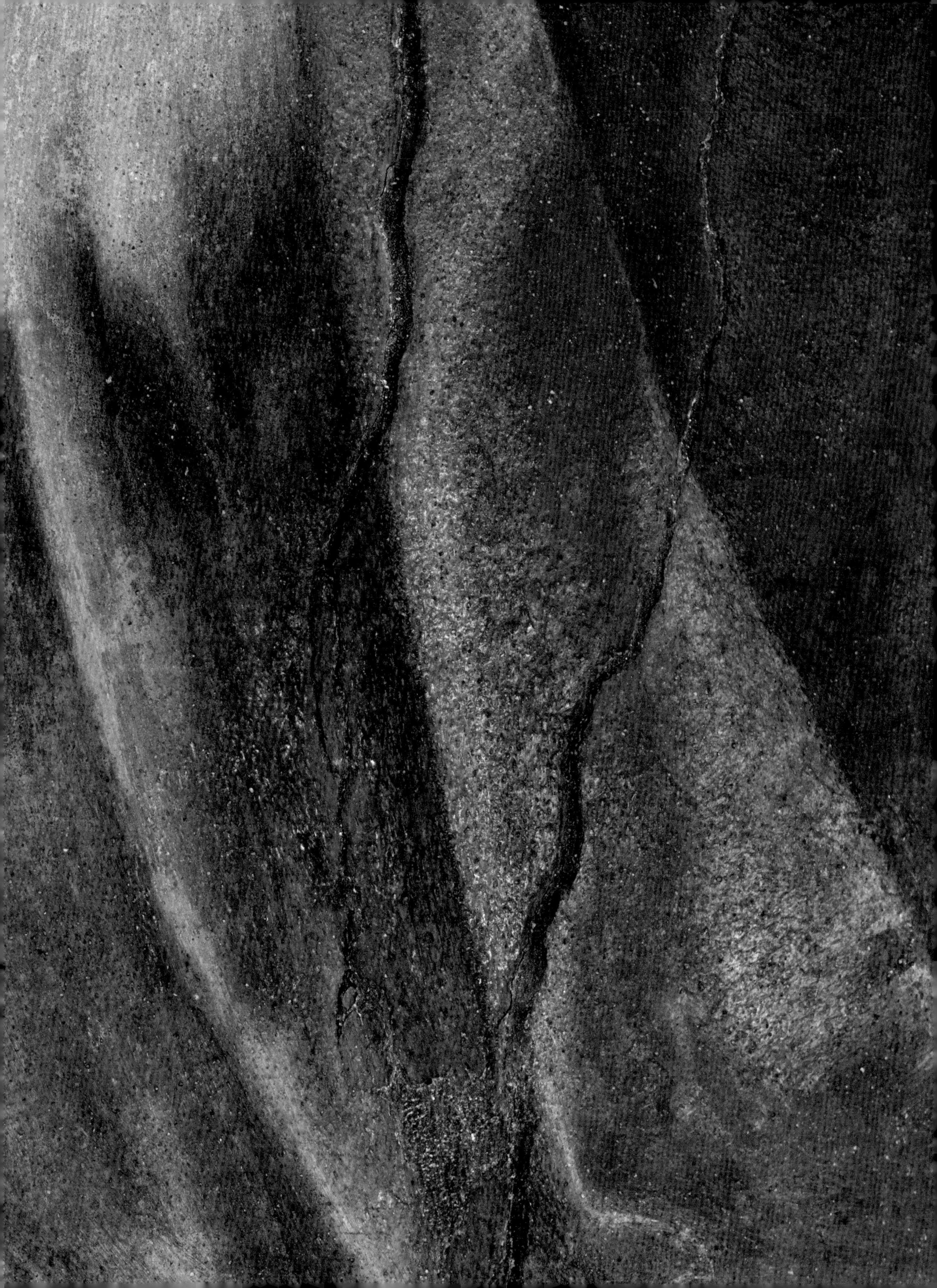

PENUMBRA

Edited by

Alessandro Rabottini and Leonardo Bigazzi
with Bianca Stoppani

FONDAZIONE IN BETWEEN ART FILM

Mousse Publishing

CONTENTS

I created Fondazione In Between Art Film to support artists, institutions, curators, and writers in the field of moving images, which is a creative domain very dear to me. I think that because art is everywhere, everything we see is potentially a video or a film, and to decide that depends only on how we look. It was to honor and expand this ever-changing space of imagination that I initiated the Fondazione, with the desire to put artists in the position to realize their visions and explore the many forms that moving images can assume as artistic media, from film and video to installation. What I love about commissioning is that you allow a new work to come to life that otherwise may not exist. It is an act of trust in the artists' vision, because you never know the final result.

Penumbra was the first exhibition conceived and produced by the Fondazione and I would like to thank the artists that accepted our invitation to create a new work for the fascinating location of the Complesso dell'Ospedaletto in Venice. We thought and dreamt together, saw the works realized, and continued to pursue their circulation. For this reason, my deepest gratitude goes to Karimah Ashadu, Jonathas de Andrade, Aziz Hazara, He Xiangyu, Masbedo, James Richards, Emilija Škarnulytė, and Ana Vaz for infusing their works with poetic rigor and political impetus, and for making us look unflinchingly at the tensions and hopes of our present.

Alessandro Rabottini and Leonardo Bigazzi passionately curated the exhibition and I thank them for carrying out such an ambitious project, from conceiving and orchestrating the dialogue between the artworks and the architecture to accompanying each artist through the different stages of the works' production. The arc of their commitment is completed with this book, of which they are attentive editors with Bianca Stoppani.

Such an inspiring historical site like the Ospedaletto needed an expert eye in order to be transformed into a temporary cinematic machine; for this reason, I was thrilled to work with Ippolito Pestellini Laparelli and his studio, 2050+, who created an unexpected viewing experience for the works that, at the same time, emphasized the many histories and narratives the building contains.

During the seven months of its exhibition, *Penumbra* originated a discursive platform that gave us the chance to listen, learn, and discuss. I would like to thank Bianca Stoppani and Paola Ugolini for curating *Vanishing Points*, the engaging public program that accompanied the exhibition and welcomed twenty-six international speakers with their informative and challenging perspectives. They were all assisted by Giovanni Paolin, whose cordial energy facilitated the realization of the program.

The visual communication conceived by Lorenzo Mason Studio allowed *Penumbra* to exist both in the digital realm and throughout the streets of Venice. Their creative interpretation of the curatorial concept helped transmit it to different audiences, as well as this last transformation into a book.

This book eloquently transposes and expands the fabric of the exhibition and it does so thanks to the collaboration of many professionals. Among them, I want to thank the writers of the eight commissioned texts—Taylor Renee Aldridge, Barbara Casavecchia, Bruno Carvalho and Ana Laura Malmaceda, Martin Herbert, Matt Keegan, Francesca Recchia, Filipa Ramos, and Giorgio Vasta—for being such sensitive interpreters of the meanings and production process of the artworks.

The entire team of the Fondazione put daily energy and care into every stage of this project, and my gratitude goes to Alessia Carlino for the dedication of her work as well as to Simona Iandoli and Chiara Nicolini for their assistance. I also want to thank Lara Facco and Sam Talbot with their respective teams for their consistent and effective work with the national and international press.

It was possible to materialize these visions as a result of a coordinated effort. I want to express my appreciation to the organizational office of *Penumbra*—Massimo Bran and Paola Marchetti of Venews C563 Arts, and Mariachiara Marzari of Ospedaletto Con/temporaneo—for being dedicated interpreters of our needs, and Lapo Gavioli of Altofragile for coordinating the exhibition setup. I also wish to acknowledge the commitment of the invigilators who ensured everyone's safety across the exhibition.

I wish to extend a heartfelt thank you to the institutions that welcomed us at the Complesso dell'Ospedaletto for the dialogue that, throughout almost two years, nurtured this project: Gianmatteo Caputo, Delegato Patriarcale Beni Culturali Ecclesiastici per il Patriarcato di Venezia, the I.P.A.V. (formerly I.R.E.), and Fondazione Venezia Servizi alla Persona.

It was an honor for me and for my team to present our work in Venice—a city that is itself a hymn to the act of seeing—and on the occasion of an event as prestigious as the Biennale Arte 2022. *Penumbra* reflected on the coexistence of light and darkness in our lives and I hope that new visions and new forms of reciprocal understanding will emerge from the shadows of our present.

Beatrice Bulgari, President
Fondazione In Between Art Film

Editors' Note

This publication marks the end of a journey that began in December 2020 with the production of a series of moving image-based works that Fondazione In Between Art Film commissioned to Karimah Ashadu, Jonathas de Andrade, Aziz Hazara, He Xiangyu, Masbedo, James Richards, Emilija Škarnulytė, and Ana Vaz. Around the films and videos conceived by these eight international artists we developed our very first institutional exhibition, *Penumbra*; its accompanying public program, *Vanishing Points*; and this titular catalogue.

Furthering the commitment of the Fondazione in expanding the discourse around moving images with editorial projects, the book reflects on the making of the exhibition as much as it offers, for the first time, in-depth essays on the thinking and production processes that led to the works presented in Venice.

The book opens with a visual essay commissioned to Venice-based photographer Giacomo Bianco. As part of the earliest stages of the exhibition's communication campaign, this atmospheric overture captures the interplay of light and darkness across the lagoon, on the facade of the Chiesa di Santa Maria dei Derelitti, and inside the Complesso dell'Ospedaletto, where *Penumbra* took place.

The essays by exhibition curators Alessandro Rabottini and Leonardo Bigazzi expand on the methodology behind the commissions, the metaphorical and spatial narrative of the exhibition, and what brings the works together inside the semidarkness of the Ospedaletto.

Mirroring the distribution of the works throughout the two floors of the building, the main section of the book is organized into eight chapters that present stills, synopses, and credits of each film, together with as many original essays commissioned to writers, scholars, and researchers. Giorgio Vasta, Taylor Aldridge, Filipa Ramos, Barbara Casavecchia, Matt Keegan, Martin Herbert, Bruno Carvalho with Ana Laura Malmaceda, and Francesca Recchia were invited to write, unusually, while the artworks were in the making, thus becoming companions and correspondents for the artists. This is the reason why the genres chosen by the writers range from the epistolary to the critical essay to the memoir, bringing a heterogeneity of perspectives that goes hand in hand with the diversity of the artistic practices. Moreover, each essay is enriched by archival images, production stills, and research materials that document both processes and moments from the conception and filming.

Between the narration of the ground floor and that of the first floor, at the very core of the book we find the installation views of *Penumbra*, preceding the essay by Ippolito Pestellini Laparelli about the scenography of the exhibition he designed with his agency, 2050+, and an essay by Bianca Stoppani and Paola Ugolini about *Vanishing Points*, the public program they co-curated.

Last but not the least, the beautiful layout of this publication is designed by Lorenzo Mason Studio, the firm also responsible for the visual identity and promotional campaign that broadcast the exhibition both online and across Venice throughout the duration of the show.

We wanted this publication to be as polyphonic as the exhibition it chronicles, and we would like to thank the many people who made *Penumbra* and its various incarnations possible with their creativity, hard work, and intellectual generosity.

Alessandro Rabottini, Leonardo Bigazzi,
Bianca Stoppani

Spaces That Transpire and Stories That Persist: *Penumbra* and the Scenic Machine of the Complesso dell'Ospedaletto

Alessandro Rabottini

Penumbra is an exhibition stemming from the desire to make tangible one aspect of the activity of Fondazione In Between Art Film, namely the commissioning and production of works of art based on moving images. The foundation, in fact, operates according to a diffused methodology: intentionally without a permanent location, it instead collaborates with different entities and in various contexts, such as institutional exhibitions, film festivals, and major periodic initiatives such as biennials. In a certain sense, the nomadic institutional model the foundation has chosen to explore incorporates—we might almost say absorbs—not just the intrinsic immateriality of the media on which we focus—moving images, as we have seen—but also their structural necessity, case after case, of finding a context and support in which to take form, to become manifest, to create a surrounding location.

Two years after the foundation was created by Beatrice Bulgari, we have felt the need to explore the medium of the group exhibition, to convey not only the results of our commitment with the artists, but also a certain way of looking at art through their work. *Penumbra* thus comes into being from this desire to encounter the audience, for the first time, through a device we can implement in all of its aspects, from the production of the works to their presentation, as well as the organization of an extensive program of conversations between the artists and international curators, researchers, philosophers, and architects. Without attempting to outline a romanticism of opportunities and a literature of inspiration, we should however recognize that *Penumbra* began to take form during our first visit to the Complesso dell'Ospedaletto, in the first moments spent inside the dim spaces of the church of Santa Maria dei Derelitti, which is also the entrance of this fascinating architectural amalgam. It was inside this church, constructed starting in 1517 and based on a design by Andrea Palladio, that an idea began to emerge: that of conceiving an exhibition that would not only draw the attention of the public to eight newly commissioned video works, but could also address darkness as the essential condition for moving images to be perceptible. Hence an exhibition that would have the works as its central focus but would also explore the absence of light as a constituent element of our chosen medium and, by extension, of the experience it requires and can offer.

Starting from the single nave of Santa Maria dei Derelitti, from the semi-darkness occasionally attenuated by the light that enters through the large windows of the left side and the vivid glow of the church's furnishings, the concept of penumbra has been taken as a narrative and spatial axis, a perspective that is both material and metaphoric. We felt that Venice would be the ideal setting to explore the mutability of darkness and the intermittence of light, and how the alternating shifts in the conditions of viewing can be understood as sites of revelation and understanding. Venice, in fact, is a city where light—natural daylight or artificial, nocturnal light—never stays still, and where darkness, like architecture reflected on water, always seems to be in a state of transition, never monolithic or impenetrable. With its fragility that has survived for centuries, Venice is also a constant warning about erosion and care, a visual ode to the transient nature of things, to conservation and ongoing mutation. Venice is a city that constantly questions the very idea of permanence, reaffirming the fragile durability of wonder in every instant. Within the uncertainty evoked by the condition of penumbra, we have attempted to grasp a complexity that seemed fertile to us: if the penumbra, in fact, is a shaded space, a place of transition between darkness and light in which neither of the two can be absolute, then the condition of doubt that accompanies what we see becomes a warning that is as optical and it is ethical, urging us to grasp the ambiguity and multiplicity of meaning in things.

The penumbra is also the result of a form of intrusion, the disruptive passage of something that interrupts the wholeness in which we are otherwise immersed when the contours of things are defined by full lighting. In this sense, we can turn to the meaning of penumbra in the field of optics: a zone—no longer light, but not yet shadow—that appears on a screen or a plane following the intrusion of a body between that surface and a light source. Once again, therefore, penumbra as a figure of exception, the interruption of a continuum, a space of perplexity that prompts us to reconsider the absolute fidelity of what we see.

If we look at astronomy, finally, the penumbra appears as an event, as a transitional, immaterial architecture, because it is the region during the course of a partial eclipse that surrounds the shadow cone. In this sense, the penumbra is simultaneously a condition of verticality and dominance (something that plunges down from above) and a space of possibility, like an unexpected resource, being the zone from which it is possible to observe an eclipse, as if it were an inverted beacon. The momentary confiscation of absolute light to which we are subjected is actually a privileged point of observation, though transitional and impermanent; but in any case it is a non-customary viewpoint, a vague observatory for uncertain times.

The works in the exhibition express a myriad of meanings that further expand the ways we inhabit this uncertainty. While with *Pantelleria* (2022) Masbedo explore the blurry space in which images of war shift from a documentary role to become an ideological tactic, transforming not only the memory but also the very nature of events, *Plateau* (2021) by Karimah Ashadu examines the obstinate persistence of the colonial past in Nigeria, and how abandonment is sometimes a form of haunting. Another unstable edge—the one that separates nature from constructed space, protection from captivity, architecture from imprisonment—is the eternally wavering zone into which we are taken by *É Noite na América* [It is Night in America] (2021) by Ana Vaz, while *Aphotic Zone* (2022) by Emilija Škarnulytė makes the total absence of light at the bottom of the sea into an ultimate boundary of human, scientific, and technological colonization.

These four works on the ground floor of the Complesso dell'Ospedaletto seem to explore the shadow zones and spaces of trauma in the relationship between human beings and the environment, between the legacies of History and the present time of bodies, between what is the object of control and what remains unintelligible. They do this through an increasingly deep inspection (almost a geological progression) of the material substance of the soil and of the ideological recesses, passing from the shelters excavated in the mountain of Pantelleria during World War II to the immersion in tin mines, from the artificial and nocturnal streets of Brasília to the remote aquatic distances of Costa Rica.

If a porosity exists in these spaces explored by the works, a principle of indetermination in the possibility of distinguishing between true and false, past and present, control and destruction, the effects that these forms of ambiguity produce in our present are not at all indeterminate, but very present and tangible.

Going up to the first floor, we find four works that appear to shed glimmers of light on psychological, existential, and political conditions that are as personal as they are collective, states of being that dwell inside individual awareness, domestic space and the urban horizon.

The distinction between body and home we can witness in *Qualities of Life: Living in the Radiant Cold* (2022) by James Richards is a malleable one: here the medical inspection of human tubing blurs into that of the plumbing of dwellings; in the meantime we grasp the perishable, mortal nature of both analog and electronic images. *House of Nations* (2021) by He Xiangyu takes us into the communal solitude in the time of the COVID-19 pandemic, inside a dormitory for international students in Berlin, with a sequence of rooms both real and imaginary, depending on a fragmentary edit that is as elusive as the inner life of the protagonist of the film, while the collective portrait of a group of homeless people in Recife brought to our attention by Jonathas de Andrade in his *Olho da Rua* [Out Loud] (2022) is crowded with individualities, as urgent as the voices they demand for themselves. The last work in the exhibition—*Takbir* by Aziz Hazara (2022)—literally plunges us into the darkness of the nights in Kabul during the taking of the city by the Taliban, confronting us with the absence of light in its most intense sonic substance, as dense as the layering of foreign occupations across the decades of Afghan history.

The visual and poetic path of *Penumbra*, then, opens with the end of a conflict from the last century and concludes with the shadows of a present regime, forming a spatial and narrative arc that extends through the two levels of the Ospedaletto complex, exploring the concept of semi-darkness as a threshold, a space of transition between one condition and another, a place of ambivalent transformation: the penumbra that gives way to the dawn, and the penumbra that comes after sunset.

To make room for the visions of the invited artists, together with the studio 2050+, in charge of the scenography, we have thought of making the entire space resonate, through its spatial potential and the narrative implications of its past. What has emerged is an exhibition that attempts to convey the spatialization of moving images, which is a practice deeply rooted in many of the artists who work with time-based media today. This is an apparently paradoxical and profoundly productive condition: in a historical moment such as ours, in which it is possible to digitally transmit images through any type of device, thus making them pervasive, immediately available, and fragmented, most artists choose to show their works in very specific spatial contexts, making perceptive and tactile use of the image itself, the technology that makes it visible, the sonic and spatial environment the images create around them.

This is the reason why we have conceived *Penumbra* as an exhibition in which it is possible to perceive images in motion as a factor of sensitivity; as a tactile matter, a show of spaces over and above stories, in which the bodies of those who observe can inhabit different situations. In this desire for spatialization of a time-based medium, we have been assisted by the architecture of the Complesso dell'Ospedaletto, a site that incorporates a Baroque space of Catholic worship, the memory of a hospital for the treatment of destitute patients founded in 1527–28, a frescoed hall for chamber music from 1776–77, and the modern extension of a rest home in operation until 2010.

Like *Penumbra* and its scenic machinery, so the Complesso dell'Ospedaletto is a place of slippage and mutation, within which the various functions across the centuries shift one into the next, just as the various temporal contexts overlap with each other. The architectural specificity of the Ospedaletto, with its collaged spatial logic, in fact, has offered us the possibility, together with the artists and 2050+, to think about a sequence of spaces, each with its own emotional and narrative temperature. Of the fragmented and conflicting present which we are going through on a global scale, the works on view convey the complexity, the unresolved difficulties and opportunities for healing, echoing the similarly discontinuous architecture of the Ospedaletto, an architecture in which moments distant in time coexist with each other in keeping with a logic that speaks both of friction and of plausible harmony. From this spatial rhythm that is syncopated at times, punctuated by rests and accelerandos, the installation appropriates the principle of ongoing interruption and resumption: the recent expansion of the rest home, in fact, intermittently cross the historical and monumental zones—like the church of Santa Maria dei Derelitti, the music room and the old pharmacy—granting the narration of the exhibition the possibility of unfolding within an alternation of decorum and functionality, horror and respite.

About Seeing and Being Seen in *Penumbra*

Leonardo Bigazzi

"Art is not a mirror held up to reality but a hammer with which to shape it."[1]
—Bertolt Brecht

A man sifts ochre sediments under the constant flow of water in a canal. He works barefoot, hunched over, his skin and clothing spattered with mud. An off-screen voice talks about the complexities and dangers of the miners' work. It could be his voice, or that of one of the other young men who work alongside him. It doesn't matter: the story belongs to all of them. The risks are frequent and inevitable, since there are no alternatives for those who live off the tin and columbite mines of Jos Plateau, Nigeria. The British colonial companies exploited them until 1985, leaving behind a polluted ecosystem drained of all its riches. The relationship between the bodies of these workers and their tormented land is portrayed in *Plateau* (2021), a two-channel installation by Karimah Ashadu commissioned for *Penumbra*. About half-way through the film, while we as spectators are just starting to get used to the intolerable, constant noise of the draining pumps, the circular, repetitive movements of the miners' hands, and the almost whispered narration of the daily tragedy of these places, something unexpected happens. For seven endless seconds, the hunched over man slows his work and looks straight at us, holding our gaze. He knows that in the future, there will be an audience behind the lens that is filming him. He seems to be aware that we are, in that exact moment, sitting there looking at him. In an instant, the geographic, social, and economic distance between him and the exhibition visitors is drastically reduced. And at the same time, it becomes painfully clear and distressing. We perceive all his dignity, his strength and determination to earn personal and collective independence through that work. But we also inevitably feel the weight of responsibility for the extraction policies at the root of the Western colonization of Africa. As spectators, we can no longer be neutral or remain passive, inert observers. We are invited to participate and reconsider our role and our privileges. That gaze is an extremely effective tool for creating a non-verbal dialogue that subverts the pre-established codes and hierarchies of the cinematic medium.[2] The artist deliberately introduces it when we are already immersed in the narration and seduced by the images. It makes us vulnerable and, in doing so, opens up an intimate space for reflection and connection with the work and its subject.

Our encounter with the gaze of the miner from Jos Plateau is not the only one that breaks the "fourth wall," transforming the screen into a permeable membrane and placing the space of the film in direct communication with that of the exhibition. The other three video works installed on the ground floor of the Complesso dell'Ospedaletto use similar strategies,

1 The origin of this quote is disputed. It is attributed to Bertolt Brecht in *Paulo Freire: A Critical Encounter*, ed. Peter McLaren and Peter Leonard, (London: Routledge, 1993), 80.

2 For an in-depth examination of this subject in film, see Marc Vernet, "The Look at the Camera," *Cinema Journal*, 28.2 (Winter 1989): 48–63.

but in these cases the exchange of gazes is with nonhuman beings. In the first room, we find ourselves reflected in the big, dark eyes of Achille, a Pantesco donkey in Masbedo's film *Pantelleria* (2022). A humble symbol of the island's ruralism, the weight of the economy of this harsh volcanic territory rested on its back for centuries. When it lost its fundamental function for local society with the mechanization of agriculture and building of roads, the Pantesco donkey began a slow decline, to the point of near extinction.[3] Within the majestic Rationalist architecture of the Hangar Nervi, its dreamlike, surreal image becomes silent testimony of an age and world that no longer exist.[4] The one in which we depended on animals in our everyday lives, as much for production as for transportation. A close relationship that was completely upended in the Western world starting in the nineteenth century, increasing our need to represent them and create artificial opportunities for encountering them, like public zoos.[5]

É Noite na América [It is Night in America] (2021), a three-channel immersive installation by Ana Vaz, is rooted in the impossibility of this coexistence in the urban context of Brasília. The Brazilian metropolis was conceived, like all other post-industrial cities, to eradicate and exclude all nonhuman species from its spaces. The destruction of their habitat has, however, forced them back into the city in search of food and shelter, exposing them to often fatal dangers. A dramatic cycle that ends when they are "saved" by the environmental police and locked up in a zoo where their fate is to become, to cite John Berger, "the living monument to their own disappearance."[6] In the film, which follows their movements in the city streets, gardens, and their own cages, these creatures seem to be on high alert for human presence. We meet a succession of fleeting gazes, like that of a little owl, a capuchin monkey deftly running along a narrow wall, and sly capybara stretched out in a field. We perceive all the suffering and fear in the eyes of a sick, disoriented crab-eating fox. But despite the close-ups, the camera seems incapable of capturing a direct gaze for more than a few moments. They look to the side, they escape, we see them but they do not really see us. A condition aptly described by Berger: "The public purpose of zoos is to offer visitors the opportunity of looking at animals. Yet nowhere in a zoo can a stranger encounter the look of an animal. [...] They have been immunized to encounter, because nothing can any more occupy a *central* place in their attention. Therein

3 The last native Pantelleria donkey died in 1985 and the species was declared extinct. In 1989, thanks to the San Matteo di Erice pilot breeding program, in partnership with Sicily's Istituto Zooprofilattico Sperimentale and the Veterinary Medicine faculty of the University of Milan, it was possible to start the process of the recovery and reconstruction of its genetic inheritance. Animals could then be selected with characteristics about 80 percent similar to the original, permitting registration on the list of equine and asinine species. In 2021, the first exemplars were reintroduced on the island of Pantelleria.

4 Designed by Pier Luigi Nervi, construction was begun in the second half of the 1930s and it became operational at the end of 1939. The Hangar is still used today for military purposes and is part of the Italian Air Force's Pantelleria Airport Detachment.

5 On the representation of animals in contemporary art, see *Animals (Whitechapel: Documents of Contemporary Art)*, ed. Filipa Ramos, (Cambridge, MA: The MIT Press, 2016).

6 John Berger, "Why Look at Animals?" (1977), in *About Looking* (London: Bloomsbury, 2009), 26.

lies the ultimate consequence of their marginalization."[7] This feeling of apparent distance is abruptly interrupted by the appearance of a majestic owl that looks straight at us. We are besieged by his threatening gaze, which is multiplied by the arrangement of the three screens in a semicircle and amplified by the pulsing light that makes him emerge from the dark. The camera lens, and so the screen, once again become the point of dialogic exchange between these gazes. A territory of negotiation that in this case probes and questions the borderline between human and nonhuman, between inclusion and exclusion. The visual encounter between the subjectivity of the Other and that of the audience becomes horizontal, equal, also because the threat to survival now seems to be tragically shared. This "*égalité du regard*" [equality in the gaze], as Chris Marker defines it in his masterpiece *Sans Soleil* (1983), inevitably provokes reflection on the need to form new alliances between species.[8] A process of re-thinking our relationship with animals or, better still, of un-thinking, as proposed by Kari Weil.[9] This acknowledgment of the Other can only happen through this shared moment, as suggested by Jacques Derrida: "An animal looks at us, and we are naked before it. Thinking, perhaps, begins there."[10]

7 Berger, "Why Look at Animals?" (1977), 28.
8 On the animal gaze in Chris Marker's films, see Kierran Argent Horner, "The Equality of the Gaze: The Animal Stares Back in Chris Marker's Films," in *Film-Philosophy*, vol. 20, n. 2–3 (Edinburgh: Edinburgh University Press, 2016), 235–49. Available online.
9 Kari Weil, *Thinking Animals. Why Animal Studies Now?* (New York: Columbia University Press, 2012), XVI.
10 Jacques Derrida, *The Animal That Therefore I Am*, ed. Marie-Louise Mallet, trans. David Willis (New York: Fordham University Press, 2008), 29.

From nights in Brasília to the darkness of the depths of the sea, in Emilija Škarnulytė's film *Aphotic Zone* (2022) the encounter shifts from our cities to the bottom of the ocean, the latest frontier of the planet contaminated by extraction policies. Here, the artist investigates the ethical, ecological, and colonial implications that reverberate below sea level, at the depth at which less than 1 percent of sunlight penetrates. We find ourselves immersed in hypnotic sequences of bioluminescent creatures, in a site-specific space created by the artist using a mirrored surface that doubles the screen reflecting it on the ceiling. But the fascination and wonder of this vision are quickly replaced by a feeling of unease. Under the beams of light from an underwater robot, we witness the disorientation of these creatures used to living in absolute darkness. Our gaze is violently forced upon them, invading the physical limits of their delicate ecosystem. Through these visual encounters, whether with overexposed animals in a zoo or the ones the human eye is seeing for the first time as in this case, we become aware of our fragility, and realize that the privilege of superiority we have claimed over other species is actually marginalizing us as well. Those who thought they were just seeing end up being seen.

Re-emerging from the shadows as we climb up the seventeenth-century staircase designed by Giuseppe Sardi, we come to the first floor of the exhibition. Here, we pass through the visual and acoustic stream of consciousness of James Richards' *Qualities of Life: Living in the Radiant Cold* (2022) and the alienating urban atmospheres of He Xiangyu's portrait of a young Chinese student in Berlin, *House of Nations* (2021). In both works, there is no direct visual contact with the audience. In the first, our gaze stays trapped in domestic settings and infrastructures that break up and re-form before us. In the second, the artist seems to have chosen a tool conceptually consistent with the need to protect the intimacy of his young subject and accentuate the feeling of isolation. His gaze brushes over us, goes past us, but the presence of the camera (and the artist behind it) should not be perceived, since this would disrupt the illusion of the truth of the document. Indeed, He Xiangyu spread the filming over two years precisely so that he would progressively disappear, getting his subject used to his presence so he could capture the naturalness of his everyday movements. In this part of the exhibition, the spectators return to feeling that their exclusively voyeuristic position is protected.

The penultimate work in the exhibition instead grew from a desire to create a participatory and collective experience in a public space. This is the work in which, perhaps more than any other, the spectator feels like an integral part of the transformative process activated on both sides of the screen. For *Olho da Rua* [Out Loud] (2022), Jonathas de Andrade worked with more than 100 members of the homeless community in his city, Recife, inviting them to take part in a series of performative actions in a park. The work is divided into eight acts, each one of which represents a theatre exercise created by the artist and partially inspired by Augusto Boal's Theatre of the Oppressed. Already in the first act, a play of gazes reflected in a mirror establishes an unexpected relationship between the subjects and their audience. Those bodies have always been there, in the streets, before our eyes; often, however, remaining invisible. Here, they instead become aware of the potential of their own image, reclaiming their right to exist, have a voice, and be heard. They invite us to welcome diversity and embrace it in all its forms. They want to finally be seen.

The ambiguity between seduction and condemnation defines the space within which the artist works conceptually. It is a subtle balance, and the—decolonized—gaze immediately becomes its main tool. Direct visual contact again puts us to the test, metaphorically breaking the camera and drawing us in. Because this process of becoming aware cannot remain confined within the frame of the screen. It needs to move beyond it and involve us as well. *Olho da Rua*, like Boal's theatre, raises questions without dictating the answers. Never didactic in its approach, it instead moves on the emotional plane of empathy through a shared learning path. Boal defined "spect-actors" as those who did not remain simple passive observers in his theatrical productions. Their role was equal to that of the performers in the dramatic action because he believed that participation increased the transformative impact of the artistic experience. According to Boal, taking on political or social issues within the safety of a creative process provides concrete tools that can be used in real life. In *Olho da Rua*, this takes place through an open exchange filled with moments of shared joy that culminate in the final sequence: *olho no olho* [eye to eye]. A single take in which we see all the protagonists of the work saying goodbye to their audience looking straight at the camera, eyes filled with expectation and new awareness.[11]

The faces from the streets of Recife are the last ones we see in the exhibition. The final work, Aziz Hazara's *Takbir* (2022), brings us back to the darkness, in both the material and the metaphorical sense, through images of Kabul after the end of the US-led NATO mission and the Taliban's retaking of power. The absence of bodies, the artist explains, stems from his difficulty representing them during this historical moment. In the dark of night of a city torn apart by the violence of war and decades of foreign occupation, there are no more gazes, just shadows, silence, flashes of light, and prayers.

Penumbra was conceived, right from the selection of the commissioned artists, to explore the capacity of moving images to reflect on the complexities of the present, activating transformative processes between different languages. Whereas at the cinema the perspective is necessarily imposed and central, in the exhibition space, where the screens multiply and time fragments, we are free to create our own encounter with this polyphony of gazes. Sight is a fluid, personal sense, constantly influenced by subjective, historical, geographic, and environmental factors. In his seminal book *Ways of Seeing*, Berger observed: "We only see what we look at. To look is an act of choice. [...] We never look at just one thing; we are always looking at the relation between things and ourselves. Our vision is continually active, continually moving, continually holding things in a circle around itself, constituting what is present to us as we are."[12] The encounters in *Penumbra* are products of their time, like the post-pandemic uncertainty, the fear of war that returned to Europe a few months before the opening of the exhibition, and all the struggles and tensions that, whether by choice or superficiality, we risk being unaware of. Most of us, "protected by privilege and by chance," to cite Giorgio Vasta, do not experience these conflicts directly.[13] But through art and the imagination, we can try to reduce our distance from those who look at us through the screens of *Penumbra*, to finally try to reposition our gaze.

11 Before its official presentation at Venice, the artist organized a special screening of *Olho da Rua*, inviting all the participants. The event became a party celebrating the shared experience of creating the work and the community it generated.

12 John Berger, "Ways of Seeing" (1972) (London: Penguin Classics, 2008), 8–9.

13 *Protetti dal privilegio e dal caso*. From Giorgio Vasta, "Immagino il dolore di Kiev per tentare di essere umano," *La Stampa*, February 26, 2022: 23. Unless otherwise noted, original texts are rendered in English by the translator.

MASBEDO

PANTELLERIA

2022, single-channel video, color, stereo sound, 19'

00:25

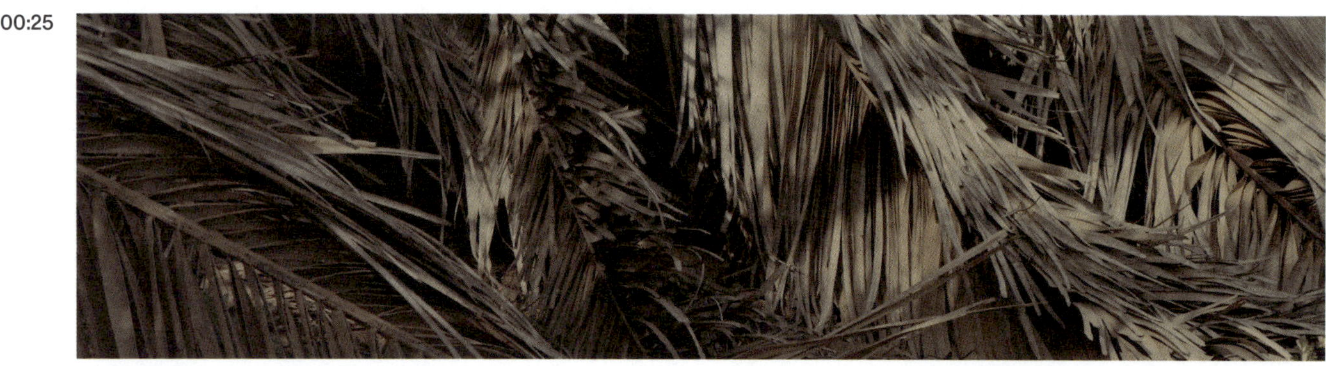

00:42

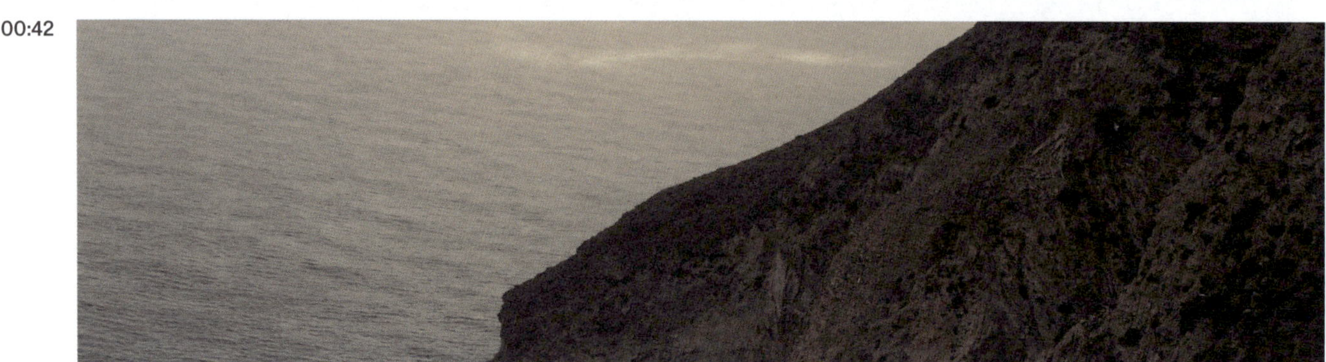

Pantelleria by Masbedo (Nicolò Massazza, b. 1973 and Iacopo Bedogni, b. 1970, Italy) engages with the historical and mythological legacy of the Operation Corkscrew: between May 9 and June 11, 1943, the Allied troops violently bombarded the Pantelleria island in their first manoeuvre to reconquer Italy. Residents recall that, a few days after the surrender was signed, some of the main village's buildings were blown up

01:22

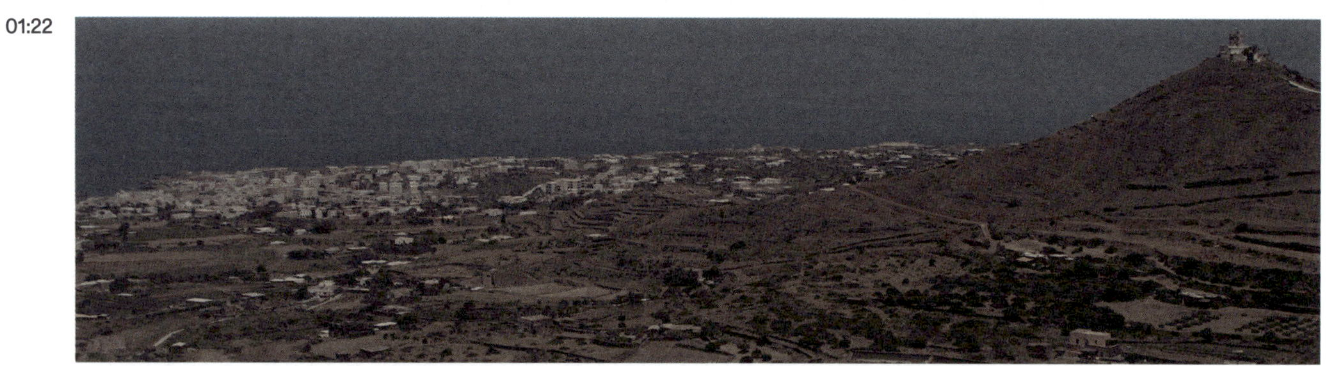

01:42

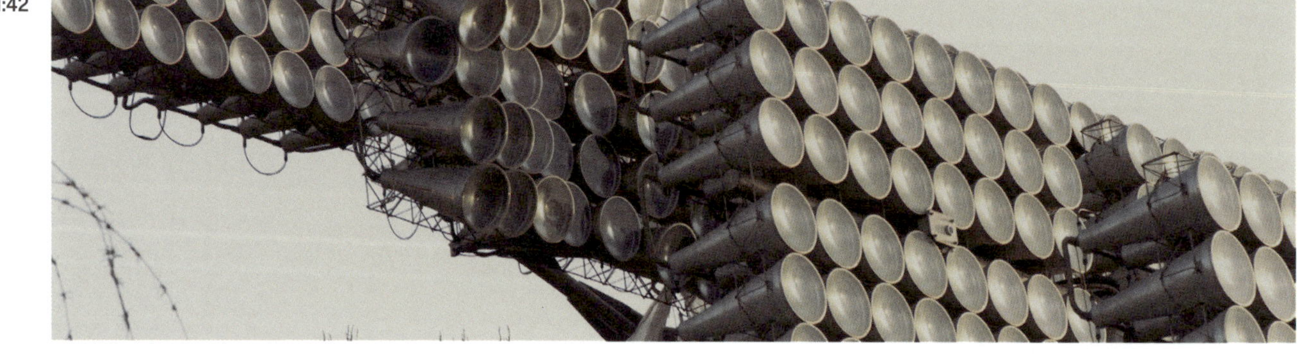

01:50

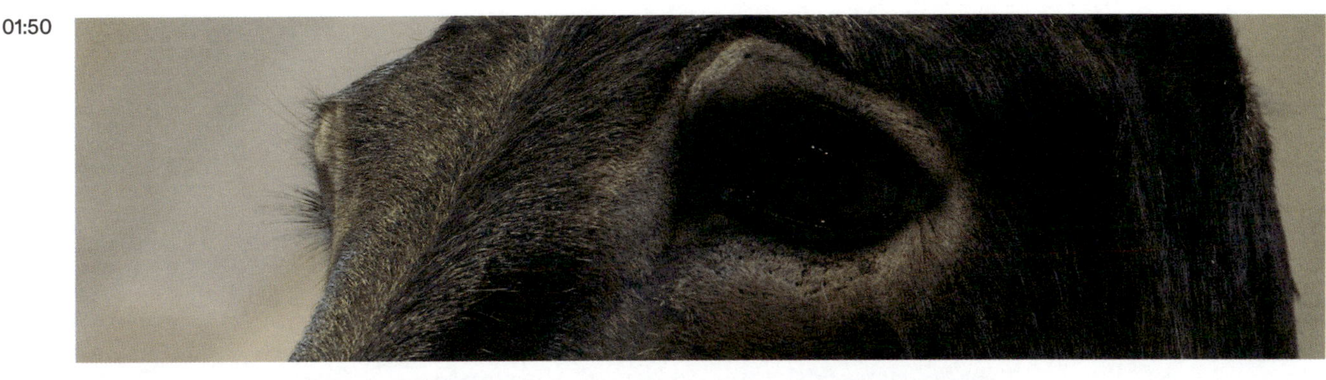

03:36

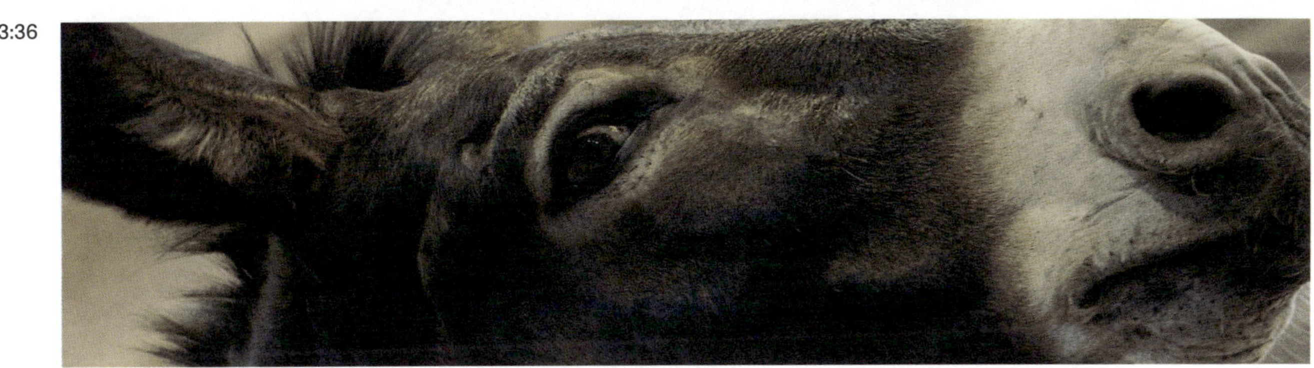

again for the cameras of a propaganda combat film. *Pantelleria* traces the memories of this episode settled in the collective consciousness of the island, and looks at the contemporary implications of an event in the shadow of official history. Through a two-years long participatory process with the residents, which included interviews, workshops, presentations, screenings, and moments of collective reflection with

03:44

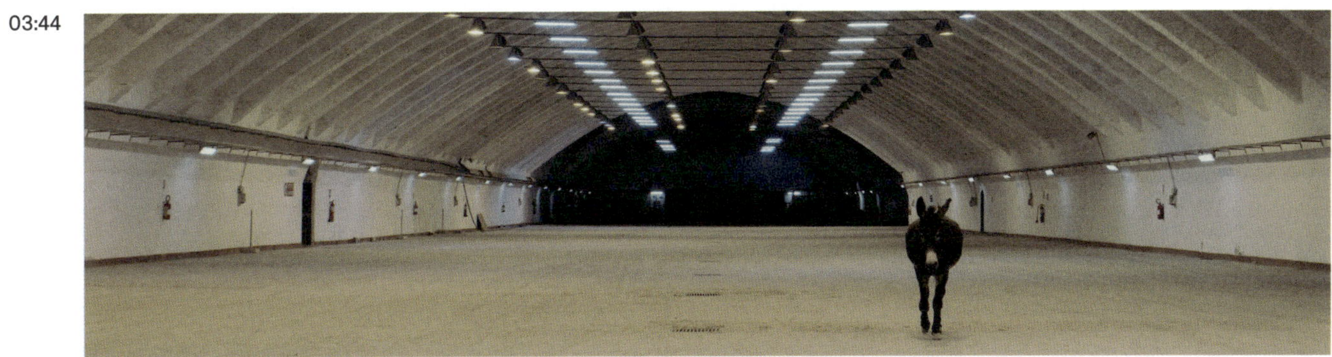

06:04

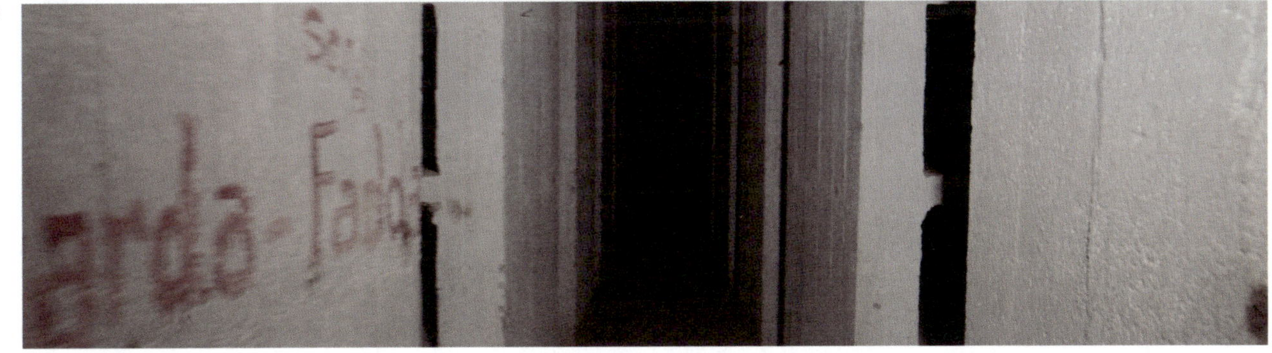

08:01

09:46

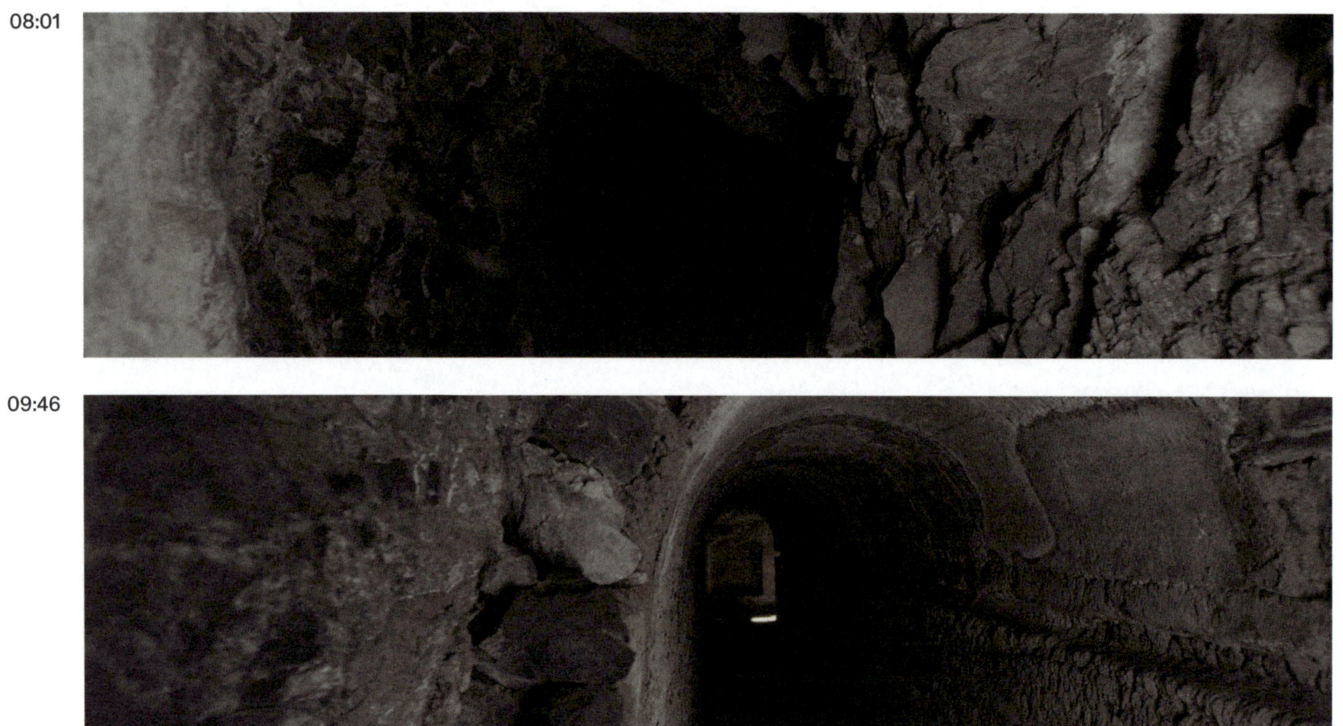

historians, musicians, and philosophers, the film explores the tension between the truth and its ideological distortion, and between the tragic reality of war and its telling through images. The hangar attributed to Pier Luigi Nervi, which still stands as a symbol of Benito Mussolini's militarization of Pantelleria, is filmed empty and inhabited by the magical presence of a local breed Pantesco donkey. The camera then travels through

10:51

11:08

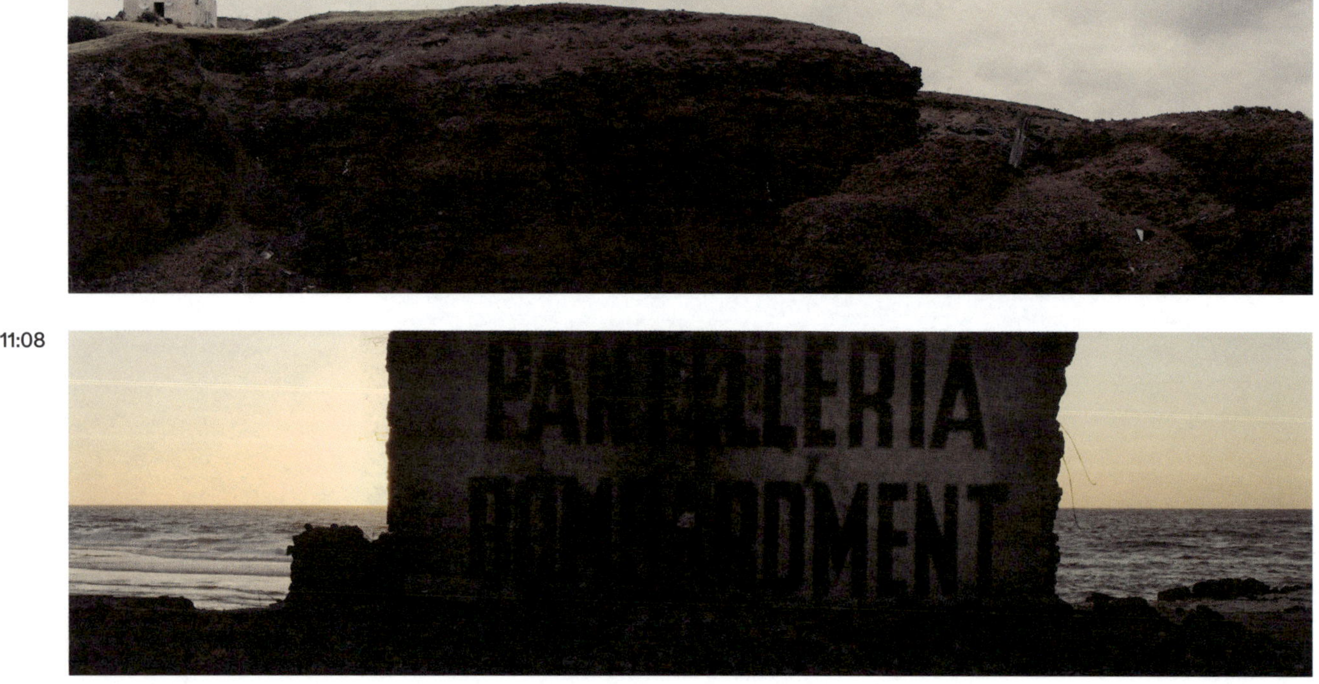

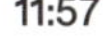
11:57

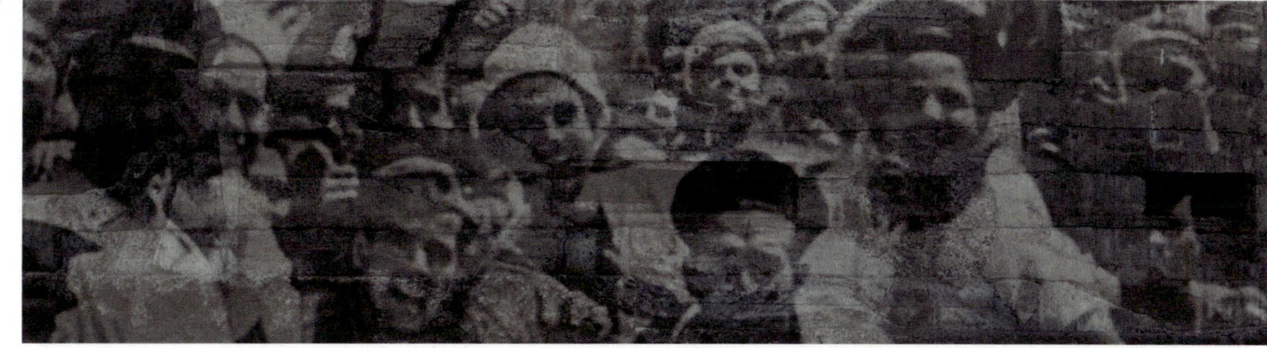

12:18

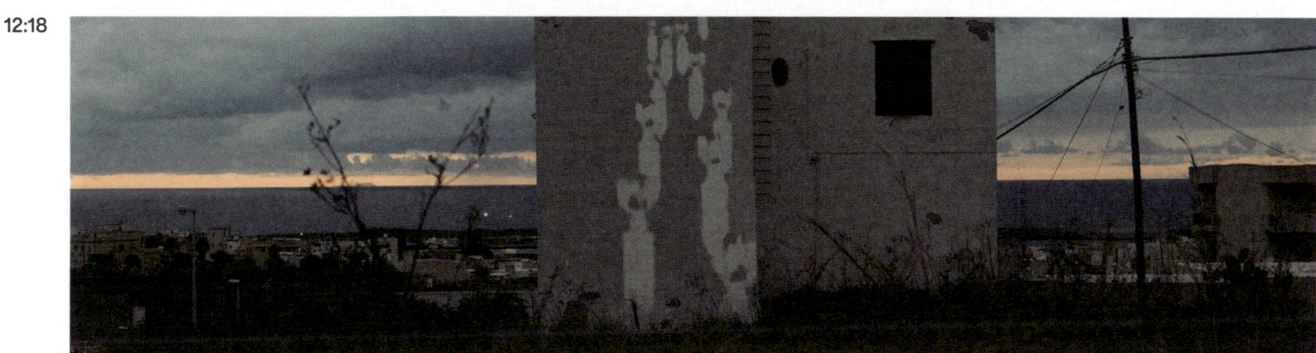

the bunkers dug deep in the rocks by the Italian army before resurfacing and observing extracts from the combat film projected onto the buildings of today's reconstructed Pantelleria. Nodding to the malleability of reality, the final masked ball is a homage to the local Carnival tradition, an extraordinary three-months long festive period held at the same time by the sixteen community centres scattered around the island.

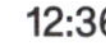
12:36

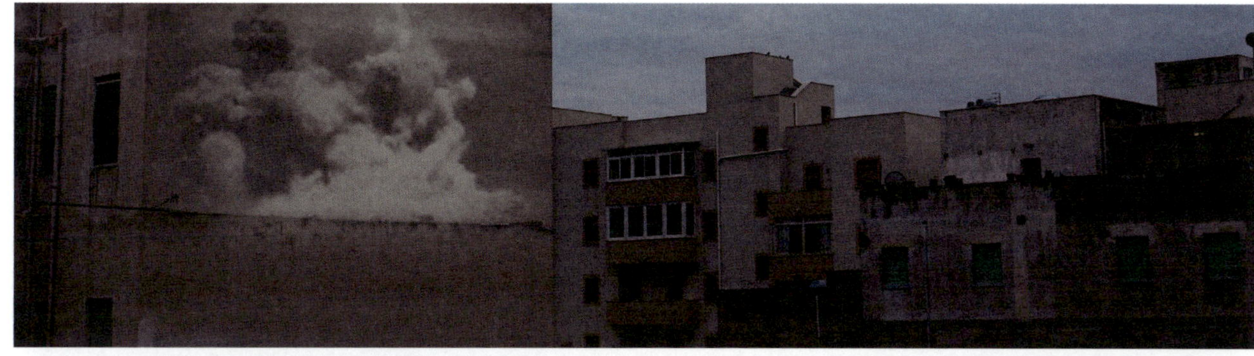

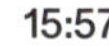
15:57

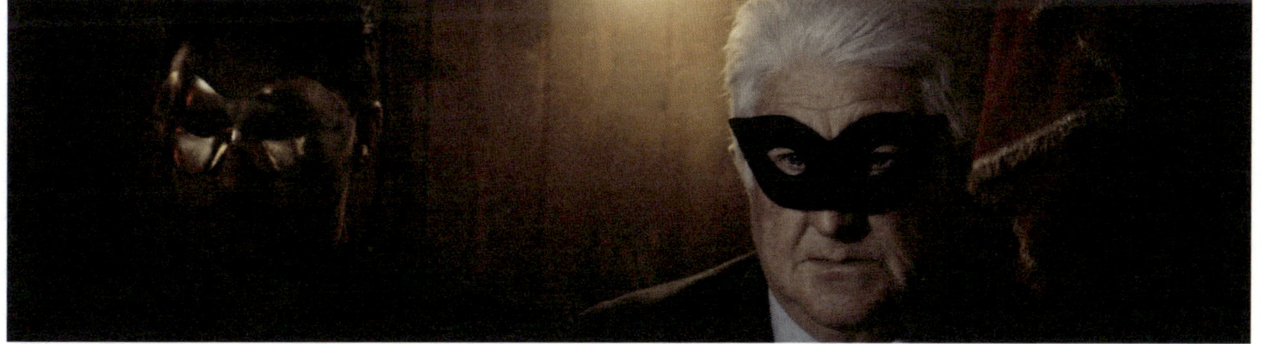

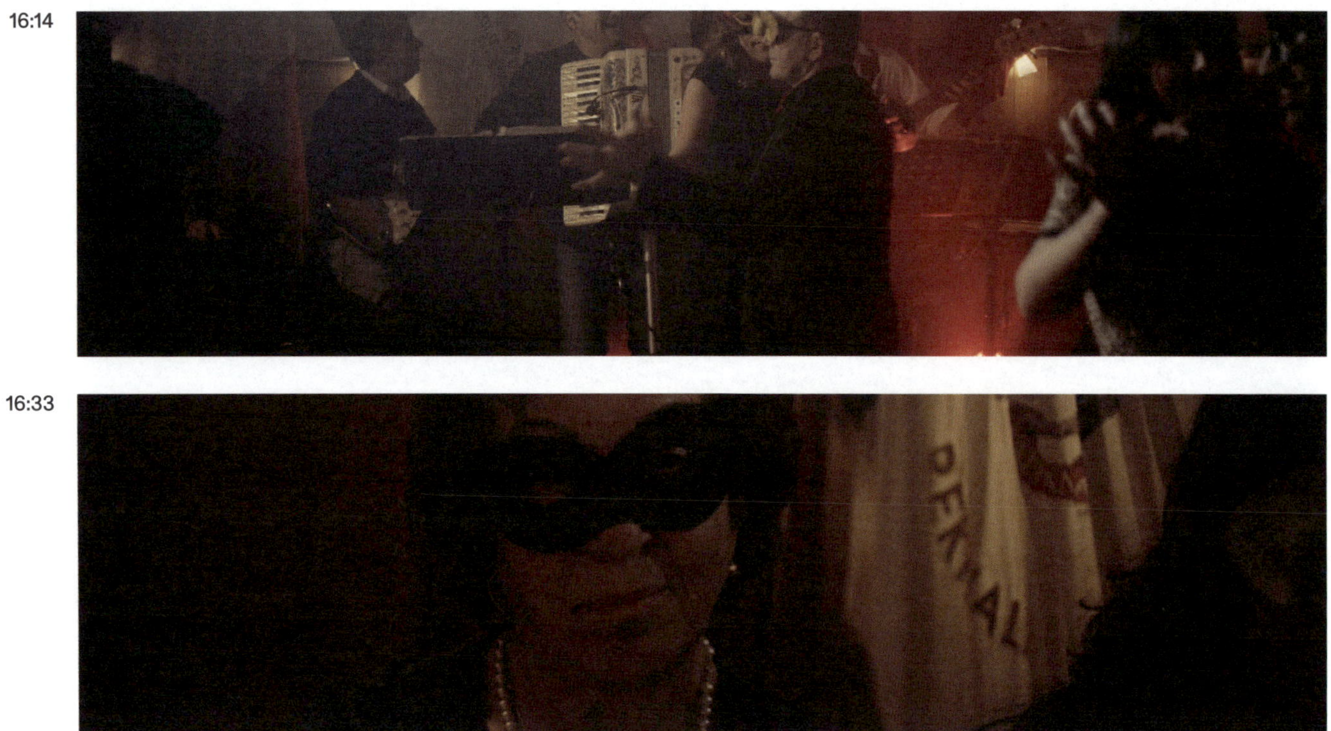

16:14

16:33

The voiceover, written and read by writer Giorgio Vasta, gives expressive form to the island's stories, while the soundtrack by GUP Alcaro and Davide Tomat distorts the recordings of the local orchestra Spata, finding in dance music a space for the reactivation of the past, and liberation in the present.

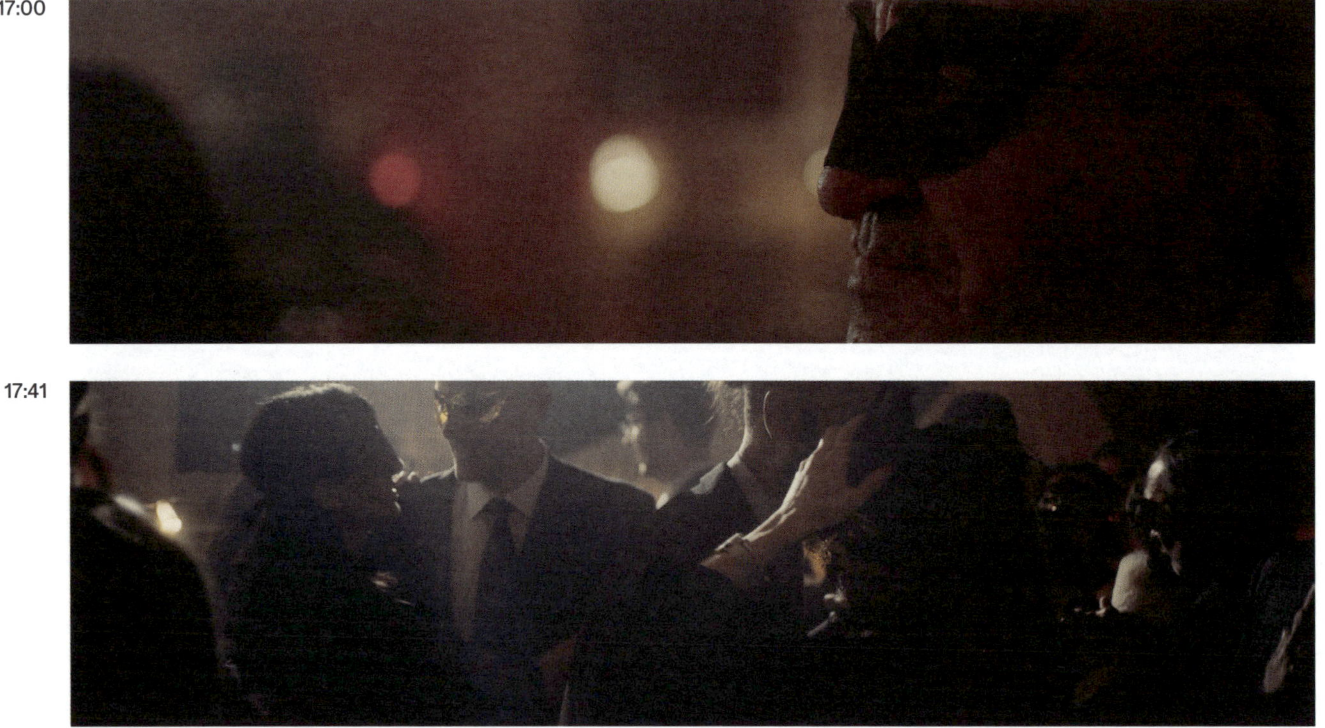

17:00

17:41

Masbedo, *Pantelleria*, 2022

Single-channel video, color, stereo sound, 19'

A film by
Masbedo

Commissioned and produced by
Fondazione In Between Art Film

Creative Producer
Leonardo Bigazzi

Text and voice
Giorgio Vasta

Editing
Valeria Ferrari

Original soundtrack
G.U.P. Alcaro and Davide Tomat

Music
Orchestra Spata (Giuseppe Spata, accordion; Salvatore Spata, electric bass; Vittorio Maccotta, drums; Giuseppe Pavia, guitar; Michelangelo Gabriele, keyboards)

Executive Producer
Luca Bradamante

Directors Assistant
Genny Petrotta

Production Assistant
Elena Castiglia

Line Producer
Alessia Carlino

Location Manager
Antonio D'ancona

Technical Director and Operator
Francesco Di Gesù

Steady cam
Lele Cerri

Focus Puller
Mauro Gianesini

Sound Engineer
Sebastiano Caceffo

Technical Rental
Co-Rent Palermo

Audio Service
Mediterranea Service S.R.L. Pantelleria

Voice recorded at
Indigo S.R.L. Palermo

Subtitles
Sub-Ti L.T.D. Londra

Partecipants to the final ball
Carmine Acierno, Antonio Basile, Giuseppe Belvisi, Cristian Billardello, Giuseppa Blanda, Francesco Brignone, Cinzia Busetta, Girolamo Casano, Laura Chiaiesi, Leonello D'aietti, Antonio D'ancona, Sonia Delli Paoli, Pierangelo Di Malta, Gabriella Di Munno, Maria Pia Errera, Fabio Ferrandes, Francesco Ferrandes, Caterina Gabriele, Giovanni Gabriele, Salvatore Gauli, Matilde Giglio, Battista Greco, Irene Greco, Anna Grimaldi, Claudio Illirico, Ismaele Illirico, Battista Impellizzeri, Simone Impellizzeri, Antonia Lopinto, Bicetta Maccotta, Lucia Marrone, Francesca Moussad, Piersimona Mura, Giovannino Pavia, Vanessa Pavia, Patrizia Polisano, Antonella Raffaele, Cristiano Raffaele, Edoardo Raffaele, Veronica Rizzo, Angela Ilenia Rodo, Mariano Rodo, Agostino Salsedo, Marino Salvino, Rosario Sanguedolce, Elena Siragusa, Enrico Siragusa, Florinda Valenza, Mario Valenza, Roberta Vitto

Special thanks to
Beatrice Bulgari, President Fondazione In Between Art Film; Alessandro Rabottini, Artistic Director Fondazione In Between Art Film; Aereonautica Militare Italiana, Stato Maggiore dell'Aeronautica – 5° Reparto "Comunicazione"; Difesa e Servizi S.P.A – Magg. C.C.R.N Michele Di Cristo and lawyer Fausto Recchia; Distaccamento Aeroportuale of Pantelleria, Comandante Tenente Colonello Francesco De Astis; Antonella Amato and the Pantelleria donkey Achille; Salvino and Salvatore Marino and Circolo Agricolo di Scauri, Francesco Marrone and Circolo Unione di Scauri; Cinema San Gaetano di Scauri; Marco Senaldi; Caterina Almanza, Livio Blandino, Rosa Brignone, Giuseppe D'aietti, Giovanni Errera, Nuccia Farina, Piero Ferrandes, Leonardo Laiti, Paolo Ponzo, Salvatore Saia, Mario Valenza; Bianca Stoppani, Paola Ugolini; Circolo Agricoltori – President Giuseppe Belvisi; Circolo Cavour – President Piero Belvisi; Circolo Cesare Battisti – President Giovanni Bernardo; Circolo Italia Redenta – President Walter Lo Pinto; Circolo Kohoutek – President Giuseppe Ferrandes; Circolo Ogigia – President Antonello Ferrante; Circolo Produttori Di Bukkuram – President Carmine Acierno; Circolo Roma – President; Giovanni Ferreri Carrubbino; Circolo Tinozza – President Maria Pia Errera; Circolo Trieste Stella – President Edoardo Raffaele; Circolo Unione Ausilio – President Battista Greco; Circolo Vittorio Veneto – President Gaetano Brignone; Unioni Produttori Di San Vito; Vanessa Pavia, D'ancona Blandino family

Courtesy of the artists and Fondazione In Between Art Film

Achilles' Heel. What I Know about a Form, When It Takes Form
Giorgio Vasta

At first I don't quite get it. On an early September day in 2021, Nicolò describes the project for me. It's hot and I'm using the phone's speaker, away from my ear, so perhaps that is keeping me from grasping the meaning. Nicolò's description is clear, but something happens along the way from his voice to my listening, the structure somehow weakens, and what should be the architrave of the narrative falls short. There is the island of Pantelleria, yes—and as I listen I recall that I met Nicolò Massazza and Iacopo Bedogni about ten years ago for another film project by their art duo Masbedo. It was set in Iceland, a strategically uncertain story that took its cue from a *pièce* by Maurice Maeterlinck. Now Nicolò is telling me about Pantelleria and it is as if we are picking up a thread that began as we imagined the absolute white of Iceland; a thread that has silently developed over the years in which we were not in contact, and now resurfaces in the radical black of another volcanic island. And inside Pantelleria there is a small piece of World War II, a month of bombing inflicted on the island from May to June 1943: the Italian-German Axis crumbles, yields, surrenders, the Allies take over. The act of surrender was signed—Nicolò tells me, and I understand what he is saying—and then there is still one day of bombing. I understand what he is telling me, yes, but evidently not: if the surrender has been signed there is a termination of hostilities, so it would be impossible for more bombs to be dropped on the island. Yet that is just what Nicolò is saying: which makes no sense, but has meaning. Or that, more precisely, this improper bombing—out of time but *in* a place—is narrated. The islanders pass this story on, the historians deny it, but the discourse of historians is inevitable partial, it takes the so-called objective truth into account, and the objective truth is just one part—a small one, all told—of what happens: it is very probable that this bombing out of time never happened, but at the same time it did take place, and they—Nicolò and Iacopo, and Leonardo Bigazzi, the curator and creative producer, and Luca Bradamante, the executive producer, and the other people collaborating on the project—want to tell precisely this story that speaks and falls silent, appears and vanishes: a story that refuses to stand still, perhaps because in reality no story stays still, but eludes us: it is here but it is also there, a wayfarer, a sleepwalker, and it is ambiguous, it is present and elsewhere at the same time.

In the moment in which I can clearly sense that I haven't really understood, I say that I like the project, since the conditions for narration are all in place. So a

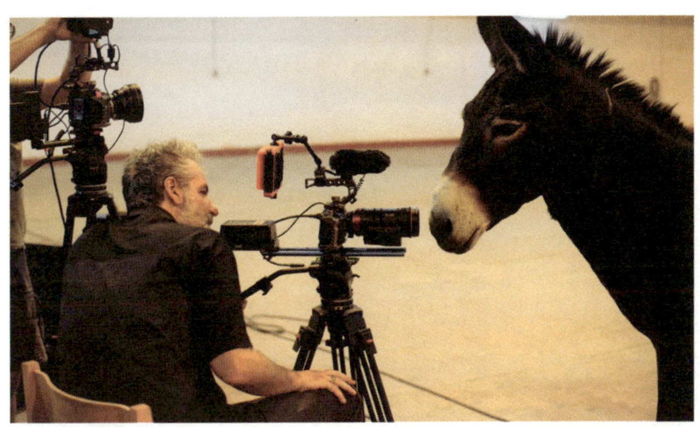

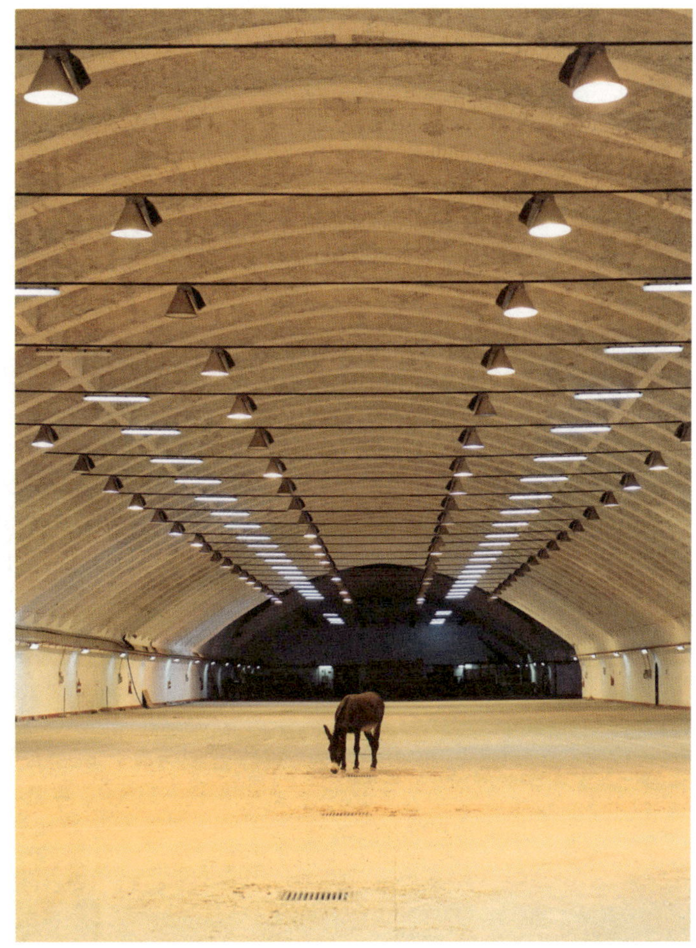

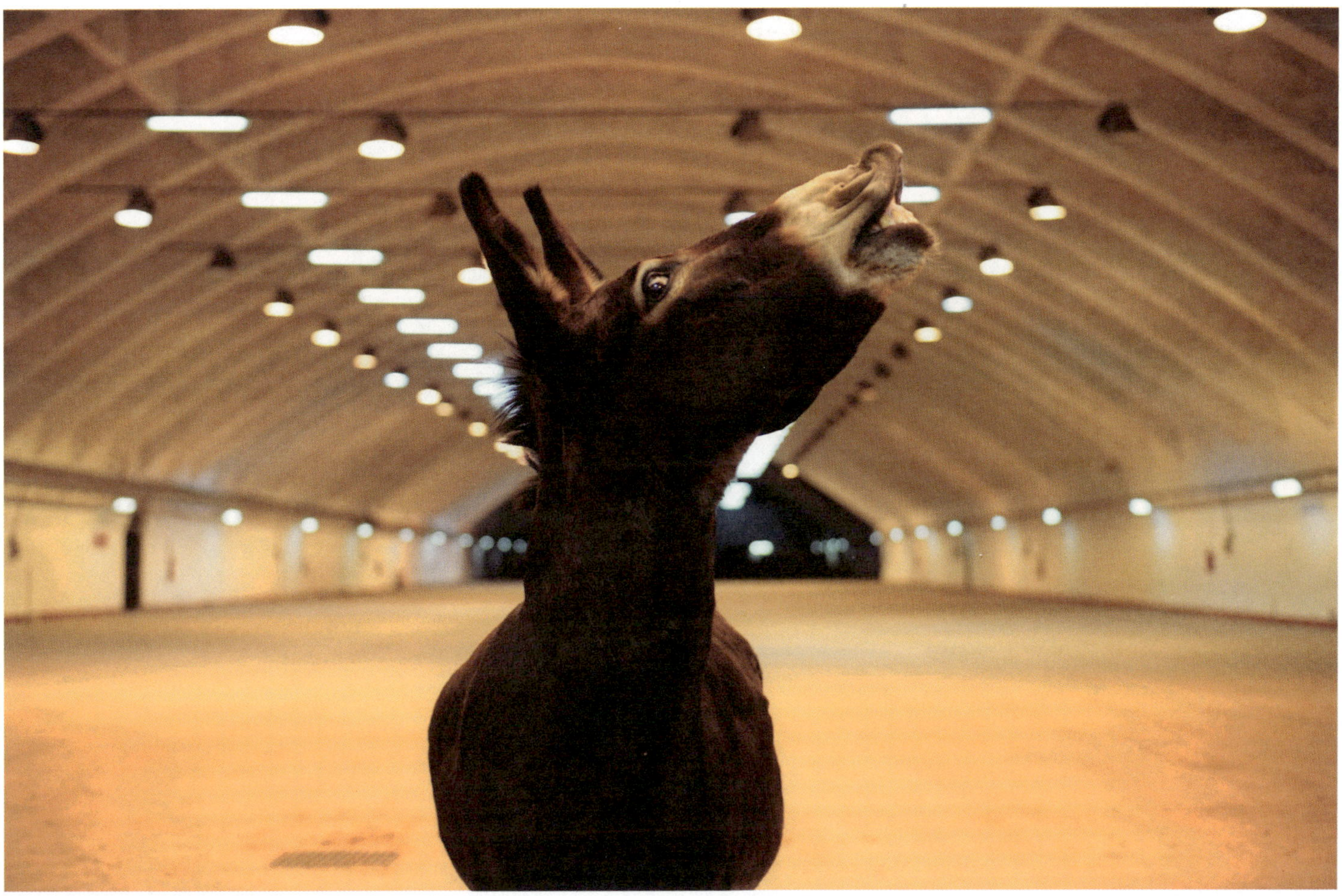

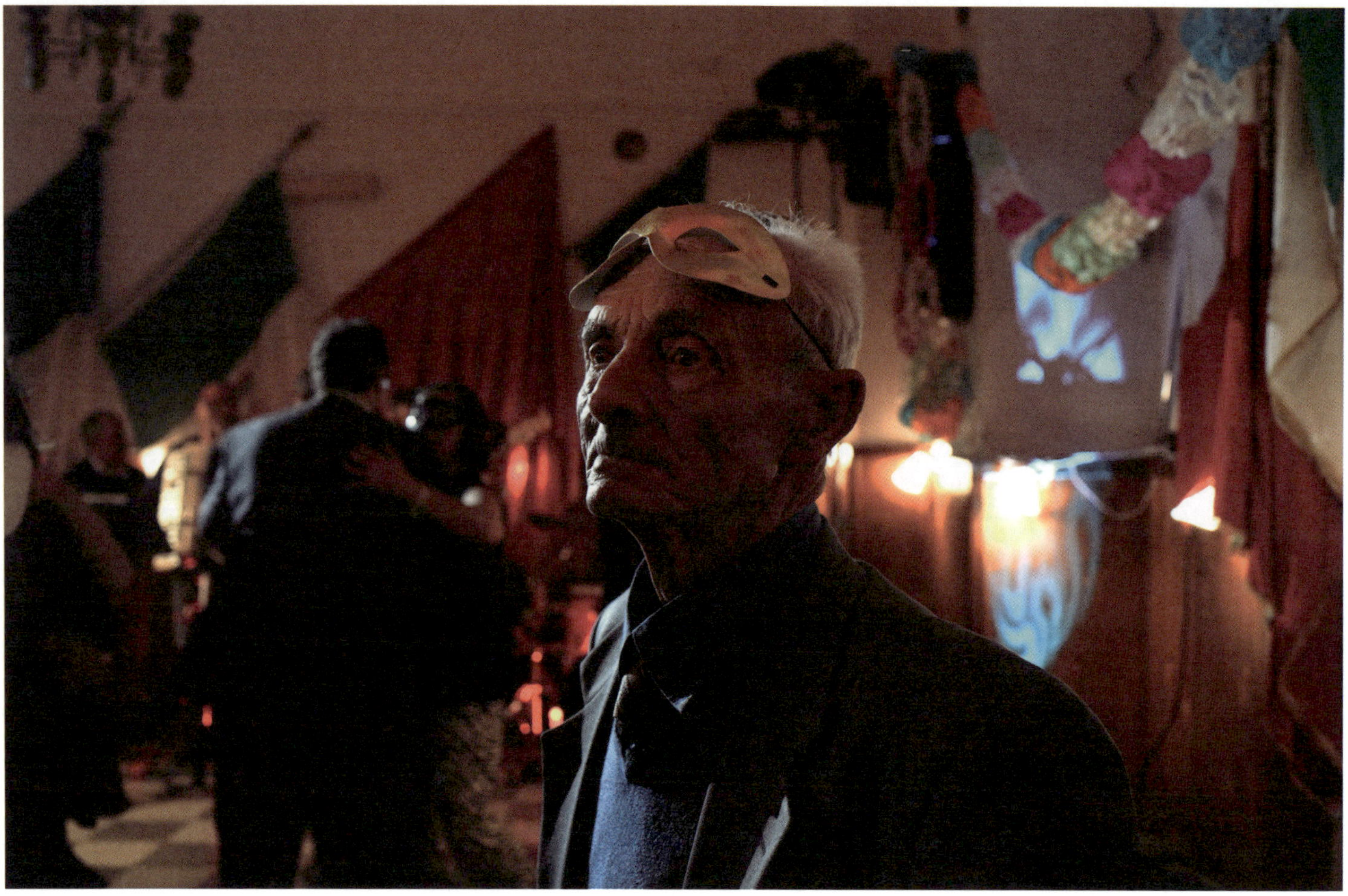

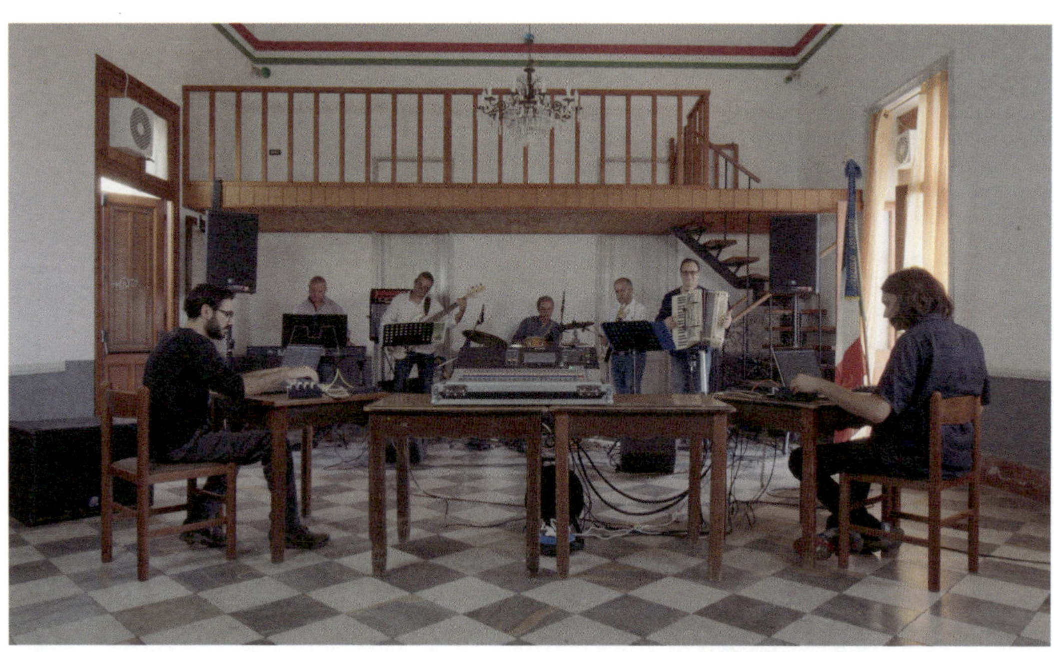

few weeks later, on October 18, 2021, we meet in Milan, and for an entire day we talk about the true false supposed indisputable bombing that happened and did not happen in Pantelleria on June 14, 1943. We watch film footage from that period, we see interviews and images shot by Masbedo on the island, we swap impressions of combat films. Listening to the stories, I take lots of notes: some have to do with what I am being told, but above all I record sudden suggestions, at times coagulated in short expressions or individual words: *sky earth water, fake boom, inventing flyers, asking forgiveness*; and then: *the syllable Pa- when the North American speaker says Pantelleria: Pa-ntelleria, the voice says, or even Pa-ntelleriua*; and then: *how many voices are needed for this story? Two, and opposing? Or would it be better to work on just one voice, but double, multiple, fragmentary diffracted psychotic?*; furthermore: *find a way to give form to an out-of-frame voice, out of context, entirely* inner, *the voice that talks in sleep, a voice without location, without counterpart, without addressee or sender.*

At a certain point on that October afternoon, shortly before parting ways, when we had been discussing things for hours and the fatigue was spreading in our bodies like twilight, a donkey appears on the screen of the computer where we had seen the footage of Pantelleria. It stands alone at the center of an enormous military hangar. It moves its torso, head, and ears; it bends, nibbling at the dust; it raises its head, looks around, takes a step, then another step: it wanders. It is one of the few specimens of the Pantesco donkeys still existing on Pantelleria, they tell me, and that space is a hangar located next to the island's airport, built during Fascism and attributed to Pier Luigi Nervi. The donkey, someone says, is called Achilles. In my notes I read: *Do donkeys have heels? Achilles, as a whole, is vulnerability and power. His gaze conveys meekness and folly, not in succession, not as alternatives, hence even less* opposites *than perhaps simultaneous*; and then: *And if Achilles were called the Story? The Story that roams in the hollow space of the hangar. An errant story. Or rather, with caps: Vague History. And so, in place of the usual presumptuous Based On A True Story, there would be the more humble and sincere Based On A Vague Story*; and then, moreover: *True and Vague should not be seen as opposites: a story is true if it tolerates levels of vagueness inside itself, just as a vague story is also made of a part of verified or ascertainable facts.*

In the days to follow, at home in Palermo, I read books about what happened and anastatic copies of documents, I watch films that address the question of the fake bombings; Iacopo tells me about a Netflix series on the combat films made by great North American directors during World War II, and I watch that too.

I spend some evenings in front of archival films on the Istituto Luce website, especially one of them that shows the arrival of the Allies in Pantelleria, the destruction in the town, the English and American soldiers, bewildered civilians observing the wreckage. Every night, after hours of watching bombs dropping out of the bellies of airplanes, falling to the earth or the water, comes a moment when my eyes see only a black and whitish muddle, a continuing explosion of something: a lingering image that comes from outside, of course, from the screen of my tablet, but is also inside my gaze: a system of origins marked by the difficulty of distinguishing between figure and ground; or, *tout court*: by the impossibility of that distinction. So I study the true false bombing of June 14, 1943, I stay up late, take some notes, doze off in front of the screen: for the moment, what I know is that there is darkness earth air water and flashes.

On November 22 and 23, 2021 we gather in Masbedo's studio in Piacenza. The physical context for the video installation is described for me, and we examine a number of photographs and renderings. We also listen to a series of audio tracks starting with songs played by an ensemble from Pantelleria. In the notes I took during that two-day session in Piacenza, I can read: *As happens with images, also for sounds, at times, distortion makes everything clearer*; *To write in a loop, in a flow, to give form to an ouroboros in writing, a Moebius strip*; *Anatomophysiology of a donkey: what is its body, the density, the coat, the odor, the gaze, and therefore the anatomophysiology of the Story: the Story says, the Story remains silent, the Story brays; the bombs, the noise of the bombs: a large part of what is called* war *is a sonic event: the silence in the moment when the bomb sinks into the sea, and then the blast of rising water, the silence that intensifies.*

At the end of those two days of meeting we realize that for all of us to go to Pantelleria together, in order to shoot the party that will conclude the video installation, we cannot wait until January as planned; it is too far away, and there is the risk that new restrictions caused by the COVID-19 pandemic might make it difficult to travel. It seems better to force the pace a bit, to gather on the island in mid-December. On the evening of November 23, during the flight that takes me from Milan to Palermo, I pull my boarding card out of my pocket and start to write what should become the framework of the text for Venice. During the trip, now and then I stop jotting because my hand hurts; I look out the window at the deep blackness, and when I resume writing I realize that after two months of ongoing thought I am still not able to put the core of the story I'm trying to tell into focus. As happened during that first phone call

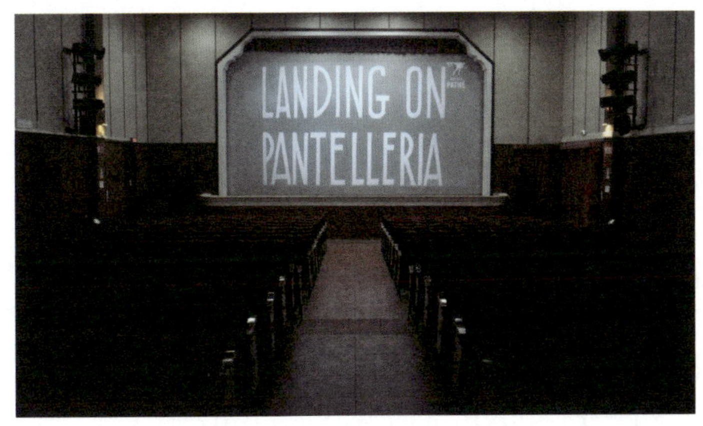
LANDING ON
PANTELLERIA

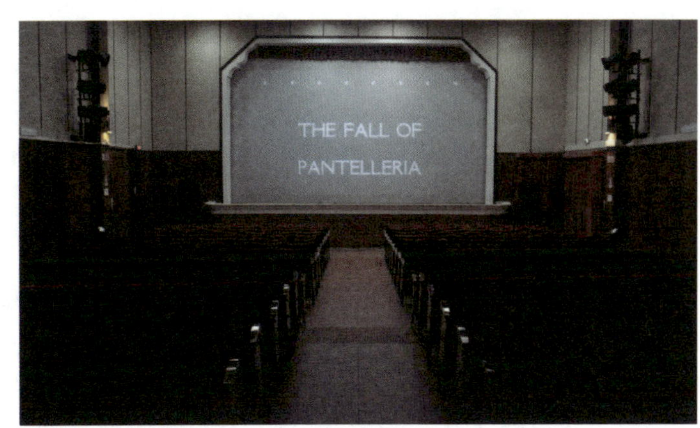
THE FALL OF
PANTELLERIA

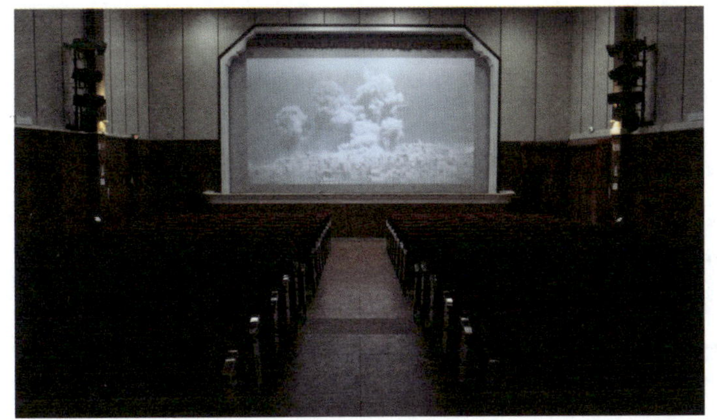

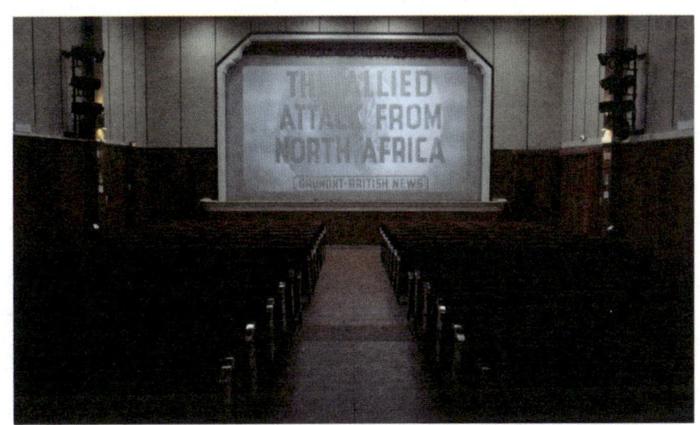
ALLIED
FROM
NORTH AFRICA
GAUMONT-BRITISH NEWS

with Nicolò, and when I observed bombings on my tablet, I am still gripped by a feeling of indestructible uncertainty.

As I write this comment, I am reading *Sotto gli occhi dell'Agnello* by Roberto Calasso. "Christ's word was sporadic, sudden, it did not create a continuity, a weave of reasoning," Calasso writes, reflecting on the Ghent triptych by Jan van Eyck.[1] The attributes of the word of Jesus—I thought as I was reading—for me, in general and in an absolute sense, are the attributes of the word in literature. A word that surfaces and simultaneously vanishes, a word that does not lend itself to continuity, or to the construction of a weave: not functional, unavailable for the purposes of argument. A word that, like the blind men in the parable, simply strides—*rises up*—and falls into a ditch. And as I thought of all this, I wondered: are these attributes only or above all related to words, or are they instead, even prior to language, the characteristic of *things*? Of what happens. Of the living, the existing. Or, furthermore, and thinking back on the bombs that fall into water and on the ground, the dust and flashes: the uncertainty, the ambiguity, the irresolvable coexistence of the so-called true and the so-called false. Are they perhaps the structure of the gaze—or at least of my gaze? Its condemnation and its privilege?

In the weeks between the meeting in Piacenza and the days on Pantelleria, I continue to make many notes. I like notes, but I am wary of them. I know that when I write I have to go through a phase in which I behave like a compulsive hoarder: everything that happens—what I see and listen to, what I imagine, conversations and dreams, everything that arises in everyday life as a marginal, infra-ordinary phenomenon, a minute fact: all the boundless marvelous odds and ends, are transformed into a possible deposit, everything *is* and *has* its potential, everything deserves annotation. These notes, when I look at them on A4 sheets of paper, tend to seem like separate points. I tell myself that at some moment a design will emerge, but in the phase of making notes this design—the form—is just a hypothesis, something I don't know, and I don't know where it is. I can recognize a *leaning toward*—a tension—but I don't know toward what. The notes, therefore, keep growing, spreading, deepening, they arise—*rise up*—and at a certain point they resemble a bundle of signs—it might be more exact to say they resemble a bundle of dreams: a tangle of visions. This process of accumulation—as I know—should be encouraged, it serves me, it reassures me on a neurotic level and at the

1 *La parola di Gesù era sporadica, improvvisa, non creava una continuità, un tessuto, una argomentazione*. From Roberto Calasso, *Sotto gli occhi dell'Agnello* (Milan: Adelphi Edizioni, 2022), 42. Unless otherwise noted, original texts are rendered in English by the translator.

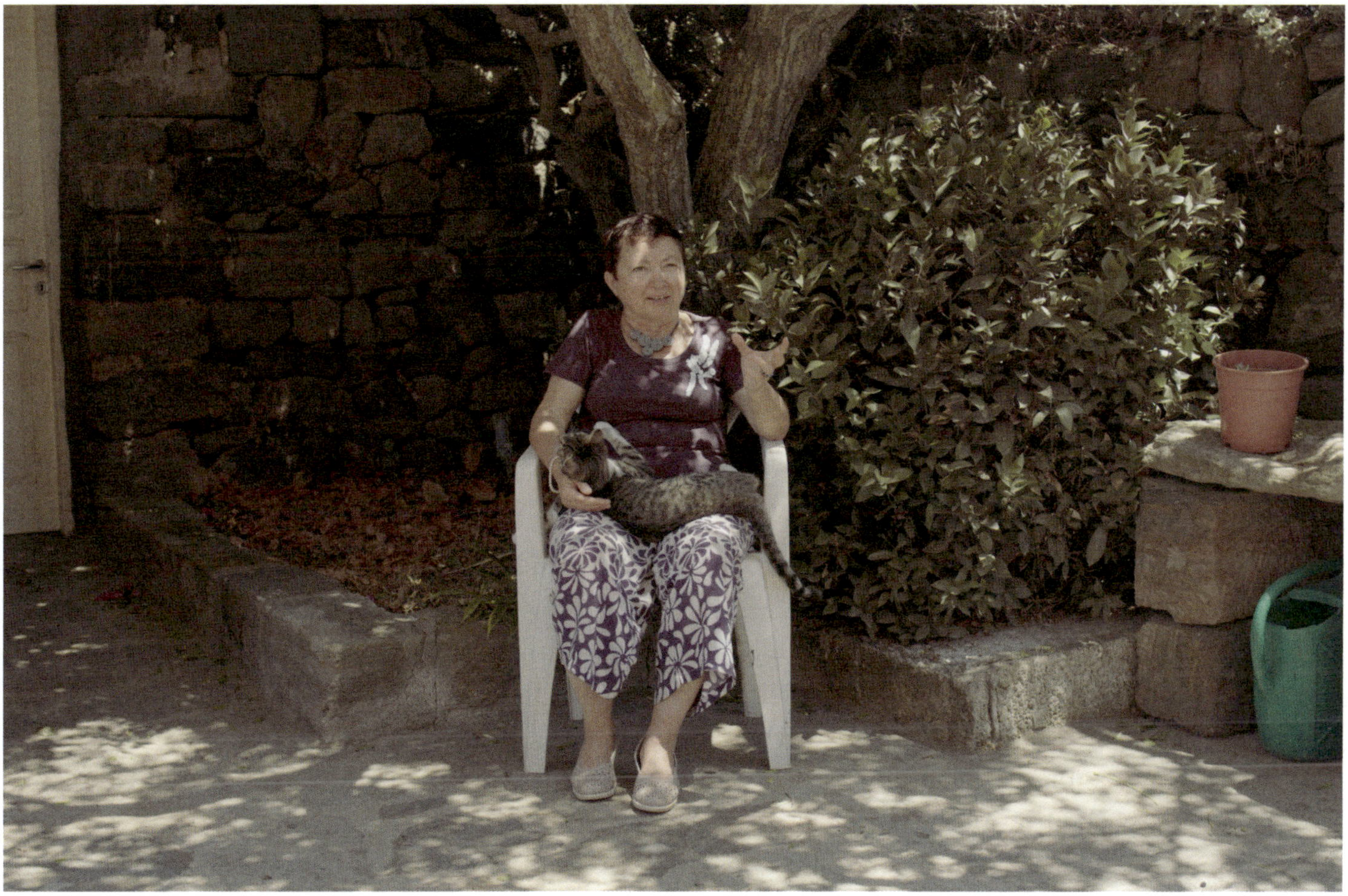

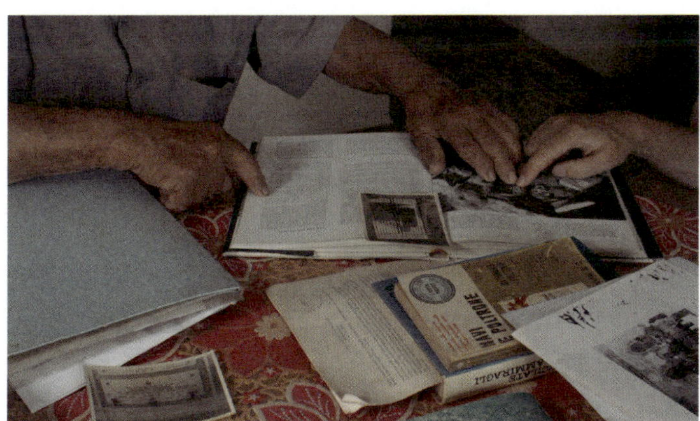
NAVI E POLTRONE
AMMIRAGLI

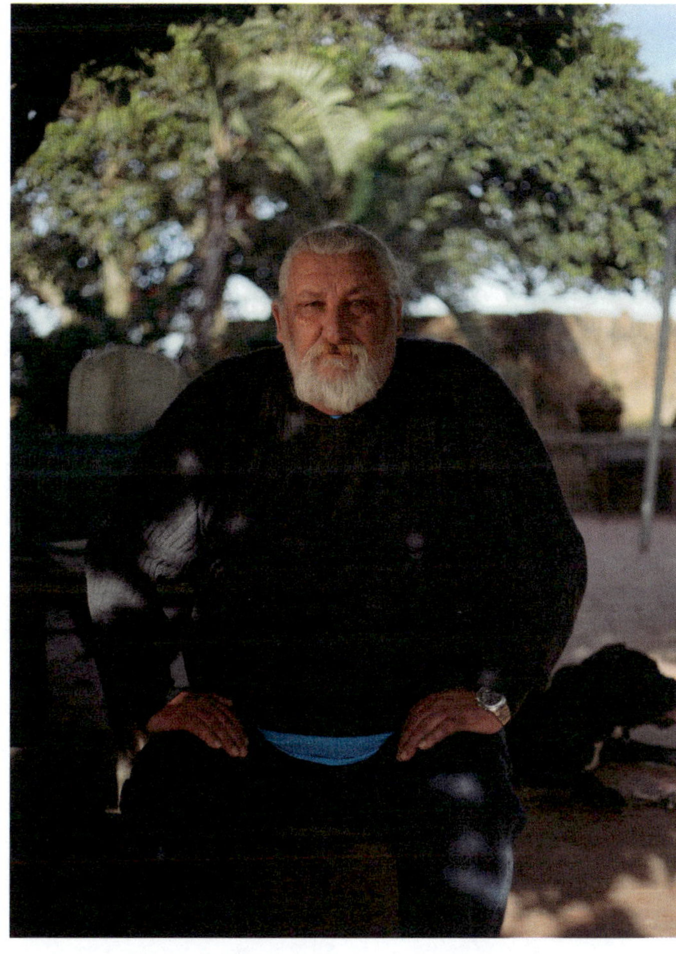

same time generates useful materials. I am aware, however, that the accumulation of possibilities, together with a sense of euphoria also triggers a sense of frustration in me: the fear—at times the certainty—that the quantity will get the upper hand over my ability to transform all that material into a form. So I try to negotiate with myself: I take an offshoot of notes and try to organize it into a sequence of phrases. And in effect something occurs. Maybe I can manage in time, manage to sort out the tangle, to transform what has been a mass up to this point into what is called *definition*, in both the training of the muscles and the experience of language.

At Pantelleria, in a break between location visits and shooting, I read what I have written for Nicolò Iacopo Leonardo and Luca. As I read my voice retreats, it's the fatigue and also a slight tension. I usually share a text when I've finished it, and I usually have someone else do the reading. This arrangement is unusual for me, though it is consistent with the collaborative nature of the project. After the reading we talk, together. We identify the nuclei, what we see as indispensable, what might be important, what instead is obscure or barely hinted or self-fulfilling. It is like working together on the making of a bas-relief: in order for the design to appear, we have to *subtract* material, to combine choices and sacrifices in order to make a form emerge. The text I am writing has to be balanced *on* the images, *amidst* the images (narrating, in this case, precisely the mystery of images).

On January 25, 2022, I send a message to Mariagiulia Colace, an illustrator friend, and ask her to do me a favor: could you draw the map of Pantelleria on the model of the so-called "duck-rabbit illusion"? Mariagiulia is kind and says yes, so now I have to manage to explain what I mean. I send her a postcard of the island, found on the web, and a drawing—also found there—of an optical illusion that fascinates and disturbs me, which for years I have utilized as a metaphor for certain things I try to say without knowing how to say them.

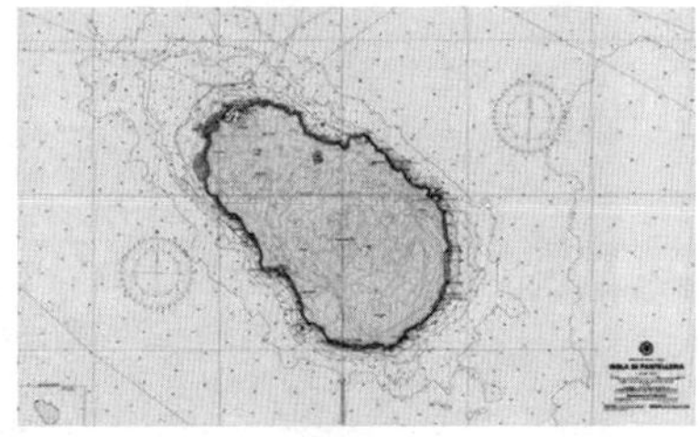

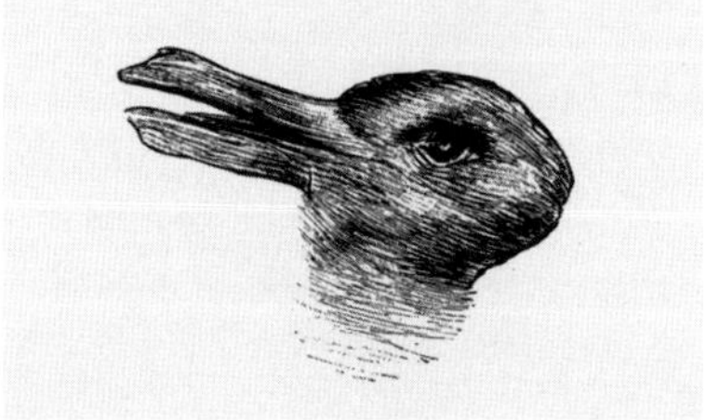

When Mariagiulia is looking at these two images, I tell her I would like her to intervene on the shape of the island, to condense two images in one and make them both perceptible.

You mean something like this?, she asks, attaching an initial sketch.

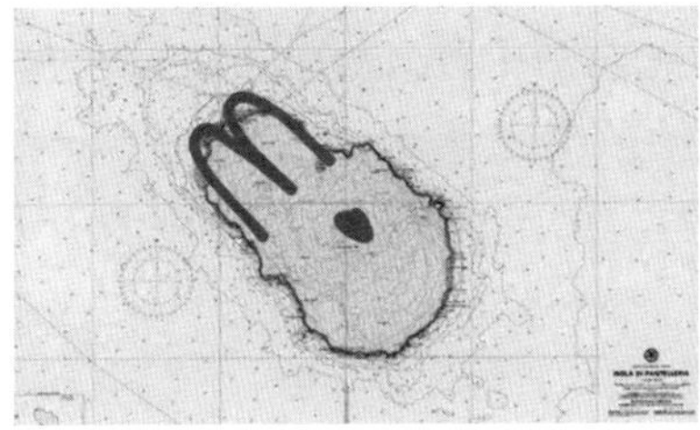

Yes, I reply, but I would like the eye, if possible, to be farther to the south. Here:

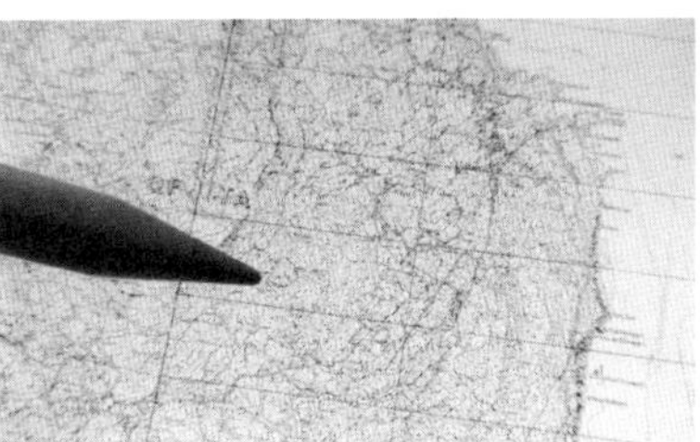

During the days Mariagiulia is transforming Pantelleria into a duck-rabbit (more of a duck than a rabbit, actually, or perhaps only a duck, with no rabbit), I write:

> *The more I try to imagine what happens, the more I realize I am still in the neighborhood of the duck-rabbit illusion. The "views" are unable to clearly exclude each other, they are not really mutual antagonists, neither one clearly prevails over the other: if anything, they tend to penetrate each other, to reciprocally allow each other to enter, becoming simultaneously available. As in the case of the duck-rabbit illusion, all this triggers a sense of disperception: the fake bombings are real, and at the same time they are forced and imagined; the demolitions after the surrender cannot be attributed to the desire of the Allies to put together images useful for a combat film, but were precautions against possible unforeseen collapses; and in any case, it would have been "absolutely normal if when the fighting had come to an end military cameramen had shot propaganda footage simulating actions of combat on the ground";*[2] *meaning that the staging is not configured as something opposite to the truth of wartime action since, if anything, it is an integral part of it: inside "the truth" of the war there is also a narrative of the war itself that is not exclusively documentary in nature, but also fictional.*

2 *Assolutamente normale che, ad azione ormai avvenuta, alcuni cameramen militari abbiano effettuato riprese propagandistiche simulando azioni di combattimento terrestre.* From Marco Belogi, *Pantelleria 1943. D-Day nel Mediterraneo* (Brescia: Liberedizioni, 2005), 181.

All human beings, when the development of their cerebral cortex permits it, understands what is fictional and is capable of distinguishing between so-called truth and so-called fiction. Animals cannot. Ever. In the eyes of an animal, everything that happens is. *Animal life happens prior to and beyond the truth-fiction dialectic, which is instead a way of thinking of human beings.*

When Mariagiulia sends me her manipulation of the map, I observe it and I tell myself that at this point I am where I wanted to be (though I continue to not really know where I wanted to be).

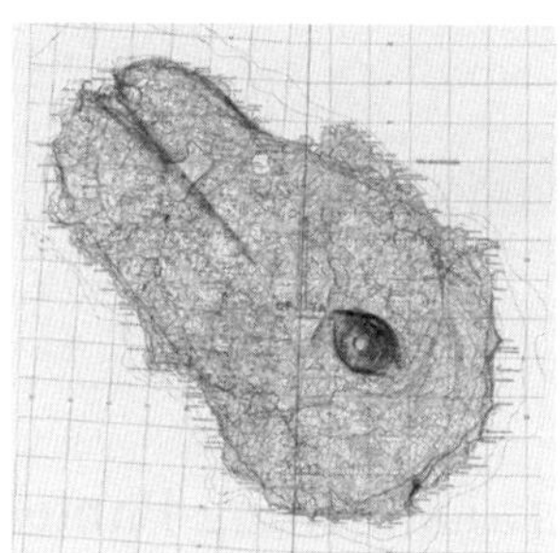

In this image that is a compendium of topography, ethology, graphic design, and narrative, the passage takes place from the *view*—what is effectively perceived—to the *vision*. If the view is a criterion that trusts in appearances—thinking that they exist and can be used to construct knowledge of the world—the vision is plural and contradictory. Therefore: the historical truth related to what happened in Pantelleria in June 1943—the bombing after the truce happened, say the islanders; it did not happen, say the historians—is now, finally, something plural and contradictory. In Mariagiulia's drawing I cannot say that I see the duck *or* the rabbit, the duck *and* the rabbit: in her drawing, as happened in October, I still see Achilles. On the screen of my tablet, I see Achilles and he looks at me. What I wanted—again: without knowing what was the object of this desire—was for the story we are telling—the Story—to have something to do with me. I wanted that meek, obtuse and luminous gaze of a donkey. I wanted the truth—the True Story—to find a way to wander—the Vague Story. Observing Pantelleria with muzzle and ears, beak and eye, I know that this *is the form* of the text. A weave of mixtures and flashes. I know that now I can finish the writing. Because now the text is open to wavering, trembling, instability, uncertainty. What is different, if not opposite, coexists, or better still it interpenetrates, the parts become indistinguishable. The image, now—always—does not know of itself, just as animal life does not know itself, just as the Story is not self-aware.

When at the start of March, with Iacopo, I enter a studio in Palermo to record the text I have written, I think back to six months earlier, when in September Nicolò told me the story of the true false bombing of Pantelleria and I had understood something, while something eluded my grasp. I think about the fact that for all this time I have continued to never have a completely clear idea about the substance of this story, or at least its mechanism. I think about how for years I have been unable to ever clearly grasp the substance of anything. Everything that happens is made of gaps; and therefore, if I try to narrate what happens, I cannot help but accept the gaps. I cannot escape from the awareness of all these missing parts. Of how much intrinsic confusion exists inside my gaze. How much vulnerability.

Every pane of shatterproof glass—as I recall, but who knows if I am truly remembering, who knows if memory is a fullness or a void—has a critical spot. A point, that is, where an impact can cause the destruction of the pane itself. A weak point, as we usually put it. A *locus minoris resistentiae*, as an anatomopathologist might way. An Achilles' heel—and here, as we know, the reference is to Greek mythology: when Thetis dips her son Achilles in the River Styx to make him invulnerable, she holds him by the heel: only that fragment of his body—the fragment with which the mother holds the son—is exposed to the fury of the world.

In the telling of a story—for example, of what happened and did not happen at Pantelleria in 1943—there is always an Achilles' heel. For me, narration does not mean managing to immerse the entire body of the story in the waters of invulnerability, but making sure the palm of the hand adheres as closely as possible to the heel: to narrate is to preserve that fragment of vulnerable skin. To protect it—knowing that protecting it, in this case, means putting it at risk. To keep it alive, i.e. potentially exposed to destruction. To narrate means considering the Achilles' heel not as a risk, even less as a limit, but as the point of greatest vitality of the form. Because the pane of glass of the story exists not *in spite of* its critical spot, but *because* of that critical spot: the pane of glass of the story is built *on* its critical spot: always open to confusion, always ready to fall to pieces.

What I have understood while working on *Pantelleria* with Masbedo is that granting form to a form—a form that not only does not deny the original confusion but, precisely, recognizes it as a legacy and protects it—for me means seeking a way to make what I do not know exist.

Images from the backstage of *Pantelleria* by Masbedo. Courtesy of the artists.

KARIMAH ASHADU

PLATEAU

2021, two-channel video, color, sound, 27'

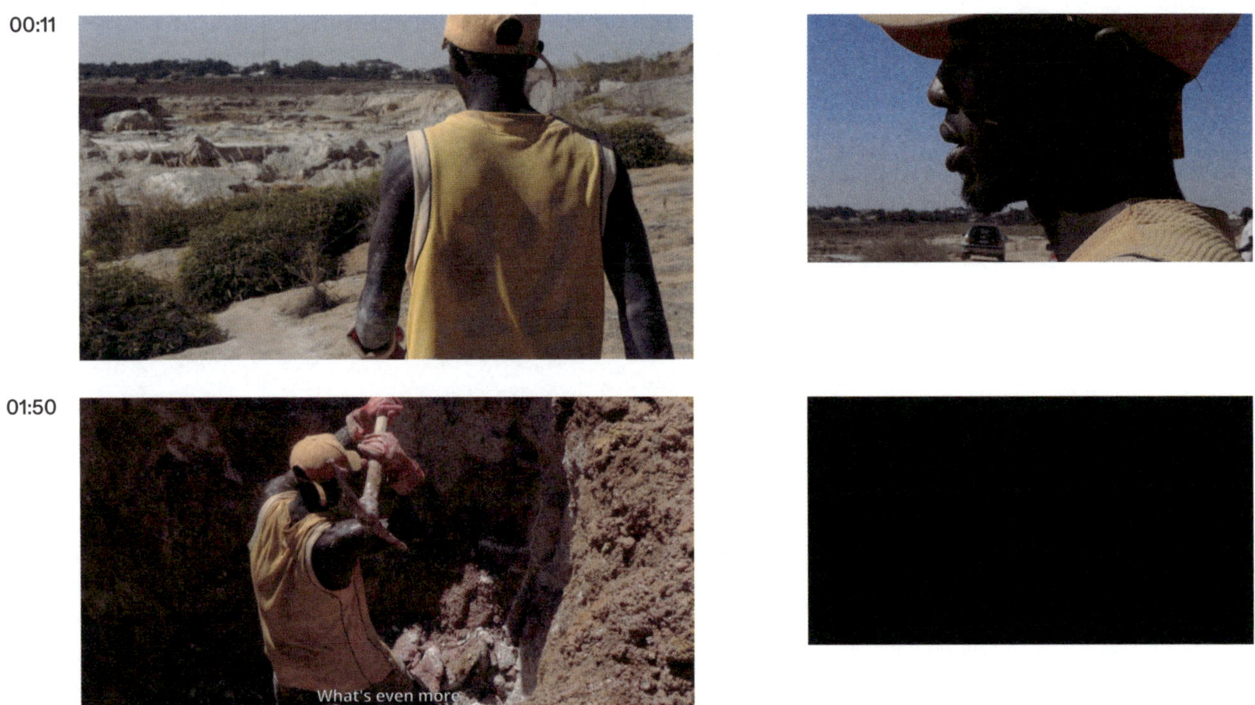

Plateau by Karimah Ashadu (b. 1985, United Kingdom) depicts a group of undocumented, self-employed tin miners who work in Nigeria's Jos Plateau region. Merging a lyrical and investigative exploration of the relation between the landscape and the corporeal, the work tells us about how the protagonists strive to make a living out of an impoverished and unstable land, and in precarious, often life-threatening,

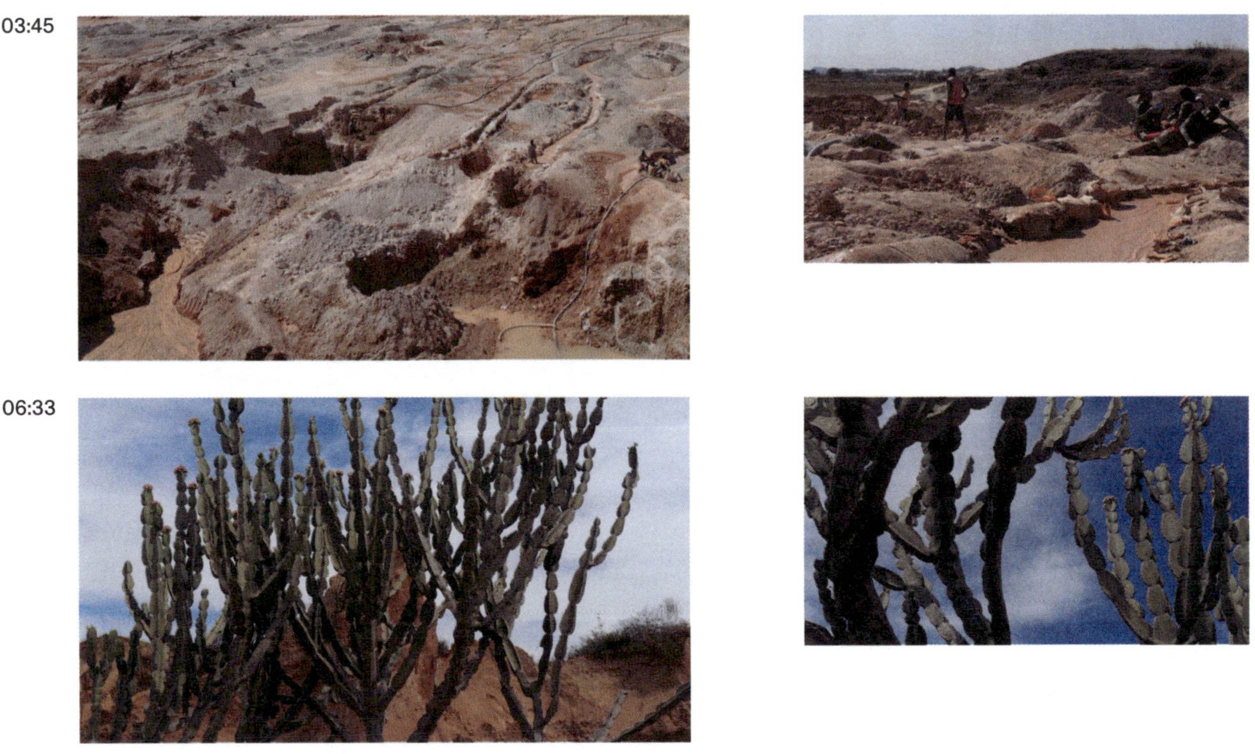

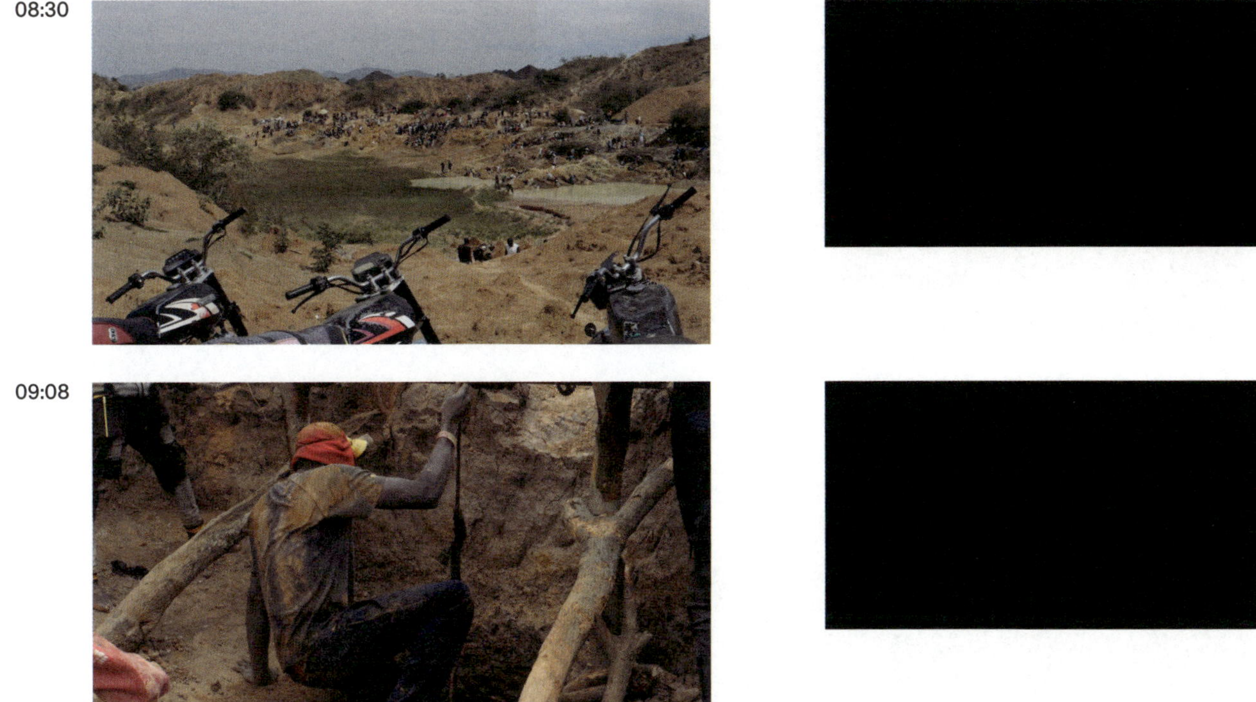

08:30

09:08

working conditions. The majestic presence of the cactus symbolically conjures both aspects in the way it endures to harsh weather. The cactus is also a cultural signifier for the Berom people—the largest autochthonous ethnic group in Plateau State—who identify with its resilience and thriving capacity despite the difficulties they may encounter. Male bodies are seen strenuously digging the land,

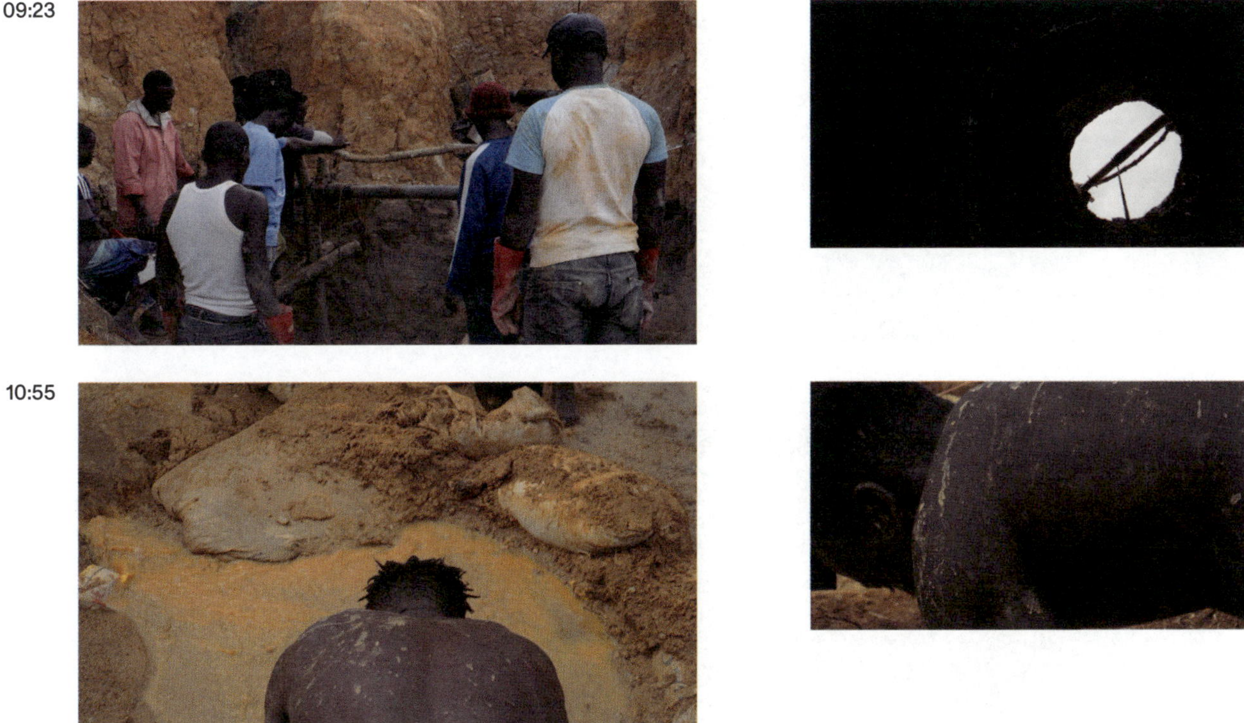

09:23

10:55

12:26

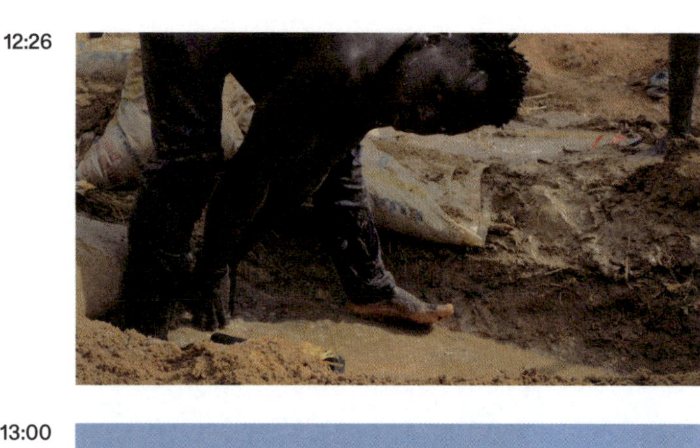

13:00

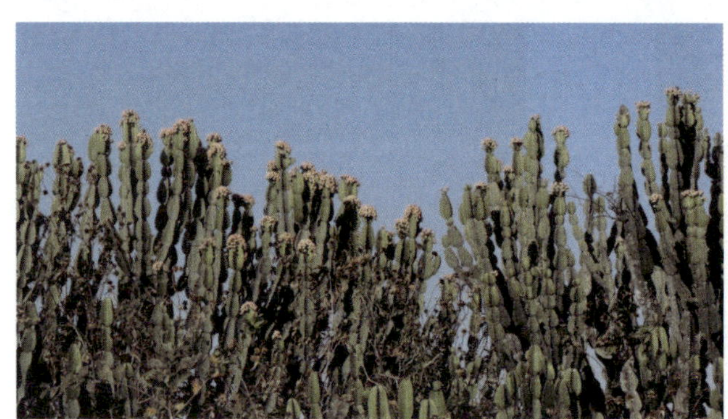

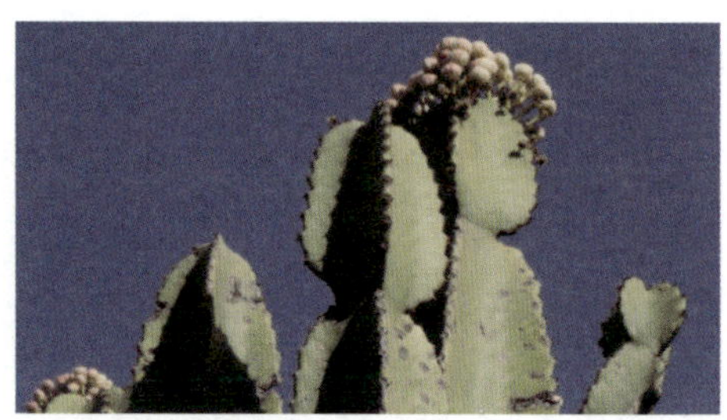

sifting mud, and moving buckets of water in repetitive, brushstroke-like gestures. They utilize inherited manual techniques to wash tin and columbite away from the soil, and what is left is then accurately sieved by women. Yet, rather than imposing a romantic gaze upon these fatigued workers, the camera stays close to their determined gestures that courageously attend the land for their survival. If during the

14:47

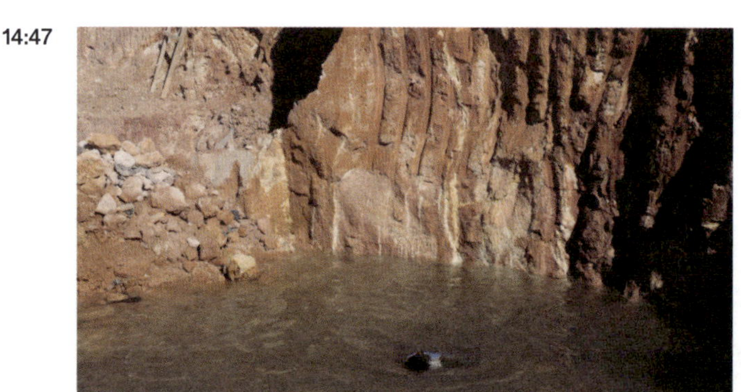

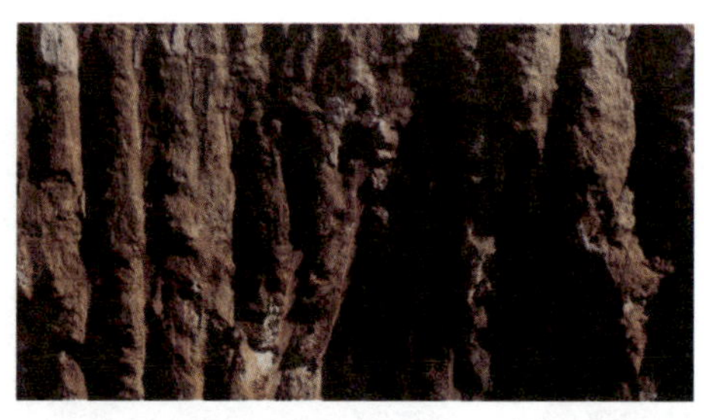

15:12

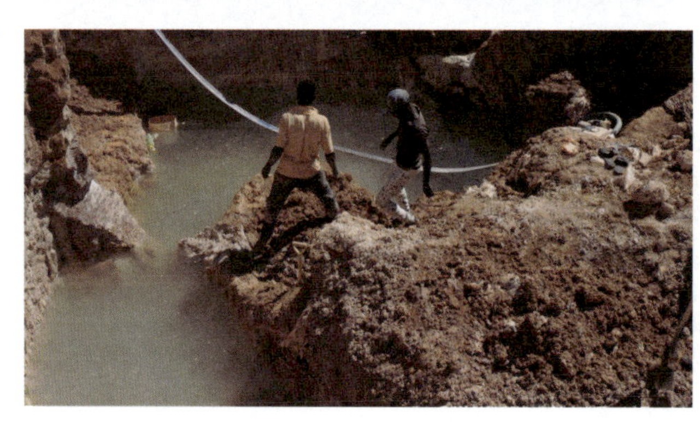

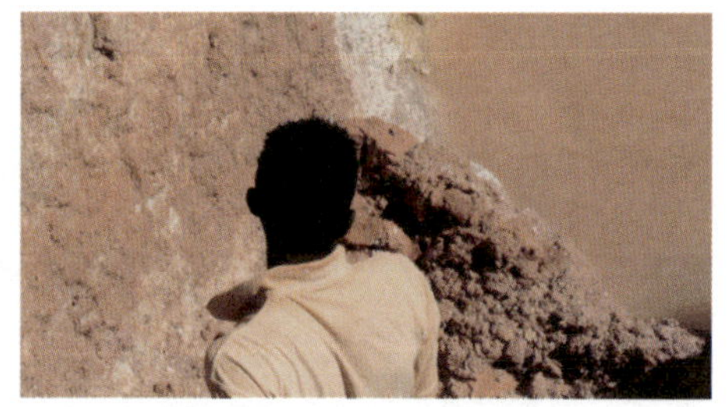

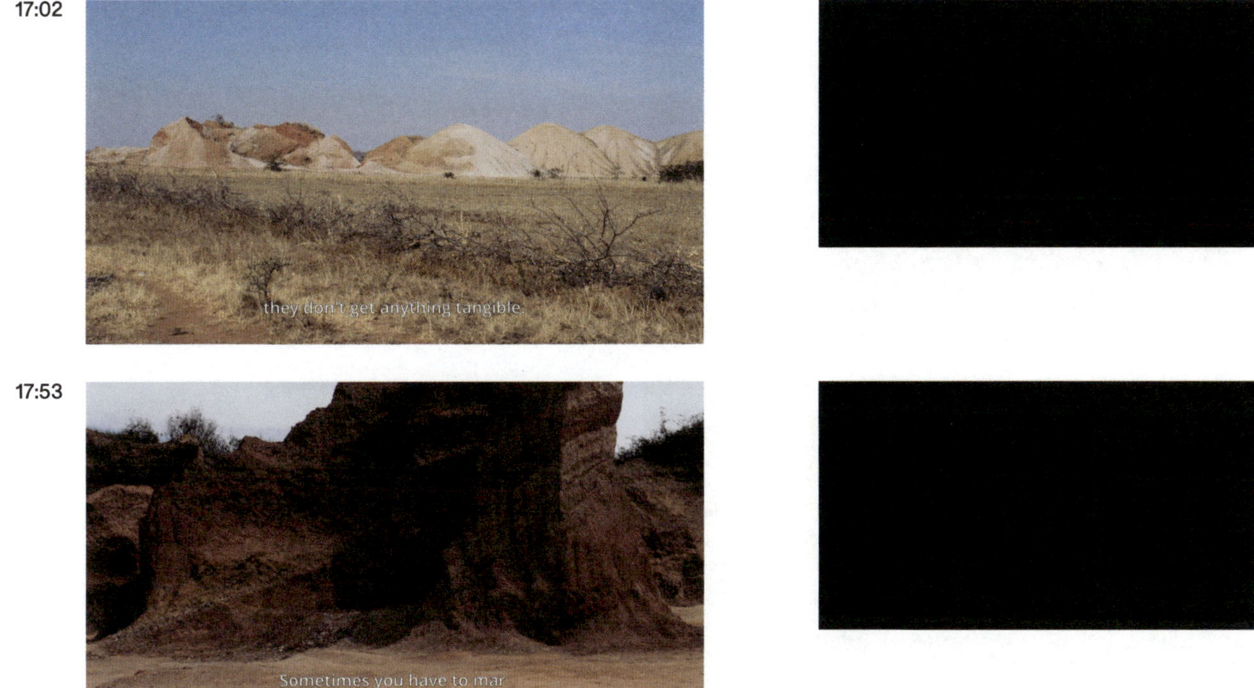

complex, century-long, violent occupation of Nigeria by the British colonial regime, miners were exploited as laborers and were given little or no shares of the wealth that the industrial mining system generated, in its aftermath they received no compensation nor investment from the Nigerian government. Hence this community find itself re-mining a damaged and dangerous landscape that is deformed with artificial

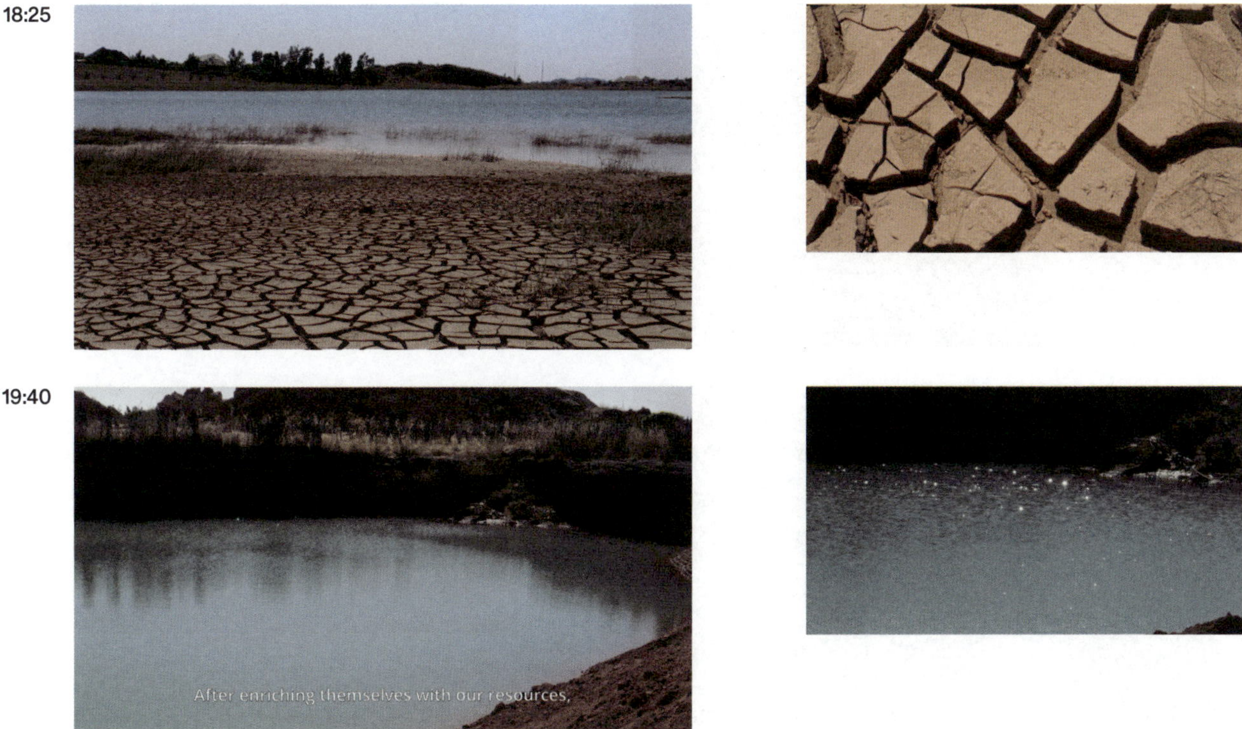

20:09

23:09

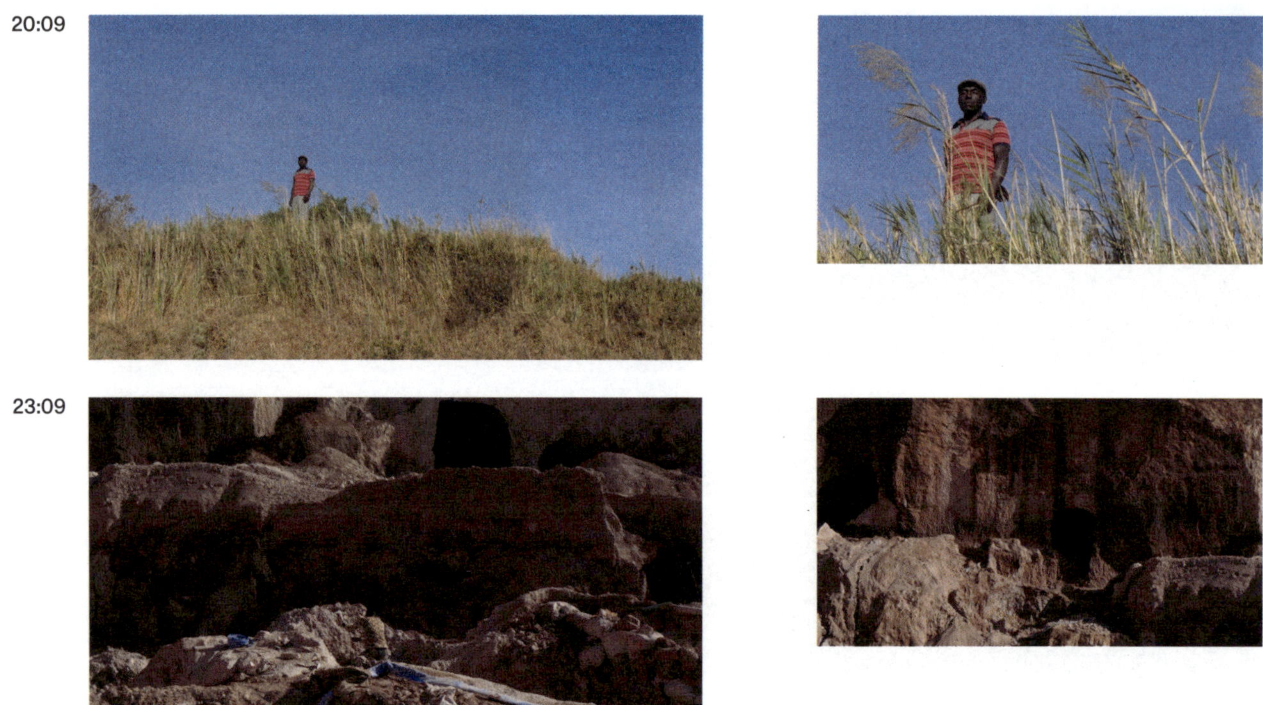

hills, open holes, channels, wells, and ponds, thus increasing the risk of landslides. The testimonies of the miners, together with those of local villagers and landowners, document the economic collapse of the region as a consequence of British corporations' decommission as well as the newly found opportunities to pursue their individual and their community's independence.

23:20

25:46

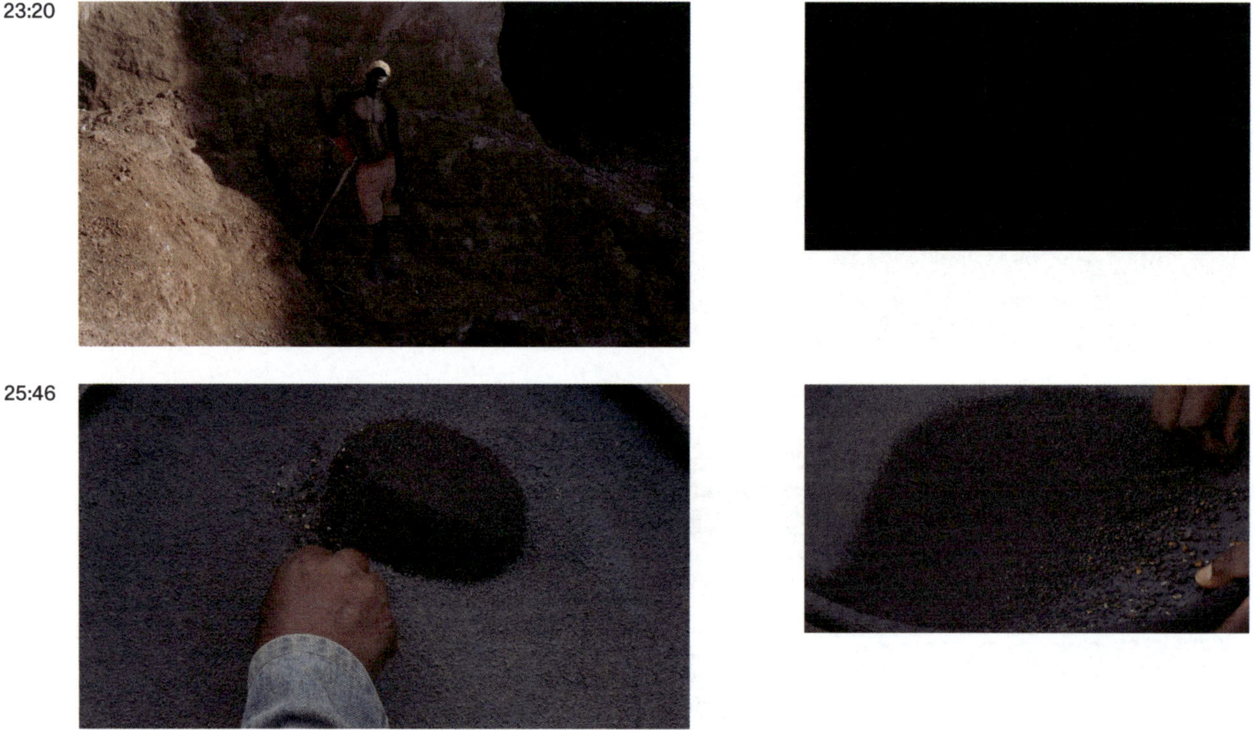

Karimah Ashadu, *Plateau*, 2021

Two-channel video, color, sound, 27'

Director and Editor
Karimah Ashadu

Camera
Aigberadion Israel Ikhazuangbe

Location Sound Recordist
Anthony Monday

Color correction and Sound adjustments
Cristian Manzutto

Credit Designer
Abdul Twebti

Commissioned and produced by
Fondazione In Between Art Film

Creative Producer
Leonardo Bigazzi

Co-produced by
Golddust by Ashadu, Germany

Supported by
African Culture Fund, Mali

With special thanks to
The miners and the location team, Beatrice Bulgari, Alessia Carlino, Alessandro Rabottini, Bianca Stoppani, Paola Ugolini, Columbia Institute for Ideas and Imagination, Paris

© Karimah Ashadu, 2022

Courtesy of the artist and Fondazione In Between Art Film

Unalienated Labor
Taylor Renee Aldridge

Tin mining began as early as 900 CE in the Bauchi Plateau of central Nigeria (now known as the Jos Plateau). Utilized by natives for many centuries, the resource became more ubiquitous during the colonial period as Sir William Wallace, of the National African Company, took notice of Nigerians' collection and use of tin material. As many colonialists did during this period of occupation, violence, and misuse of land, tin became industrialized by the British who had invaded Nigeria. By 1909, a company by the name of Tin Fields in northern Nigeria began explicitly exploiting the Bauchi Plateau for the sole purpose of collecting and distributing the material. Other companies followed, producing thousands of tons of tin by 1937, at a value of over £2.5 million.

The history of the Jos Plateau is mostly rural, consisting of the Berom people who were known for hunting, both for use and recreation. Tin mining was one of the major resource-gathering activities pervasive among the people of this region. One early paper on tin mining history in this central Nigerian rural landscape notes a spiritual lore that revolves around the metal resource and its abundance. It declared that tin ore can reproduce itself, and that tin mines were formed through the alchemy of shamans and metaphysics.[1]

It is through this mining and celestial lineage that we can locate the film work of interdisciplinary artist Karimah Ashadu, entitled *Plateau* (2021). In the film, the artist has engaged several tin mining workers in contemporary Jos Plateau, to explore labor as a practice of independence and self-determination. Through a series of vignettes, Ashadu documents multiple testimonies shared by the all-male cast of tin miners. The filmmaker creates a record of the multi-century resource of tin and its impact on people's ability to access both capital and autonomy.

After the cessation of the International Tin Miners Agreement in 1985, the residual tin mining corporations abandoned the region as the market collapsed and economic precarity ensued. The absence left gaping holes in the landscape, but also an opportunity for the self-employed tin mining community of Berom to mine the product. However, instead of employing great bulldozers, often used

1 Sir Godfrey Fell, "Tin Mining Industry in Nigeria," *Journal of the Royal African Society* 38, no. 151 (April 1939): 246–58.

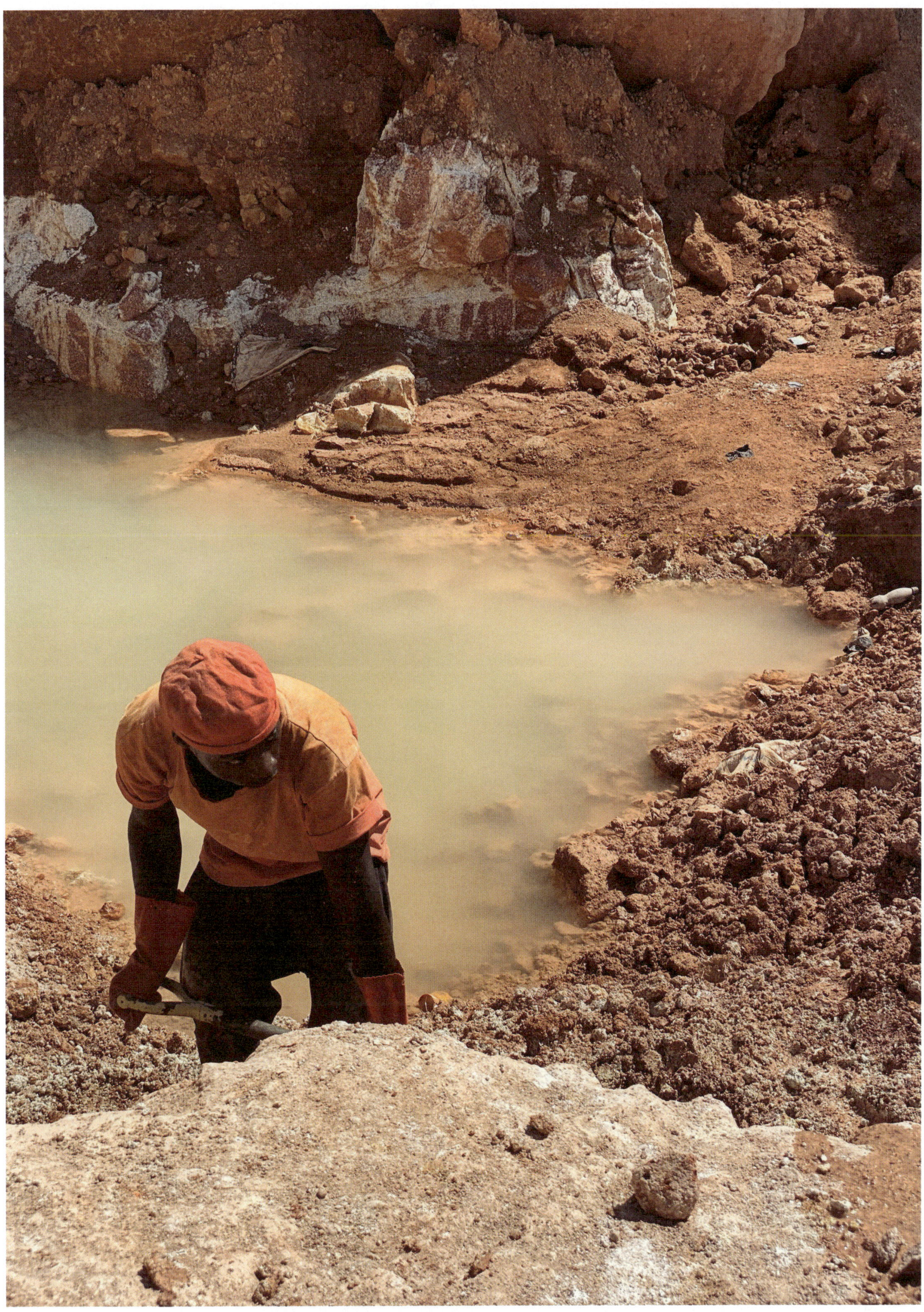

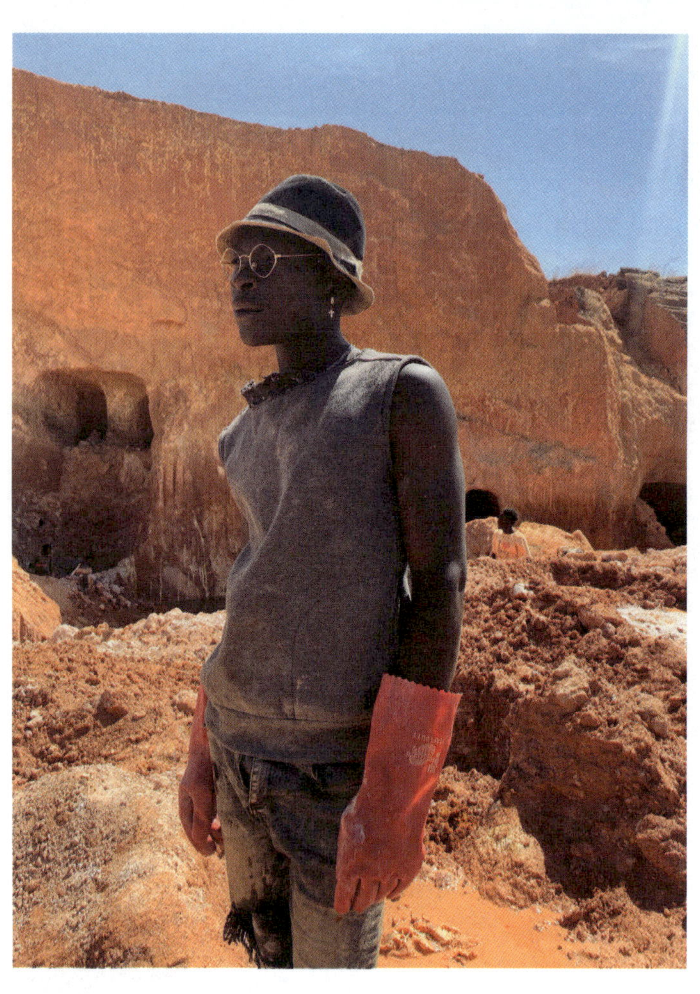

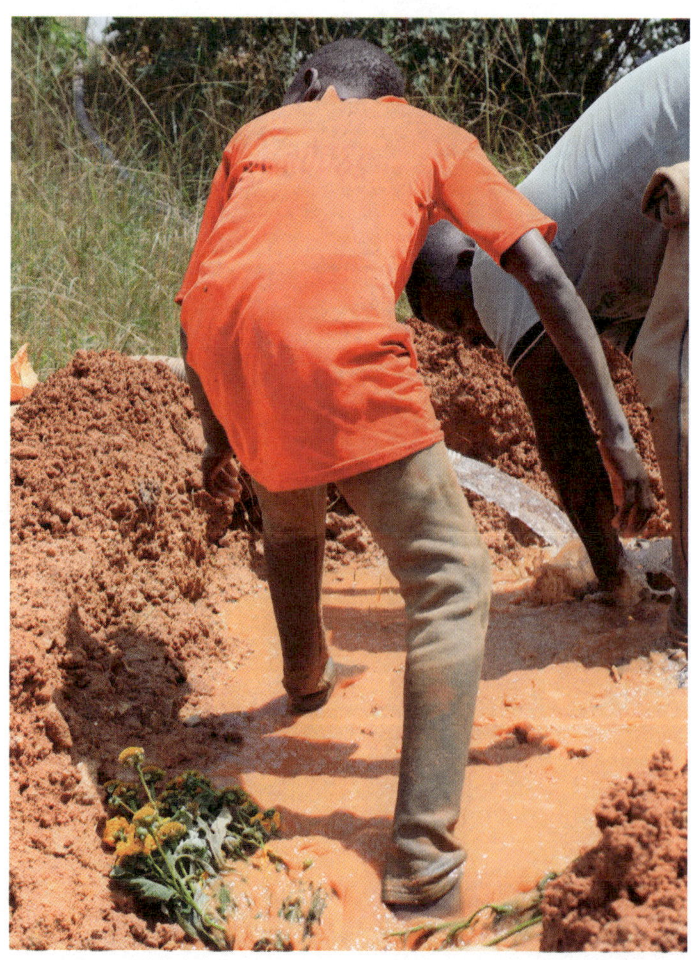

by the corporate tin mining companies throughout the height of its excavation, these small communities of tin workers scour the brown, muddy surface for tin with their own bodies; their handheld tools and prowess often inherited by their familial predecessors.

In her twenty-seven-minute film, we learn that these entrepreneurial miners are often under threat of potential landslides, at the mercy of tin buyers who insist on setting their own prices, and open to conflict with other rival miner groups. Despite the risks that are guaranteed, the miners acknowledge these potential challenges while also romanticizing the freedom that the work provides under the absence of massive, industrialized economies run by foreign individuals. In this mundane work of tin excavation, miners sift out the metal material to sell on their own. The workers operate as an industry in and of themselves. Their labor is not alienated or estranged. The value they produce through their own labor efforts are solely theirs and does not belong to the faceless leader of a corporatized entity.

Images of tall and robust bunches of cacti appear throughout the film. The appearance of this resilient plant embodies the possibility of thriving in extreme conditions. In *Plateau*, Ashadu captures the severe work that these laborers commit to, in what appears to be excruciating heat. Tin mining requires a tremendous amount of movement, and is a corporeal commitment that is risky, which Ashadu's work explicitly conveys. In the film, miners wade through knee-deep water, using both arms to stab away at the crust of the earth with a planting hoe, and loosening the claylike gravel under the water to sift out the desirable tin matter. The work is arduous, physically demanding, and done throughout a variety of harsh weather conditions. In the monotonous rigor of their mining work, however, there is also grace. Ashadu captures the workers in intimate portraits—the camera functions as a witness, or like the perspective of a tin miner in training, as well as a personal diary belonging to each of the men featured. Viewers are often presented with their backs, as they shovel through the earth's crust. Some scoop out small amounts of water with paint buckets. In other scenes, the camera captures the portraits of the men, their faces tightened in response to the light of the sun. Chiseled cheekbones and dark eyes are revealed. And then there are brief moments of play; a worker swims in a body of water for his own pure delight. Although extremely onerous, this profession in contemporary Jos allows for a specific kind of freedom in production, which allows workers to dictate the terms of their labor and how and when they will mine.

While the British presence in Jos has been long gone for decades, the major colonial tin mining companies from the early twentieth century are still ever present. Through decades of massive digging and deterioration, their mark is left indelibly on the land's surface. Ashadu makes clear that the land is perceived to have one sole purpose: to collect tin, and nothing else. One worker in *Plateau* declares: "The land is dug and left open, resulting in open gullies, ponds, and wells everywhere . . ." Another worker in the film names the ecological effects that the industrial mining systems have had on the land: "The land is good for nothing." To mine, the whole of the land's surface has been ruptured, excavated, and destroyed to locate the product. In this particular framing and consideration of the ecological effects of the industry, Ashadu subtly marks the material and detrimental effects of mass industrialization on the Plateau region and writ large. As we learn in the film, many of the workers have inherited mining strategies from their parents, as their parents did from *their* parents. The land is their inheritance, an opportunity to never have to surrender to supplication. And yet, *Plateau* names an irony brought on by colonial presence; contemporary workers have inherited a dying landscape to find their autonomy within.

Trained as a painter, Ashadu has transcended the genre and utilized some of the more formal techniques of painting to fabricate works in other mediums such as film, and more recently sculpture. In the traditional film genre, viewers are often placed in the role of spectator while viewing subjects and narratives for interpretation. However, throughout Ashadu's oeuvre she plays with perspective's physicality, layering points of view and making the position of the viewer elastic. Her film work could be defined as a metaphorical impasto, the heavy layering of content to produce a tactile surface. The film is something that you want to touch; it encourages haptics. For instance, in *King of Boys (Abattoir of Makoko)* (2015), the artist placed her camera within a pellucid red beer keg to establish the film's point of view through a commodity. In another work, *Lagos Sand Merchants* (2013), the artist attached a camera to a drum-like device to create a revolving and disorienting effect. Ashadu's *Plateau* continues in this effort of placing the viewer within the specialty of its subjects, as opposed to sole observation of them.

Plateau could be seen as part of a lineage of documentary photography and moving images that aims to render the interior lives of laborers and the contradictions they experience. Particularly, we might consider the work of Allan Sekula who is renowned for his film essays on globalization and labor conditions, such as *Performance Under Working Conditions* (1973) and more recently *The Forgotten Space* (2010). Ashadu's *Plateau*, however, can be seen

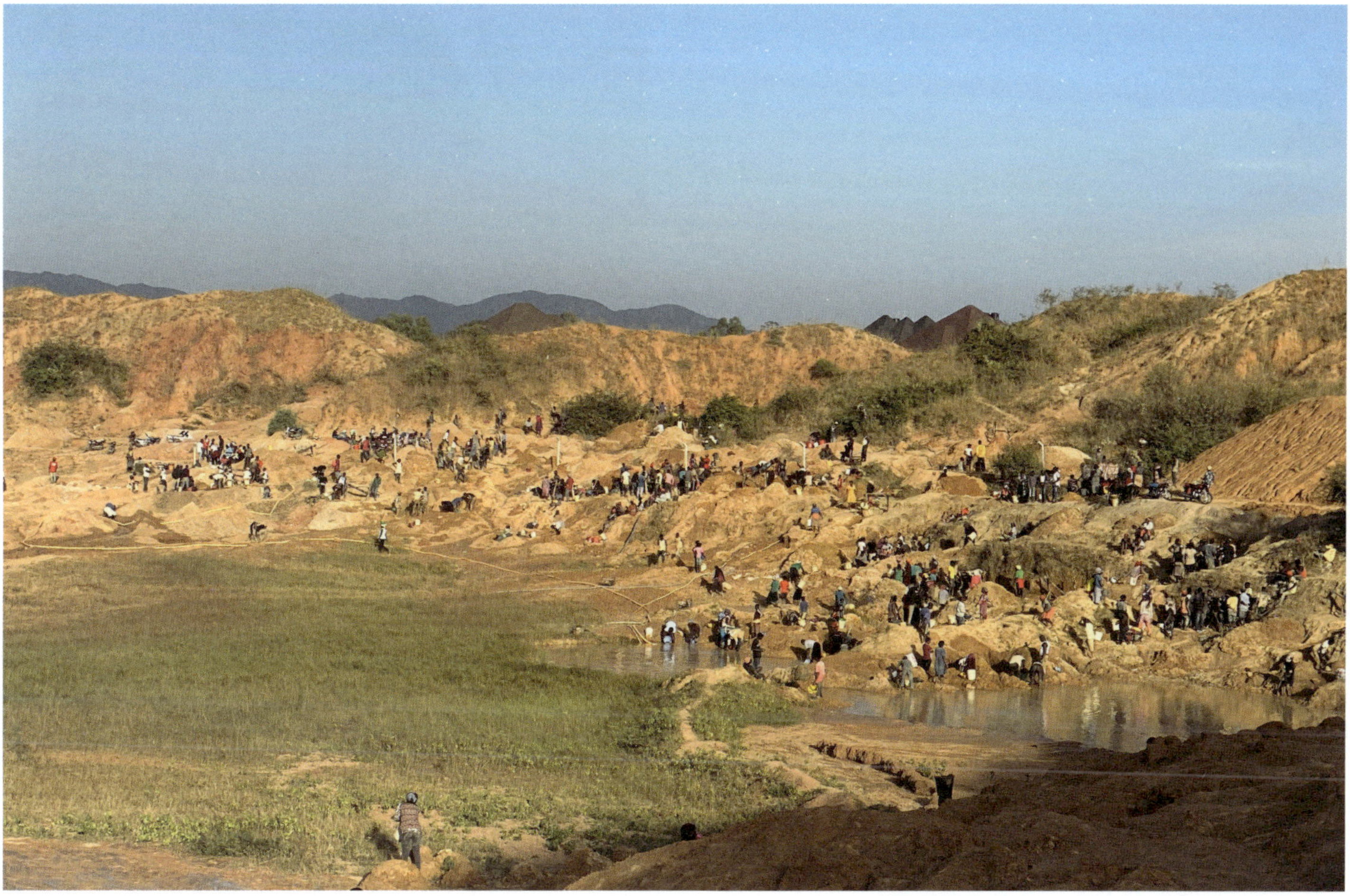

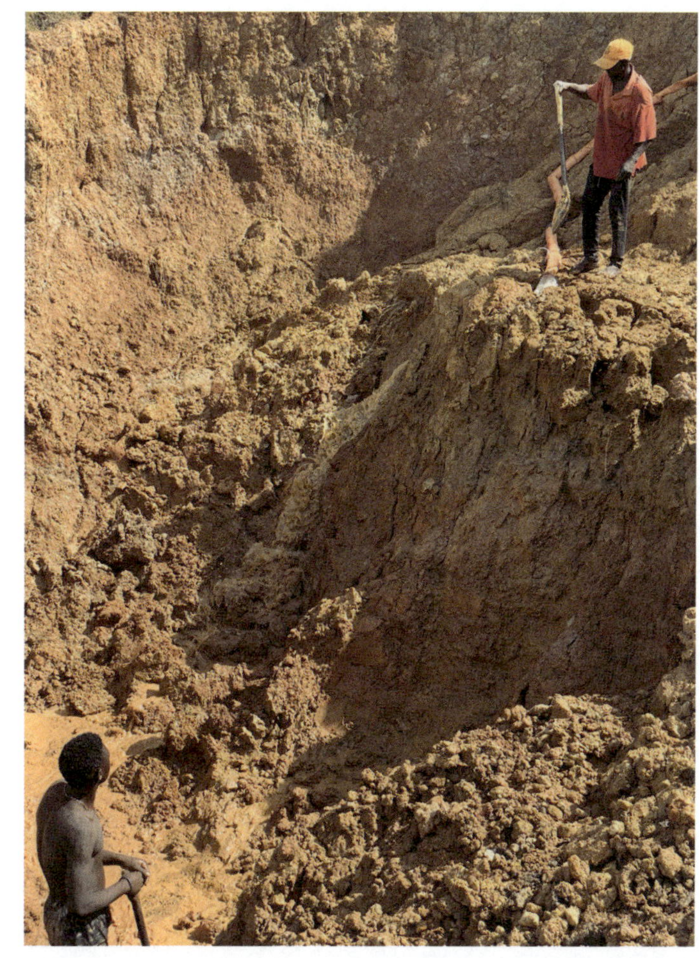

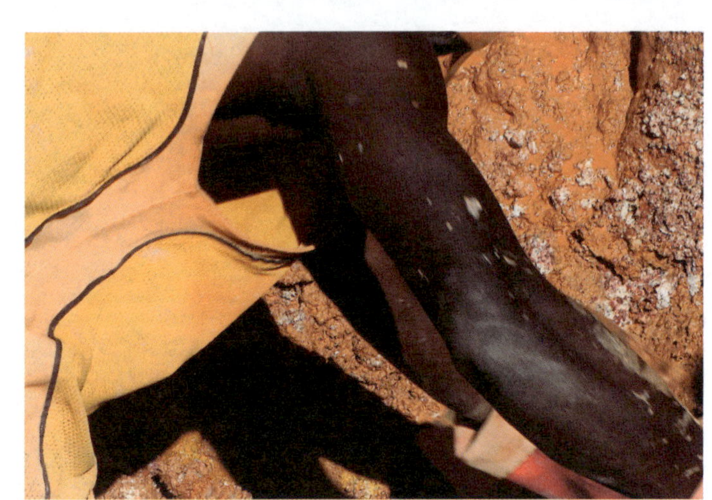

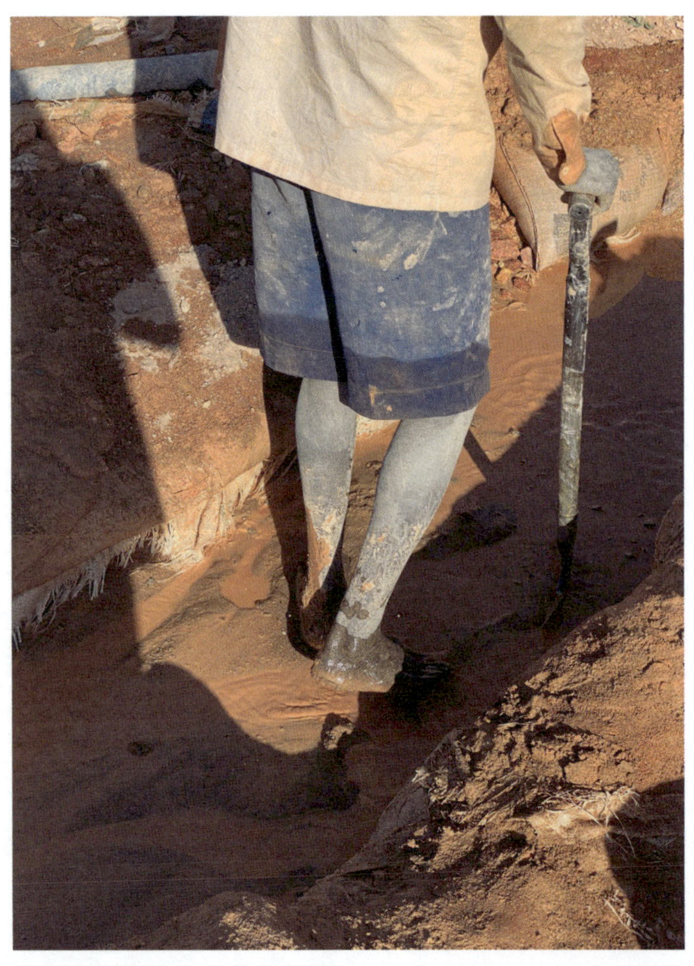

as tangential to traditional documentary films on labor. The work presents no distinct point of view from the maker. There is no narration, no additional text that encourages us to consider a critical analysis in tandem with the workers' testimonies. Viewers are given no context other than what the workers provide through an audio diary. Instead, as viewers, we are encouraged to arrive at our own conclusions with their testimonies.

One of the narrative threads that appears to rise to the surface more acutely is a correlation made between the lineage of Nigerian independence from British colonial rule and the liberation of the work of Jos Plateau native miners from British colonial industrialists. Toward the end of the film, a miner recalls that his own elders worked alongside colonialists to mine tin. His parents and grandparents were paid at the end of every week for their work; compensated only enough to pay for food. That testimony is followed by a contemporary elder figure, a Nigerian man who has been able to purchase land in Jos where he allows younger workers to mine tin. In the two-channel presentation, the man stands on a hill, looking down at the camera. He has persevered, and is the product of an accessible upward mobility and independence that so many of the contemporary tin miners work toward. At this moment, viewers are able to consider that colonizers not only excavated physical matter from the Nigerian landscape, but also the possibility of labor autonomy for multiple generations throughout the twentieth century. The presence of tin in this region of central Nigeria not only symbolizes the possibility of capital for its natives, but also emboldens past, present, and future complications with posterity for Indigenous Jos miners.

Despite the failure of legislation in 1946 that was meant to repatriate land to and benefit the Indigenous people of the Jos Plateau, contemporary tin miners utilize their own self-determination, and resources outside of the confines and failures of state and federal legislation, to manifest their own destiny to capital and work. The presence of mass industrialization and hyper-capitalism has routinely alienated workers from the value of their labor, perpetually benefiting the leaders of the corporations they work for. However, in Jos, and through Ashadu's tender portrayal of contemporary tin miners, we are able to reimagine the joys and possibilities of autodidactic labor. Work leveraged into capital that ultimately aims to reciprocate resources back into the community it is extracted from. *Plateau* is a postindustrial narrative, imbued with speculative musings for how we might engage with work on the precipice of industrial capital collapse and climate change.

Images from the backstage of *Plateau* by Karimah Ashadu. Courtesy of the artist.

ANA VAZ

É NOITE NA AMÉRICA

2021, three-channel video, 16mm transferred to HD, color, sound, 44'

00:17

00:44

"A young anteater found dead by the side of a road, a maned wolf is found in a farm in Sobradinho II, a small owl is rescued in the Radio Center district, a capybara swims in the water mirror of the Itamaraty Palace. The question is: are animals invading our cities, or rather are we occupying their habitat?"

09:44

11:08

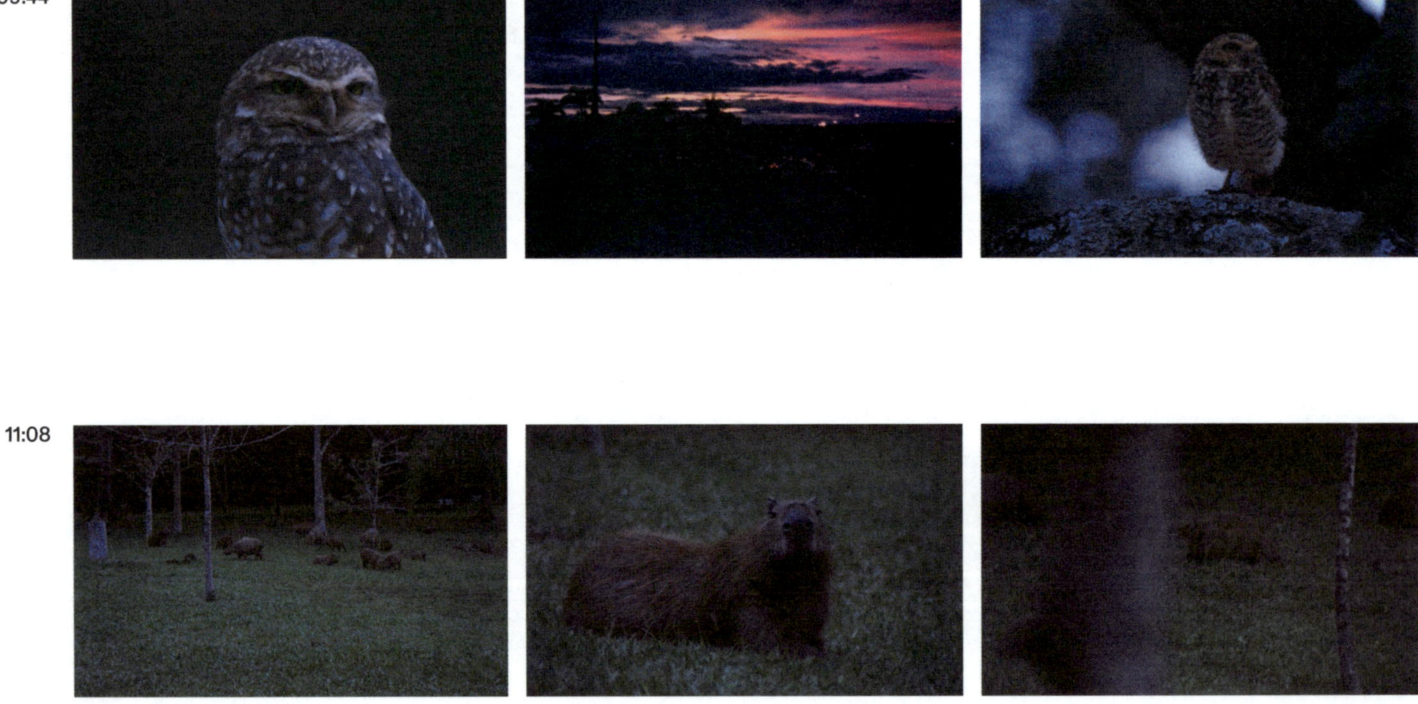

12:03

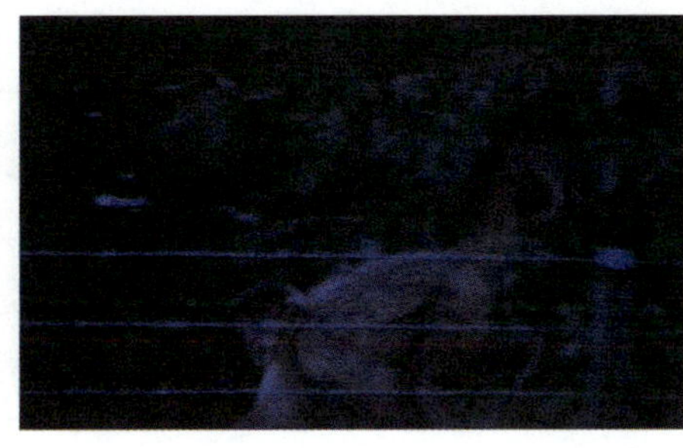
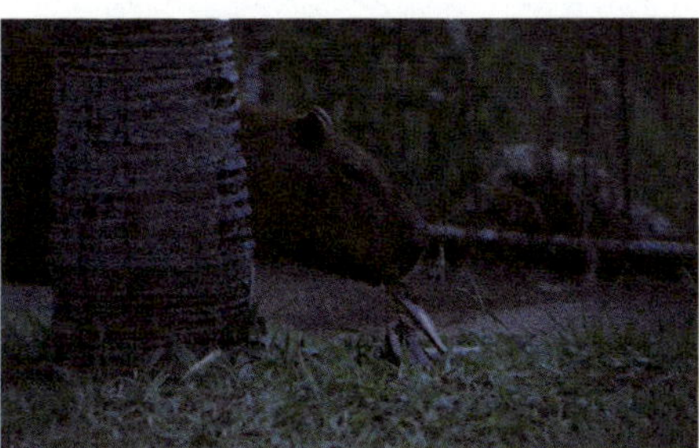
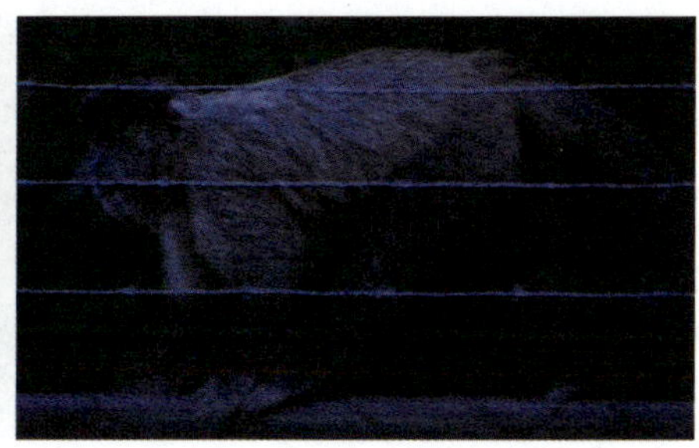

12:46

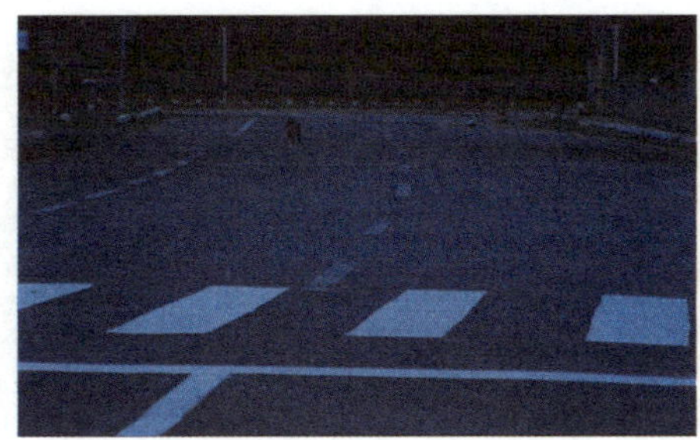
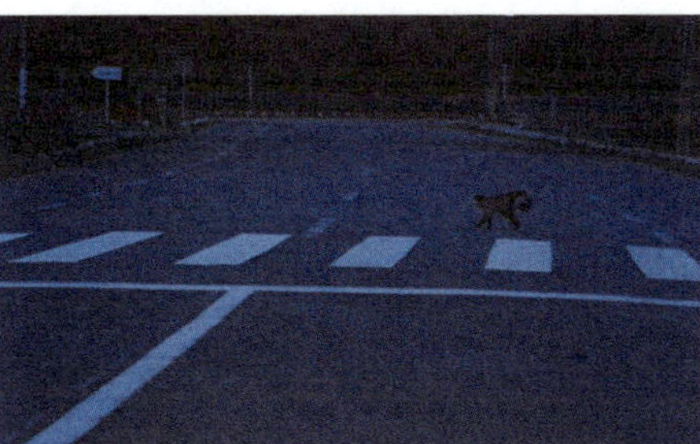
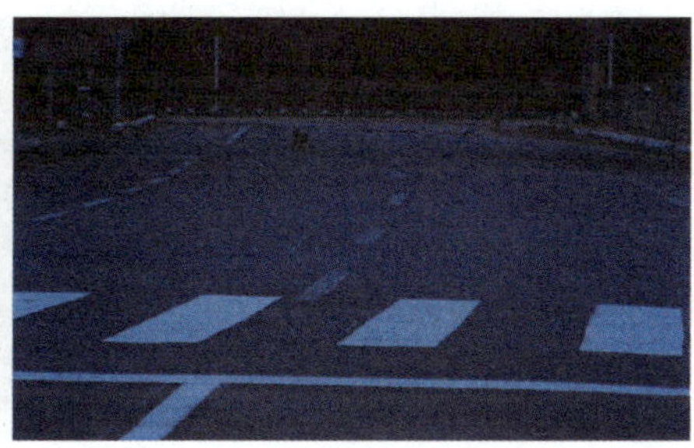

(*Correio Braziliense*, February, 2021). On the wings of Brazil's aeroplane-shaped capital city—a necropolis transformed into an oasis by architects—thousands of trapped lives seek refuge in its gardens. *É Noite en América* [It is Night in America] was filmed at Brasília Zoo, habitat of hundreds of rescued species fleeing

14:24

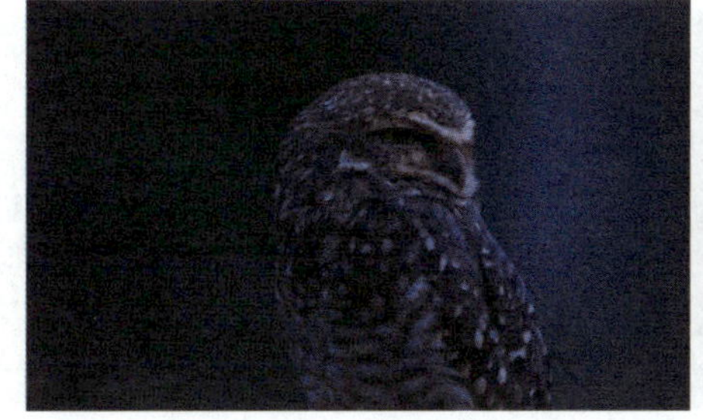
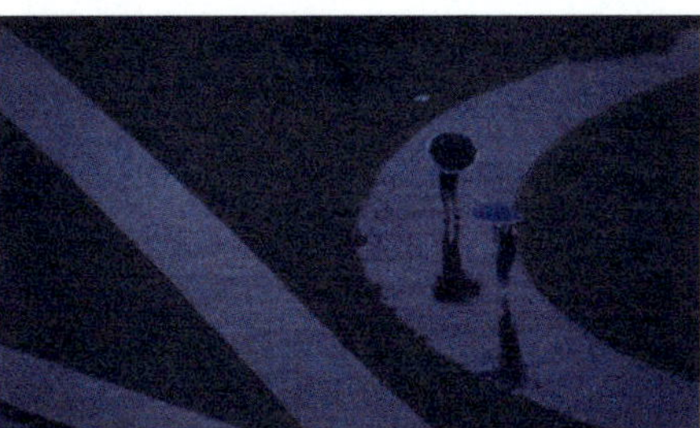
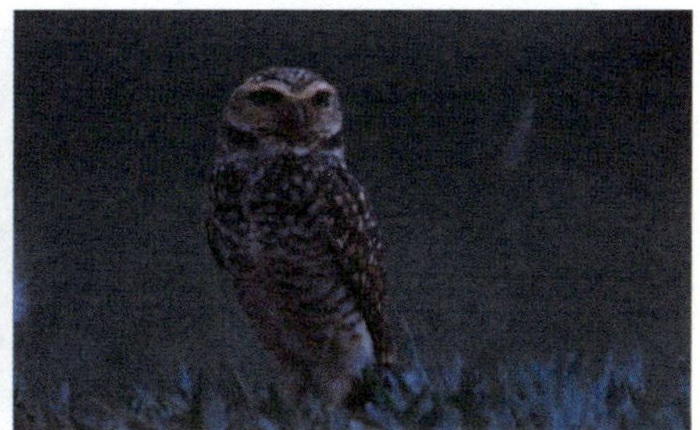

16:05

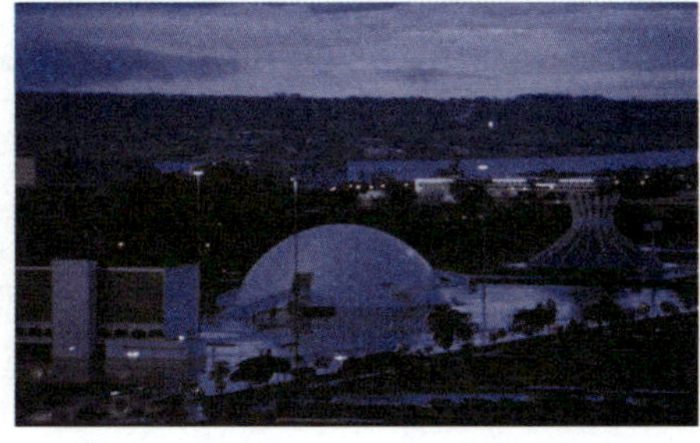
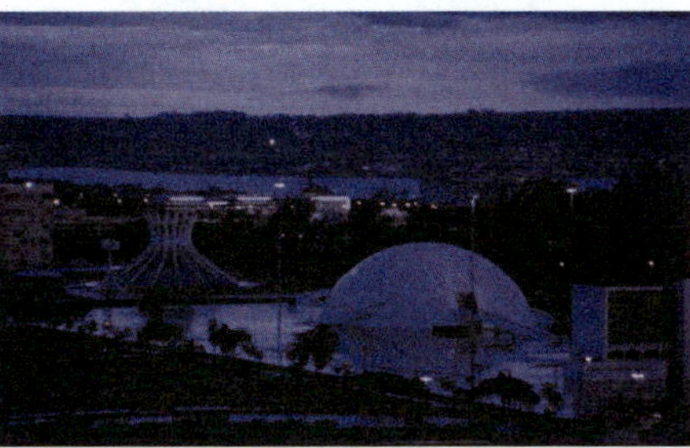
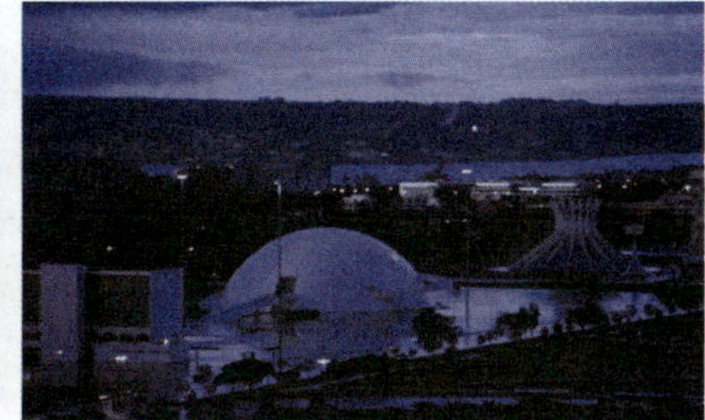

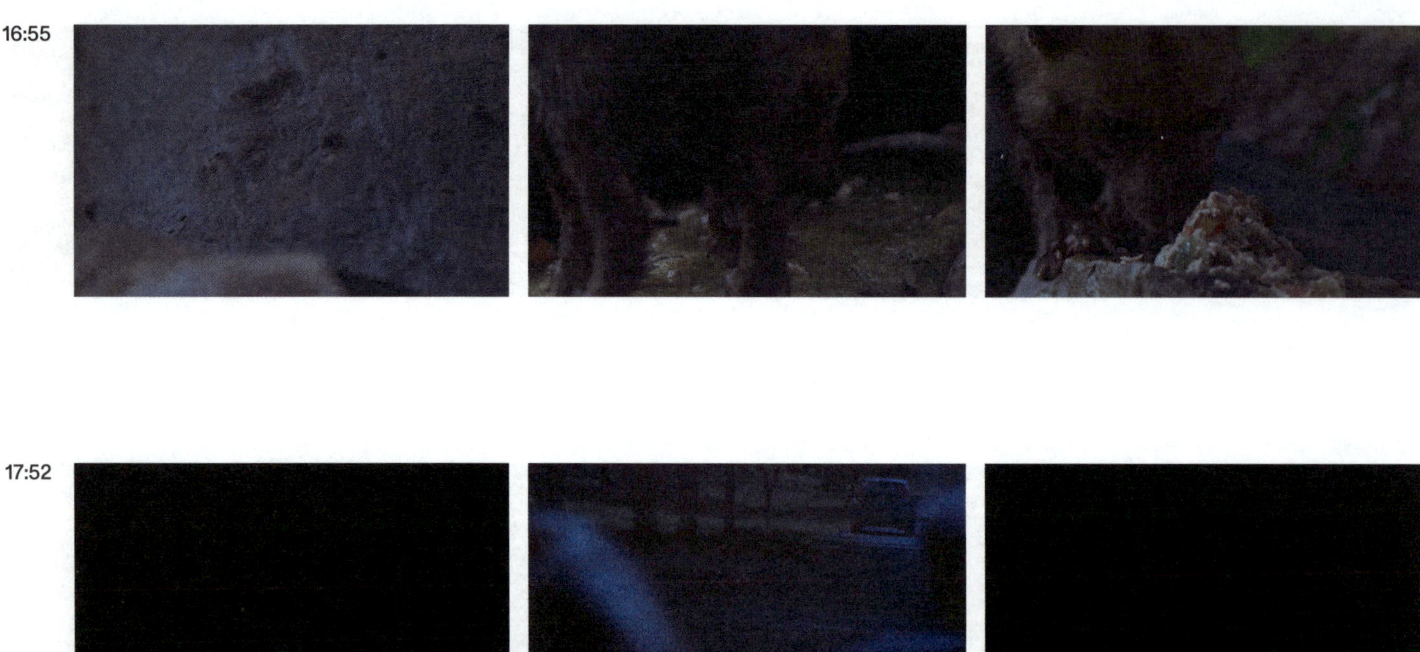

the violence of agribusiness, urbanization and the pollution of the Brazilian cerrado. As a nocturnal feast filmed on expired 16mm—a material also in danger of extinction—, this immersive installation casts an animalistic spell with shades of eco-horror, wildlife fictions, and documentary, subverting the limits of

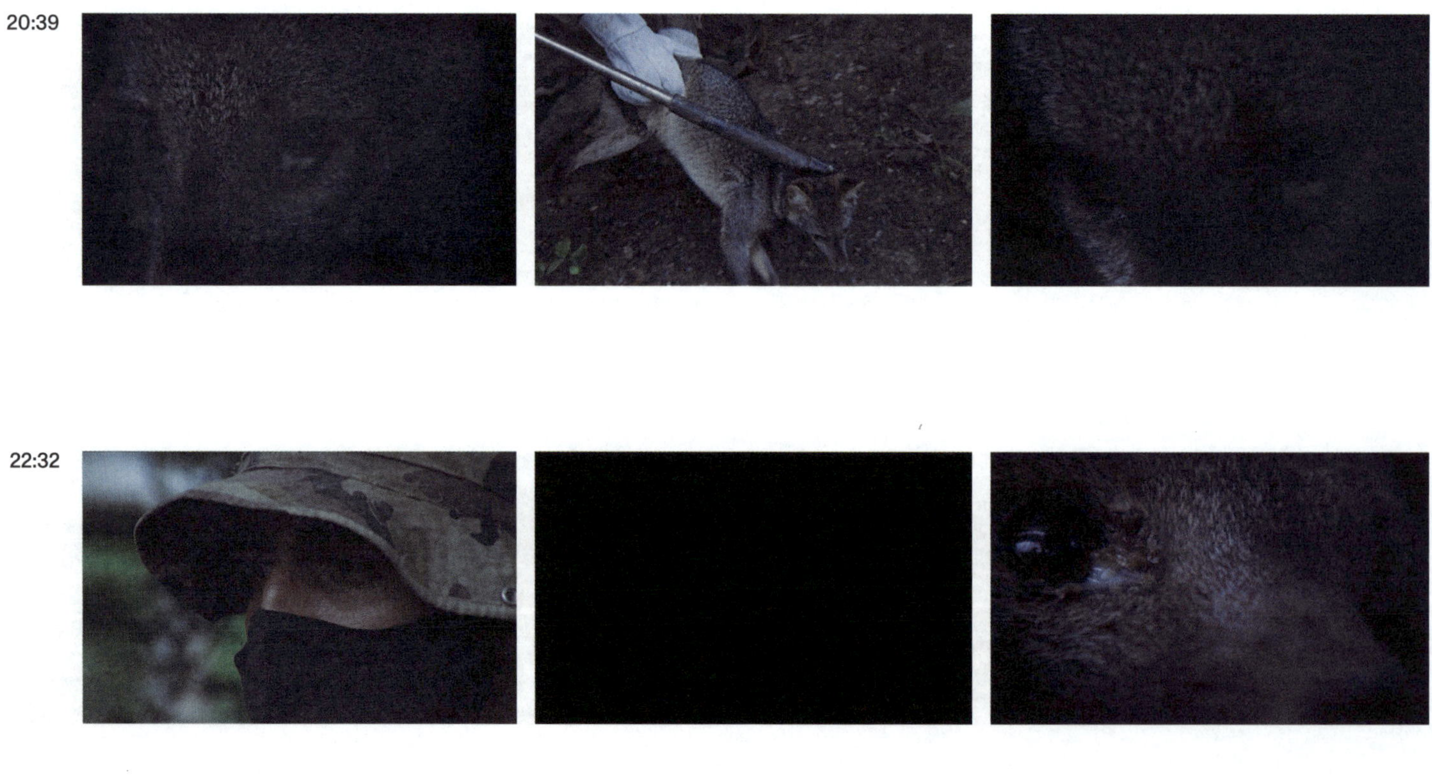

25:03

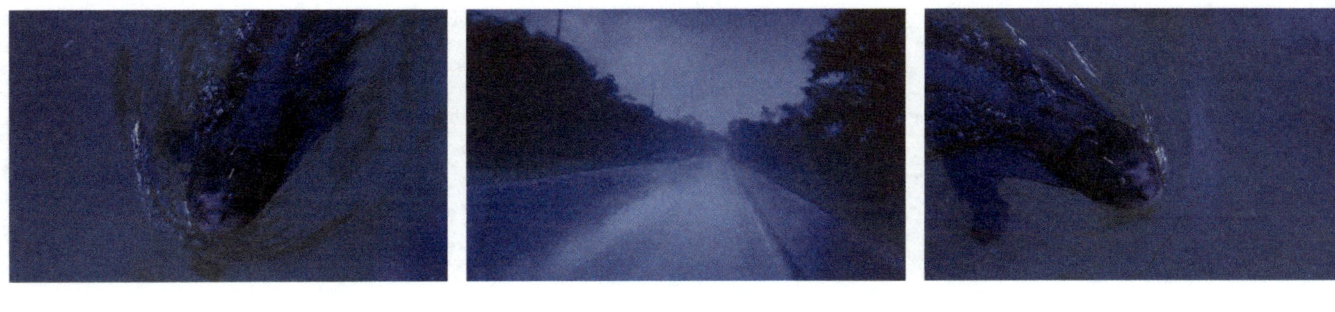

26:26

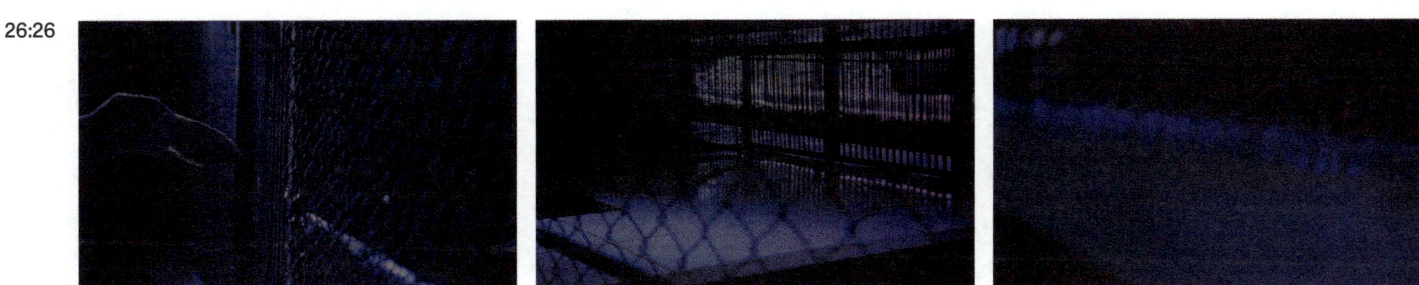

cinematic genres. Giant anteaters, otters, maned wolves, owls, and capybaras meet with veterinarians, caretakers, and the environmental police in a sombre plot where the challenges of preserving life weave a web of intersecting perspectives. In the end, who are the real captives?

27:30

28:32

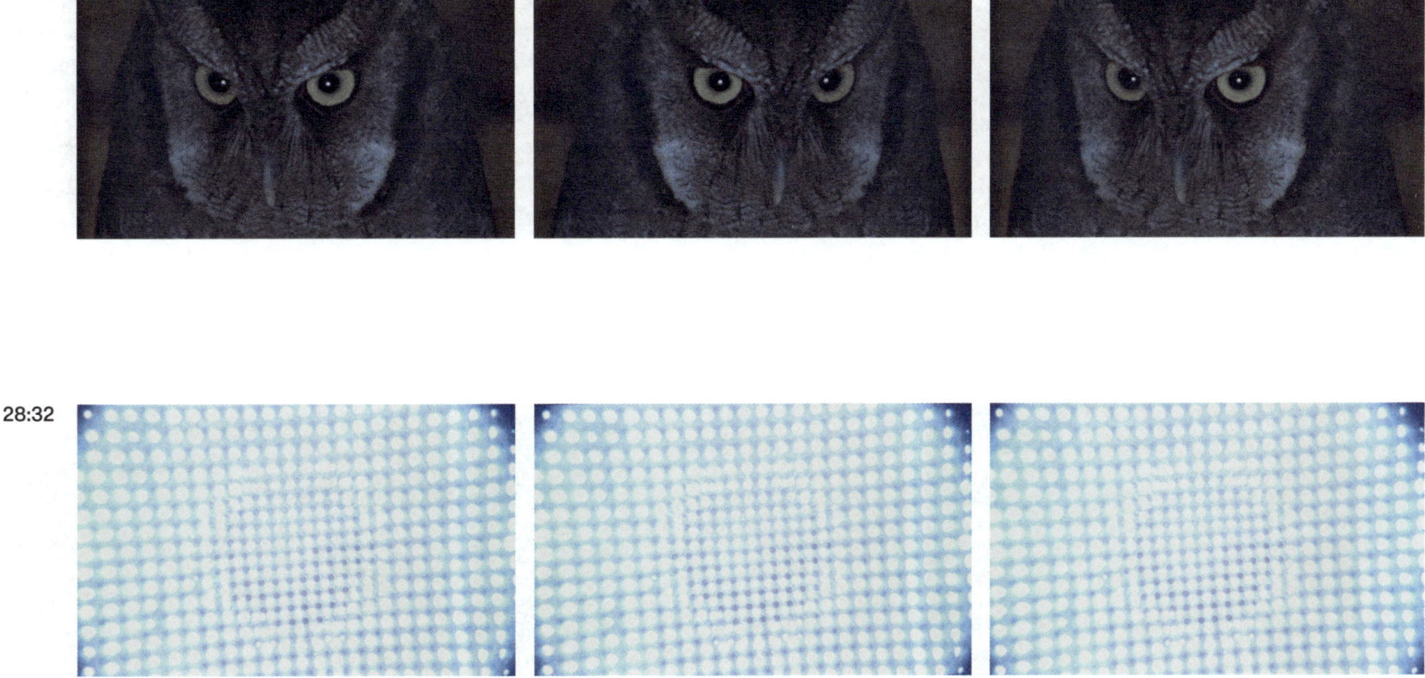

31:32

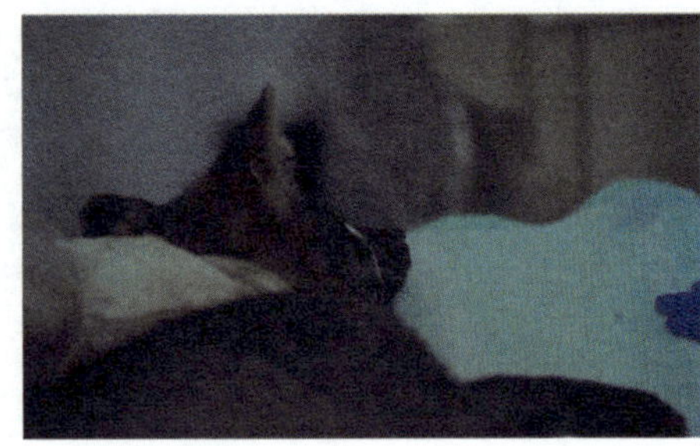
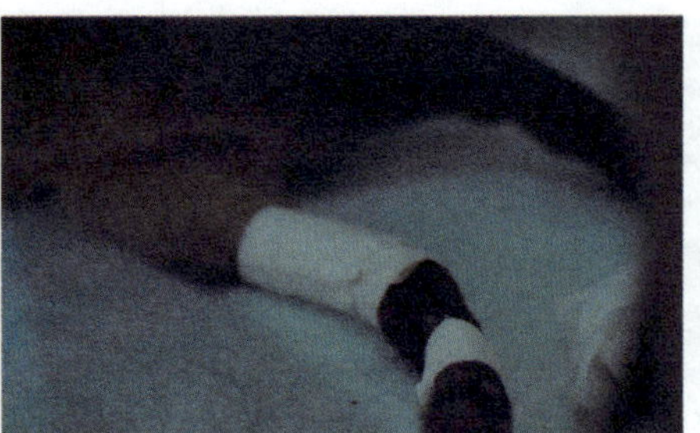
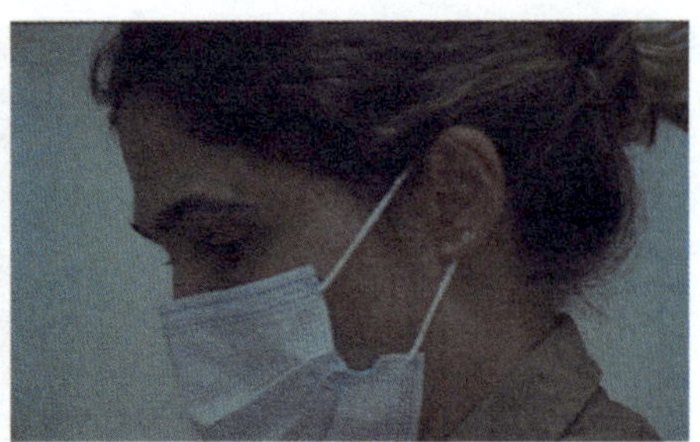

33:38

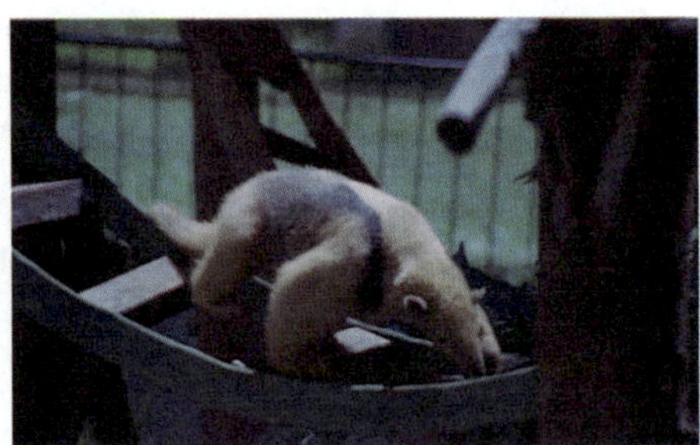
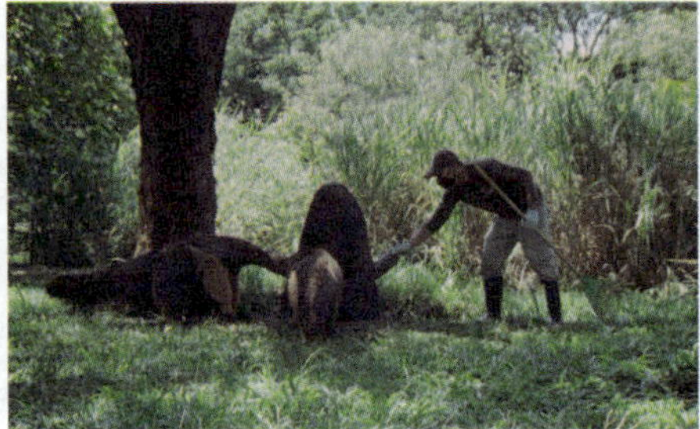
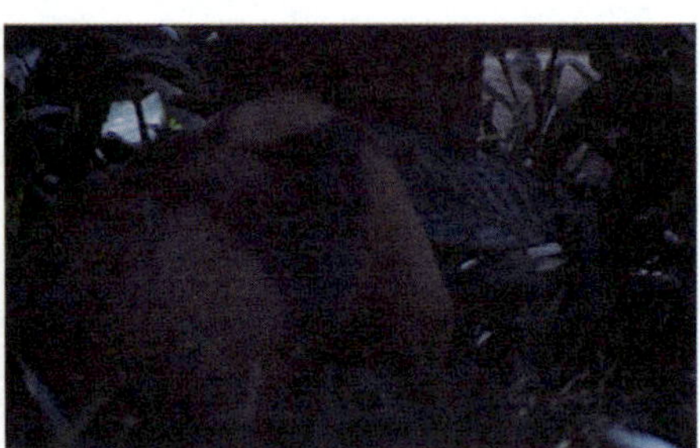

36:07

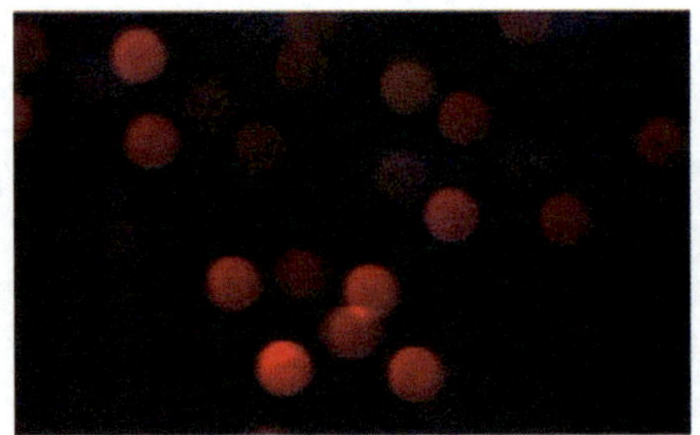
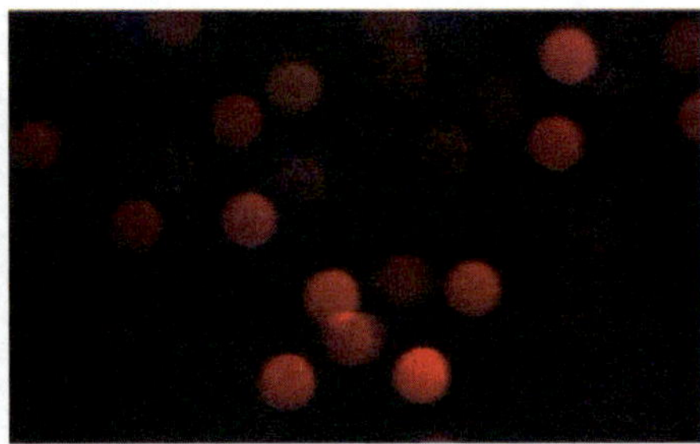
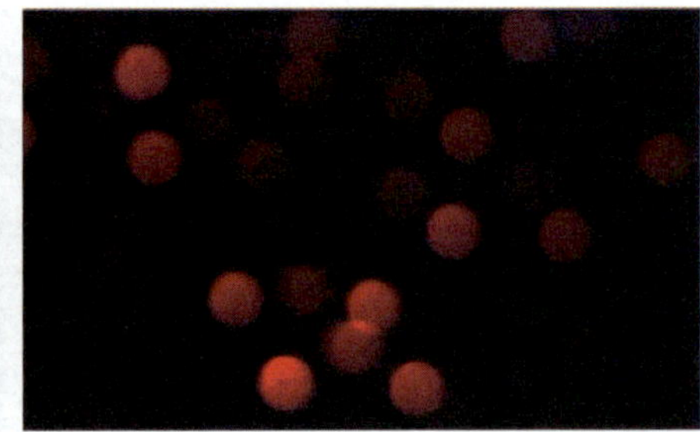

40:38

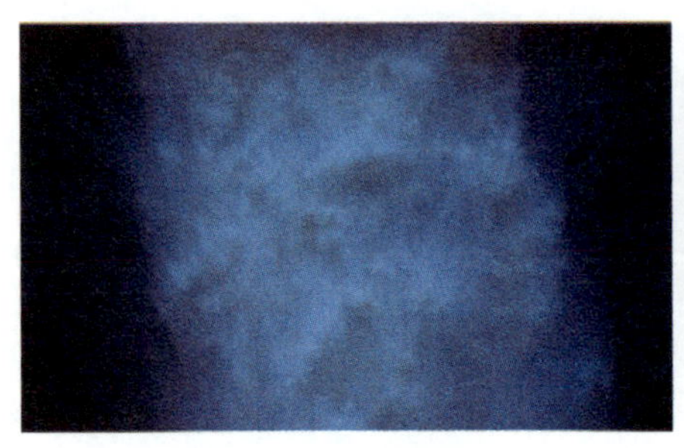
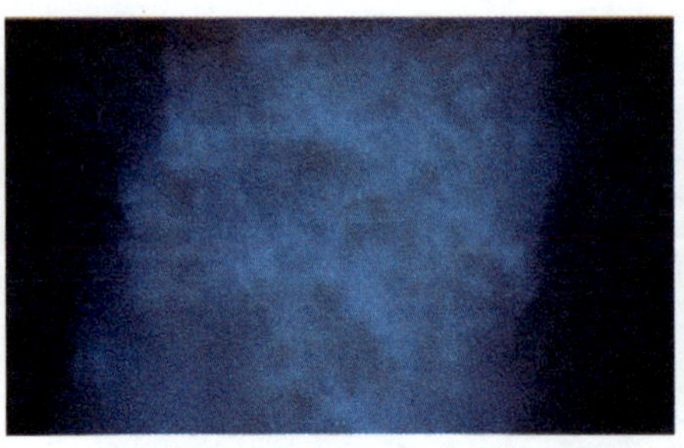
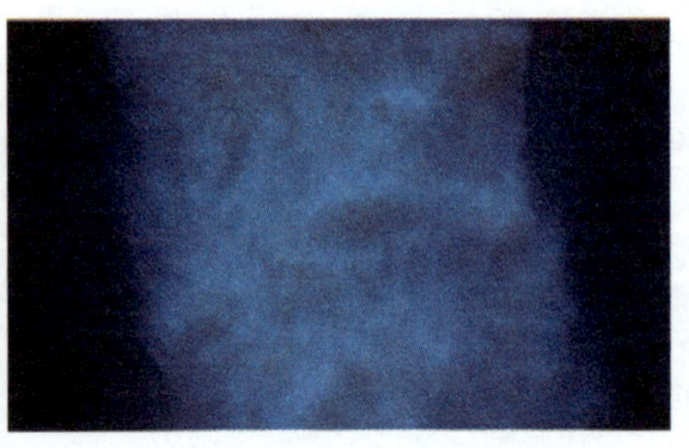

Ana Vaz, *É Noite na América*, 2021

Three-channel video, 16mm transferred to HD, color, sound, 44'

With
Macau (Ptenoura brasiliensis), Amanda and Jair (Chrysocyon brachyurus), Xingu (Speothos venaticus), Caramelo (Tamadua tetradactyla), Quim (Cerdocyon thous), Megascops choliba, Athene cunicularia, Betânia Borges (Homo sapiens sapiens), Legolas and Ploft (Myrmecophaga tridactyla), Isabela Abritta (Homo sapiens sapiens), Macacos Bugius (Alouatta seniculus), inhabitants of the Brasília zoo since their rescue during the construction of the Belo Monte dam, Pará

Narration in Gualin
William Dimpa

Support at Brasília zoo
Igor Morais, Thiago Zuryp

Directed by
Ana Vaz

Cinematography
Jacques Cheuiche, ABC

Camera Operator
Ana Vaz

Sound
Chico Bororo

Field recordings
Nuno Da Luz

Music
Guilherme Vaz

Editing
Ana Vaz, Deborah Viegas

Sound editing
Ana Vaz, Nuno Da Luz, Erwan Kerzanet

Color
João Nunes

Sound mixing
Olivier Guillaume

Camera Assistant
Bacco de Andrade

Line Producer Brasília
Carolina Wotjila

Grip
William Dimpa

Driver
Gilberto Fernandes Menezes

Translation
Catarina Boieiro, Miguel Cardoso, Tristan Bera

Translation Gualin
Olivier Marboeuf, Claire Finch

Freely inspired from
A Cosmopolítica dos Animais by Juliana Fausto

Photographic archive
Jardim Zoológico de Brasília

Photographs
Joaquim Firmino, Luiz Lemos, Brito

Music
Panthera Onca from the album "O ANJO SOBRE O VERDE" (2001) composed by Guilherme Vaz. Trombone played by Paulo Silva; tuba played by Alisson; percussion played by José Roberto Gaivão. IPSA SONANT ARBUSTA

With thanks to:
Poliana Pieratti, Clara Terra, Clémence Seurat, Tristan Bera, Coyote, Gabinete C, Brian Sewell, Eduardo Guimarães, Sônia Wiedemann, Catarina Boieiro, Lisa Merleau, Jorge Veras, José Saraiva, Olivier Marboeuf, Fernanda Brenner, Juliana Fausto, Deborah Viegas, Bacco de Andrade, Laís Cheuiche, Jacques Cheuiche, Lineu Palaia, Maíra Gadelha, Wilma Pereira, Nuno Da Luz, Guilherme Vaz, Cláudia Pereira, Aki

Polícia Ambiental DF
Major Maidana, Major Roseneide Tenente Ramalho

Zoológico de Brasília
Igor Morais Thiago Zuryp, Isabela Abritta, Betânia Borges

Fondazione In Between Art Film
Beatrice Bulgari, Alessandro Rabottini, Bianca Stoppani, Alessia Carlino, Paola Ugolini

Commissioned and produced by
Fondazione In Between Art Film

Creative Producer
Leonardo Bigazzi

With the support of
Pivô, Fernanda Brenner (Artistic Director)

Production São Paulo
Carolina Câmera, Equipe Pivô

Co-production
Spectre Productions, Ana Vaz

With the support of
Centre National des Arts Plastiques

With additional support of
Jeu de Paume, Paris

Technical support
Fabrika Filmes

Filmed in
Brasília, DF and Salto de Itiquira, Goiás

Flmed on 16mm film
Kodak 50D (2011), Kodak 100T (1999-2007), Kodak 200T (2001-2007), Kodak 250D (1999-2007), Kodak 500T (2004-2005), Kodak 640T (1996), Fuji 125T (1999), Fuji 64D (2003-2009), Fuji 250T (n.d.), Fuji 400T (n.d.)

Courtesy the artist and Fondazione In Between Art Film

Midnight in the Open-Air Prison
Filipa Ramos

"When I died, one day I opened my eyes and there was Brasília. I found myself alone in the world [. . .] I waited for the night, like someone waiting for shadows in order to steal away unobserved. When the night came, I perceived with horror that it was hopeless: wherever I went, I would be seen [. . .] A prison in the open-air. In any case, there would be nowhere to escape to. For anyone escaping would probably head to Brasília."[1] —Clarice Lispector

Heading to Brasília, Ana Vaz's *É Noite na América* [It Is Night in America] (2021), started off ten years ago with a sunrise.

The artist captured this moment in real time, filming that magical transformation of shadows into form that happens anew every morning but always feels like a mystery. She left the footage unedited, clean, evolving from the appearance of the first ray of light until the fat, round star was suspended high above the horizon. She presented viewers with the unmediated experience of the sun gradually covering the land below with its veil of warmth and color, a rare event for those who live too distant and too disconnected from the places and times where the uninterrupted transition from dawn to day can best be seen.

Vaz's sunrise evolved into a scorching savanna day in which green landscapes performed a bygone rainfall, and arid geologies a long process of anthropogenic transformation of land into stone and stone into human things. With radical changes of scale, she portrayed tiny insects and large quarries with the same attention, care, and precision, while her unique sensibility to sound flanked tropical birdsongs and mechanical noises as complementary creatures who inhabit these lands of rocks and clouds.

Interrupting that brown and green horizon of dust and foliage, a strange bone-like structure defied the film's relationship to truth, imposing itself like an impossible form that was being built out of nowhere and for no one.

1 *Quando morri, um dia abri os olhos e era Brasília. Eu estava sozinha no mundo* [...] *Esperei pela noite, como quem espera pelas sombras para poder se esgueirar. Quando a noite veio, percebi com horror que era inútil: onde eu estivesse, eu seria vista* [...] *Uma prisão ao ar livre. De qualquer modo, não haveria para onde fugir. Pois quem foge iria provavelmente para Brasília.* From Clarice Lispector, *A descoberta do mundo* (Rio de Janeiro: Rocco, 1999), 292–95. Originally published in *Jornal do Brasil*, June 20, 1970. Unless otherwise noted, the original texts are rendered in English by the author.

This presence shifted the film's angle, tone, and direction, posing questions of veracity, sense, and purpose that concerned both punctum and picture. What began with a sunrise ended with the edification of a wreck, echoing the lyrics of singer Caetano Veloso's famous song "Fora da Ordem" [Out of Order], "Here everything still seems under construction and is already ruin."[2] Vaz's *It Is Night in America* also started off ten years ago with a ruin.

The abovementioned site where the initial sunrise and ruin of *It Is Night in America* appeared was called *A idade da Pedra* [The Age of Stone] (2013), a twenty-nine-minute, single-channel film shot in the far west of Brazil. It is a work in which Vaz explores, among other things, how the interdependency of expansion and decay, life and death, history and fiction, nature and culture defines her hometown of Brasília and its surrounding territories. Brasília, the federal capital of Brazil, the "airplane-city" as Vaz calls it, is a place she keeps returning to, equipped with a camera and many questions. When she is there, she visits kin of blood and affect—some of them growing, as *The Age of Stone* actress Ivonete dos Santos Moraes; some ageing, as Vaz's beloved grandmother; and some manifesting themselves for the first time, even when dead. Such is the case of the tamandua she saw on the road, "a dead body in the middle of the pavement," as she describes in the film, who "ran over her" when she least expected it. This encounter prompted an ethical dilemma: "How to watch over this dead body?" she wonders in her mourning, "the body of the cub strayed away from a grieving mother." Endowed with the pain and sadness she inherited from this event, Vaz sets off to meet those creatures who traverse the fringes of the city: animals looking for the food and land that was taken away from them, searching for their pathways and migratory routes and weakened from the poisons of humanity's debris.

The first night of her quest starts with a panorama across a tall, dry city. A barcode of a city, whose limits were set by a dark mountain that imposed a wall of darkness and shadows. Like the margins of a giant crater, these gloomy mountains prevented the city from further expanding, placating its dreams of growth and multiplication, of transformation of soil into concrete and of sound into noise. The buildings this city is made of host no visible life within them. The wind cries, howls, and despairs, carrying with itself haunting oaths that curse this place of concrete and wire. In this first night, everything spins in blue. Toxic blue. Poisonous blue. Cobalt blue.

2 *Aqui tudo parece que é ainda construção e já é ruína*. Caetano Veloso, "Fora da Ordem," 1991.

The second night of her quest evolved like on a road trip at dawn. Or was it dusk? You can't tell. But it doesn't matter because you also don't know where you are or where you are heading. Is this city the same as the one before? Here there are no buildings or houses, only traffic lights and small fires lighting up in dark, abstract roads. Endless asphalt snakes that zigzag above any geography—they are gravitational forces that attract to burn, obfuscate, and obliterate.

In this journey, Vaz also ends up following those who follow the ones astray, the Federal District's Environmental Military Police, responsible for the rescue and detention of wild animals in peril. Such militarization of conservation is not uncommon. In Kenya, the white rhino Sudan was permanently surrounded by transmitters, watchtowers, fences, drones, guard dogs, and trained armed guards. Images of the lonely animal being escorted, fed, and caressed by his guards were widely circulated, revealing his abyssal loneliness. But Sudan wasn't only alone, he was also a token of his own finitude.

In *It Is Night in America*, Vaz observes Brasília's management of the presence of wildlife in its territory. The city, which Ukrainian-Brazilian writer Clarice Lispector called "an open-air prison," offers a paradigmatic example of biopower in action, as the same forces that originally transformed, dispossessed, and oppressed wilderness are now stepping in to further marginalize, ostracize, and criminalize it through legitimized practices of control and discipline. Vaz reveals this by showing how, once captured, the wild animals that enter and traverse Brasília's urban perimeter end up in that prison that some call the Zoological Garden. With some back-and-forth moments, the three-channel film installation gradually moves from images of the city's constructions, roads, and highways to the space of the zoo. A particularly telling scene documents a group of capuchin monkeys agilely running and jumping across a wall with a barbed wire fence. It is impossible to tell whether the monkeys are in or out of the zoo. Most likely they are in and out of it. But regardless of where they have chosen or have been forced to live, the ways in which their daily life has been materially conditioned by these violent, obstructing devices are made obvious. Concepts such as those of domesticity and wilderness are redundant here. The artist ignores these distinctions to instead focus on the complexity of animal life and its forms of adaptation, at once impressive and tragic.

Dogs bark. Owls scan the horizon with their periscopic gaze, entangling a tribute to that major owl lover, filmmaker Chris Marker, with Vaz's own signature panning techniques. A sick crab-eating fox is captured with wires and cages.

Visibly unwell, we later learn that he is suffering from canine distemper, a viral disease particularly contagious to wild animals who come in close contact with dogs and human dwellings. Freedom and vulnerability walk hand in hand, paw in paw, while healing and tameness also come together: the medical alleviation of dependency.

Indeed, once wild and unruly, these creatures whose mere existence—symbolic and concrete—challenged the civilization process of the West are now, once in the zoo, subjected to systematic forms of debilitation, repression, and censorship. They must comply with a precise apparatus of regulation, visibility, and punishment that ensures they exist within well-defined norms of occupation, circulation, and hygiene; they are exposed to a permanent scrutiny that prevents them from having intimate, unruly behaviors; they are forced not only to remain behind bars but also to be exhibited as such.

Despite their condition, they remain mesmerizing prisoners. The images of Macau, the male *ariranha* filmed by Ana, coming in and out of his swimming pool, cause both pain and pleasure, grief and excitement, contempt and attraction. The tension between the giant otter's enclosed condition and his fascinating body—dark, shiny, soft, bendable and with an incredible torpedolike shape—and face (yes, face, contrary to Emmanuel Levinas's anthropocentric reduction of the face to humankind), at once expressive and expressionless, funny and bizarre, familiar and uncanny—is difficult to resolve. This difficulty largely emanates from a conundrum: we can see this animal because he is exhibited and he is exhibited because he is detained. Vaz acknowledges such conditions by allowing the zoo's enclosures to actively enter the film. Metal bars impose themselves between the camera and the animal and between the animal and the keepers, revealing how the zoo is a site where exhibitionary, penitentiary, and authoritarian regimes coexist.

But by focusing her (and the viewers') gaze upon this giant otter in an aquarium and subsequently transposing such experience of observation onto an exhibition and cinematic space, Vaz is not merely illustrating this situation. She is also complementing and complexifying these reflections on the genealogies, legitimizations, and traditions of the dualisms between the visible and the invisible, submission and order, death and life, confinement and spectacle. By being captured inside an aquarium and re-presented through a projection, the giant otter becomes a double captive, once in the aquarium and twice in the screen. With such an operation, Vaz highlights this condition and exposes some of the characteristics of the device of captivity in which Macau finds himself. She does so by reinforcing the aquarium's one-way optics and transposing it into a film installation in which it is obvious that the spectators are seeing without being seen and are granted permanent access to the animal, who is always exhibited, exposed, and visible, existing at once as a commodity, a prop, a decor, and a performer.

This fragment, alongside those that follow it, in which present-day images of Brasília's zoo are paired with archival photographs of its construction and early years, reveals how the modes of exhibition of the zoo not only expand the logic of the carceral apparatus but also magnify and distort it. The zoo (and in the giant otter's precise case, the aquarium) offers the illusion of access to wilderness while actually presenting its opposite. While pretending to organize a sample of the giant otter's environment—broken but diversified, partial but rich, participatory but alienating—the zoo builds a fiction that informs a pictorial imaginary of "the wild," confirming and reinforcing visual expectations and common places informed by long-standing traditions of representation and display of animal life. As Vaz's installation attests, the individuals the zoo exhibits reify and decorate its composition in ways that make it both more and less real; more real because they attest, with their own existence and movement, to the truth and livability of this mise-en-scène; less real because they fail to correspond to a spontaneous density and composition of the animals' ecology, especially in the present times where, for instance, the giant otter's natural environment—the Amazon river—has been largely emptied of life. Unlike the carceral apparatus—which is opaque, inaccessible, invisible to the outside—this other spectacle of incarceration, pain, and forced labor that is the zoological garden (when it also drastically restricts the animals' movements in space, engendering "biopolitical techniques to render their bodies more productive and at the same time more docile," to quote author Alex Mackintosh) relies on transparency, accessibility and visibility.[3] Vaz's installation reveals how this space follows the three features of the instances of confinement identified by philosopher Michel Foucault—intervention in the spatial distribution of individuals, intervention in their individual conduct, and reinforcement of a vertical apparatus of power—now applied to animals instead of individuals.[4] But in addition to this condition of visible public confinement and biopolitical subjugation of the confined/exhibited individuals, the zoo's mode of detainment is

3 Alex Mackintosh, "Foucault's Menagerie: Cock Fighting, Bear Baiting, and the Genealogy of Human Animal Power," in *Foucault and Animals*, ed. Matthew Chrulew (Boston: Brill, 2017), 180.

4 Michel Foucault, "The Punitive Society," in *Ethics: Subjectivity and Truth (Essential Works of Foucault, 1954–84, Vol. One)*, ed. Paul Rabinow (London: New Press, 2000), 30–31.

not temporal and contingent, but permanent. It is not aimed at merely displacing the detained subjects from the context from which they were extracted but also at assuring their longevity and eventual reproduction within a panoptic model of life where a permanent and repetitive accessibility is imposed upon them. The zoo, like other instances of confinement, transforms animals, but not as a form of regeneration; on the contrary, it transforms animals to the point of rendering them incapable of returning to and surviving in their original habitats.[5]

Breaking this moment of visual access to the giant otter's confined life, another animal enters the screen. It is an owl, or better yet three versions of this same owl, one per screen. The animal's gaze is intense, sharp, almost angry. Accompanying these one and three owls is an ensemble of trombone, tuba, and percussion playing a syncopated melody that stirs anticipation. These sounds have been heard before, in the film's opening scene and in some of its key interludes. They will reappear again, as a grand finale of night and shadows to this American night, a title that alludes to another kind of night, as the *nuit américaine* is a cinematographic technique for shooting outdoor scenes that are supposed to take place at night during the day as a way to induce the illusion of night while taking advantage of the visibility of daylight. But when they reappear, these sounds belong to yet another past, that of the artist's own history. They echo the composition *Panthera Onça* (1990) by artist and composer Guilherme Vaz, the late pioneer of Brazilian conceptual art and concrete music and Vaz's father. Guilherme's original score was composed to accompany filmmaker Sérgio Bernardes's film of the same title, an experimental documentary that raised awareness for the massive killing and endangered state of the spotted jaguar in the Pantanal wetland area of Brazil. Here, the melody stretches itself over time, uniting new and familial environmental concerns and love for film, art, music, and animals.

The magnificent owls and their trumpets gradually give way to visions of a pen of tamandus, some of them being moved around by caretakers, and to images of the crab-eating fox being treated. A story starts being told in *gualin*, a vernacular mode of speaking that consists of the inversion of syllables whose coded messages are only understandable to those who know its logic. The term *gualin* is the inversion of the Portuguese word *lingua*, or "language," its literal English translation being *guagelan*. *Gualin* is an intentional process of creolization, an exercise of transformation and adaptation of a known language that allows

5 As in the human penal apparatuses studied by Foucault, the regenerative capacity is often a legitimizing framework that doesn't necessarily fulfil the logic it purports to enforce.

a community of individuals to estrange themselves from their context and thus reconstitute their sense of comprehension and cohesion, and to speak in a freer way. To speak *gualin* is to become another through the reshaping of linguistic, social, and affective codes and bonds. Vaz's inclusion of *gualin* in the context of this film connects it with a liberation that acts as an incipient form of subversion. In its incomprehensibility, the *gualin* heard in the film becomes a spell, an incantation, a ritual to revert that upmost manifestation of human cultural entitlement that is verbal expression.

Hopefully, departing from language, this process of reversion will contribute, in a slow but steady way, to upturn conceptions of human distance and superiority from all those that, throughout an equally long process of edification of modernity, have been othered by that myth of the age of reason that is the white man. Guilherme Vaz once said, "Freedom is measured in seconds."[6] May the animal frames and images contained in *It Is Night in America*, scanned and paced by Ana Vaz's own spatial and filmmaking sensibilities, initiate a much-needed process of emancipation and liberation of the many living bodies that generated them, freeing even that "open-air prison" of Brasília from itself.

Images from the Brasília Zoo Public Archive, 1957–87. Photographs by several artists, including: Joaquim Firmino, Luiz Lemos, Luiz Cruvinel, Brito and others not identified. Courtesy of the Brasília Zoo Public Archive.

6 Guilherme Vaz, interview with Franz Manata and Saulo Laudares, Rio de Janeiro, May 27, 2015. From *Guilherme Vaz uma fração do Infinito*, exh. cat. Rio de Janeiro: Centro Cultural Banco do Brasil, January 2013–April 4, 2016, 11.

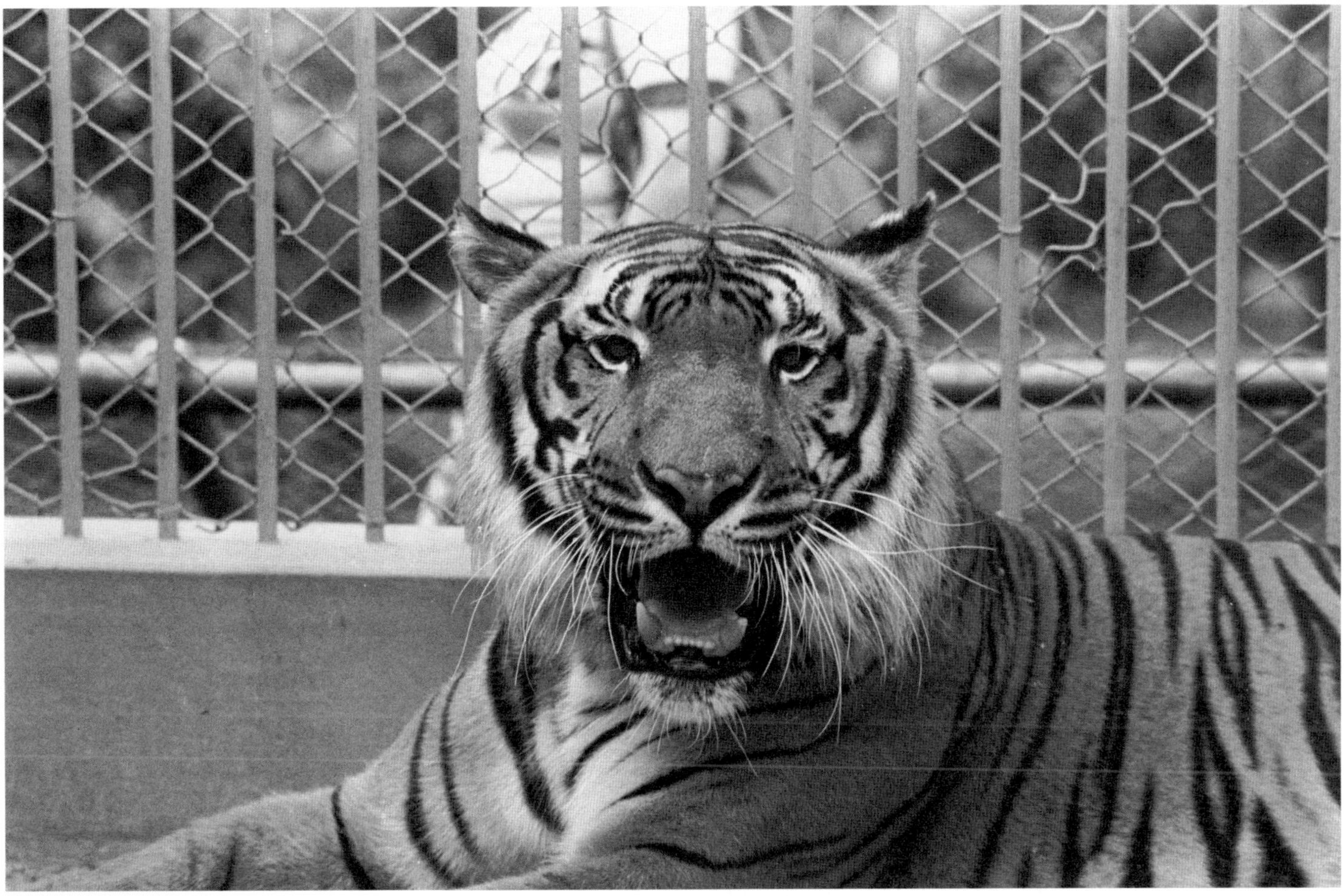

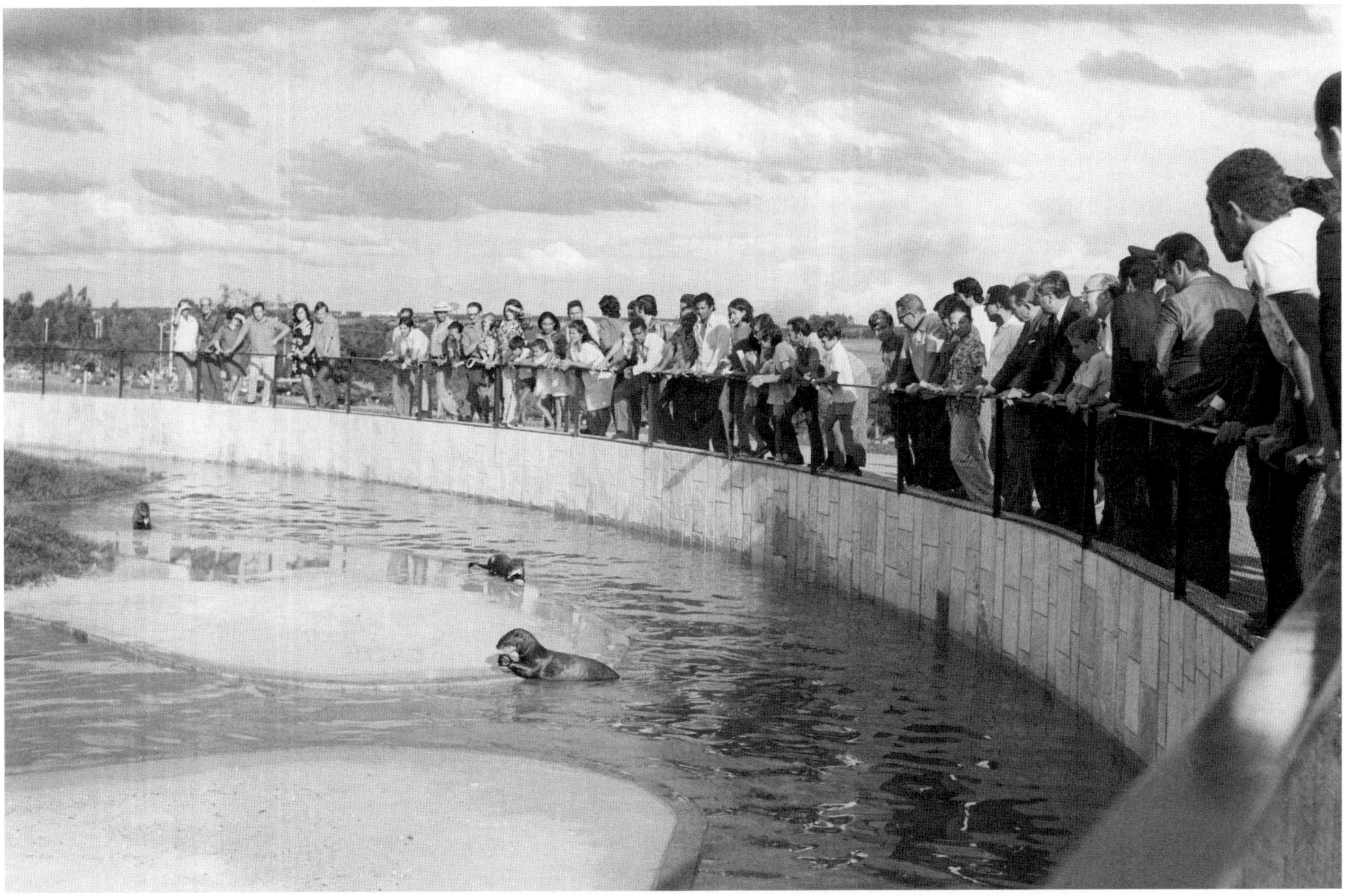

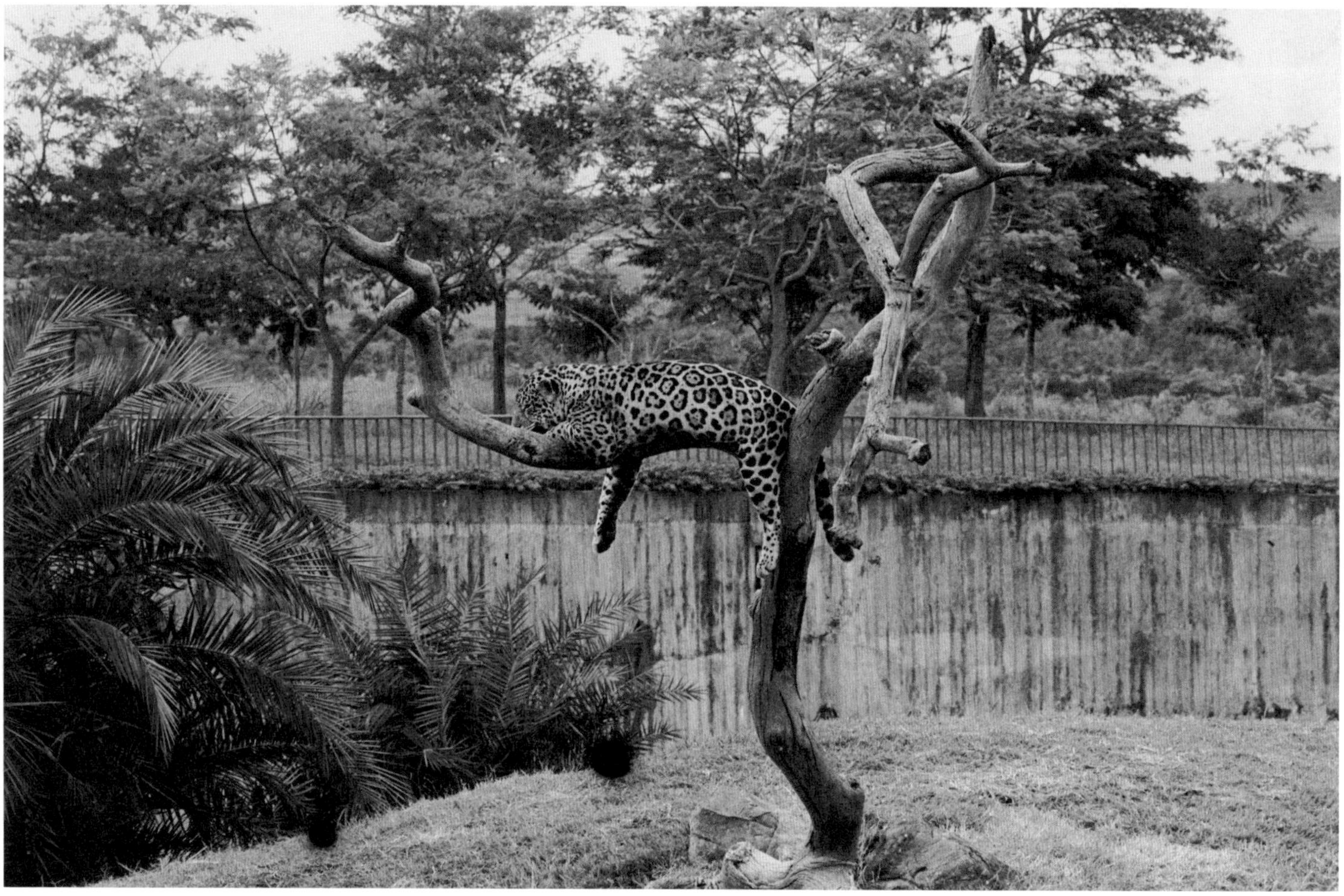

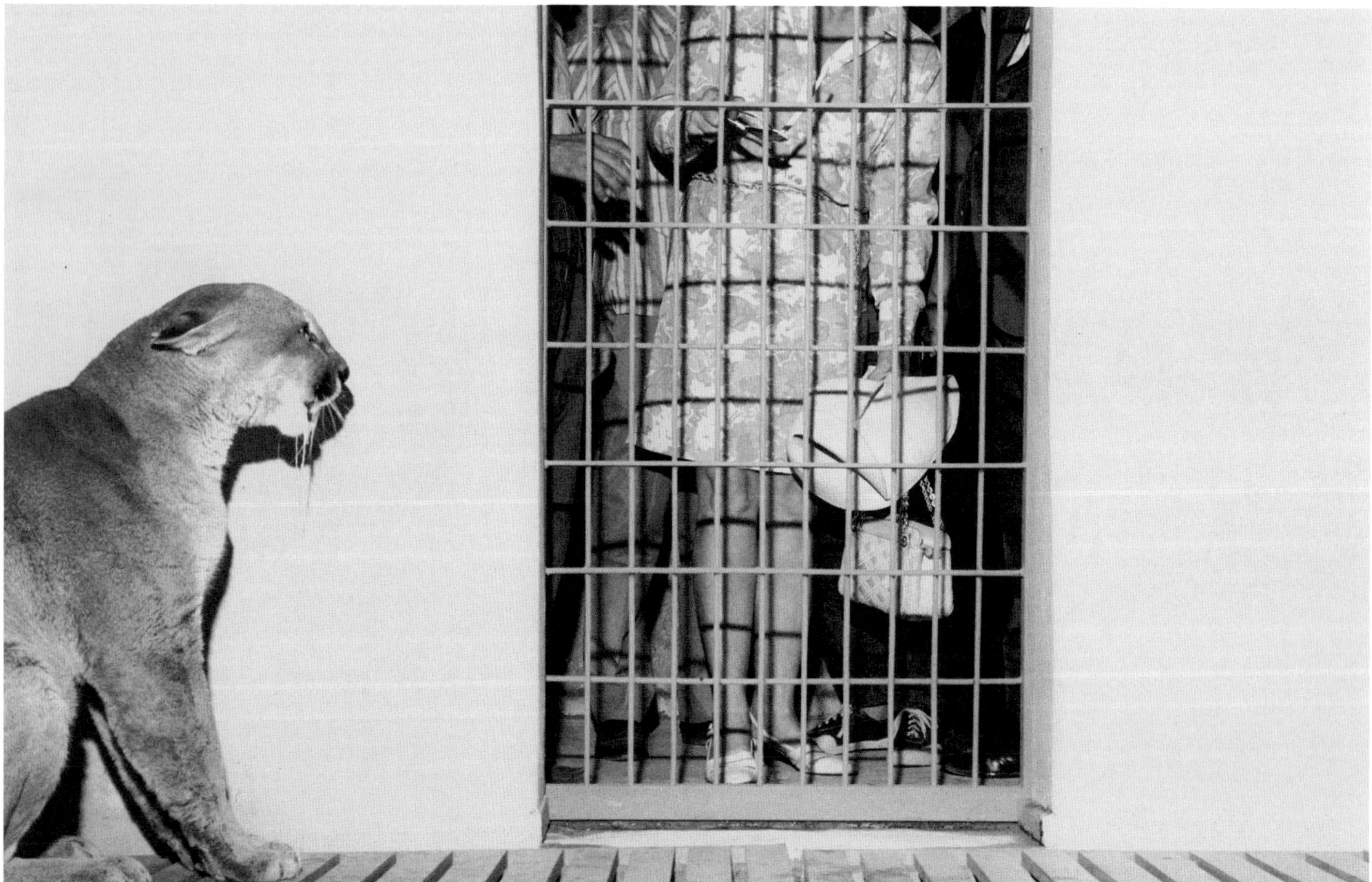

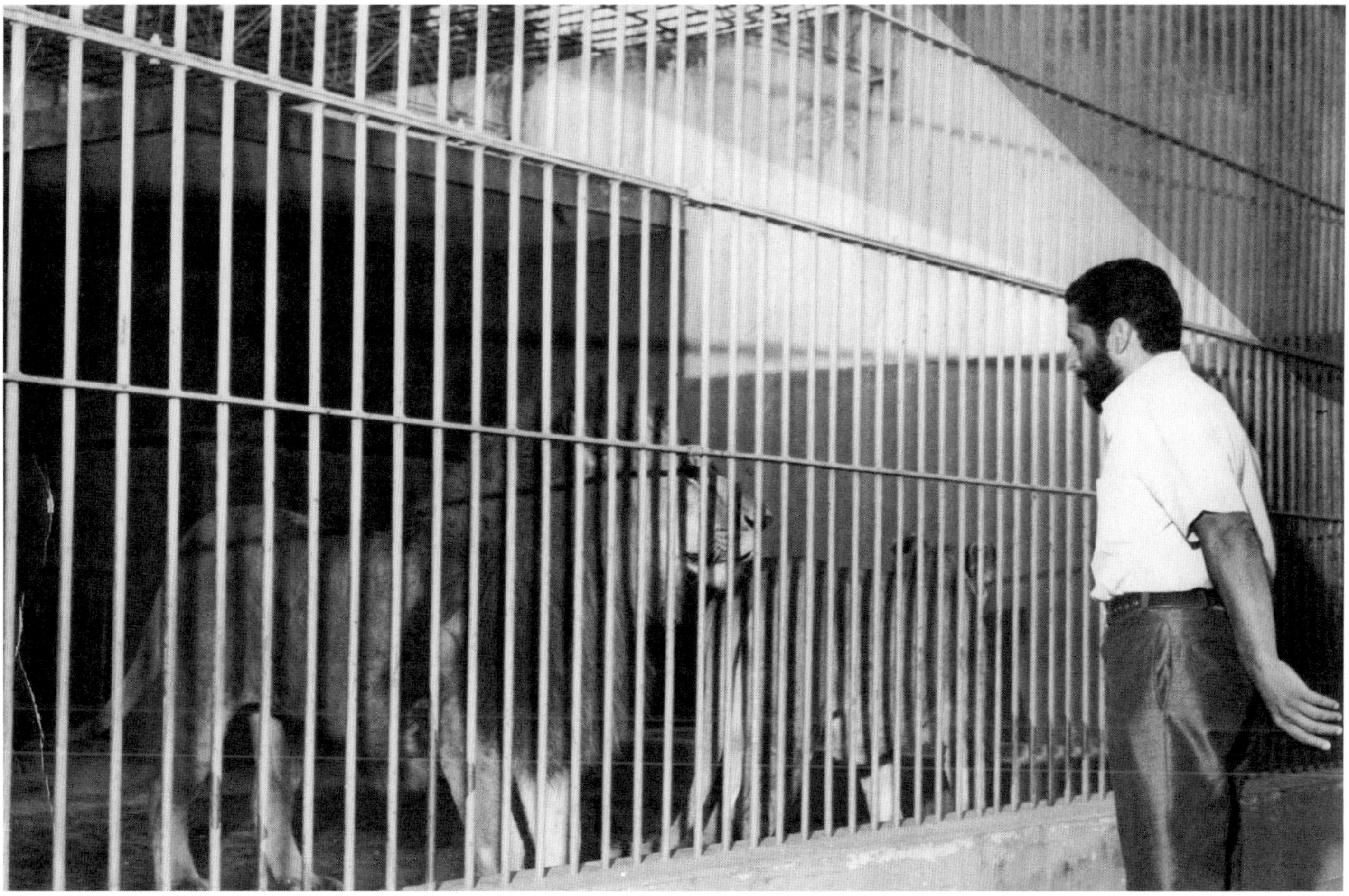

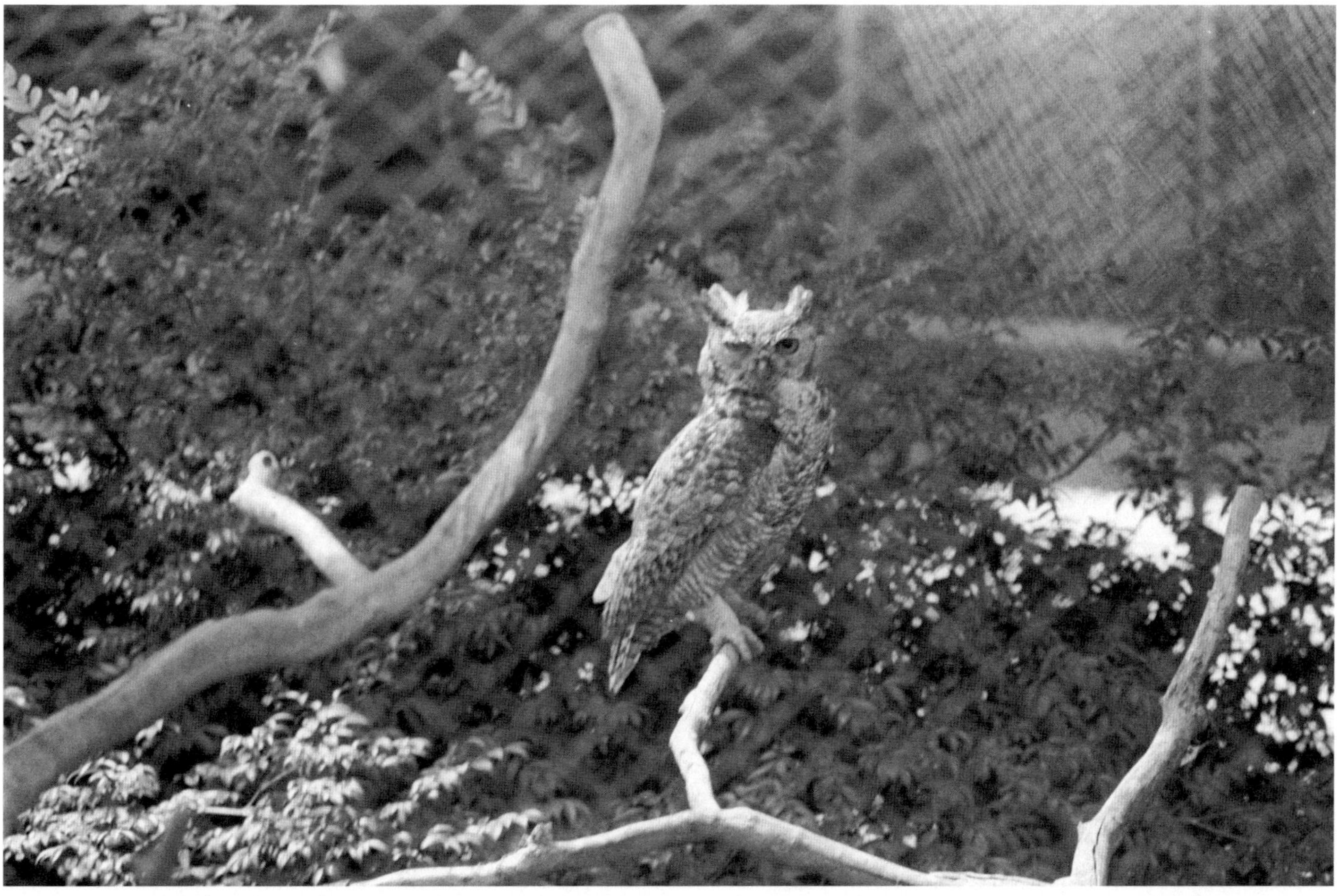

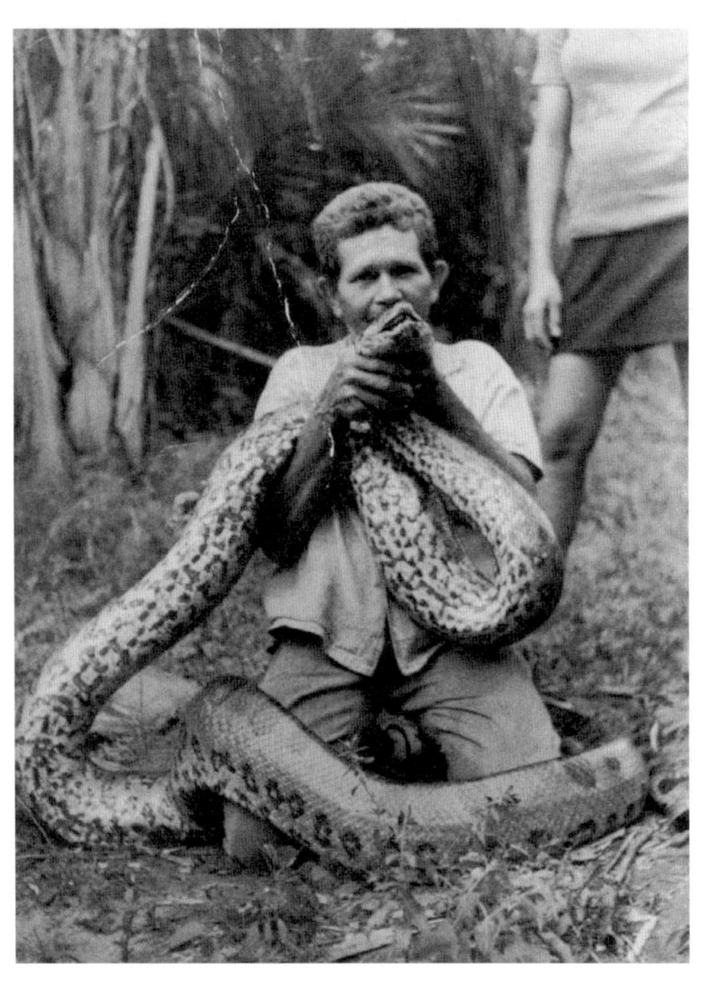

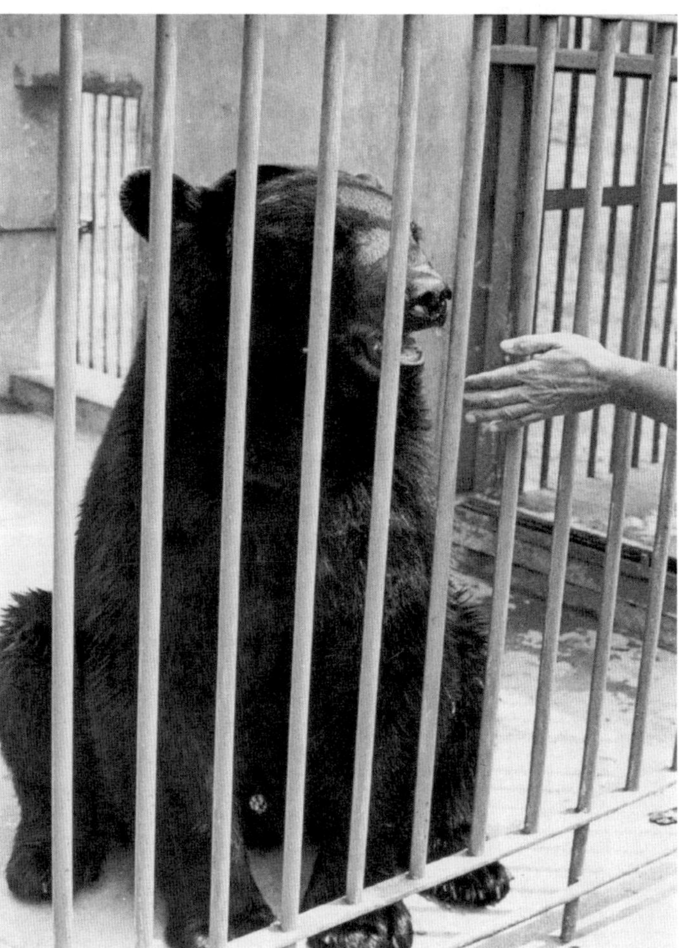

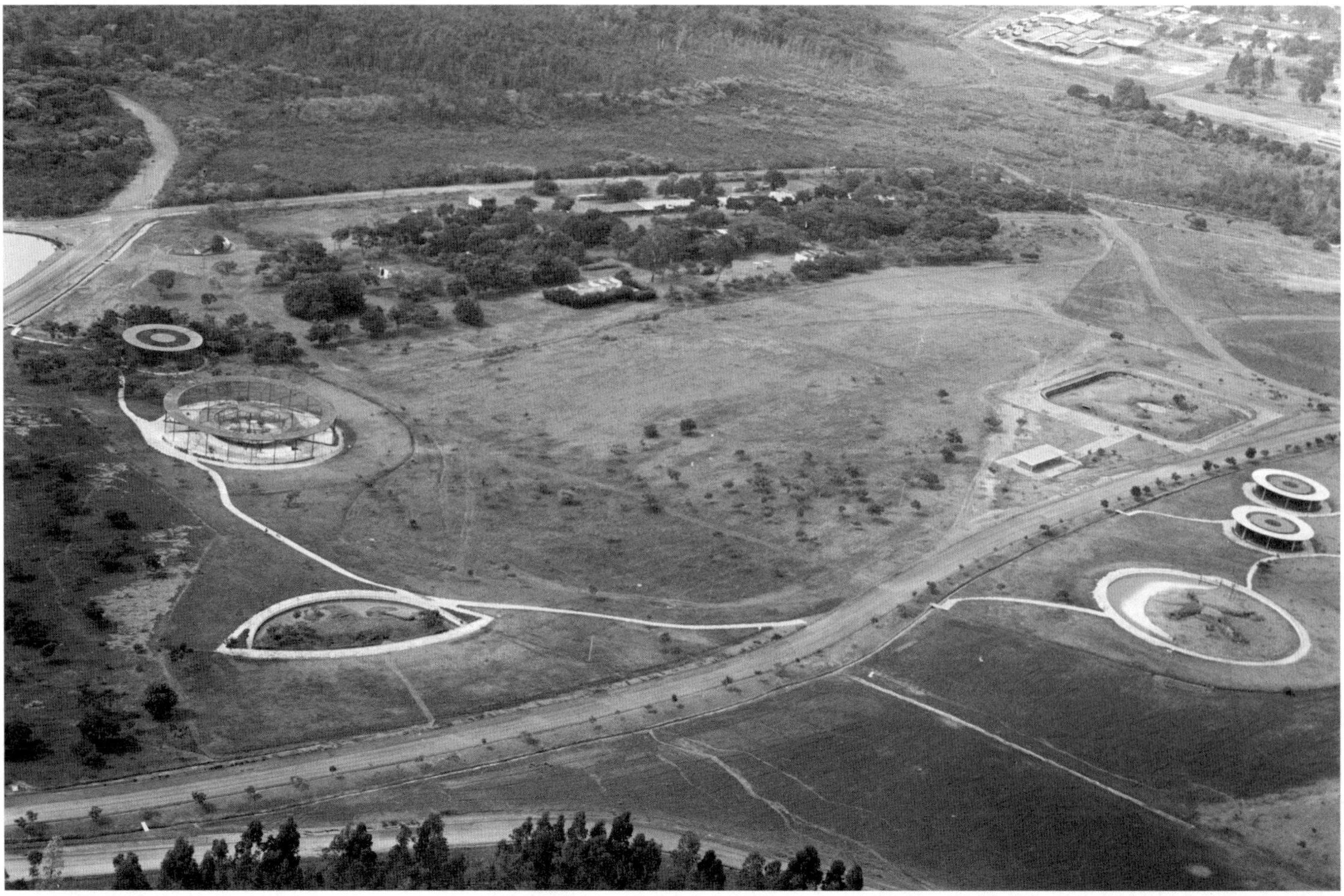

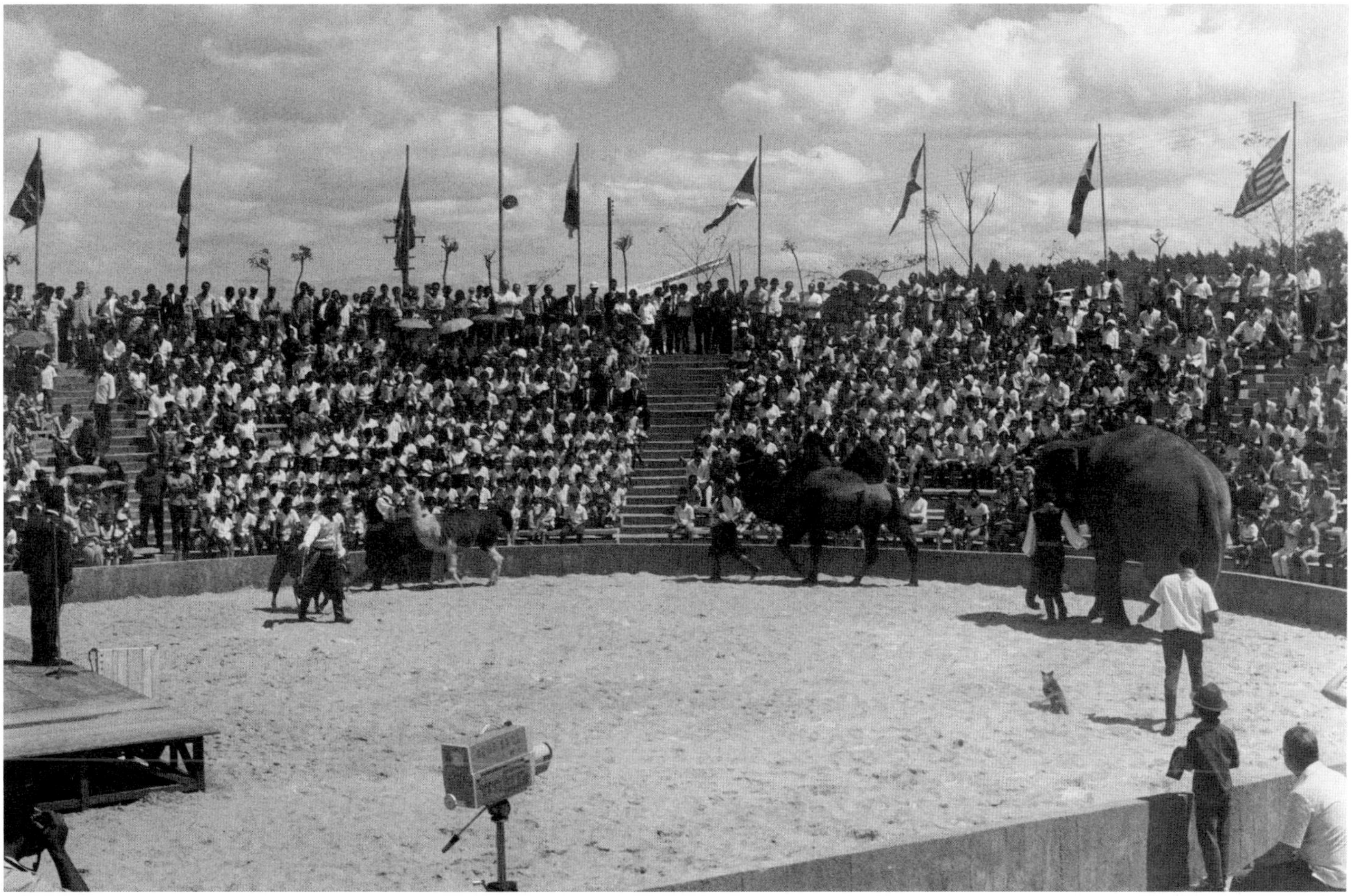

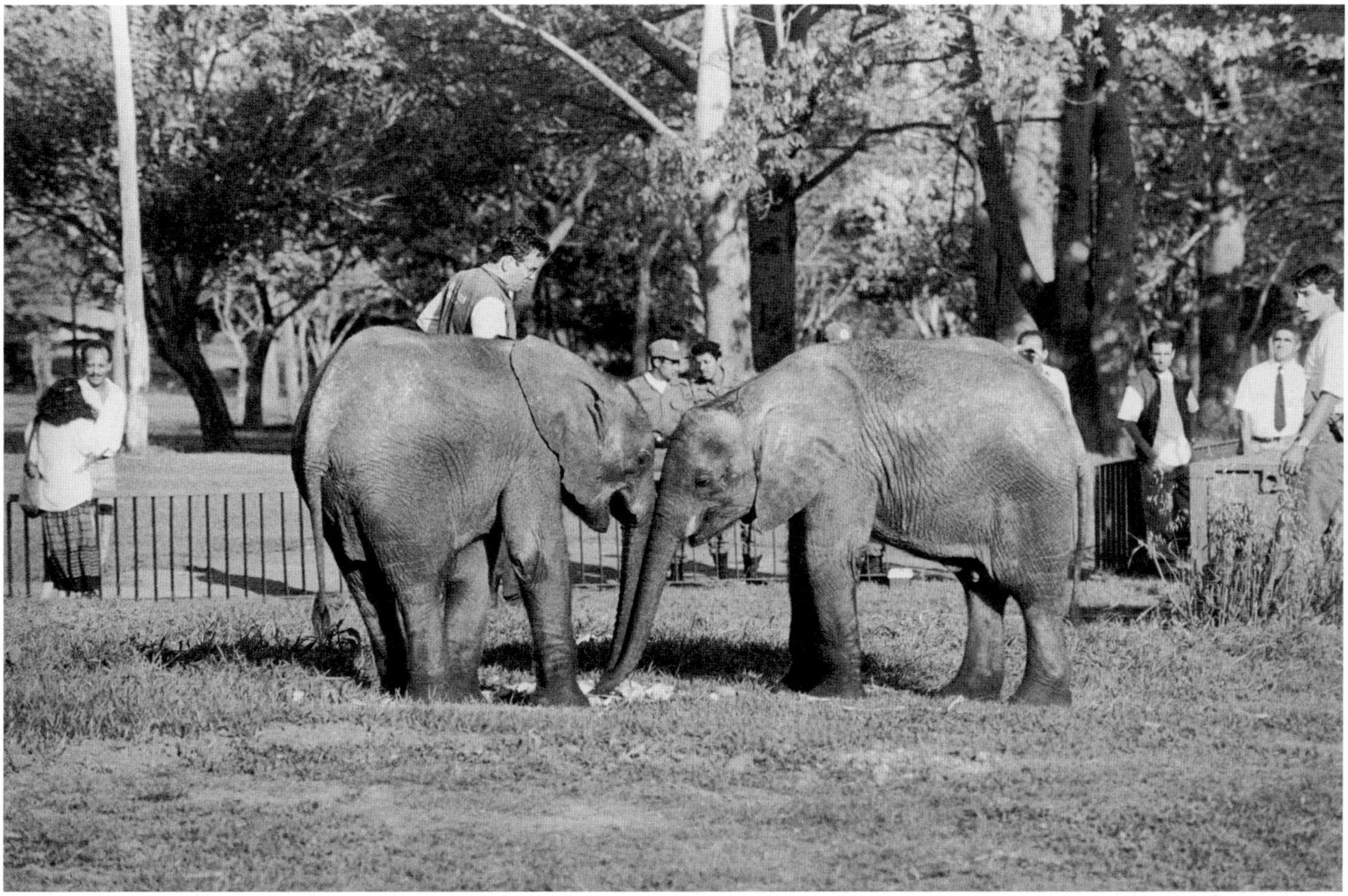

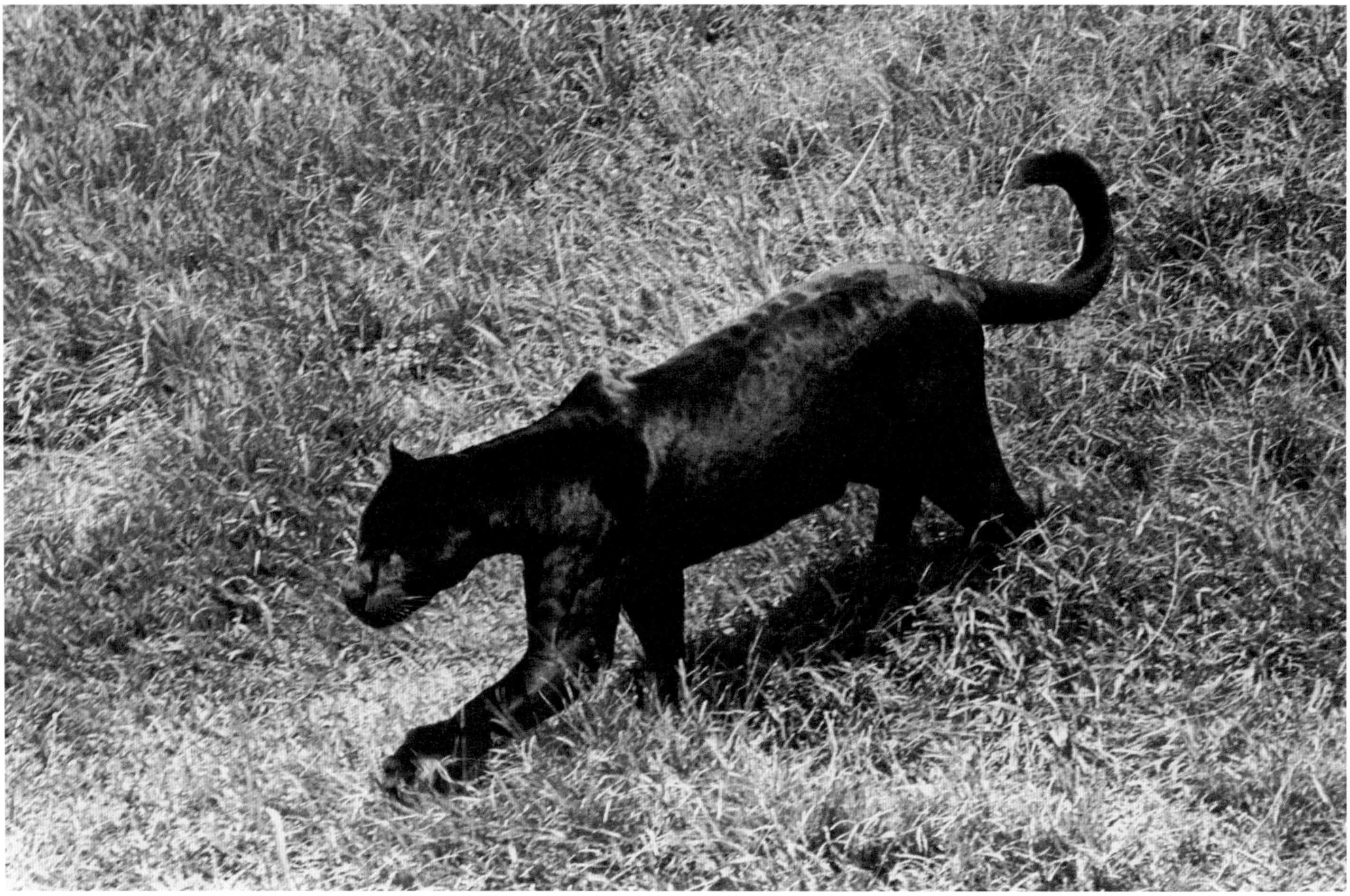

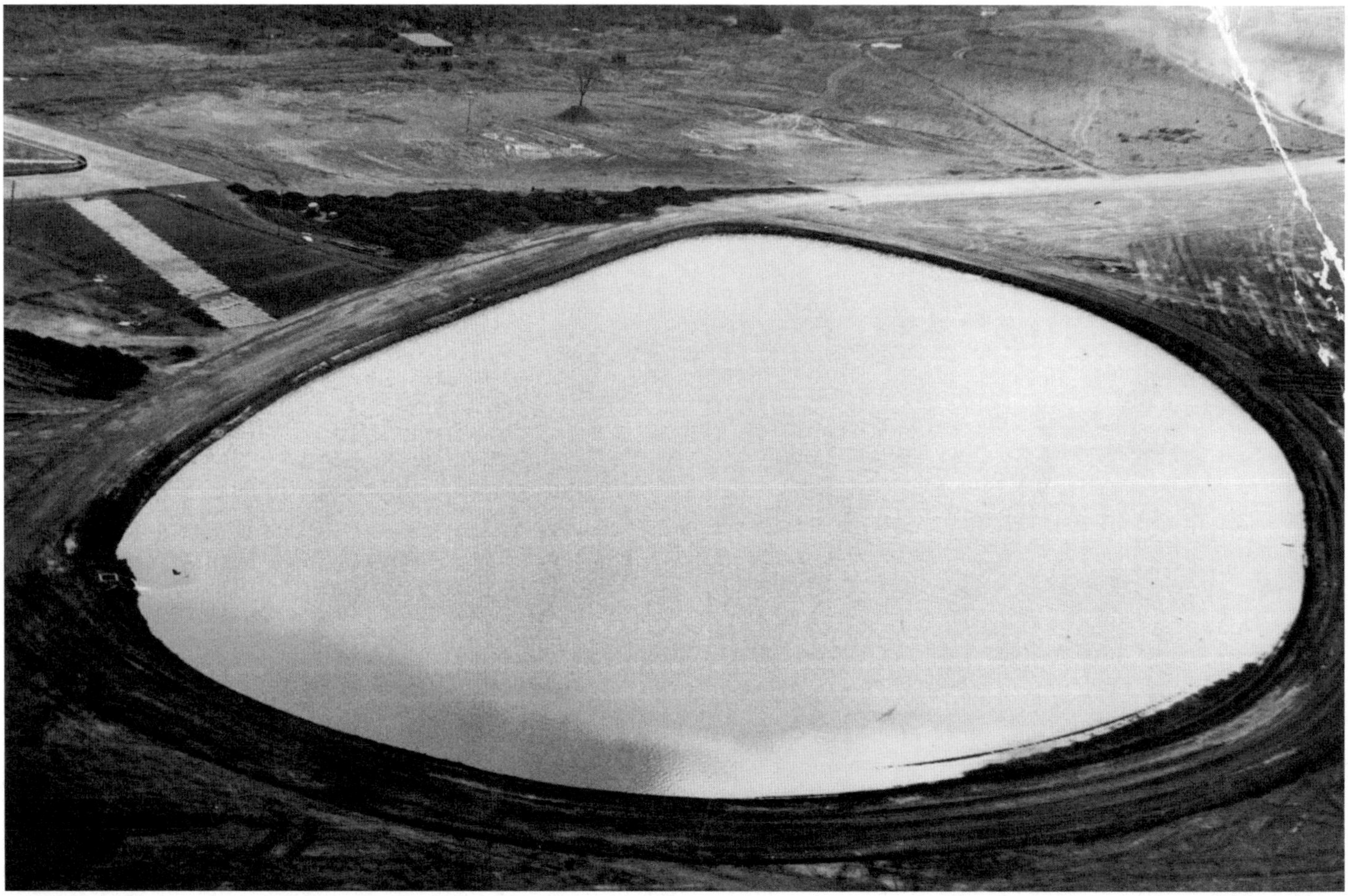

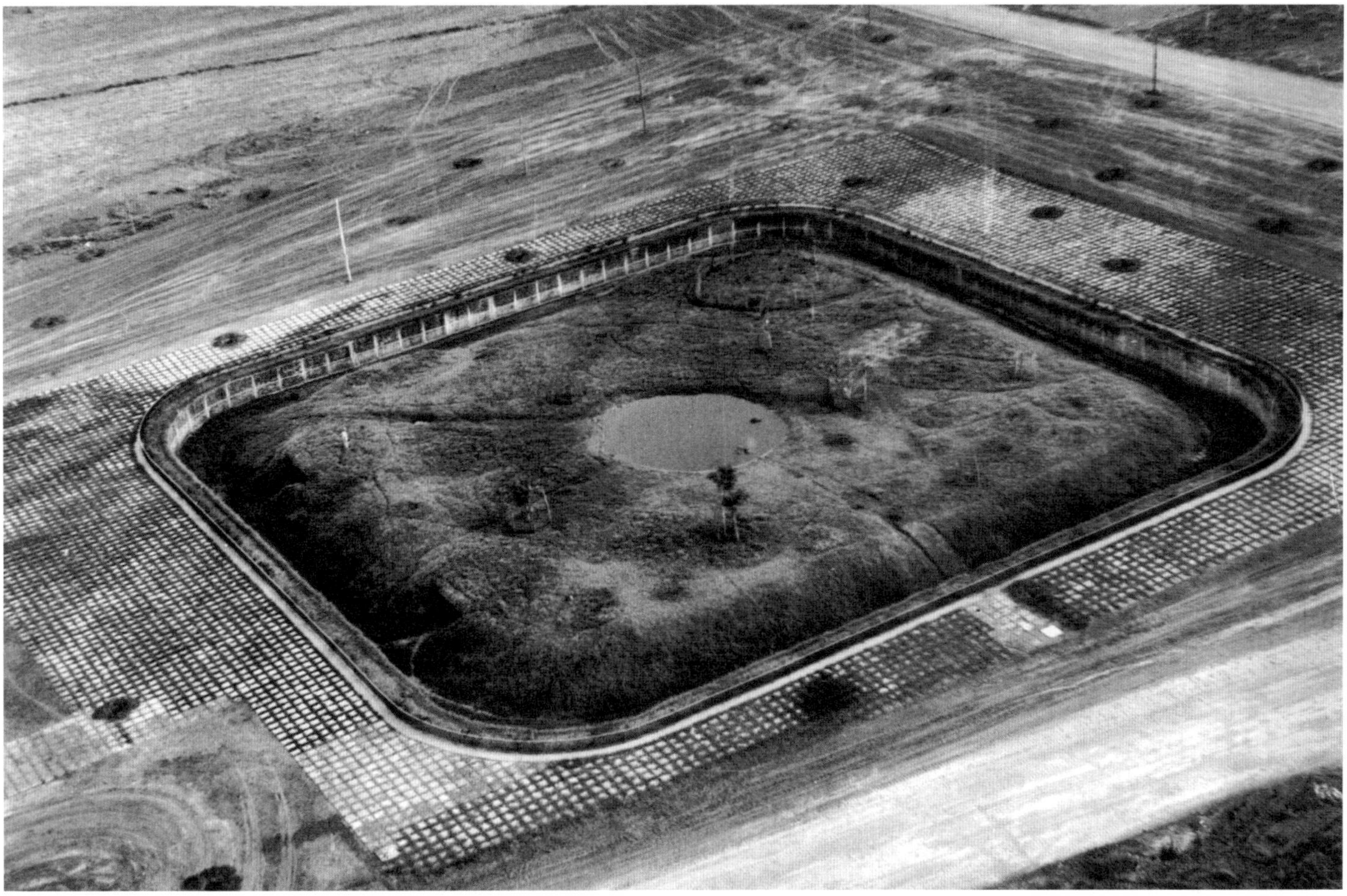

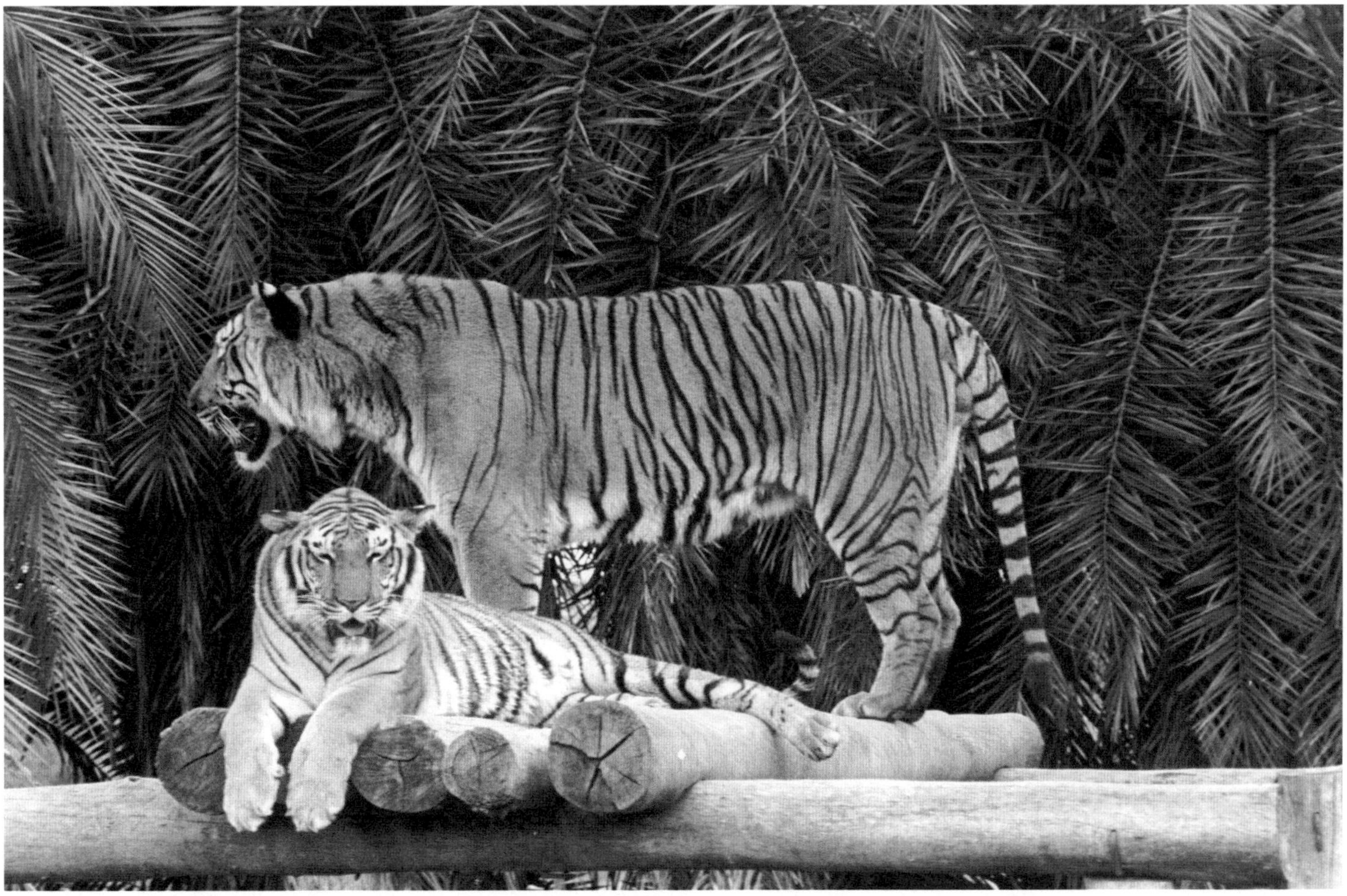

EMILIJA ŠKARNULYTĖ

APHOTIC ZONE

2022, 4K digital video, color, 5.1 sound, 16'

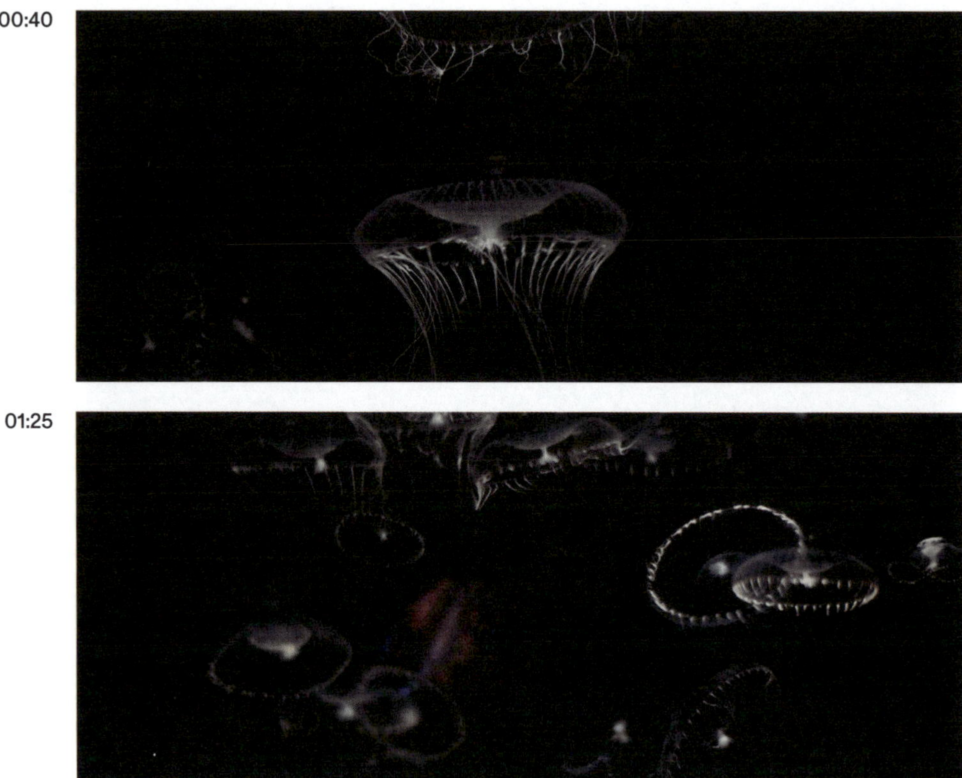

00:40

01:25

As a cinematic journey across abyssal spaces and times, *Aphotic Zone* by Emilija Škarnulytė (b. 1987, Lithuania) locates the mythological as much as the critical aspects of scientific research and its ventures into worlds beyond the human scale. This poetic video crosses an oceanic trench at 4 kilometers depth to reach the pitch black (or, aphotic) zone of the Pacific seamounts of Costa Rica on the other side. In these

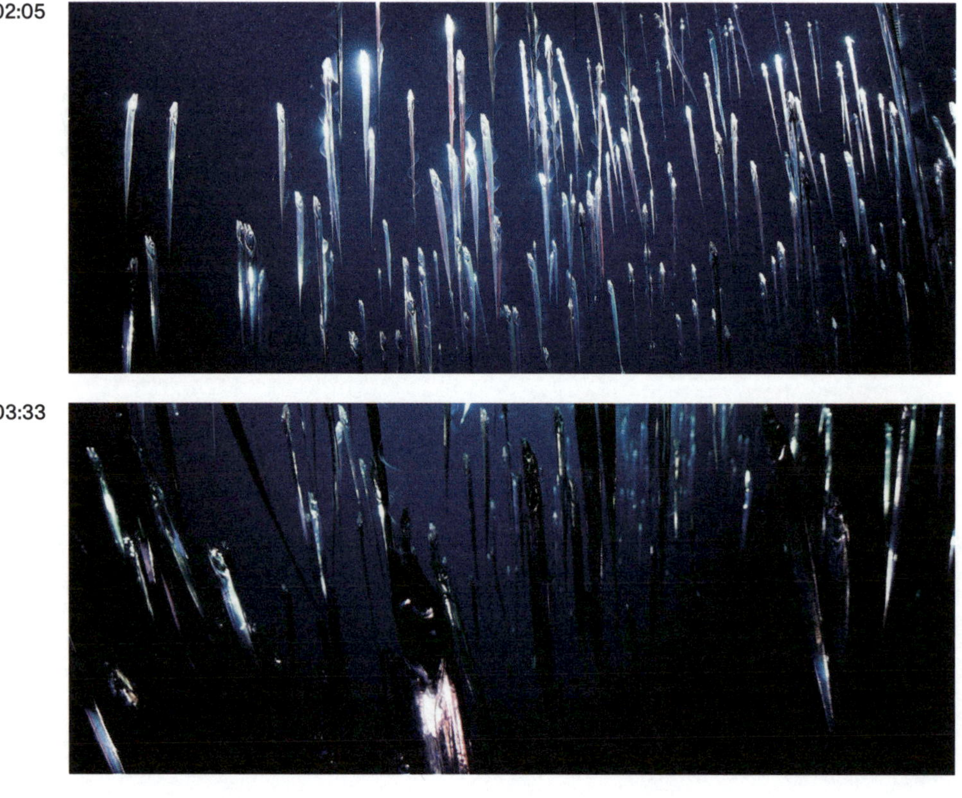

02:05

03:33

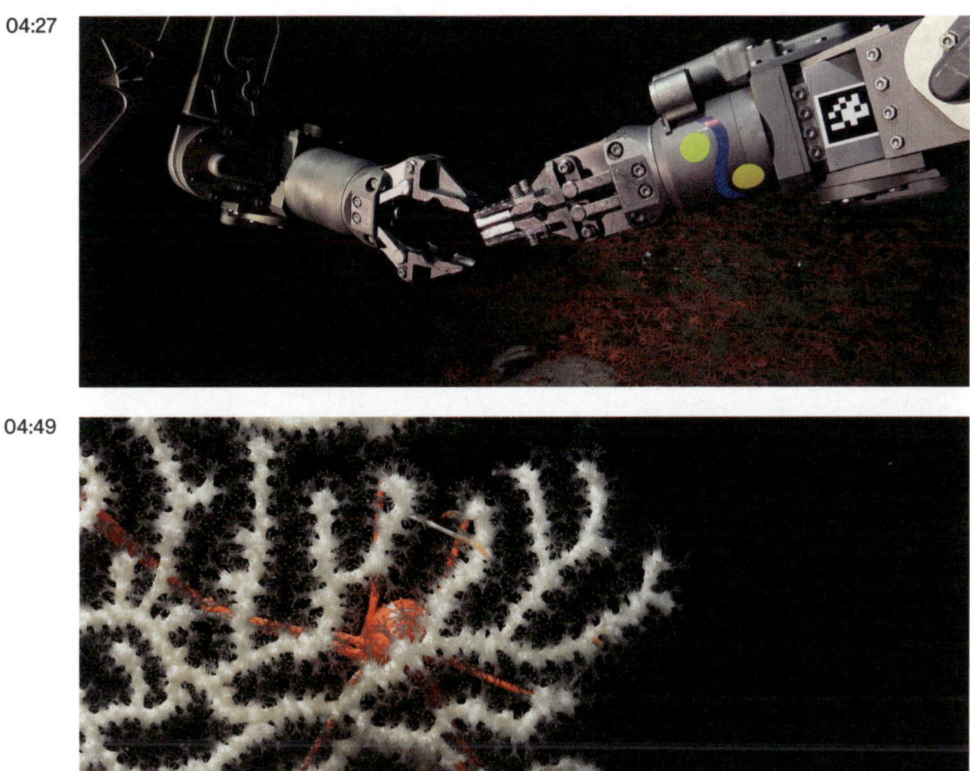
04:27

04:49

inky depths, the only visible lights beam from strange, bioluminescent sea jellies, or from the chromed skin of a school of cutlassfish when illuminated by the underwater cameras. Drawing from documentary footage realized by Dr. Erik Cordes and his team of marine biologists at the Schmidt Ocean Institute, we see Subastian, their Remotely Operated Vehicle, sampling deep sea corals, rocks, and small organisms living

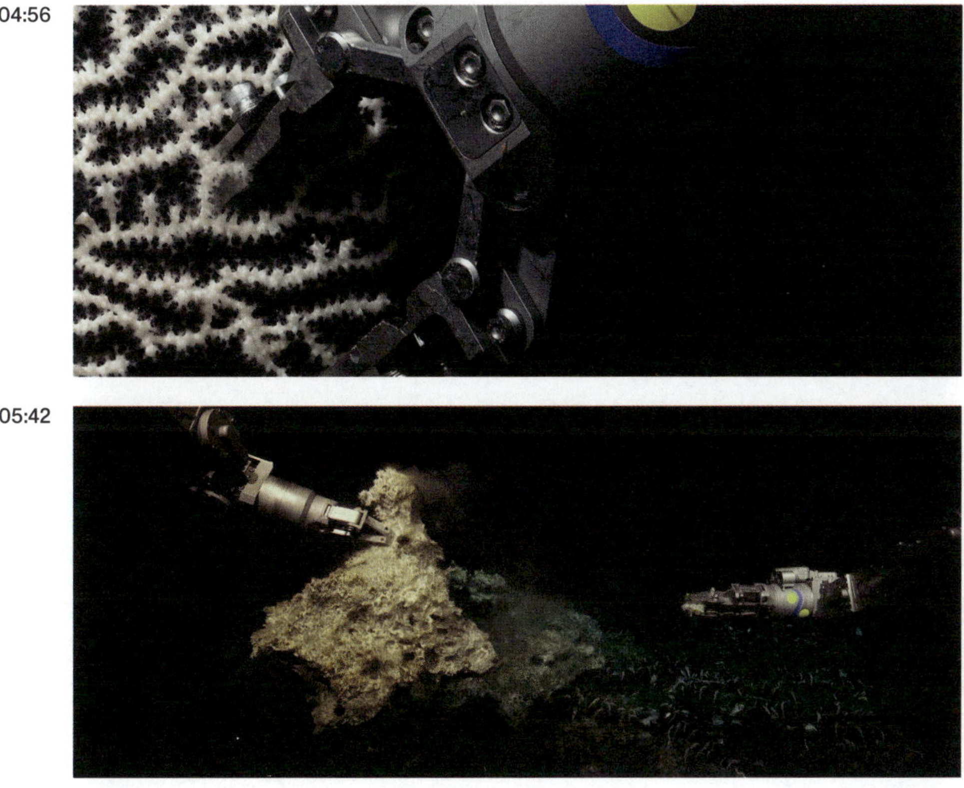
04:56

05:42

06:01

06:35

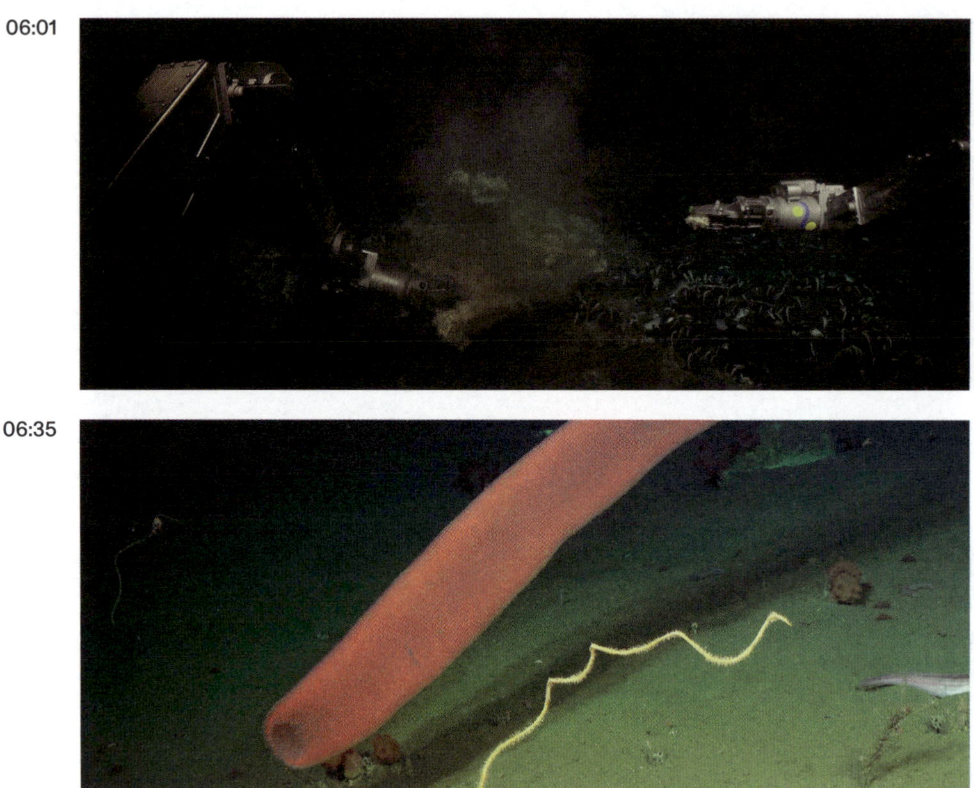

in the seafloor with its robotic arms and sucking hose. Yet *Aphotic Zone* takes the imagination further into an oneiric landscape of prehistoric creatures and advanced technology, combining images of a mountainous seabed generated from 3D laser scanner data with an undersea Duga radar (a towering, Soviet-era missile defense system near Chernobyl), and digitally animated phytoplankton organisms.

06:39

07:14

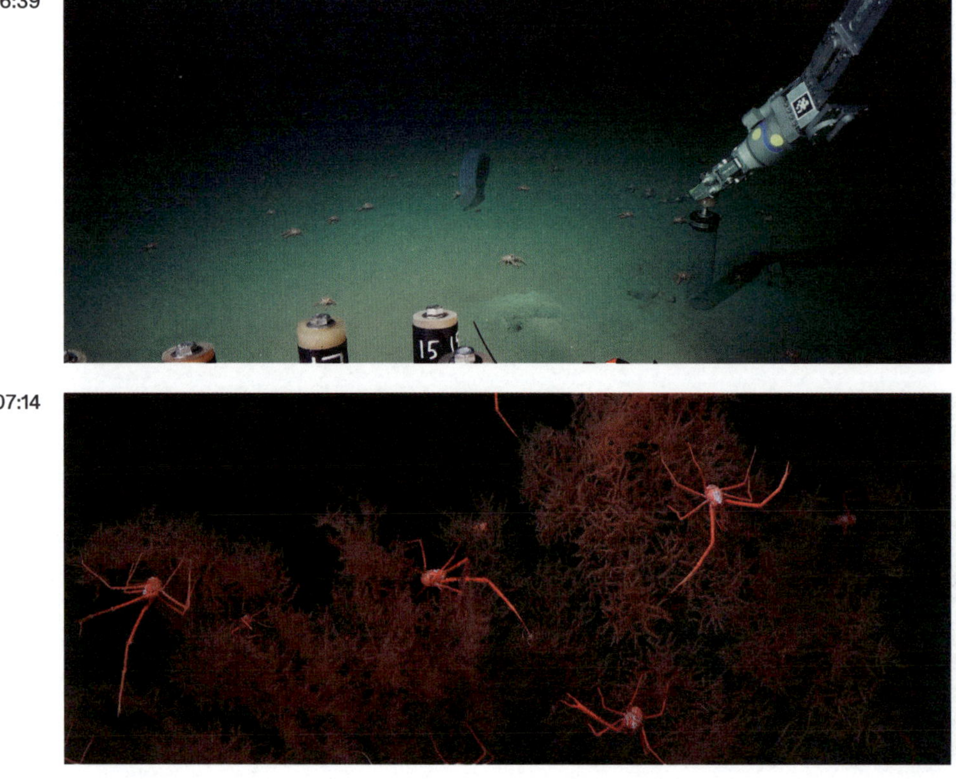

07:17

10:09

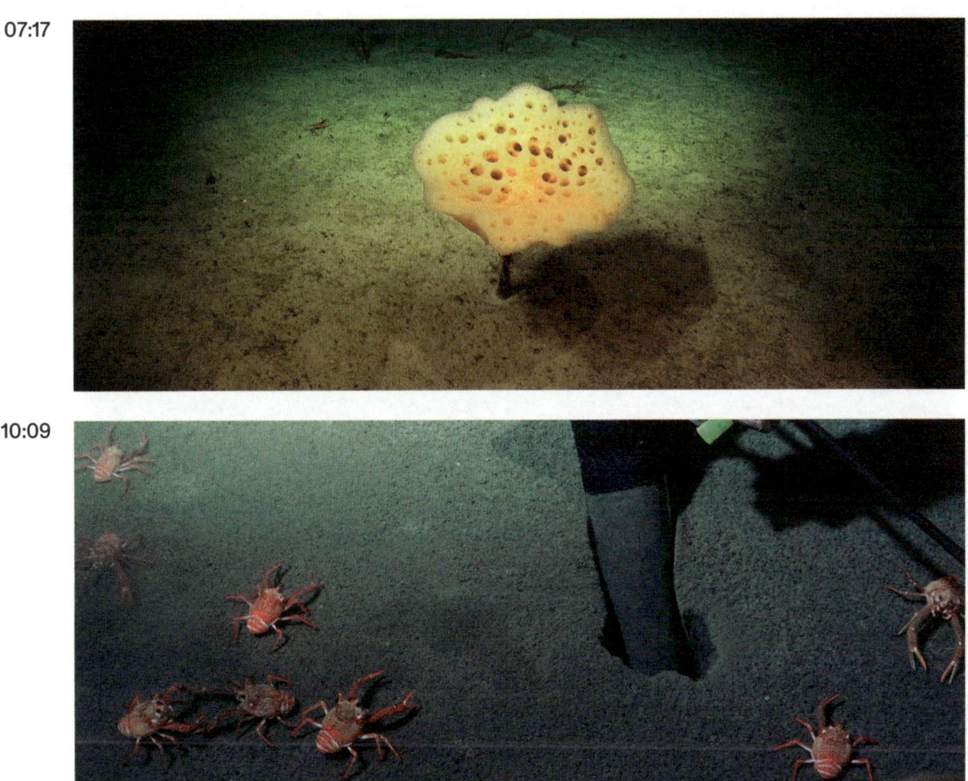

Here, more-than-human and machinic agencies weirdly coexist with the sonic memory of a distant civilization: mixed by Oscar-winning engineers Jaime Baksht and Michelle Couttolenc, the sound was recorded in Mexico City's main plaza during the commemorations for the 500th anniversary of Spain's bloody conquest of Tenochtitlan. The former capital of the Aztec Empire becomes a sonic ghost

11:39

12:11

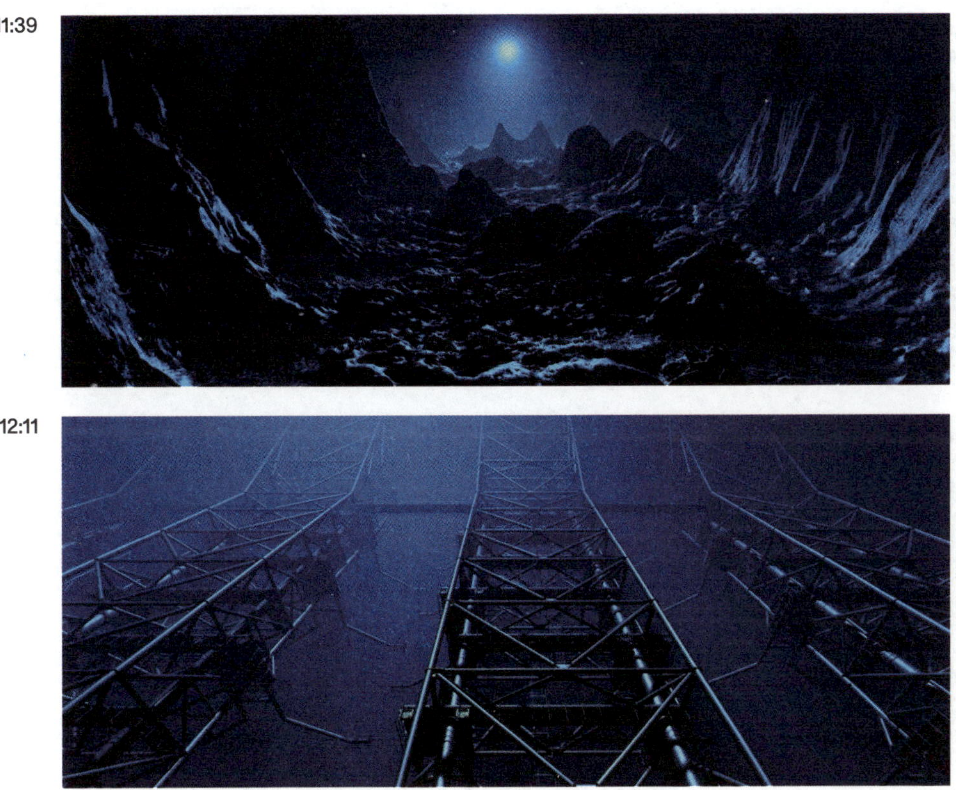

13:33

13:57

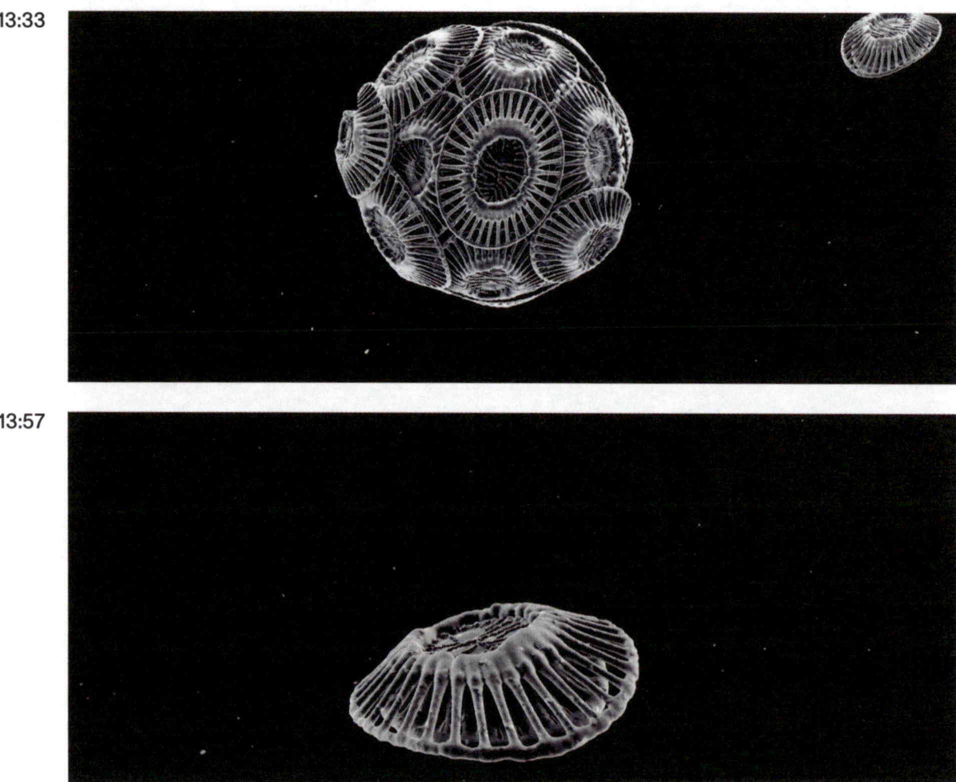

reverberating with, and warning us against, the recent and contemporary destructions of societies and ecosystems. *Aphotic Zone* imagines the future as its vantage point with the aim of looking back into the present amid the threats of climate crisis and economic extractivism; the idealistic prospects of science; and what will survive the ravages of human greed.

14:28

14:33

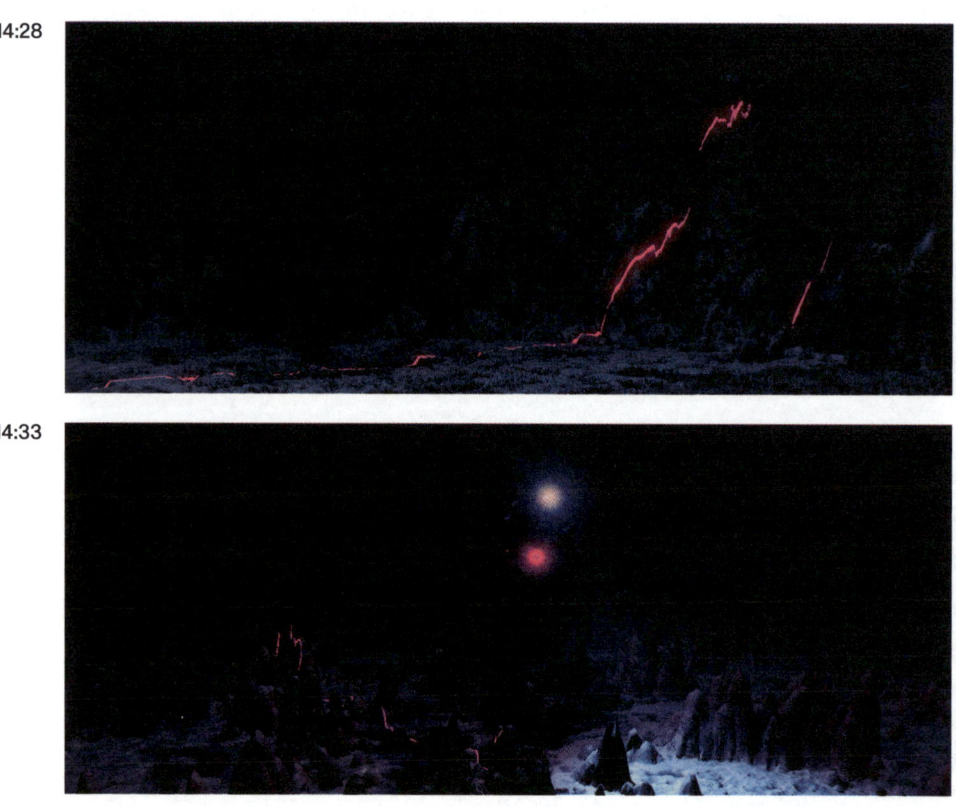

Emilija Škarnulytė, *Aphotic Zone*, 2022

4K digital video, color, 5.1 sound, 16'

Written and directed by
Emilija Škarnulytė

Commissioned and produced by
Fondazione In Between Art Film

Co-produced by
Emilija Škarnulytė / Mirror Matter Productions

Creative Producer
Leonardo Bigazzi

ROV
Dr. Erik Cordes and the Schmidt Ocean Institute

CGI
Gregory Blunt

Editor
Vytautas Tinteris

Colorist
Vytautas Tinteris

Composer
Jokūbas Čižikas

Sound design
Gerardo Artemio Islas Bulnes

Additional music
Emilija Škarnulytė, Vytautas Tinteris

Re-recording mix
Jaime Baksht, Michelle Couttolenc

Post-production studio
Astro Studios Mexico

Mastering
Vytautas Tinteris

Title design
Vytautas Volbekas

Assistant
Viktorija Smailytė

Consultant
Barbara Casavecchia

Legal services
Martin Heller

Distribution
Mirror Matter Productions

Footage courtesy of
Dr. Erik Cordes and the Schmidt Ocean Institute

Featuring locations
The Pacific Seamounts of Costa Rica

Music
Deep Sea Dweller (2022) composed by Jokūbas Čižikas; *Aphotia* (2022), composed by Emilija Škarnulytė

Thanks to
Beatrice Bulgari, Alessandro Rabottini, Alessia Carlino, Bianca Stoppani, Paola Ugolini, Dr. Erik Cordes, The Schmidt Ocean Institute, and The U.S. National Science Foundation

Courtesy of the artist, Dr. Erik Cordes and the Schmidt Ocean Institute, and Fondazione In Between Art Film

Dear Emilija: Three Letters across Remote Proximities
Barbara Casavecchia

Dear Emilija,

I am writing across time and space, since our schedules away from the keyboard often do not align. You travel so much, so often. I remember a long conversation shared together last year via phone and then FaceTime (Do we question enough what we are using, and how much these forms of remote proximity are impacting us all, as individuals and inhabitants of the planet?) on our mutual fascination for underwater infrastructures, such as the telescopes anchored to the bottom of the Mediterranean Sea to detect and observe neutrino fluxes from cosmic origins. Deep sea and deep space share the same darkness, where humans cannot live, nor see, and it's from that darkness—the same, deep lightlessness of dark matter—that they are trying to extract answers.

Here are some fun facts, to let our imagination swim faster. The ANTARES detector, positioned at 2500 meters depth, 40 kilometers off the coast of France, was switched off on February 2022, after sixteen years of data mining on high-energy cosmic neutrinos. The new KM3NeT-It (about 80 kilometers off Cape Passero in Italy) and KM3NeT-Gr (off Pylos, in the Greek Peloponnese) detectors will operate at an unprecedented depth of 3500 meters in order to capture Cherenkov radiation, the blue or violet glow emitted by muon neutrinos while they pass through the water faster than light. The subaqueous telescopes, like silent predators, try to capture it. They can be blinded by the wrong twinkling: natural bioluminescence generates enough light to require background-suppression methods.

You know, underwater telescopes do not look like their terrestrial cousins at all. They have a grid shape that reminds me of the nets traditionally used for catching tuna or cultivating mussels: hundreds of long, vertical strings of high-speed electro-optical cables hold in place thousands of pressure-resistant glass spheres called "digital optical modules" (DOM), each around 43 centimeters in diameter and containing several photomultiplier tubes that convert photons into electrical signals. With my eyes closed, I see giant strings of iridescent eggs akin to those of cuttlefish, each one alive with its mechanical pupil. I think I've seen them in your video *Mirror Matter* (2018), based on the Super-Kamiokande neutrino observatory in Japan. Behind my eyelids, I see floating forests of giant kelp, embroidered with

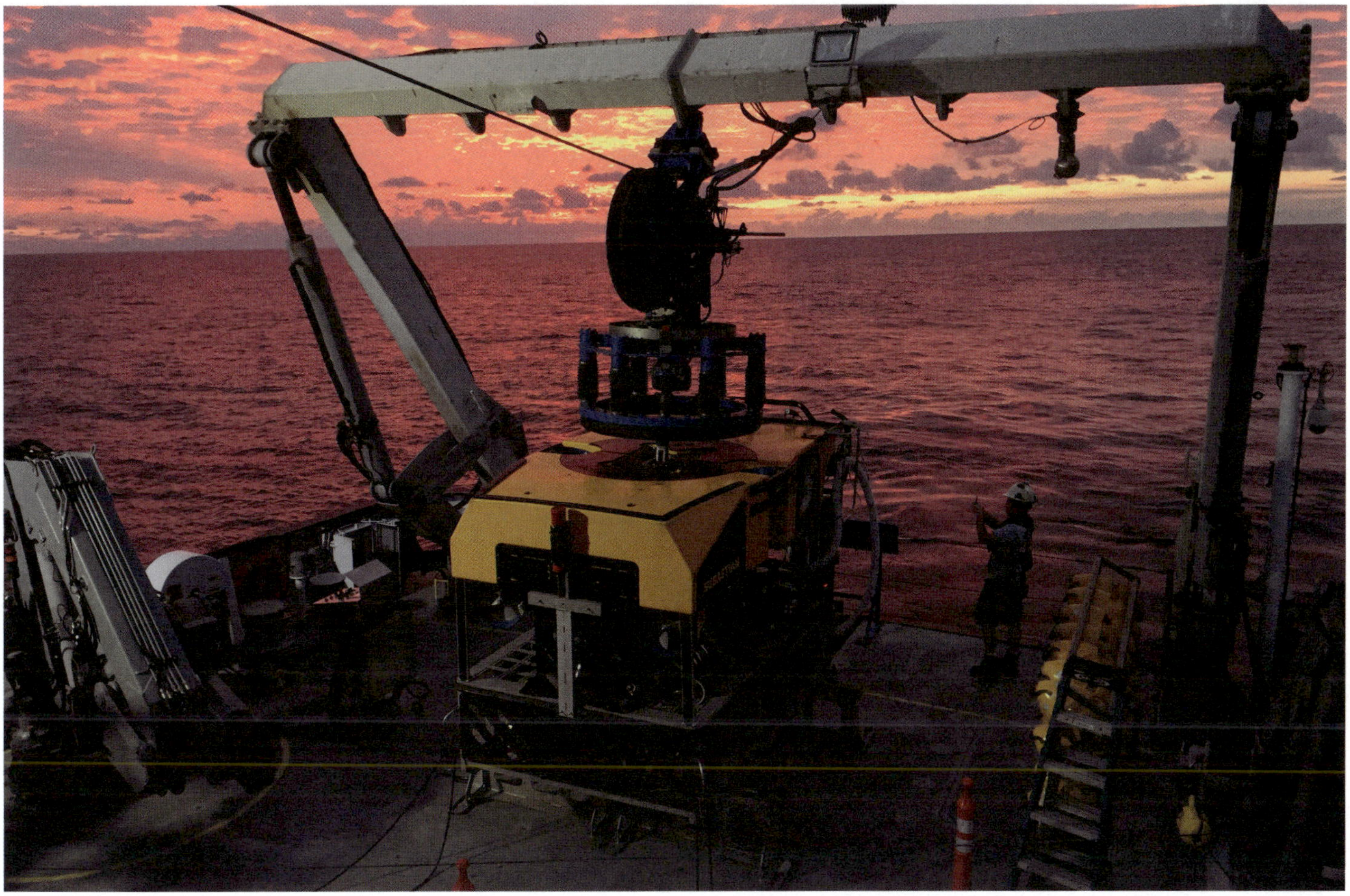

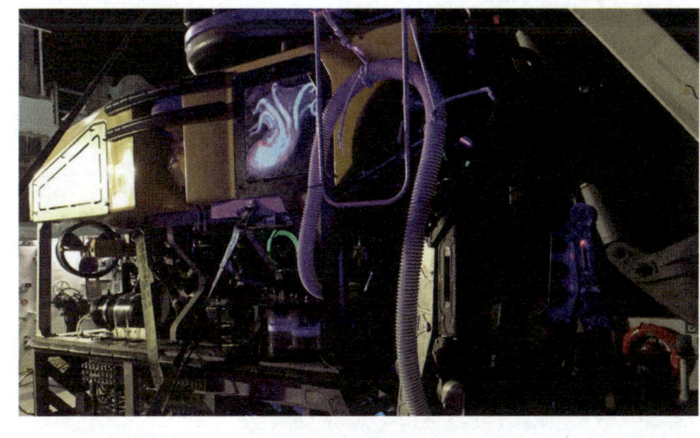

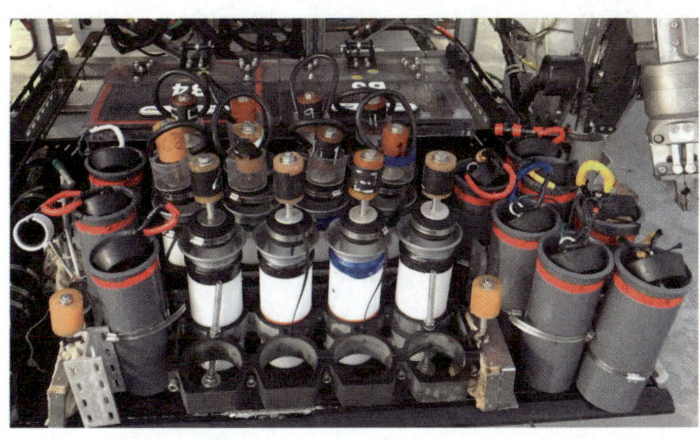

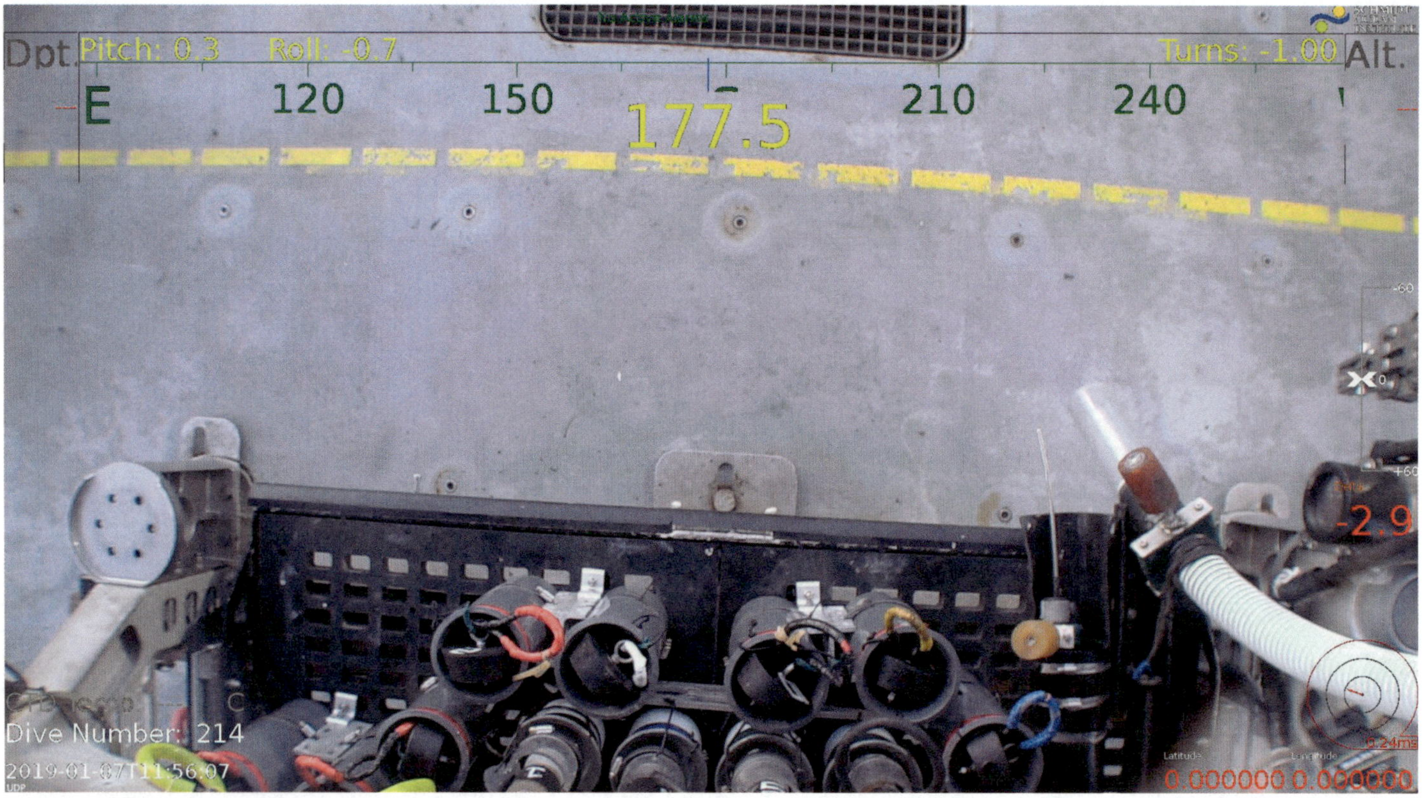

Dpt. Pitch: 0.3 Roll: -0.7 Turns: -1.00 Alt.

E 120 150 210 240

177.5

-2.9

Dive Number: 214

2019-01-07T11:56:07

Latitude Longitude

0.000000 0.000000

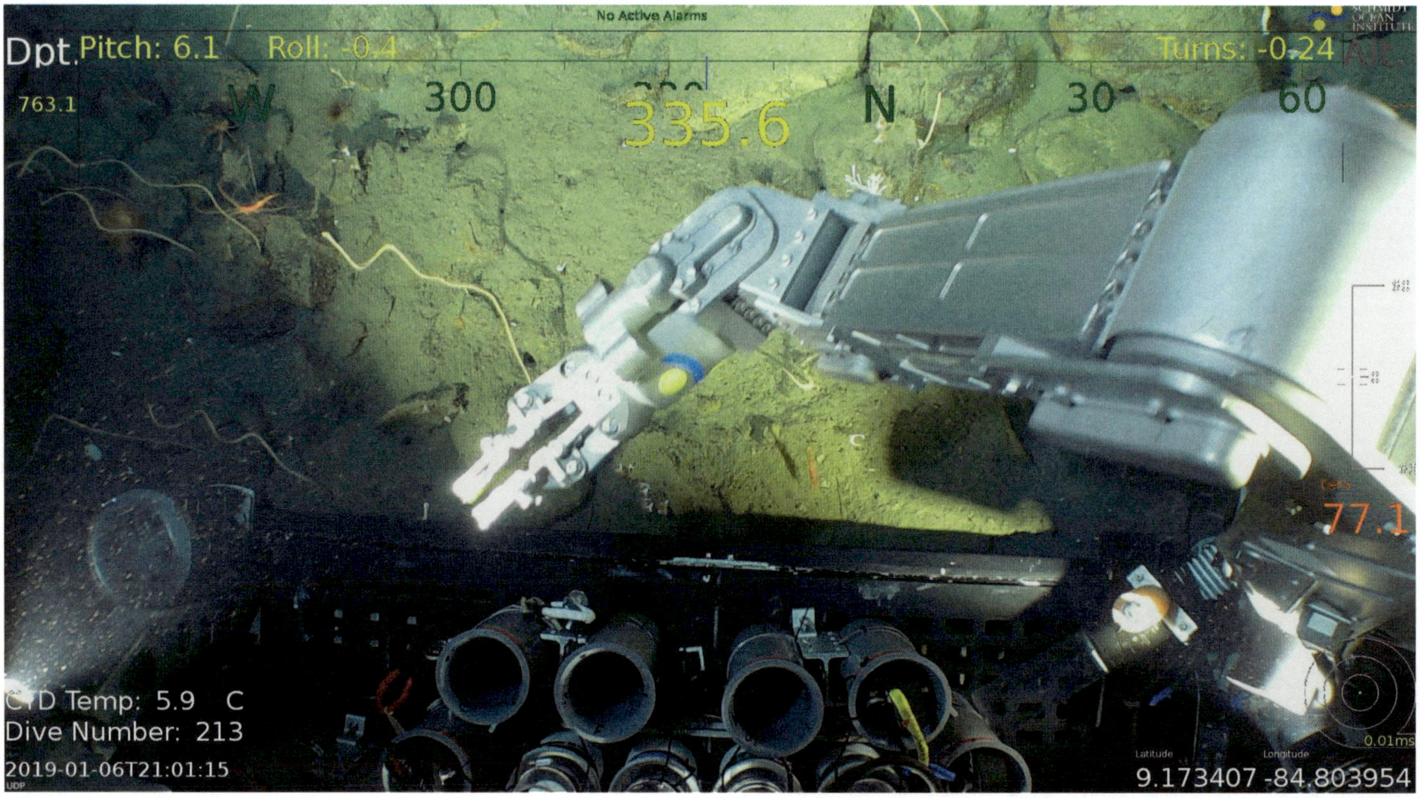

No Active Alarms

Dpt. Pitch: 6.1 Roll: -0.4 Turns: -0.24 Alt.

763.1

W 300 N 30 60

335.6

77.1

CTD Temp: 5.9 C

Dive Number: 213

2019-01-06T21:01:15

Latitude Longitude

9.173407 -84.803954

pearly globes, peeping into a pitch-black Mediterranean Sea. Jules Verne and his Captain Nemo's description of an underwater plantation are still haunting me.[1]

You too, in your eponymous film, have looked in the aphotic—from the Greek prefix *ἀ-* (without) + *φῶς* (light)—zone, where less than 1 percent of sunlight can penetrate, to find inspiration and moving images: between the Gulf of Mexico and the Caribbean Sea, around 4000 meters deep, where a submarine projects cones of luminosity around them just to make visible to humans what nonhumans and machines are perfectly capable of perceiving otherwise. Blinded by that intrusive, impossibly bright light, the inhabitants of the zone are severed, captured, extracted, and separated from their world, just to allow humans to perfect their knowledge on the resilience of corals. And to perfect control, and domination. The webpage of the Schmidt Ocean Institute explains that the research of Dr. Erik Cordes, who led the mission, "is focused on understanding the areas of the deep sea that support the highest biomass communities: deep-water coral reefs, natural hydrocarbon seeps, and hydrothermal vents. He studies these ecosystems at all levels of organization, from energy flow in ecosystems and patterns of community assembly, down to gene expression and microbial processes."[2] The new frontiers, science says.

I remember that during that call I was in Norway, surprised to be traveling again after two years of COVID-19 pandemic *moratoria*, and close to the same Baltic waters where you have plunged into many times and continue to explore, also as part of New Mineral Collective. A few days later I was—very shockingly, to my Mediterranean self—snorkeling in an icy fjord in the Lofoten, and couldn't stop staring at the corals, and the incredible density of life in those brackish waters, so similar to a starch soup. Wherever I'd turn my head, shafts of light from above would reveal minuscule shapes and forms—jellyfish, plankton, algae—and living beings I do not know. Human eyes see so little, besides what matches their own scale: they need microscopes and super-resolutions to begin to understand biodiversity.

In *Aphotic Zone* (2022) and elsewhere, you have zoomed in on the Coccolithophore, a minuscule unicellular marine alga whose peculiarity lies in its spheric shell made of calcium carbonate scales. As it is photosynthetic, it can live only in the photic (sunlit) zone of the ocean, and has a crucial role in the

1 See part 1, chapter 17 of Jules Verne, *Twenty Thousand Leagues under the Sea*, trans. F. P. Walter (Paris: Hetzel, 1870).
2 See "Our Team: Erik Cordes, Principal Investor," Schmidt Ocean Institute, available online.

marine food chain. Their scientific name is *Emiliania huxleyi*, and we have both shared jokes about it. You told me you're planning to use it as a pseudonym for the release of your first music album. Fossilized coccoliths, piled at the bottom of the oceans since primordial times, are the main components of chalk (think of the White Cliffs of Dover). By studying layer samples of those sediments, scientists can look into climatic changes over deep time. Bodies, no matter how large or minuscule, have been accumulating in the lowest strata of the oceans forever. They are part of water, as much as water constitutes the majority of our bodies. Do we see this? Can we think across scales and with them?

Yours,
Barbara

Dear Emilija,

Are you close to the sea? Are you diving? I woke up thinking of your mermaid tail and fin in action, with dreamy moves, in *Sirenomelia* (2018). Immersions, immersivity: they are both part of your life and works. To me, everything is connected by the ear. I can explain. When I was thirteen, I popped my ear drums while breath-hold diving with a friend. For a few seconds I could not tell whether I was swimming toward the bottom or the surface of the sea. That forever changed my relationship with acoustics and orientation: strong noises are unbalancing and loud drones almost annihilating, and invariably followed by tinnitus. Underwater sonic pollution is as intense and disruptive as other forms of pollution, but even more invisible to us. Sound travels much faster in water than in air, and noise levels in the oceans are believed to have doubled every decade since the mid-twentieth century. Scientific evidence suggests that fish and marine mammals like whales are learning to raise their voices, in order to communicate with each other across the deafening frequencies humans are generating at an increasing rate. They shout, researchers say, as we do in rowdy places when body language does not suffice. We find it even harder to listen, as we don't know how to. I am copy-pasting an excerpt from an article by David George Haskell on the physical impact of sonic slow violence on marine life: "Aquatic animals are immersed in sound. Sound flows almost unimpeded from watery surrounds to watery innards. 'Hearing' is a full-body experience. For most whales, and for many fish and invertebrate animals, eyes are only occasionally useful.

In the abyssal depths, the animals swim in ink. Along coasts, the water is so turbid that animals see, at most, a body length ahead. Sound reveals the shapes, energies, boundaries and other inhabitants of the sea."[3]

Do you feel it, when you swim below the surface? I know you've been at work with a community of blind divers.

In *Wild Blue Media: Thinking through Seawater*, Melody Jue writes: "If writers, artists, and theorists have traditionally been situated at a table in front of a computer to reflect on representations of the ocean from a distance, what form of thought might take place from within the water column, pressed on all sides by the fluid salinity of seawater? To what extent might the ocean operate as a necessary 'disorientation device' for theory and philosophy, a milieu that denatures our normative habits of orienting to the (terrestrial) world through language?"[4]

I think again of your video *Aphotic Zone*, the images of the robot's mechanical arm plucking corals, hovering and sampling life forms whose life condition would be crushing for human bodies, are not accompanied by the sound generated by that extraction—underwater video recordings and live streams from oceanic depths are often silent. The soundtrack you have created for it comes from Mexico City. You recorded a walk you took across the city center, departing from the Zocalo, on August 13, 2021, during the ceremonies for the quincentennial anniversary of the Fall of Tenochtitlan, as the city was called in precolonial times. Below its modern urban surface, it is still there. You often use your body to measure space and time, and connect the many layers of past and future, so entangled. On the same occasion, Mexicans were also celebrating other twenty-ones: the year 1321, when the Mexica (Aztec) Empire was founded in situ, and 1821, marking the end of the wars of independence fought by the so-called New Spain to free itself from the old one. The coat of arms on the Mexican flag reflects the foundation myth of the ancient, now sunken capital: an eagle holding a rattlesnake is perched on a prickly pear cactus, stemming from a rock surrounded by water. *Tenochtitlan* means "a cactus on a stone," because it was erected on the spot where an eagle performing the same action was first encountered, in the middle of the once vast and prosperous Lake Texcoco.

3 David George Haskell, "An Ocean of Noise: How Sonic Pollution is Hurting Marine Life," *Guardian*, April 12, 2022, available online.
4 Melody Jue, *Wild Blue Media: Thinking through Seawater* (Durham, NC: Duke University Press), 23.

Stories keep being told, as well as untold and unlearned. The *conquista* of Tenochtitlan was first chronicled, in triumphant tones, by the self-appointed Spanish "conquerors"; Indigenous authors offered different versions, where local warriors—mostly Tlaxcallan—outnumber the Western colonizers. Moving from the Gulf Coast in 1519, Hernán Cortés headed for the island city of Tenochtitlan. After the capture and death of Emperor Motecuhzoma II in 1520, an Aztec revolt drove the invaders from the city, but Cortés forged new ties with his allies, built a small fleet of ships to control the lake, and sieged Tenochtitlan for three months, while starvation and smallpox decimated its population. On August 13, 1521, the city surrendered and was destroyed. The conquistadors compared Tenochtitlan, built on artificially expanded and interconnected islands and surrounded by water canals, to the Italian city of Venice, the only equivalent they could conceive of or understand. Nowadays, there is almost no trace left of Lake Texcoco: over the centuries its body of water was brutally drained, and it finally succumbed to the drought and water shortages that rule the Anthropocene. You told me that, to you, fall and fallout are connected. According to geologists, one of the markers of the global advent of the Anthropocene is the presence of traces of nuclear fallout after bombing and nuclear tests carried out in the second half of the twentieth century in all the strata collected in very different parts of the world. Other scholars argue that the Anthropocene started with the *conquista* of the Americas and the global expansion of colonialism and its extractive horrors.

Maybe this story will not be told for much longer, if the extractive machine keeps on grinding, alienating, and atomizing planetary resources and forms of life and kinship?

Yours,
Barbara

Dear Emilija,

Did you read Carlo Rovelli's *The Order of Time*, in the end? I remember we were talking about it at some point. During my summer trip along the fjords, I was reading his other book *Helgoland*, on the birth and evolution of quantum physics. It's very thin but very dense, and I can be very slow when it comes to science; it took me a month to finish it, as if time began flowing at a different speed

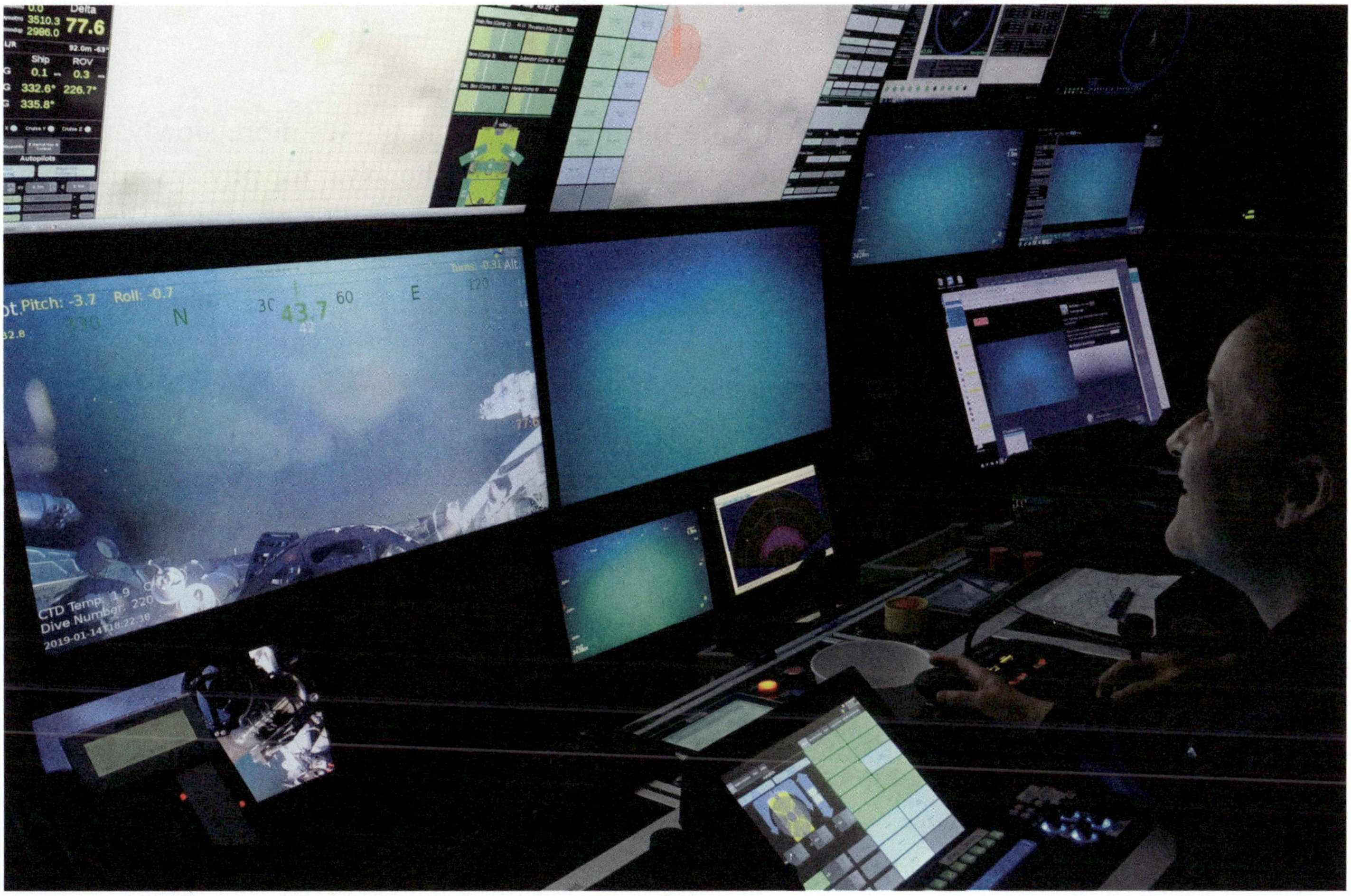

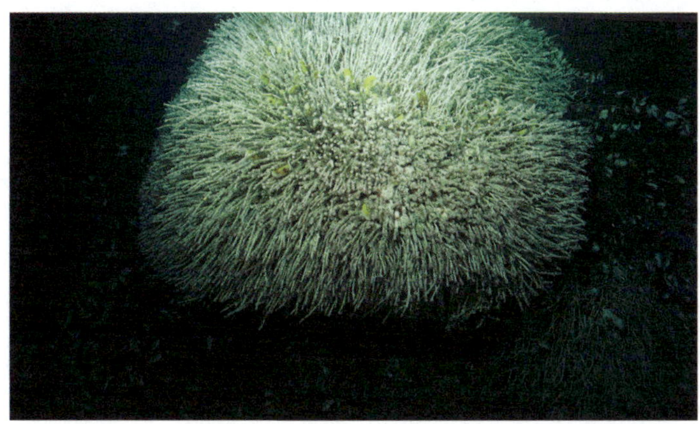

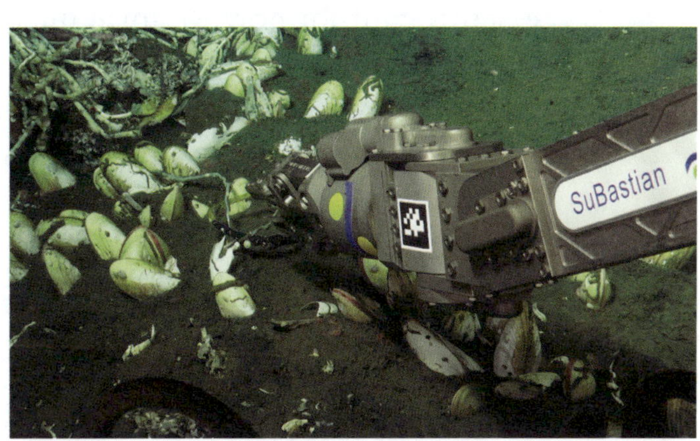
SuBastian

around its margins. For those who are on the move, time passes more slowly, Rovelli demonstrates. There is no such thing as "now," he says, for physics and philosophers alike—the idea of a universal present is just an illusion. He writes: "If I ask whether two events—one on Earth and the other on Proxima b—are happening 'at the same moment,' the correct answer would be: 'It's a question that doesn't make sense, because there is no such thing as 'the same moment' definable in the universe.' The 'present of the universe' is meaningless."[5]

To explain the "now," Rovelli refers to the "here," something that makes sense only when situated in a given spot, from an individual point of view, although I am certainly oversimplifying. My "here" and your "here" are not the same, they coexist with and within us simultaneously. In the last pages of *Helgoland*, the solidity of reality melts like an iceberg facing global warming, to the point that the author feels compelled to remark that each time we start seeing something apparently solid as liquid, the flowing of our lives becomes sweeter. The vast majority of Earth is occupied by water. It is more liquid than solid, although as humans we adopt very terrestrial perspectives and gravities. To move underwater challenges not only our physical limitations, but also our apparatuses of knowledge and our ways of seeing. To gaze at the bottom of the ocean, where sediments have rested for countless eras, feels like looking at deep time. To dive into it means to actually position ourselves in a condition of liquidity.

I am sharing another quote from *Wild Blue Media*, as I suspect you may like it. To me, it translates into your research almost wave by wave, fin stroke by fin stroke, as we follow you "modern undine" (as Quinn Latimer writes, ever so beautifully) underwater, to the dark and constantly changing depths of our postmodernities: "By offering entirely different conditions than land—increased pressure, three-dimensional movement, light refraction and magnification, and the inability to tell the direction of sounds, to name a few—the ocean is a material and imaginative space for the conditions of perception that we have taken for granted. Milieu-specific analysis acknowledges that specific thought forms emerge in relation to different environments, and that these environments are significant for how we form questions about the world, and how we imagine communication within it. However, the challenge with milieu-specific analysis is not to reify the ocean as a stable object, since what the ocean 'is' is also a matter 'for whom.' There should also be a historical consideration, since the way

5 See chapter 3, "The end of the present," in Carlo Rovelli, *The Order of Time* (New York: Riverhead Books, 2018).

we come to know the ocean is through many accumulated moments of contact through our bodies, cultural practices, and technological instruments. Thus, instead of seeing the ocean as a decodable structure that determines thought, we can think of it as a dynamic milieu whose characteristics manifest by actively moving within it (as a human, octopus, plankton, or other) and through mediated forms of contact."[6]

It's through your body, I think, that you always try and measure space-time. Whether you do it by walking along the noisy streets of Mexico City in a here and now that could also be the here and now of centuries ago, or by swimming toward the bottom of a sea, where sunken cities[7] and once-modern infrastructures are submerged by bodies of water in constant movement, it doesn't seem to matter. Am I right?

Good night, dear, take care.

Yours,
Barbara

Images taken by Dr. Erik Cordes.
Courtesy of Erik Cordes and the Schmidt Ocean Institute.

6 Jue 2020, 3.
7 See, for instance, Emilija Škarnulytė's work *Sunken Cities* (2021).

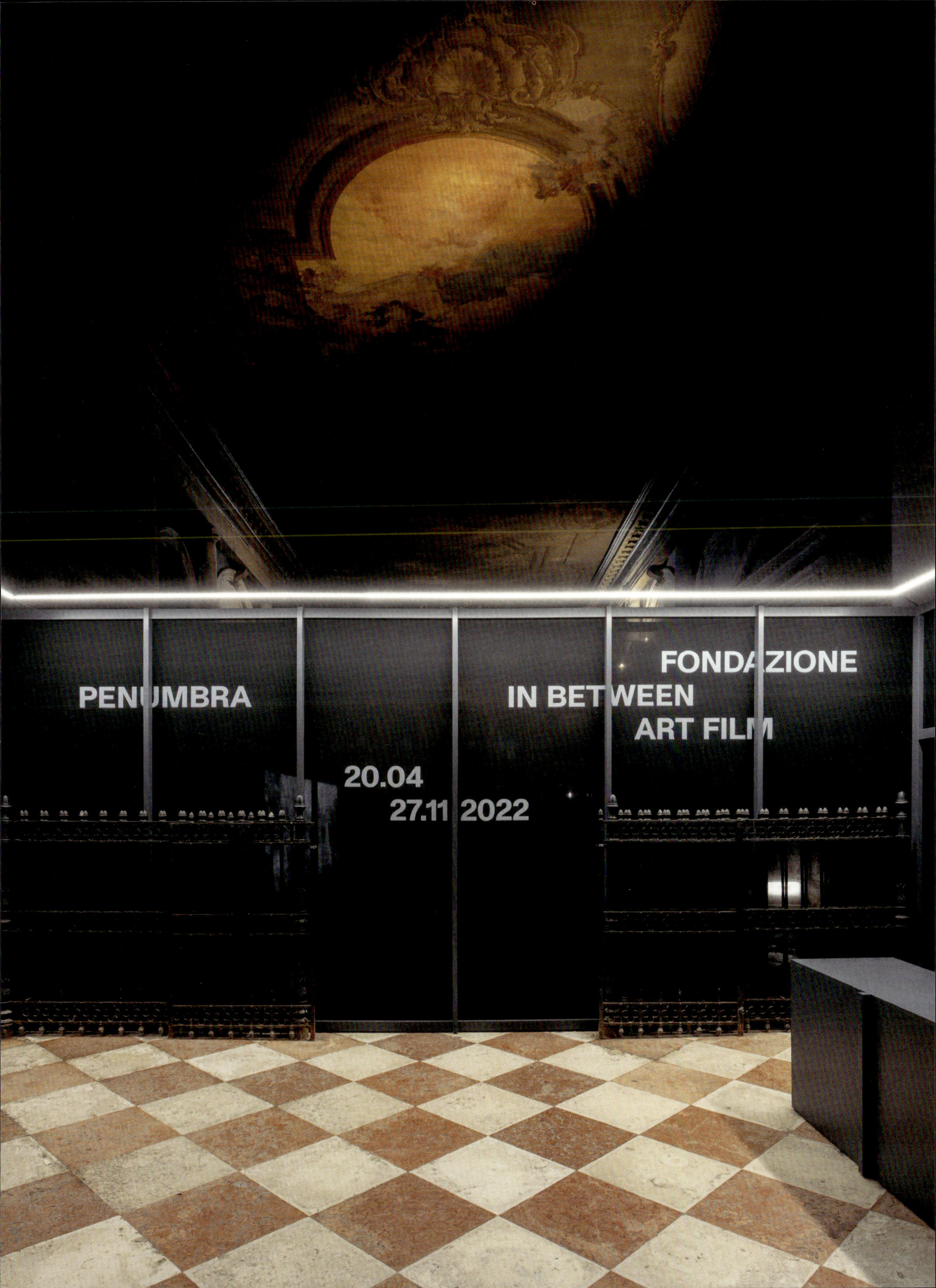
FONDAZIONE
PENUMBRA
IN BETWEEN
ART FILM
20.04
27.11 2022

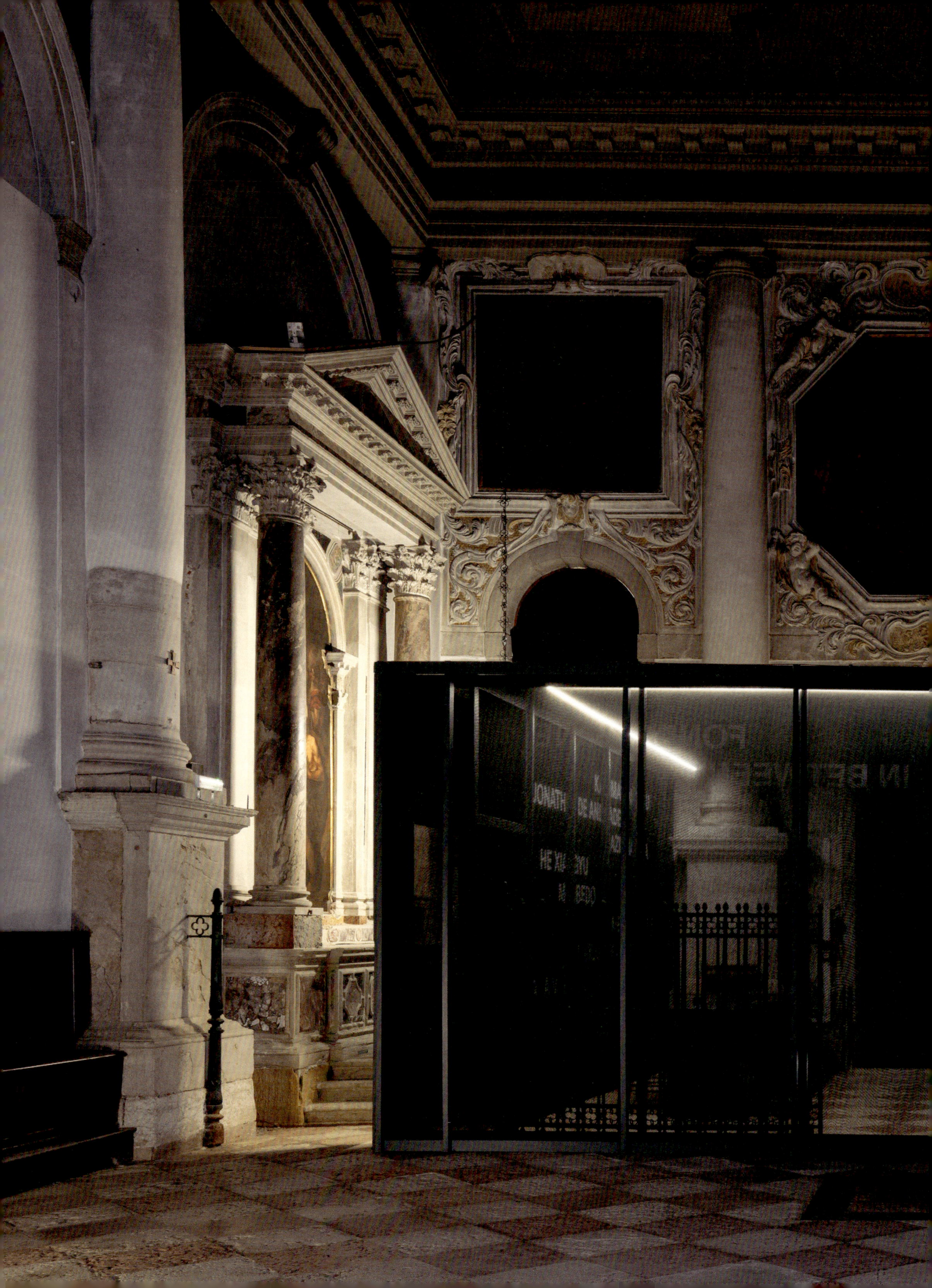

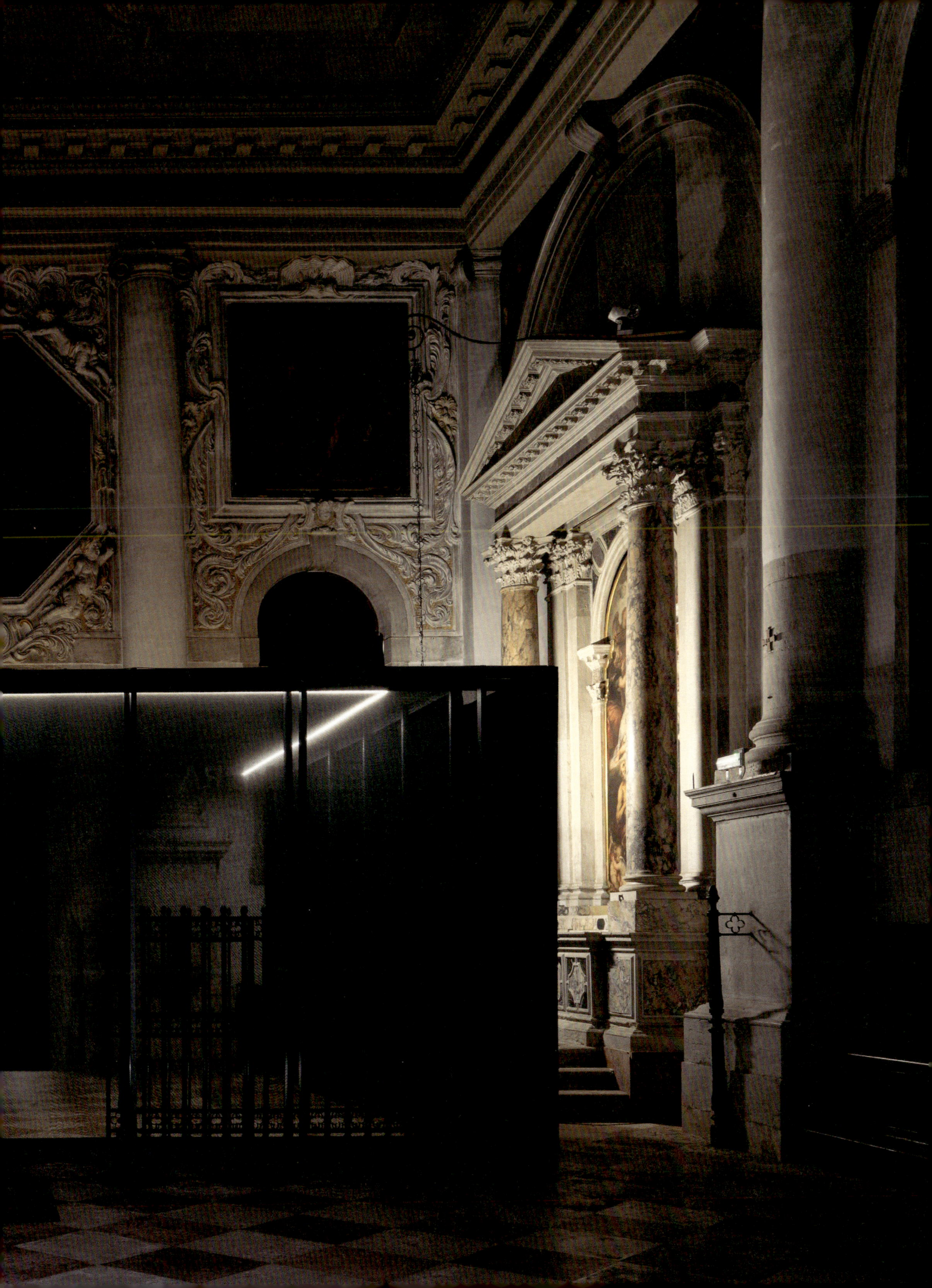

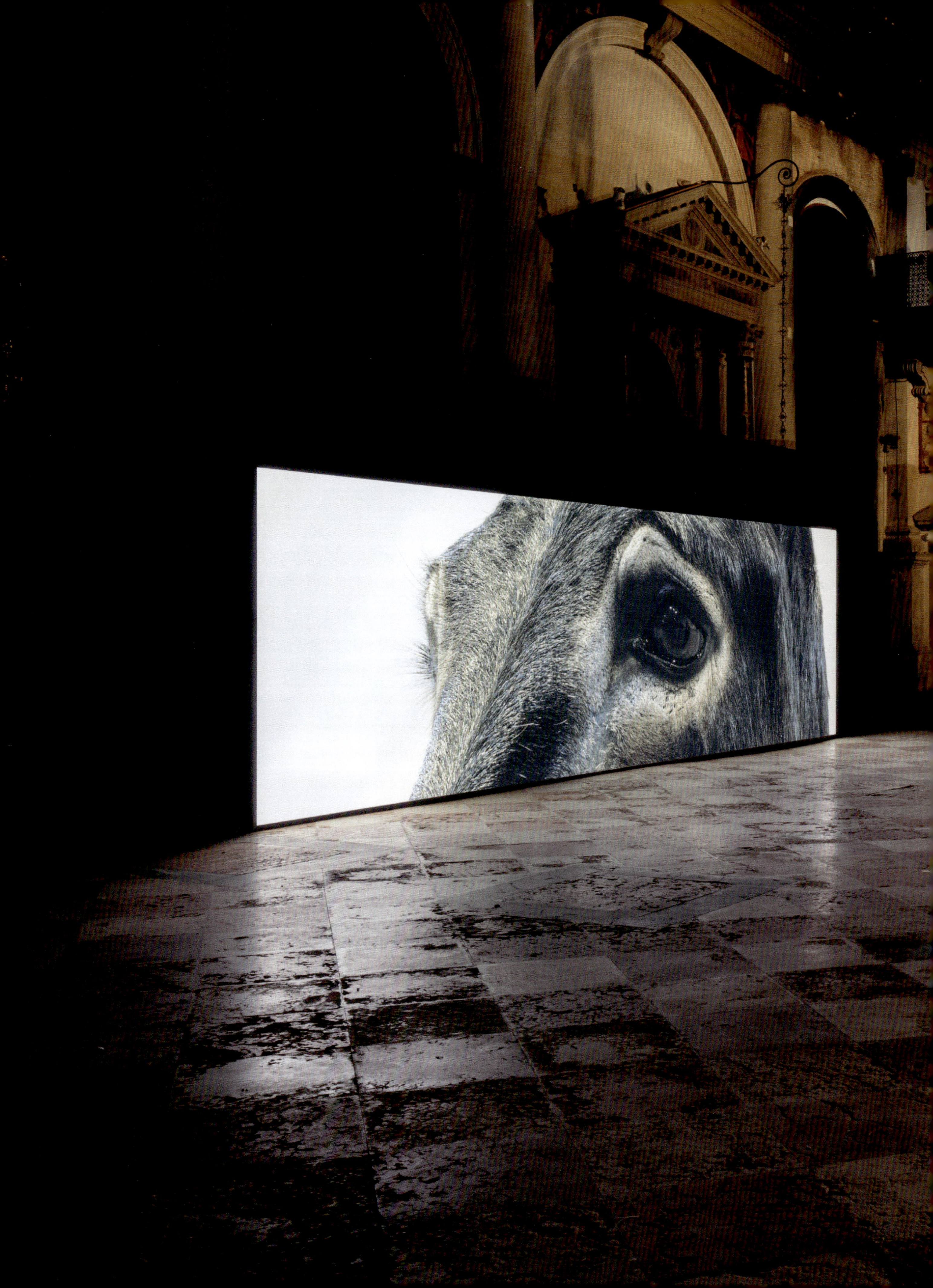

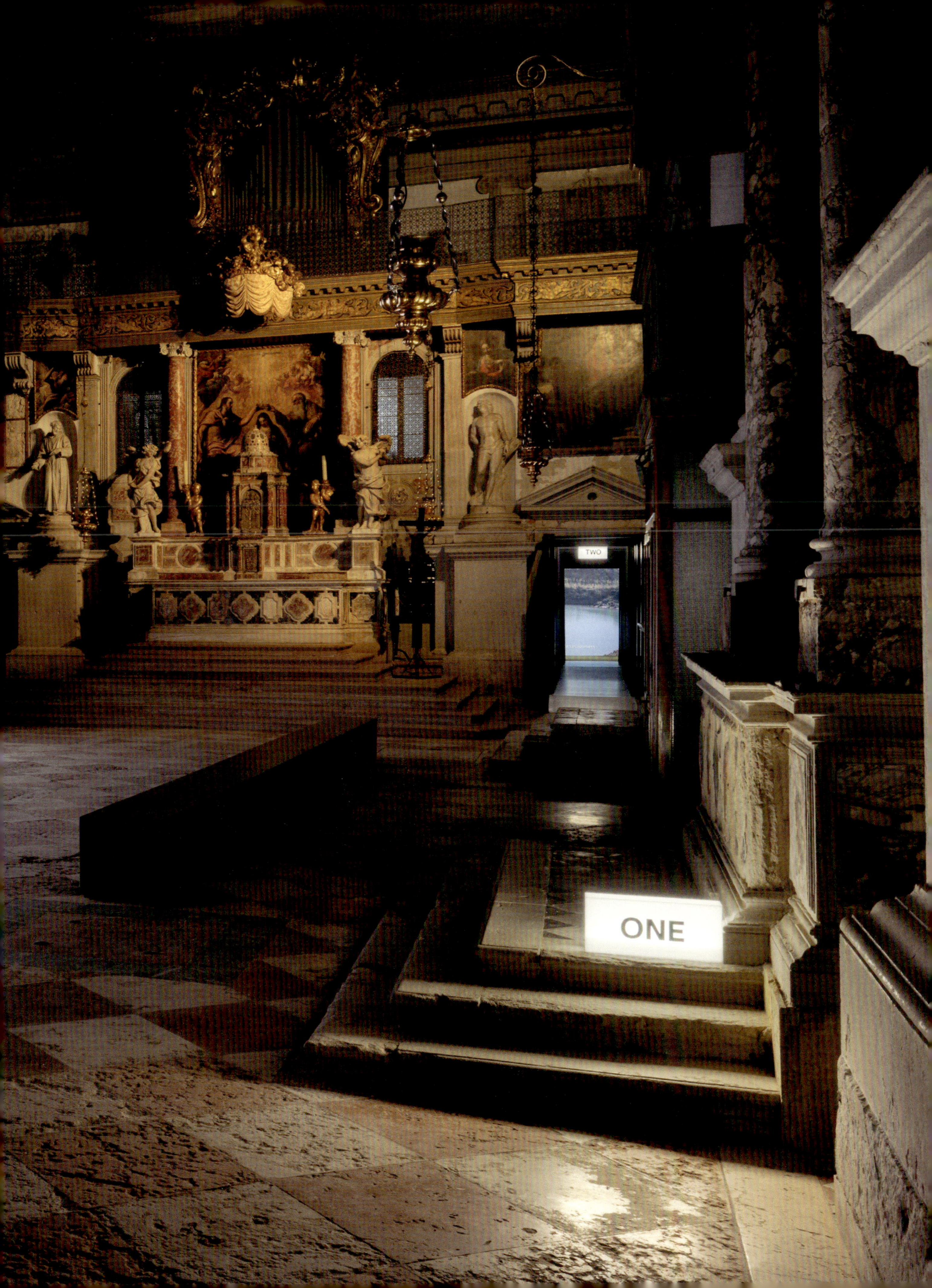

TWO
ONE

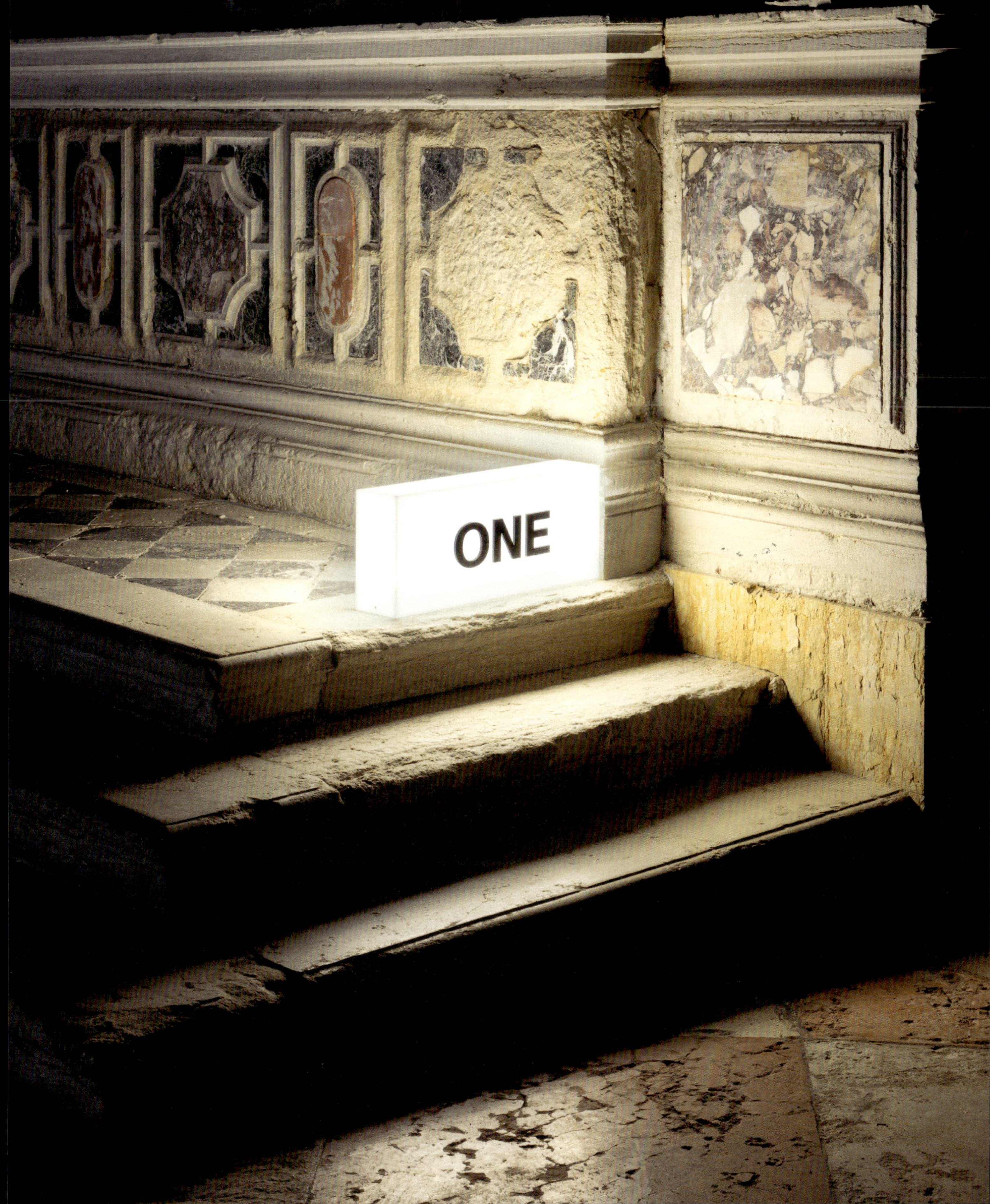
ONE

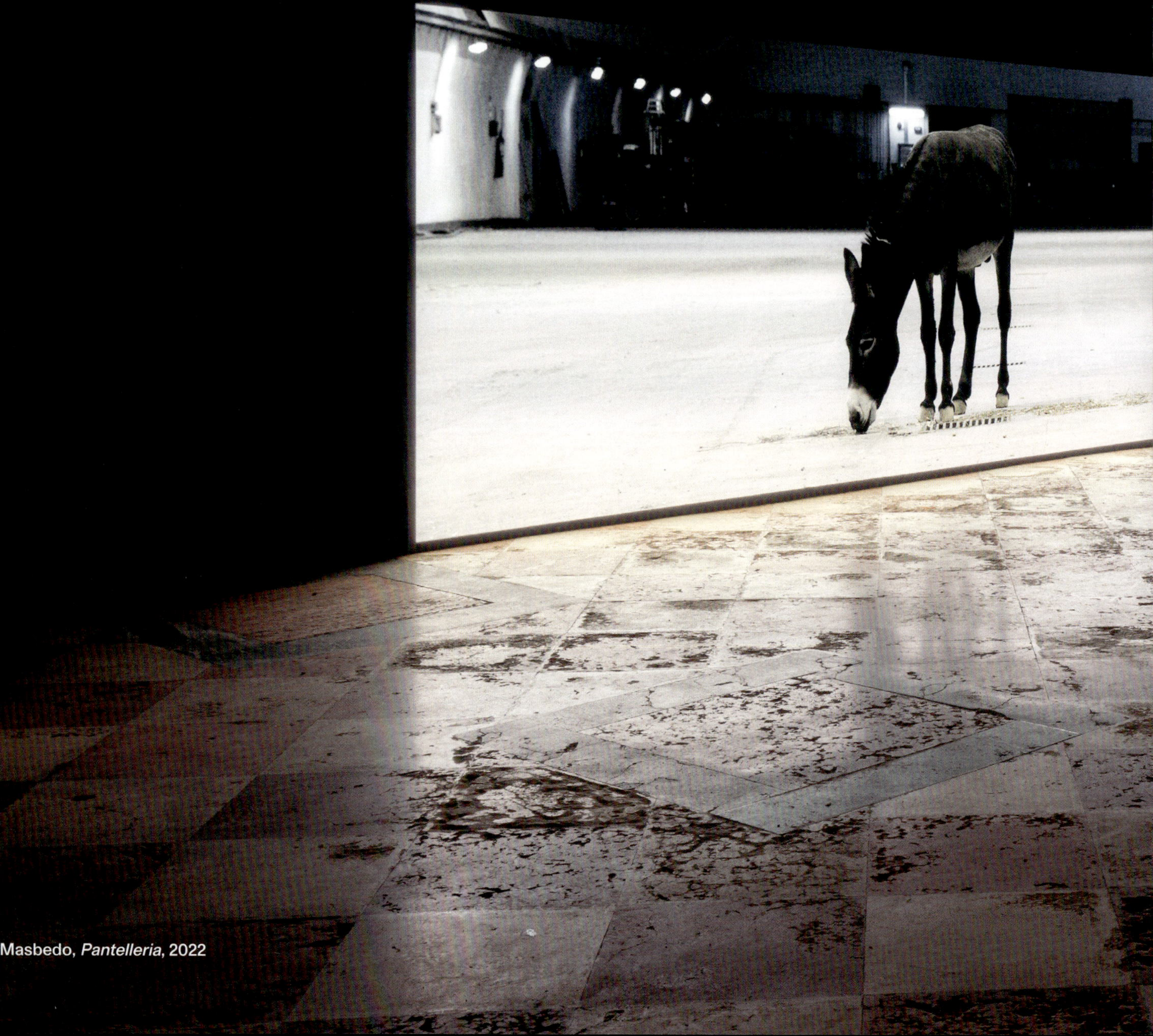

Masbedo, *Pantelleria*, 2022

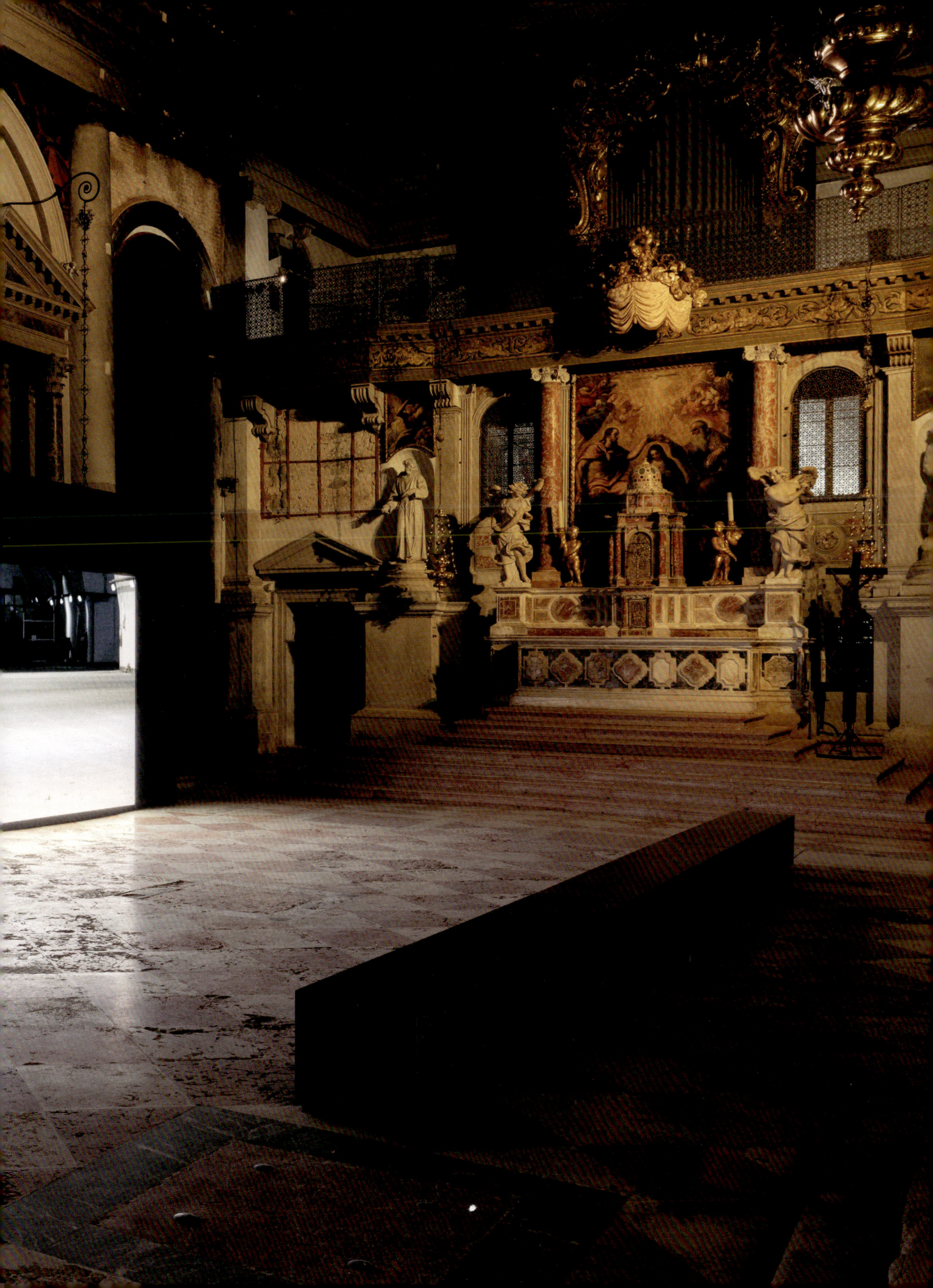

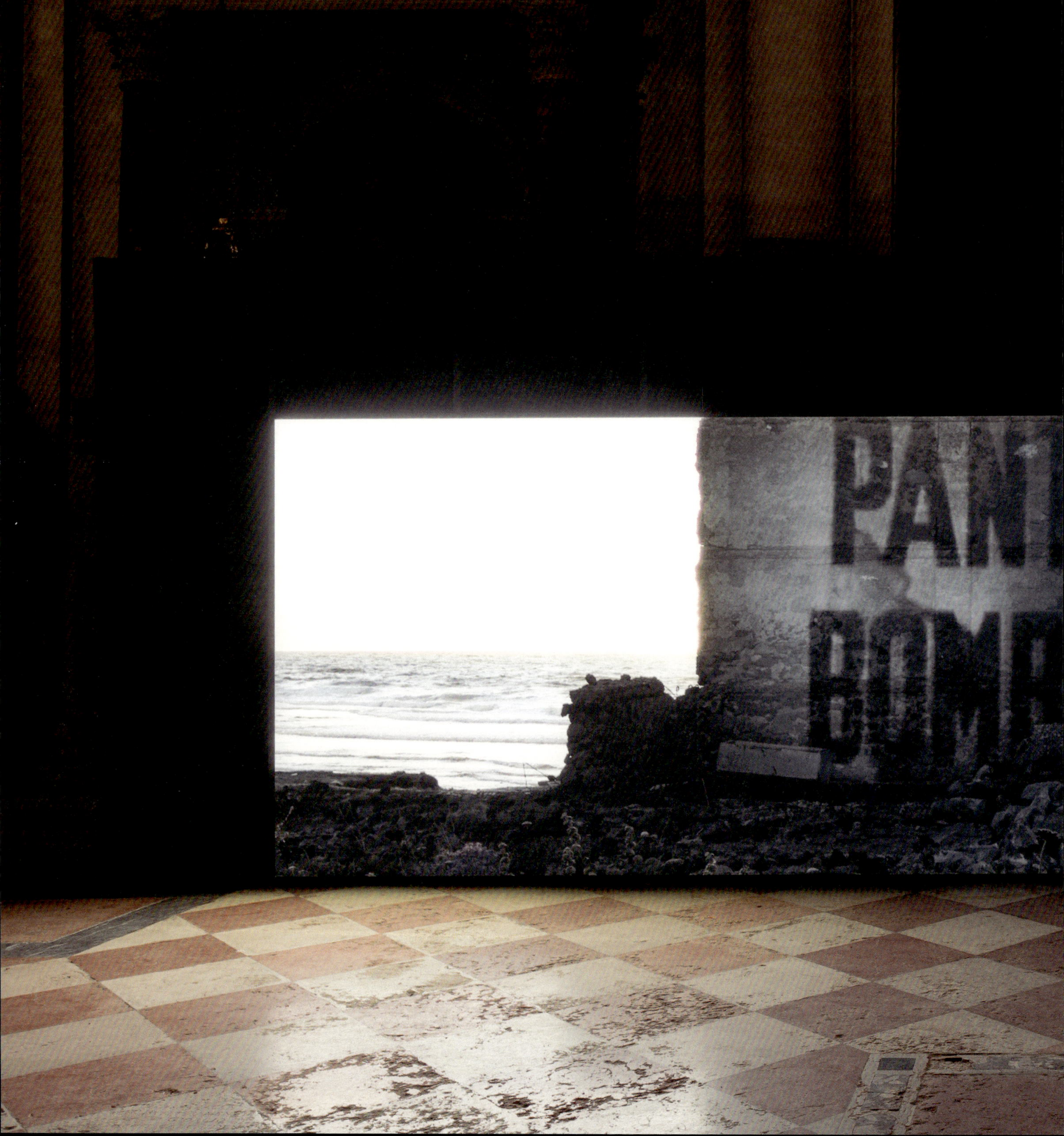
PAN
BOM

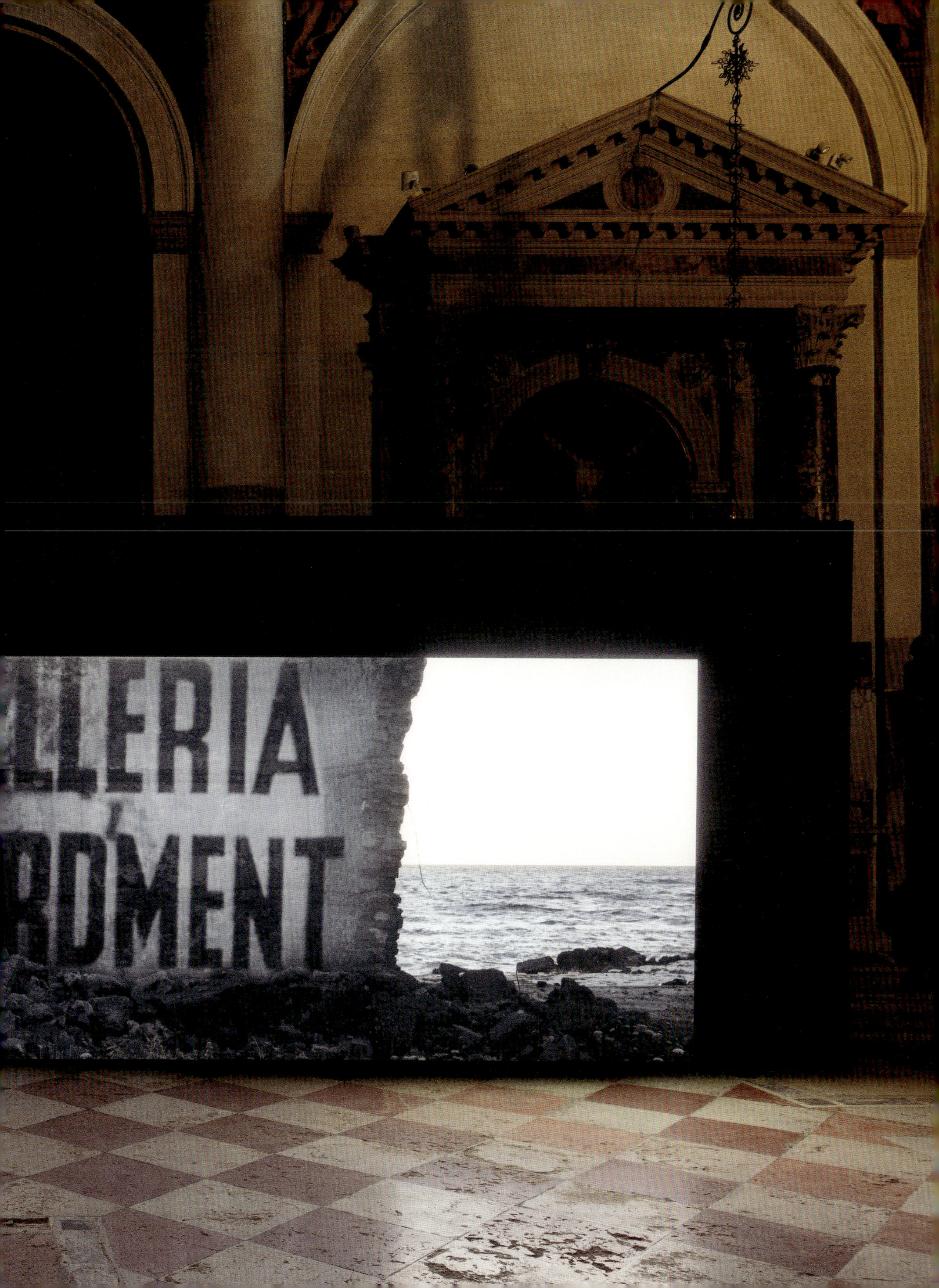

LLERIA
RDMENT

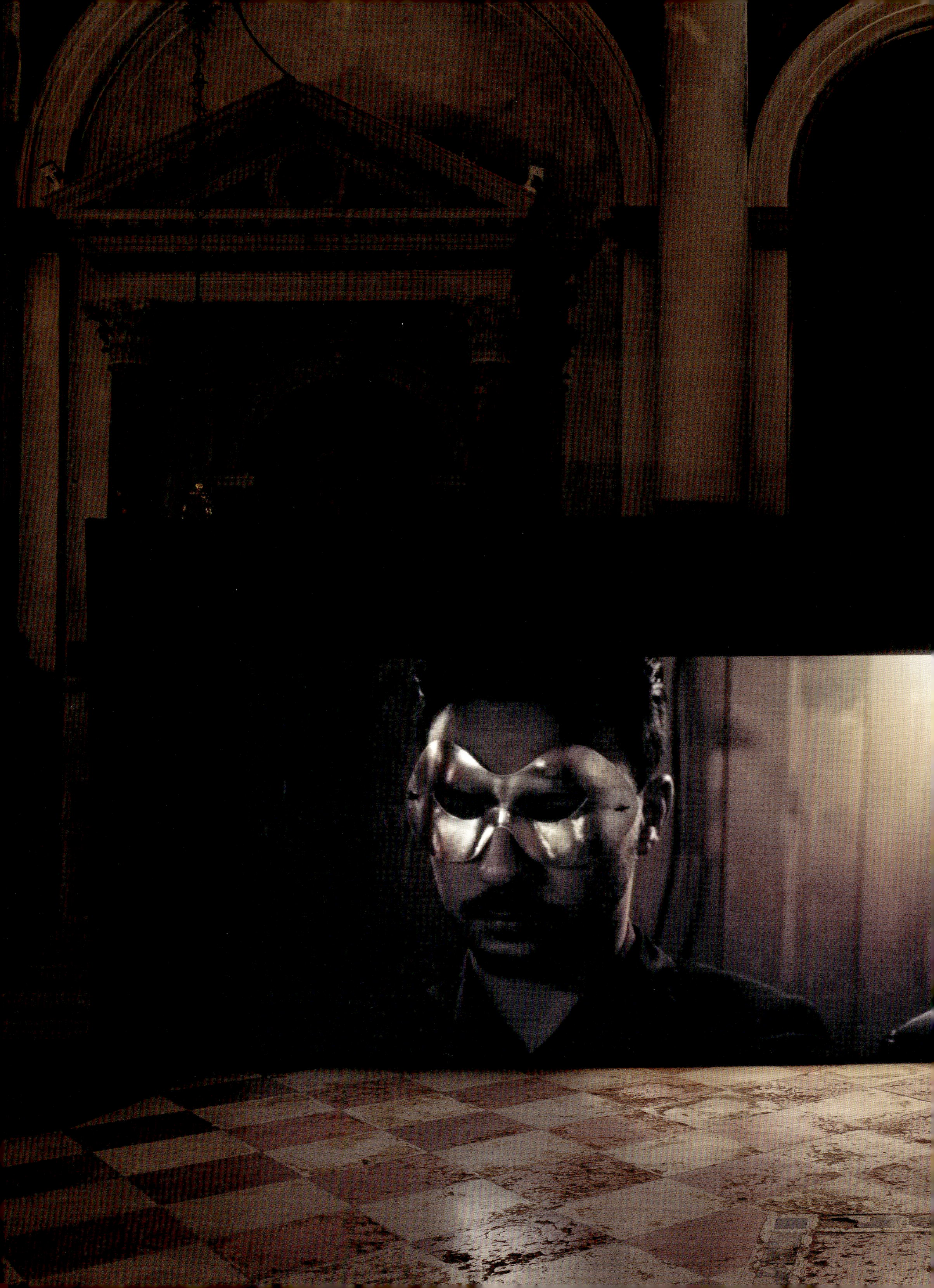

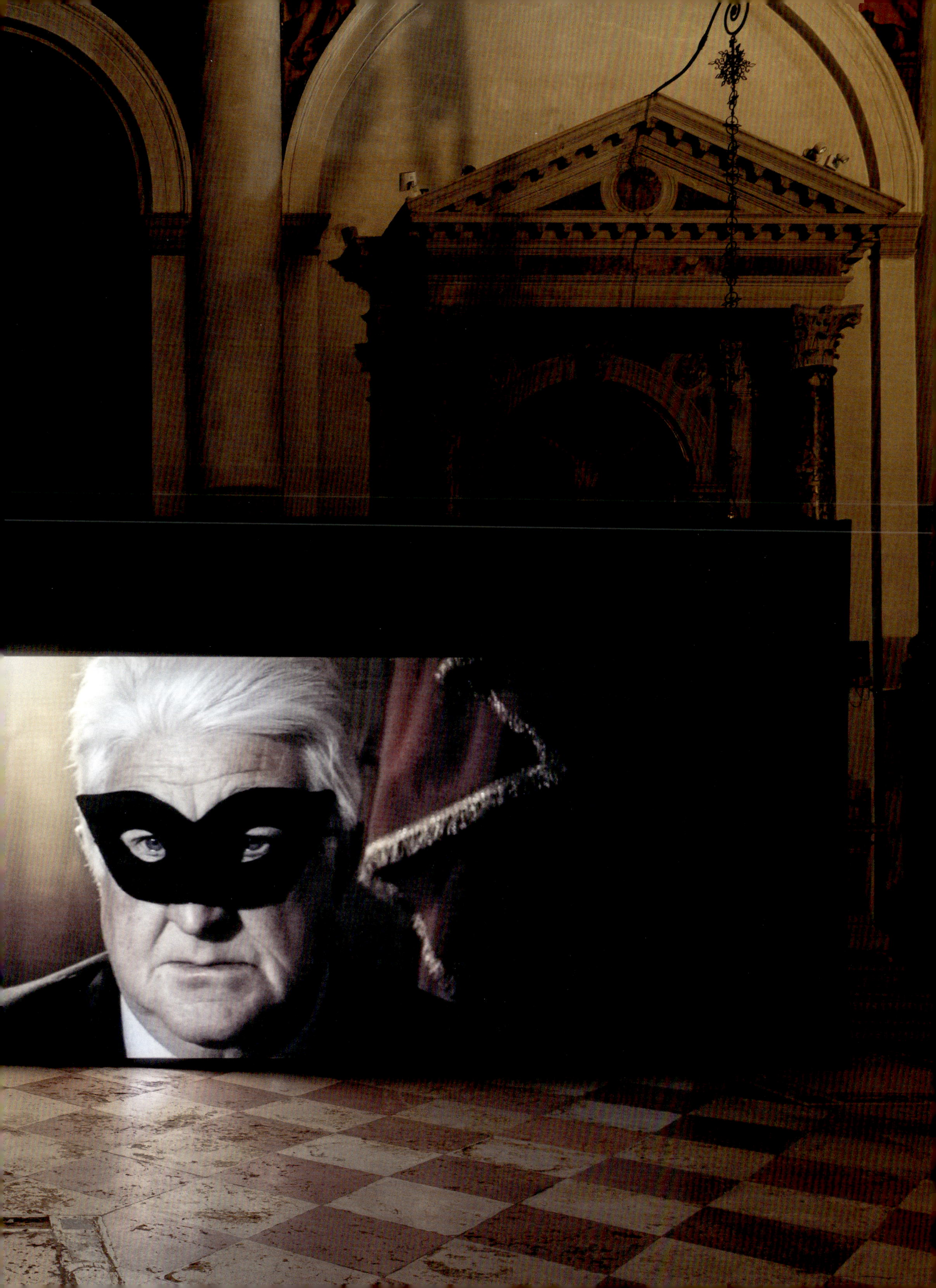

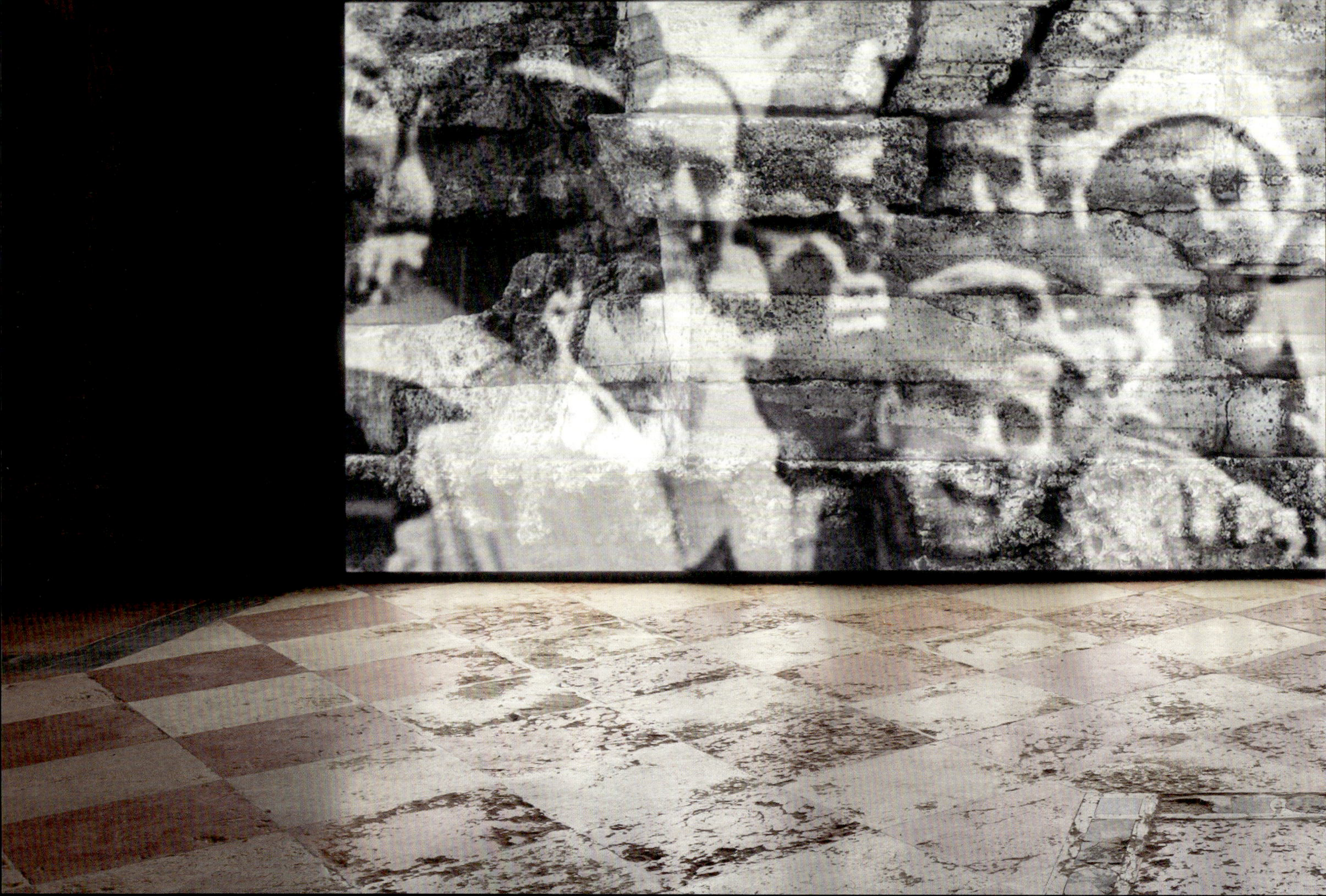

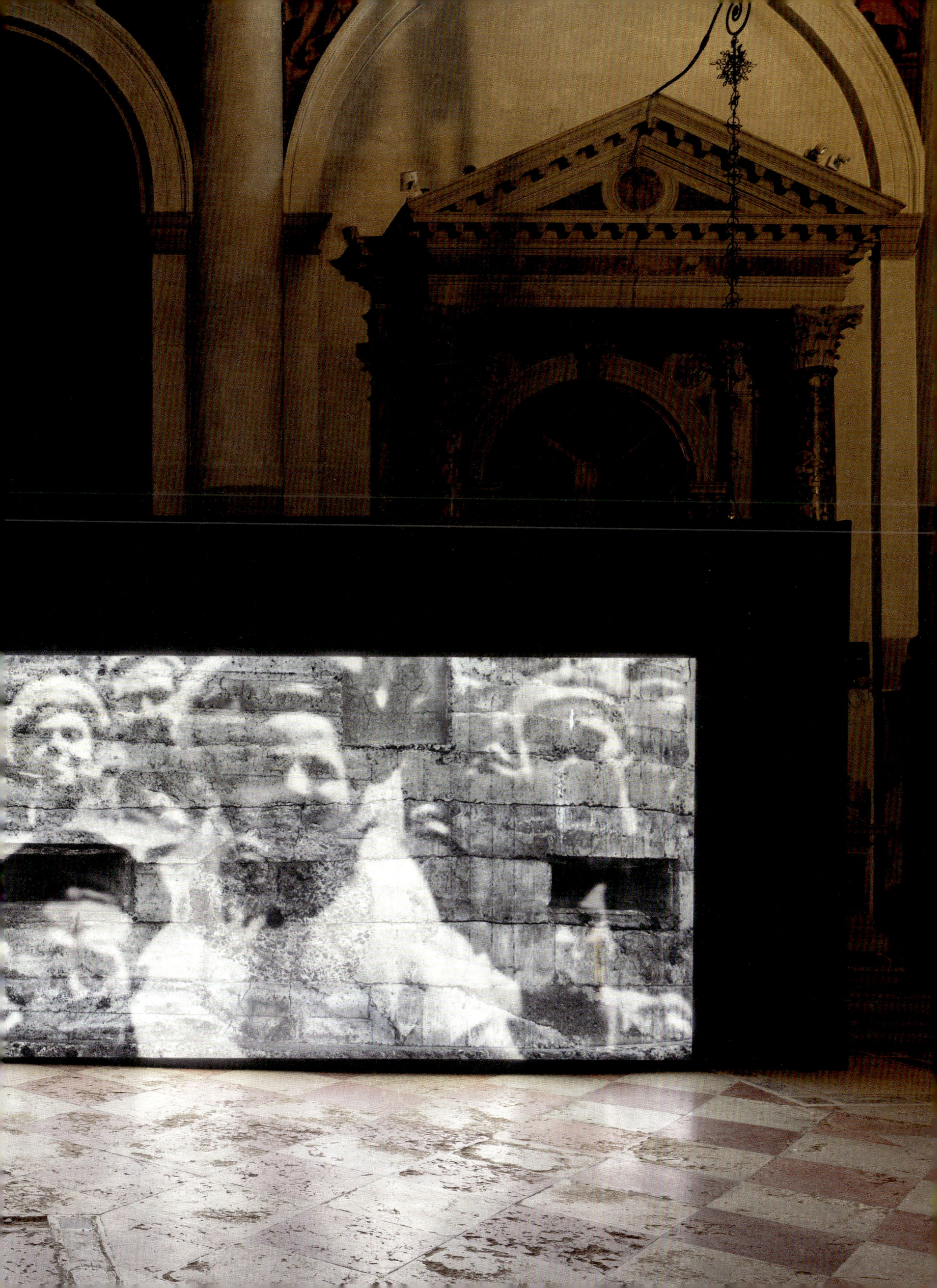

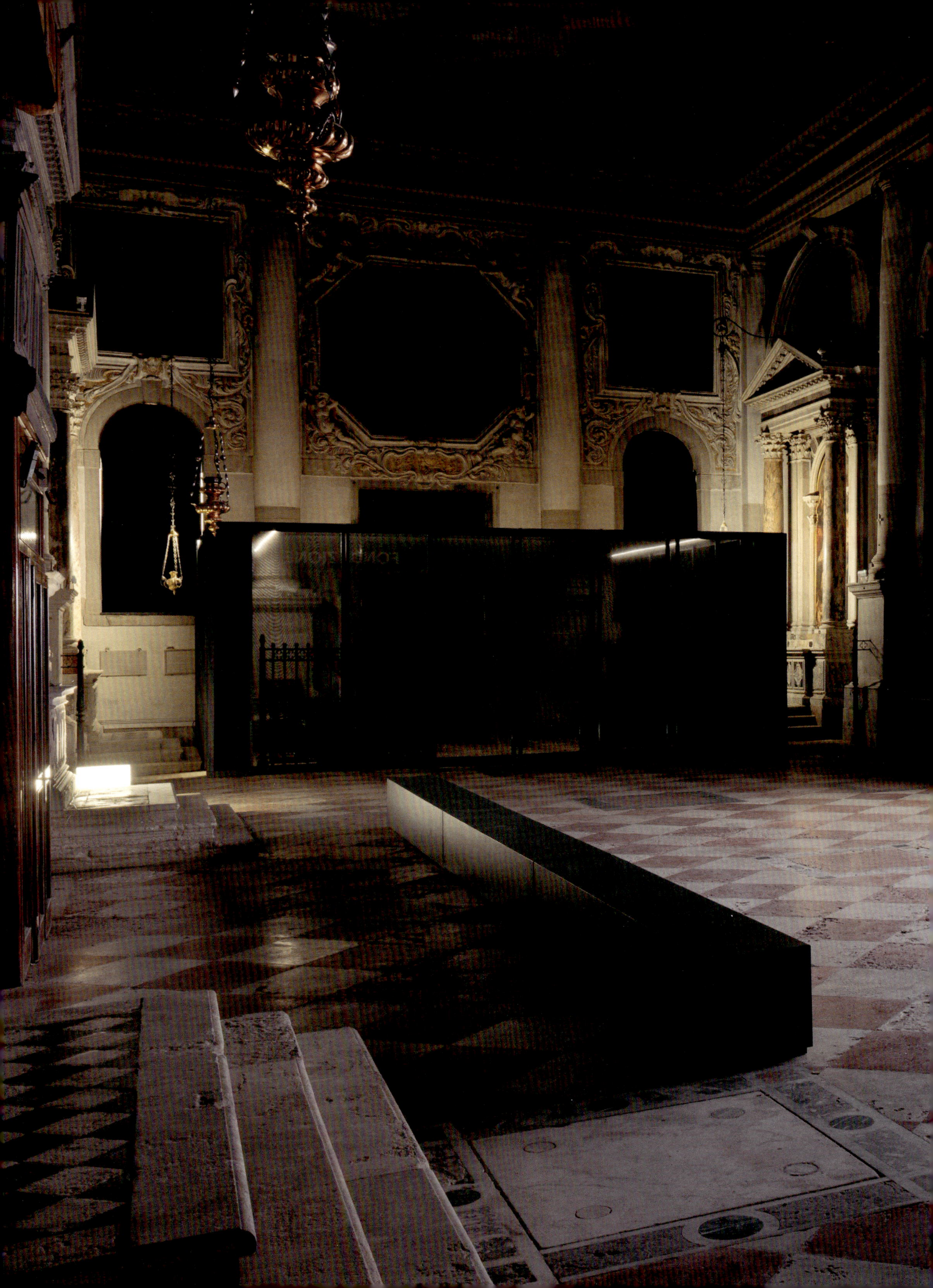

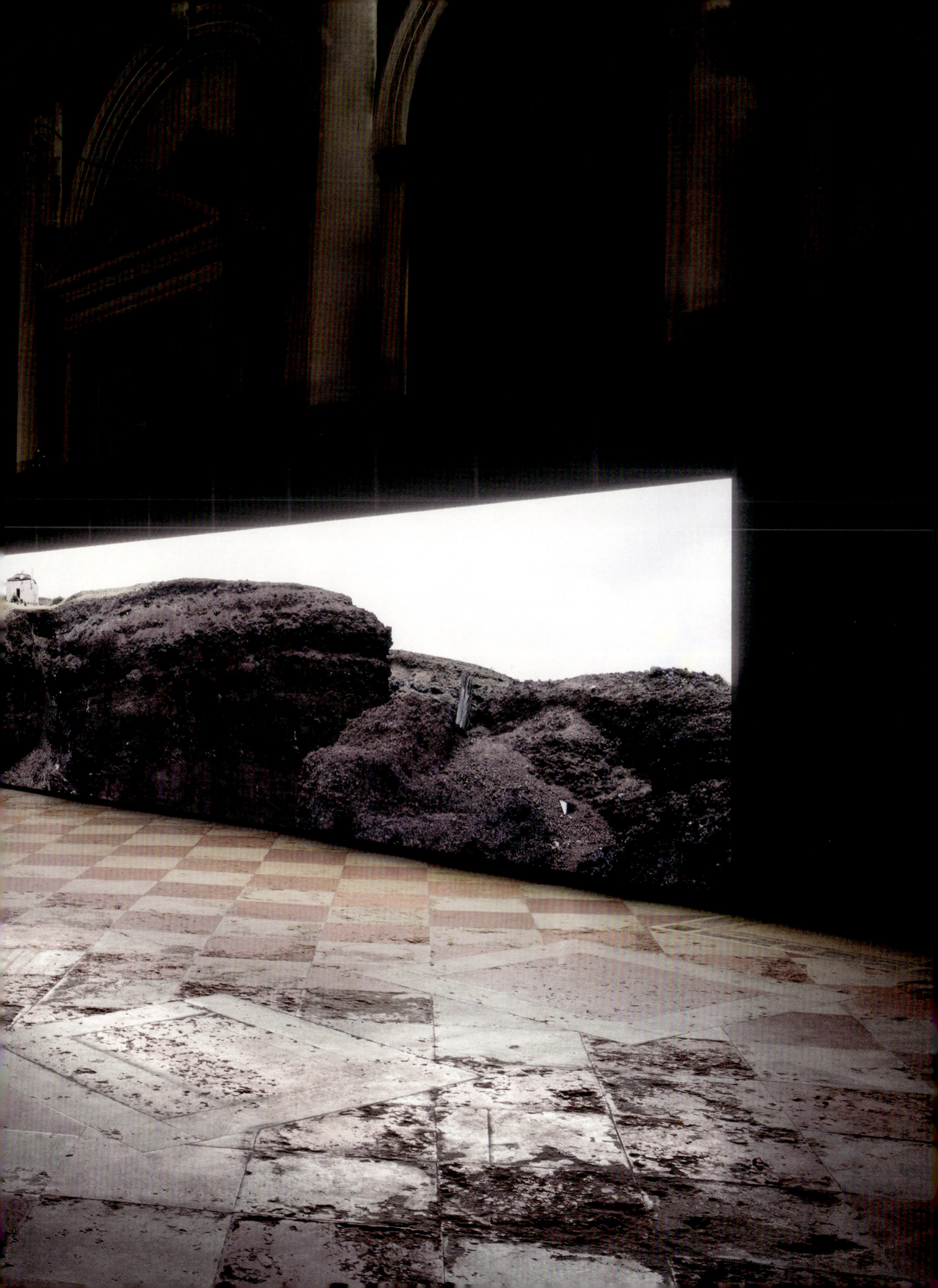

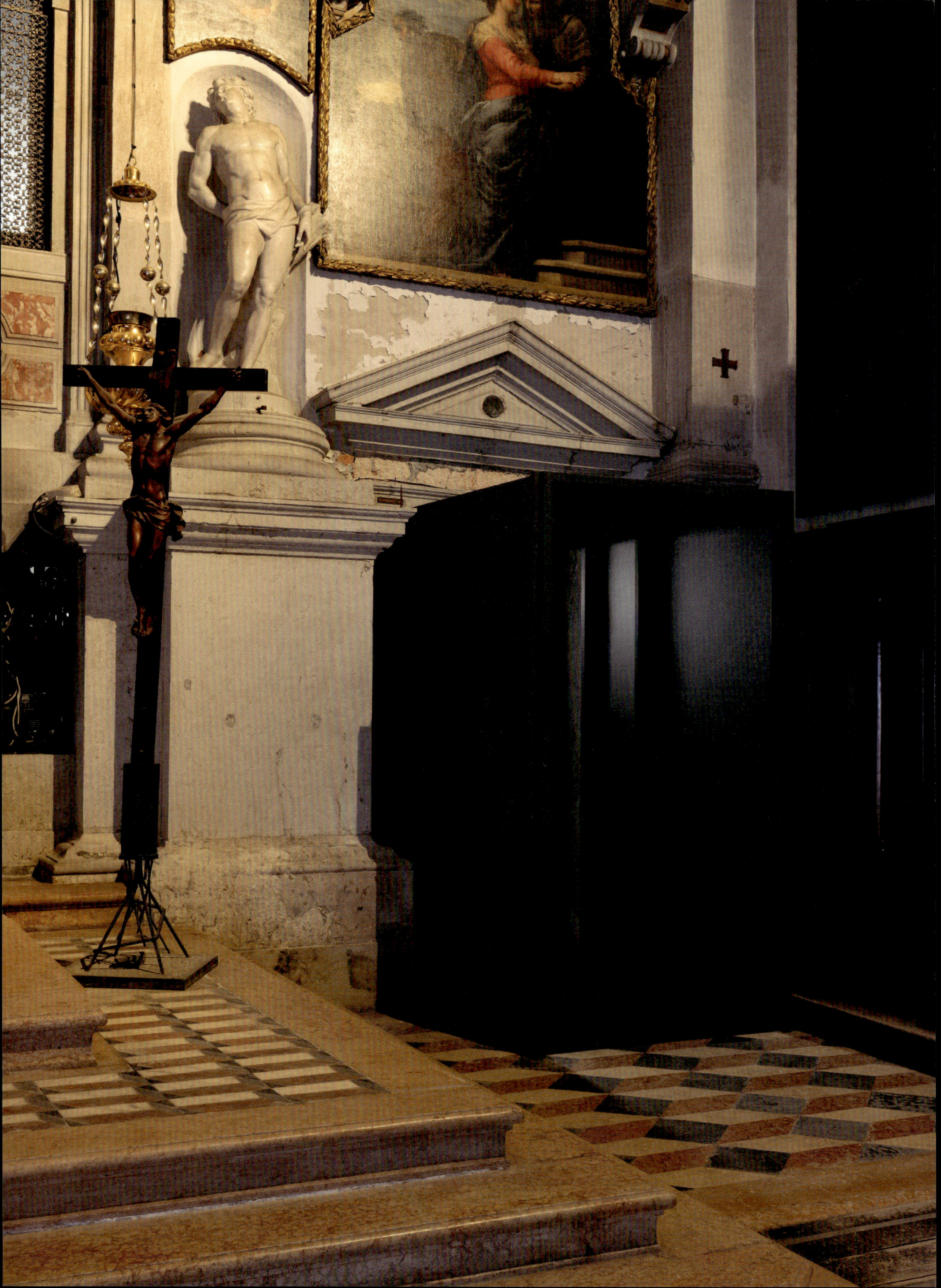

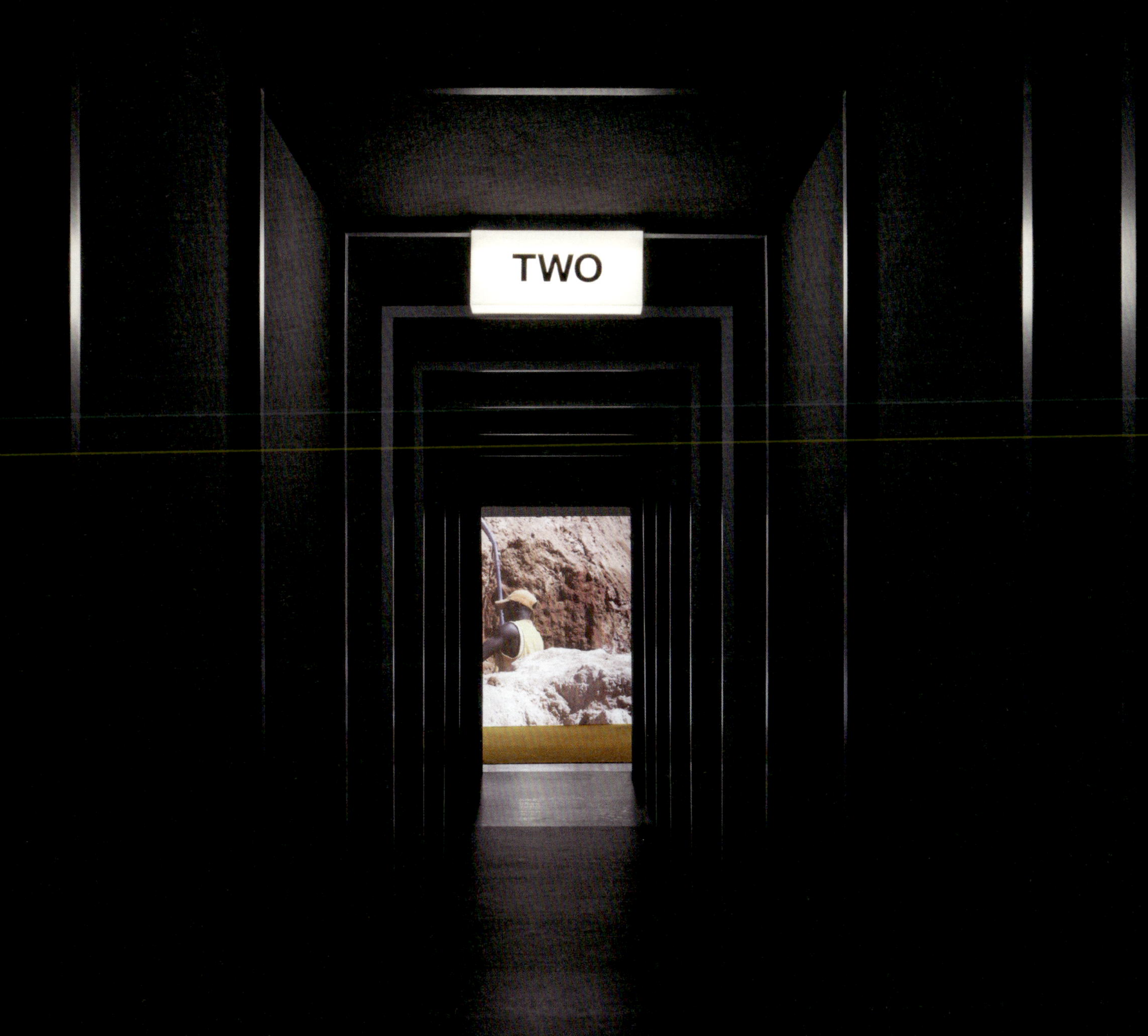
TWO

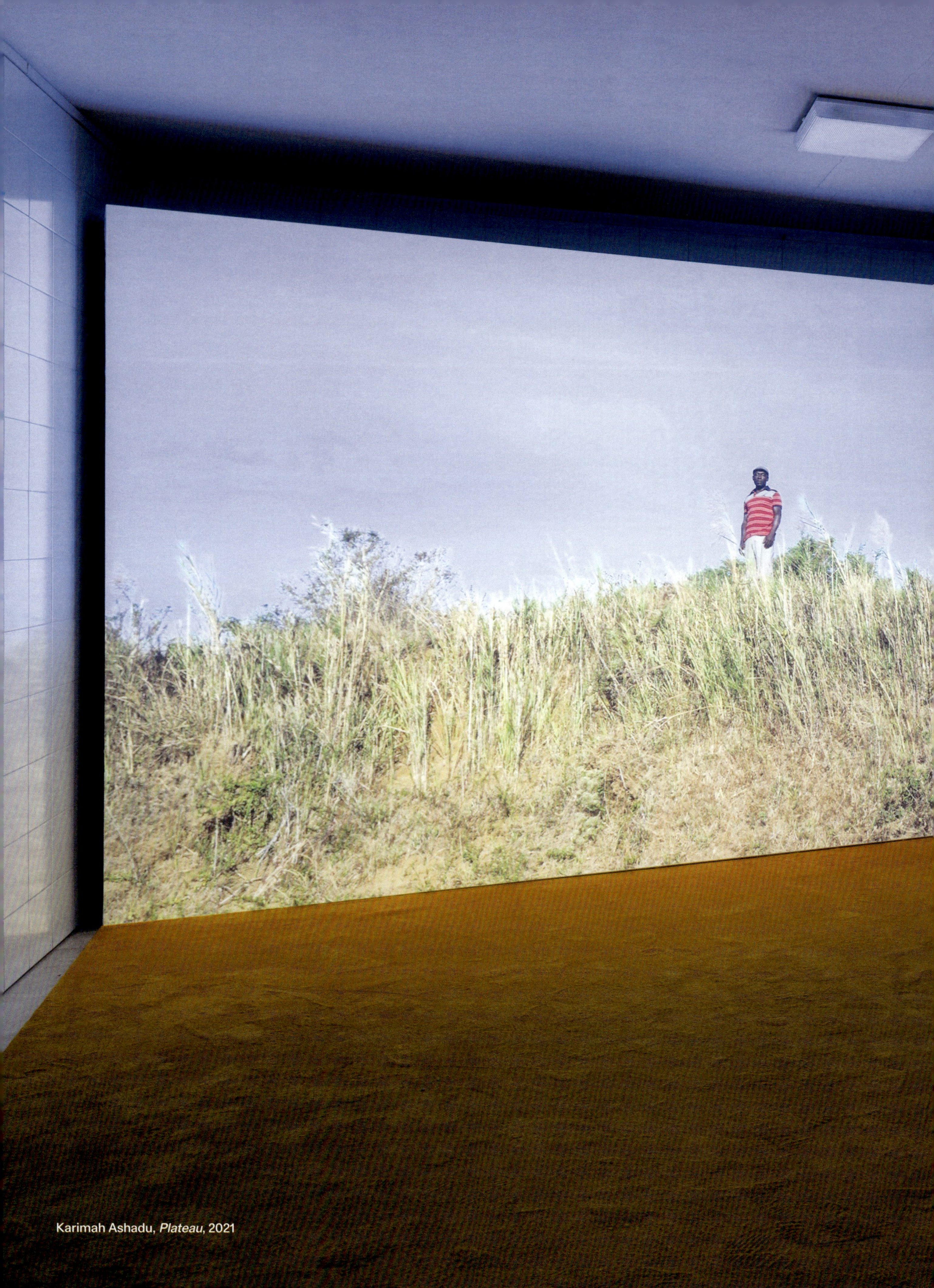

Karimah Ashadu, *Plateau*, 2021

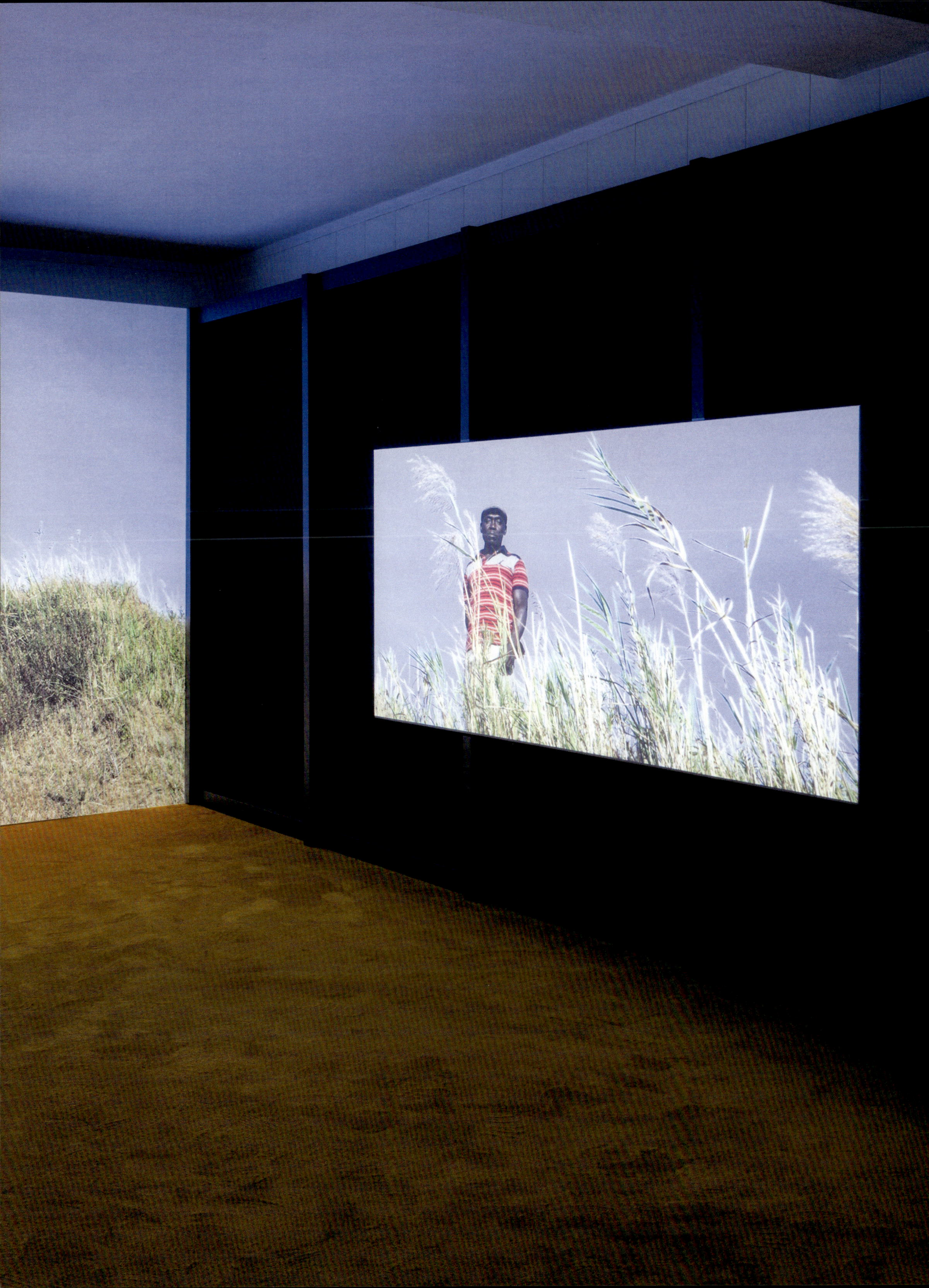

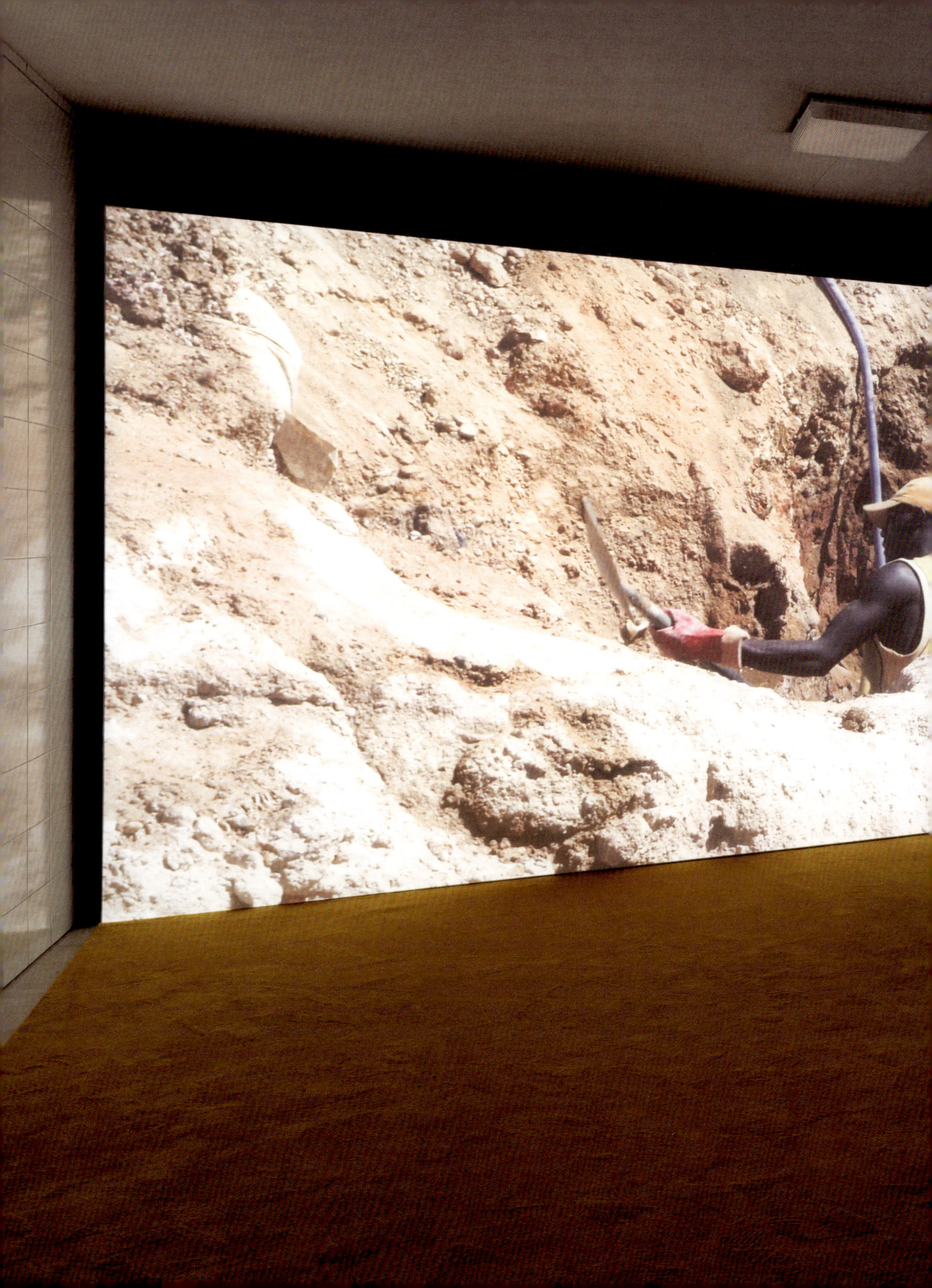

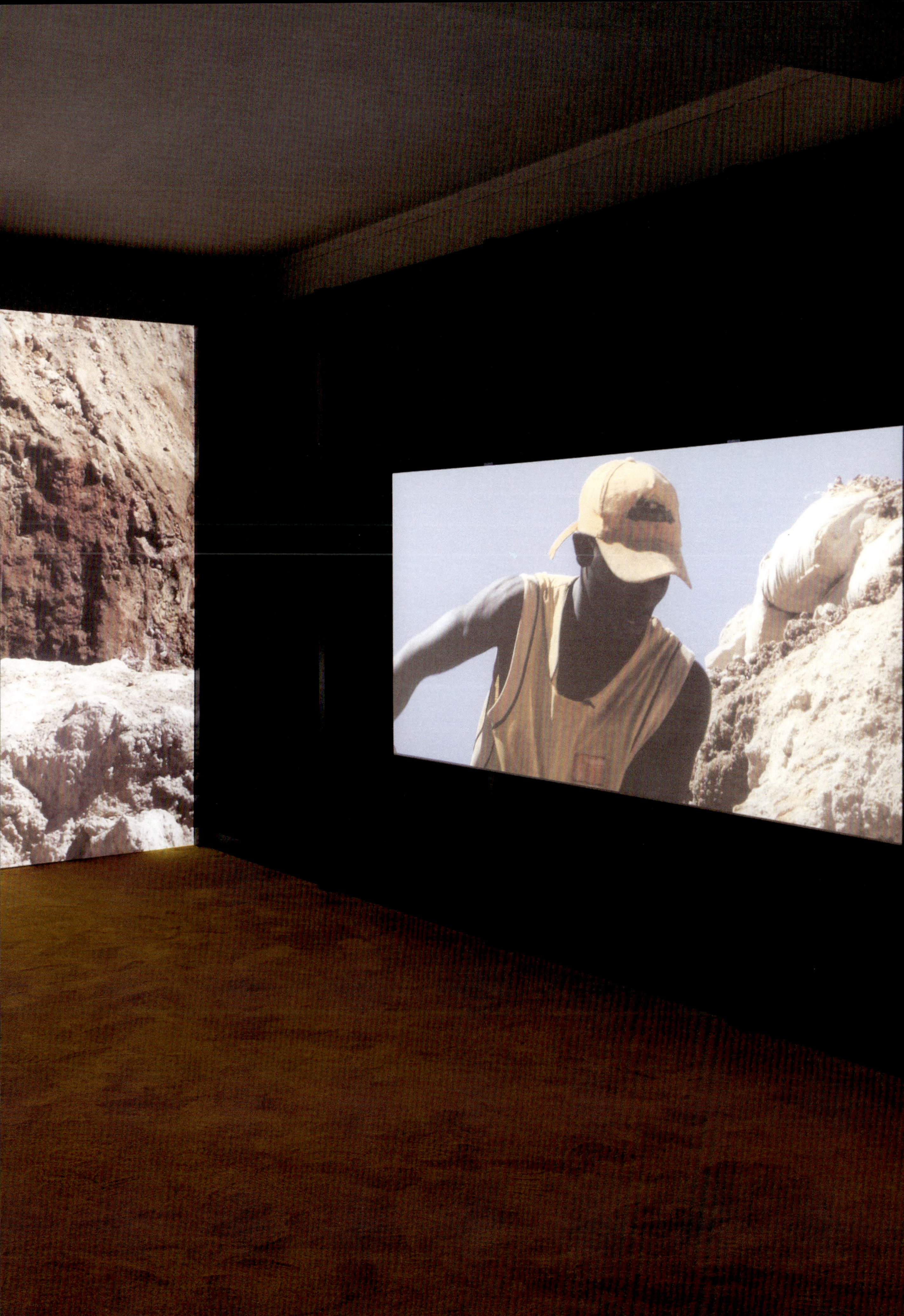

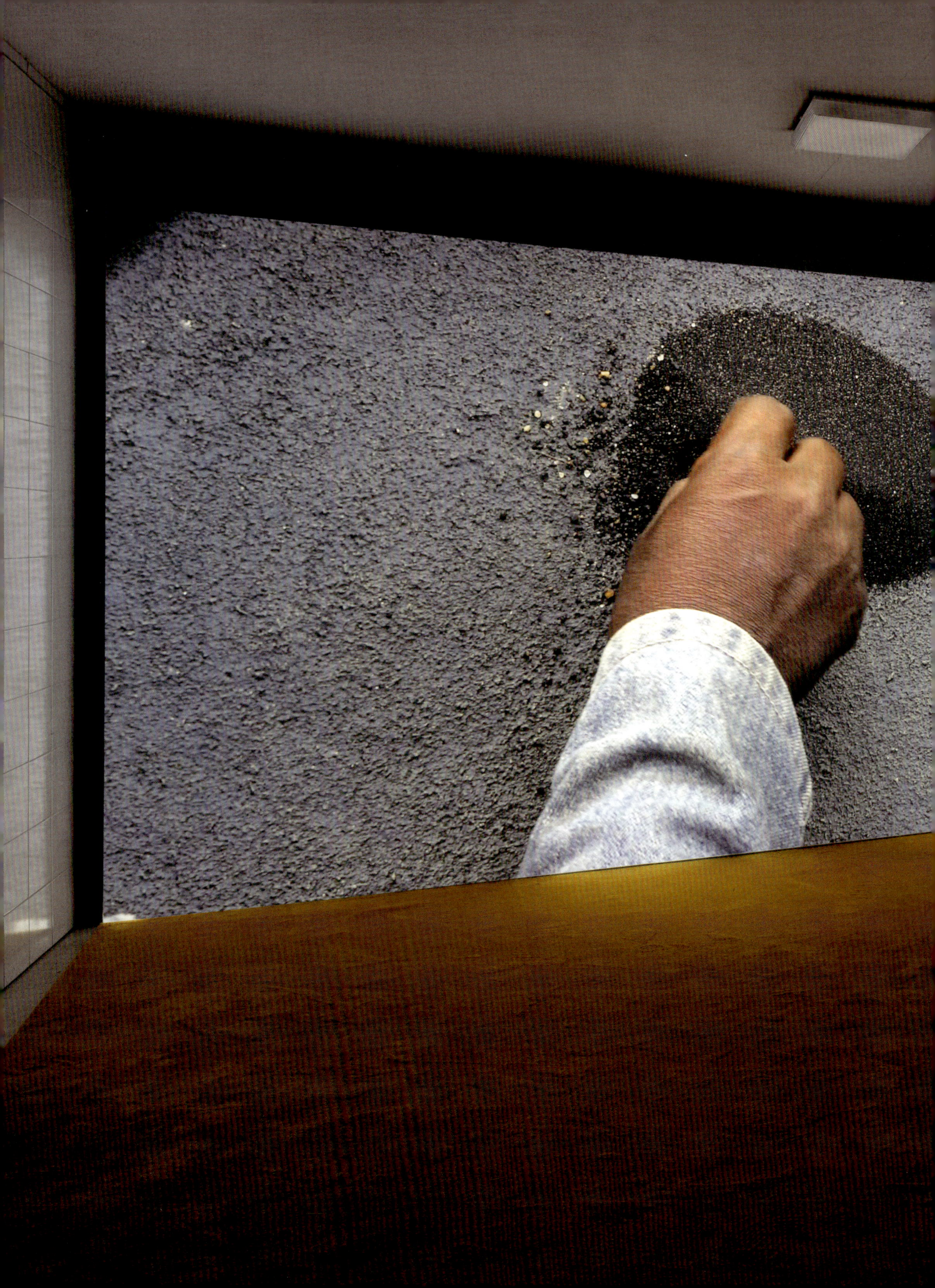

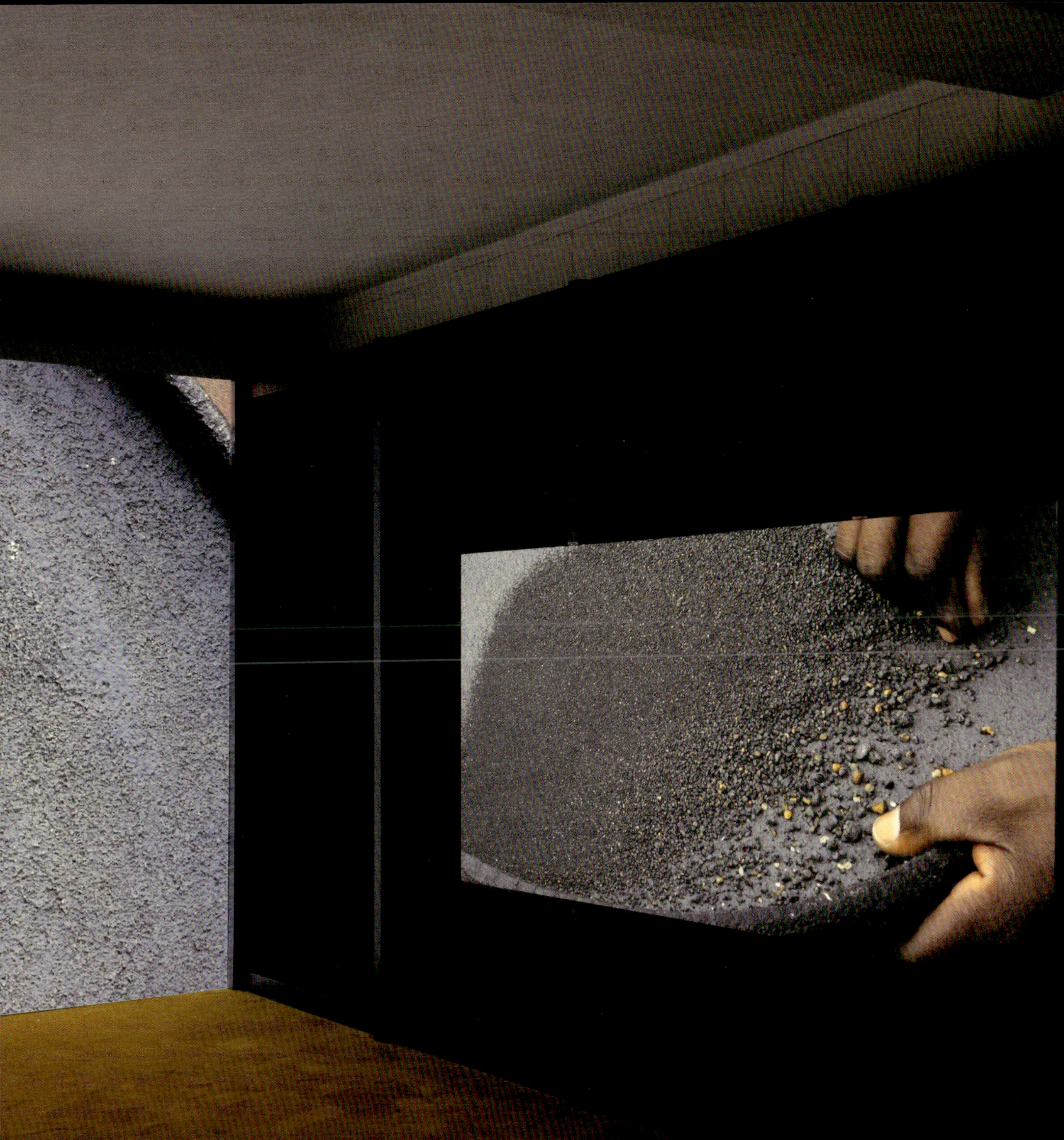

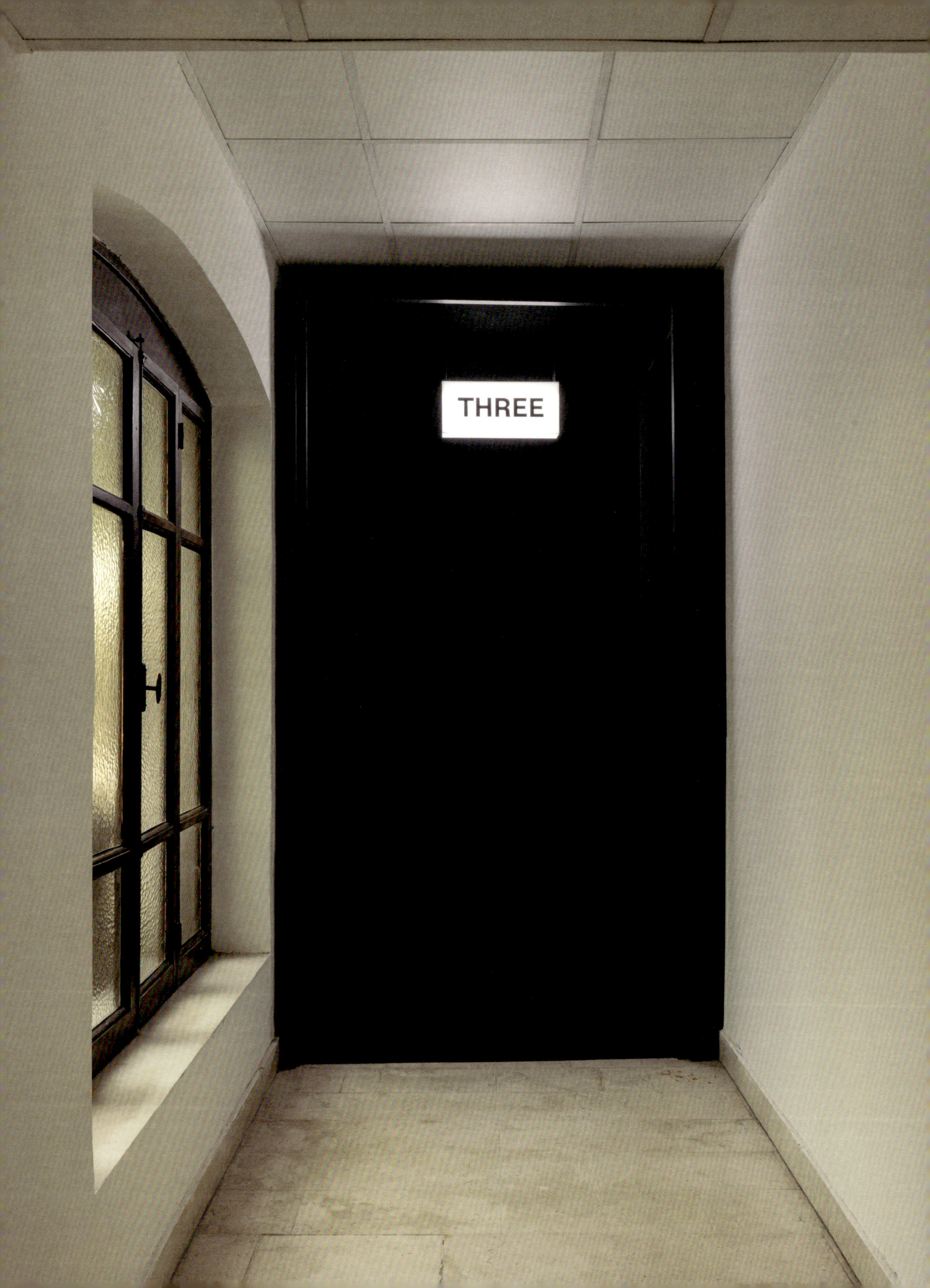
THREE

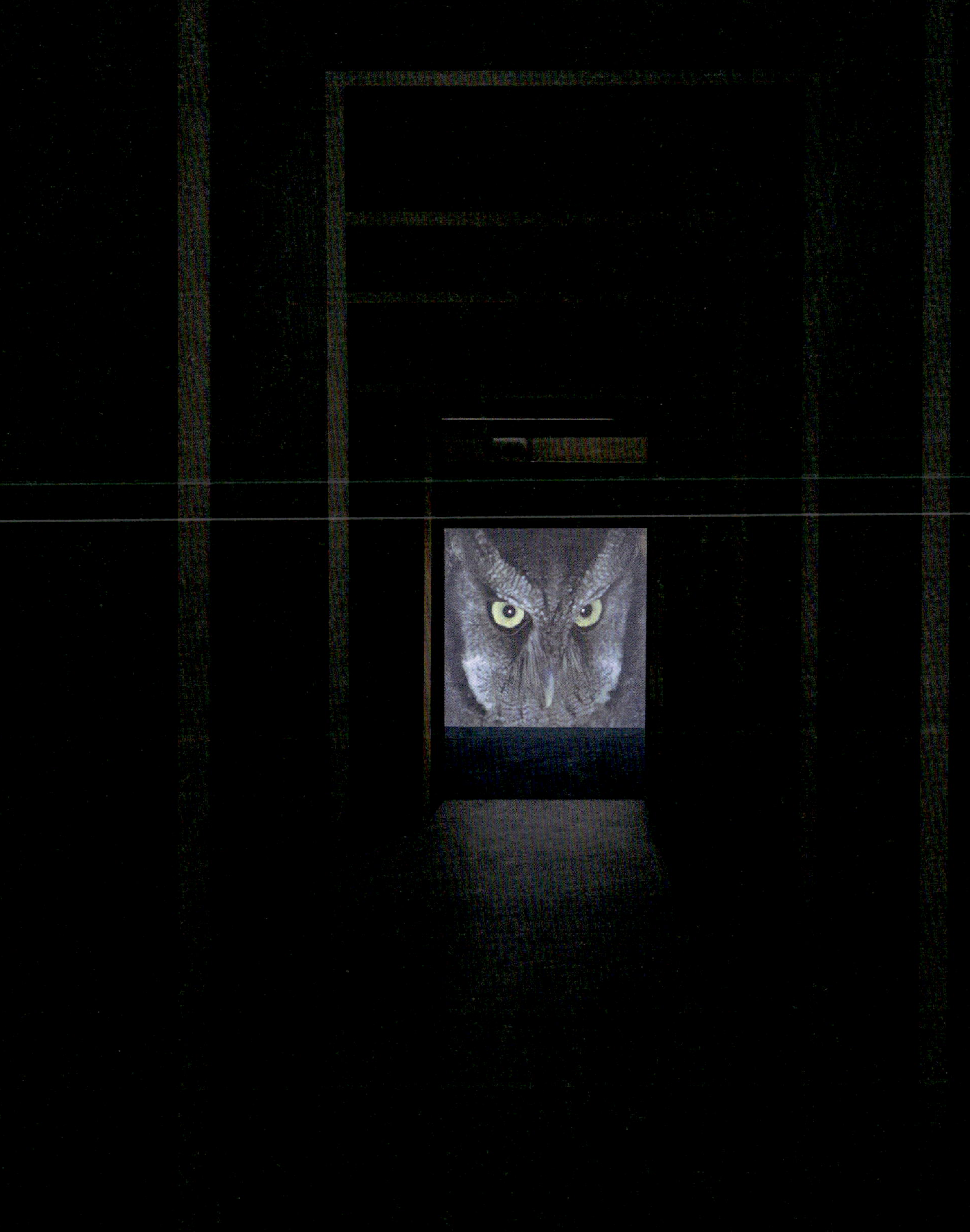

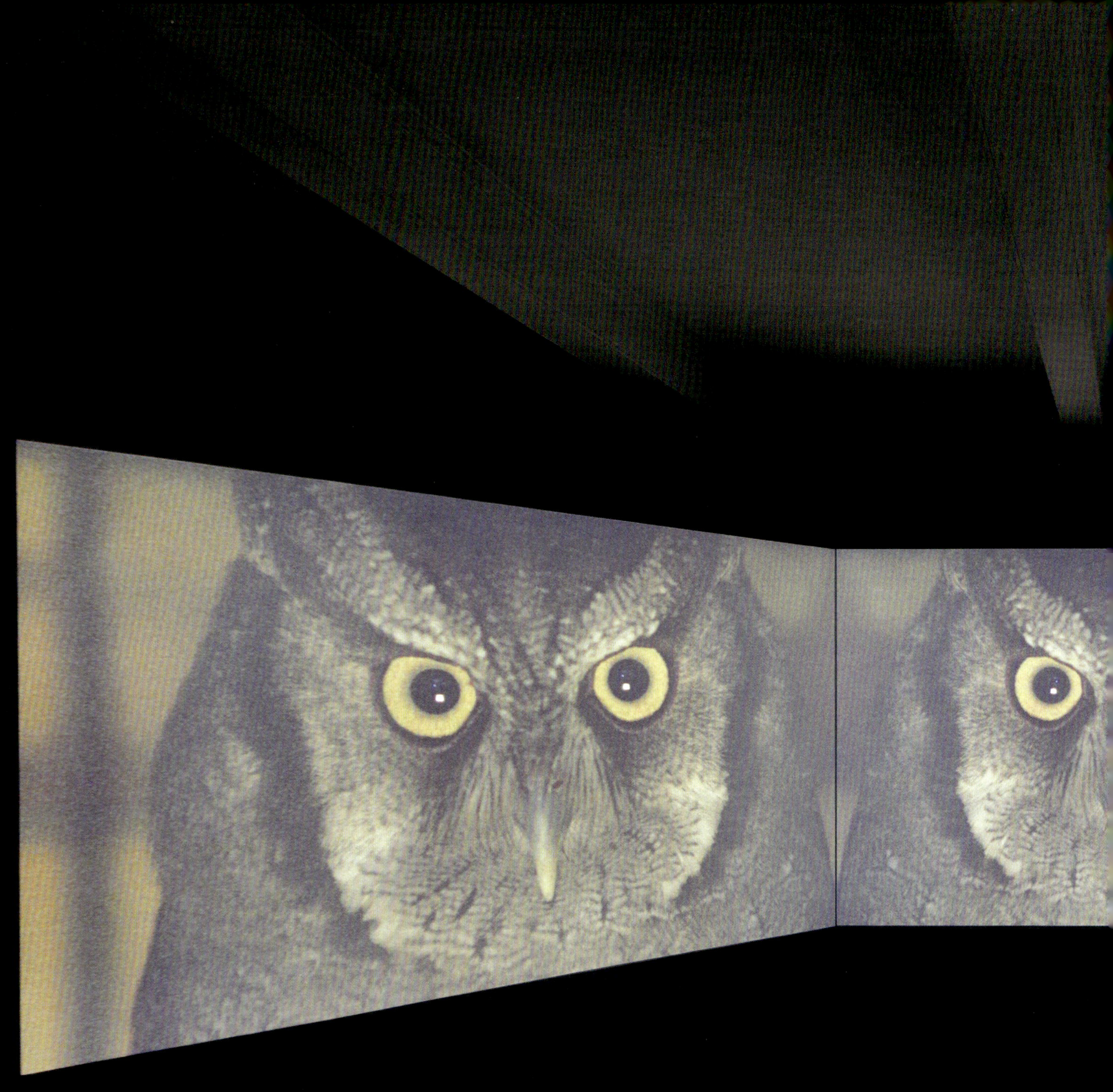

Ana Vaz, *É Noite na América*, 2021

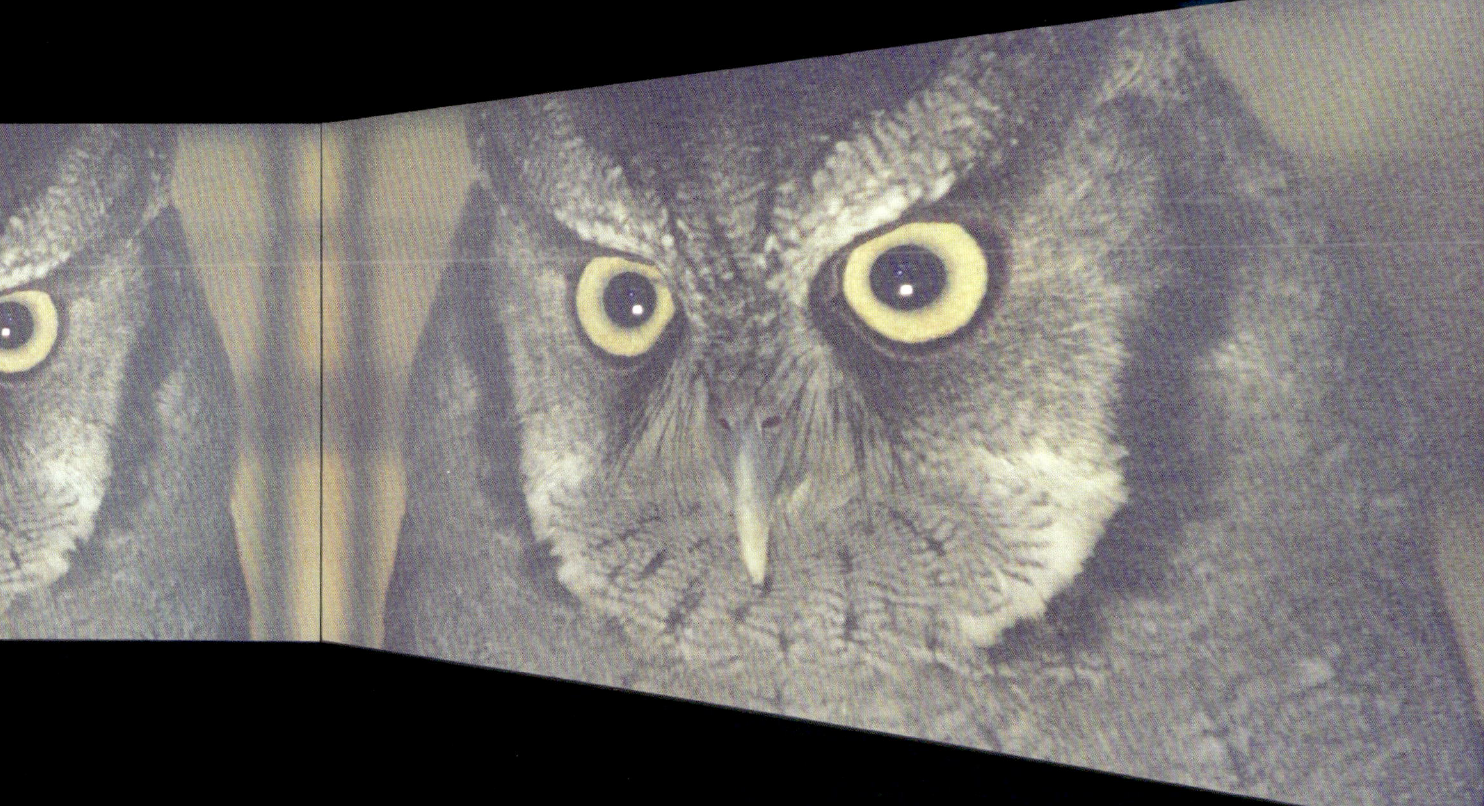

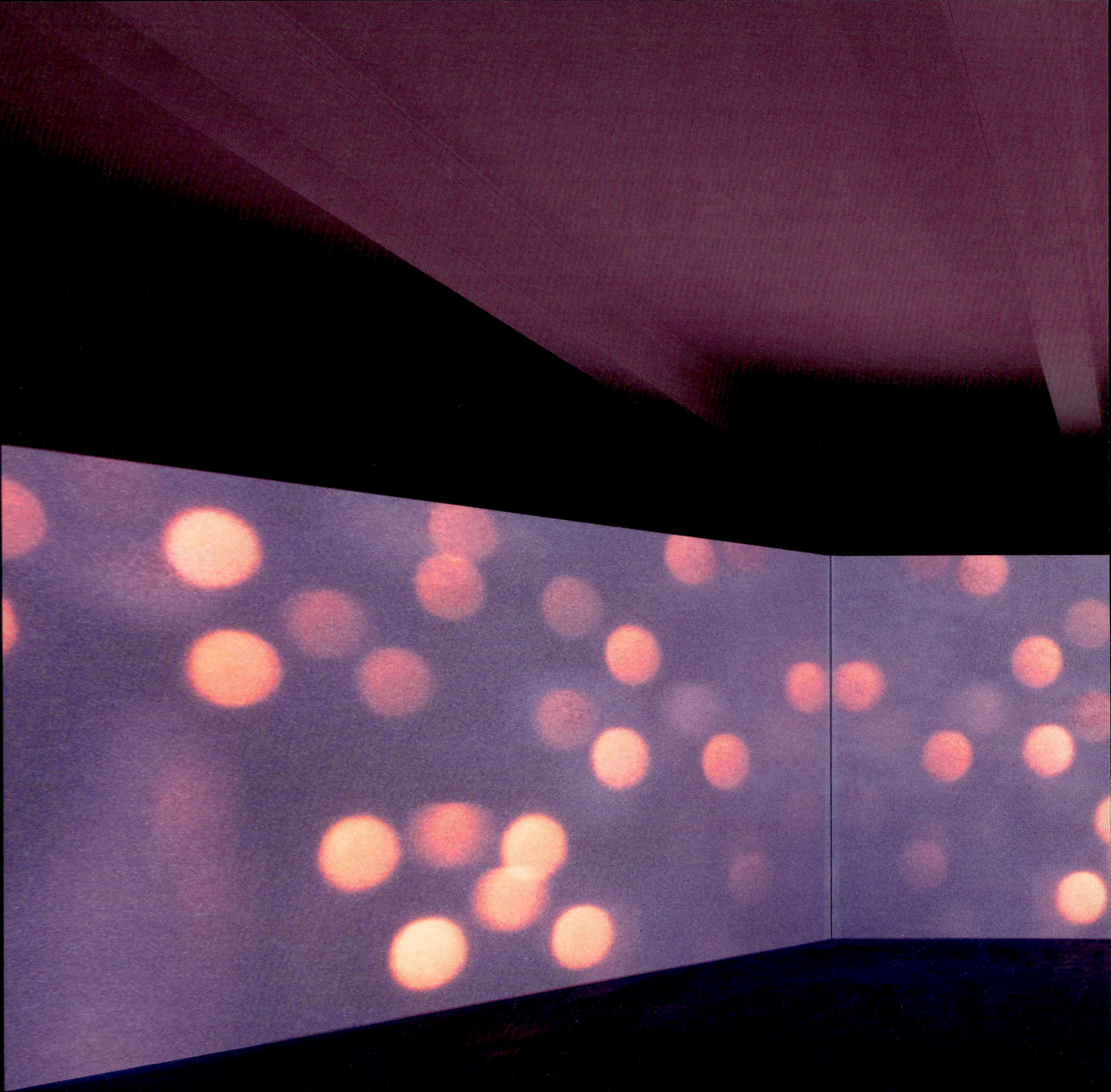

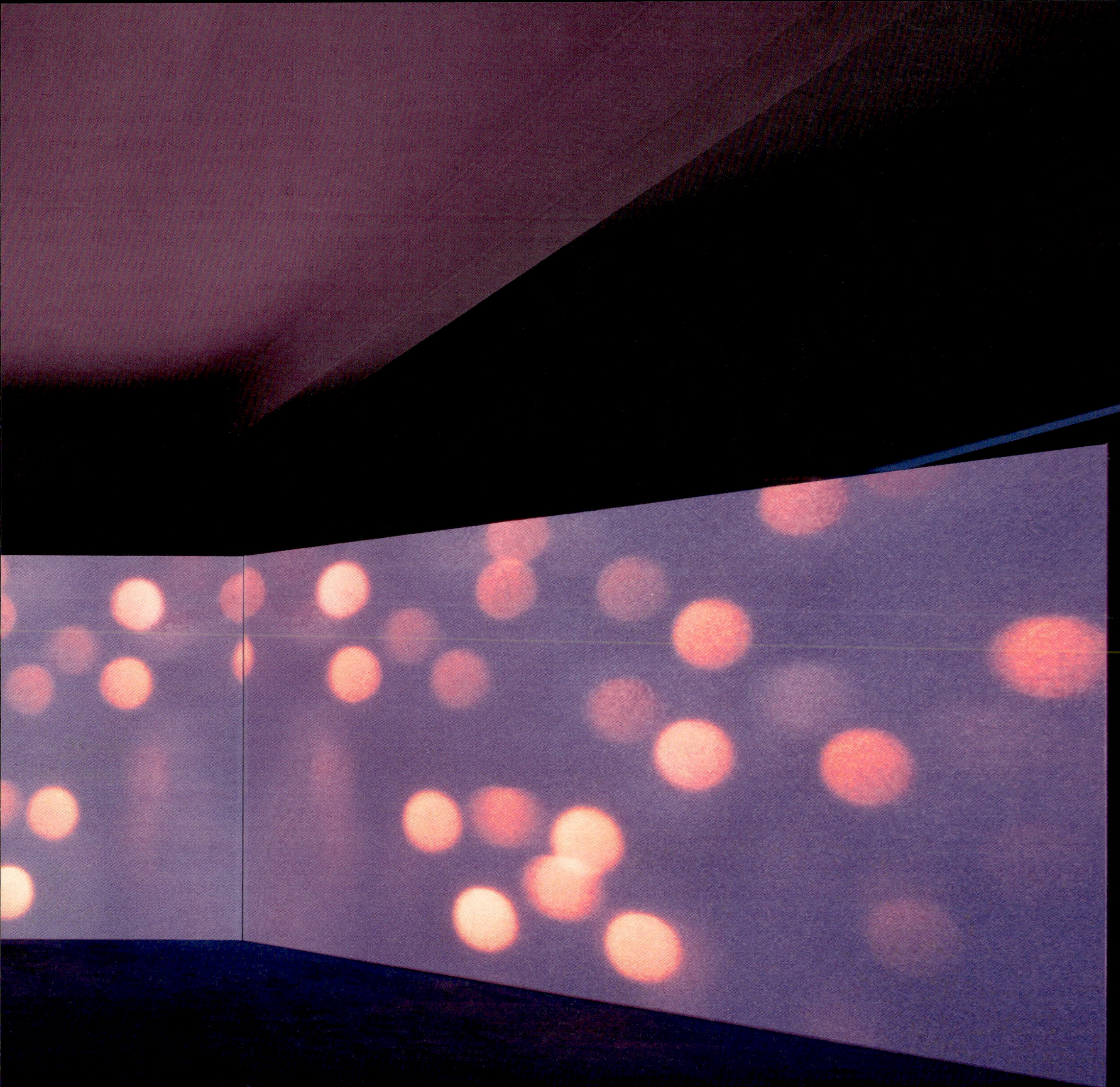

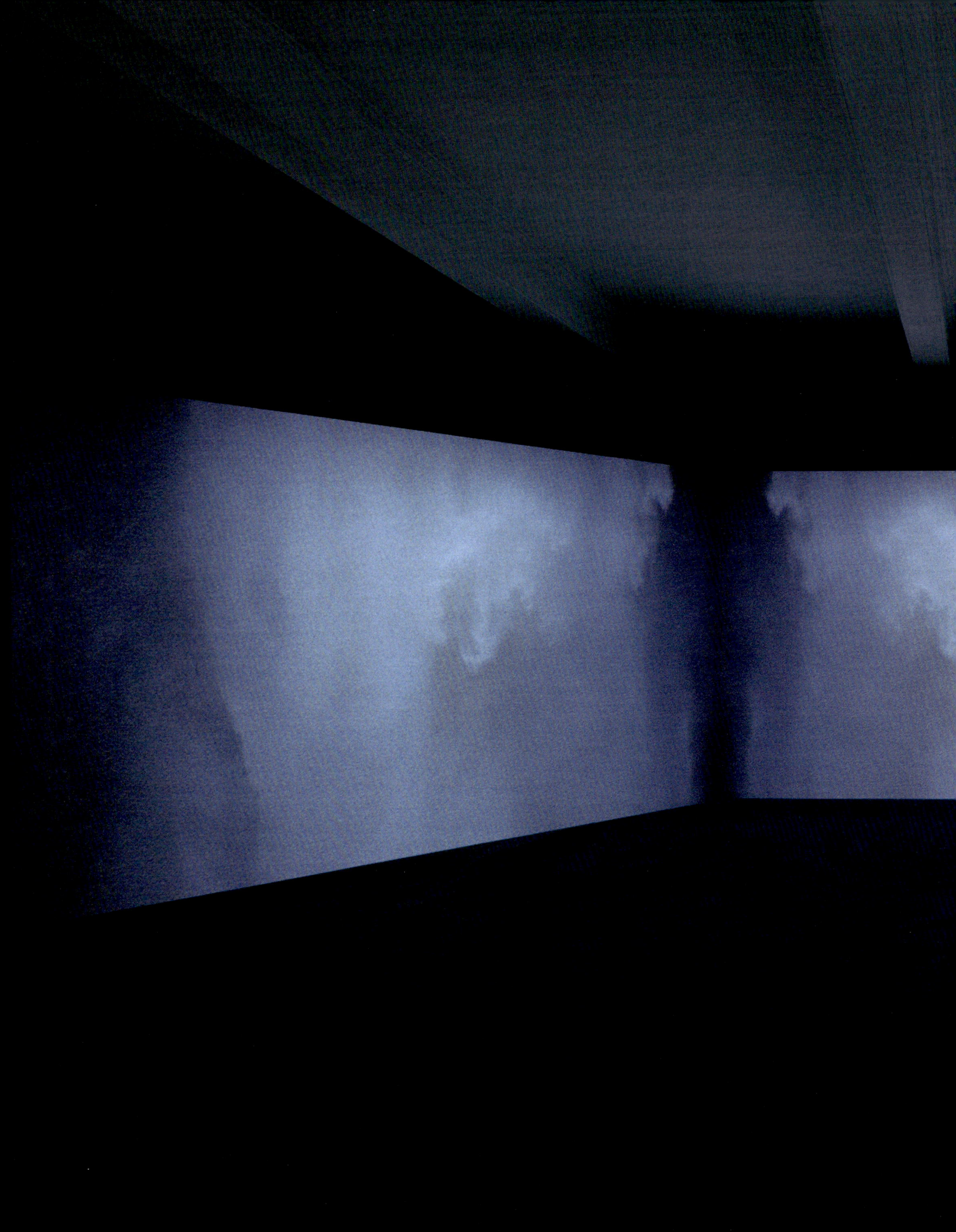

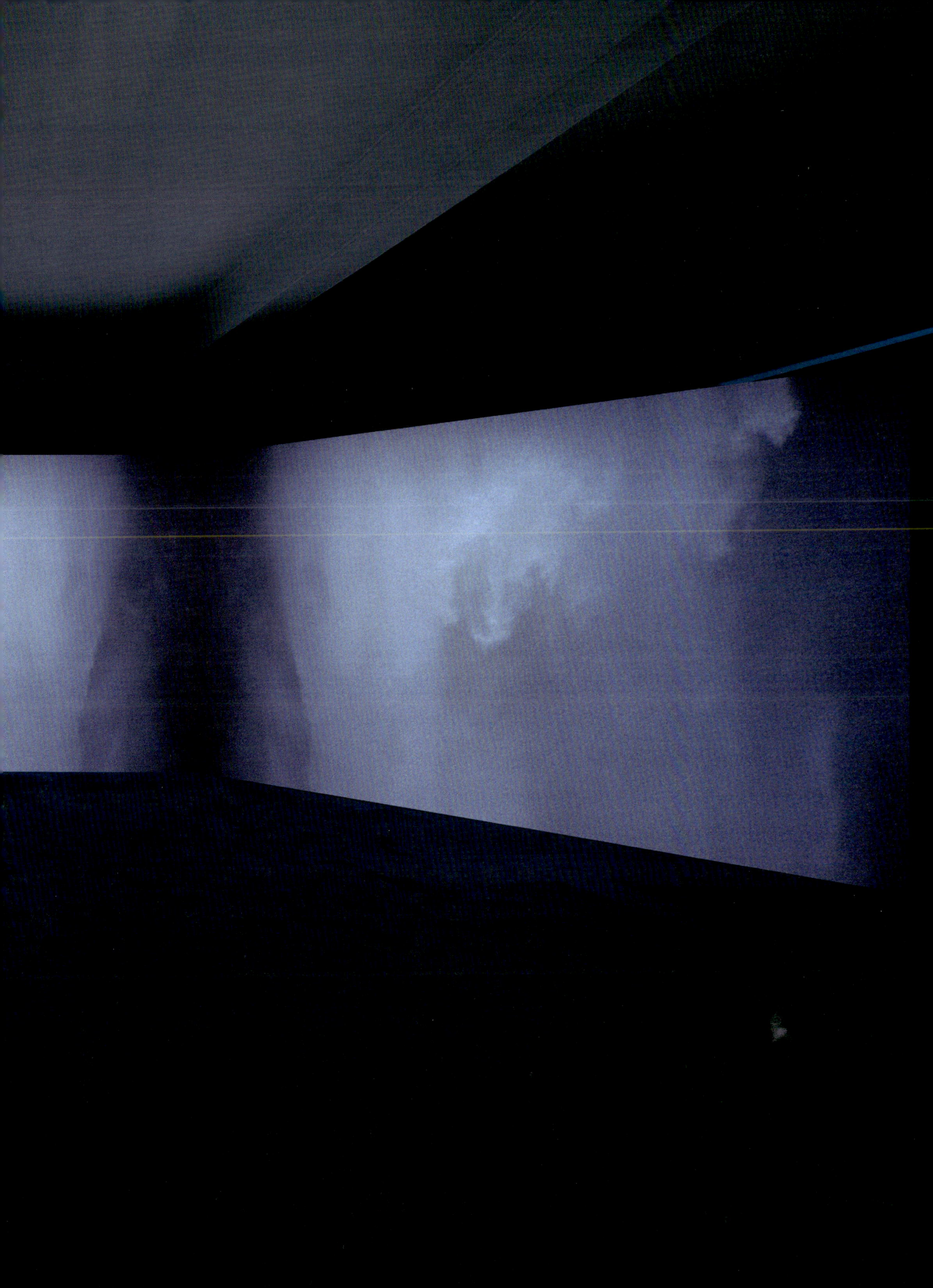

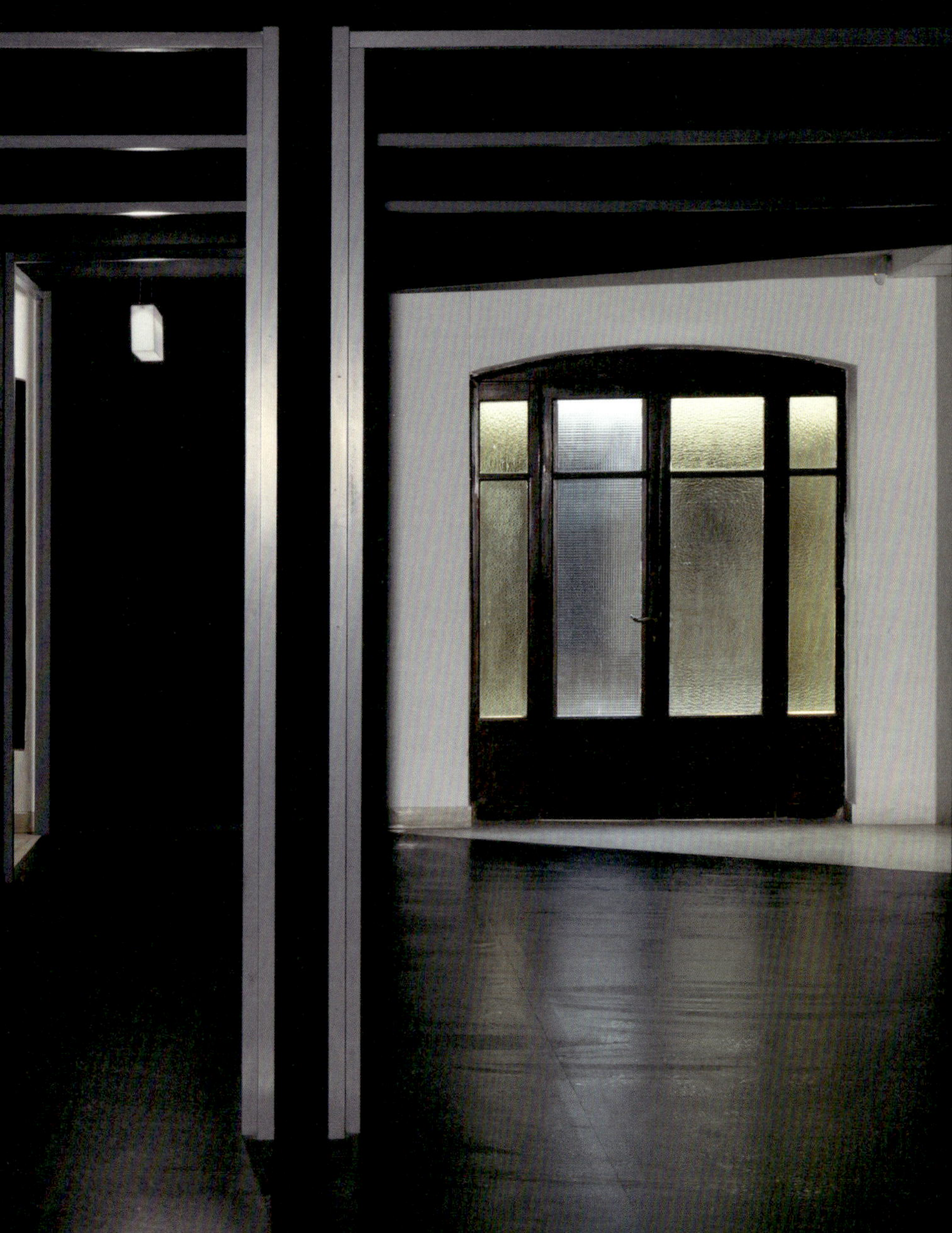

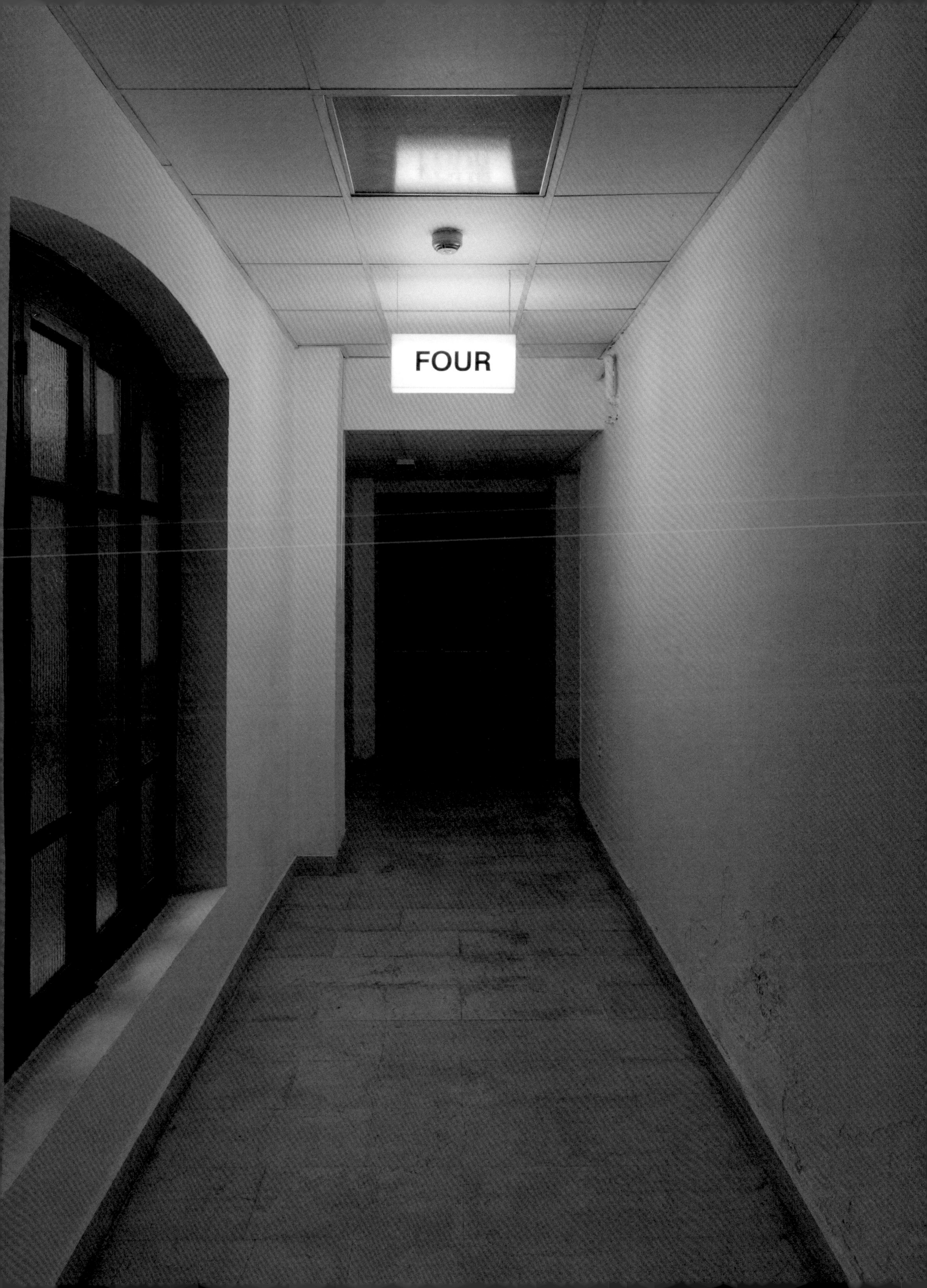
FOUR

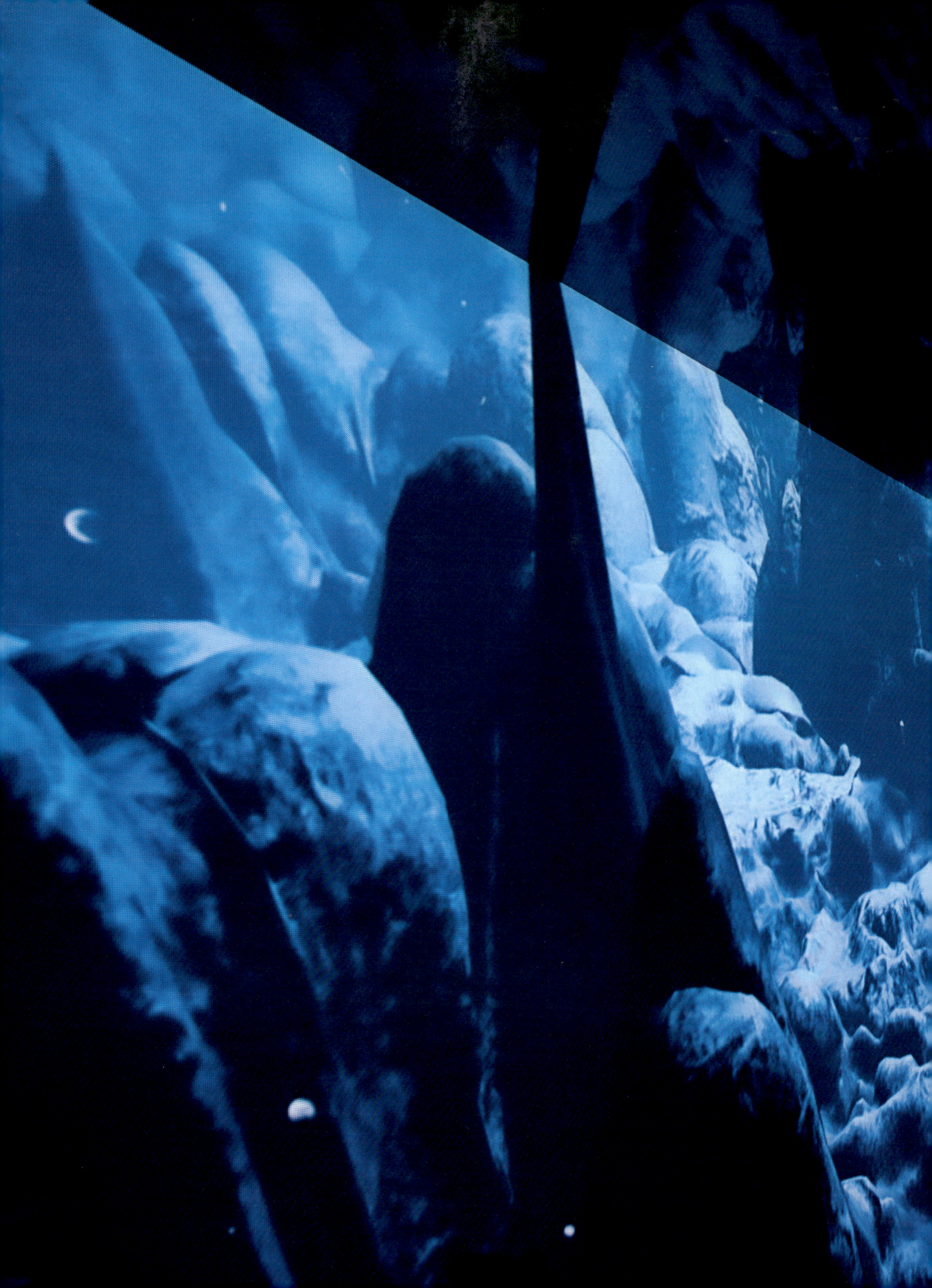

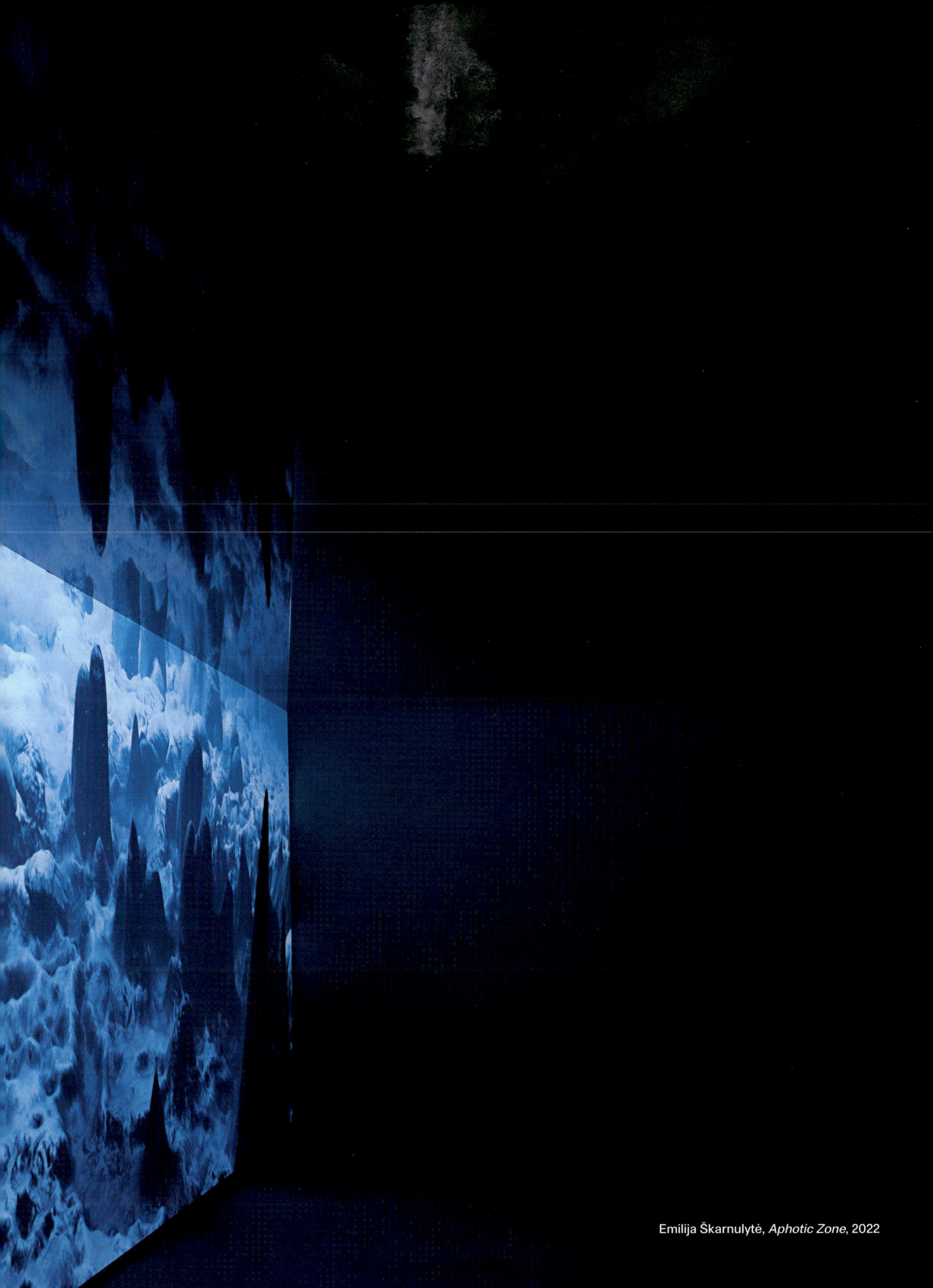

Emilija Škarnulytė, *Aphotic Zone*, 2022

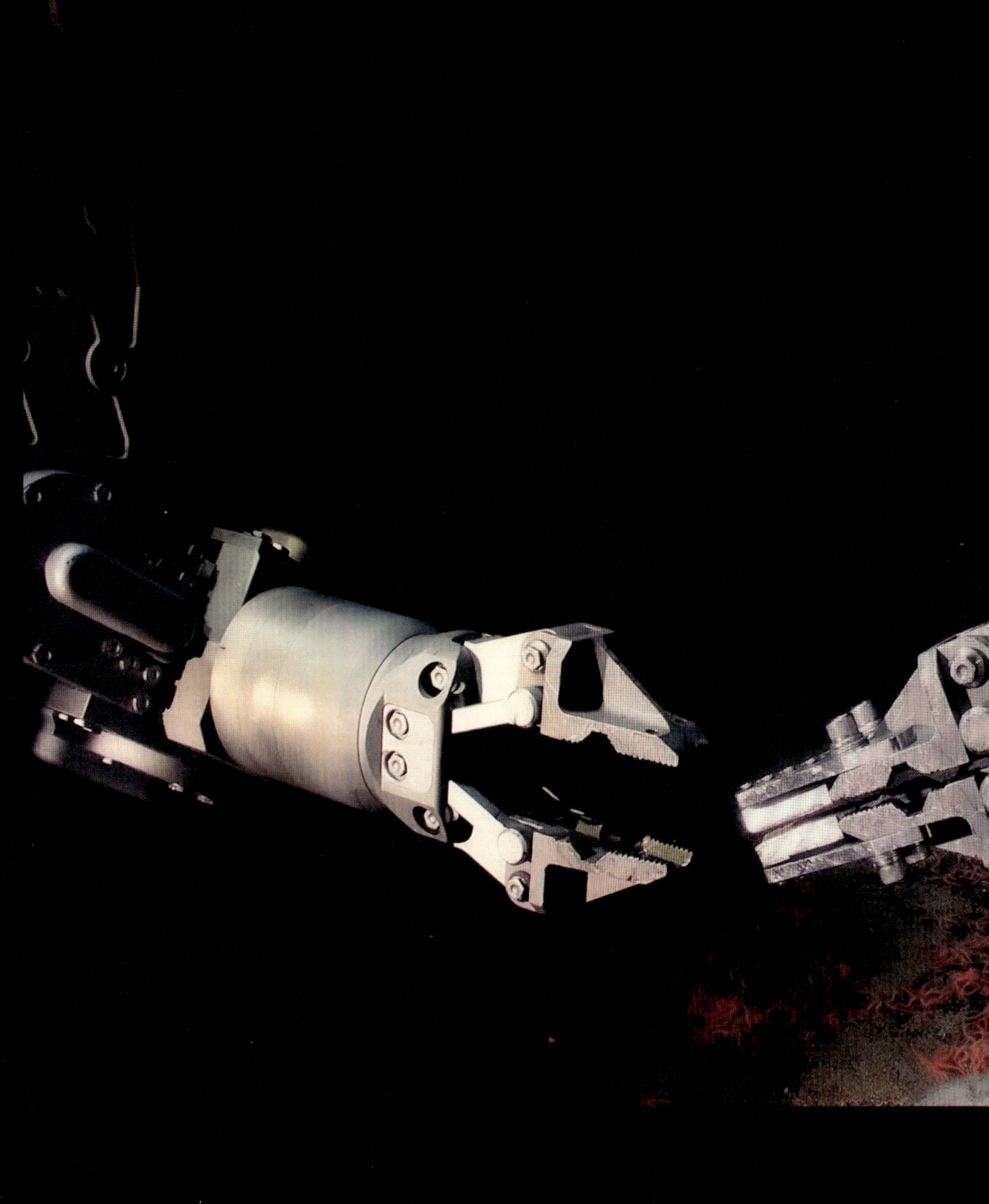

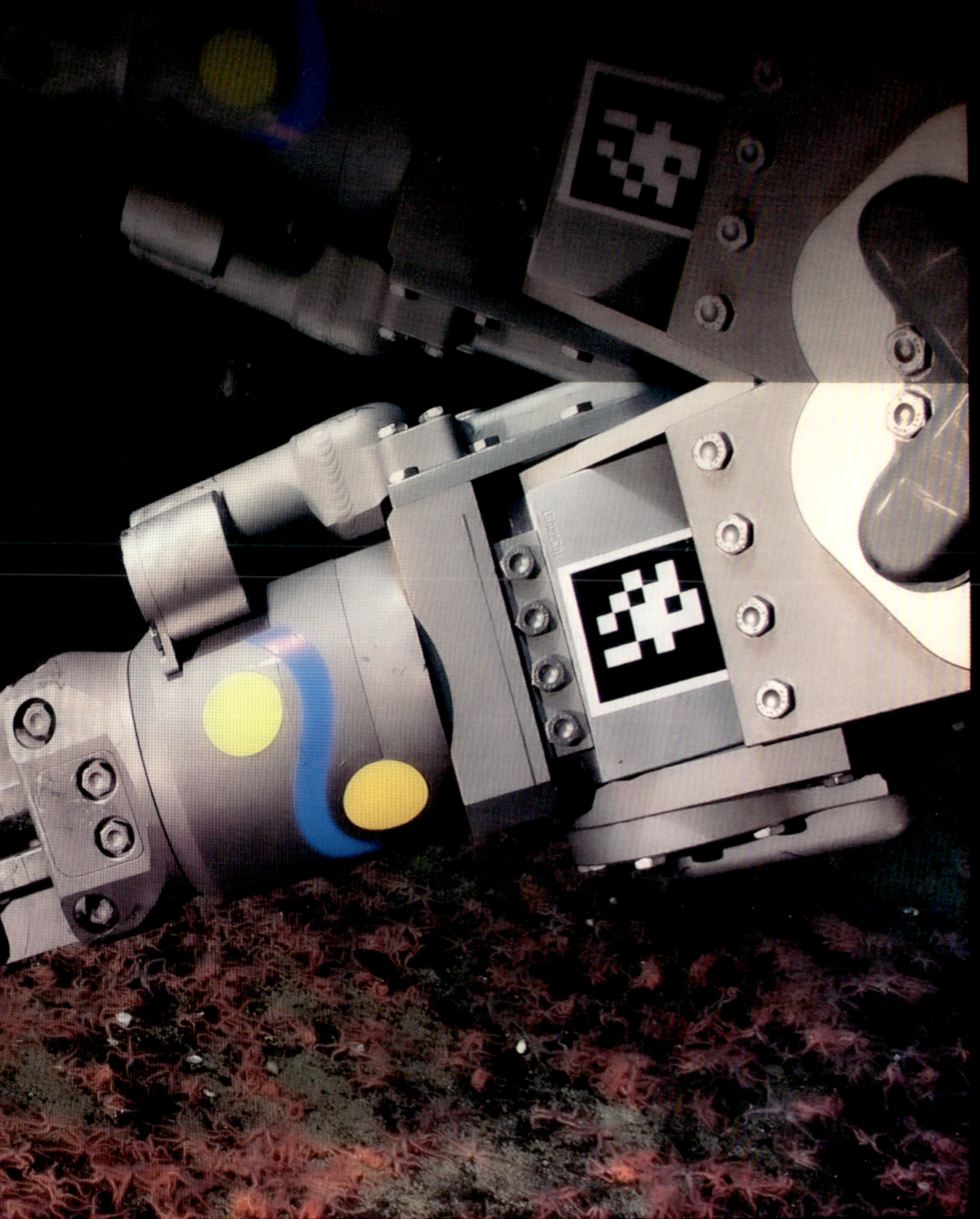

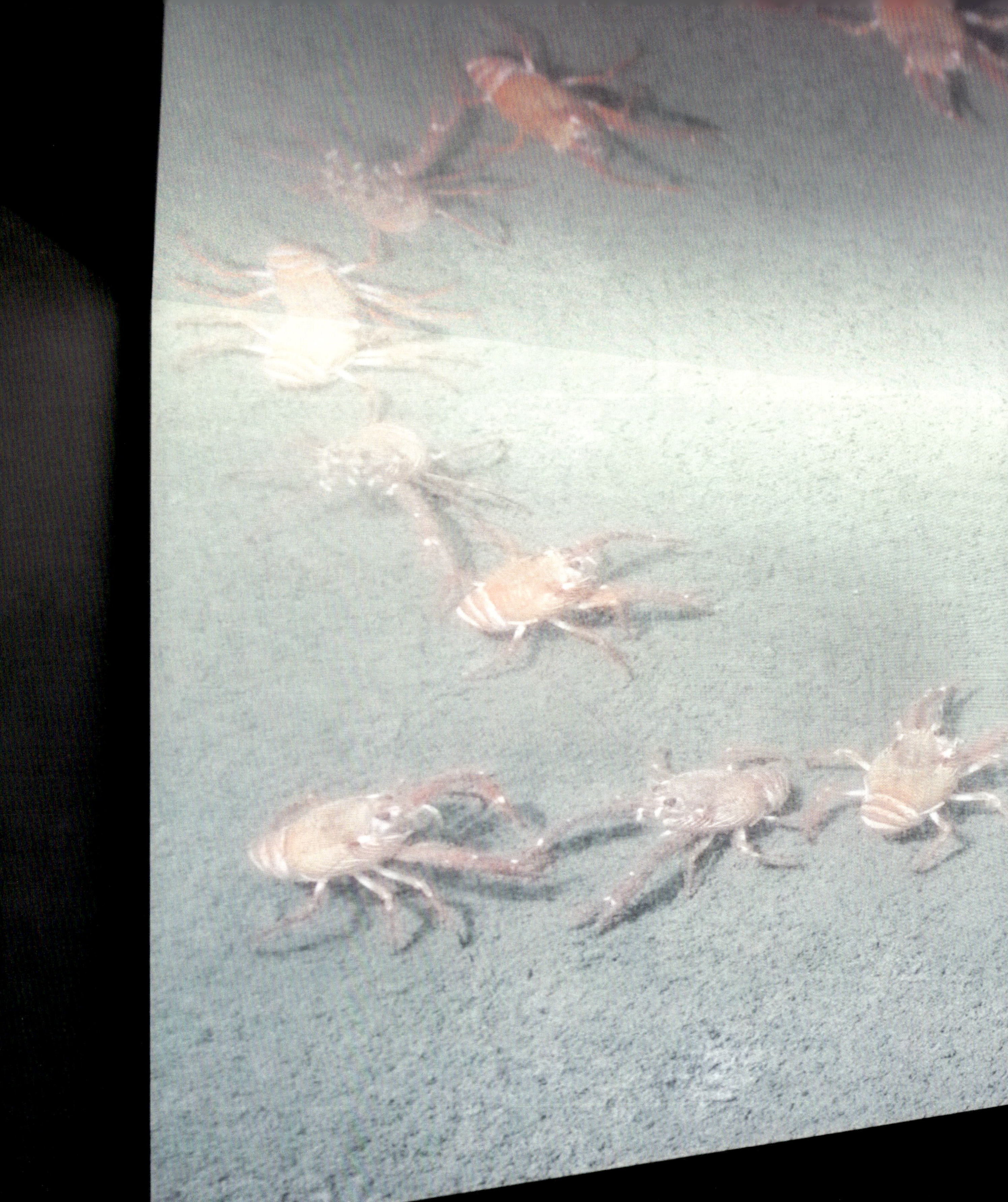

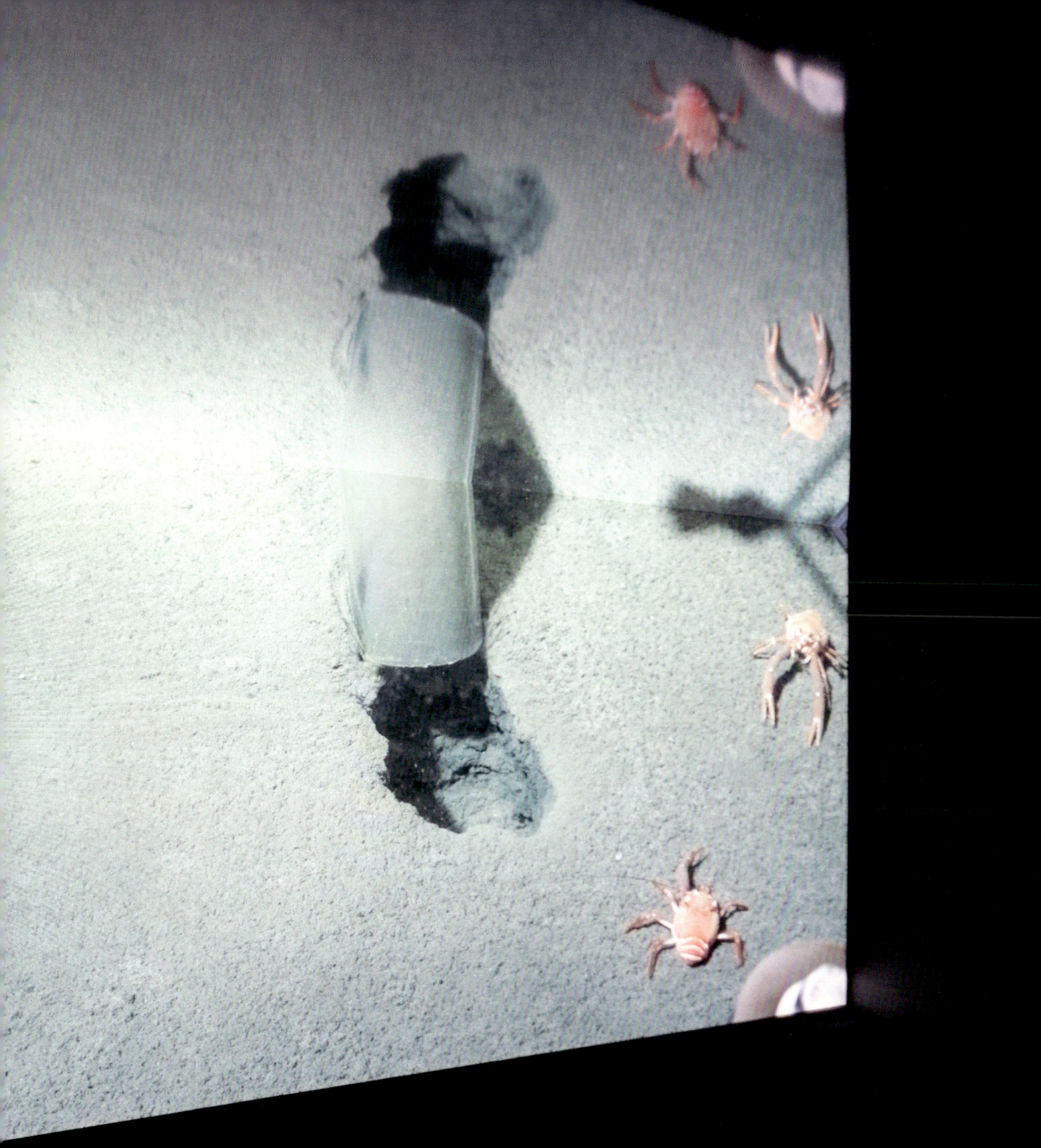

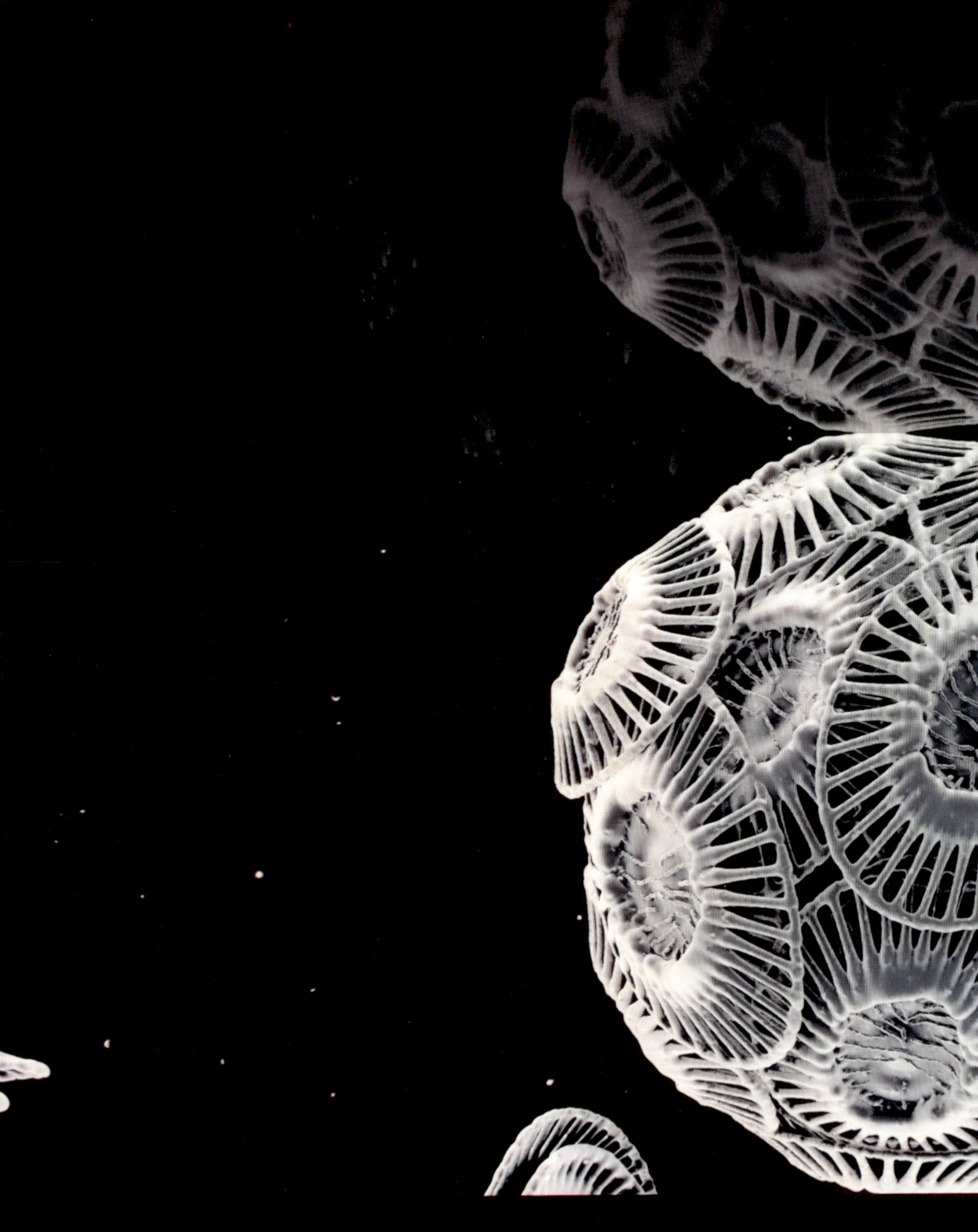

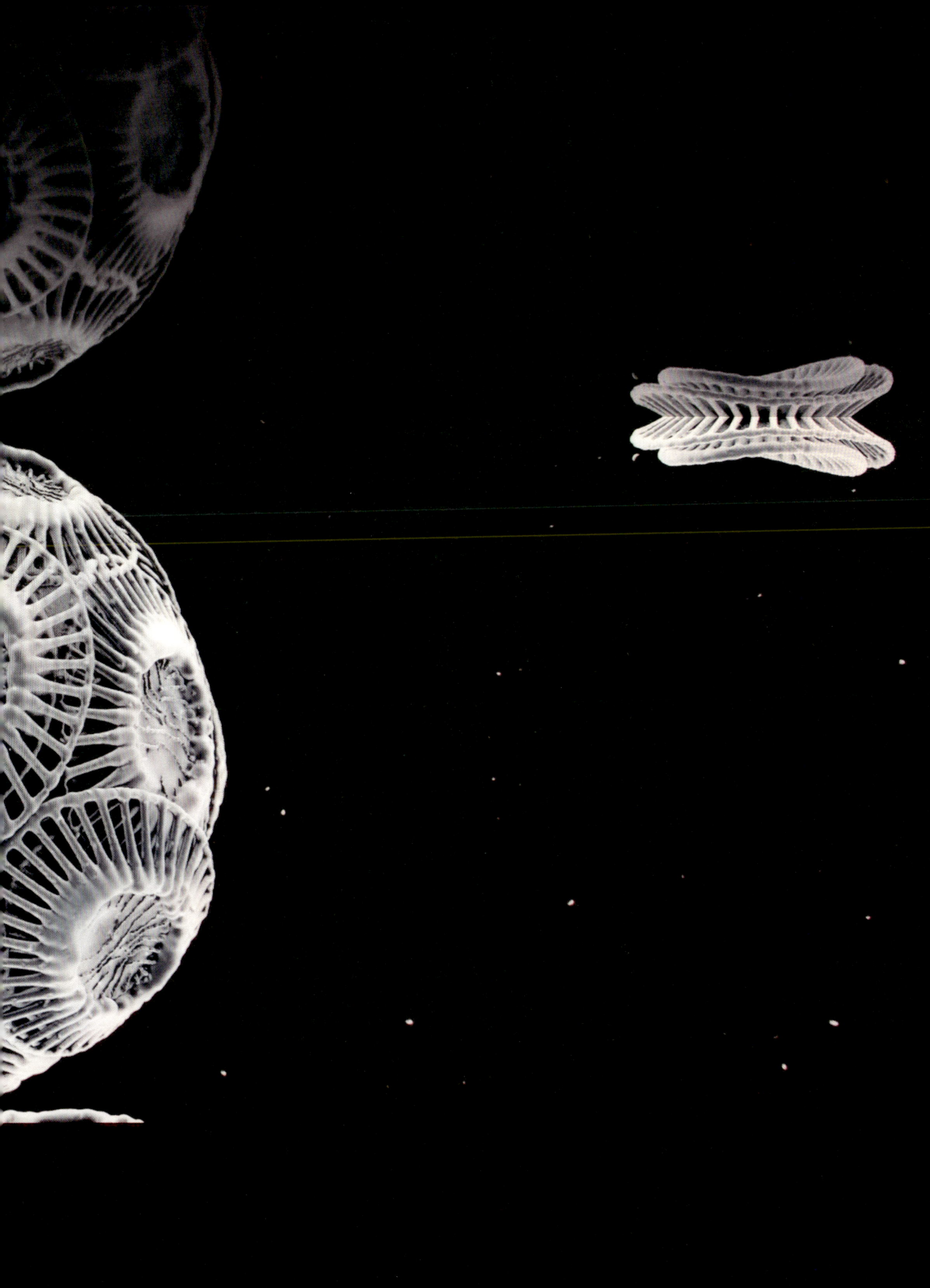

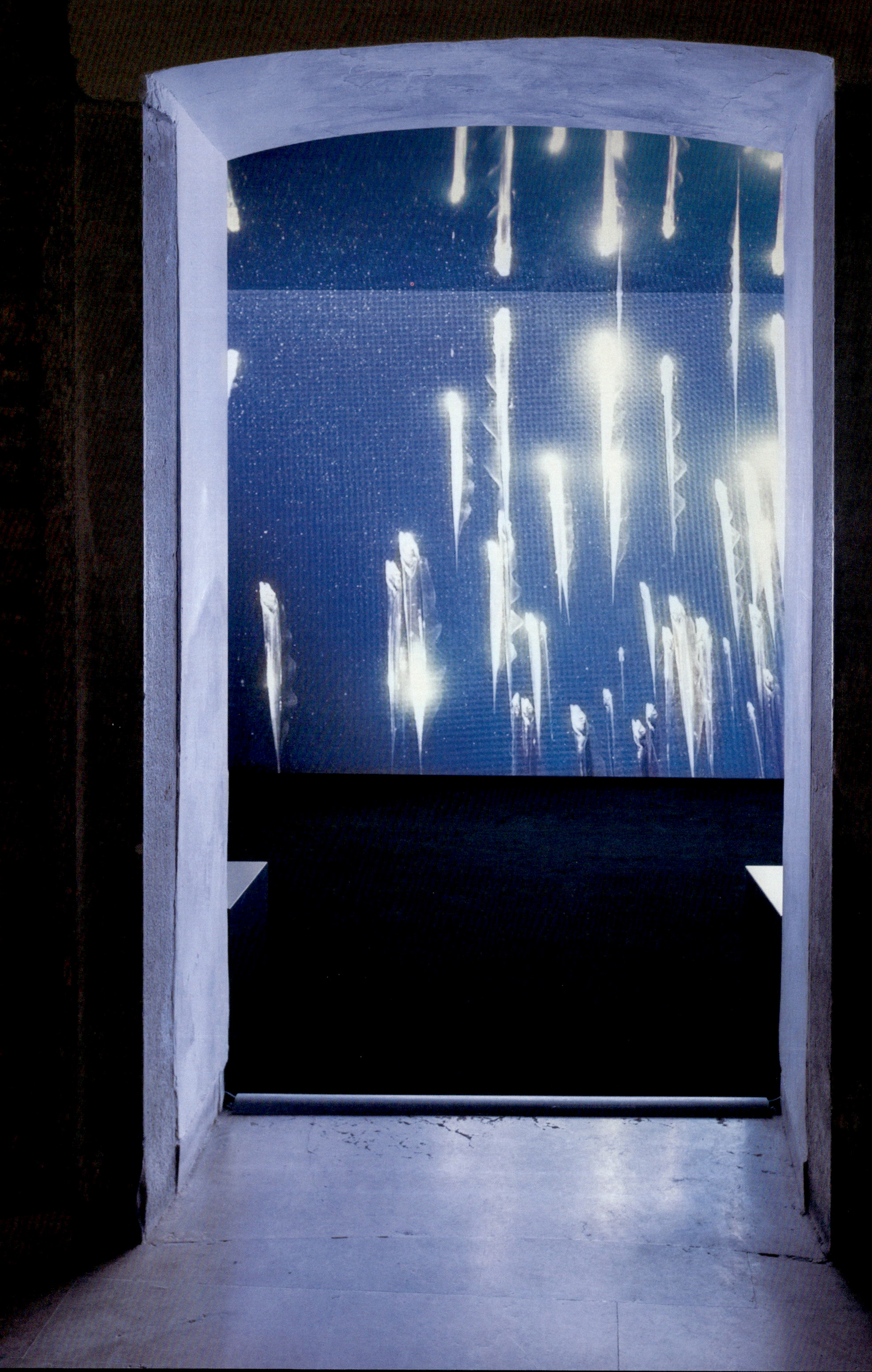

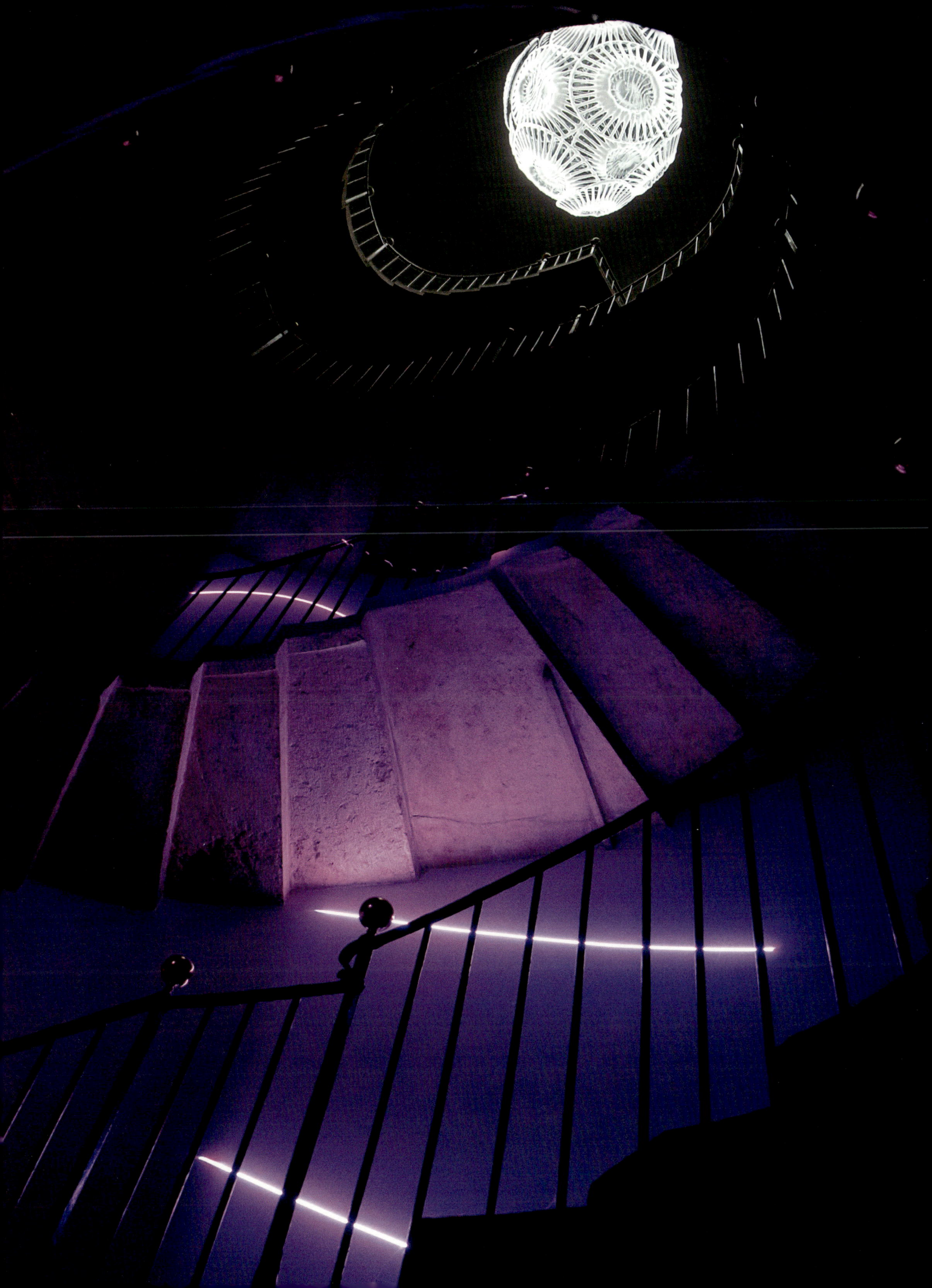

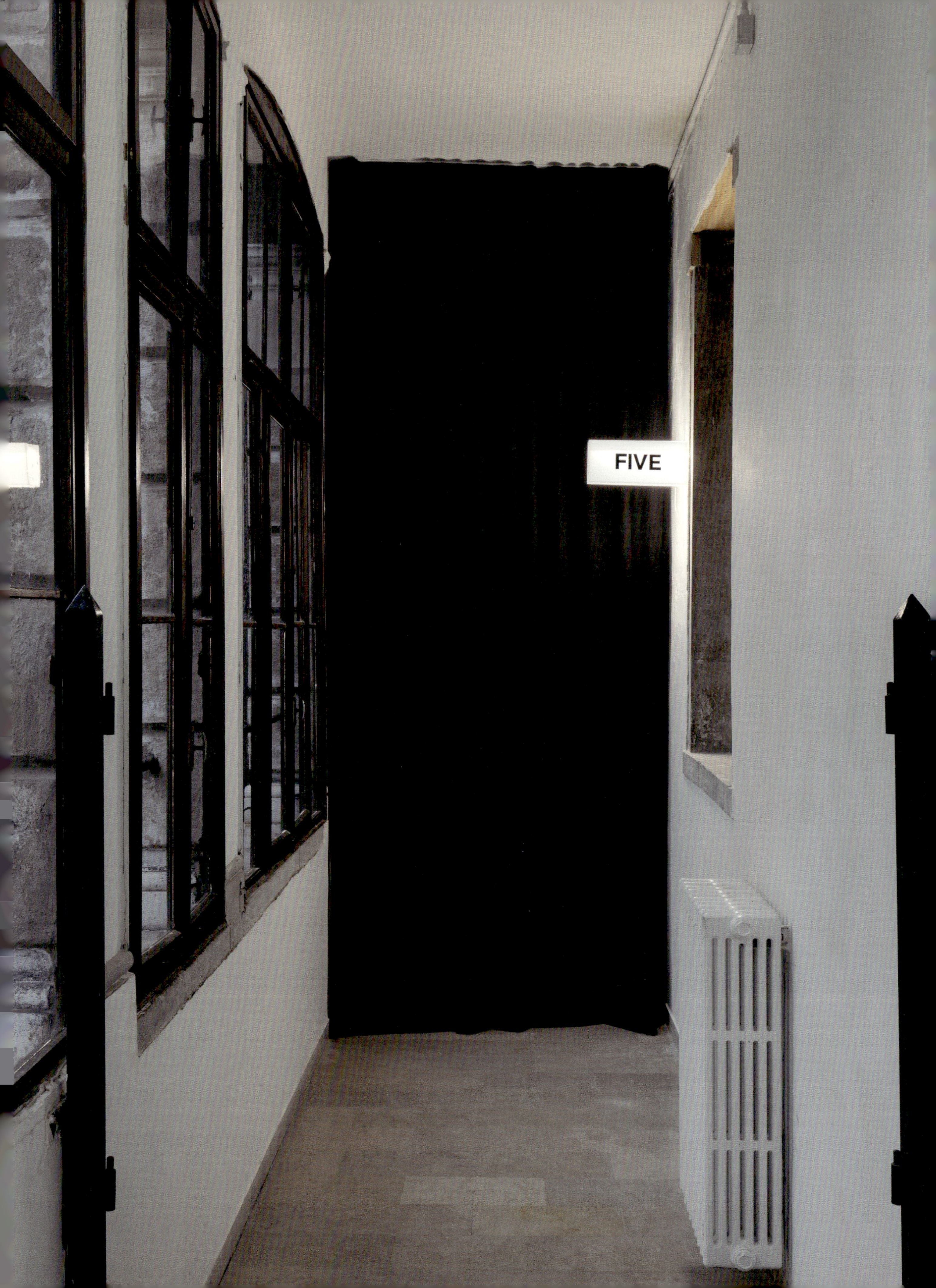
FIVE

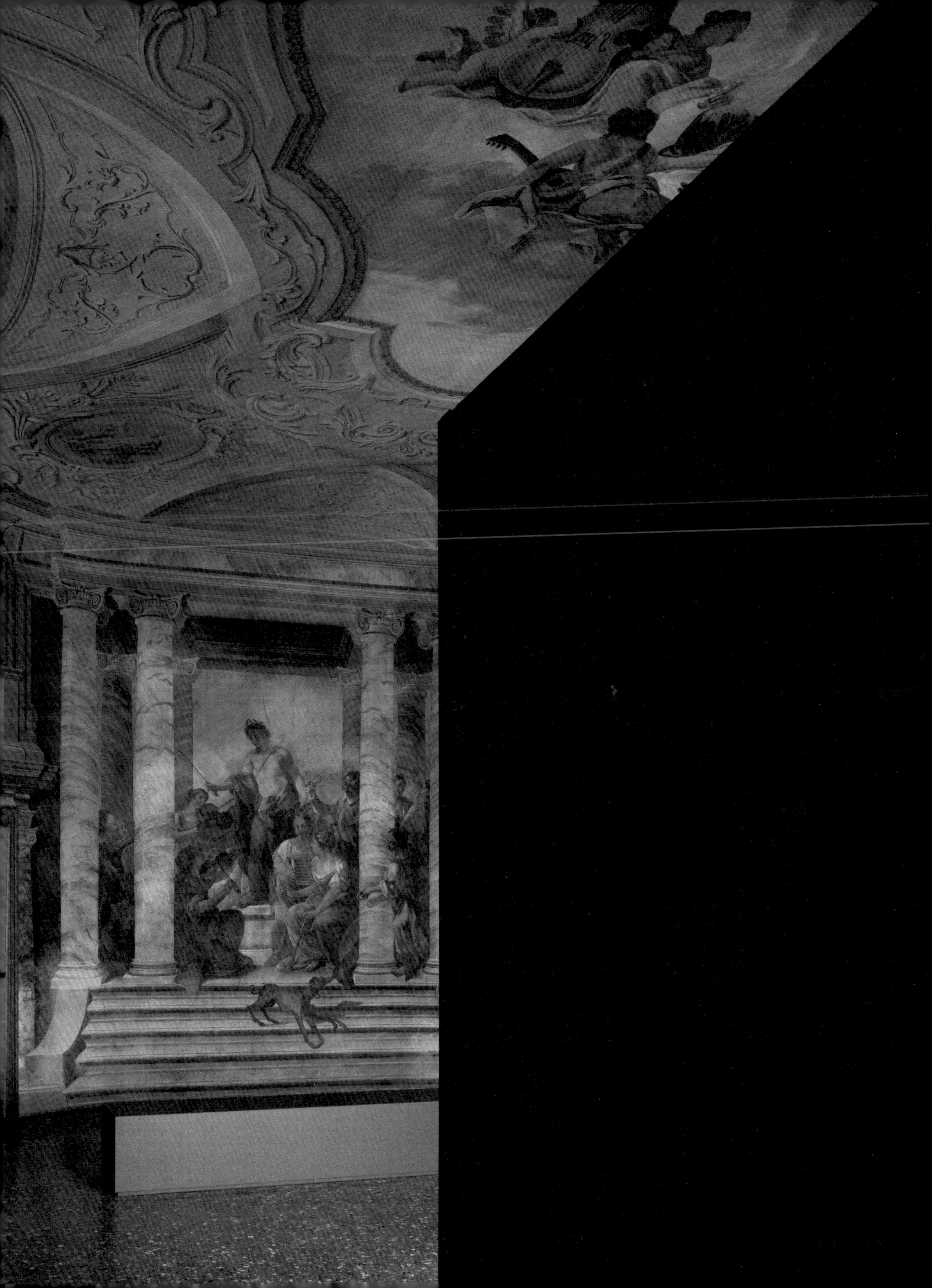

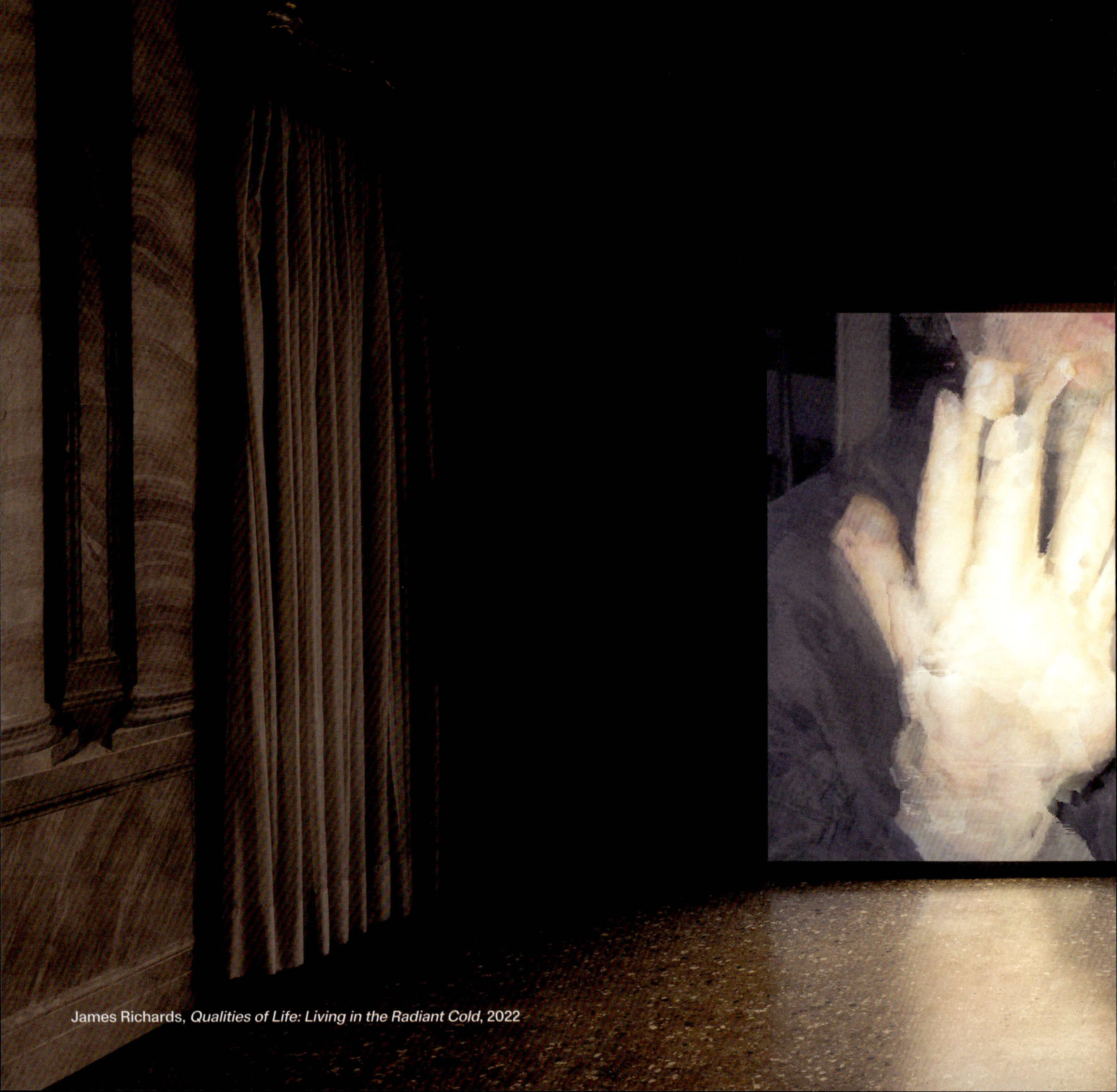

James Richards, *Qualities of Life: Living in the Radiant Cold*, 2022

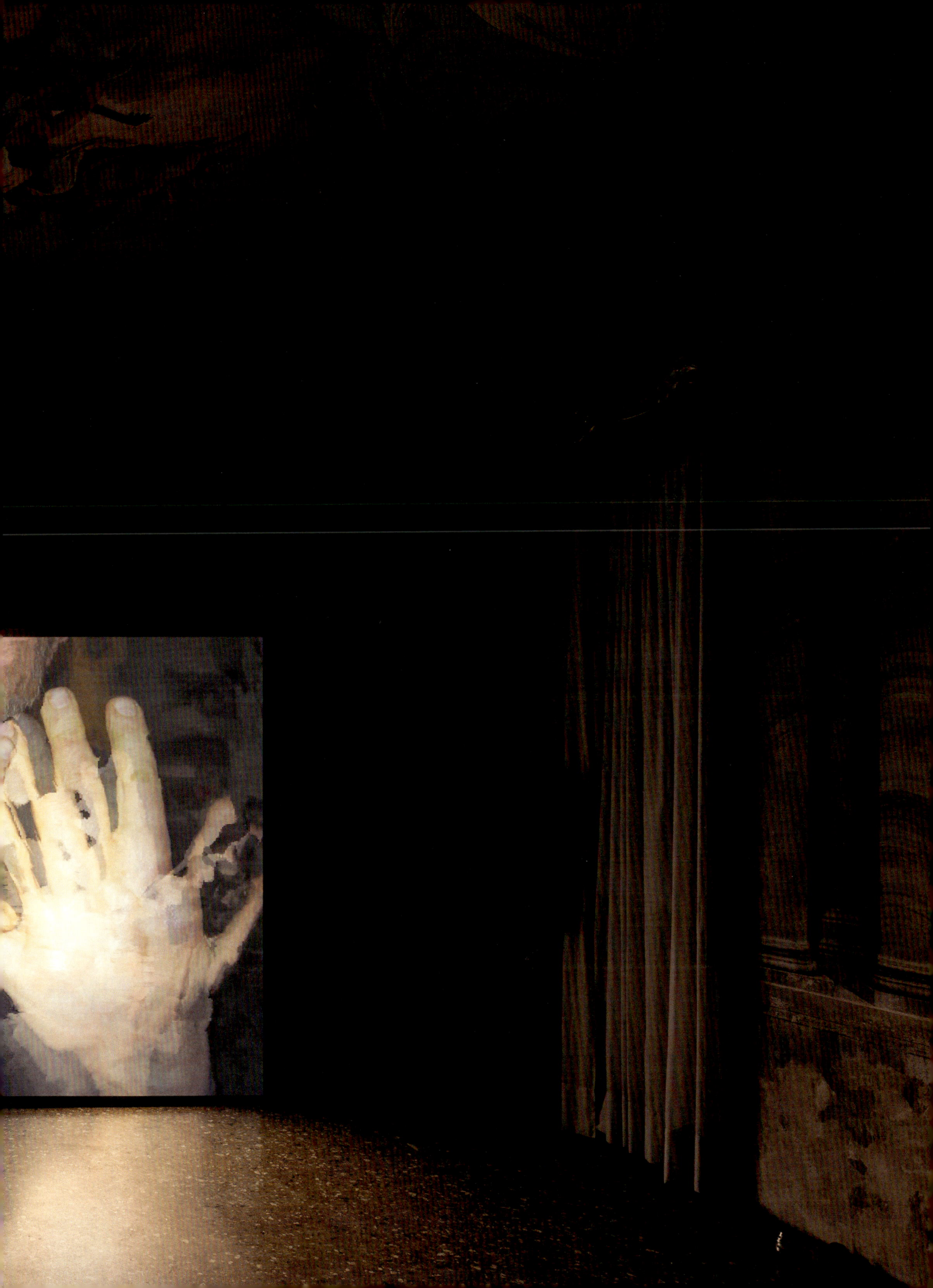

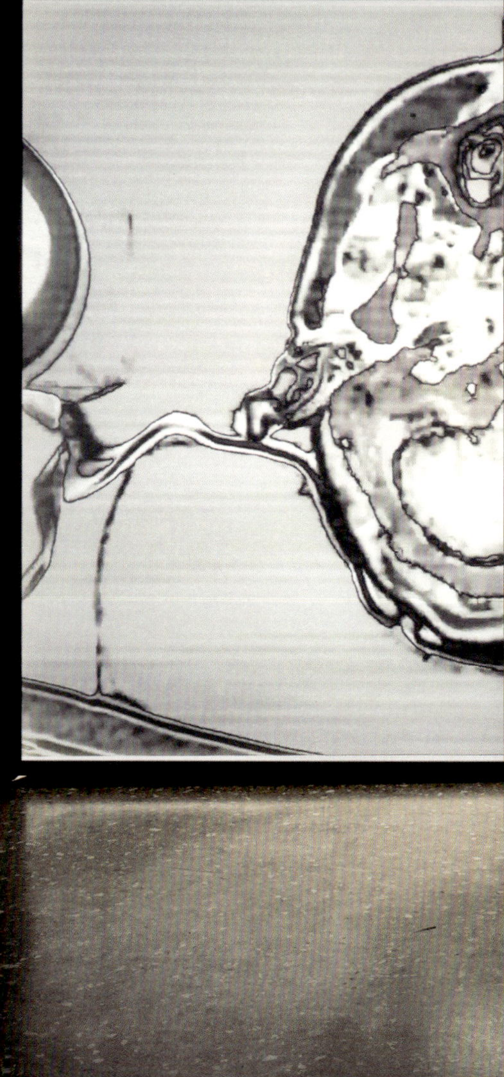

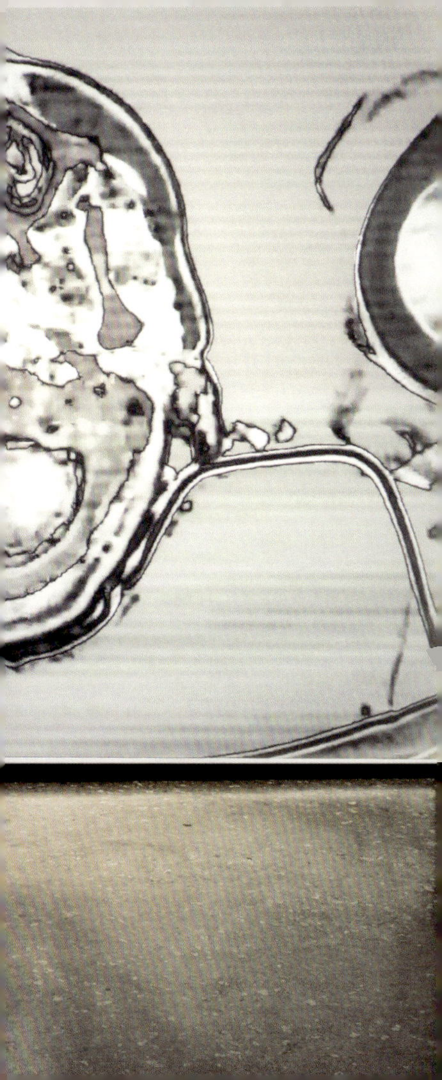

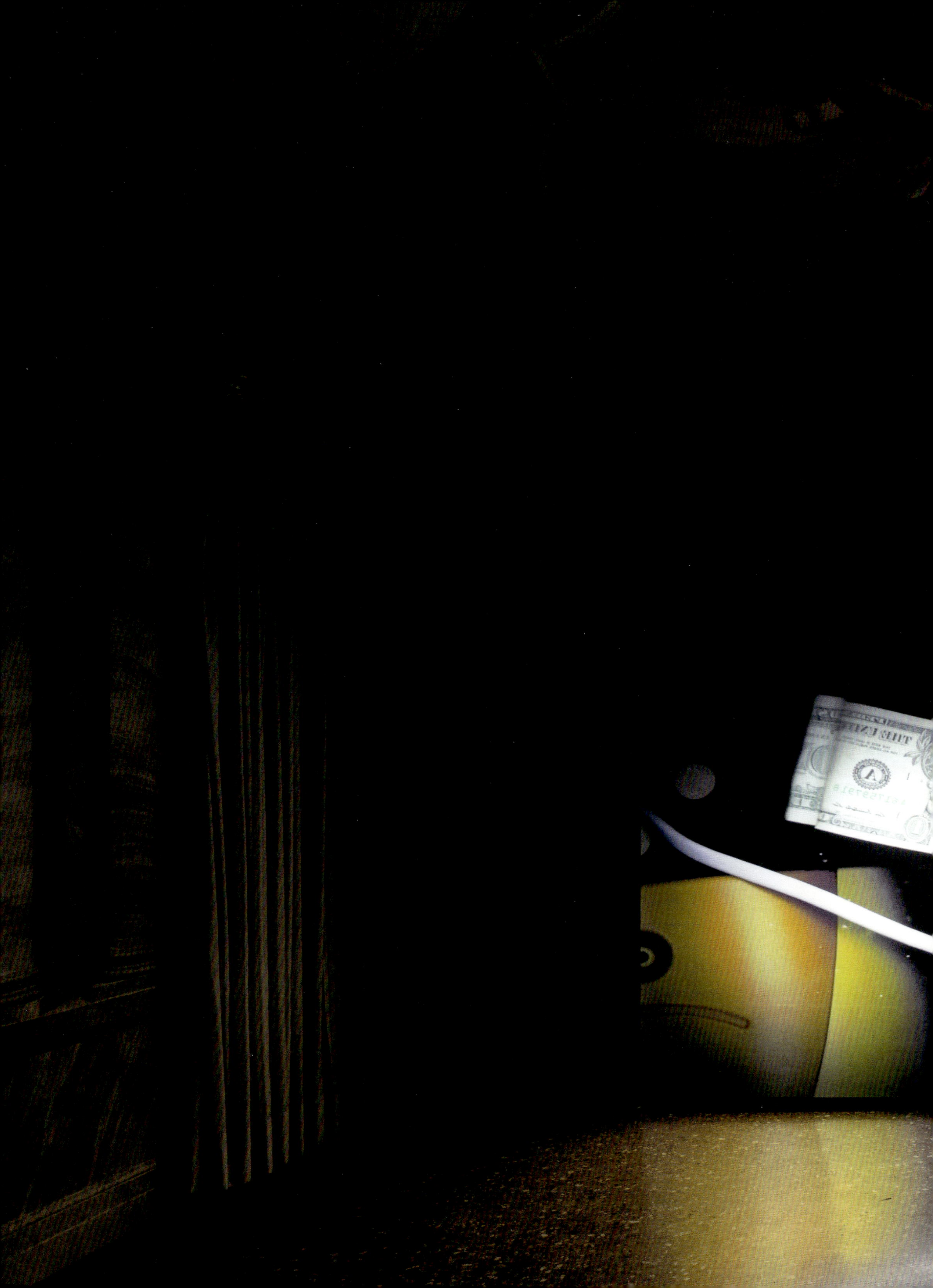

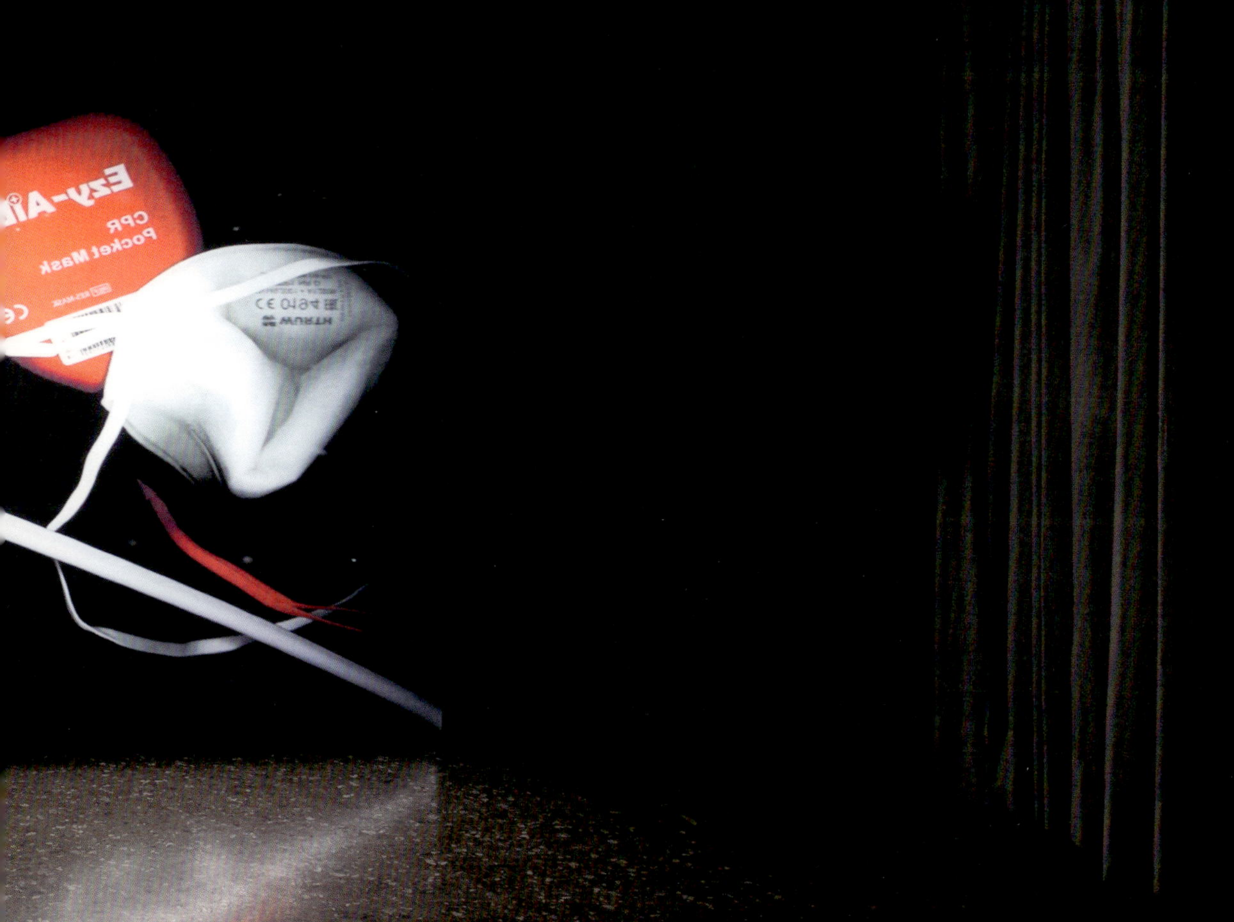

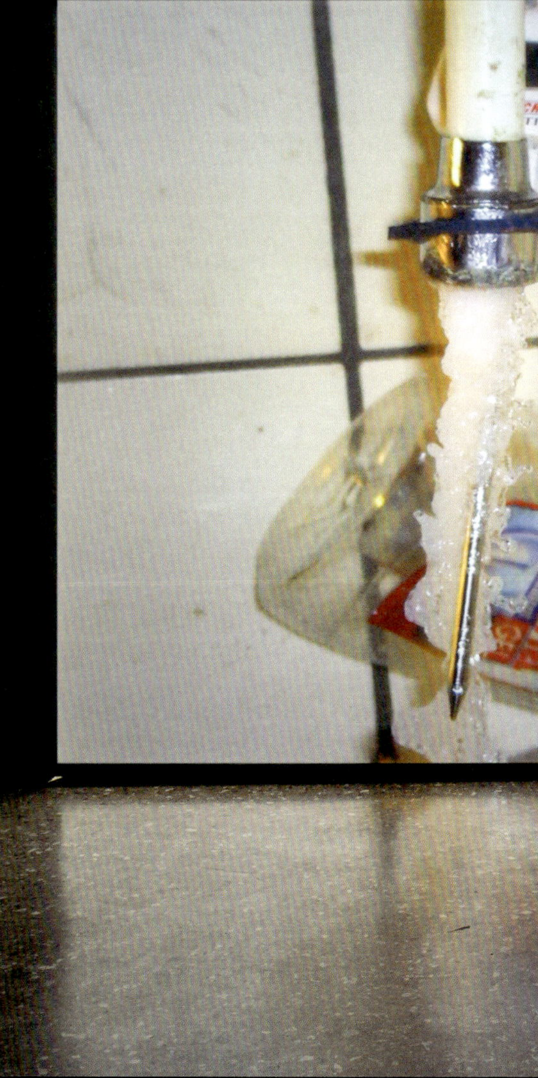

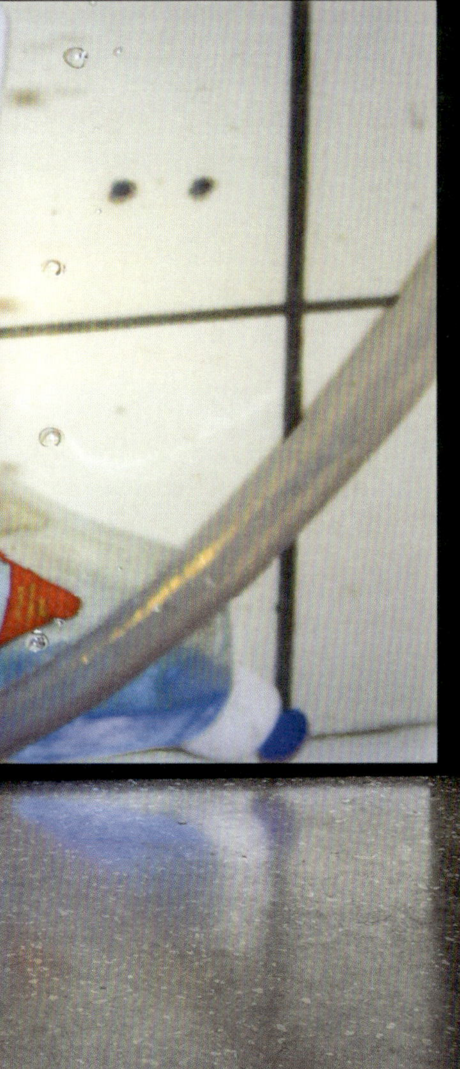

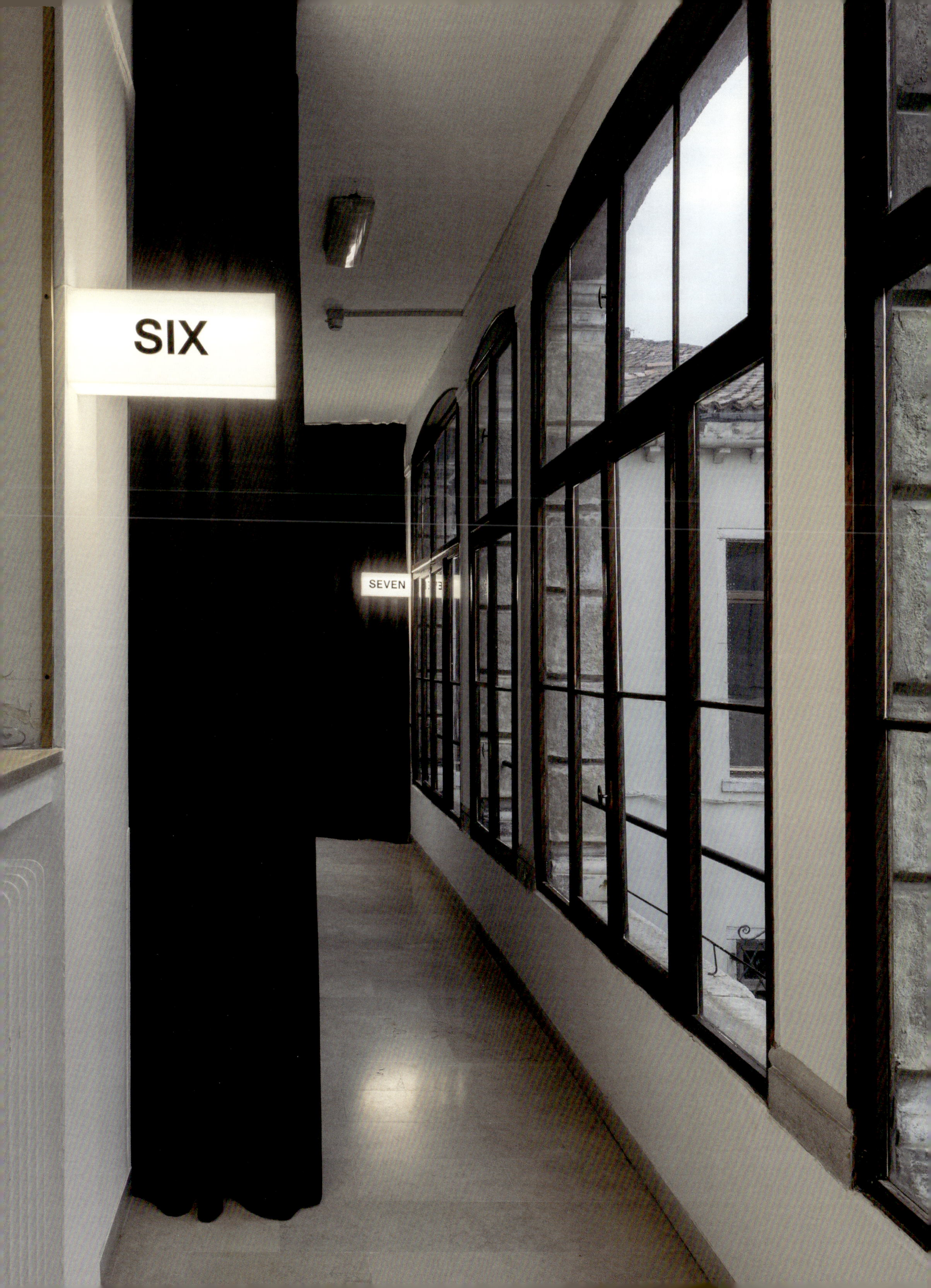
SIX
SEVEN

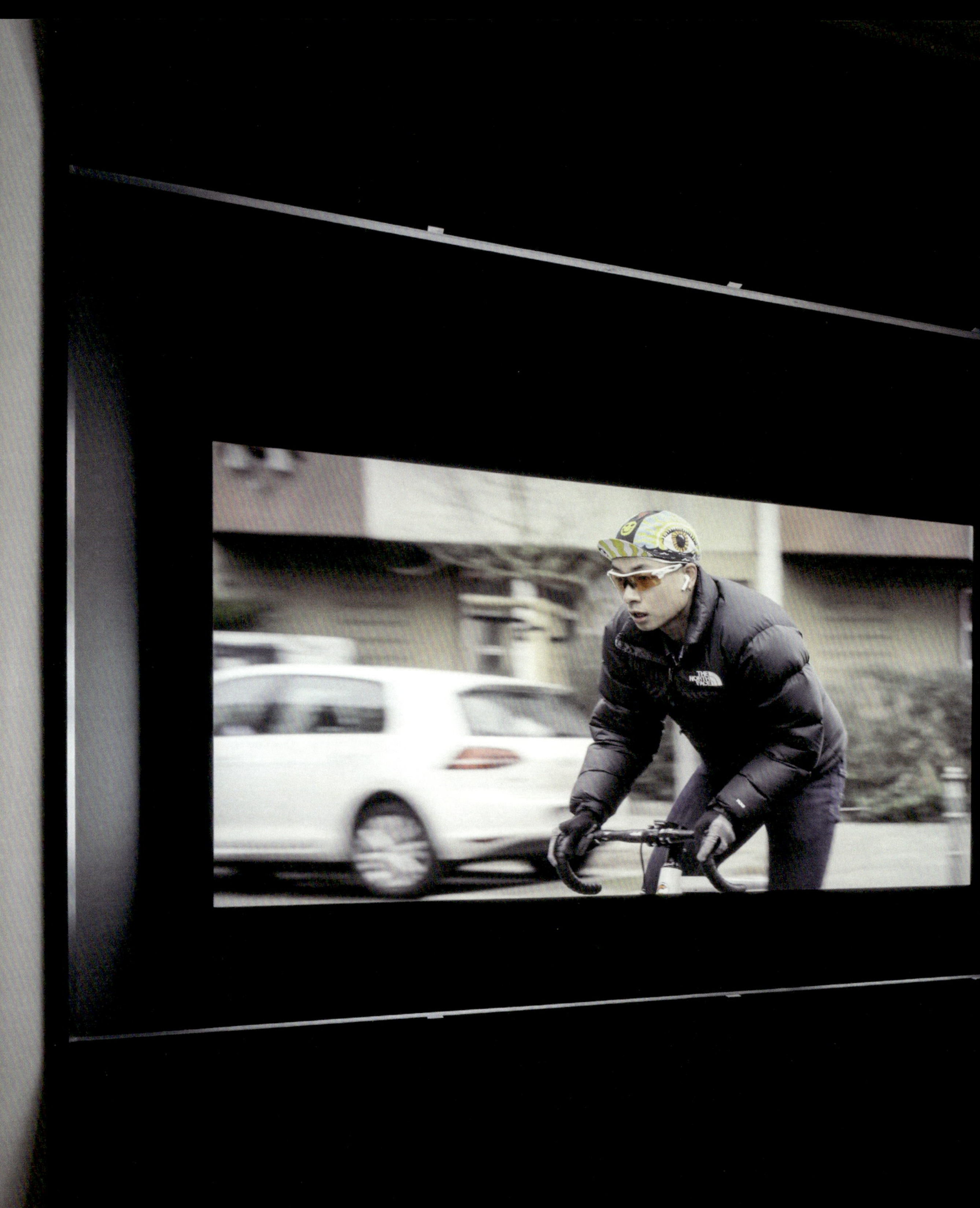

He Xiangyu, *House of Nations*, 2021

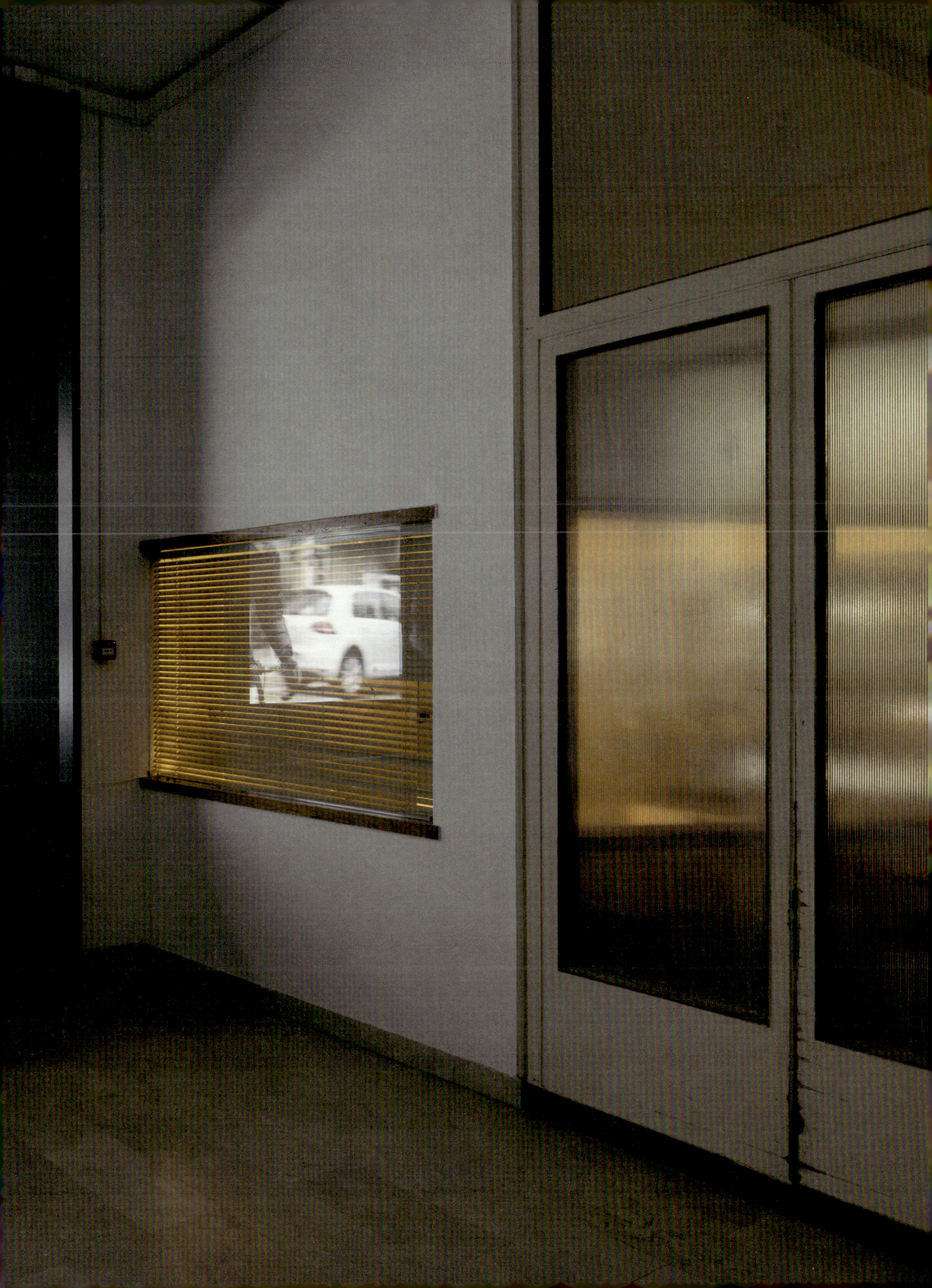

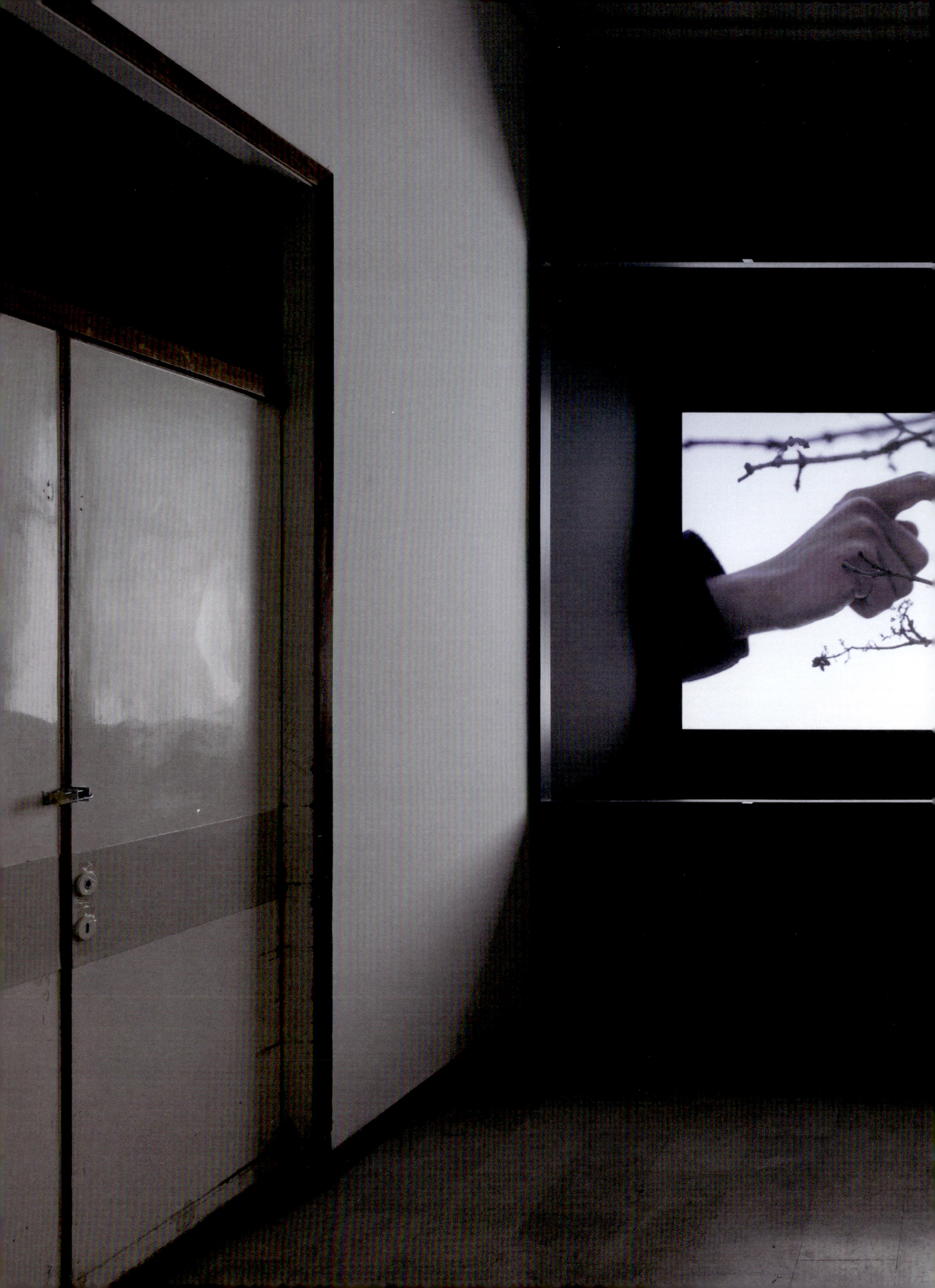

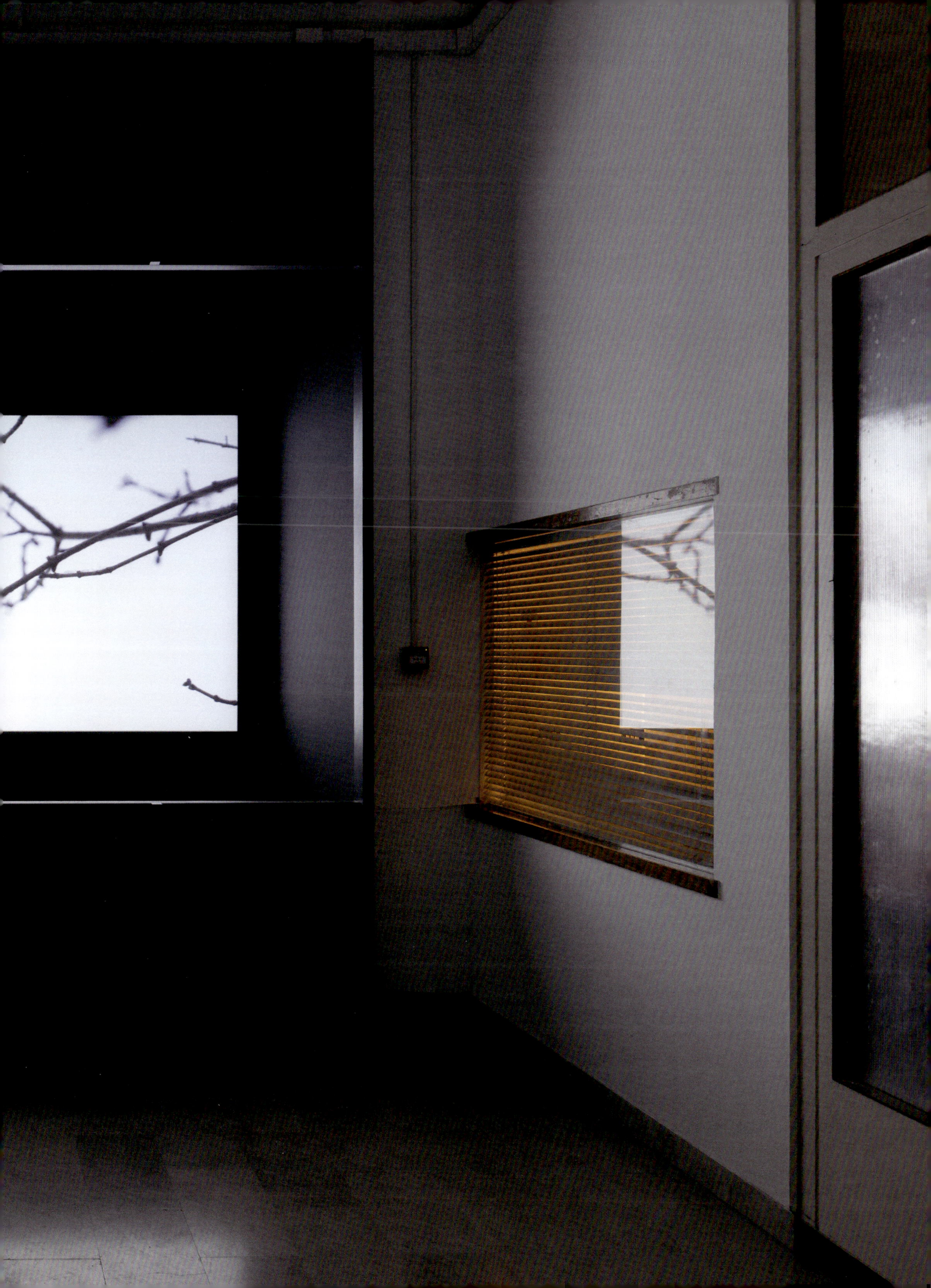

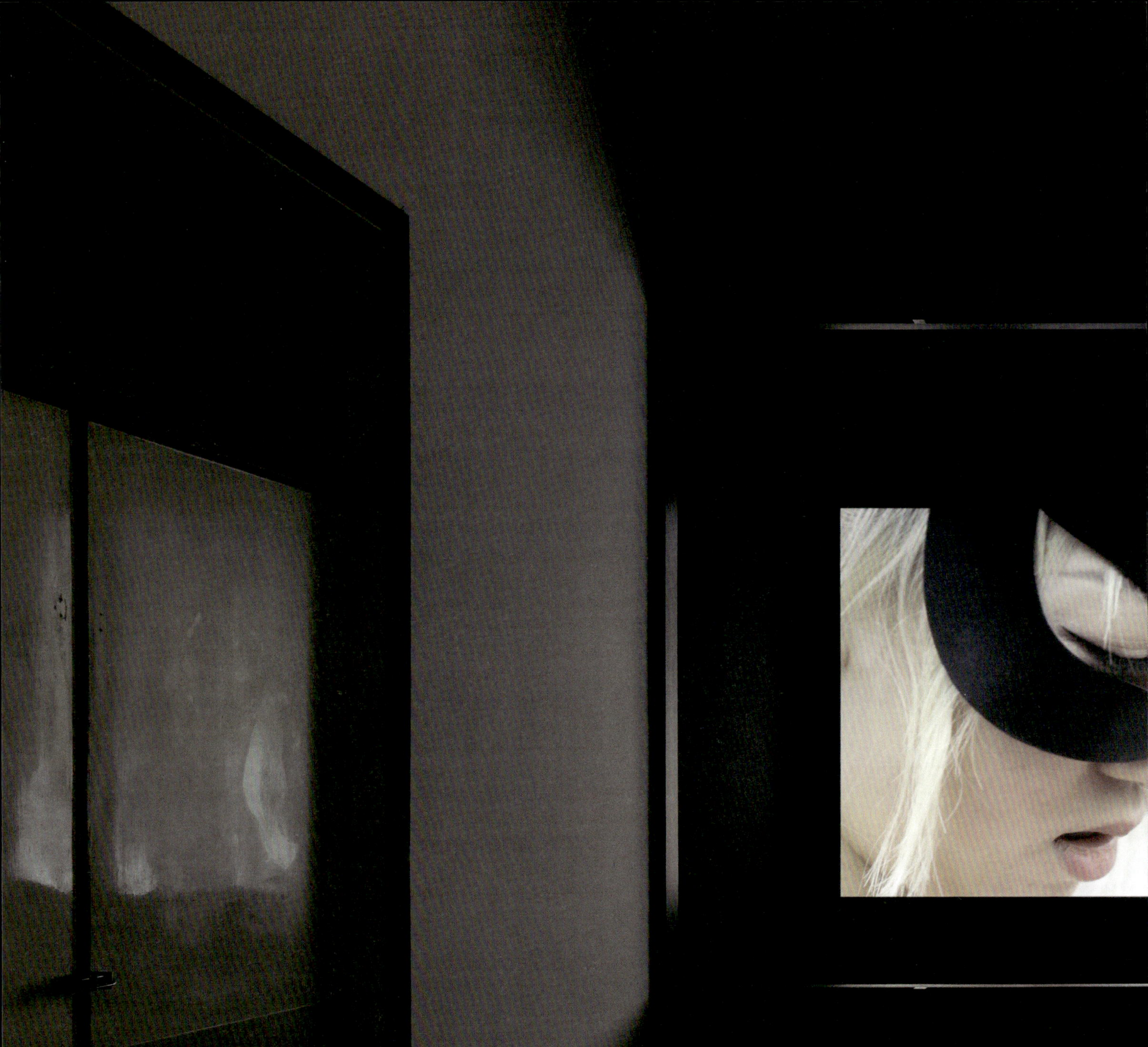

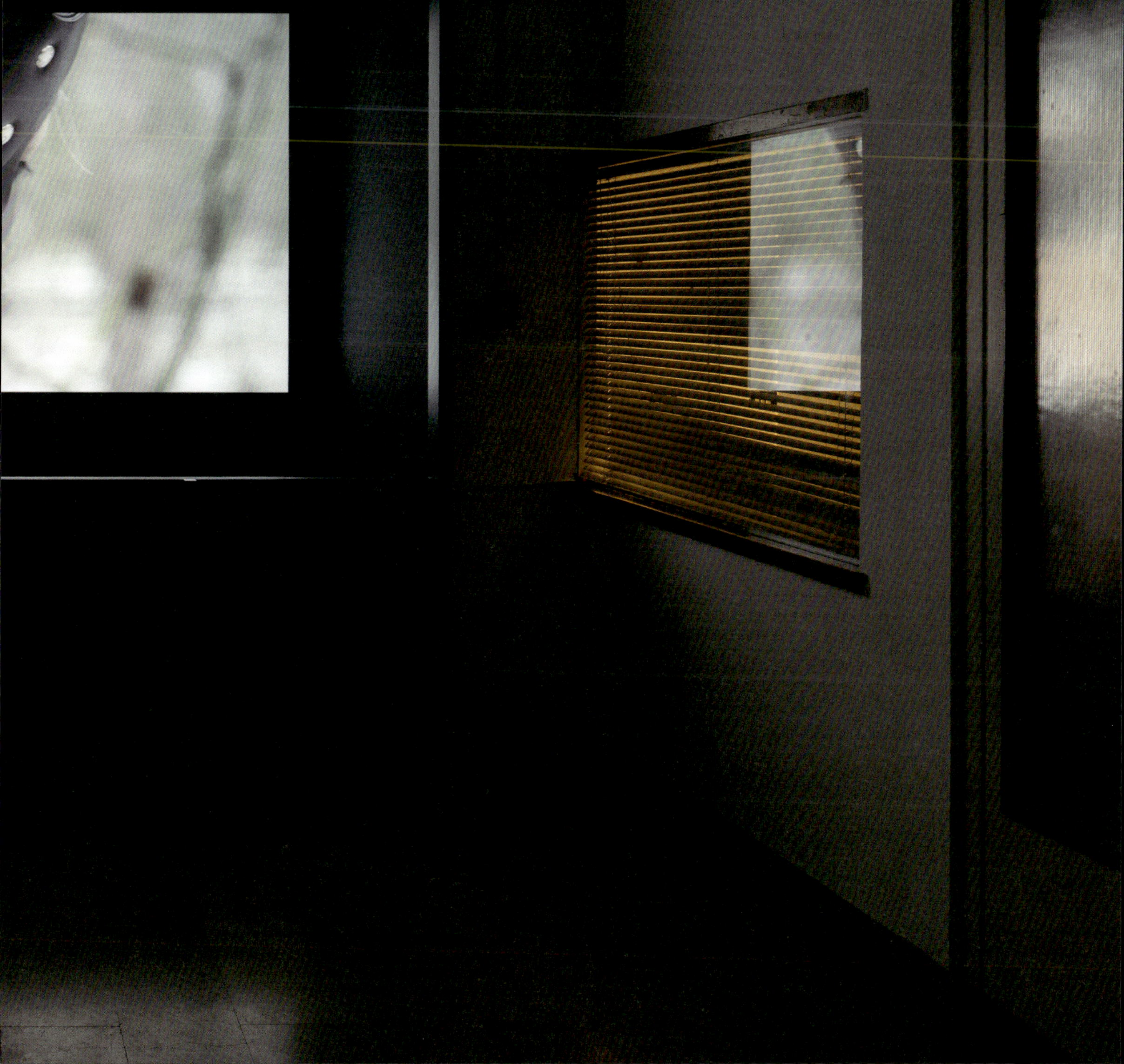

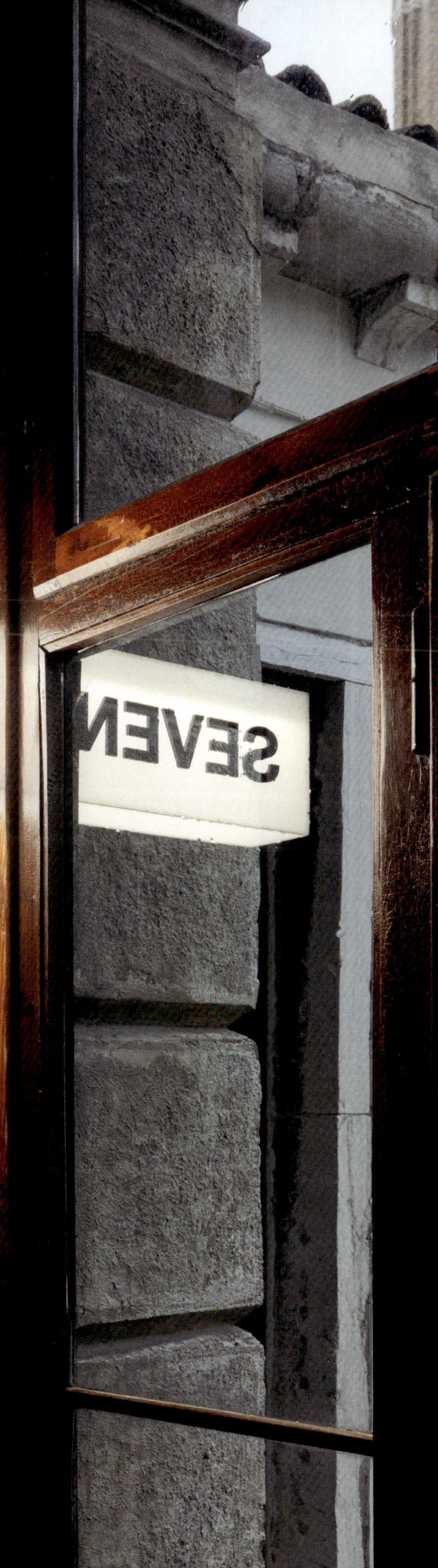
SEVEN

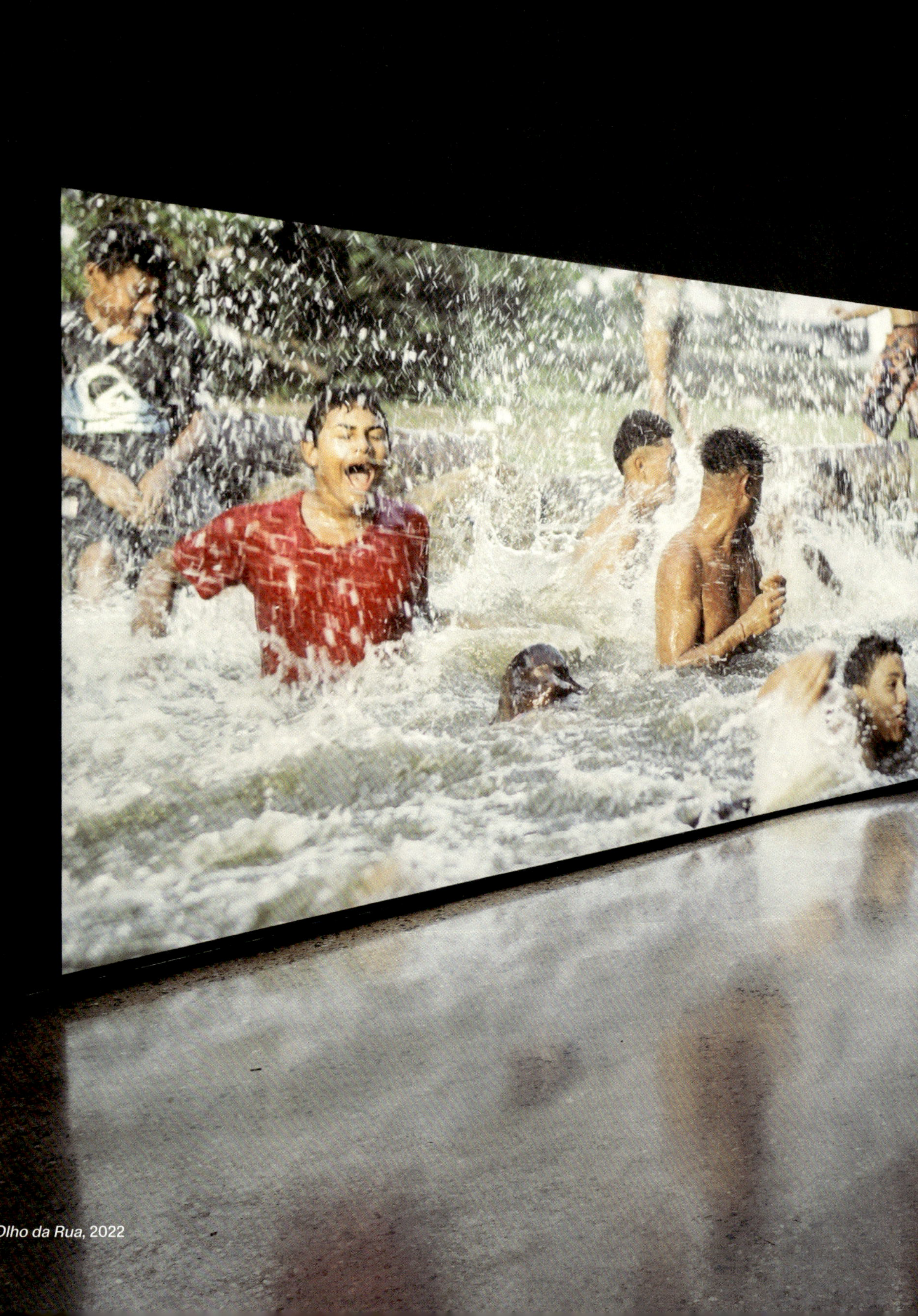

Jonathas de Andrade, *Olho da Rua*, 2022

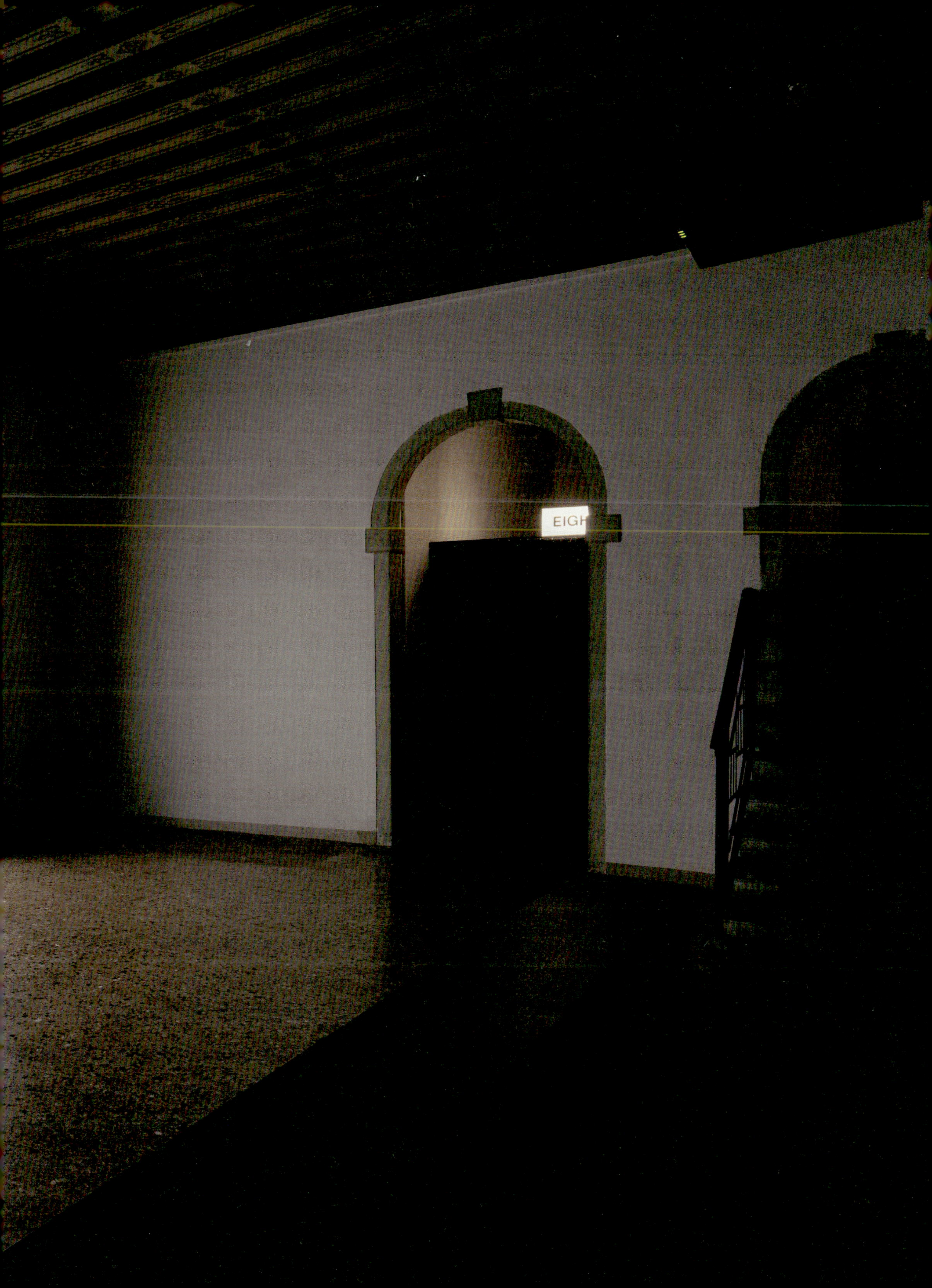
EIGH

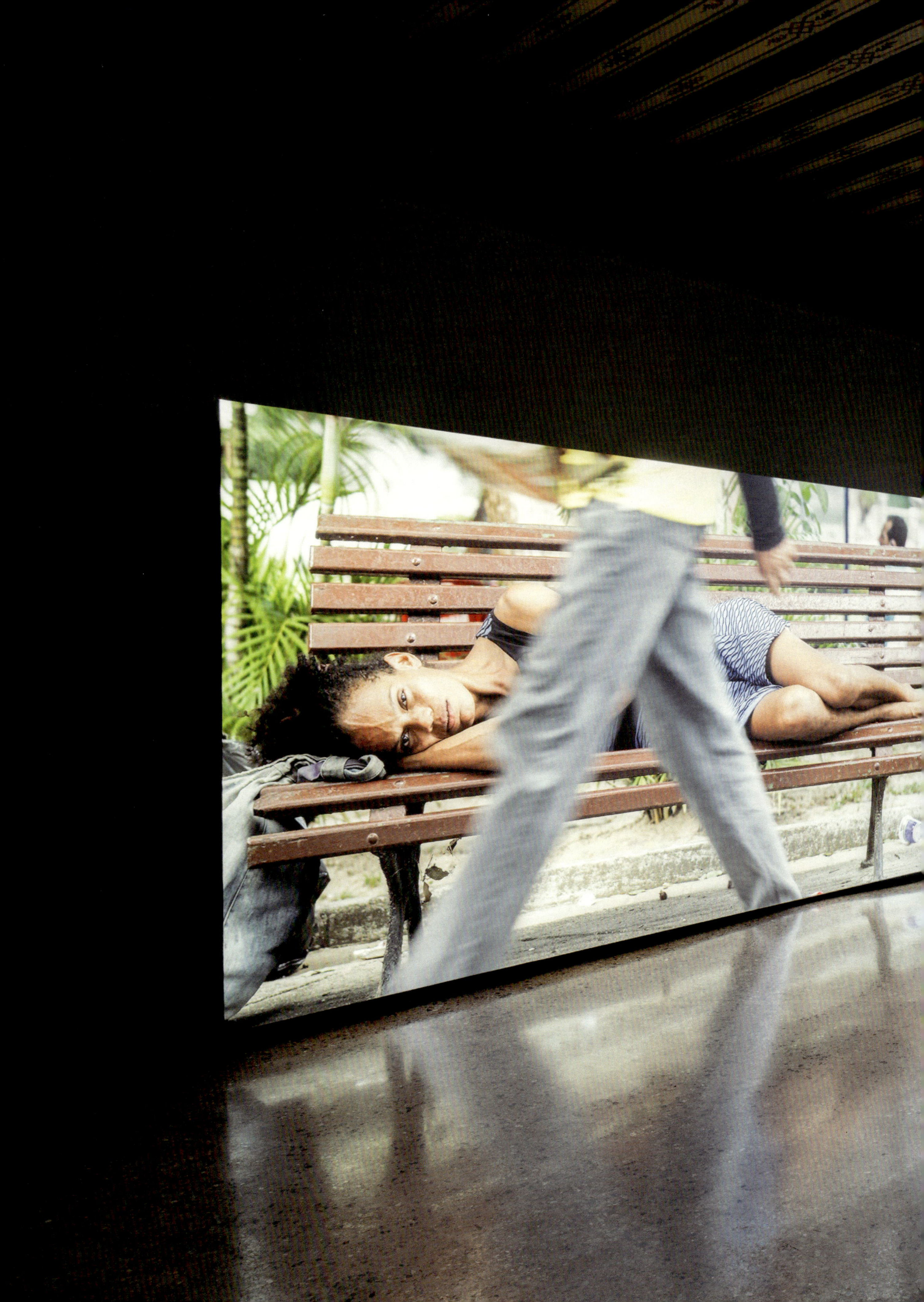

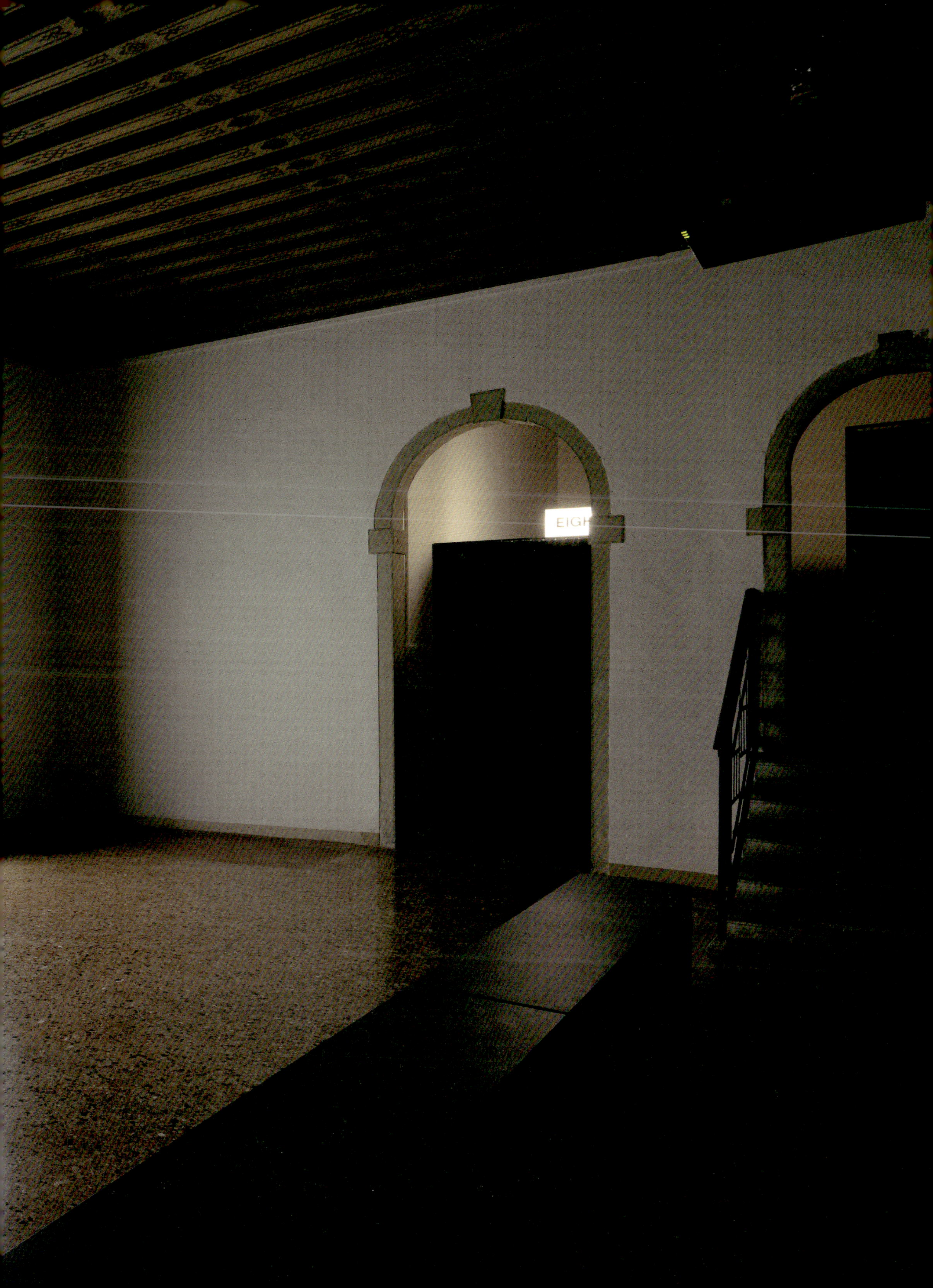
EIGH

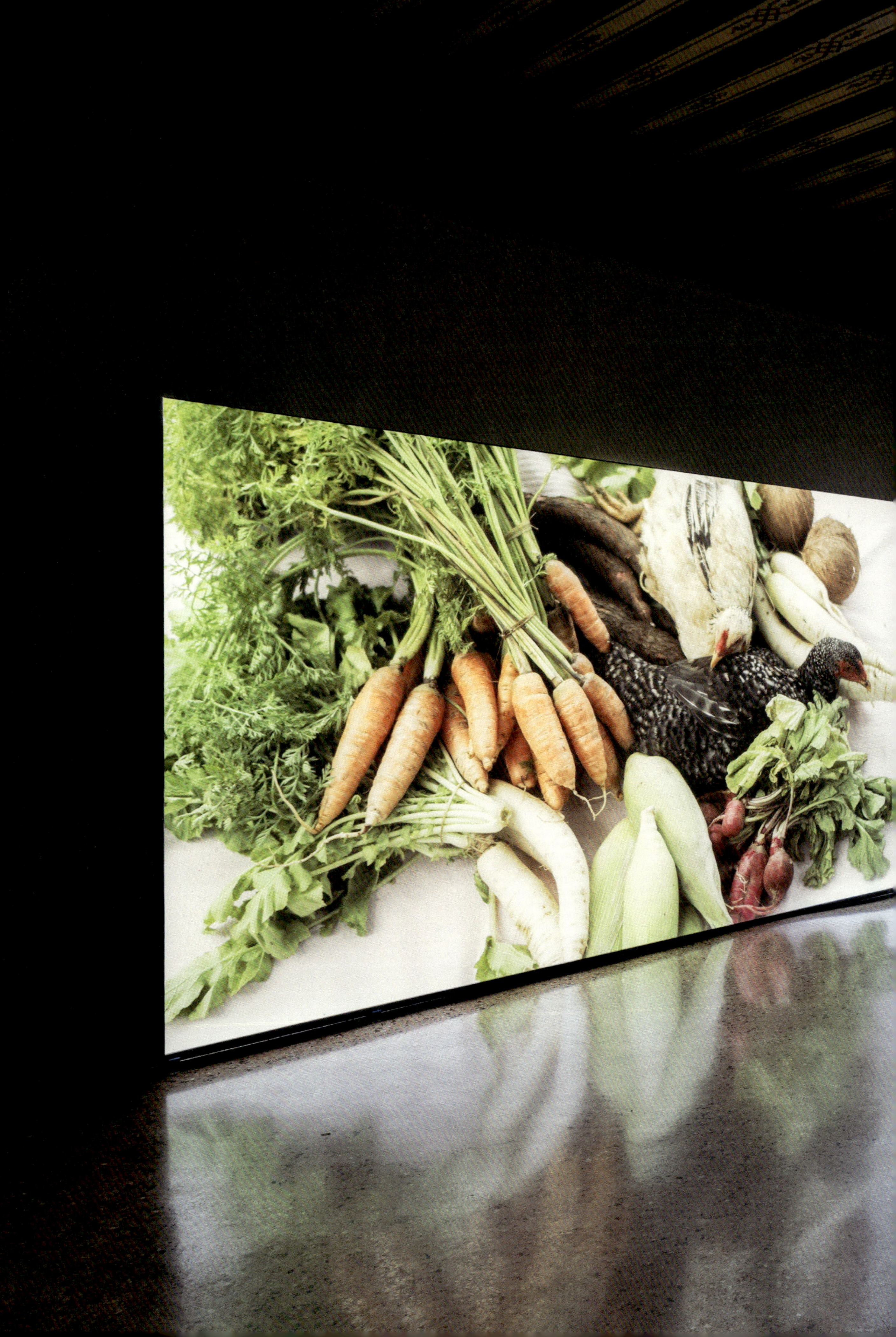

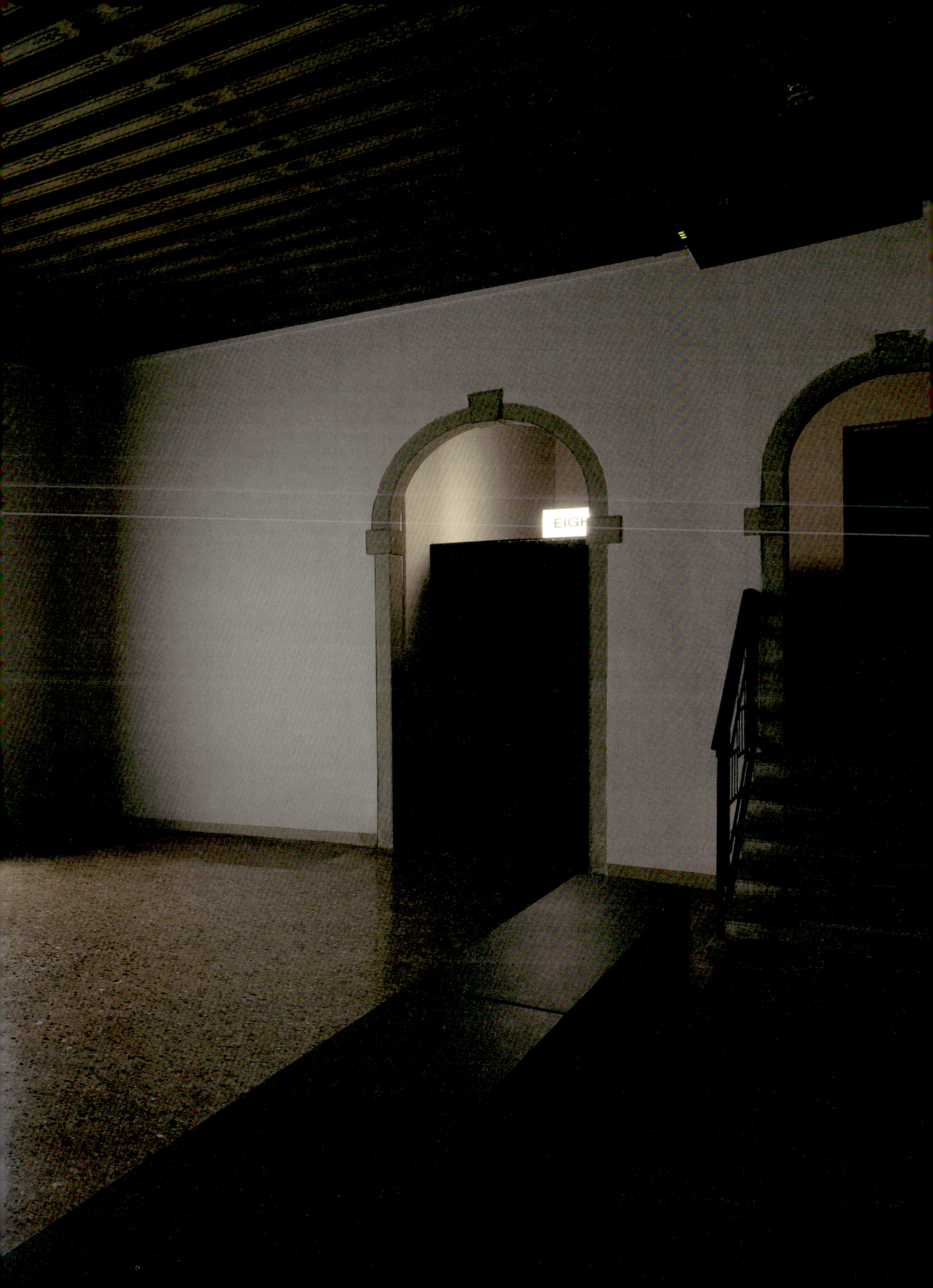
EIGH

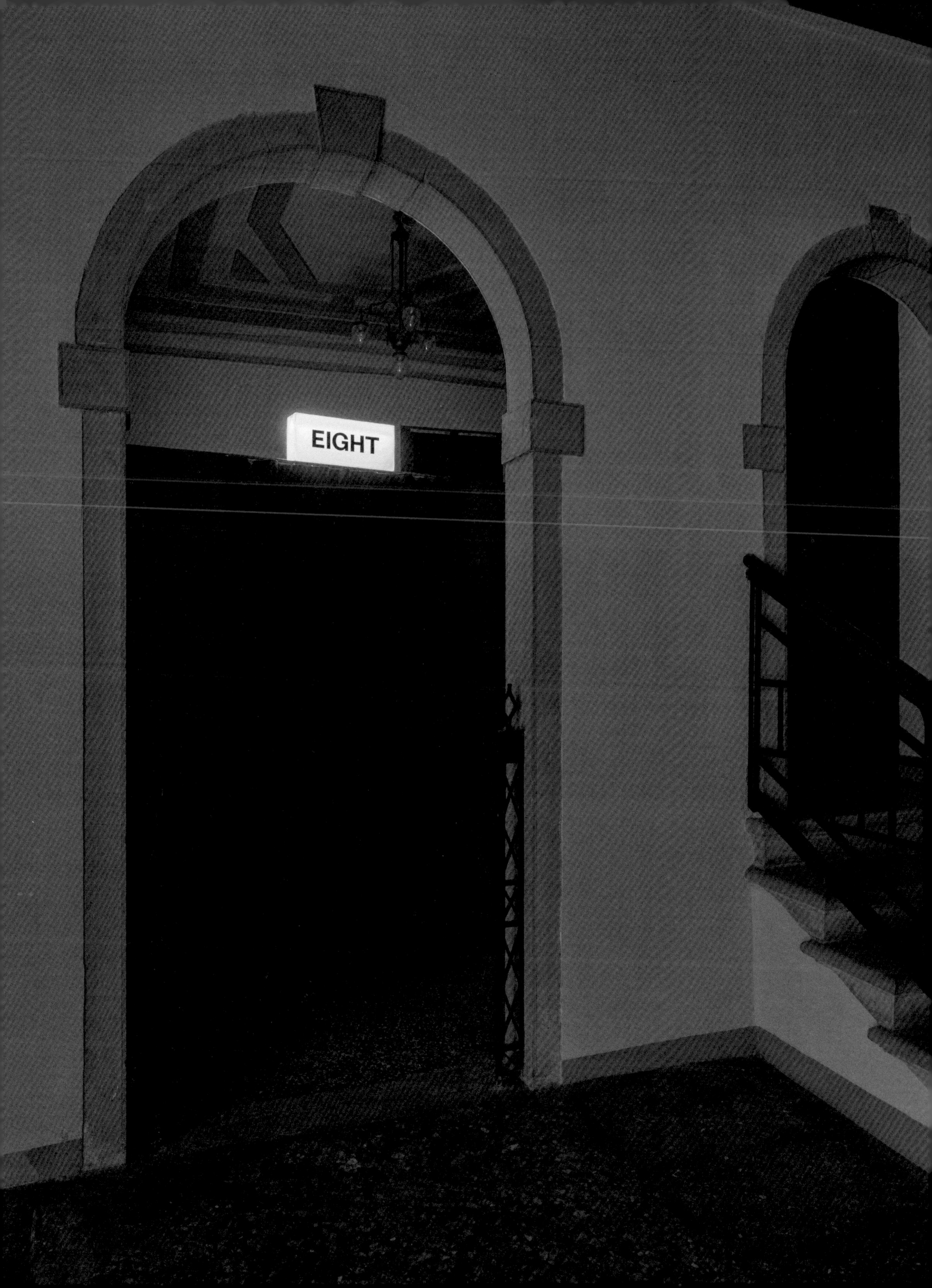
EIGHT

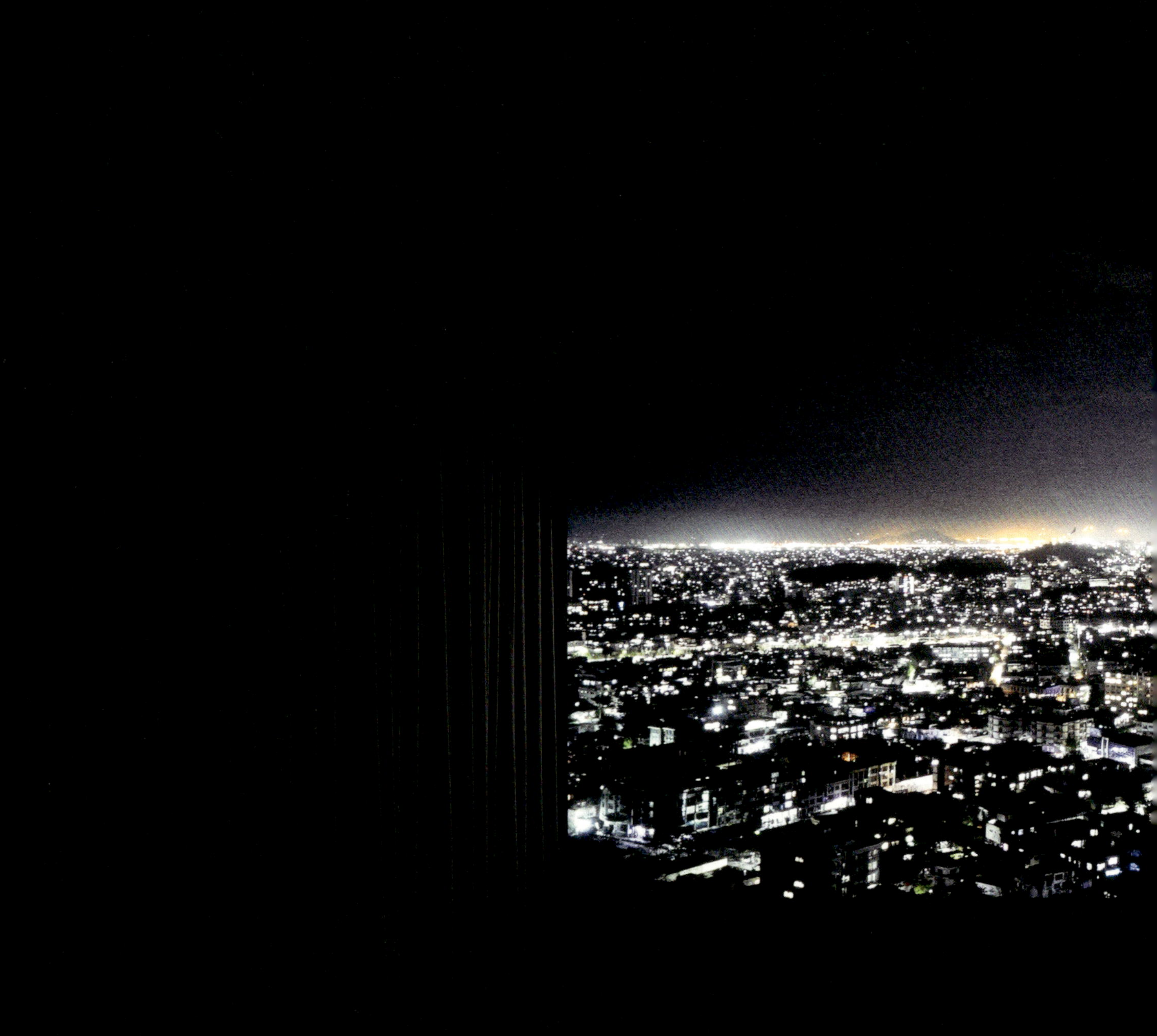

Aziz Hazara, *Takbir*, 2022

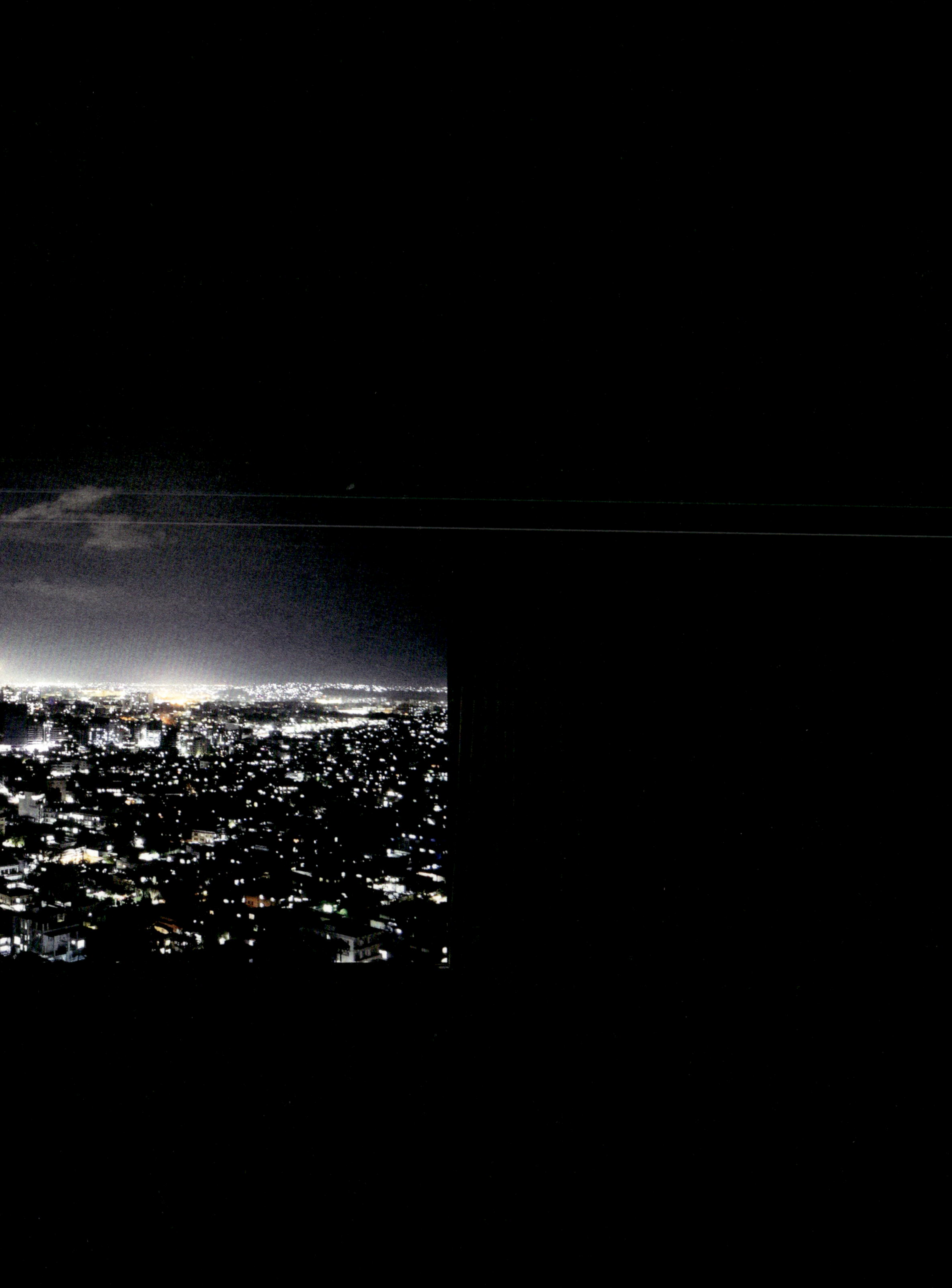

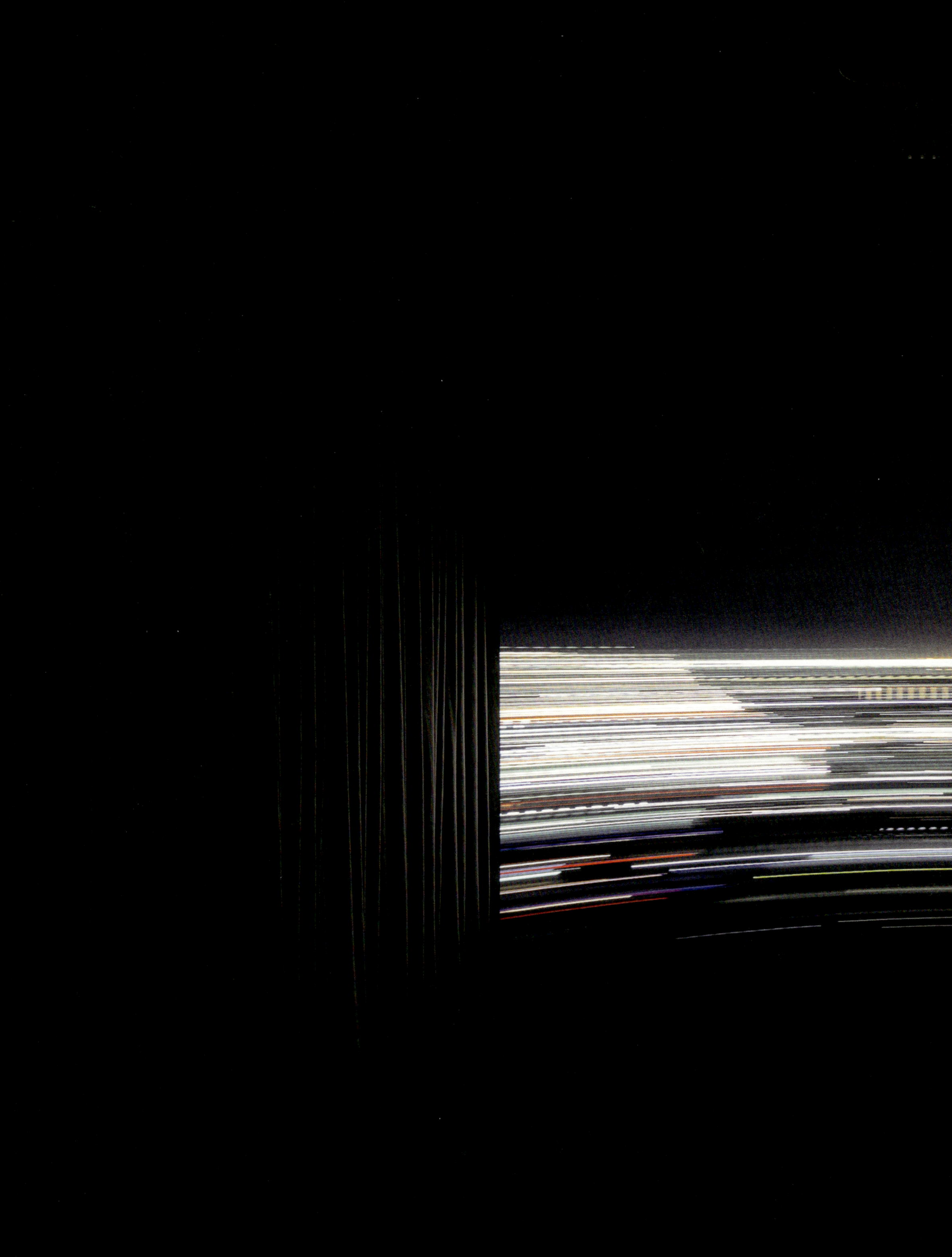

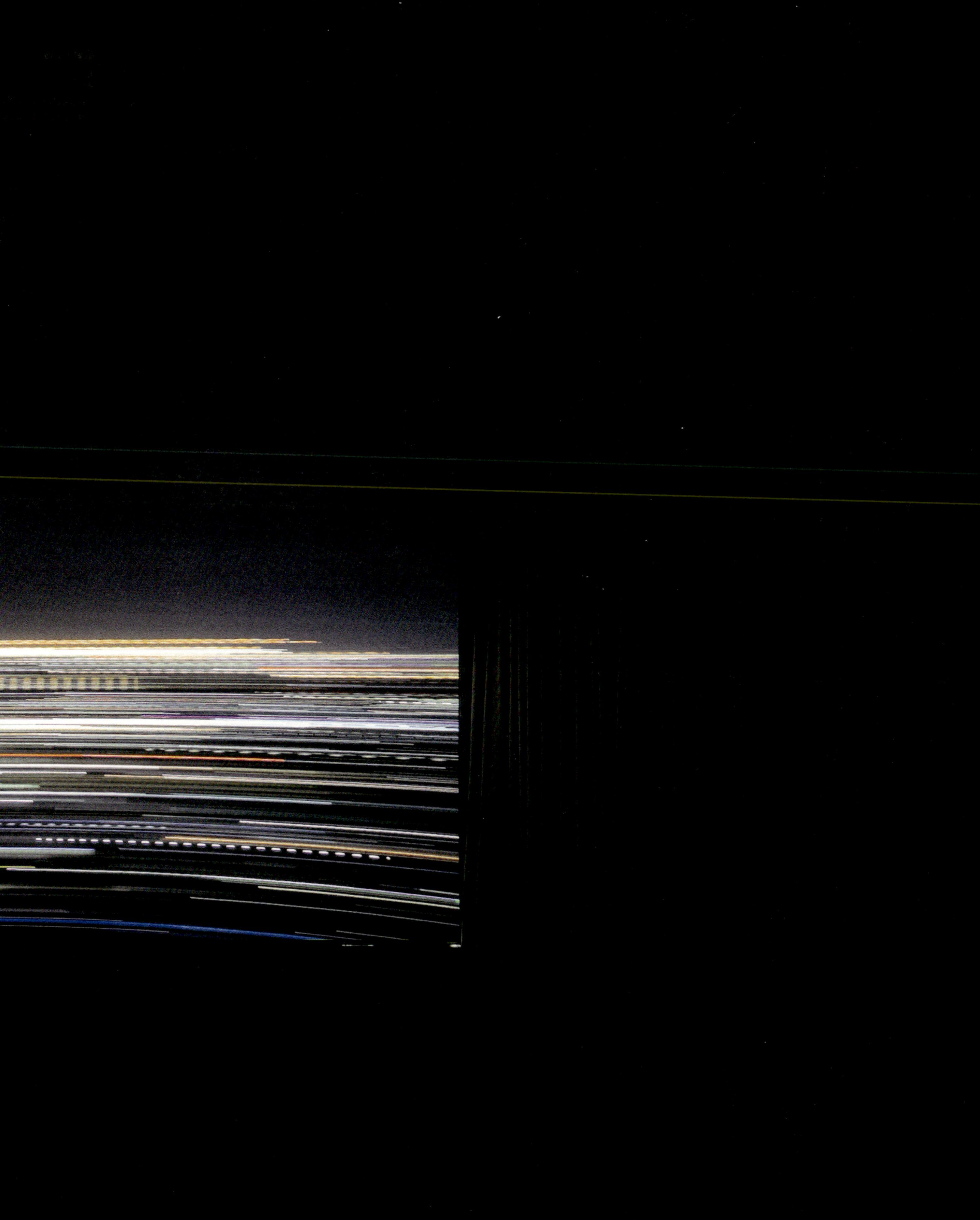

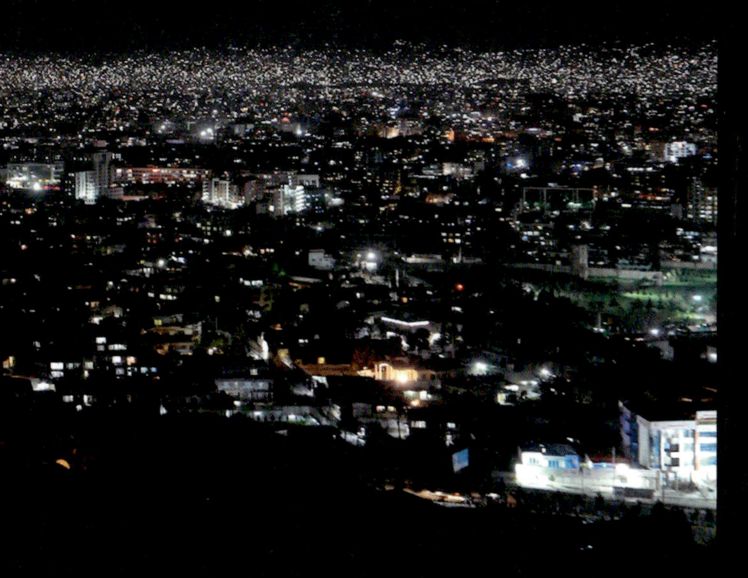

JAMES RICHARDS

QUALITIES OF LIFE: LIVING IN THE RADIANT COLD

2022, 2K video, color, stereo sound, 17'29"

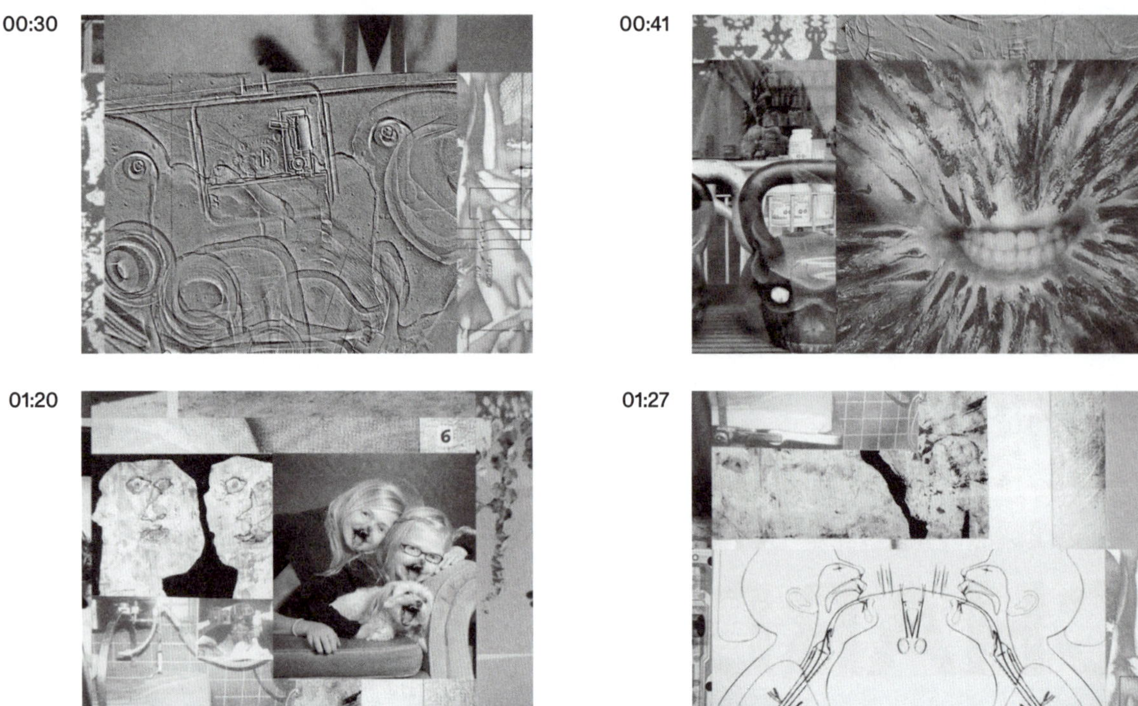

Qualities of Life: Living in the Radiant Cold by James Richards (b. 1983, United Kingdom) records and compiles domestic still lifes, radiological images, cultural detritus, and civic sewage systems into a poetry and music suite. The aim of this material and metaphorical endoscope is to look closer at the private and public dimensions of decay, hygiene, and contagion. Over its sections, that the artist conceives as stanzas,

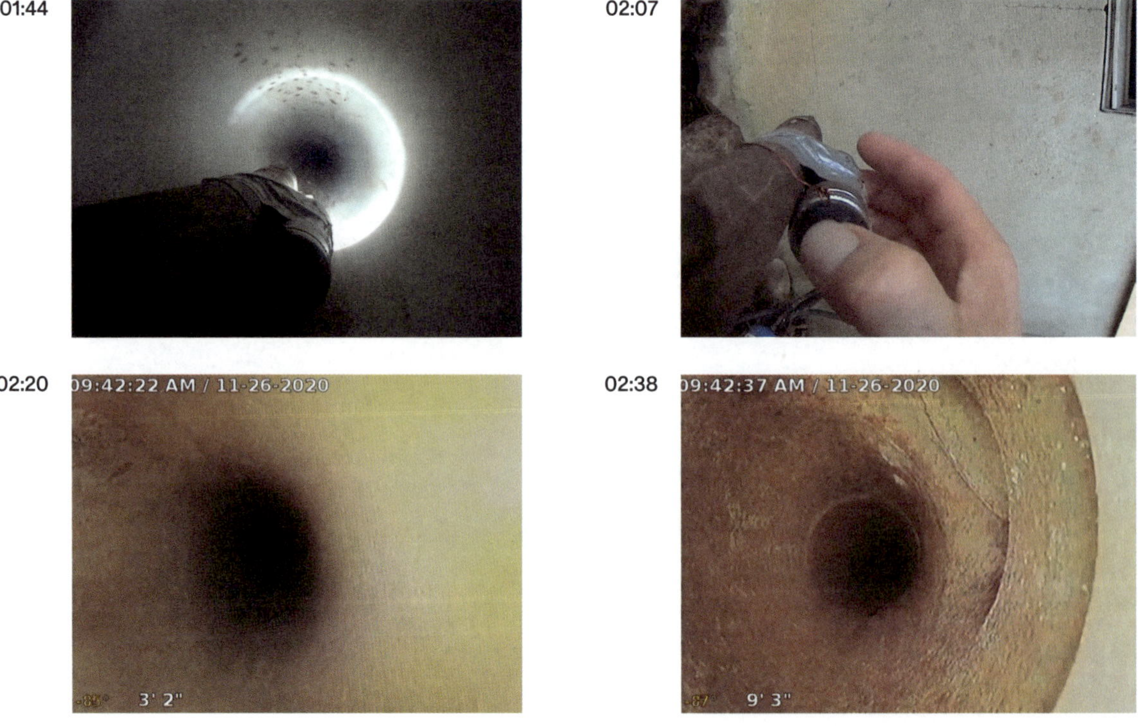

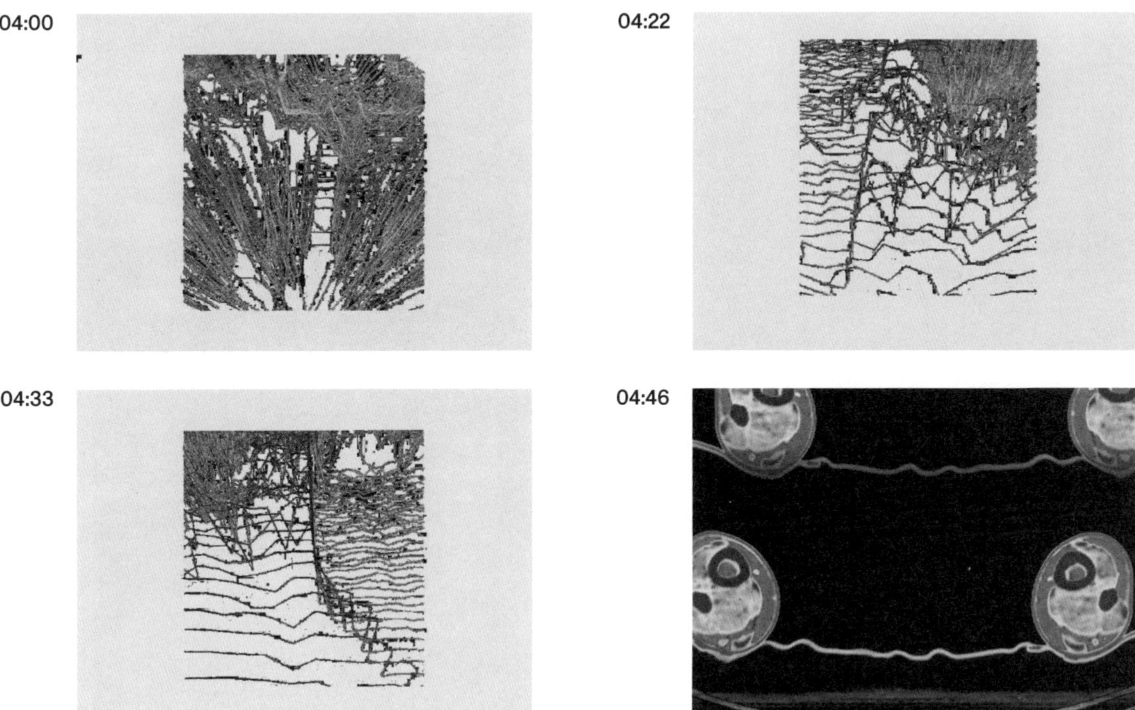

it focuses with granular attention on the different materials it collects, as if involved in the anamnesis of a self, a body, a house, a city. The scalability in the visualization of phenomena from the micro to the macro is taken further by grafting an extract from *Hemlock* (2021)—originally shot by artist and often collaborator Leslie Thornton—where a young boy in the shape of pulsating waves explains the millennial evolution of

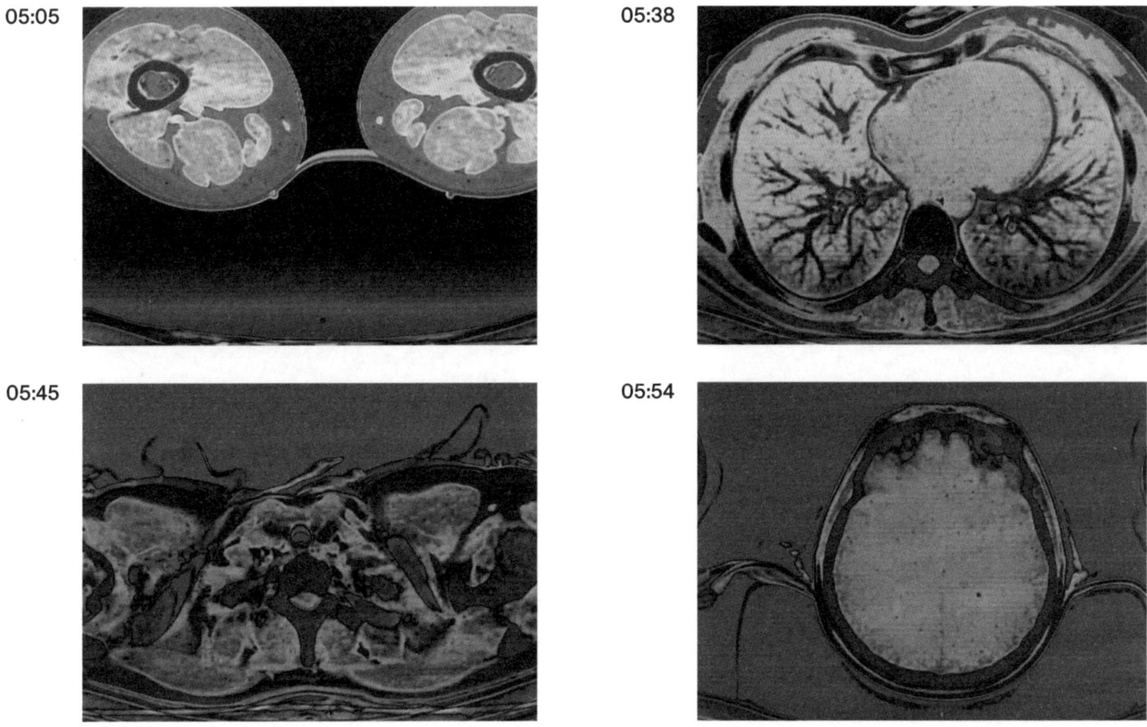

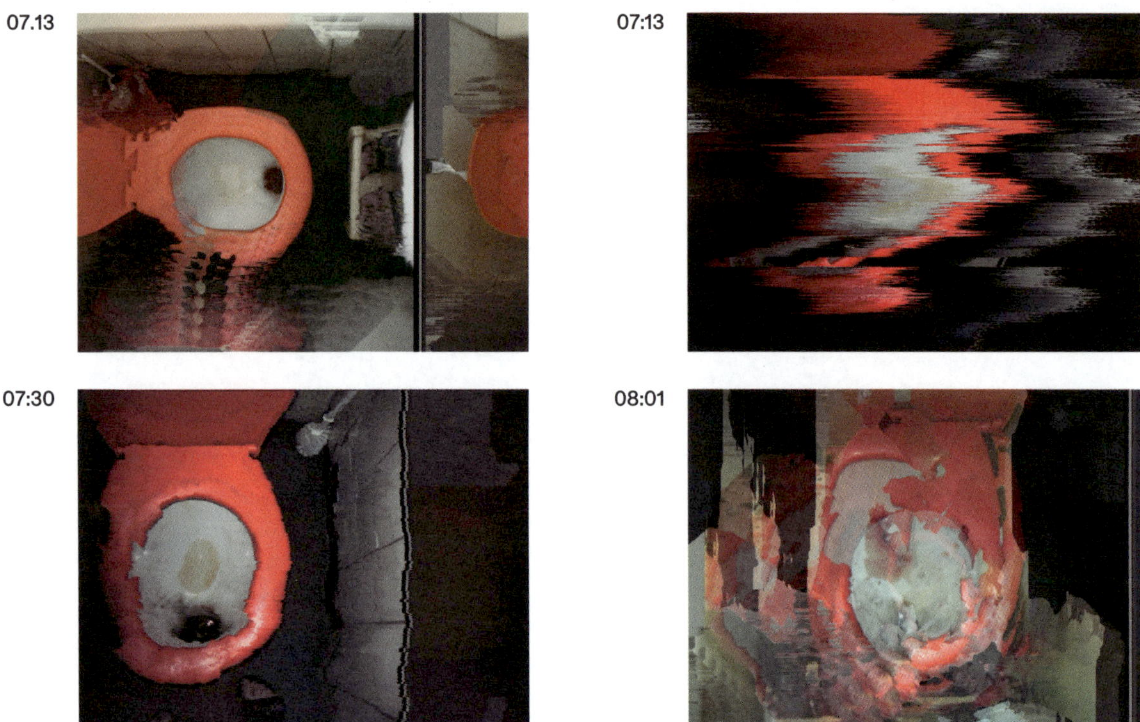

bees' social structure. One of its guiding forces is the series of *Daily Photos* and *Observational Photos* (both, 2000–07) featured from the archive of Horst Ademeit (1937–2010), whose obsessive, multi-decade imperative was to register the detrimental impact of radiations (or invisible, "cold" rays, as he called them) on his body and his surroundings. In another stanza, various erotic, narcotic, and nostalgic paraphernalia

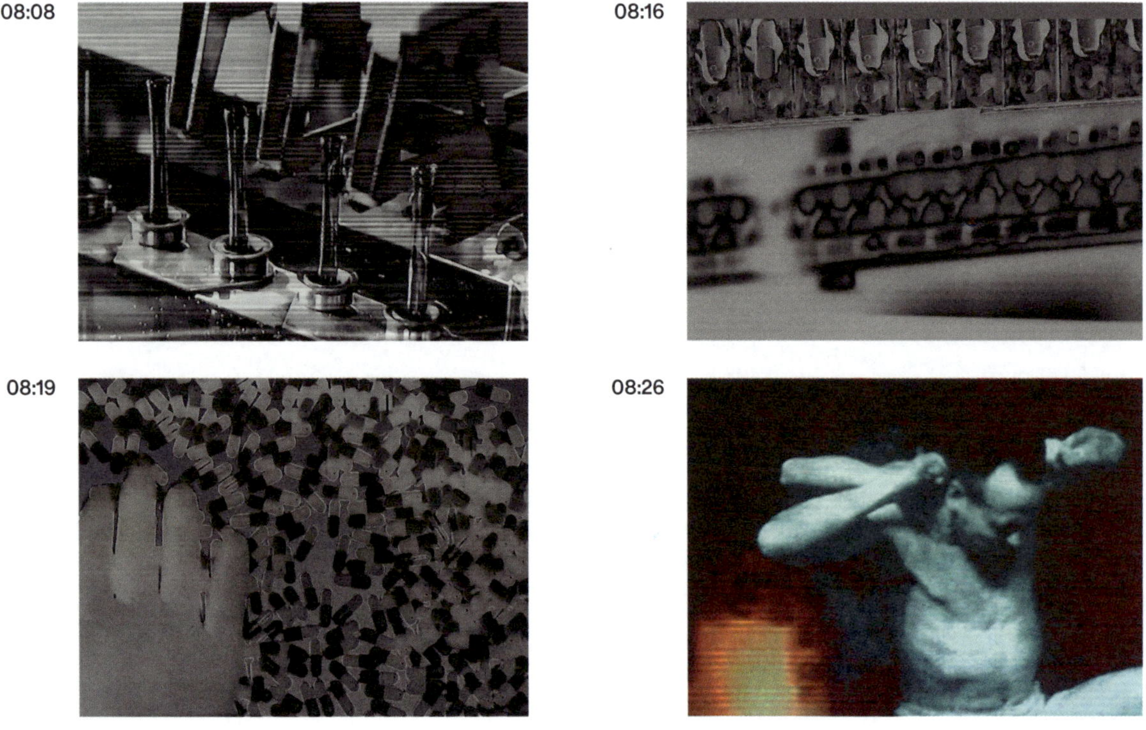

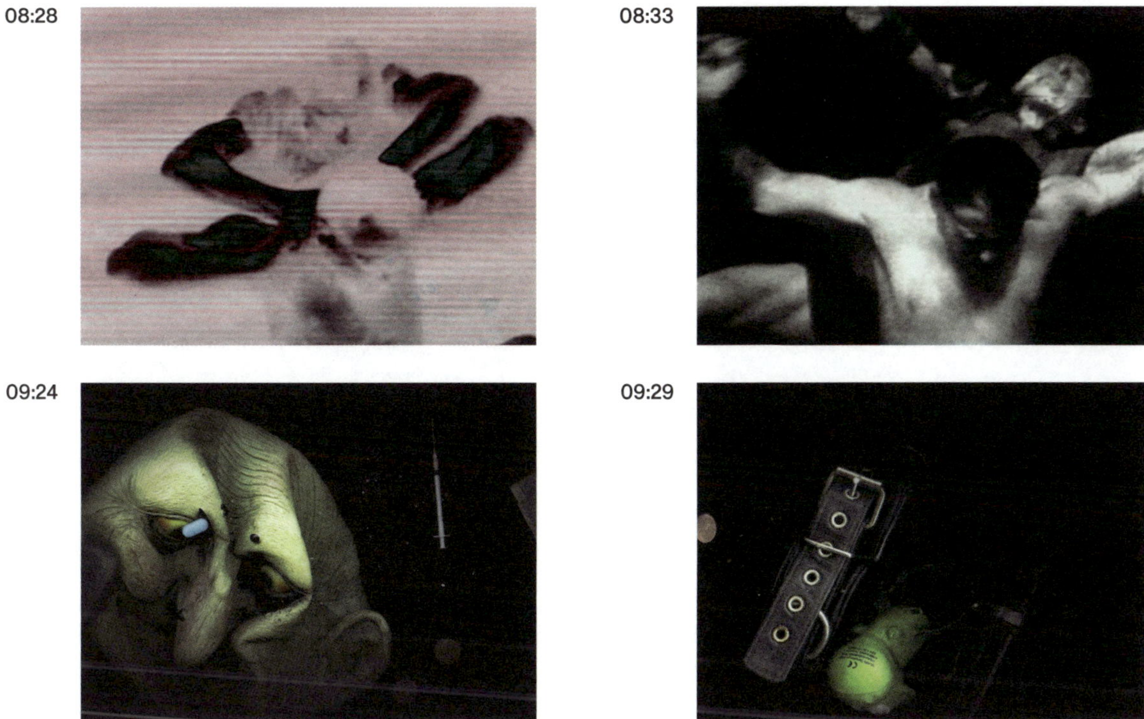
08:28 08:33 09:24 09:29

from Richards' apartment and studio are gathered, scanned, and animated into mental conglomerates shipwrecked in a dark, viscous space. Throughout the film, objects and subjects, bodies and images, voices and sounds manifest as intimately vulnerable, only solidifying for a moment before smearing their borders, and drifting into something else. Voices and percussions developed with musicians and actors

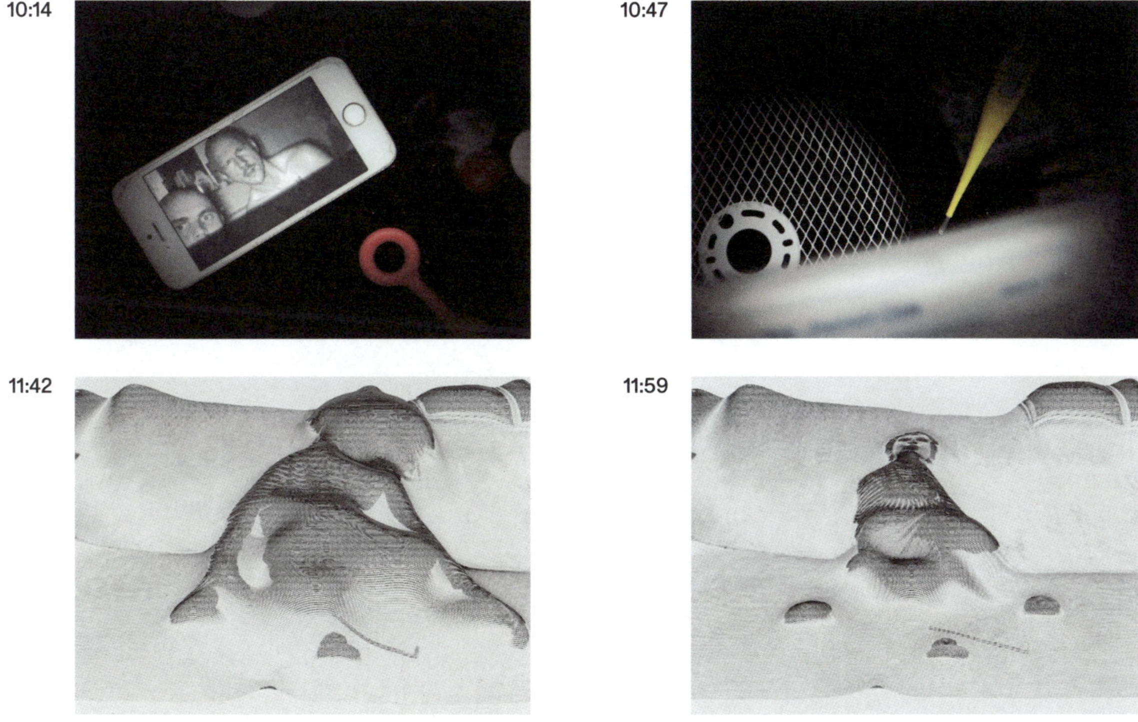
10:14 10:47 11:42 11:59

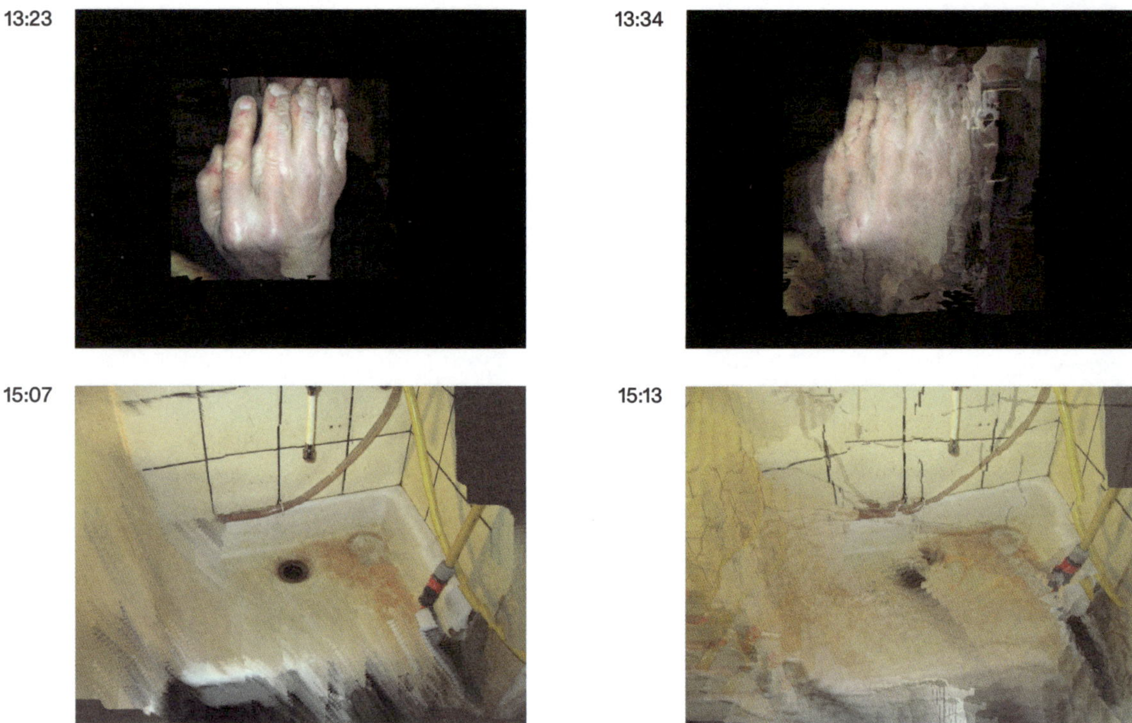

rhythmically emerge and submerge together with sampled sounds, causing novel interferences throughout the collaged materials. The video poses a survivalist dilemma on images and media, or maybe a trick, in the subtly mundane and infrastructural dimension that it traverses.

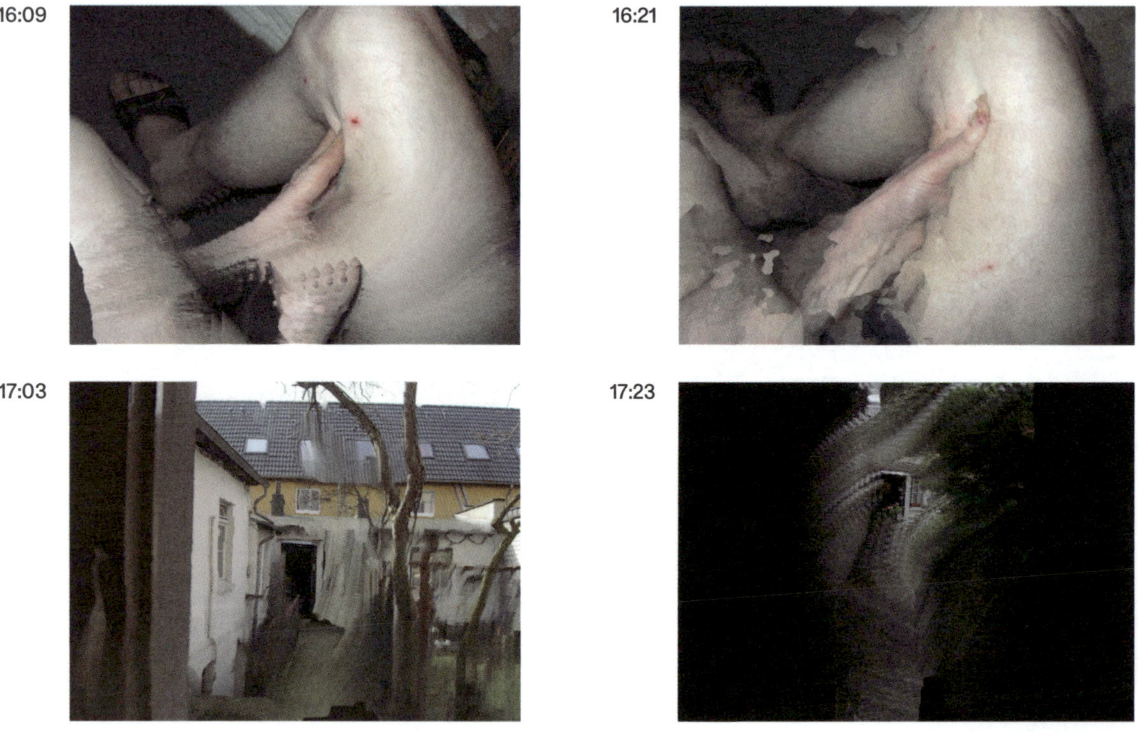

James Richards, *Qualities of Life: Living in the Radiant Cold*, 2022

2K video, color, stereo sound, 17'29"

Commissioned and produced by
Fondazione In Between Art Film

Creative Producer
Alessandro Rabottini

Cinematography, editing, sound design
James Richards

Additional animation
Ben Brix, Roy Hamilton-Sturdy

Voices
Vocal Juice

Featuring
Daily Photos and *Observational Photos* (both, 2000–07) by Horst Ademeit (1937–2010), an extract from *Abyss Film* (2020) by Leslie Thornton and James Richards, and from *Hemlock* (2021) by Leslie Thornton.

Special thanks to
Fatima Hellberg

Thanks to
Beatrice Bulgari, Leonardo Bigazzi, Alessia Carlino, Bianca Stoppani, Paola Ugolini

Courtesy of the artist, the Estate of Horst Ademeit, and Fondazione In Between Art Film

Fellow Traveler
Matt Keegan

When I wake up in the morning and go to the bathroom, my cat, Earl, arrives toilet-side to solicit head pets. My proximity to the ground comforts him. My normal verticality and busy human behavior fall away, and he sees me as a fellow animal shitting in proximity to his litter box. Recently, I have been making drawings of the plumbing in my bathroom, thinking in part about cleanliness due to augmented COVID-19 hygiene but also about the plumbing's complex infrastructure linking my body and the privacy of my apartment to the elaborate sewage system that runs throughout my neighborhood and wider city. The construction of New York City's sewers and waste removal started in 1849, in response to a major cholera outbreak, and by 1902 most of the city had a functioning sewer. Two years later, NYC's first underground subway began operating, visually overlaying the intestinal structure of plumbing onto the network of trains.

In James Richards's video commission *Qualities of Life: Living in the Radiant Cold* (2022) for the Fondazione In Between Art Film, we continuously encounter solid and liquid waste and the various systems that circulate them. We see feces and wastewater being sucked from a large rectangular sewage hole and multiple sequences of cameras snaking through pipes to find blockage, a visceral transposition of the now routine endoscopy. We see an array of unlikely objects floating in water, repeated washing, sinks, a red-seat toilet that shifts from containing bloodied water to resembling an open wound. In Jim's broader practice, he often utilizes an associative logic in the assembly of archival material alongside his own footage to tell us stories rooted in and about the body. *Radio at Night* (2015), a commission for the Walker Art Center, comes to mind for its affinities with this new work. Reflecting on this earlier video, the writer and curator Mason Leaver-Yap writes, "*Radio at Night* is a work suffused with openings, holes, and voids: eyes, mouths, viewfinders, geysers (as well as violent openings: surgical incisions and bullet holes). Whether literal or metaphorical, bodily apertures are both the subject of the work and the tools for its reception."[1] These are not instructional works; instead logic and meaning emerge only within and from the intuitive and nonlinear order of their sequencing.

1 Mason Leaver-Yap, "James Richards: Radio at Night" *Crosscuts*, June 1, 2015, available online.

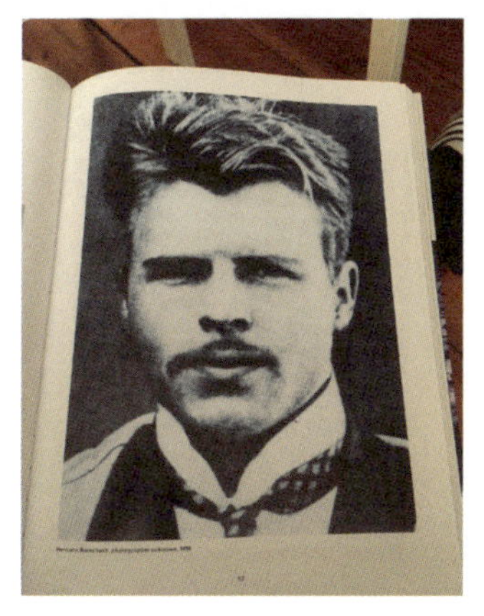

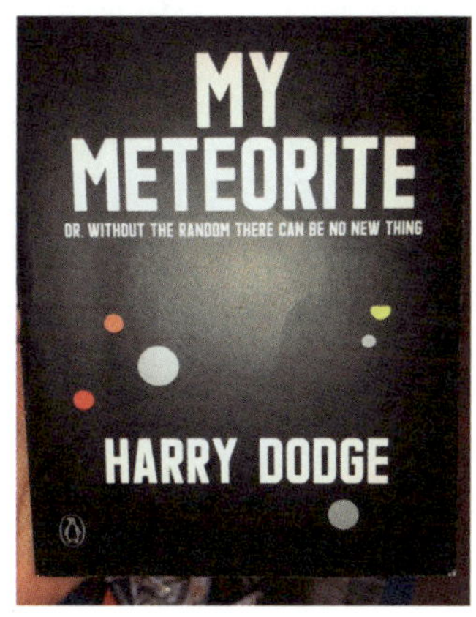
MY
METEORITE
OR, WITHOUT THE RANDOM THERE CAN BE NO NEW THING
HARRY DODGE

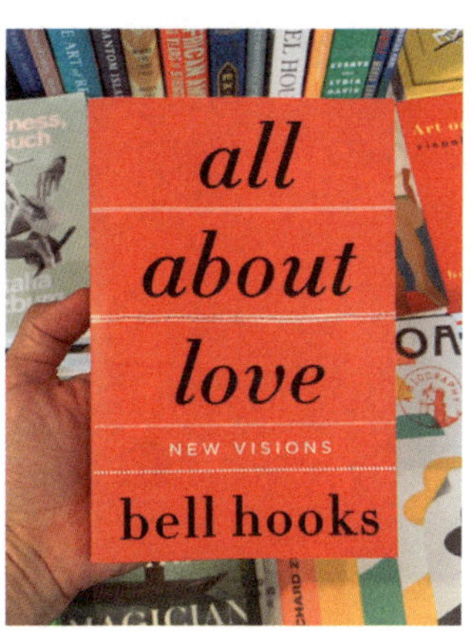
all
about
love
NEW VISIONS
bell hooks

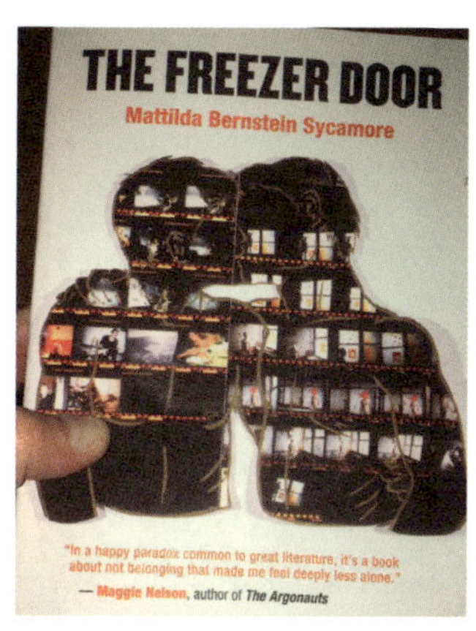
THE FREEZER DOOR
Mattilda Bernstein Sycamore
"In a happy paradox common to great literature, it's a book about not belonging that made me feel deeply less alone."
— Maggie Nelson, author of The Argonauts

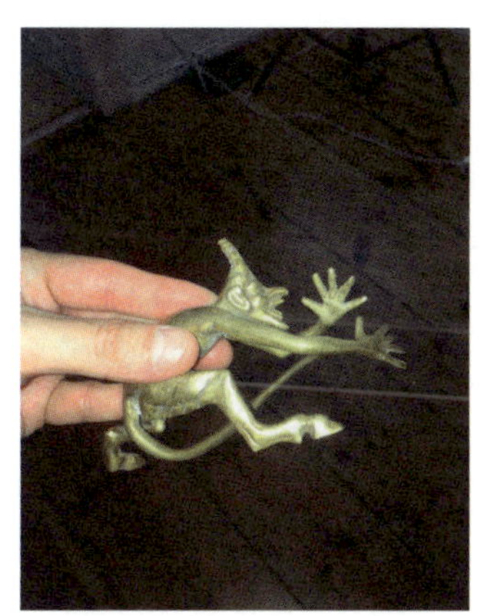

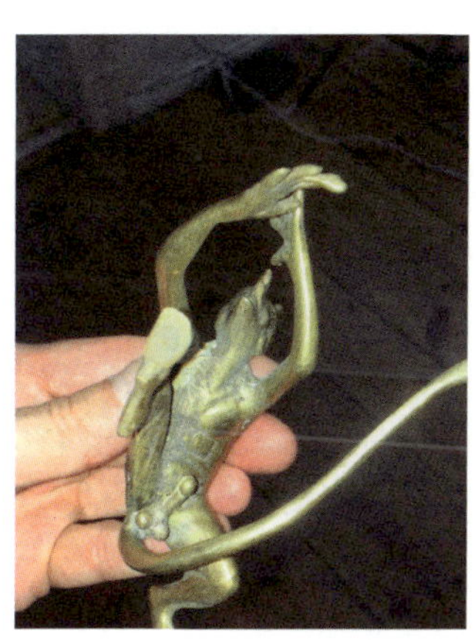

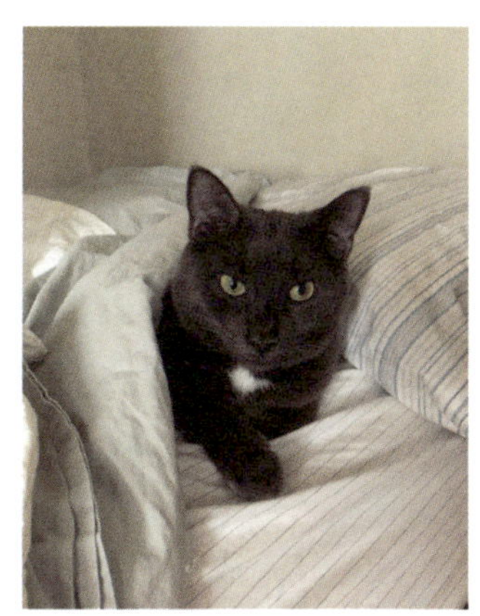

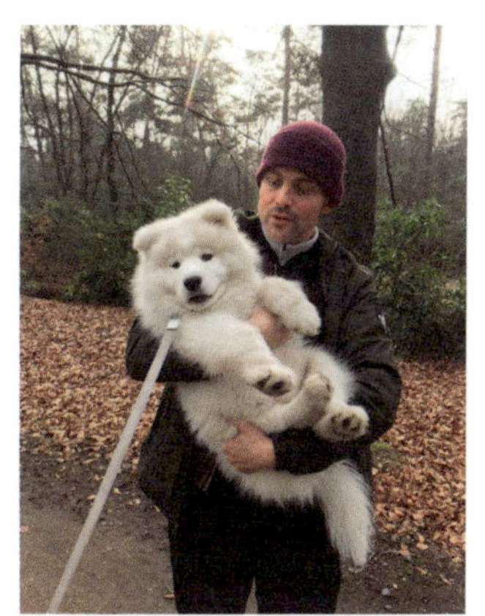

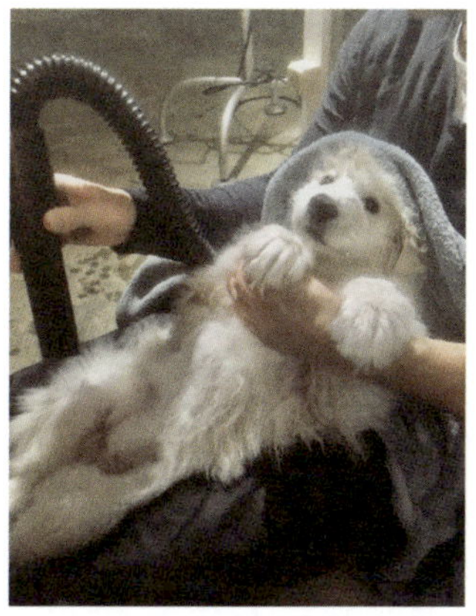

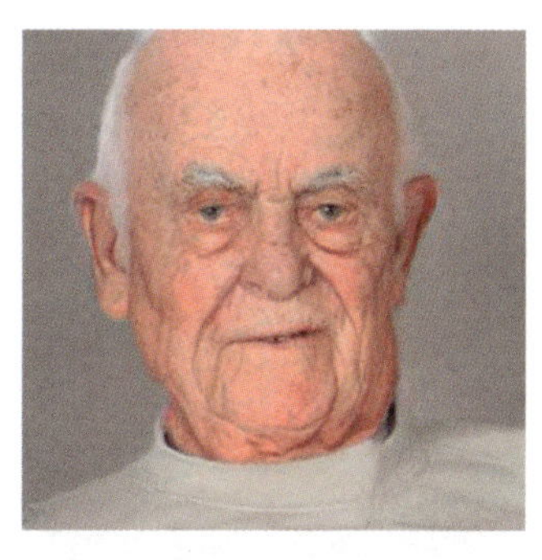

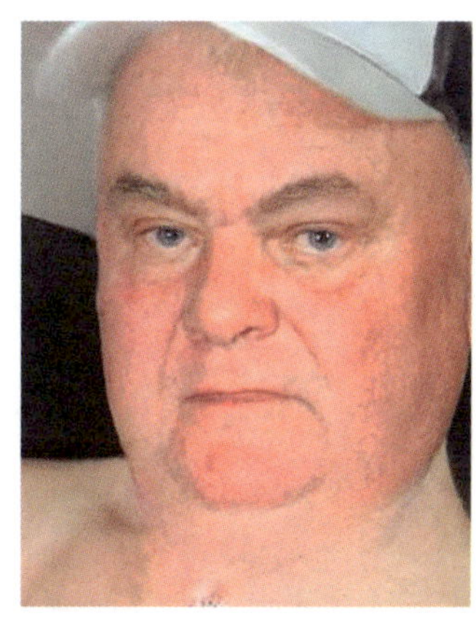

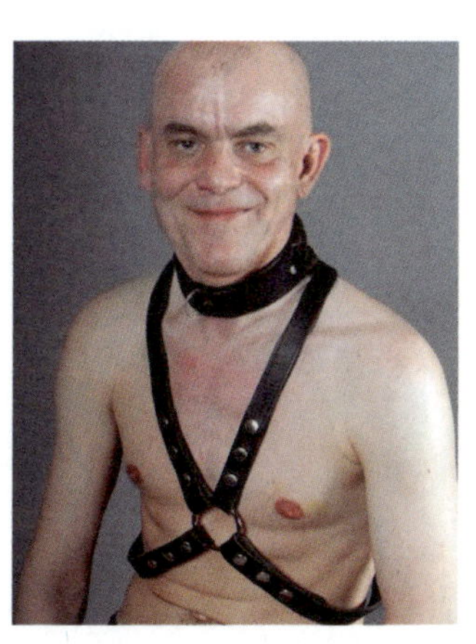

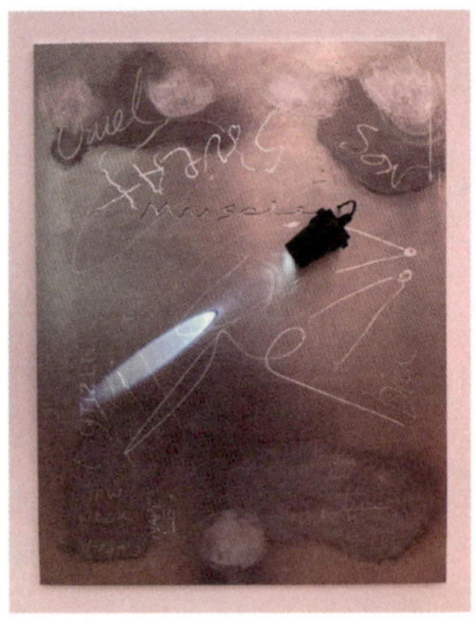
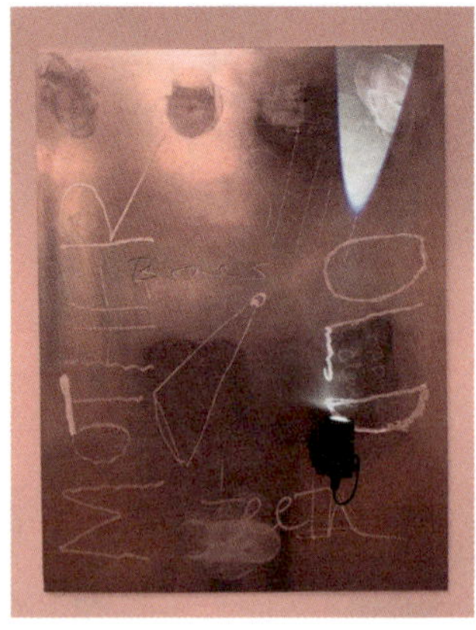
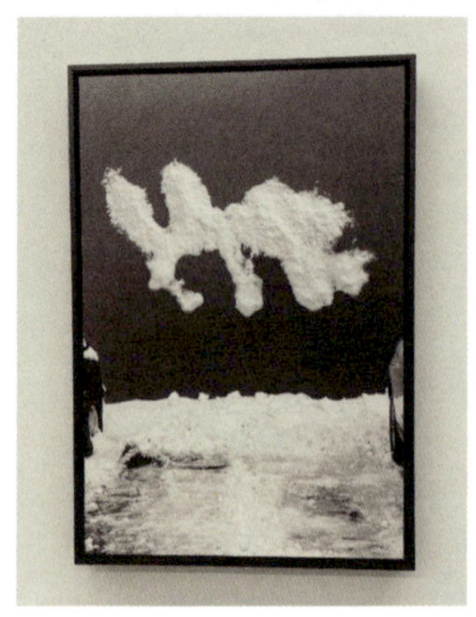
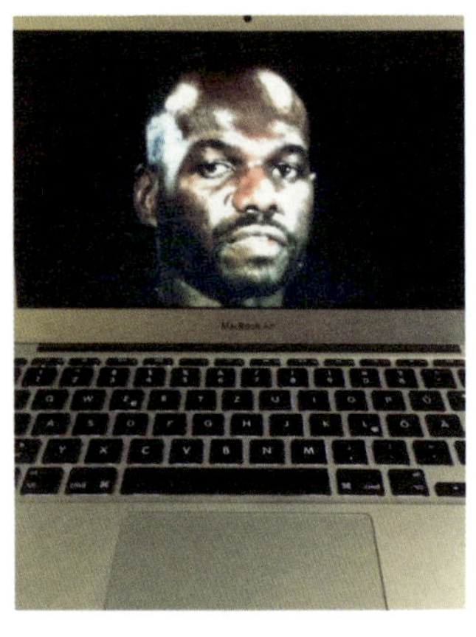
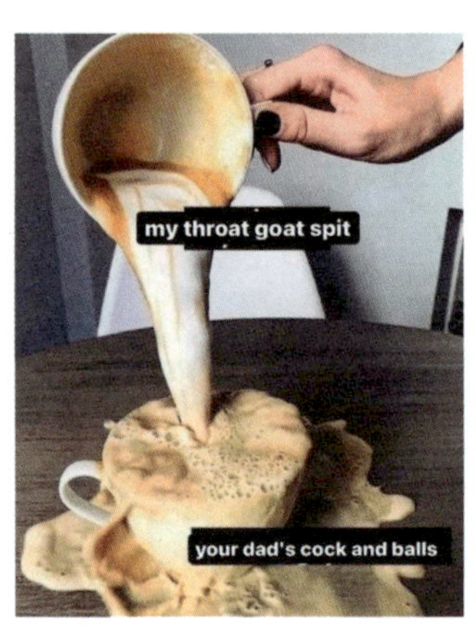
my throat goat spit
your dad's cock and balls
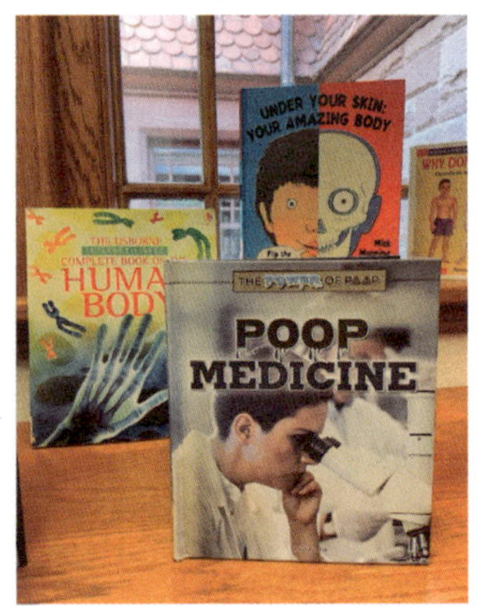
UNDER YOUR SKIN: YOUR AMAZING BODY
POOP MEDICINE
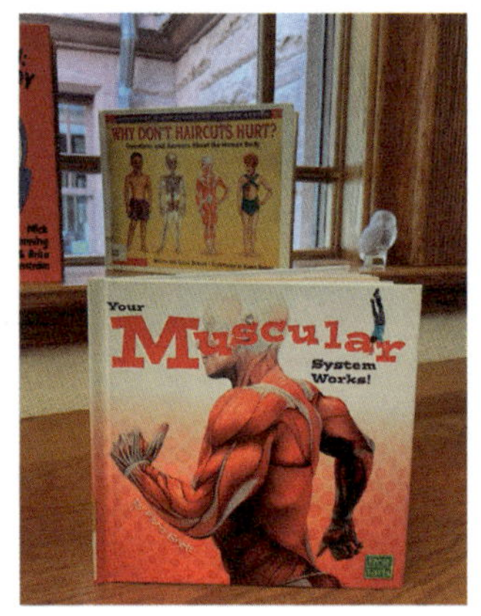
WHY DON'T HAIRCUTS HURT?
Your Muscular System Works!
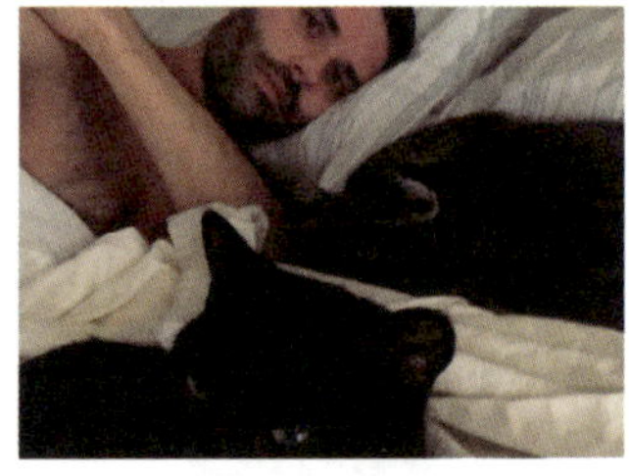
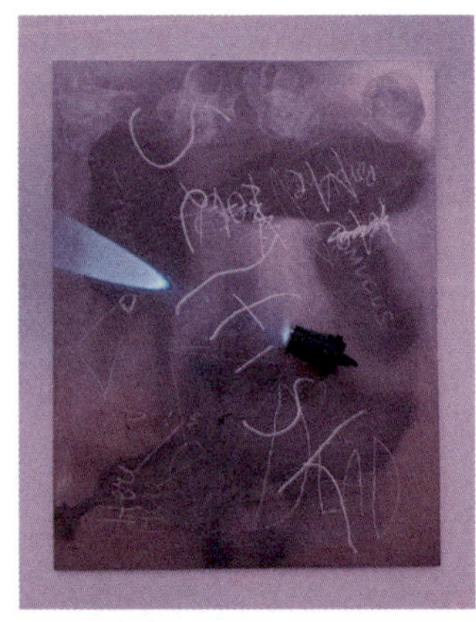
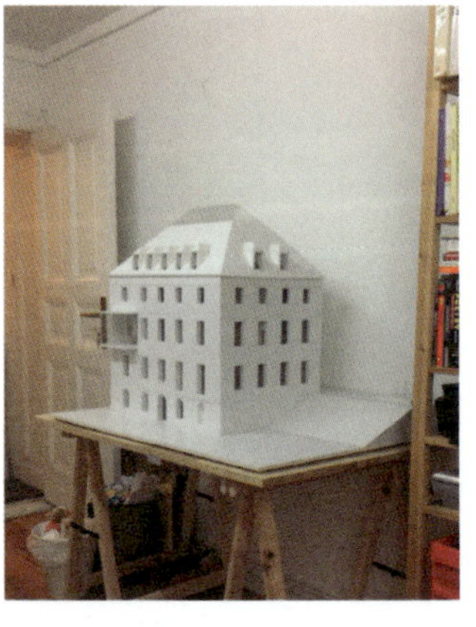
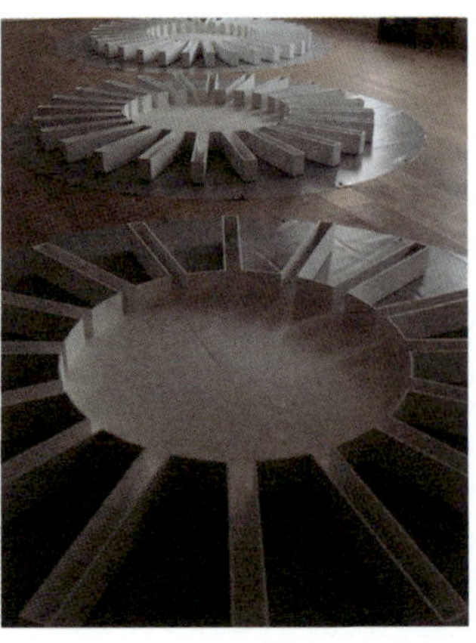

When Jim asked me to write about his new work, I thought about the fact that our relationship mainly takes place over the phone and on WhatsApp, from our homes in Berlin and New York. I decided to write this essay between the locations of home and work, during my twice weekly train commute to teach art students. I take the subway to Grand Central, a commuter train hub that brings passengers to the northern parts of NYC and into Connecticut, where I teach. The Metro-North New Haven Line brings me to my eventual destination; the line was absorbed into New York's Metropolitan Transportation Authority in 1983, the year Jim was born. Greenwich, Stamford, Stratford, and Milford are stops I pass on my way to New Haven, and all these towns have corresponding locations in the United Kingdom. I google the train travel time between Cardiff, where Jim grew up, and London, where he went to college, and am surprised to read that it is nearly identical to my journey from Grand Central to New Haven. These spatial and temporal parallels affirm my mobile writing structure. The trains that move me from home to work and back again provide focused space for me to think about Jim's previous videos and current research in relation to his developing commission.

I met Jim in the spring of 2009 at the opening of the New Museum's first triennial exhibition, unfortunately titled *Younger than Jesus*, where our work was featured. Jim presented a single-channel video, *Active Negative Programme* (2008), which played on a monitor flanked by two speakers and faced by two rows of black institutional chairs, all on a raised platform. The speakers were nearly as large as the monitor, establishing the centrality of audio within Jim's work. *Active Negative Programme* foregrounds the process of looking and listening, and begins with found footage of a teacher instructing a viewer how to draw eyes. Over a twenty-five-minute run time, it focuses on the visual and aural processing of information presented in formats that profess to teach, such as lighting tutorials and voice training. It centers on a simple psychophysiological process of eye and ear: the transmission of visual and aural information to the brain via the optic and auditory nerves. It is a basic process that ultimately undergirds the synaptic logic of Jim's assembly of found material alongside his own footage for optimum sensorial effect.

The work I included for the triennial grew out of an artist's book I made in 2008 called *AMERICAMERICA*, looking back at the end of Ronald Reagan's presidency just as George W. Bush's tenure was ending. Through archival material, interviews, and commissioned writing, the book maps how the AIDS crisis came into public view in 1986 in tandem with a burgeoning social conservatism activated by Reagan. After I shared this book with Jim,

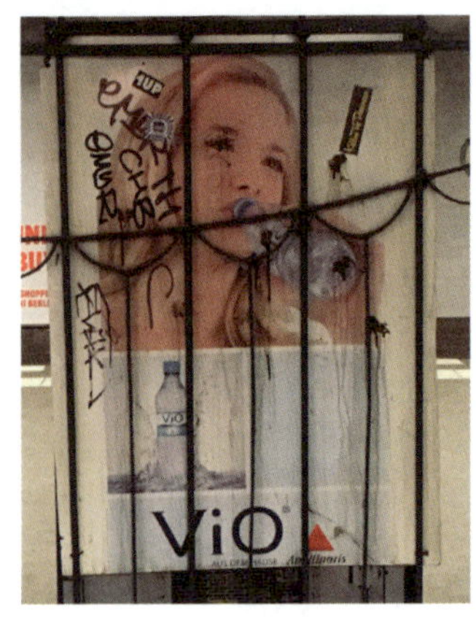
ViO

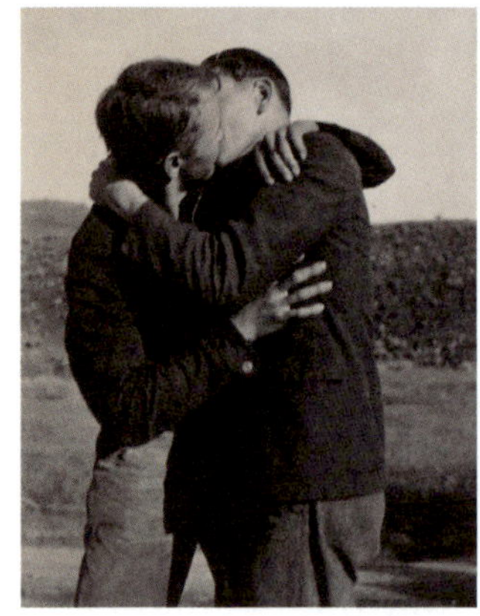

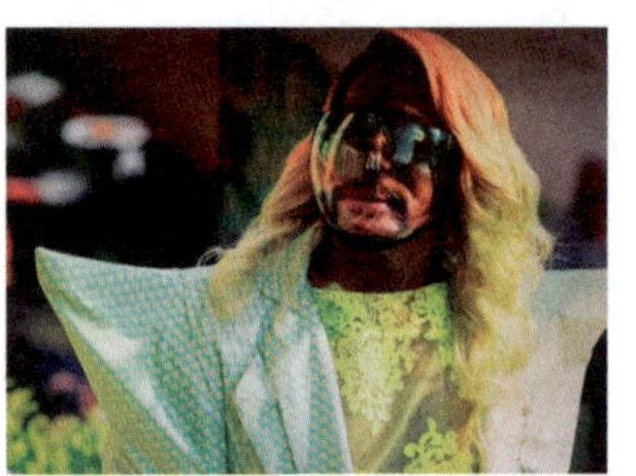

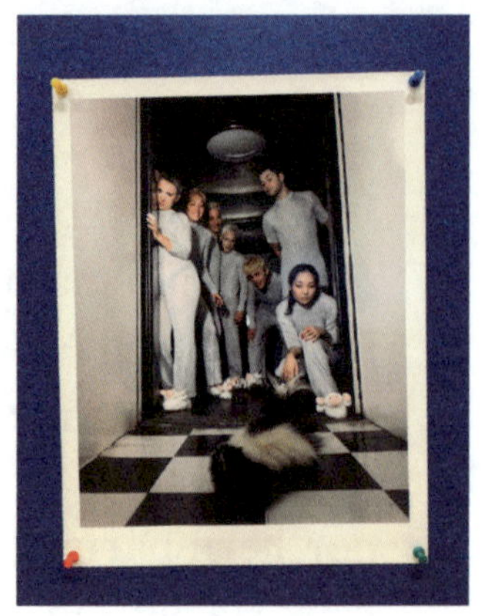

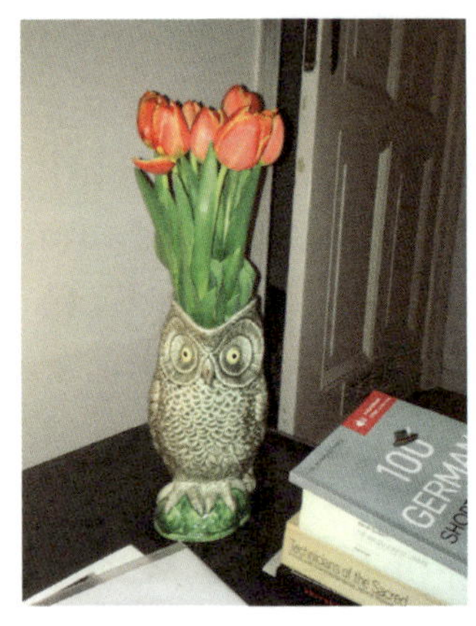

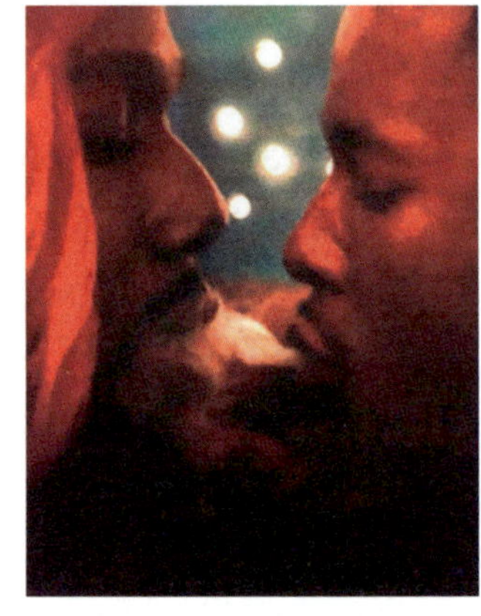

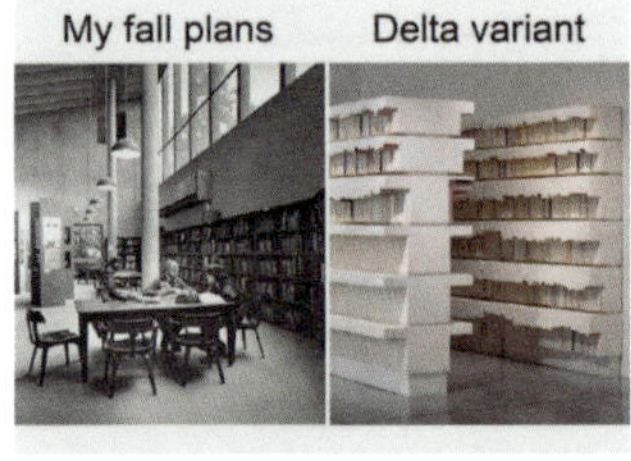
My fall plans
Delta variant

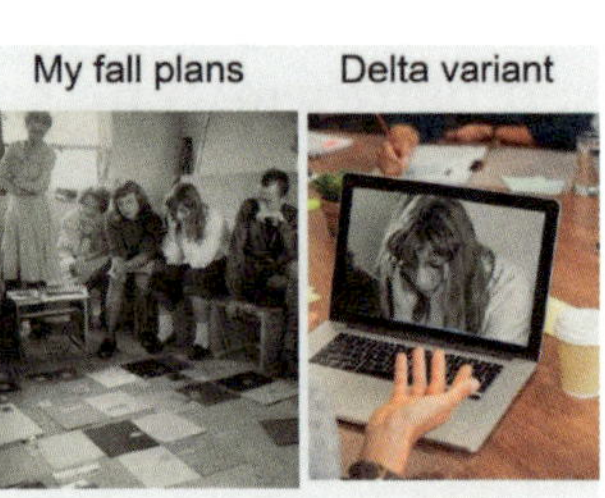
My fall plans
Delta variant

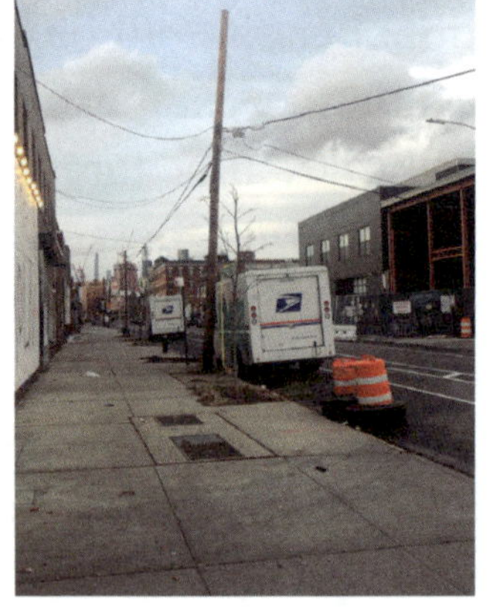

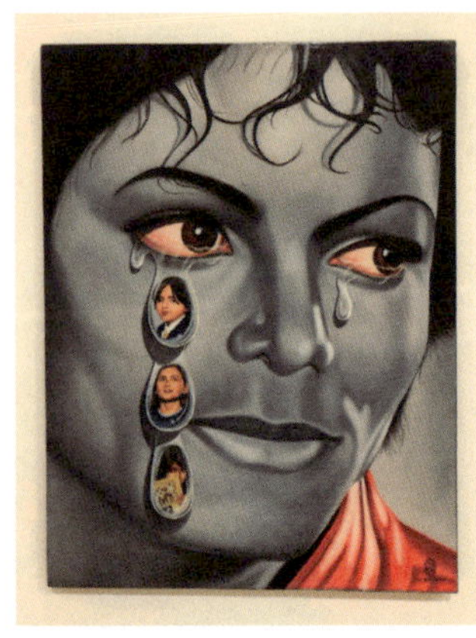

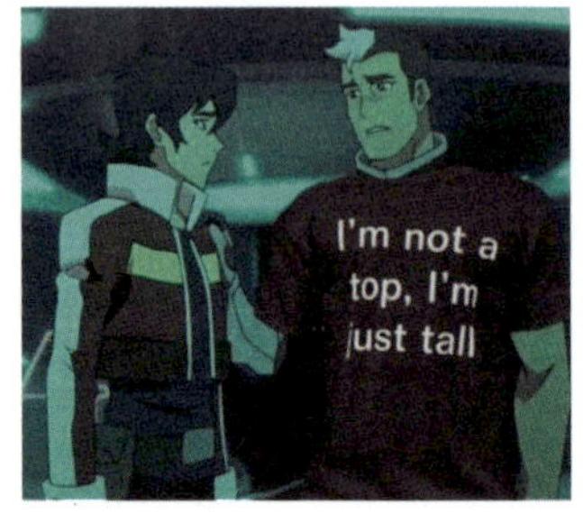
I'm not a
top, I'm
just tall

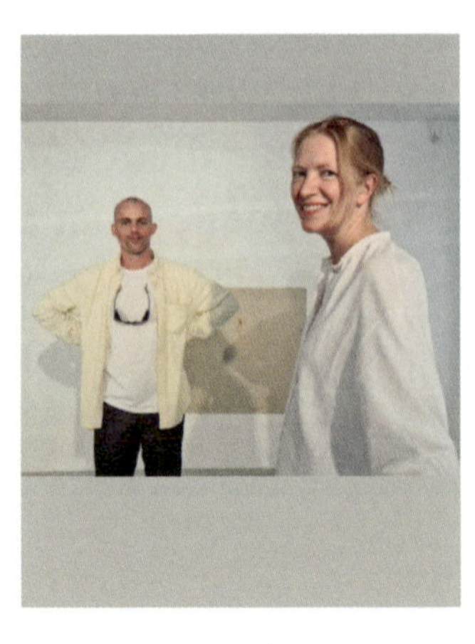

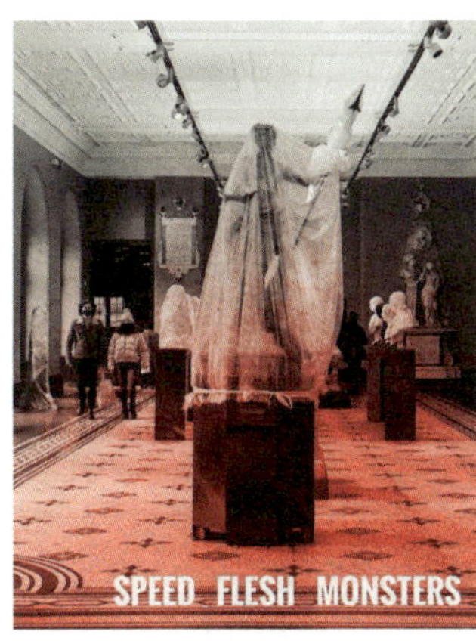
SPEED FLESH MONSTERS
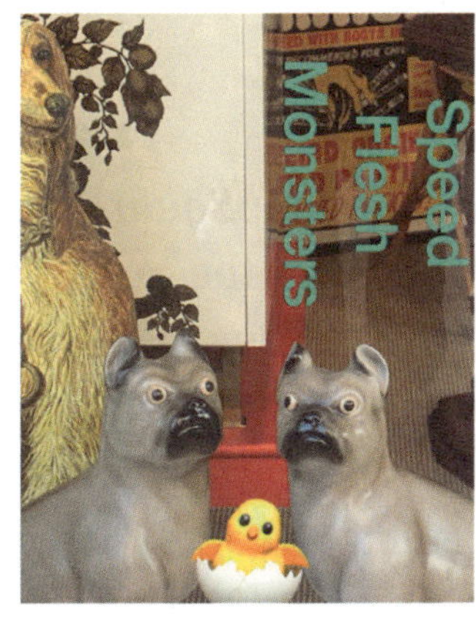
Speed
Flesh
Monsters
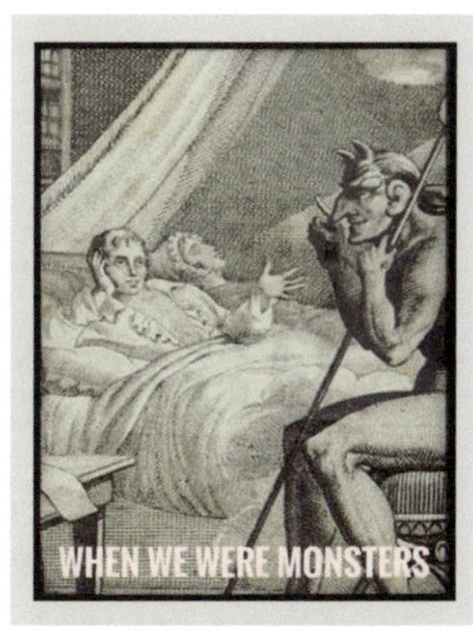
WHEN WE WERE MONSTERS
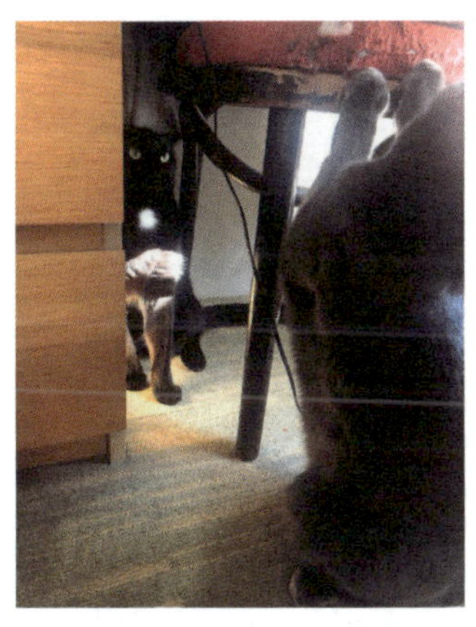
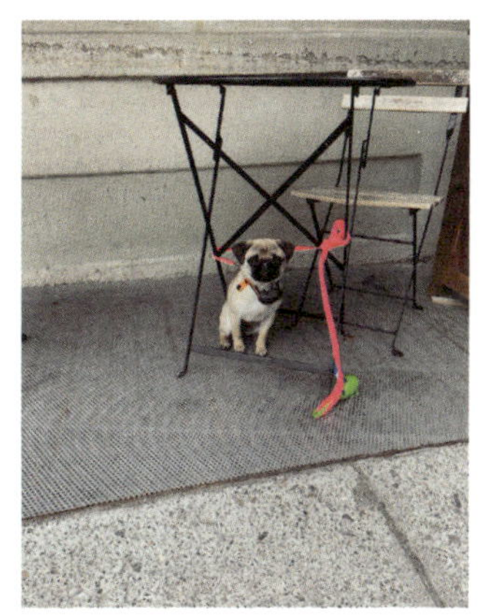
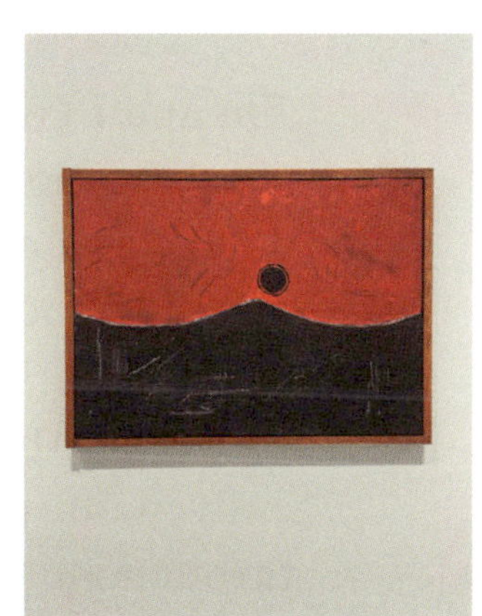
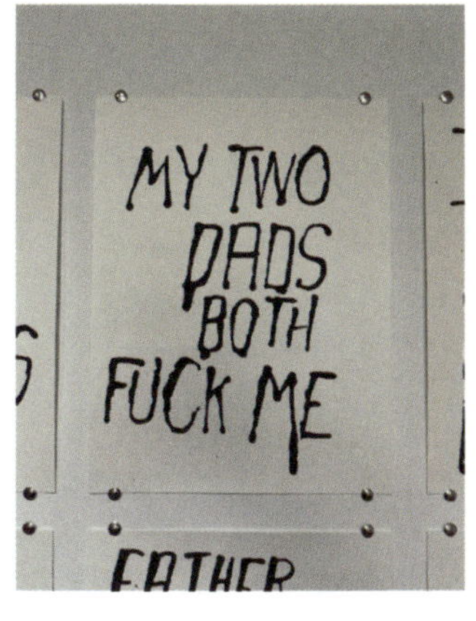
MY TWO
DADS
BOTH
FUCK ME
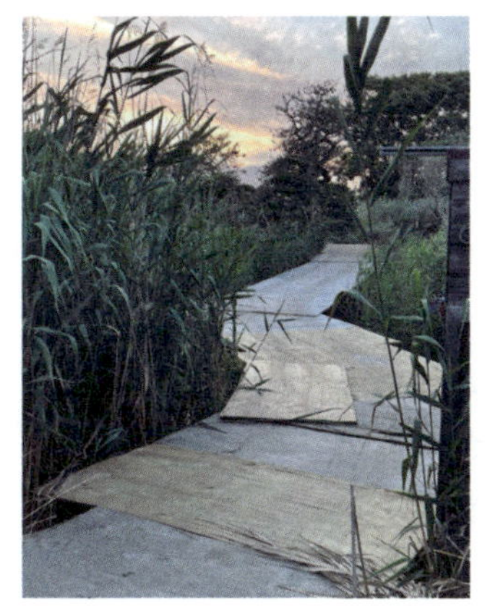
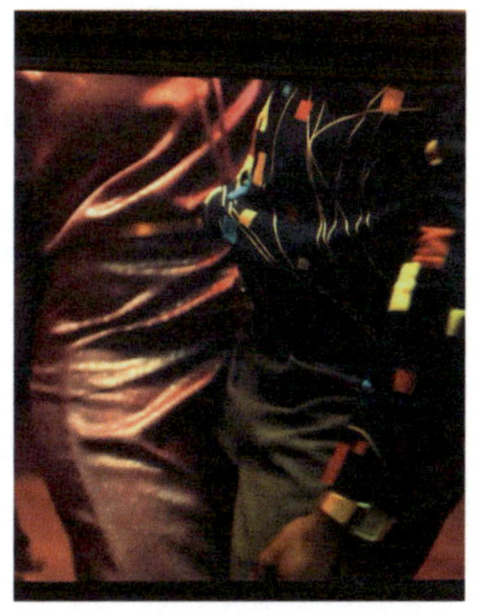
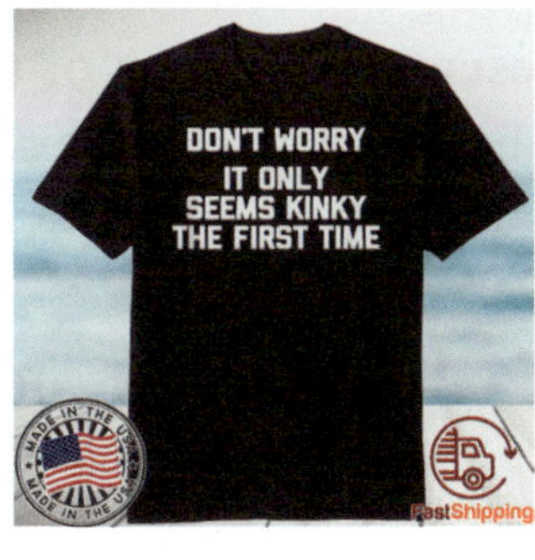
DON'T WORRY
IT ONLY
SEEMS KINKY
THE FIRST TIME
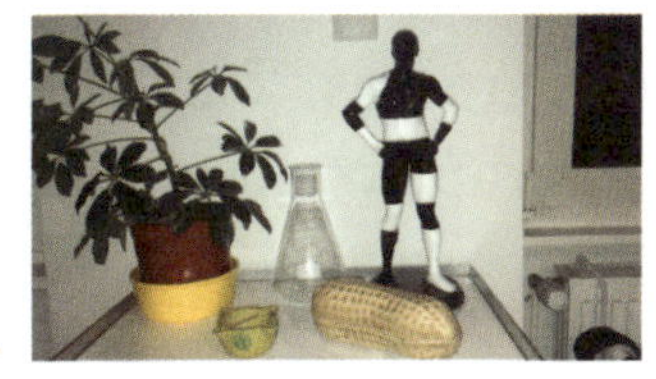

he recommended that I read Samuel Delany's *Time Square Red, Times Square Blue* (1999). In his preface, Delany establishes that the book's two essays "look at aspects of New York City affected by the Times Square Development Project [...] The city has instituted not only violent reconfiguration of its own landscape but also a legal and moral revamping of its own discursive structures, changing laws about sex, health, and zoning."[2] Through personal reflection ("Blue") and critical analysis ("Red") spanning the 1960s–90s, Delany creates a deeply felt and articulated book; he foregrounds the need for "interclass contact and communication" that amongst other reasons is often tethered to sex.[3]

Jim and I grew up in the wake of the early years of the AIDS crisis and the gentrification that followed in London and New York City, where we both lived during and after art school. AIDS completely rewired our understanding of our own bodies as permeable to a disease that could kill us through casual sex. Like in most queer relationships, talk of sex permeates our friendship as we WhatsApp about our crushes, love affairs, and the well-endowed men that enliven our pandemic days and nights. The imprint of AIDS can also be found throughout Jim's work, including this current commission. We see blue PrEP pills, empty pill casings, syringes, home testing equipment, and alcohol swabs all floating in water. The cameras that move through throat-and anus-like plumbing canals underscore the body's vulnerability. The initial minute of *When We Were Monsters*, Jim's 2020 video realized with his long-term collaborator Steve Reinke, alarmingly addresses this vulnerability: a gruesome strobing montage of bodies, inside and out, visually marked with a wide variety of physical afflictions, dramatically accentuating the body's ability to become infected and its need for constant care.

As Jim's work began to develop, he shared with me a cache of research, including images made by Horst Ademeit, a German artist born in 1937 who created an elaborate system of photography and notation to document his daily life. Ademeit died in 2010, just months after the inaugural US presentation of his work at White Columns, where I first encountered his confounding Polaroids; the images were adorned with meticulous writing akin to the writer Robert Walser's microscripts, filling out the white frames. The work presented was part of a vast archive of thousands of photographs and notes that began in the 1980s and continued to nearly the end of the artist's life.

2 Samuel R. Delany, *Times Square Red, Times Square Blue* (New York: New York University Press, 1999).
3 Ibid.

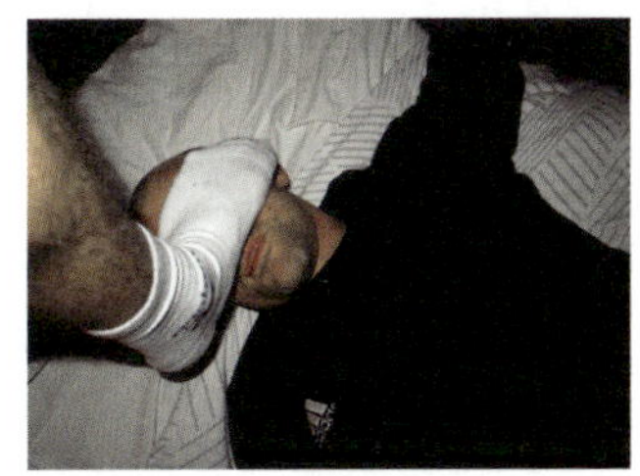

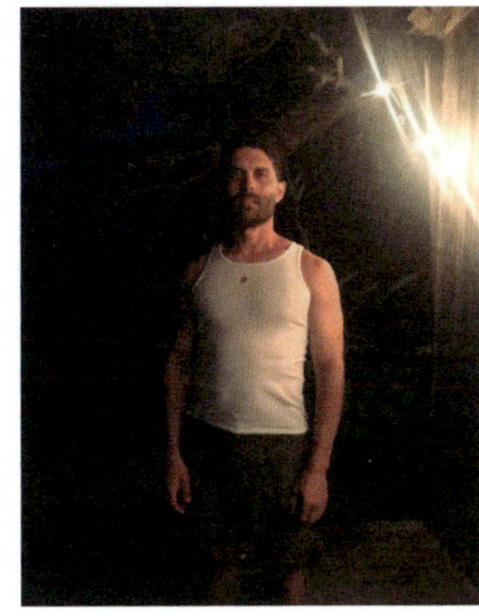

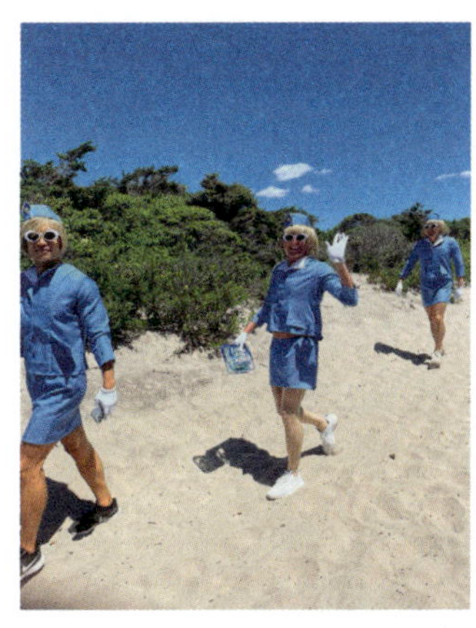

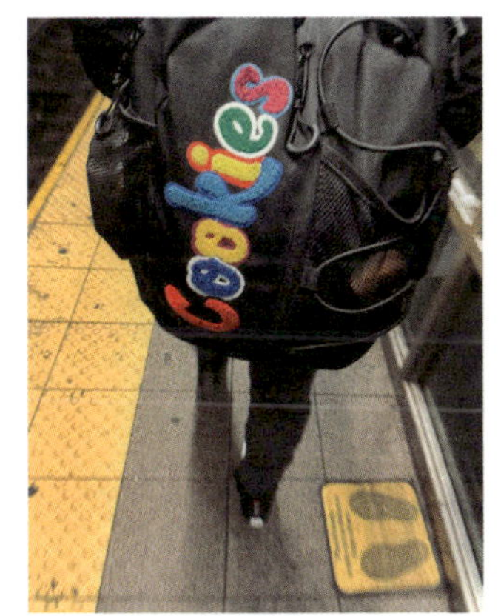
Cookies

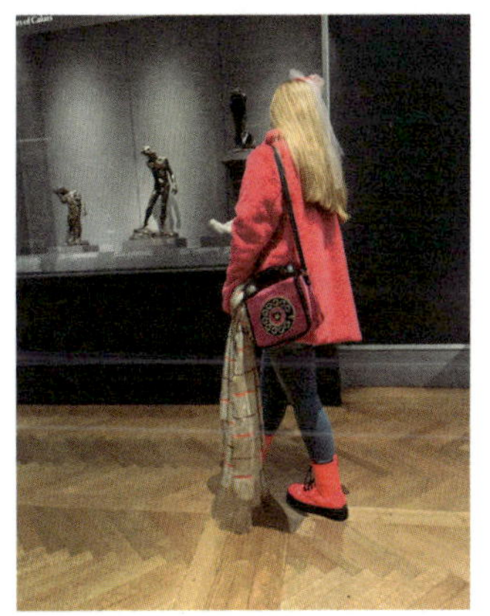

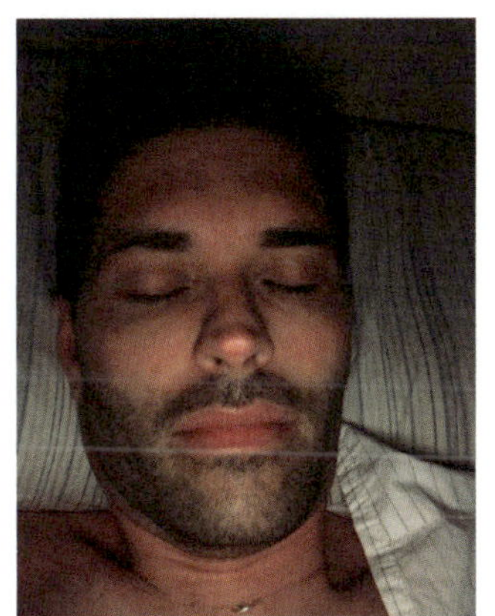

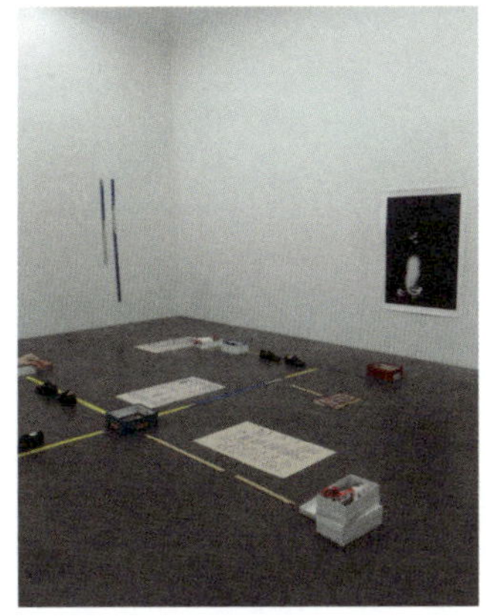

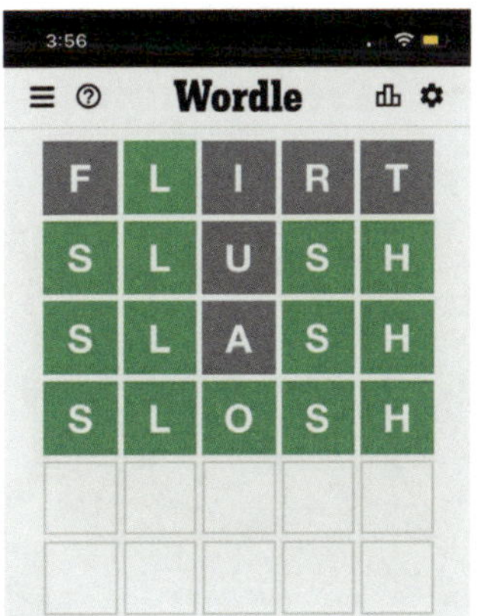
3:56
Wordle
F L I R T
S L U S H
S L A S H
S L O S H

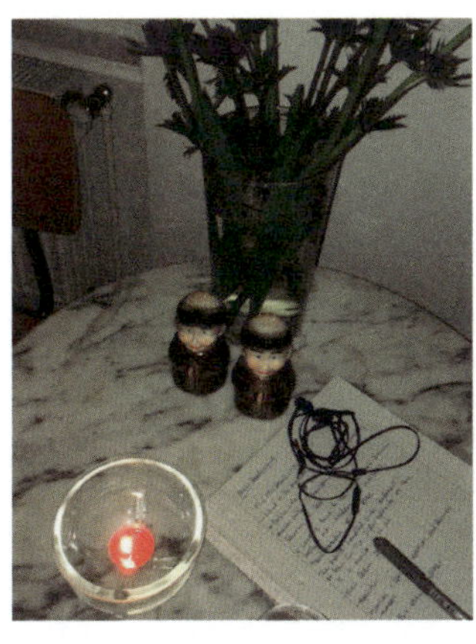

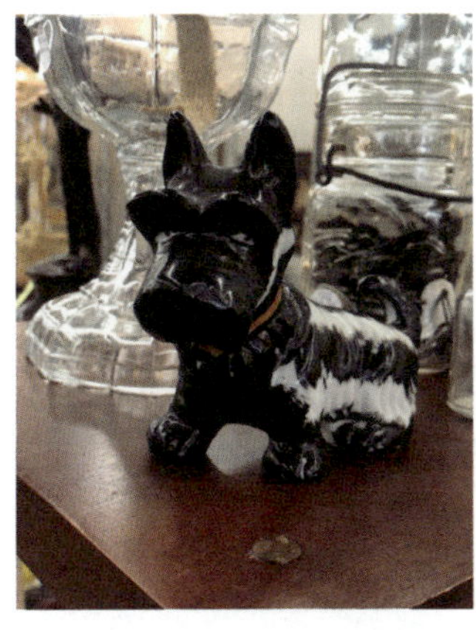

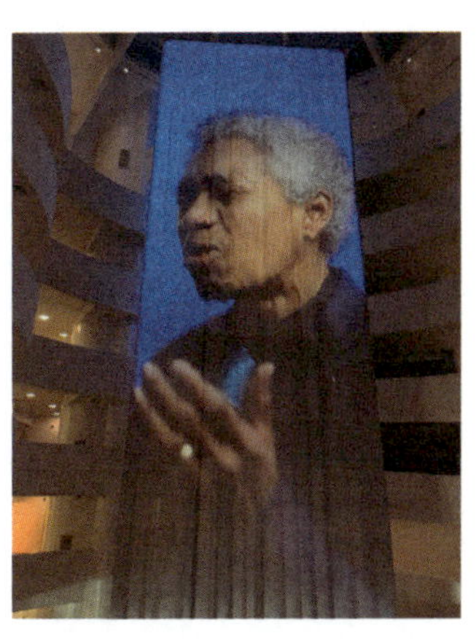

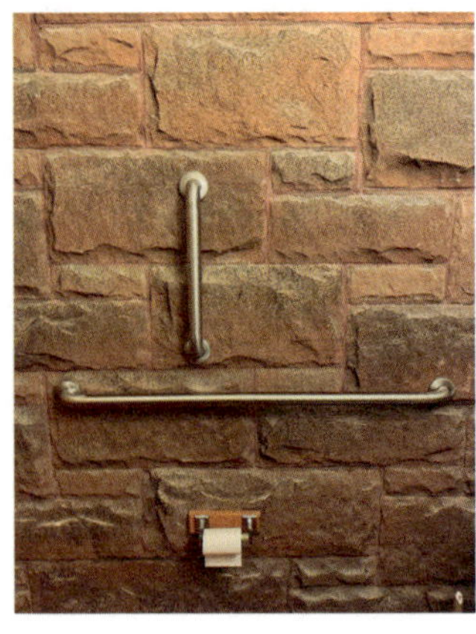

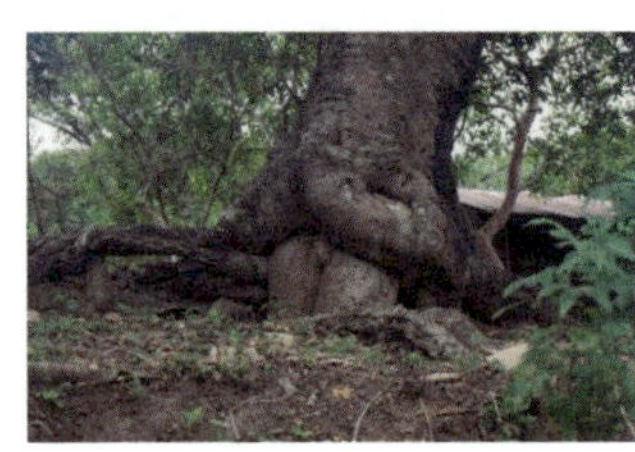

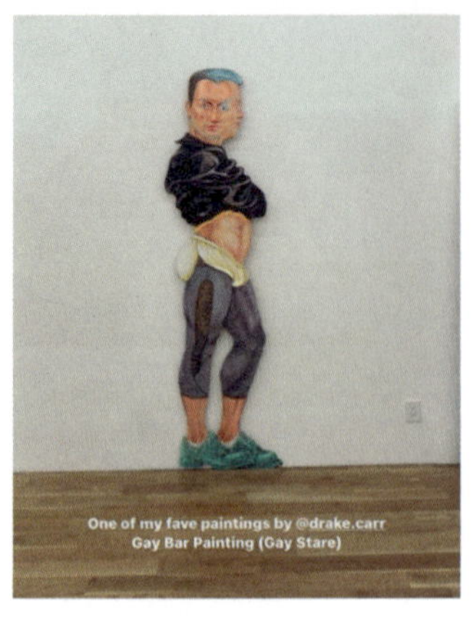
One of my fave paintings by @drake.carr
Gay Bar Painting (Gay Stare)

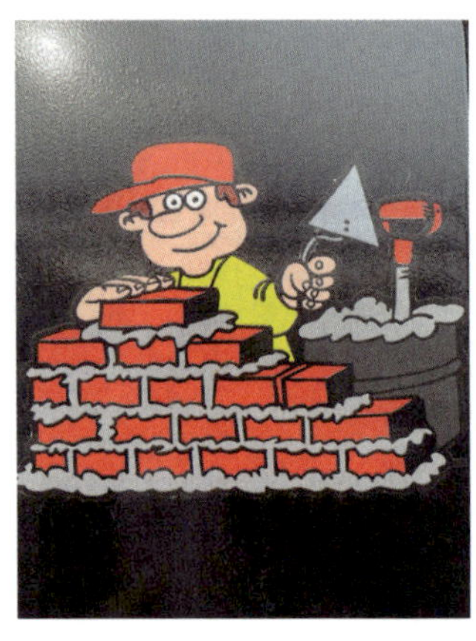

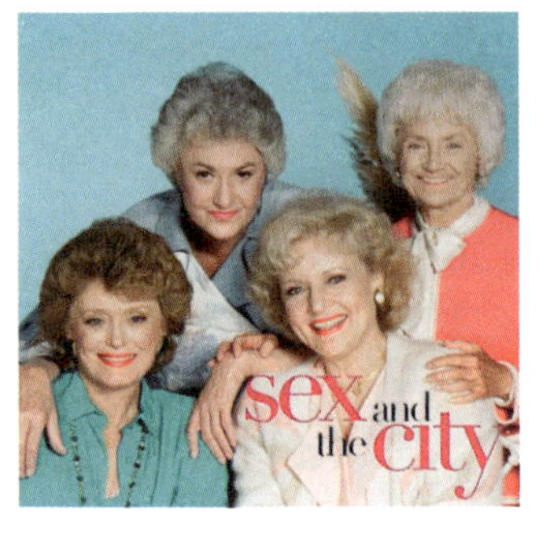
sex and the city

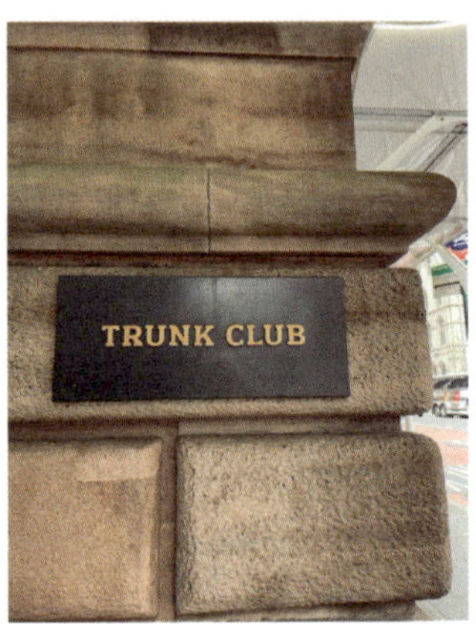
TRUNK CLUB

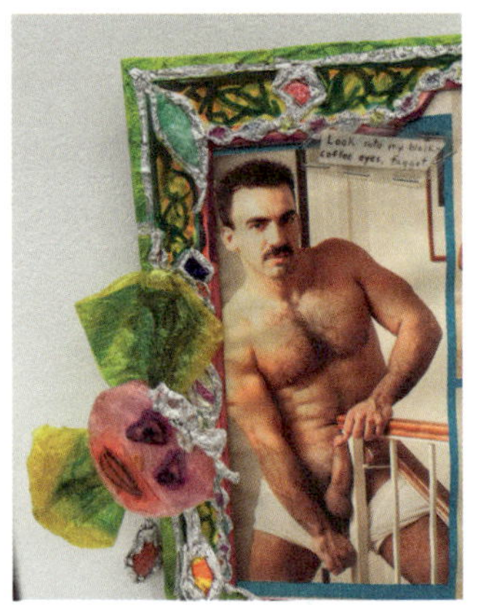

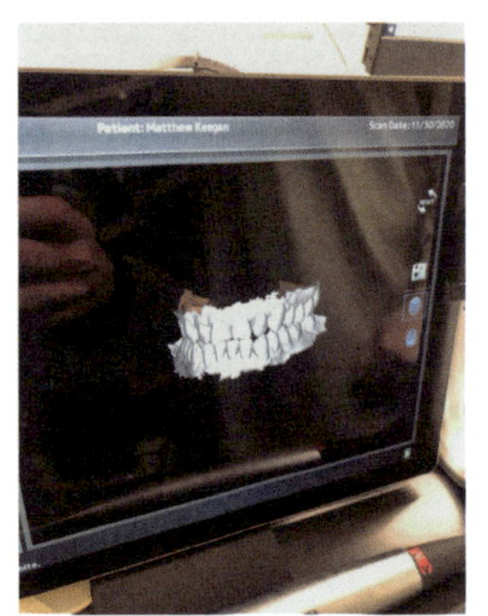
Patient: Matthew Keegan

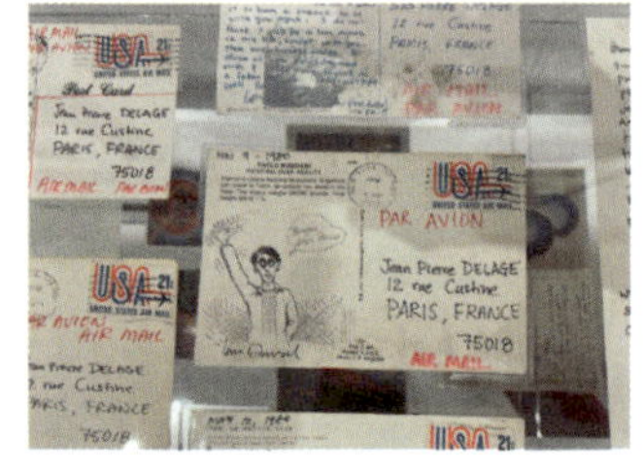
PAR AVION
Jean Pierre DELAGE
12 rue Custine
PARIS, FRANCE
75018

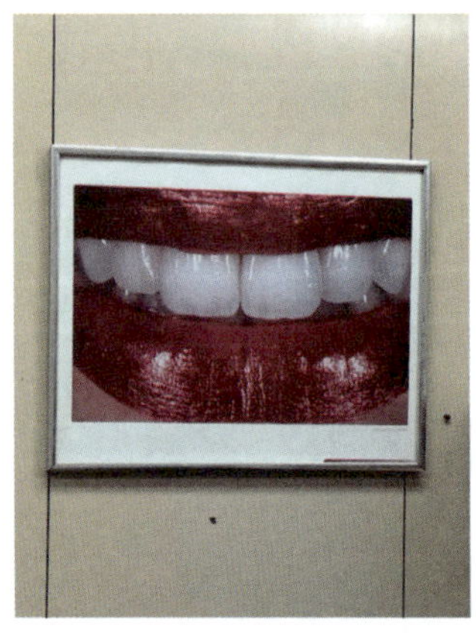

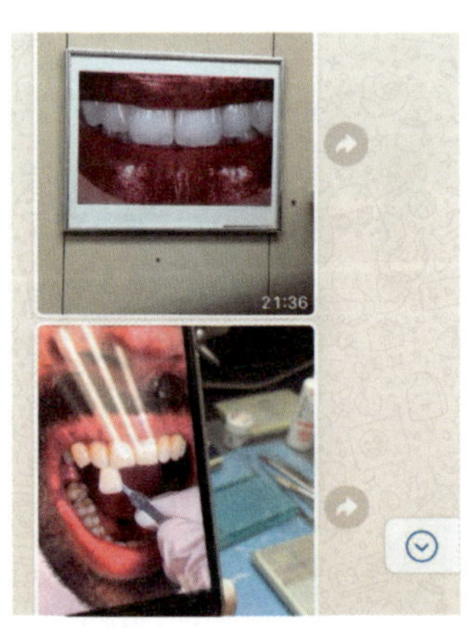
21:36

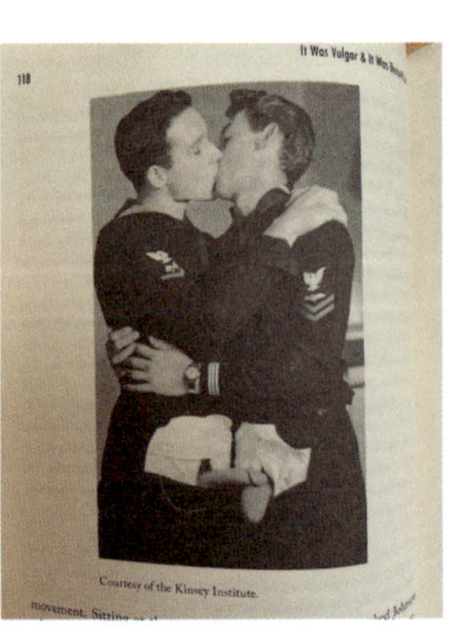
Courtesy of the Kinsey Institute.

The photos and elaborate system of note-taking documented what Ademeit categorized as "cold rays": environmental phenomena that had a direct impact on his day-to-day life. The documentation spanned from the chronicling of his body to the cataloging of his apartment, his broader neighborhood, and daily newspapers. The exhibition press release states that Ademeit's system of notation was "typically augmented with gauges, thermometers, compasses, clocks, and other measuring devices. In tandem he made notes that recorded distances and other quotidian phenomena, as well as recording things beyond visual perception: smells, sounds, atmospheres, moods, etc."[4] Such recording of things beyond visual perception for esoteric and even neurotic ends is translated into the insistent nature of Jim's own methodology, specifically how his photographs and stills generate their own parallel architecture. In postproduction, these initially static images get distorted, expanded, and repeated to complicate what they originally documented, transforming them into imaginative and often hallucinogenic spaces.

Having recently read about Ademeit's work and the daily mapping of his life over decades, I am struck by encountering Ralphie on the subway to Grand Central. He is someone who has marked my twenty-three years in New York, as I have ridden the L train with him since the summer of 1998. I have mainly lived in Brooklyn during this time and witnessed a wide variety of people on the subway who are performing, selling or giving away food, seeking work, or usually just in need of money. There are people that I have encountered with more frequency, but Ralphie is the only person that I have seen regularly for over two decades. He used to introduce himself by saying: "My name's Rafael but my friends call me Ralphie." He had a tick that has faded: in between talking, he would make a sort of *tsst tsst* sound. He now introduces himself only as Ralphie. He was selling books and I could not make out their titles. He used to sell a newspaper called *Good News* that sounded Christian, so I avoided it. Ralphie emphasized that he is not feeling so good and mentioned that he was in the Navy when he was younger. A detail I did not recall from before. Ralphie did not look good. Skinny. Torn clothes. I had not seen him in a while and used to see him nearly every week. I remember he would refer to people who did not give him money or buy his papers as PCPs and always wondered what this abbreviation stood for. After this past year of COVID-19 precautions, the public space of the subway, in which people live in front of one another with unusual physical proximity, is brought into further focus by Ralphie, fragile and aged over an incalculable number of subway rides.

4 White Columns, "White Room: Horst Ademeit," March 5, 2017, available online.

My Metro-North train commute from Grand Central to New Haven is two hours. Feature film length. Most people prefer to ride the train facing the direction traveled. I prefer the backward re-view, reflecting on what has passed. I am reflected in the large glass window that frames my view, more visible in low light, wearing glasses and a disposable medical mask. I also see the person sitting across from me. Lots of men heading to finance jobs in Greenwich and Stamford, either wearing athleisure or button-downs and pants with sneakers. Autumn's arriving so sweaters and zip-up fleeces are prevalent. Ads inside the train promote the benefits of Norwegian Wool. The pace of the train allows me to ascertain class structures of passed-by neighborhoods. Bigger backyards, a dog hotel and spa, covered boats, car dealerships, multifamily homes on top of one another, generic apartment buildings, offices, various businesses (Wayne's Auto Body), mini-malls, graffiti, a Fuck Biden flag, shuttered factories, so many cars and trucks. People in their cars. Adjacent roads, highways, and street signs. Very few pedestrians. A dad pushing a stroller. Kids playing basketball. Parking lots with graphic grids. Train stations. Water. The stutter of trees. Neighborhoods that I will never experience and their residents whom I will never meet.

Within the research file shared by Jim, I read "Box" and "Phrasing" written by Rae Armantrout, an American poet associated with the language poets, who emerged in the 1970s. I was not aware of Armantrout nor her affiliated group with its deadpan name. I learn that their name comes from the magazine *L=A=N=G=U=A=G=E*. My friend Shiv Kotecha, a writer and poetry teacher, coincidently wrote his undergrad thesis on "lang po" and texts me that these poets are the first-generation readers of then-recent English translations of continental philosophy and are heavily influenced by semiotics and poststructuralism. Jim adds that Armantrout's poetry engages more with traditional lyricism and tends to be more personal than analytical. Shiv further notes that language poets think of the reader as co-creator, a position echoed by Jim in his work. When I watch Jim's videos, I am acutely aware of his prioritization of the viewer and the generosity of his work: he requires the audience to fill in the gaps. In a recent lecture, Jim spoke about how, in his videos, we often enter a scene just before or right after the action, forcing a viewer to parse out what may be happening. A definitive reading that the full audience can agree upon is not the goal.

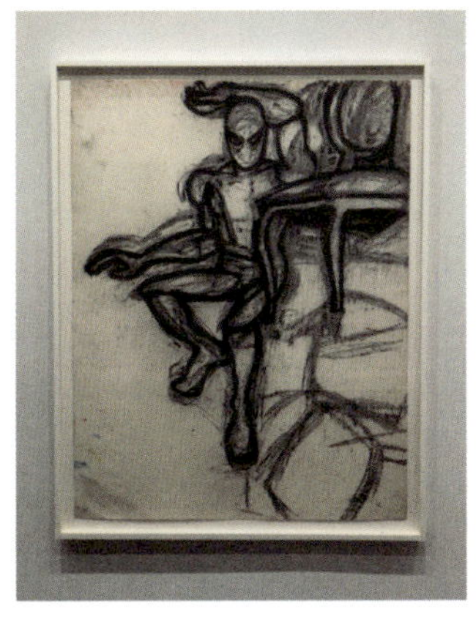

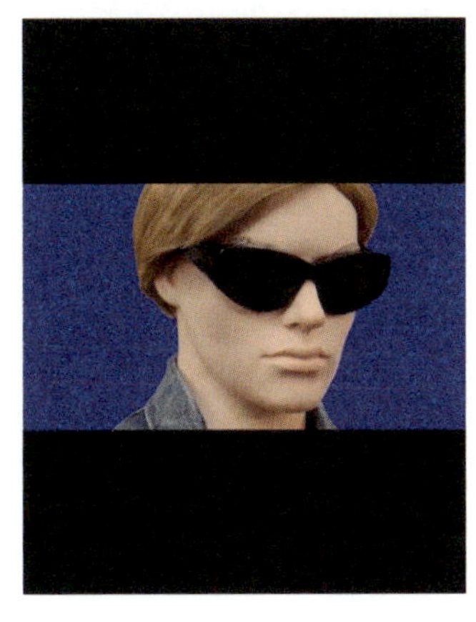

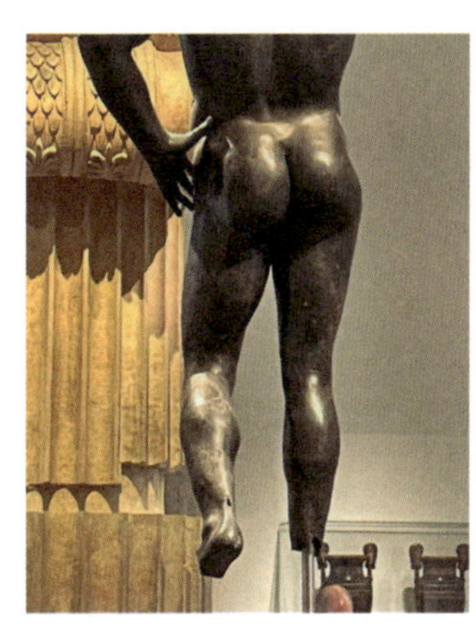

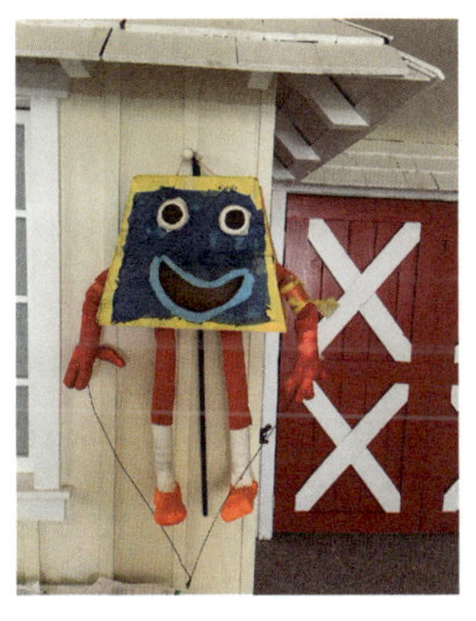

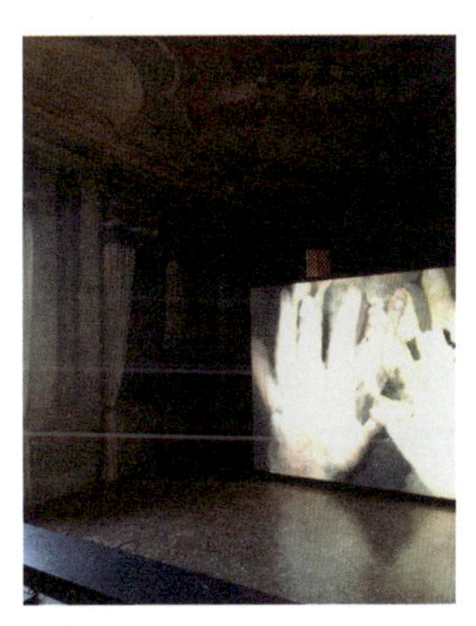

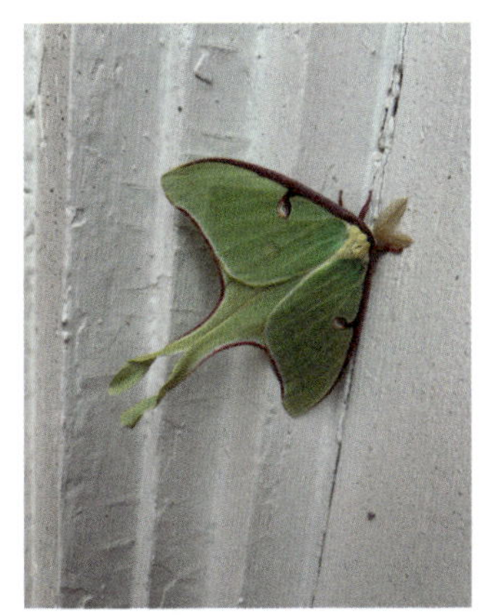

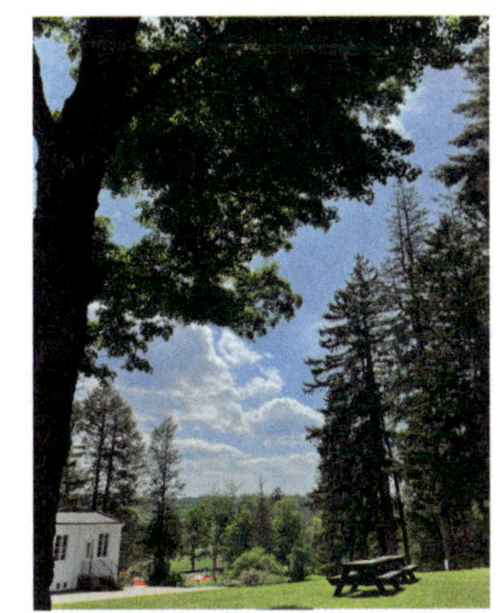

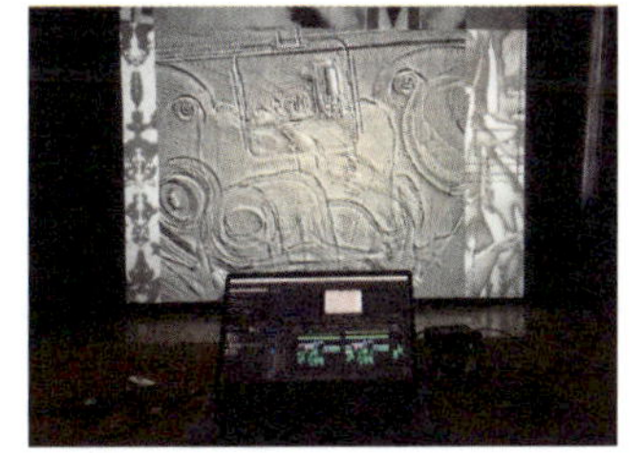

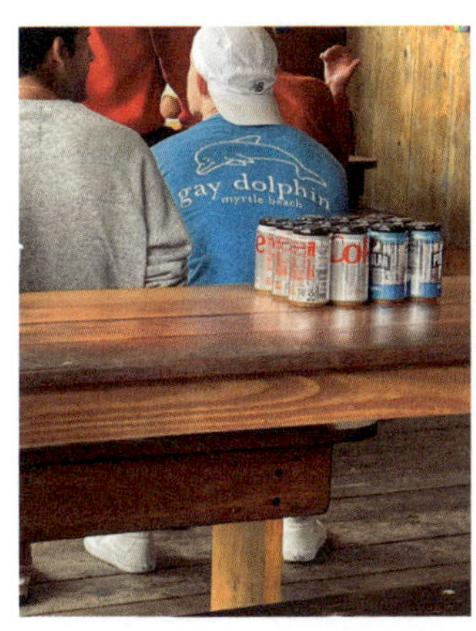
gay dolphin

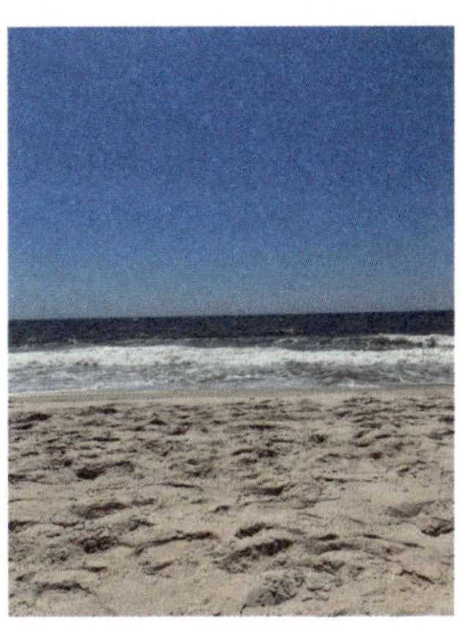

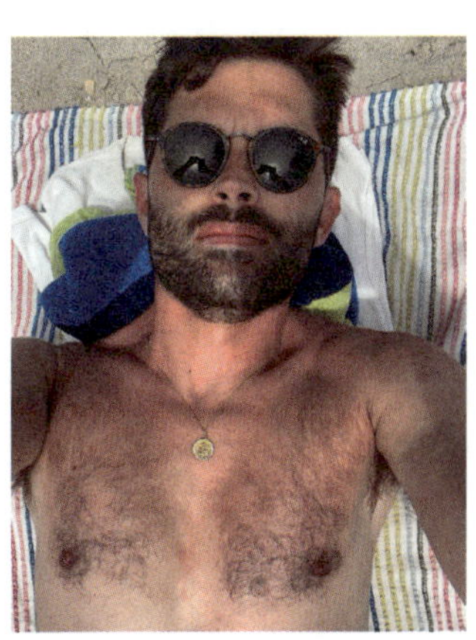

Armantrout's "Phrasing" closes with this text:

> I'm in between
> two states
> and can't be interrupted,
> between two points
> and can't be found,
> waylaid

Included within Jim's shared drive were his tracking shot experiments with Tolia Astakhishvili that confuse and conflate an industrial location with interspersed two-dimensional planes. The camera steadily scans from a fixed central point of rotation: industrial space butts up against collaged walls that hold reproductions of drawings and photos. Overlaid music sounds as if someone is strumming the interior mechanisms of a piano, becoming more emphatic, like the escalating score in a thriller when the villain's approaching. A female vocalist singing octaves briefly disrupts the crescendo and we encounter Jim as a still image, looking down at the camera with an intense unblinking stare. Although the eyes and ears are parallel receptors, they are often separately catered to in Jim's work, with scores that are developed in tandem with the visual elements but not beholden to them. The images often bend and morph in response to the audio track as if having an emotional or psychological response to its sound.

Jim's videos have mapped the technologies of his lifetime, from the appropriated VHS footage in *Active Negative Programme* to cutting-edge cameras, scanners, and imaging software in his ongoing collaboration with Leslie Thornton. But even as he incorporates new technologies, the old remains equally weighted; everything is up for grabs in terms of assembly. This nonhierarchical organizing principle is woven into Jim's broader archival instinct to voraciously collect found footage and audio and store this material alongside what he shoots in his day-to-day life. This way of working is linked to Jim's time at a London-based film and video archive and distributor, LUX, where he was employed during college. This experience certainly influenced the way Jim works and introduced him to many artists and filmmakers, including Steve Reinke. Walking through the archive, a young and keen Jim came to see the expanse of material as not simply a preservation of the past but as rich material for a moving-image artist. This eventually led to the construction of his own archive of hundreds of hours of footage, all reconfigurable in endless subsequent edits. In a recent essay on Jim's work, the art historian Joseph Henry writes, "Instead of mastering the image, controlling its semantic meaning, exposing its ideological constructs, or even emptying its affective determinacy, Richards submits to its potential, in turn generating new 'coalitions,' as it were between subject and image and image and image. Richards's is in this sense a queer montage, expanding its modernist dialectics beyond a dichotomy into a less geometric, more pulsating field."[5]

To begin making this present work, Jim delved into his reserve of preexisting footage. This process of remaking is a constant within his practice and underscores the way his work generates a reflexive archive; he builds a vocabulary in which meaning changes based on how clips are paired together as well as via the adverb-like impact of an audio track or a visually augmenting postproduction overlay. This iterative way of working is akin to the physical process of mastication in preparation for digestion. Mastication, or chewing, is an automatic process that, like breathing, has a pace that can be sped up, slowed down, or stopped. This process resembles the embodied editing and pacing of Jim's recycled material. He chews his material as if saying a word over and over and over again until it becomes dislodged from meaning and new with possibility. This metabolic reprocessing and redigesting is not a minimalist exercise of distillation. Instead it yields a baroque visual and aural amalgam revealing how the body sees and hears, learns, changes, feels, and fails.

Images exchanged online by James Richards and Matt Keegan.

5 Joseph Henry, "The Camera Feeds," in *When We Were Monsters*, ed. James Richards and Johanna Markert, (Dortmund: Verlag Kettler, 2022), 181–91.

HE XIANGYU

HOUSE OF NATIONS

2021, 2K video, color, 5.1 sound, 28'58"

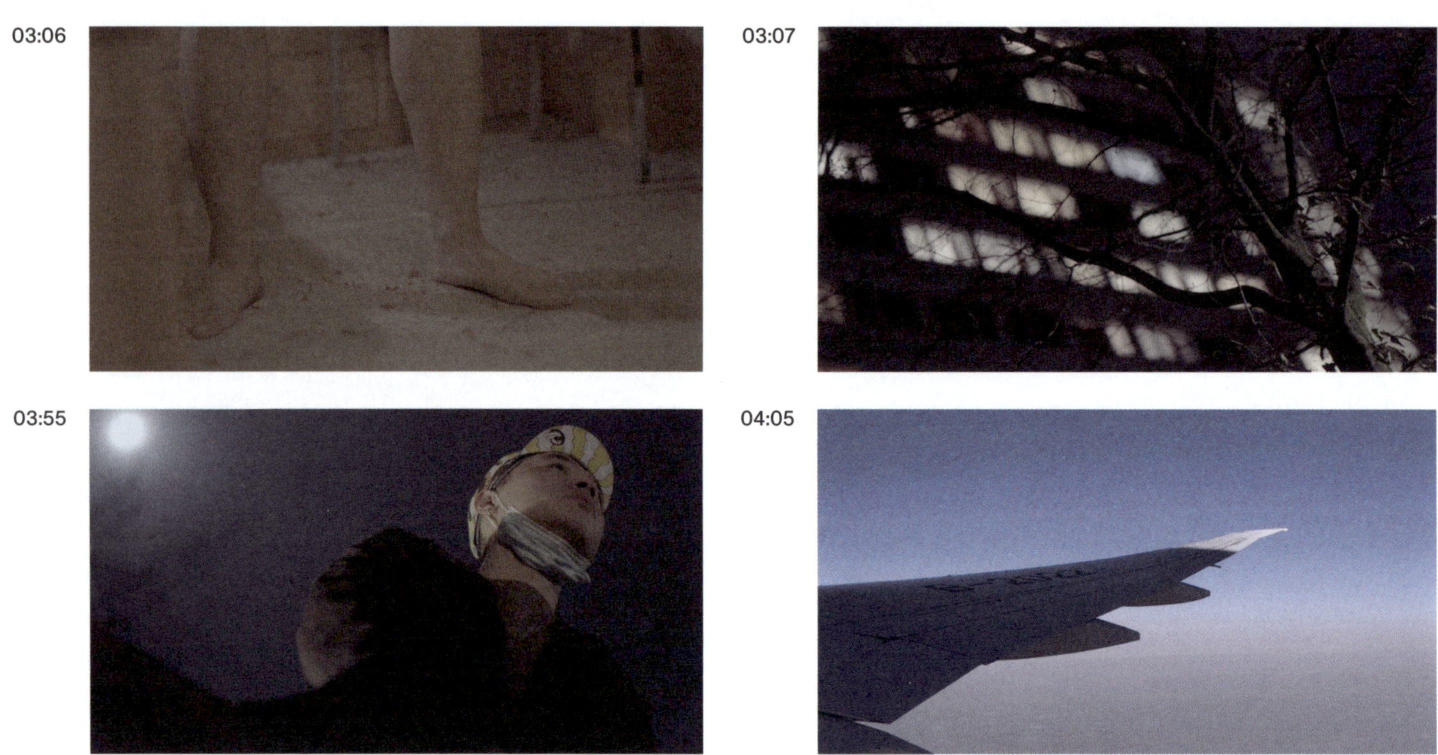
03:06 03:07 03:55 04:05

Set during the COVID-19 pandemic, *House of Nations* by He Xiangyu (b. 1986, China) is an intimate and elusive portrait of a young Chinese man who lives in a Berlin dormitory compound with approximately 700 rooms for international students. The video closely follows the protagonist and studies his surroundings over two years: we see him taking care of his very small studio flat and daily errands on his bicycle,

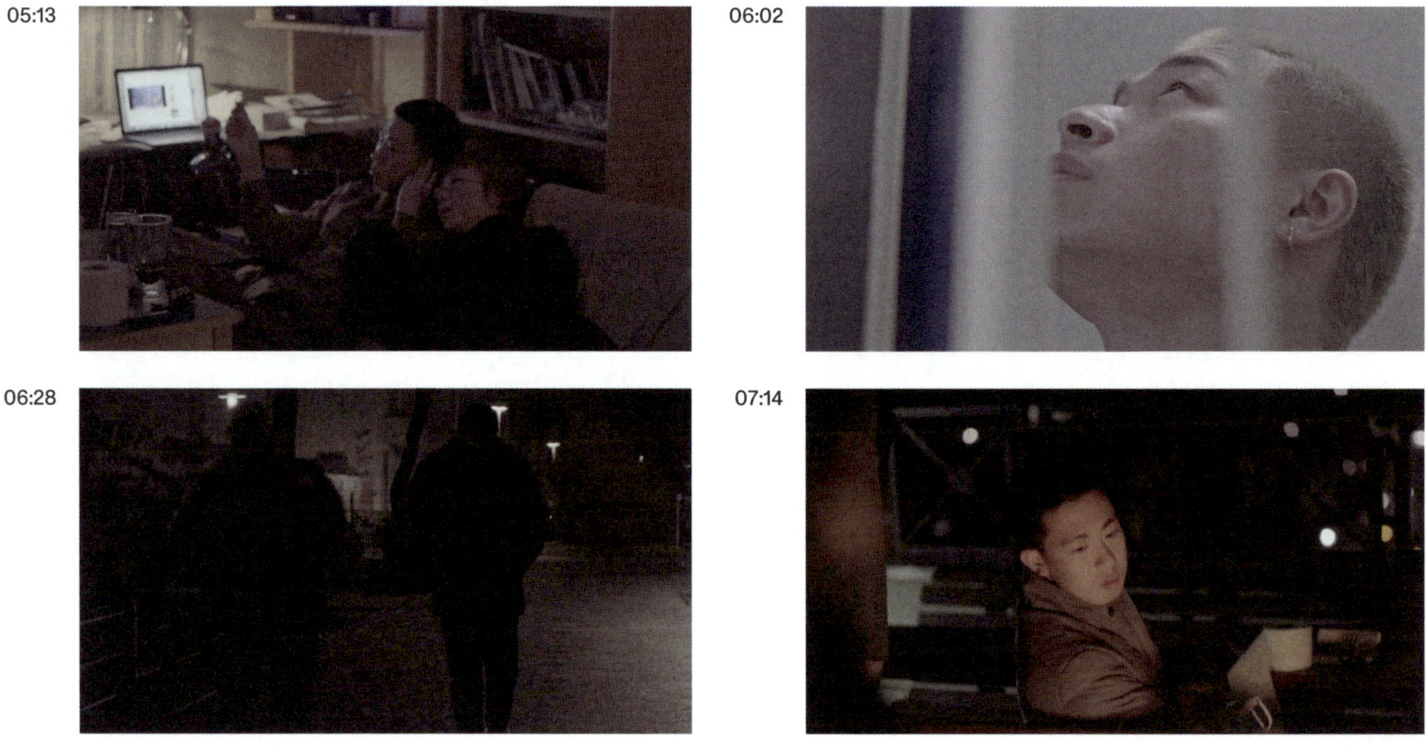
05:13 06:02 06:28 07:14

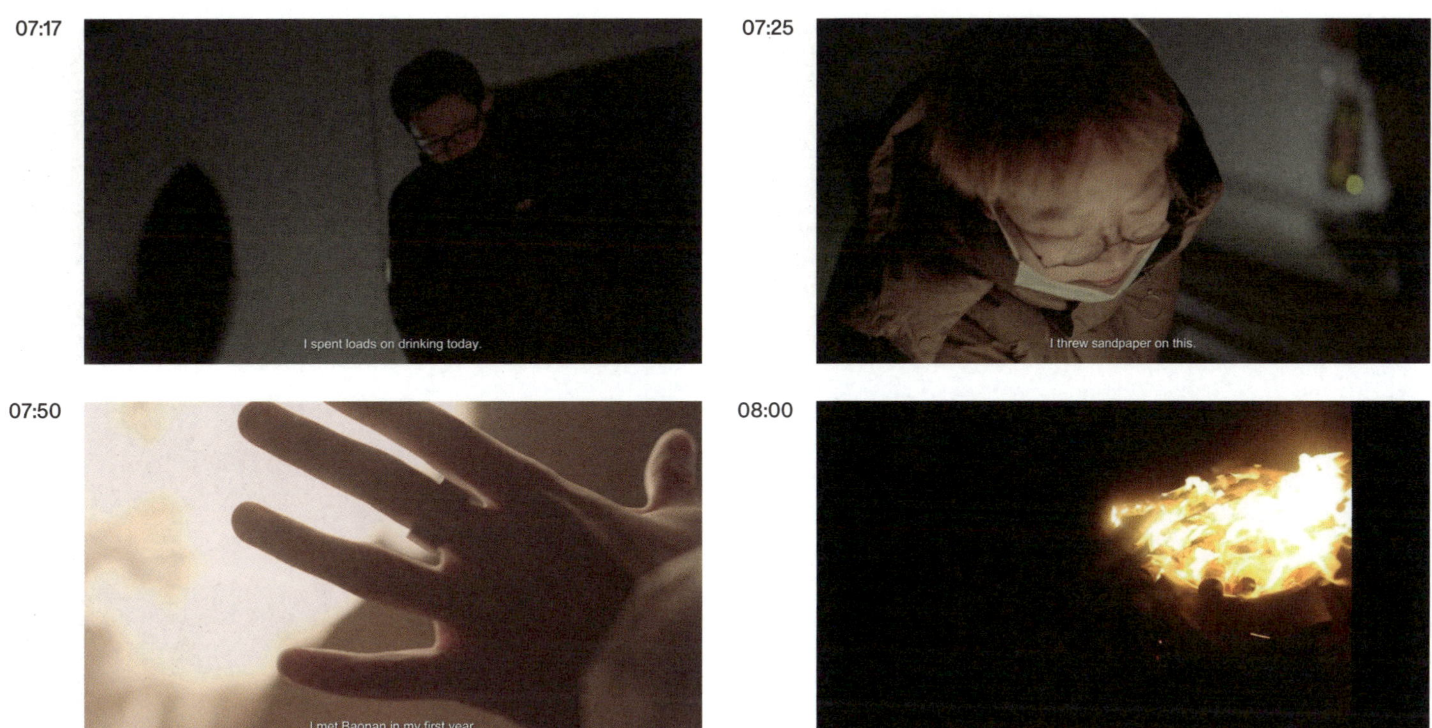

07:17 07:25

07:50 08:00

gathering and drinking with his social bubble, praying at a temple, and moving around the city amid the invisibility that the urban context places upon the life of individuals. No major events happen around him. Yet a series of minor specks of dust—a lonely look in his eyes, a sense of disconnection in his body language, an obsessive quest to feel something, anything, really—creep in and suggest the existential

08:01 08:26

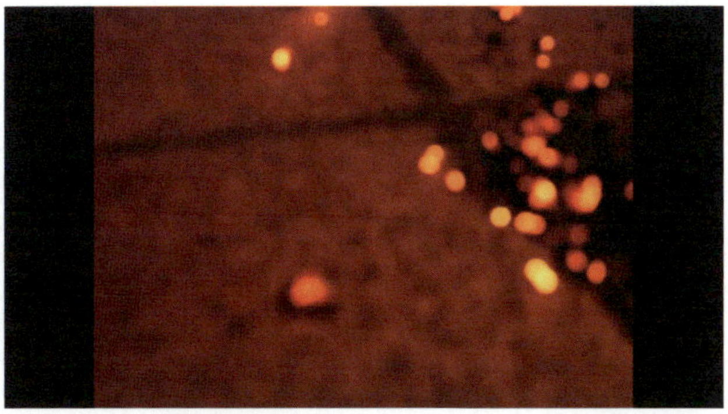

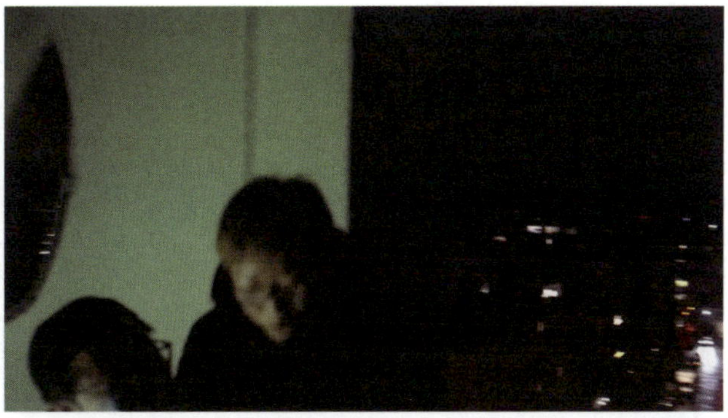

08:34 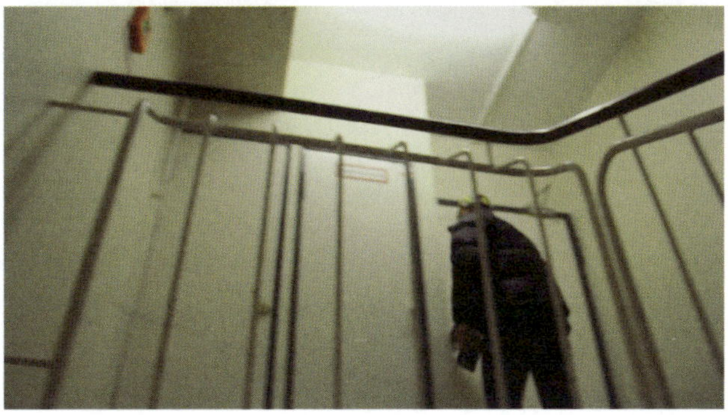 08:41

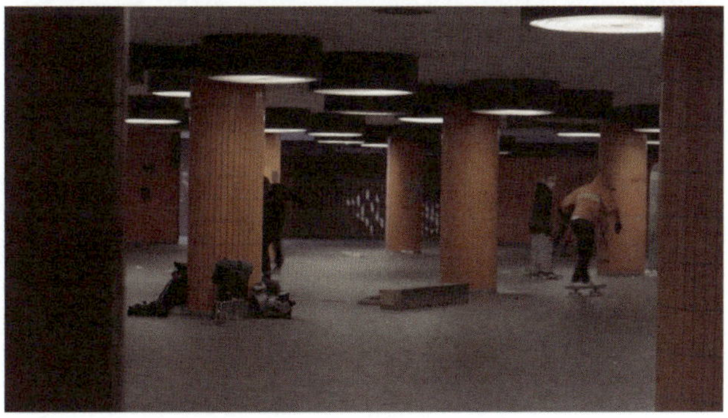

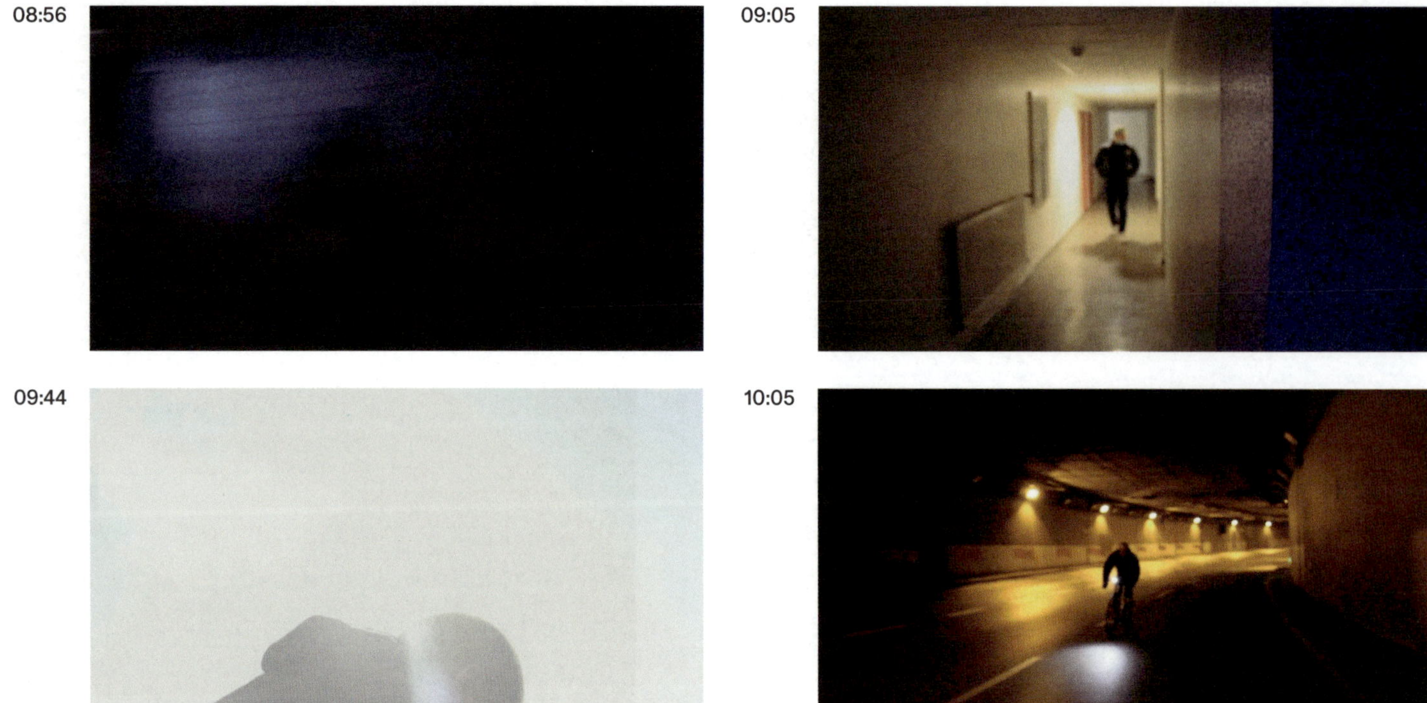

aspirations and uncertainties he is grappling with. Many of the young students living at the House of Nations—the artist was told—responds to their conditions by alienating their identity either from the local context or from their home countries. Tactile sensations such as the warmth of a bonfire, the cold of a skinny dip into a lake, the dryness of his hands when rubbed together, the soft harshness of a rope during

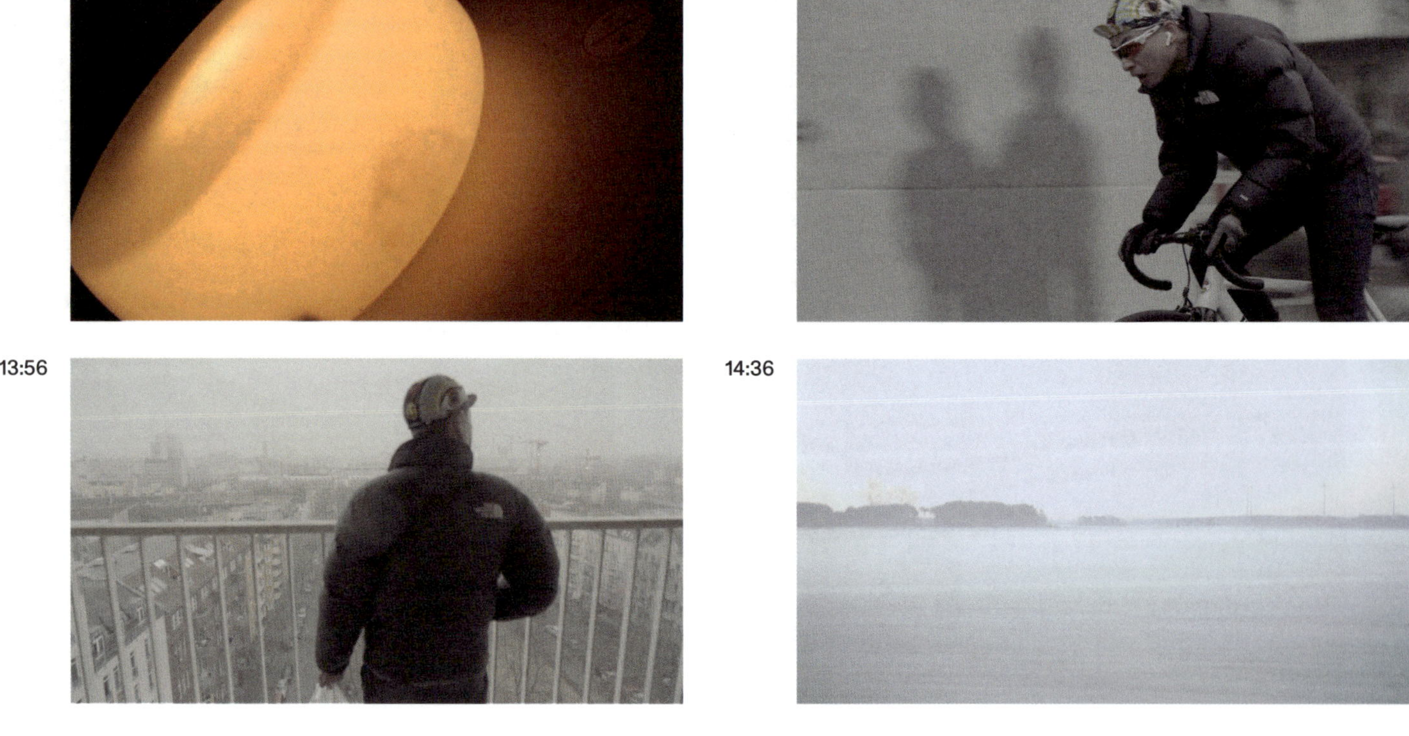

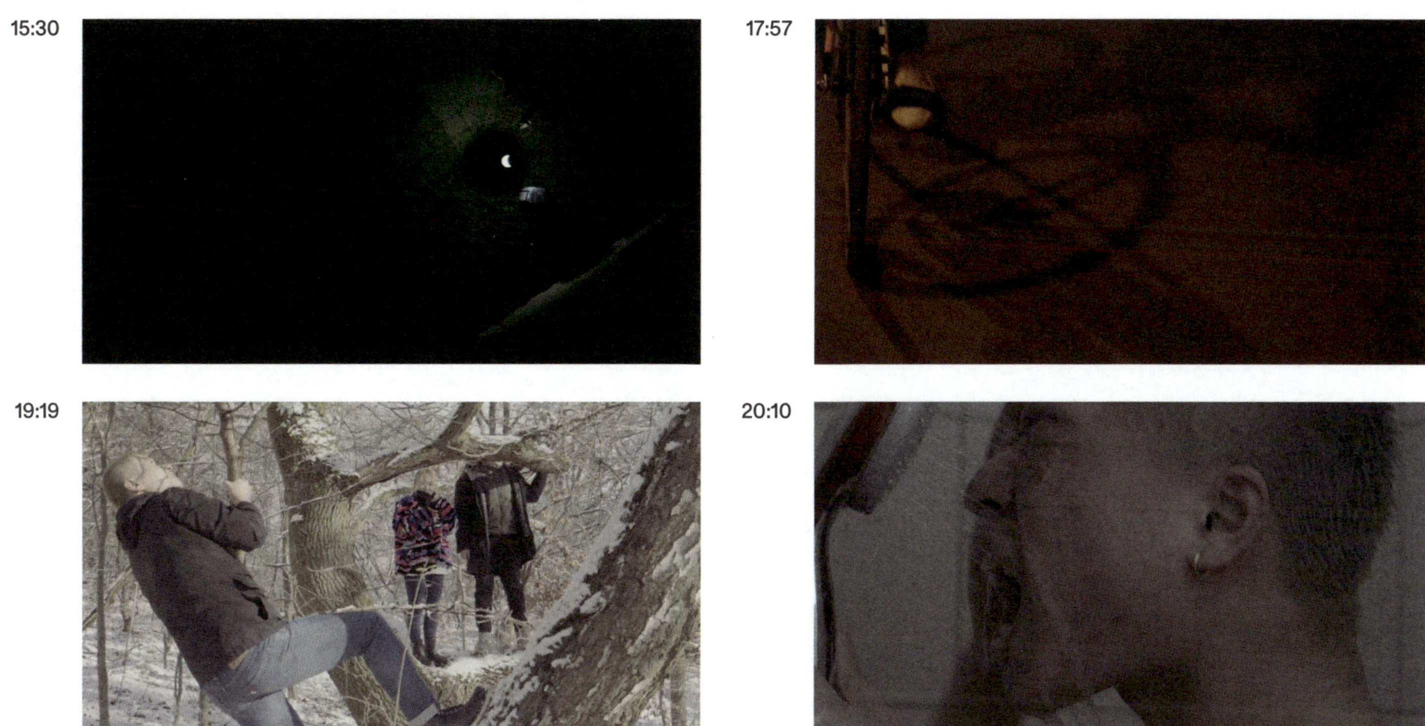
15:30 17:57 19:19 20:10

a bondage session serve as a compass to navigate the spectrum of the protagonist's psychology. At the same time, the doors of the House of Nations' nondescript building that recurringly open and close gesture toward those attempts at translation of his experiences as well as at transgression of the boundaries between what is inside him and what is outside. With its cinema verité approach, the video offers a space

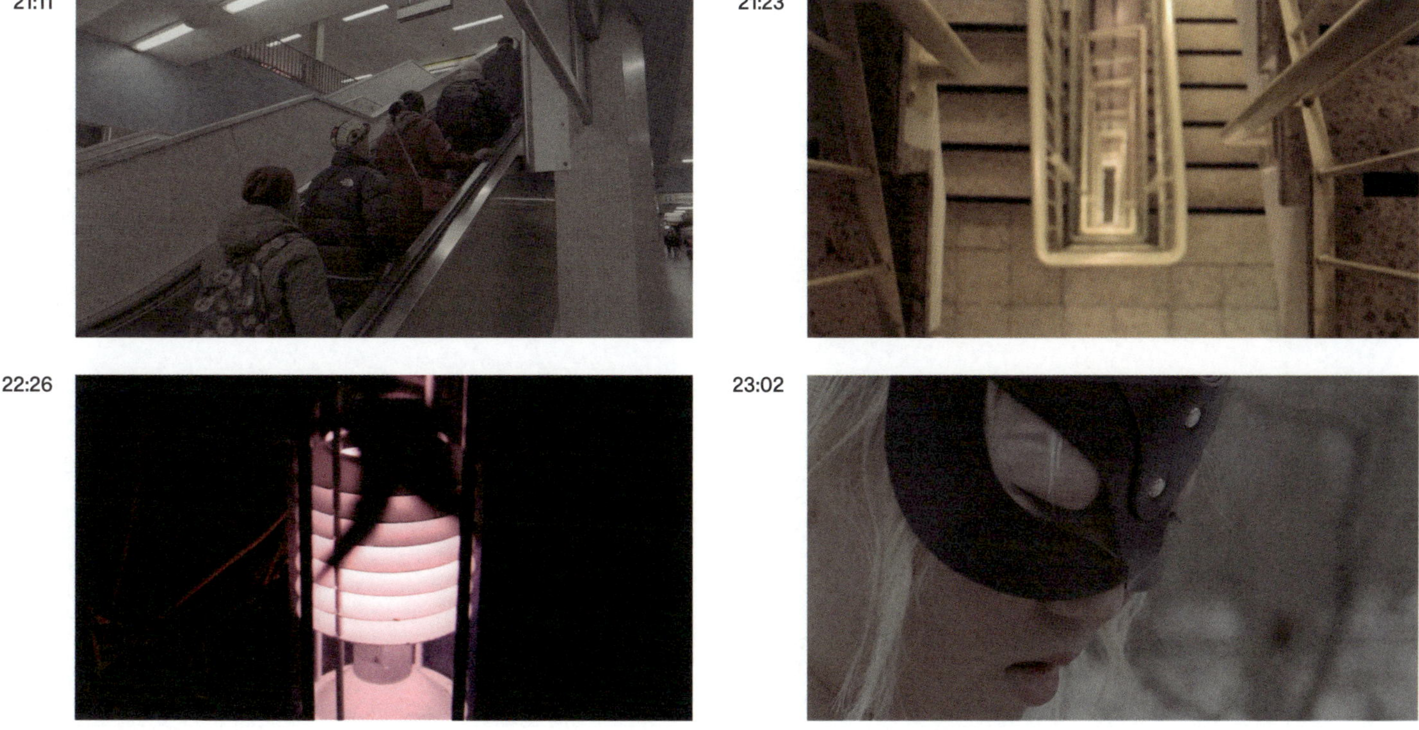
21:11 21:23 22:26 23:02

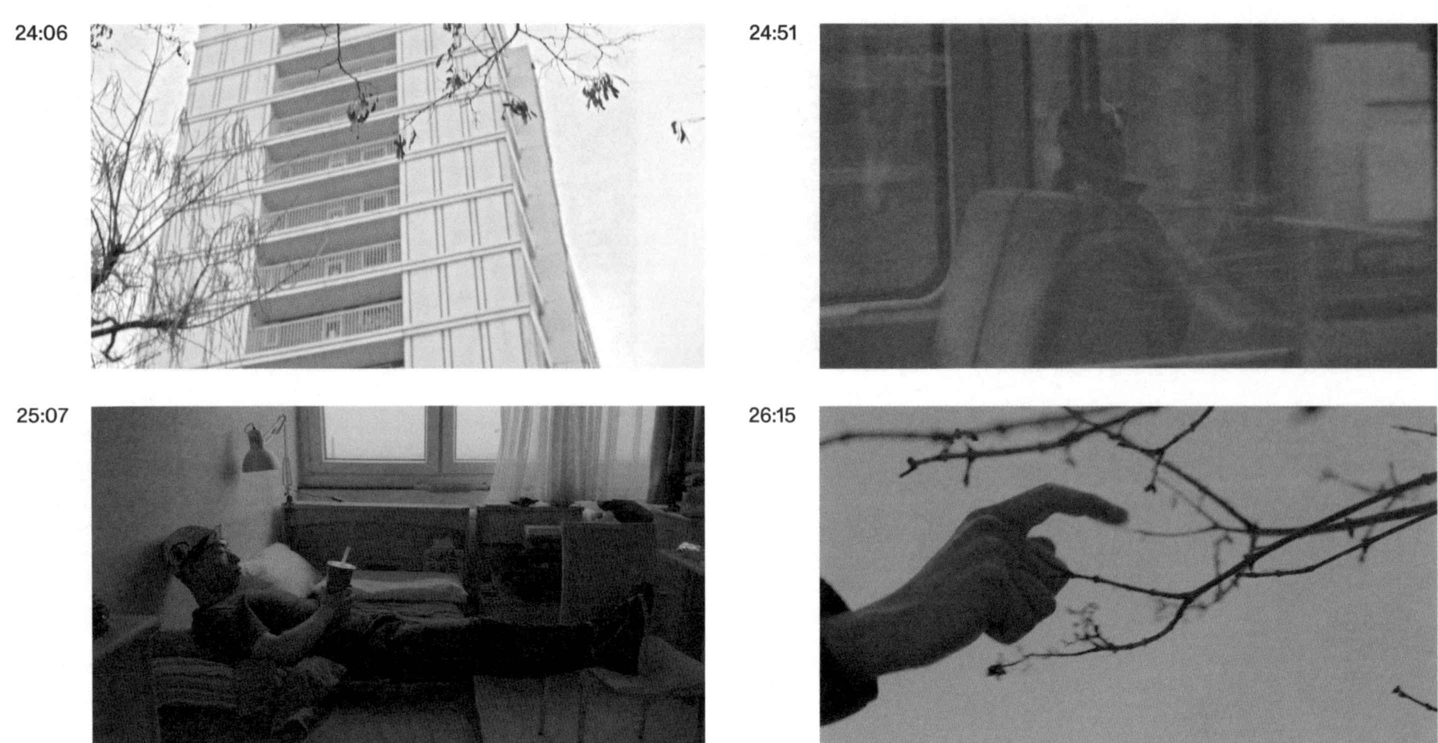

of storytelling to all those lives that would otherwise be deemed anonymous, while exposing the impact of the paradoxes of globalization on individuals and communities in its false claims of a borderless world and seamless displacements.

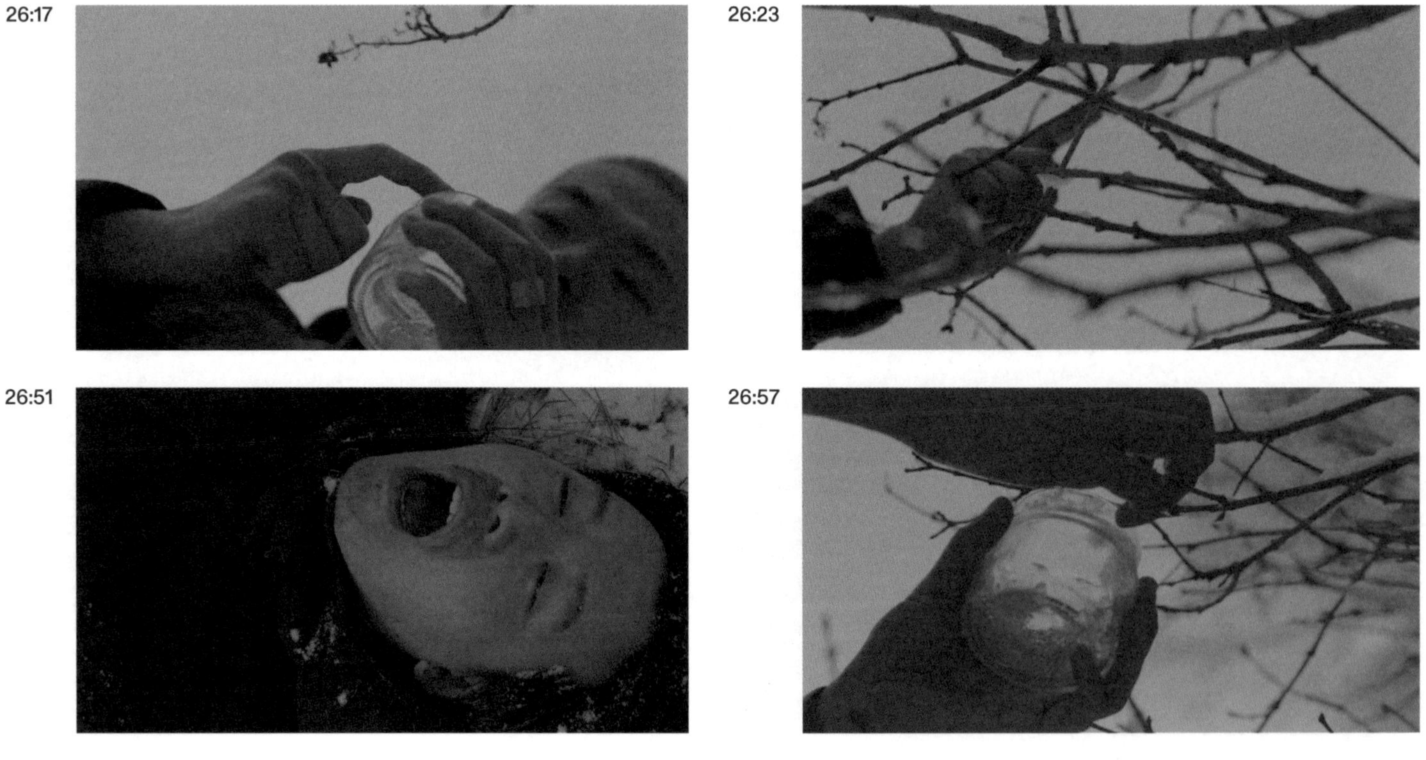

He Xiangyu, *House of Nations*, 2021

2K video, color, 5.1 sound, 28'58"

Commissioned and produced by
Fondazione In Between Art Film

With additional support from
the Gesellschaft für Deutsch-Chinesischen kulturellen Austausch e.V.

Co-producers
He Xiangyu, Zhang Yu

Creative Producer
Alessandro Rabottini

Cameraman
Shu Chou

Local Producer
Hao Yiming

Cast & Crew
Hao Yiming, Yuan Wenze, Zhang Chi, Li Luci, Chen Manli, Chi Chengwen, Shen Han, Wu Qiuyu, Bao Qianru, Lu Cong, Darryl Leung, Liu Haoyu, Wang Yongwei, Mia Madlen Jacobs

Post-production coordination
Zhao Fan

Editors
Karl Riedl, Mario Battistel

Assistant Editor
Sebastian Köcher

Digital Colorist
Yov Moor

Sound design
Roman Dymny

Foley recording
Louise Canguilhem / La Puce A l'Oreille post-production

Graphic design
Ingo Maak

Proofreaders
Zhou Congshan, Chen Siran, Han Junyi, Moira Barrett

Subtitles
Aya Kouamé / Babelfisch Translations

Original music
Dance of Consciousness, *Mind is Relative 2*, and *Dissolve the Violence*, all composed by Ding Ke

Special thanks to
Beatrice Bulgari, Leonardo Bigazzi, Paola Ugolini, Alessia Carlino, Bianca Stoppani, Simona Iandoli, Chiara Nicolini, Zhang Yu, POLY SON post production, La Puce A l'Oreille post-production, Cine Chromatix post-production Berlin, Fo- Guang-Shan-Tempel, Berlin e.V., Songs United Publishing e.K. / Joerg Fukking Musikverlag, Jiang Dingding, Joanna Gemma Auguri, Oakfield Mastering, Patrick Long, Patricial Feldmann, Martin Herbert, Cao Yang, Zhang Di

Courtesy of the artist and Fondazione In Between Art Film

Inside Out

Martin Herbert

For artists, every medium is a time-based one. Even the static object or image that, in an exhibition, can be seen all at once—if not necessarily understood—took time to make. That is doubly true if, like He Xiangyu, you happen to work with moving images; your films involve a crew, logistics, et cetera; and the work is made amid the production of other kinds of art. And it is triply true if your films are made in an exploratory fashion, with the narrative being a process of discovery, evolving, and revealing itself over months alongside the deepening relationship between the director and the people being filmed. The upside is that, in making such efforts, you can broach something like terra incognita. The first time I went to Xiangyu's studio, a short walk from where I live in Prenzlauer Berg, Berlin, he showed me some wall-based works that "represented" the upper palate of his own mouth as he visualized it while moving his tongue over its curves and ridges. The mouth, of course, is an interior; and you might say—Xiangyu's latest film, *House of Nations* (2021), affirms it—that one thing he is deeply interested in is how the concealed inside of a person is represented and brought to light. Imagine, now, that your task is not to do that to yourself but to another person. If both parties are sincere, then it will take as long as necessary.

Like Xiangyu's film *Terminal 3* (2019), which concerned itself with a group of African acrobats in Wuqiao, China, *House of Nations* focuses on an ad hoc, self-contained community abroad. *Terminal 3* developed over four years; *House of Nations* between two winters. But whereas the former film cleaves more closely to the conditions of documentary, the latter is a stylistic hybrid. It is set in the House of Nations in Wedding, Berlin, a rooming house for international—predominantly Chinese—students. Beyond this, the film focuses in on Hao Yiming, a graphic designer who, says Xiangyu, has been looking for work but unable to find it, one of many wants. Yiming's character (if that is the word) blooms and complicates over its twenty-nine-minute running time, as the film itself morphs. During its course we peek into Yiming's daily life, via intimate handheld filming, particularly as he participates in the micro-community within the building. In the film's opening minutes, we see him dragging a carpet back to the building, which will be cut up and shared with others; soon after, he is at a drinks and bonfire party; then cycling around, cooking, shopping for food, praying at a Taiwanese temple. We might think of the film, up to this point, in the context of the COVID-19 pandemic (signified by face masks) and its

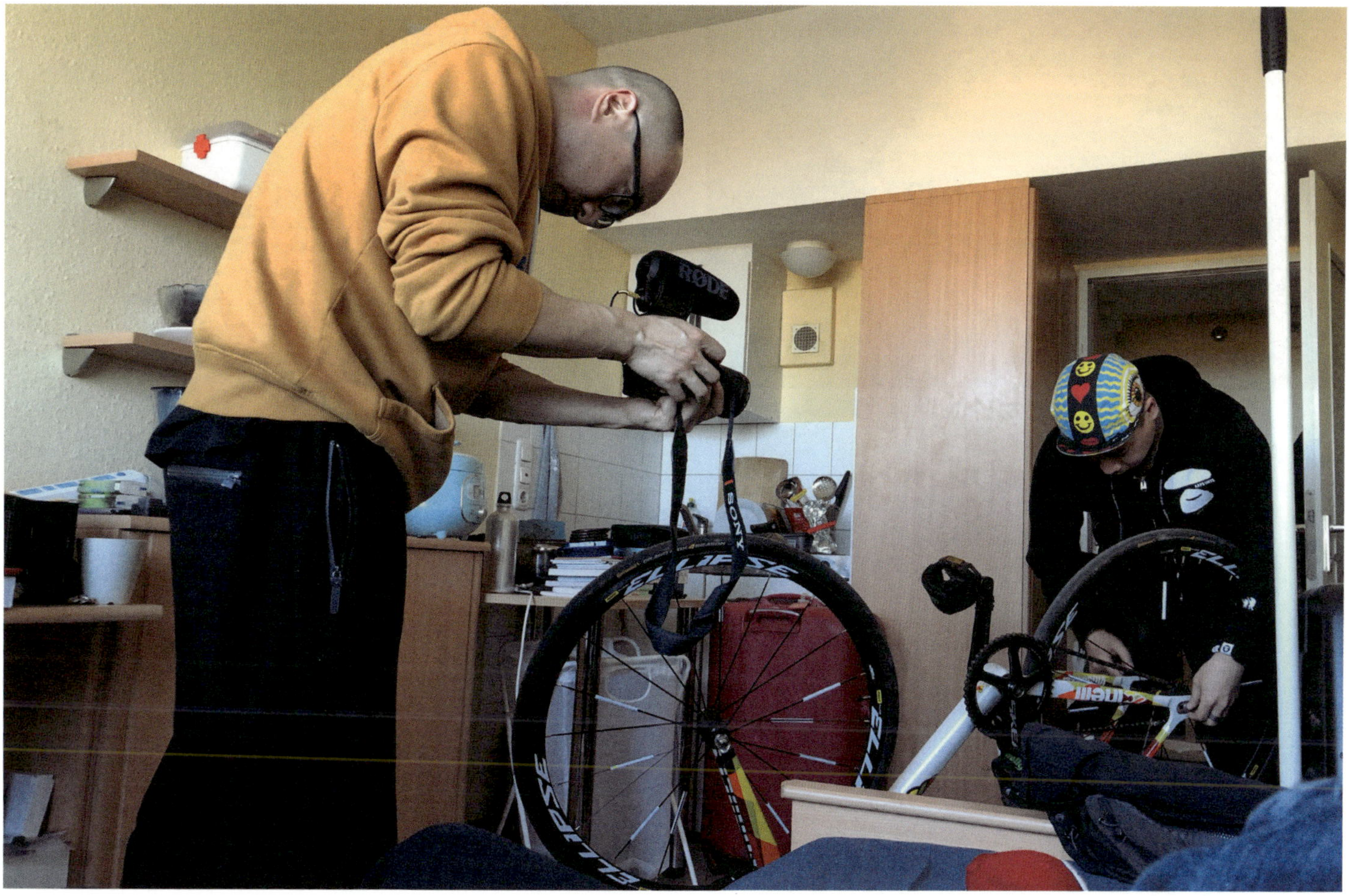
RØDE
SONY
ELLIPSE

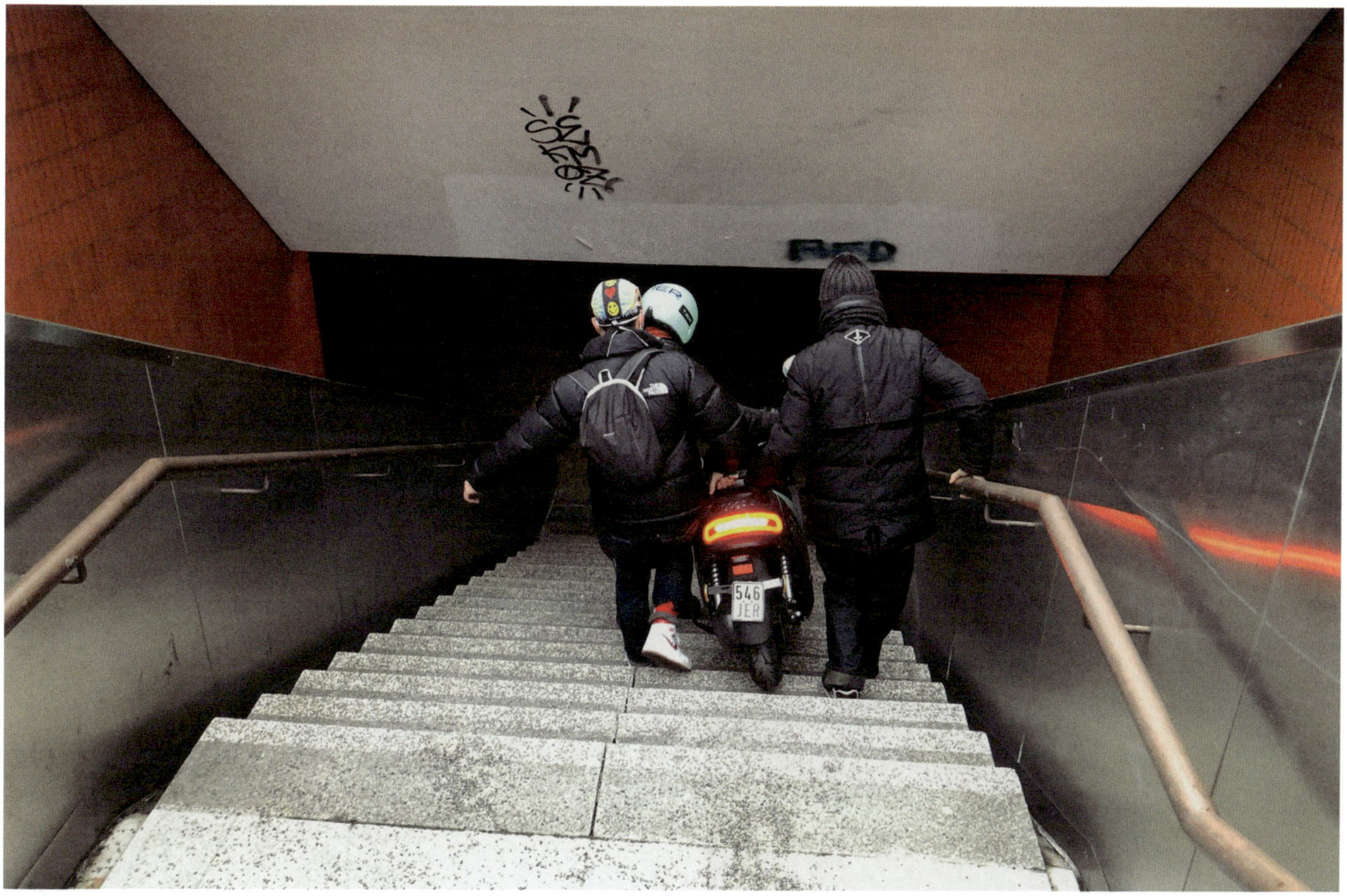
546
JER

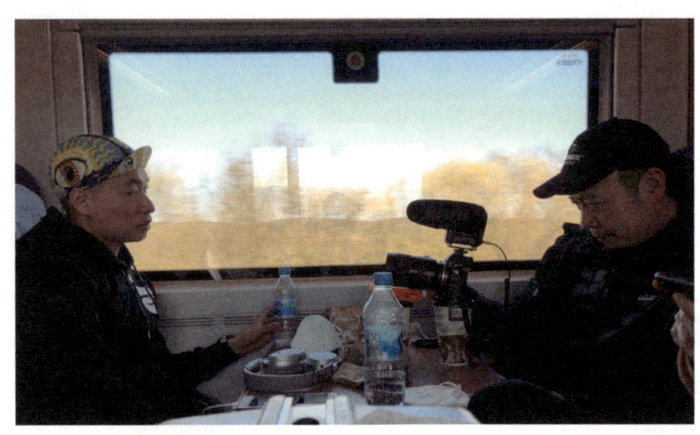

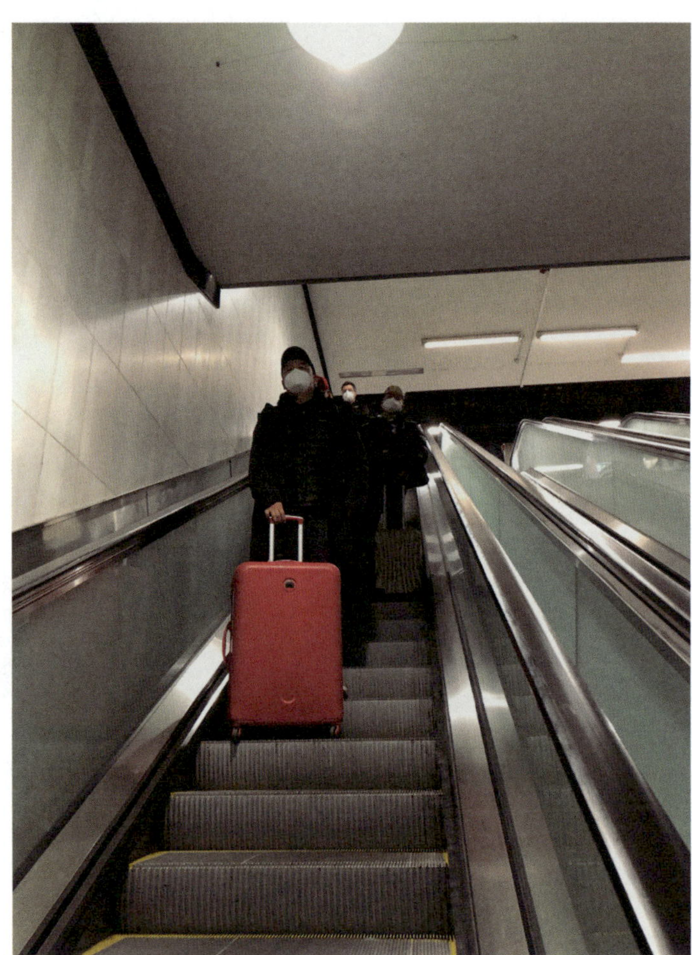

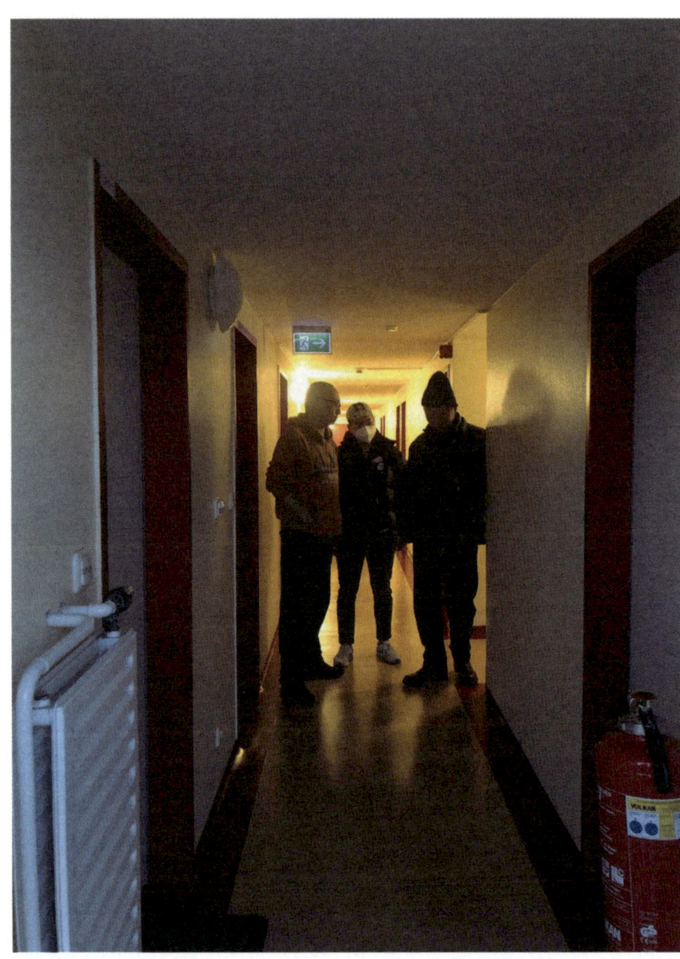

relation to isolation—the students already seem bundled up in their own tight group, and lockdowns presumably only added to the constraint. Constriction, though, brings tensions to the surface—at least, it does so here.

Xiangyu could have made a sociological study of the House of Nations, a rich one—*Terminal 3* attests to his subtlety in exploring community in this regard—but the film progresses from stepping inside a building to stepping inside a mind. Increasingly, between shots of Yiming's impassive face, we get glimpses of what he's thinking about, in scenes that might be happening in reality or might not. While he mopes on a stairwell, a blonde girl—who will become significant later—throws an item of clothing past him; elsewhere, we see a female hand stroking a male one. There are foreshadowing shots of a lake. In some images he has green-blond hair, in others his natural brown, as if there were (at least) two of him. He cycles through the city (notably, he has both a real bike and a dream bike, which we see on his computer screen), through streets and underpasses. At another party, he observes the girl and glugs alcohol, a salve. He does not speak. Much of this, over the course of editing, was reshuffled and augmented—for this viewer, seeing new drafts throughout some nine months, it was something like playing the tray game, where items on a tray are removed and you have to remember what has gone, made more difficult by new items being added. A song appeared and disappeared, considered too on-the-nose and explicatory, and too beautiful. Ambient music rose in the mix, as did disorienting, near-abstract footage, and a changeable emphasis on lights. A relatively binary structure became, it seemed, a subtler one. Over multiple versions, the film never stopped being both fascinating and elusive, like a poem, albeit one whose sentences kept mutating; or like getting to know someone, if never fully.

As he told me, in conversations over tea at his studio along with his assistants and film editor (and, later, over whisky—by nice coincidence, my favorite brand), Xiangyu wanted Yiming to be an active collaborator, opening his film out to the wild card of another's subjectivity. This is an expansion, if you like, of the format of documentary itself: documenting the thoughts—and, it turns out, bodily desires—of your main "character," who is, or is being played by, a real person too, and whose inner life will in turn drive the narrative, seemingly switching the format to fiction. Except, if the ensuing scenes reflect the fantasies and needs of a real person, *are* they fictional? Are they not, like Xiangyu's drawings, a way of bringing insides out? Arguably, just as by necessity this very text requires a hybrid form of critical writing and memoir of getting to know an artist, *House of Nations*' formal ambiguity keeps the viewer in engaged uncertainty.

Even in its early and most ostensibly documentarian stages, Yiming is "styled" by the director—a ruse to make him stand out to Western audiences, Xiangyu says—with colored hair and earrings. (He also has a fancy hat, which he chose himself because, says the artist, "He likes to be cool.") The very format of the film suggests a desire for something, something other than the normative of documentary form, a different reality breaking out.

To return to the interior/exterior narrative, it seems to shift decisively after the character has attended the temple. Religion puts moral limits on what people can do, so it is notable that what develops then is a kind of release, albeit one involving further constraint. We see Yiming jump a fence in the street, and then the scene changes to a bondage scenario of which there has been a brief hint earlier—a scenario that, again, is *real* in the sense that it is a reflection of a true desire: when Xiangyu asked his lead what he wanted to do in the film, Yiming said he wanted to try bondage. On the one hand, this seems fairly opposed to the aspect of the character that is spiritually active. On the other, as Xiangyu pointed out when I asked, a person who goes to temple must have a lot of control over his spirit. Nevertheless, Yiming's character contains multitudes, for toward the end of the film there is an abstracted fight scene in a snowy forest (for which Yiming, like a warrior, prepares by taking a nude dip in an icy lake), maybe a battle for the blonde girl's affections, and certainly a suggestion of latent violence within him. Again, this fantasy wraps itself in truth—not least during lockdown periods, people ripple with suppressed desires and conflicts. Through the course of the film, the character has an arc. He appears to learn something about himself, about different kinds of aggression that exist within him (both soft and hard); what he wants; and how shaded and striped his personality is.

To hear him tell it, Xiangyu films in a deliberately loose way—in the sense that he does not go in for many takes and told his character what he wanted him to do just before shooting—and edits almost like a painter: a little more of this here, balanced by a little less of this there, feeling his way forward while also trusting his inner compass. He shot, by his own admission, a fair bit more quotidian material (a trip to the dentist, for instance) before alighting on the atemporal structure described above. Then, once the latter was in place, he kept tweaking the film's emotional texture. For instance, we discussed—he was open-minded enough to consult me—whether a certain sequence should be retained that showed the character in a relatively bad light, and one that prefaced some ambiguous scenes. I thought it should be excised (if you lose the viewer's sympathy for the character, they might be less inclined to follow you, and him, through some

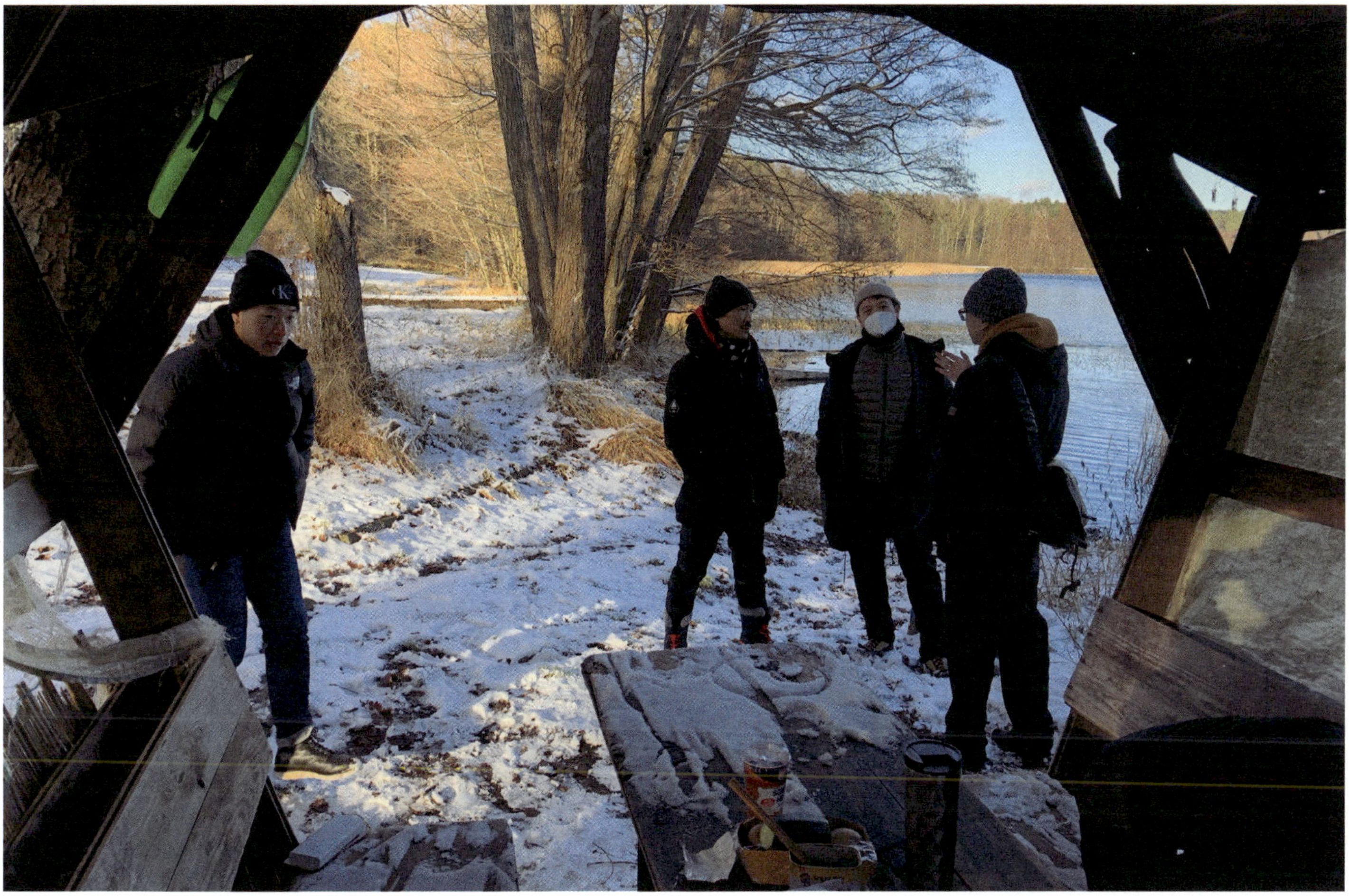

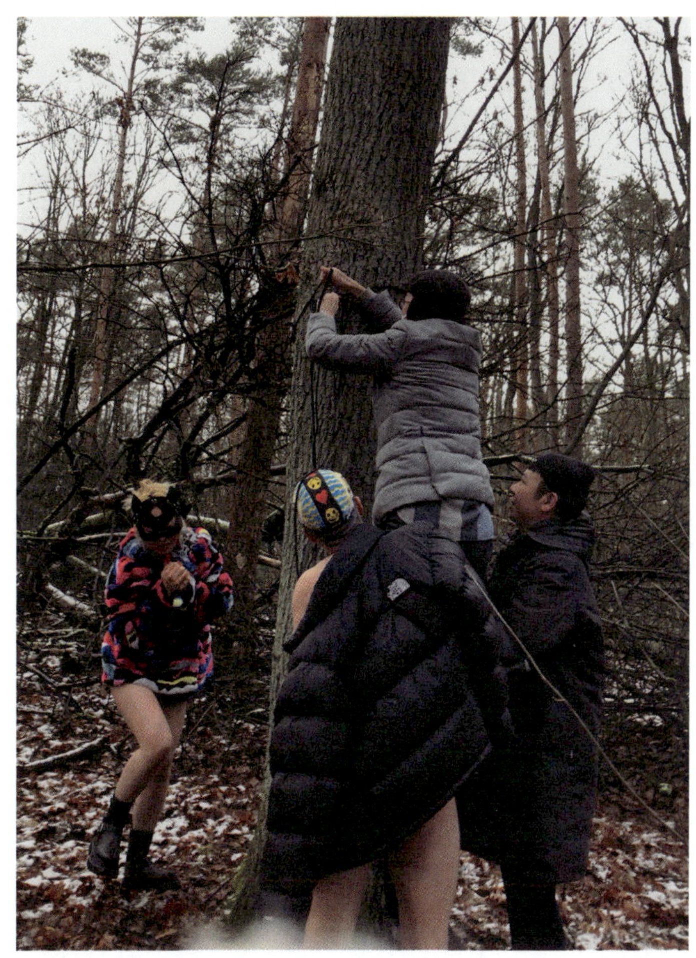

narrative thickets), and so did Xiangyu. Generally, as is known, the critic is not involved in the creative process; they turn up to perform the postmortem. I studied art—and made some films—but at a certain point I stopped, and any time I jump the fence myself it feels strange. At one point, a few years back, I mentioned the name of a Renaissance painter to a sculptor whose work reminded me of the painter's characteristic way of rendering drapery; later, the artist named a work after the painter. The oddity of that, to me, revealed boundaries that I have set up within myself. I tend *not* to ask for advice on much of anything. Xiangyu reminded me, here, of the virtues of doing so, of pooling opinions.

In any case, the very fact of his inquiry points to something both productively humble and organic and innately collaborative in his process—he will listen to an actor and even, god forbid, an art critic, and clearly he will also listen to his instincts, his gut. Having witnessed the development of the film only after shooting stopped, but while the editing was still going on, I would guess that one quality of Xiangyu's personality that brings so much out of his crew and actors is his personal warmth, generosity of spirit, and, indeed, general generosity. From personal experience, he is a person who will invite you to drink a high-end tea with him and, when you enjoy it, send you a large cake of the same delicious tea. It is going to last me a while, this tea, and I doubt I will drink a single cup of it without thinking of Xiangyu and, by extension, *House of Nations*.

Sociability, indeed, is where the film's roots lie. Xiangyu first knew Yiming on a personal basis. They met, hung out, Yiming helped him in his studio, and he also showed Xiangyu his home in the House of Nations—its multicolored floors, its myriad inhabitants. Xiangyu got to know the community inside the place, which operates like a miniature city—you can change Chinese currency to Euros, for instance—built predominantly on mutual support. The film, then, unfolded in at least two ways. Xiangyu got to know the context and the person—that is, two related insides. Much of what drives the film, you would have to imagine from outside, is a kind of trust for which there are no shortcuts. Yiming, Xiangyu readily says, is his friend, and as a result what you see onscreen has a quality of authenticity about it, of mutual risk-taking and support, since the director wants to portray the person that he knows, and the latter is encouraged to bare himself and take risks. Of course, there is a history of filmmakers working with nonactors and actors without scripts, the films being tailored to their known personalities—to Xiangyu I mentioned John Cassavetes and Mike Leigh; he countered with Abbas Kiarostami—but I cannot think of a prior example where a film switchbacks like *House of Nations* as a way of entering into a space the viewer has not been in before: first, through the door of the House of Nations; secondly, deep into the psyche of one of its inhabitants.

There are, in the later scenes of *House of Nations*, events that are equivocal enough in their montage that the viewer is thrown back fulsomely on interpretation. In these stretches, the film reminds one that it is a hybrid of not just documentary and fiction but of both those things and art, which is always to a degree unfixed and a collaboration with the subjective audience. The film is not limited by its cultural context, either. Insofar as it is a work about isolation, inward desire, the need for community, and the contradictions that can be seen to coexist in one person, it is a prism for, well, most likely anyone who sees it, because these are things that we have all experienced at one time or another, and have maybe experienced more of over the last couple of years, as the pandemic has thrown us back on our own inward resources and given us more time with our own thoughts. If, as a film, it feels like a true portrait, it is because Xiangyu did not stop until he and his character had arrived at the latter's multifarious inner self. The House of Nations can also be one person, Xiangyu said to me during our conversations—a statement that is itself open to interpretation. But here are two related ways of seeing it. A person can stand in for the other people that the camera lingers less upon—all of whom, no doubt, could have their own film illuminating their inward complexity. And that person, as *House of Nations* makes fulsomely clear, can contain nation-sized expanses within themselves.

Images from the backstage of *House of Nations* by He Xiangyu.
Courtesy of the artist.

JONATHAS DE ANDRADE

OLHO DA RUA

2022, HD video, color, stereo sound, 26'

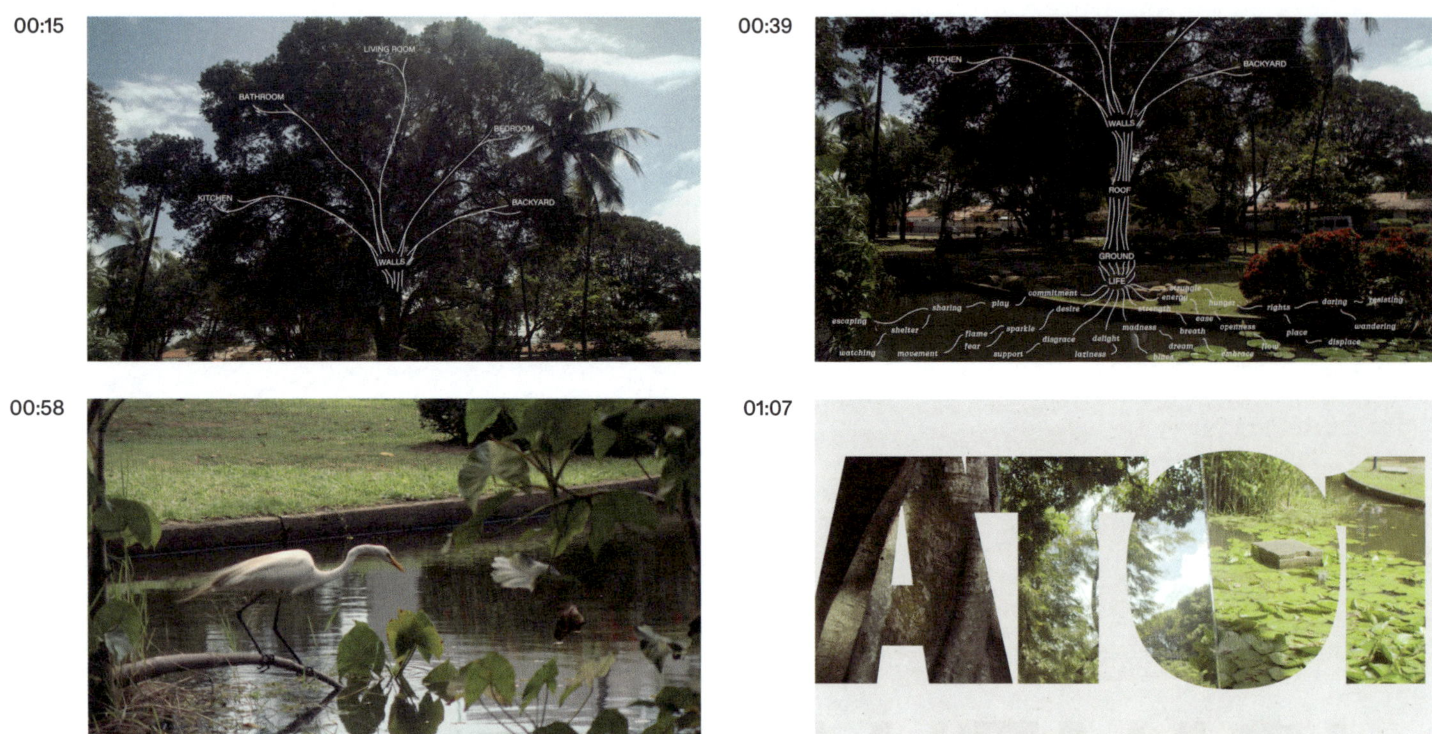

Olho da Rua [Out Loud] by Jonathas de Andrade (b. 1982, Brazil) casts a temporary community of homeless people living in the streets of downtown Recife, where the artist is also from. Inspired by the techniques of theatre practitioner, theorist, and activist Augusto Boal's Theatre of the Oppressed, the video opens with the diagram of a tree that metaphorically connects, from its crown to its roots, the structure

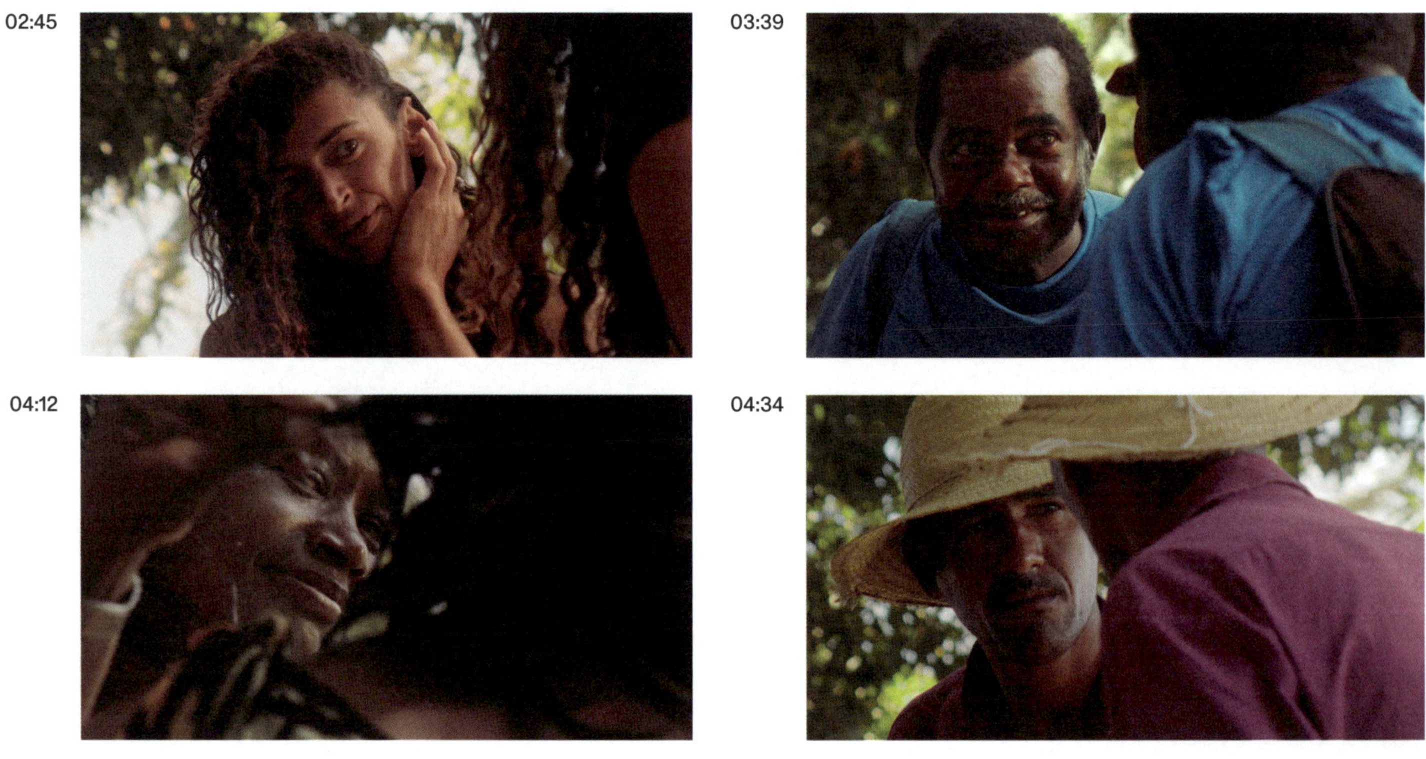

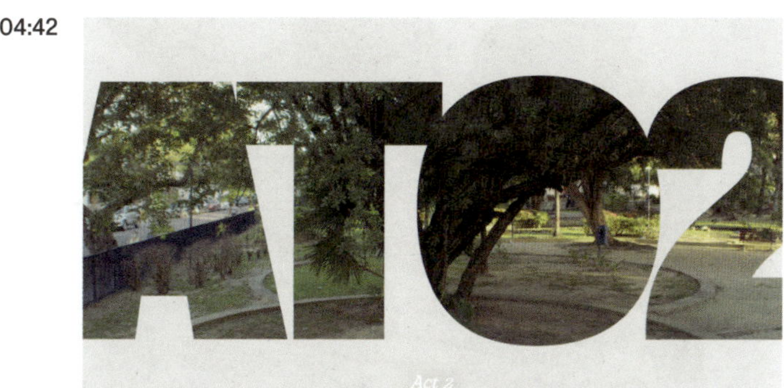

04:42

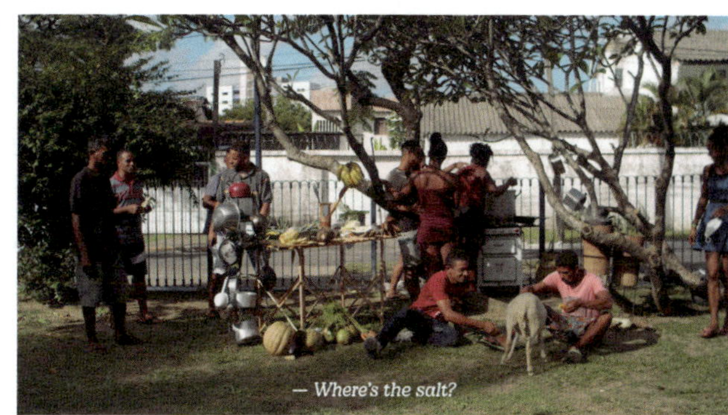

06:09

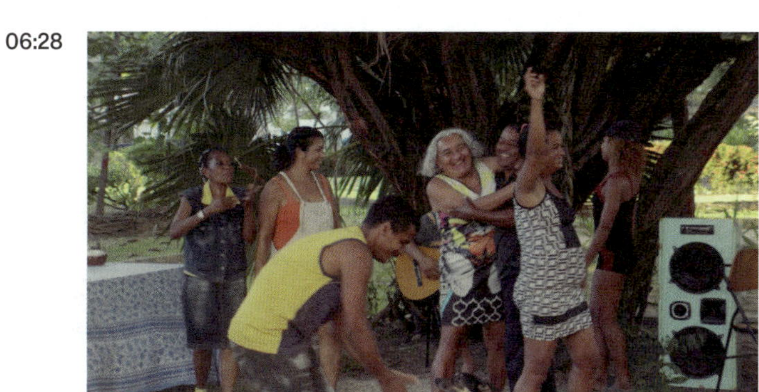

06:28

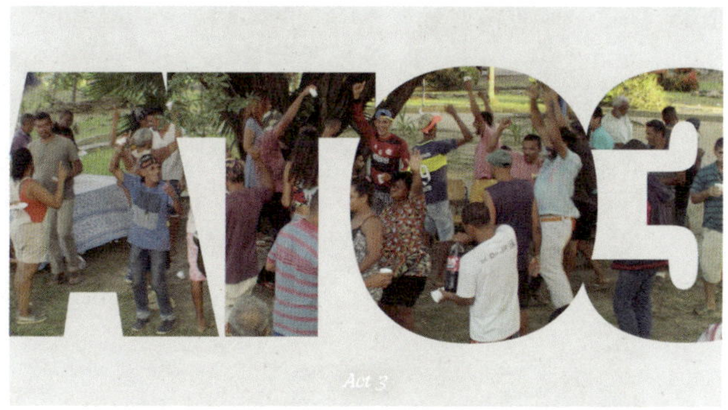

06:51

of a house to the emotional experiences of the cast in relation to housing and lack thereof. It then stages a series of eight performative acts that focus on collective dynamics, power structures, and exercises of gaze in a recently gentrified public square. The cast is seen confronting one's image in a mirror, cooking for each other, enjoying a feast, resting, playing with tree trunks, sitting in a circle to share their struggles

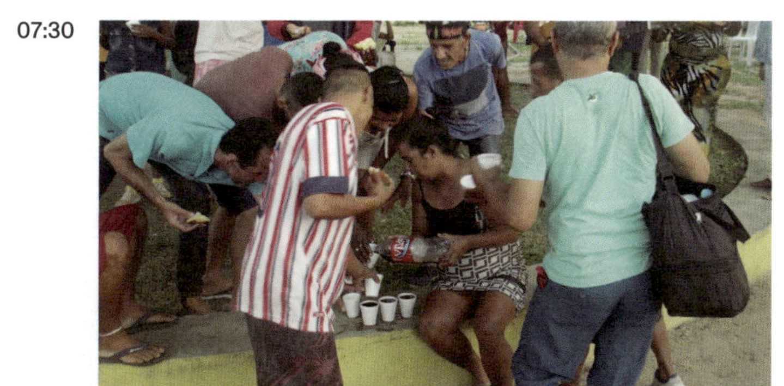

07:30

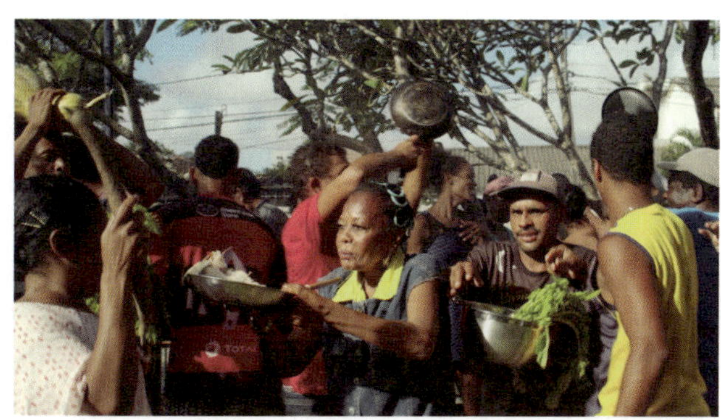

07:37

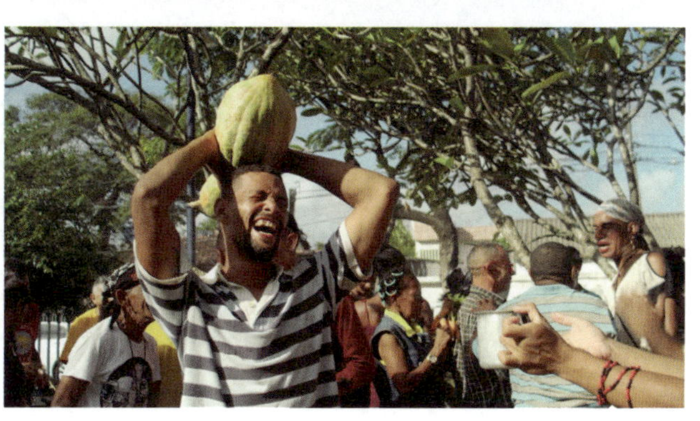

07:44

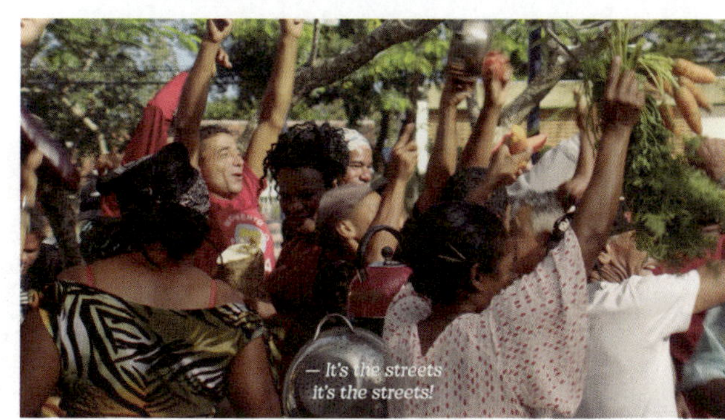

08:07

08:11

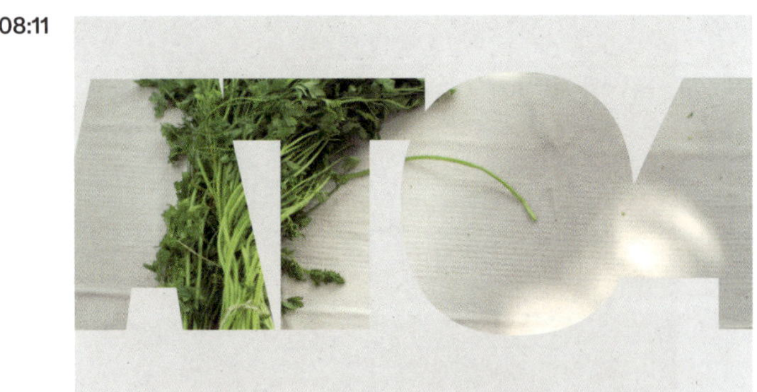

08:50

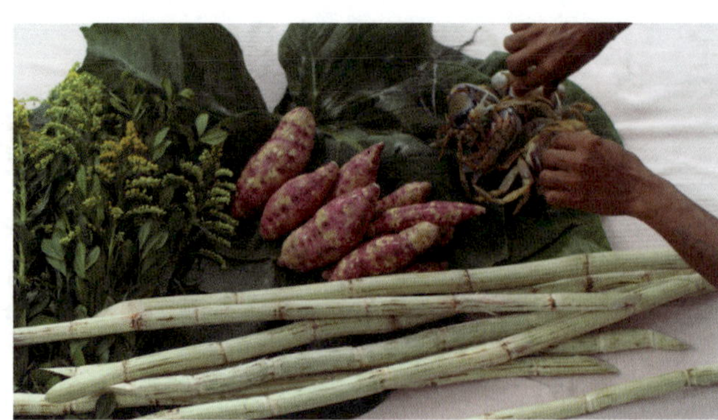

09:05

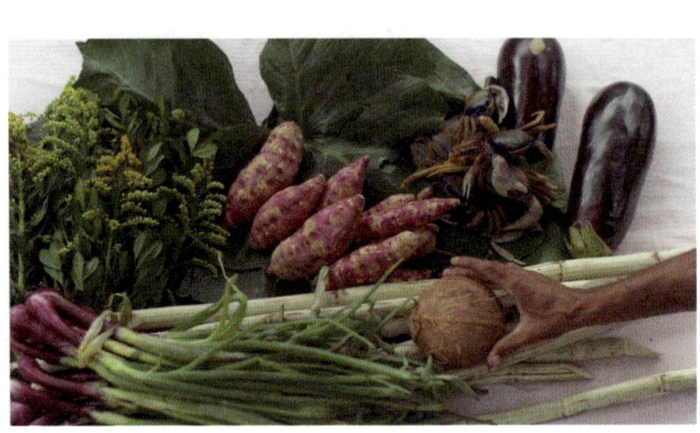

09:21

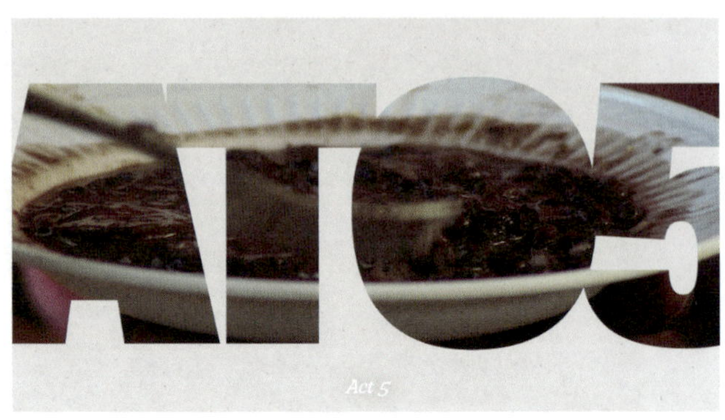

and make demands, throwing a party as well as staring back at the camera that observes them. Bordering fiction and nonfiction, the aim of this participatory project was to engage the cast of nonprofessional actors in conversations around identity, care, family, class consciousness, and socio-political visibility through actions and words. Out of the script, the images are delicately receptive to the cast's personality and

09:47

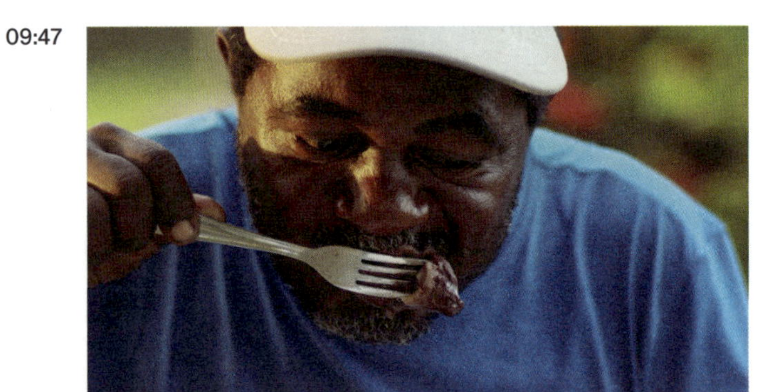

10:18

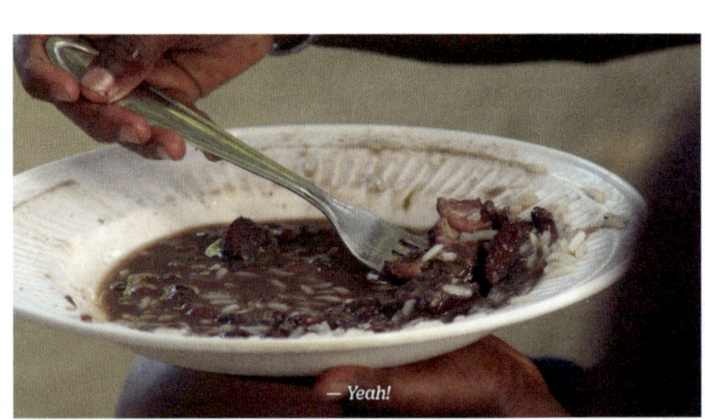

10:25

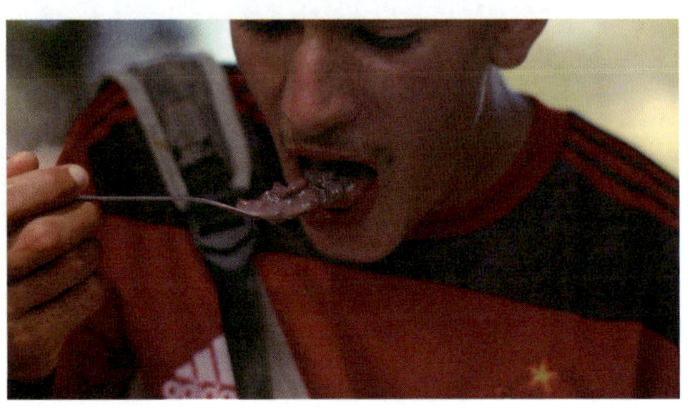

11:56

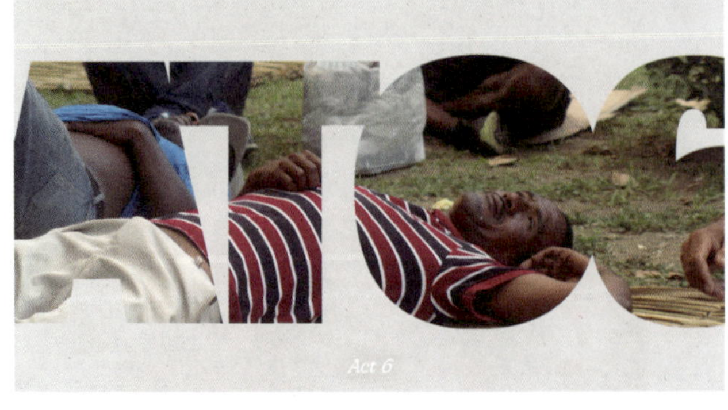

12:16

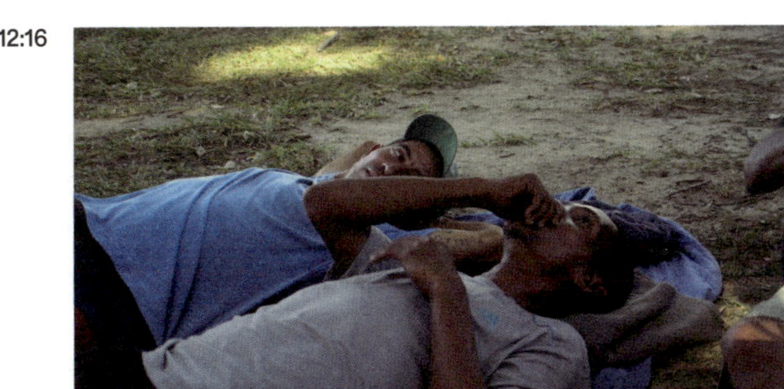

12:41

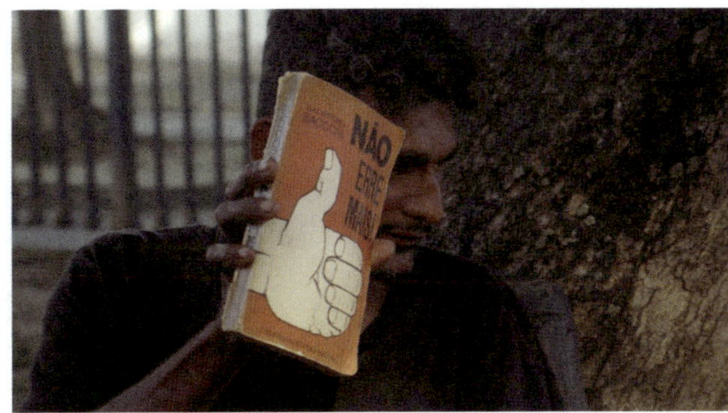

13:03

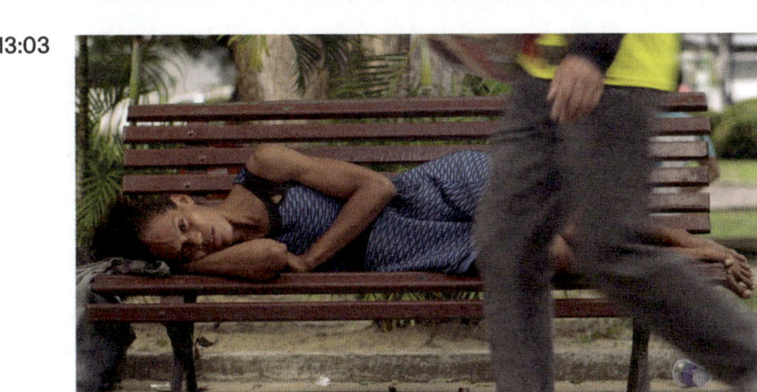

14:57

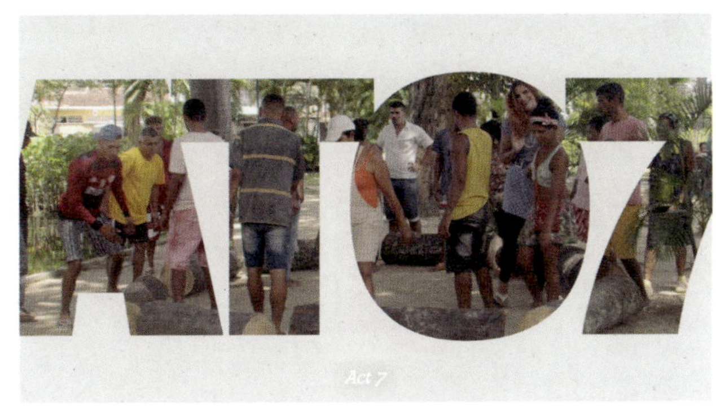

emotional worlds, and stand as a powerful testimony of contemporary Brazil, with its rich multiculturalism and structural inequalities. To accompany them is a hypnotic soundtrack by percussionist Homero Basílio that uses instruments traditionally rooted in Northeastern Brazil, such as djembe drums, shakes, seeds, and clay flutes. The video is not only a reflection on power dynamics rooted in colonialism—and on how

15:50

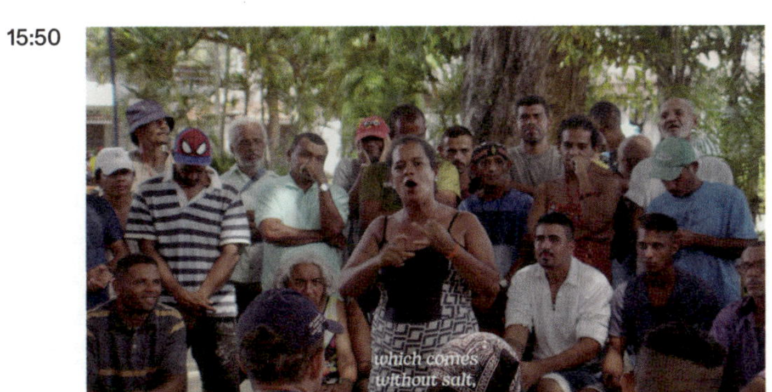

16:30

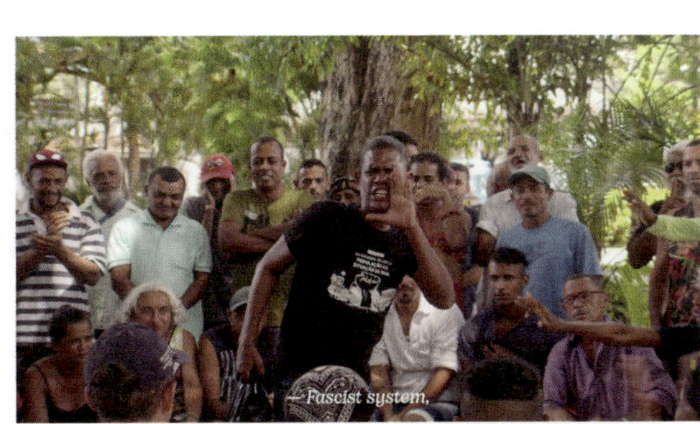

16:34

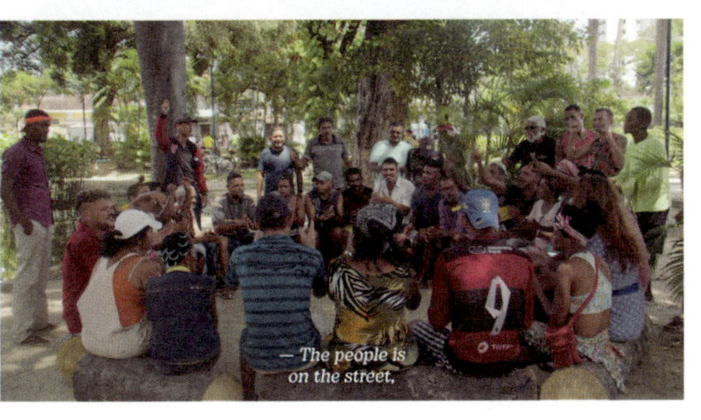

16:41

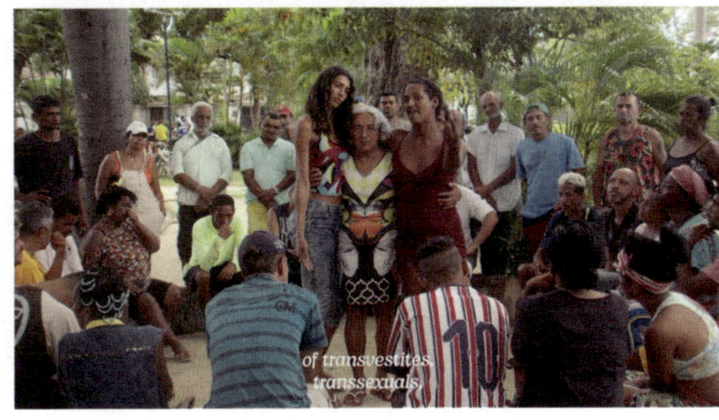

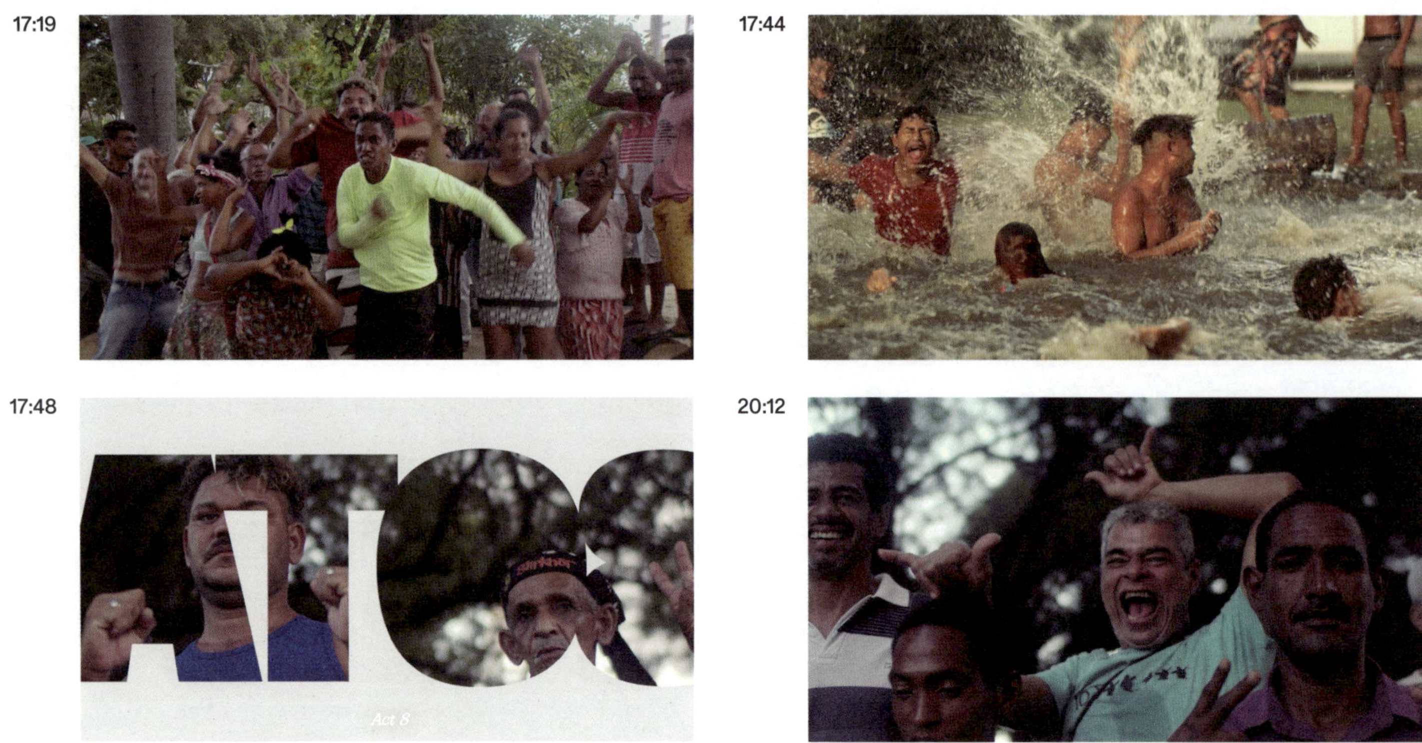

these may be tied to whoever holds the camera—but also a provocation to whoever looks. Using art and radical pedagogy as tools to reposition the stories of people who are marginalized and made invisible, the work fosters ways to collectively rethink reality and imagine alternatives.

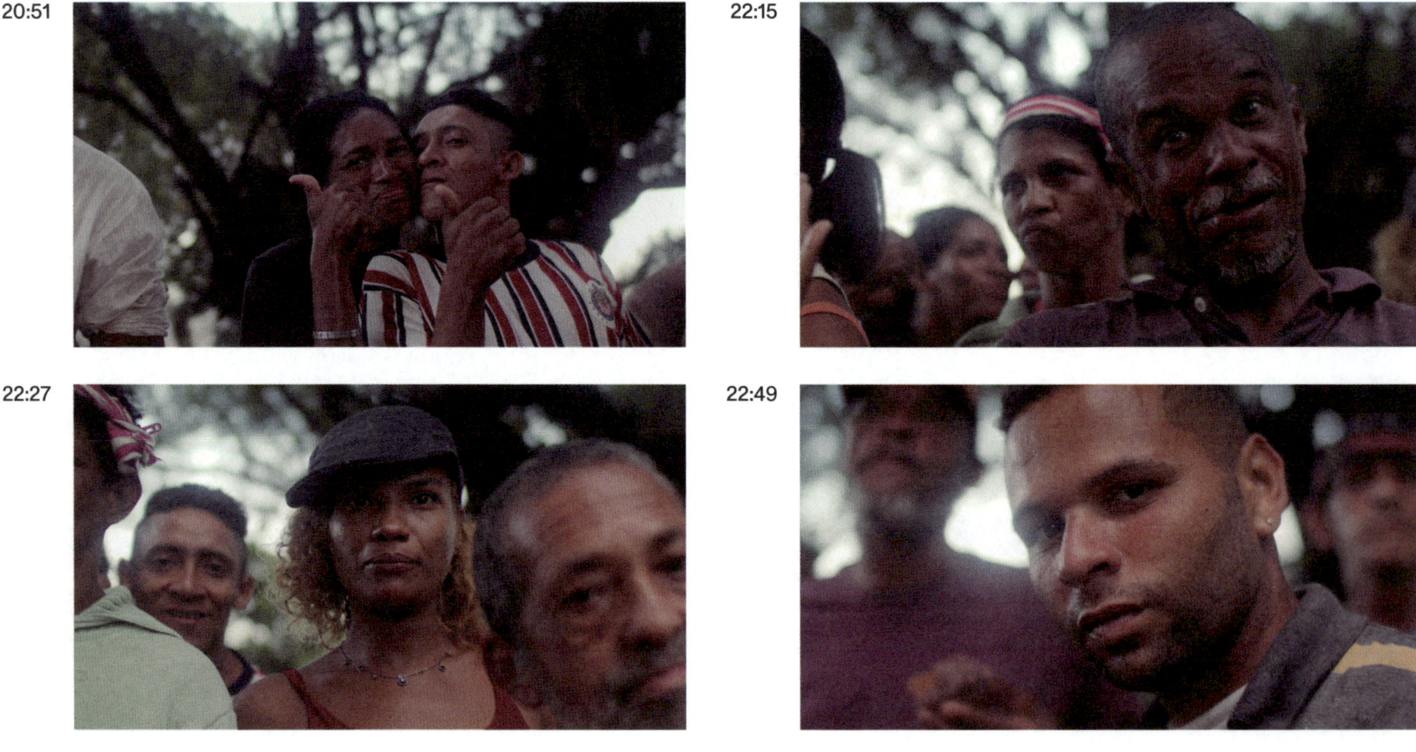

Jonathas de Andrade, *Olho Da Rua*, 2022

HD video, color, stereo sound, 26'

Cast
Adamis Soares da Silva, Adriana Júlia Guerra da Silva, Adriano Leonardo dos Santos, Aécio da Costa, Aguinaldo Santos da Silva, Albino Cabral da Silva, Alessandro A. R. Santiago, Alice Maria Bernardes da Silva, Amaro Pedro da Silva Santos, Anderson Oliveira dos Santos, Angela Maria da Silva, Antônio Fernandes Dias, Ary Jerry, Bráulio Gomes de Oliveira Júnior, Brenda Close, Brian Barros de Oliveira, Carlos Alexandre de Lima, Carlos André F. da Silva, Carmelita Cebile Ribellino, Cibele Gracielle da Silva, Cigana da Silva, Claudemiro José Batista, Daniel Lira de Carvalho, Daniel Menezes Costa, Djair José de Oliveira, Edilza da Silva Gomes, Edson André B. da Silva, Edson Policarpo da Silva, Elídio Flávio da Silva, Elizângela Maria dos S. Monteiro, Eric Henrique S. Silva, Evandro C. de A. Júnior, Everaldo José de Oliveira, Everton Francisco Vieira, Fábio Rogridues de Souza, Fausto de Oliveira Gomes, Fávio César N. de Aquino, Fernando Mota de Lima, Gabriel da Silva, Gata Molhada, Genildo Santos Silva, Hayk Ferreira Gonçalves, Heraldo Rocha G. da Silva, Isaias Cavalcante de Lima, Ivanildo Antônio Barbosa, Ivison Anacleto, Izabele Félix de Souza, Jailson José dos Santos, Jaison Batista da Silva, Jamesson T. da Silva, Jeferson Alves Ferreira, Jefferson, Carneiro da Silva, João Aparecido Luciano, João Vitor Francisco da Silva, Jonatan Antônio da Silva, José Hebert dos S. Silva, José Inácio da S. Filho, José Medeiros da Silva, José Zildo R. do Nascimento, Josenildo do N. Ferreira, Luciano José da S. Santana, Luciano Soares dos Santos, Luciene Maria Torres, Luiz Alves Vera Cruz Neto, Luiz Carlos dos S. Silva, Márcio Favoreti de Souza, Márcio Moniz C. de Andrade, Marcone Alves da Silva, Maria Glimara da Silva, Maria Gomes da Silva, Mário José de Oliveira, Mario Santiago Amorim Júnior, Matheus Oliveira Souza, Moisés Ferreira da Silva, Nailton Leonardo Ferreira, Renê Araújo, Ricardo de Souza Barbosa, Robson da Silva Pessoa, Rosangela Soares Cardoso, Rosinete Nascimento Santana, Sidnei Martins dos Santos, Tarcísio Silva Pinheiro Vasconcelos, Thiago Augusto Aevedo, Vera Lúcia Conceição Santana, Vera Lúcia F. da Silva, Wagner Pereira G. dos Santos, Wanderson Felipe, Wilames Oliveira da Silva

Script and direction
Jonathas de Andrade

Creative Producer
Leonardo Bigazzi

Executive production
Juliana Soares

Director of photography
Gustavo "Tijolinho" Pessoa

Art production
Joana Claude Migeon

Mounting
Fábio da Costa, Gustavo Campos

Direct sound
Joelton Ivson, Catharine Pimentel

Script consulting
Gustavo Campos

Filming script consulting
Letícia Simões

Executive Production Consultant
João Vieira Jr

Assistant Director
Jerônimo Lemos

Cast preparation
Clébia Sousa, André Marinho

Production direction
Amanda Guimarães, Gabriela Alcântara

Casting producer
Ingrid Farias

Plateau
Anderson Villar

Plateau Assistant
Wilkson Souza

Production assistance
Victor Hugo Oliveira Santiago

Free School for Harm Reduction
Cibelly Silva, Larissa Karla, Virgílio Vasconcelos

Sound design and mixing
Guga S. Rocha

Soundtrack
Homero Basílio

Color correction
Fábio da Costa

Graphic design
Priscila Gonzaga

2nd camera unit
Tiago Calazans

Photography and still assistant
Vito Carvalho

DIT
Victoria Drahomiro

Head of machinery and electrical
Milton Torres

Machinery and Electrical Assistant
Fernando Marinho, Bruno Miranda Ramos

Still
Emanuel da Costa

Costume
Babi Jácome

Stagehand
Bryan

Cakes and animals
Cristiano Lenhardt

Drivers
Paulinho, Alessandro (Dinho), Severino Gomes

Catering
Armazém do Campo (MST)

Safety
Pitbull Segurança

Radio rental
Livre Acesso

Equipments
Cabra Quente

Special thanks to
Abrigo Noturno Irmã Dulce, Autarquia de Manutenção e Limpeza Urbana do Recife – EMLURB, Escola Livre De Redução De Danos, Anamaria, Carneiro (Escola Livre), Arturo Escobar (Escola Livre), Fran Silva (Escola Livre), Priscilla Gadelha (Escola Livre), Rafael West (Escola Livre), JEA Laboratório De Análises Clínicas, João Paulo, Malu Moraes, Maria Helena Alcântara, Movimento dos Trabalhadores Rurais Sem Terra (MST Brasil), Movimento População de Rua de Pernambuco, Padre Julio Lancelotti, Paulo Mansan, Programa Consultório na Rua, Rafael Oliveira, Secretaria de Defesa Social de Pernambuco, Vó Nalva, Beatrice Bulgari, Alessandro Rabottini, Alessia Carlino, Bianca Stoppani, Paola Ugolini, Ana Maria Maia, Cristina Gouvêa, Cristina Fino, Marília Nepomuceno, Tita, Vanessa Barbosa

Commissioned and produced by
Fondazione In Between Art Film

This film was created with the participation of a cast of homeless non-professional actors who live in the city center of Recife, Brazil

Recife, Brazil 2022

Courtesy of the artist, Galleria Continua, Galeria Nara Roesler, and Fondazione In Between Art Film

Heart of the Street

Bruno Carvalho and Ana Laura Malmaceda

First, we see a tree against the bright sky and a superimposed diagram referencing the parts of a house. We are in an urban park. There is a street in the background. Public spaces in traditional urbanism could function as extensions of domestic space. Someone sits on a bench. The birds we hear might make a home out of the branches. A shaker plays over the breeze. The world seems to be in harmony; a vast, shared living room. We cut to the image of a white heron, with an ominous sonic cue. Not so fast—the bird appears set to launch after a fish. This is an adaptable species, widespread in urban Brazil. This is not just an innocent still life. It cannot be, with the metallic drums. It cannot be, in the modern world we have built. There is always more than meets the eye. As the opening shot pans down, the diagram includes underground roots. We read a list of values and qualities that sustain life. Some shape it: energy, strength, desire, commitment, hunger, openness, rights. Others give the world meaning: place, laziness, delight, embrace, madness, play, grace.

The tree as a diagram had been how Augusto Boal explained the Theatre of the Oppressed. It is rooted in solidarity, supporting the trunk of concrete intervention, creating a canopy that projects onto the future an ongoing revolution toward greater justice. Most of us do not know much about this park, at the outset. The film is called *Olho da Rua*—its literal translation would be "eye of the street." In Brazil, the idiomatic expression can denote the condition of being jobless: to be cast out onto the eye of the street. The eye might be observers, society, or in this case, the camera. Street is a metonymy for the city. We see an urban space that could be in any Brazilian town or metropolis. We know where it could not be. Such public spaces, sites of spontaneous or curated encounters between people of all stripes, slipped through the cracks of modernist dreams. The urbanist Le Corbusier had called for "the death of the streets" in the 1930s. He argued that streets and parks like these were obsolete, that highways could be more efficient, avoiding unproductive and unseemly mixtures. Le Corbusier had many disciples in Brazil. These images are in fact filmed in the Praça do Hipódromo, part of a neighborhood in Recife surrounded by tower in the park-style developments. They have enclosed, private open spaces and parking garages.

These images are from Jonathas de Andrade's work *Olho da Rua* [Out Loud] (2022), where he stages and films a drama in his hometown, Recife. There is a plural milieu that we are going to see, which also pervades much of his art. It is always, in his work, both milieux and universe, local and global. In *Eu, mestiço* [Me, Mestizo] (2017), he subverted eugenicist tropes in postwar studies of race in rural Brazil. *O Peixe* [The Fish] (2016) pushed the boundaries of connections between humans and fish. His art walks the razor's edge. It can cut toward misery or joy, histories or futures, commonalities or stratification, document or imagination, agency or control, coexistence or violence. Yet, Andrade's protagonists are consistently those pushed out of circuits of power.

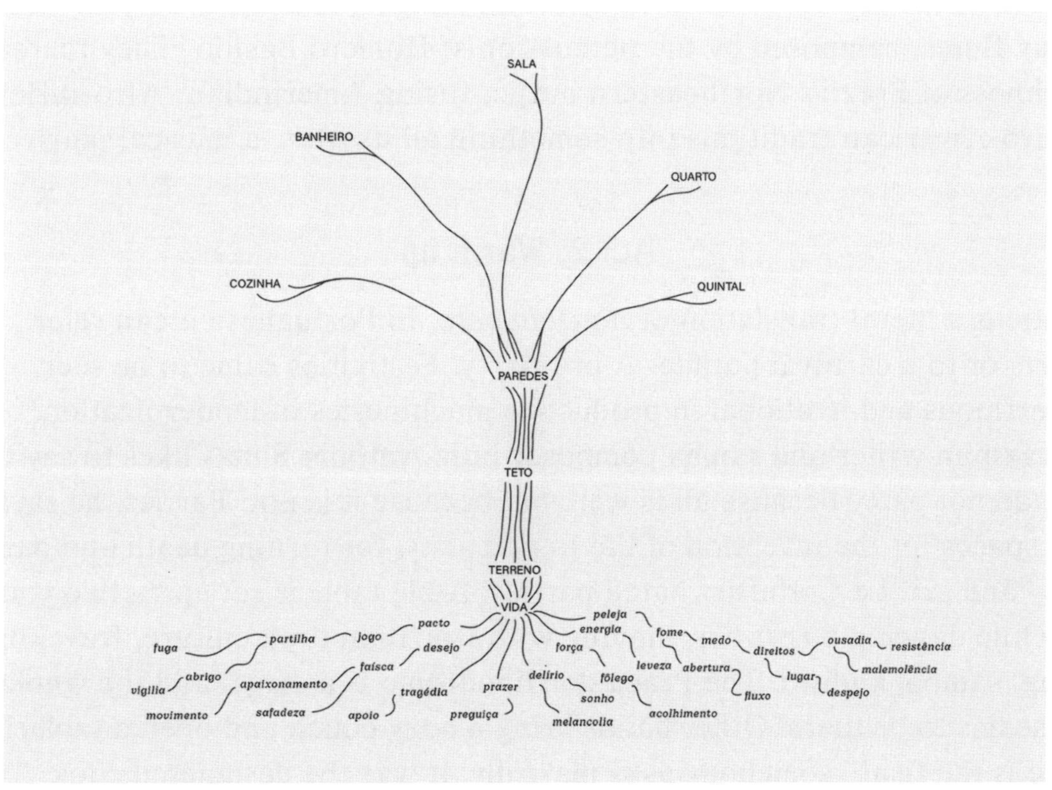

Act 1: Prismatic

The language of beautification and embellishment permeated transatlantic urban discourse when this neighborhood first developed in the nineteenth century. City planners and their lettered circles absorbed scientific racism and Eurocentric norms about beauty. Associations between Afro-inflected cultures and ugliness, dirtiness, and backwardness tightened. Yet, from the ground up, this city reflects the people that made it. Sometimes, in spite of who it had been made for. They contemplate their own beauty in the mirror. They were not supposed to be beautiful, back then. Or even in the picture. But here we are. Smiles, intimacy, flirtation out loud.

Imagining a way out of the project of killing the streets leads to the question "What is life?" These images touch the political body of a street; they show paths that could always be dangerous for those who cannot be seen as fully human (and beautiful) by technocrats, oligarchs, and so on. Instead of projecting fear, a mirror in the middle of a park becomes a crossroad between fiction and possibilities of affection. A woman's eyes play with the performance of seeing and being seen in her own image, reflected through the open camera lenses. Desire and recognition felt like an equal right. A prismatic act: when the hunger to see and be seen makes way for the pleasures of living in plentifulness. We are immersed in the sounds of congas, djembes, bongos, shakes, seeds, clay drums, and clay flutes, composed by the percussionist Homero Basílio. They recreate the richness of Brazil's Northeastern music, fusing Amerindian, Afro-inflected, and Euro-American traditions into something all its own, a musical pluriverse.

Act 2: Warm up

This title is a literal translation of *aquecimento*. In Portuguese it can refer to sports or to a carnival parade. A pre-party. Festivities came to be seen as superfluous and irrational in productive machineries of modernization. The Brazilian writer and samba composer Luiz Antônio Simas likes to say that people do not party because all is well, but because it is not. Parties, he says, create spaces for the invention of life in precarity, for turning death and pain into joy and art. Le Corbusier hated parties. A big table is set up by two young men, while dancing *passinhos*, moving with Brazilian funk culture, frevo, break dancing, samba, kuduro. The Praça do Hipódromo is a stage, and the whole world seems to be there. Other hands bring a cozy couch and open a tablecloth. "Where is the fish?" somebody asks playfully. It was the designated cook. "Still being fished?," comes the worn-out punchline. The fisherman laughs along with his rod and sexual innuendo, playing a part in the great communal drama. The classical guitar, portable speakers, and cake all arrive. The party is warming up. "Today it's just party and joy," someone hopes.

Act 3: Community

It has heated up now, with frenzied dancing. Utensils become percussive instruments. We hear Brazilian pop music, bringing bodies together. The sounds and food are shared. They belong to no one and to everyone at the same time—perhaps the best definition of the commons, or of public spaces. Somebody serves a local soda called Viva, which means Hurray, Live, or Alive. Somebody else says over the lyrics: "It's the violence of a plate with no food." This is humanity at its most serious. We celebrate not because all is well and the world is just, but to renew our commitments to each other, to life. A community that struggles together parties together, when it can. From the hodgepodge, a chant emerges: "It's the street." "The street is us, and will always be," as a refrain from rapper Emicida puts it. Le Corbusier rolls in his grave, but who cares?

Act 4: Full life

In the original, *natureza farta*. Abundant nature. Nature might be so, but it hangs by a thread. Its diversity is as wide as the concepts we make out of it. Dominant modern understandings assume humans to be in opposition to nature. Nature as the nonhuman. Western art has a longstanding interest in *vanitas*, which gave us vanity. In the representation of still life, nature was captured in order to show the transience of bodies, the futility of pleasure, the certainty of death. That Christian imaginary is set aside from the table, maybe overcome by something less morbid: the crab and fowls move. We see the diverse shapes of yams, collard greens, and freshly picked carrots creating another visual and conceptual frame for nature: full, alive, in motion. Like cinema.

Gathered by many hands, the harvest displays colors, textures, artfulness. Agogos, a reco-reco, and drumbeats suggest the atmospheres of Afro-Brazilian religions, like Candomblé, Jurema, or Xangô de Pernambuco. There is a deliberateness in the placing, as if these are offerings. The screen is a canvas, and art resignifies. If that guineafowl had been a pet, it is now food, or sacred. This is widely known in Brazil as *galinha-d'angola*, Angolan chicken. No other country has been shaped as much by the African diaspora. Around 4.8 million enslaved people arrived in the ports of Brazil, to cities like Recife—as many as 45 percent of those taken as captives to the "New World." Brazil was the last country in the Americas to abolish slavery, in 1888. The abundant collard green leaves and the religious legacies can remind us of the full lives behind systems that tried to reduce nature to commodity, and people to property. Cinema, like ritual, can translate material elements to the realm of the sacred, and vice versa. The fowl on the tablecloth and screen is known as *Etù* in Candomblé. It is an entity of connection to deities (*orixás*), a medium between life and death in their intermittent cycles. Full life, pointing toward meanings beyond what meets the eye.

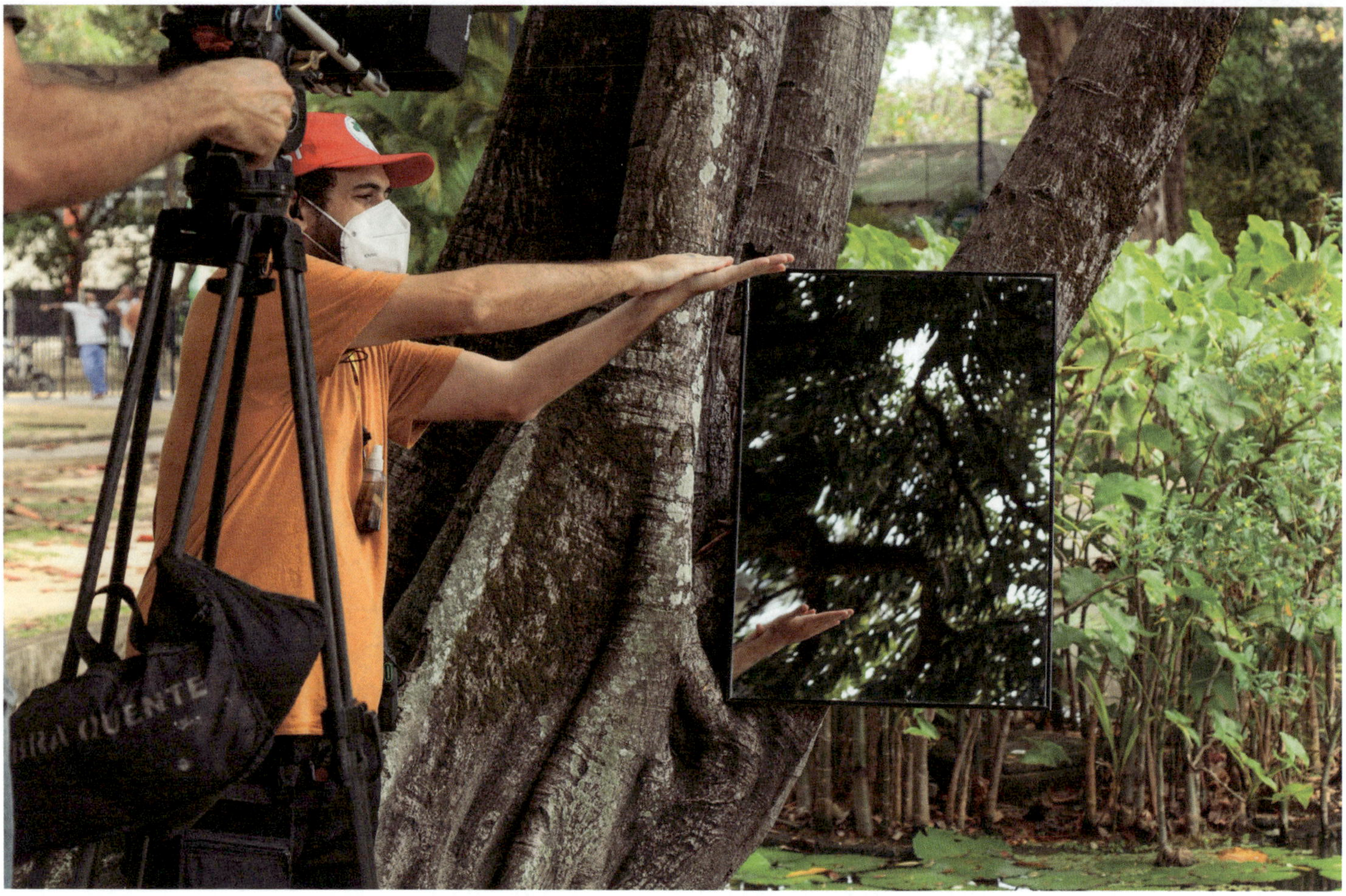

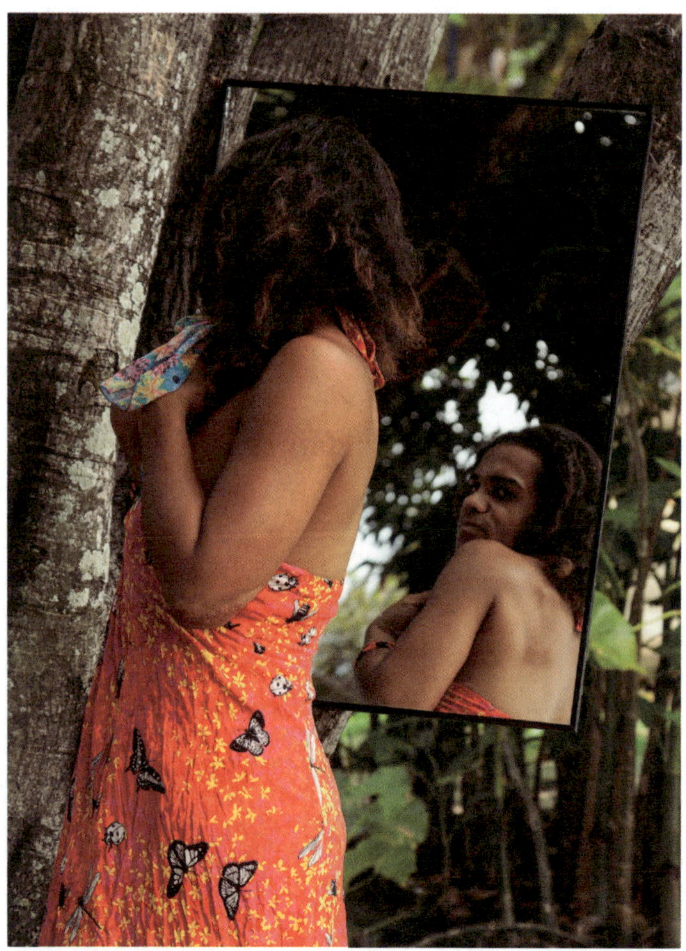

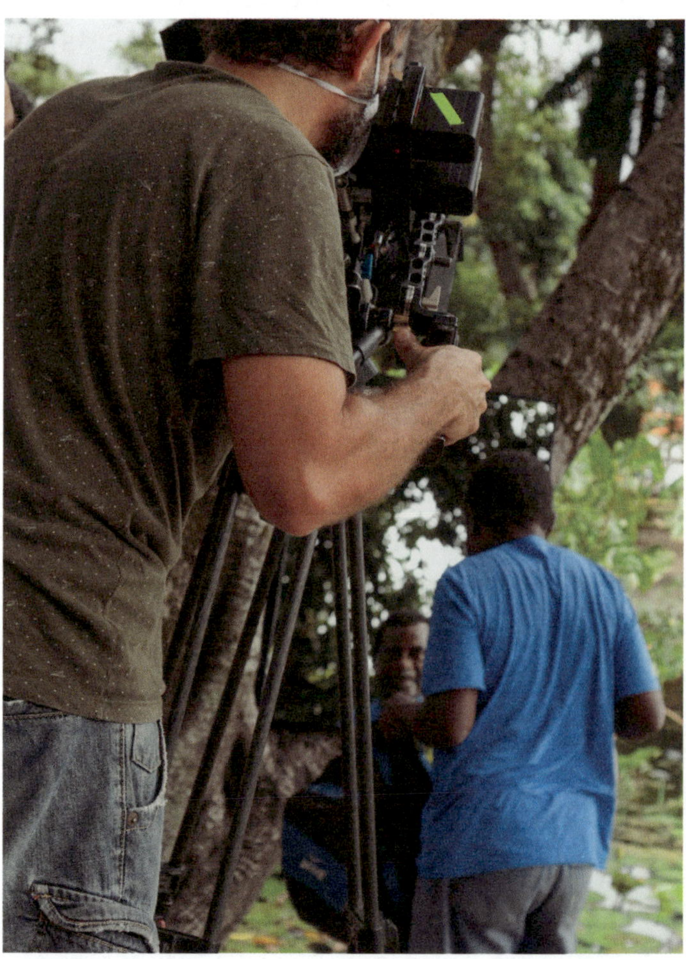

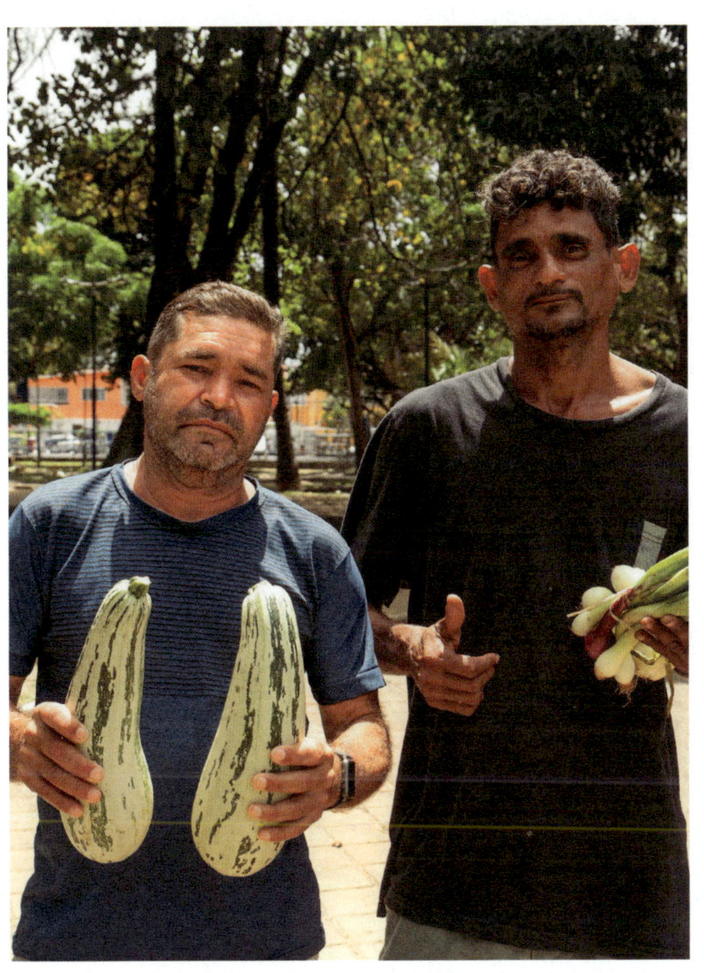

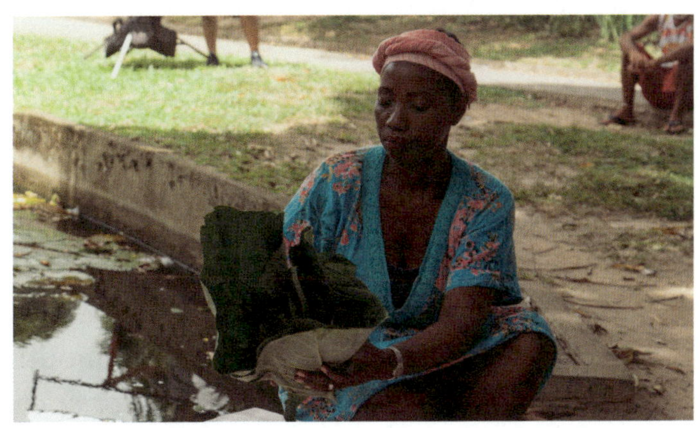

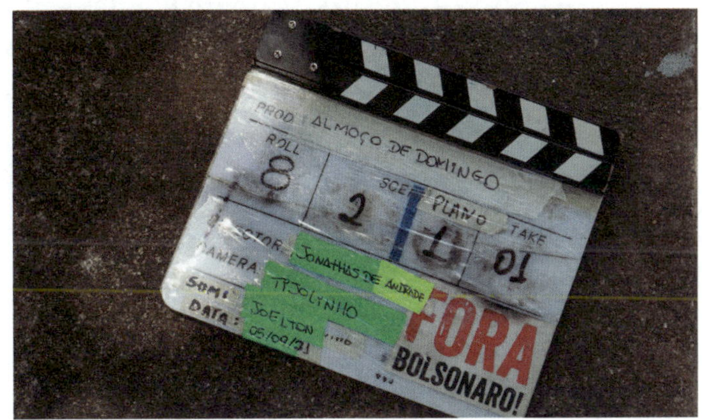
PROD ALMOÇO DE DOMINGO
ROLL
8
2
PLANO
1
TAKE
01
CAMERA
JONATHAS DE ANDRADE
SOM
TIJOLINHO
DATA
JOELTON
05/09/21
FORA
BOLSONARO!

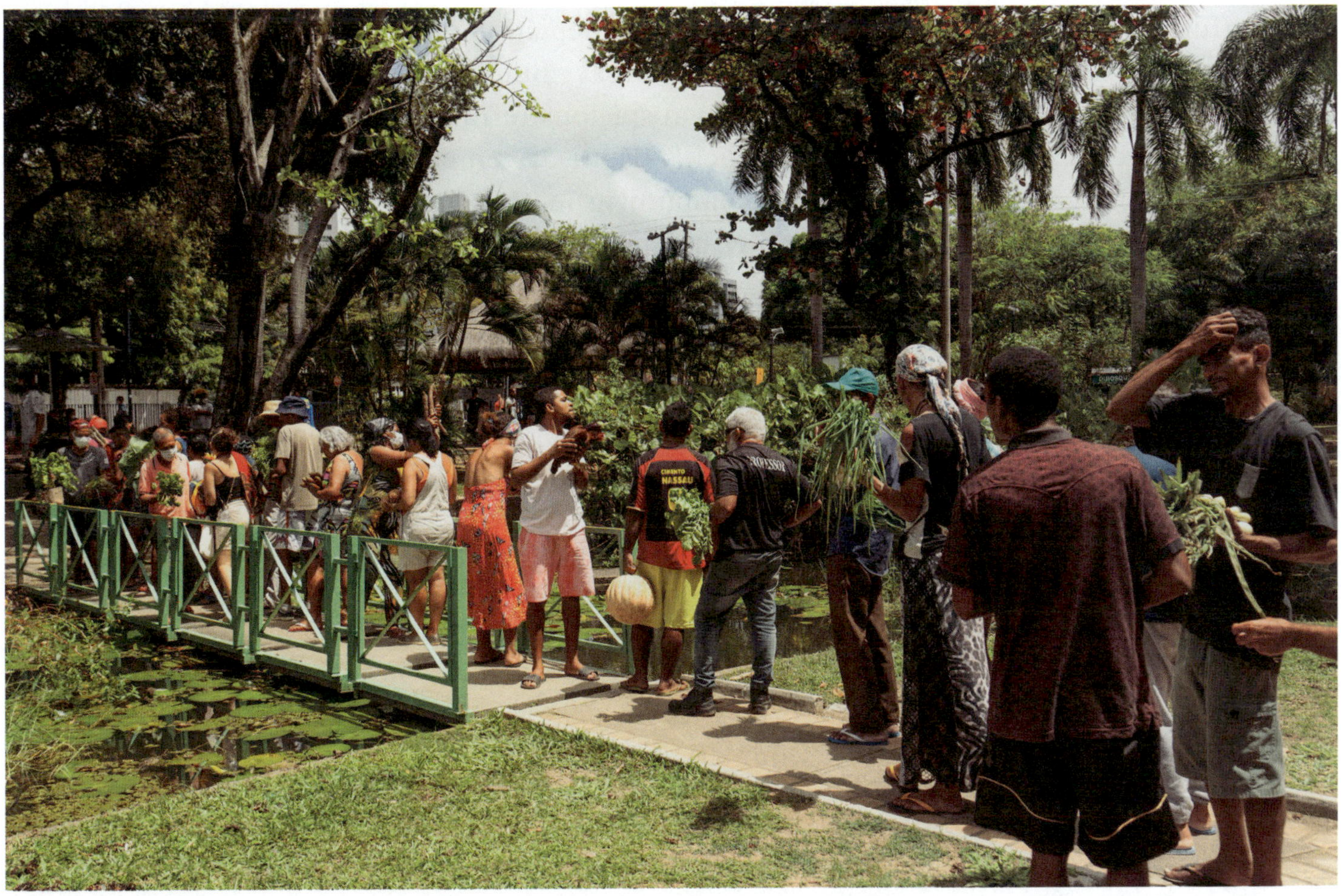

Act 5: Mouthful

In the original, *boca cheia*, full mouth. The phrase can denote a boastful attitude. Rice and beans run inside a zoomed-in mouthful of satisfaction, suggesting that the work of art metabolizes into something else. We see plates passed from hand to hand, utensils from hand to mouth, cameras from mouth to mouth. In the background, a brash and tender speaker shifts without missing a beat from denouncing a low salary to asking for her soda: "Love, come my gorgeous, mama waits for you." No reason to think she speaks to her son. Now unashamedly devoured, nature transforms itself into action through the body, and on film. We see more mouths than eyes. Chewing, swallowing, smiling. That same voice refers to someone else: "She is community ... That one is a warrior." The ultimate compliment. Marriage comes up. Eating is sexual. In Brazil, the languages of food and sex are never far apart. We eavesdrop. Small talk is abundant. Life goes on.

Act 6: Bellyfull

In Portuguese, *bucho cheio.* This is an idiomatic expression for being satiated, common in Brazil's Northeast, in which the stomach is compared to the intestines of other animals. There is no futility in a *bucho cheio.* There's the fulfillment of necessity and pleasure in this depiction of eating. Under the shade of canopies, as birds sing, it's time for a break. But life goes on. Someone raps to the beats of Carioca funk, with an auspicious refrain, "*Fora Bolsonaro*" [Out Bolsonaro]. There is no rest with such a death-driven president. But there can be no enduring struggle without community, poetry, improvization, and joy. One of the men sings while another beatboxes, under encouragement: "We are here on the street, we have ..." This verse fizzles. But it brings to mind a popular proverb: "The voice of the streets is the voice of God." If this is an MC battle, they call out the more powerful but lesser performer: "He's on television to move up in the polls, but everyone knows he is a fraud."

Another man holds a worn-out book—*Não Erre Mais* [Stop Making Mistakes]. This work promises to teach readers the erudite version of the Portuguese language, so they can sound educated. The interlocutor responds: "I don't know how to read." The one holding the book points out the thumb up on the cover. The title becomes practical life advice. "*Vamo simbora*," he says, in a delicious and colloquial version of the formal *vamos embora*, "let's go." The author would roll over in his grave at this grammatic betrayal, but who cares.

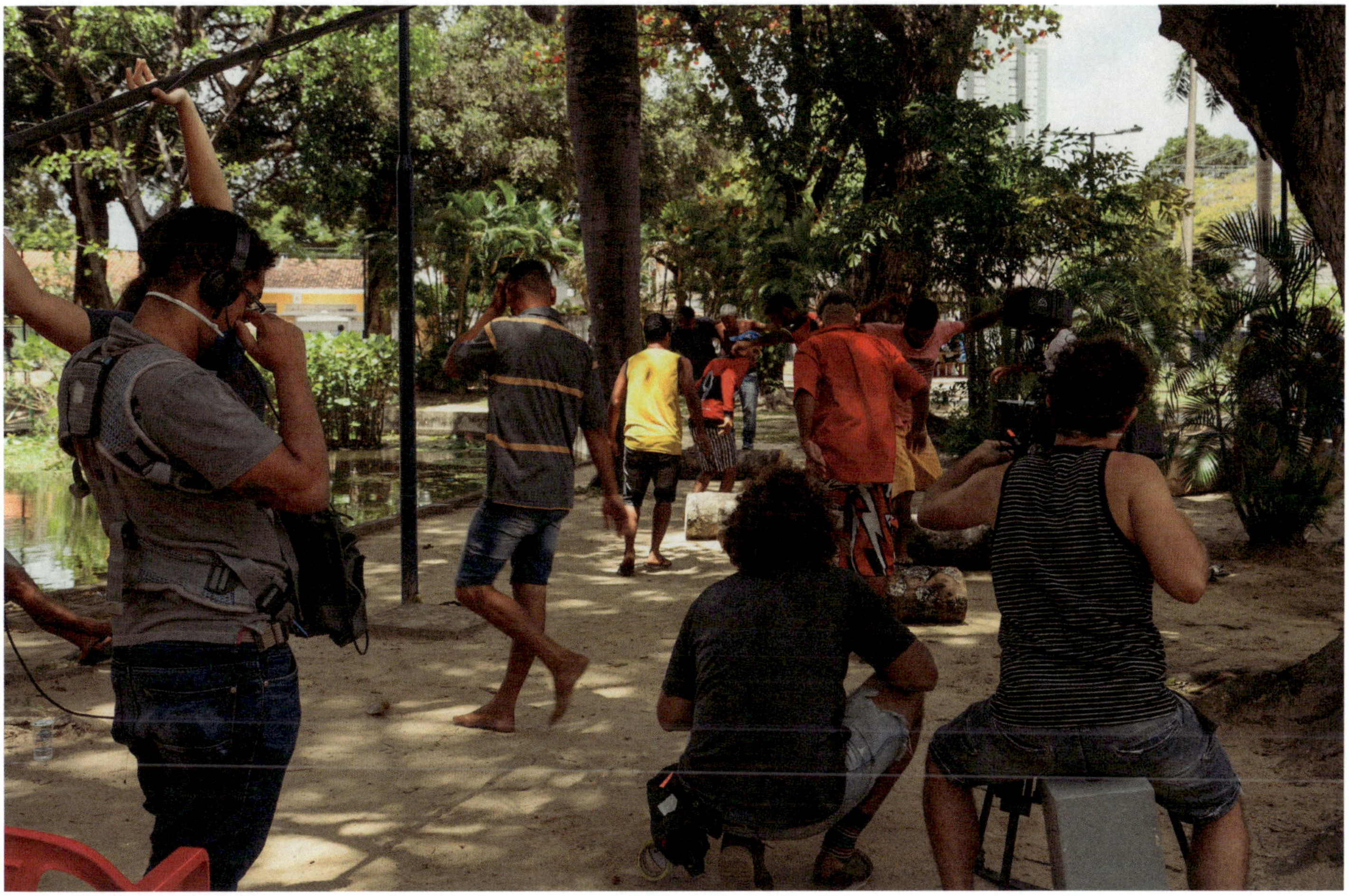

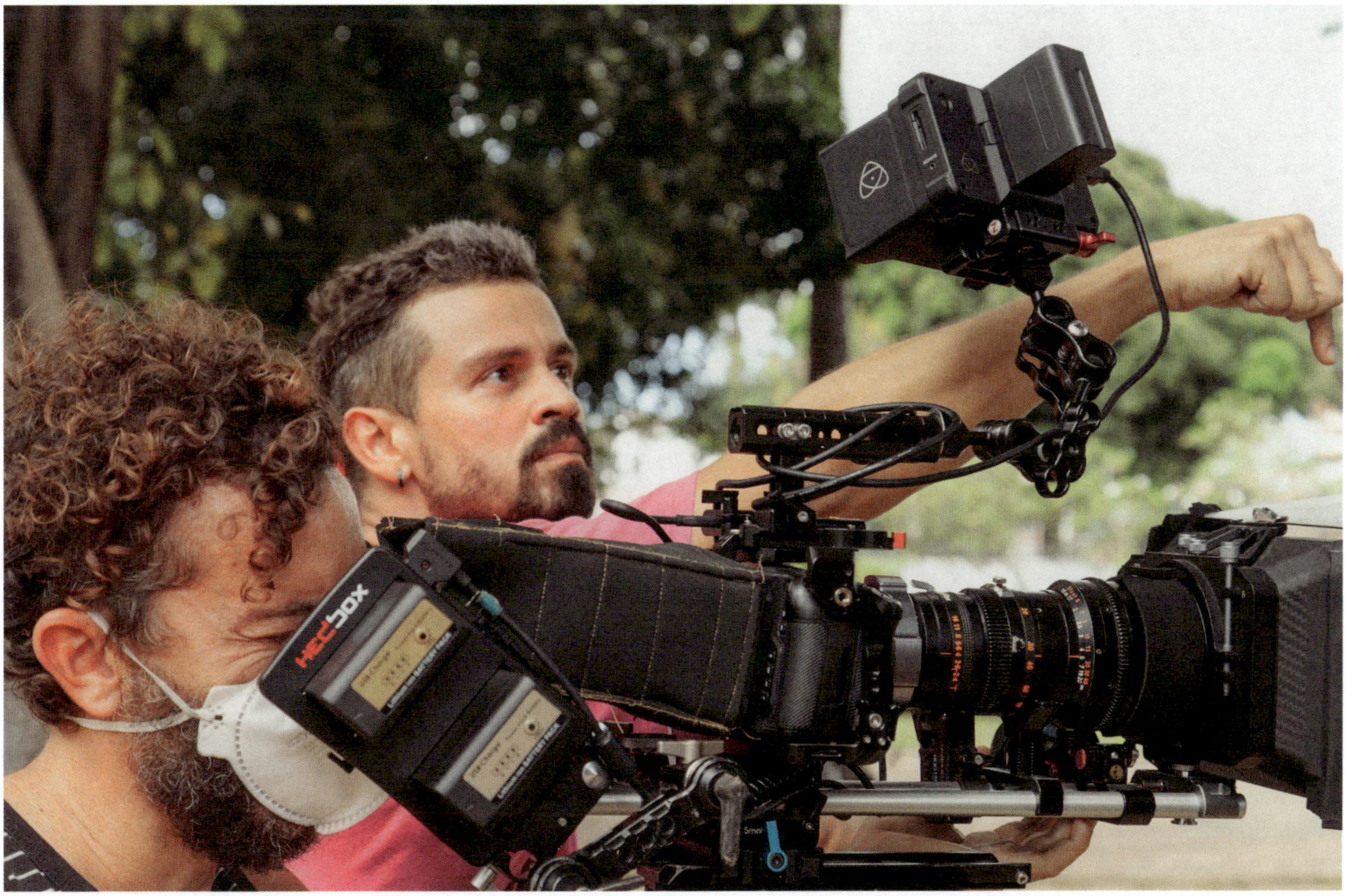

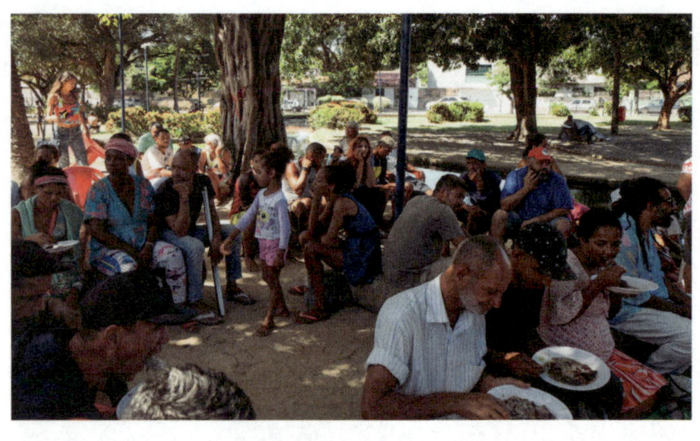

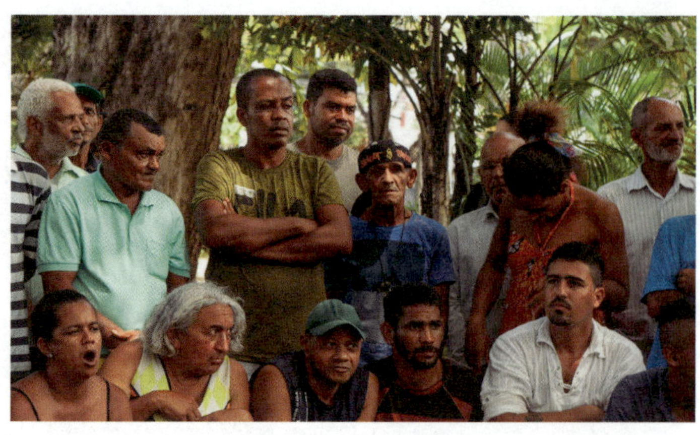

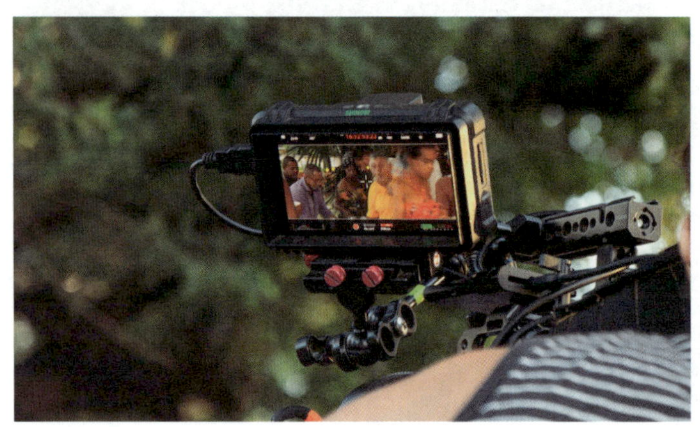

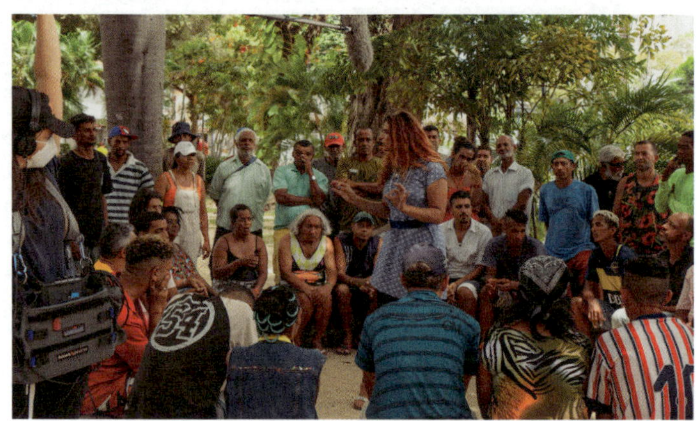

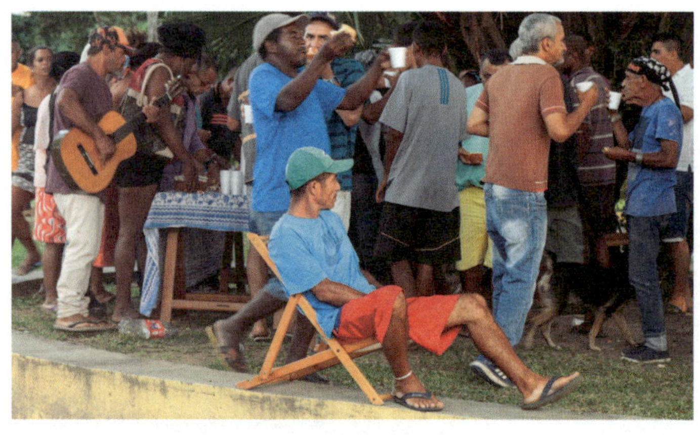

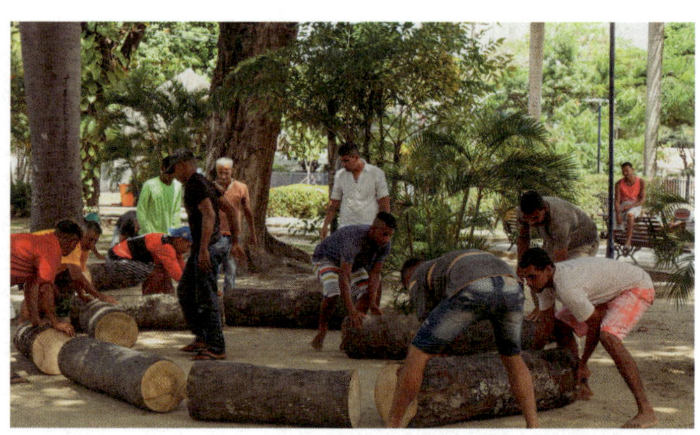

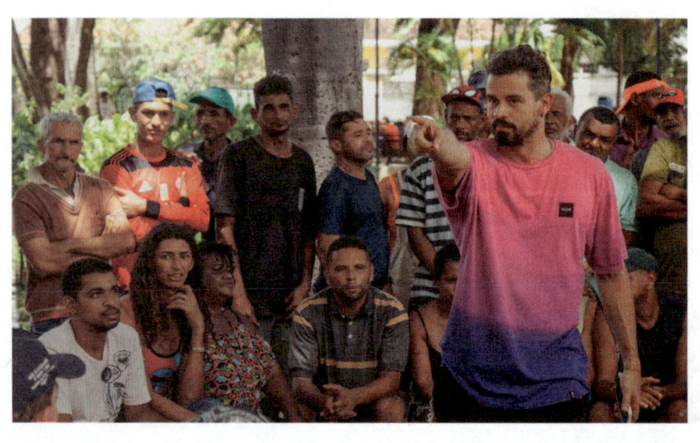

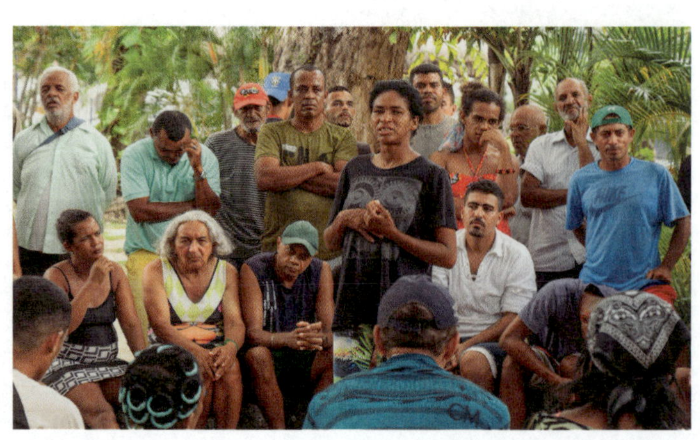

The man complains: "You only think of community." Others nap, some wake up. We hear samba, and an accelerated pace. Another scene of nature in transformation: log rolling, trees turned into seats.

Act 7: Out loud

In Portuguese, *boca livre*, literally "free mouth." A *boca livre* is not quite a metaphor. The expression refers to an event: it requires a physical presence, and a certain disposition. It might be used to describe somewhere where free food is being served. Here, we see it transform itself. Out loud, on-screen, there is a space where freedom of expression meets visibility. The tree trunks become a *roda*, a forum around a circle, another structure inspired by Boal's theater. Each person has a place to express what should be heard by all. Someone asks for "respect for all Black women" and asserts the humanity of drug users: "They are not dogs." Others speak against war, fascism, sexism, and anti-trans violence, laying out an ethic of solidarity and care. They chant age-old rallying cries, and some specific to these times: "The people are on the streets / Bolsonaro it's your fault!"

There is a sense of joy in their collective indignation, a contrast to the affective misery of online activism. There is hunger for life. Someone with a non-Brazilian accent says: "You, who are listening to me, do not need to look at me with bad eyes: embrace, welcome, and do not punish." The street is a metonymy of a country of mixtures and inequalities, traumas and aspirations. As someone calls for a group hug, another states: "This is our Brazil." They chant: "Street, street, street." The park's manicured pond, made to be looked at, becomes the site/sight for the party's culmination: bodies splashing on the waters.

Act 8: Eye to eye

Boal used to say that to make theater is to dominate one's pain, to be an agent of resistance instead of a victim. The Theatre of the Oppressed stages a collective struggle in which the itinerant actor bridges different opinions in a given group of people, recreating scenes of responses to communal issues. Representation becomes a shared creation, a dialogue instead of an evangelizing or sanctimonious monologue. It is reflected collectively through the sensorial and political bodies. This living theater questions how we regard others, and seeks to transform colonial or modern gazes that reduce people to inferior conditions based on gender, race, class, language, looks, and so on.

The Theatre of the Oppressed asks actors to give unrestricted access to their eyes, exercising the full openness of the gaze as an ethos. The last shot pans left in slow motion, showing the actors of *Olho da rua*. A still portrait is proposed by the camera, each person frozen in their chosen poses. This goes against the tradition of ethnographic or scientific representation, in which bodies were staged by the photographer's direction, catalogued and classified in taxonomic systems. Here each person gets to say goodbye, leaving a gesture to the camera's eyes and a moment of contact with their eyes. Vital connections are made and registered. Closed fists, kisses, thumbs-ups, peace signs, a salute to show respect. There are soccer jerseys, a T-shirt for the heavy metal band Slipknot, and another that reads "LGBTphobia is a crime, This Struggle is Ours." Performances of authenticity and authentic performances, with no meaningful line between documentary and fiction, life and theater, politics and affect.

Among the cast of cocreators listed in the film credits, there are multiple people called "Silva." This surname is a type of metonym for the world of *Olho da Rua*: the Northeast, favelas, popular parties, public parks, or street life. And the dignity and potentials of this Brazil, in turn, can be understood as a metonym for planetary futures. However the Brazil of Silvas goes, so will also go the health of ecosystems, social fabric, cultural effervescence. Streets have refused to die. May their life renew the possibilities for greater tomorrows.

Images from the backstage of *Olho da Rua* by Jonathas de Andrade.
Courtesy of the artist.

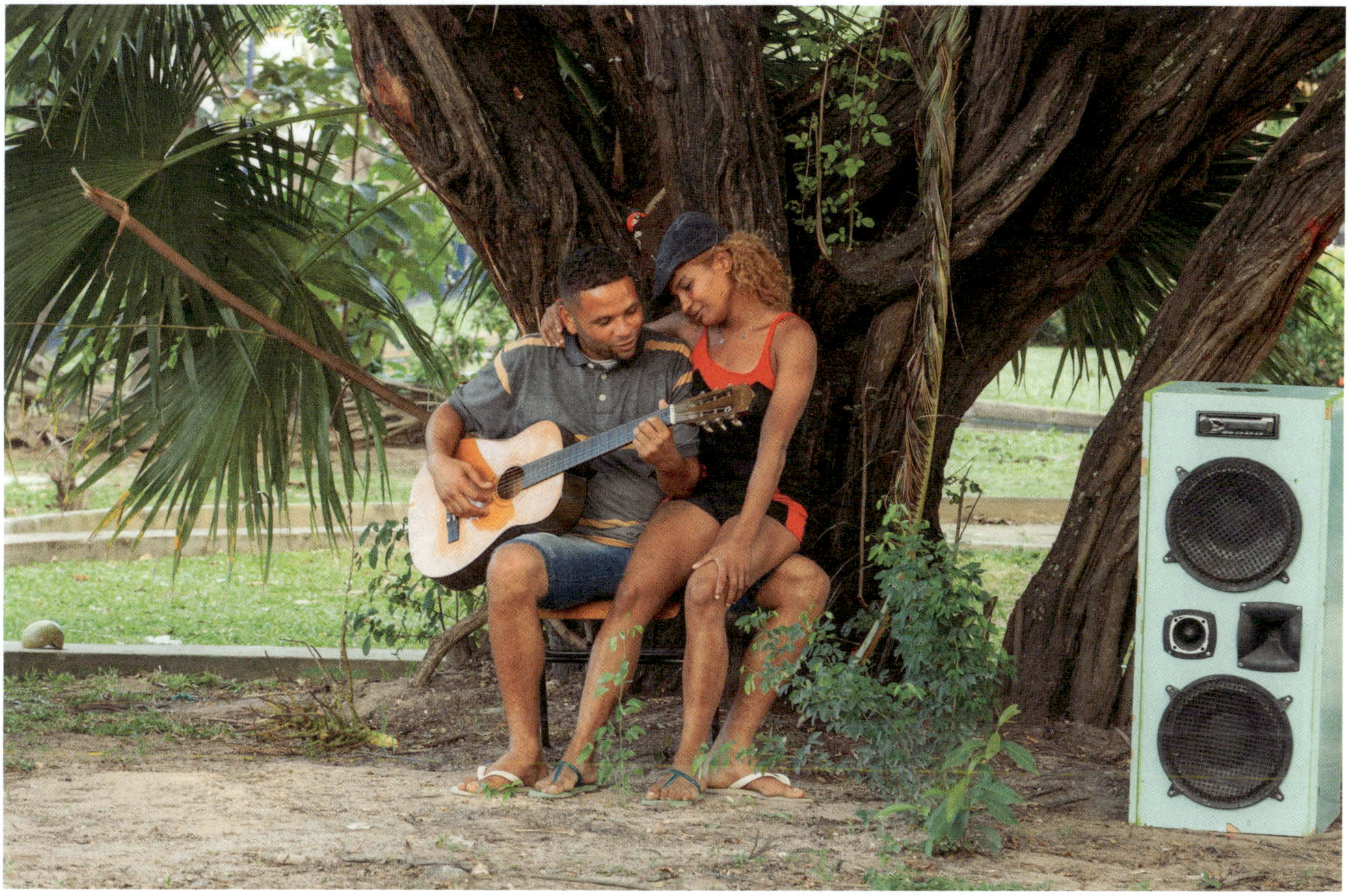

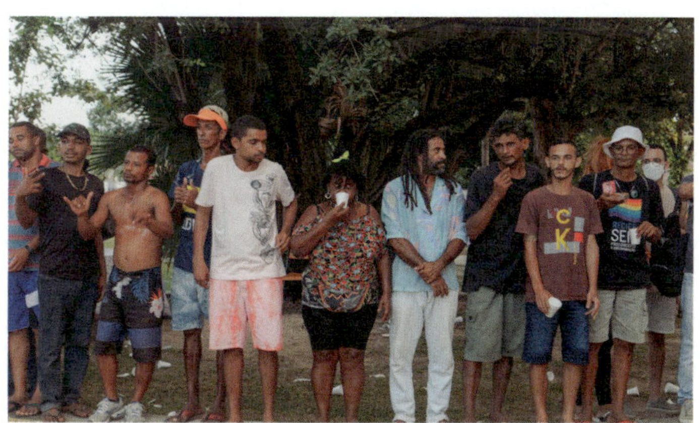

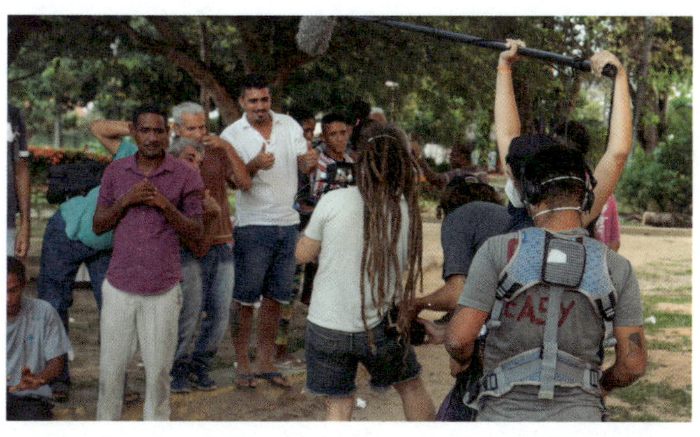
EASY

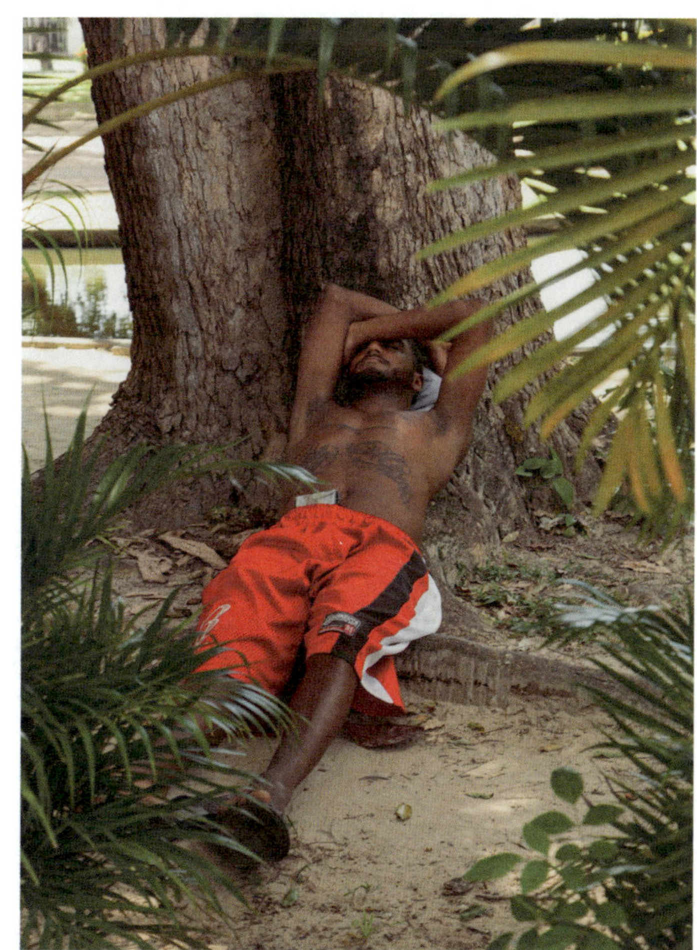

AZIZ HAZARA

TAKBIR

2022, HD digital video, color, 5.1 surround sound, 9'58"

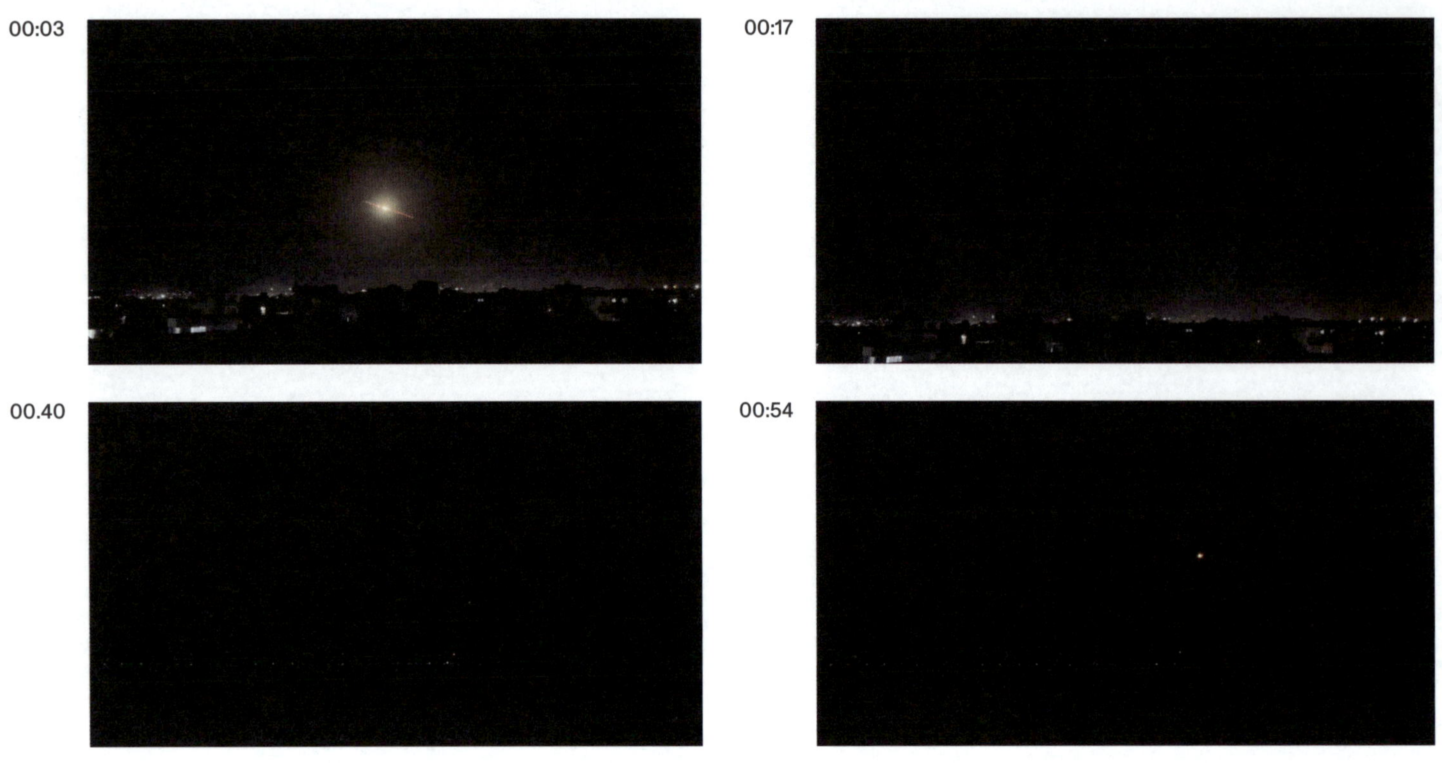

Takbir by Aziz Hazara (b. 1992, Afghanistan) observes darkness and light, sound and silence as perceptual and metaphorical devices to dissect the transformations brought about by the War on Terror. It conjures the beauty of a busy city like Kabul—its buildings and streets buzzing with life and glimmering in the night—with the cruel consequences of normalized violence. In this context, which is part of the lasting material

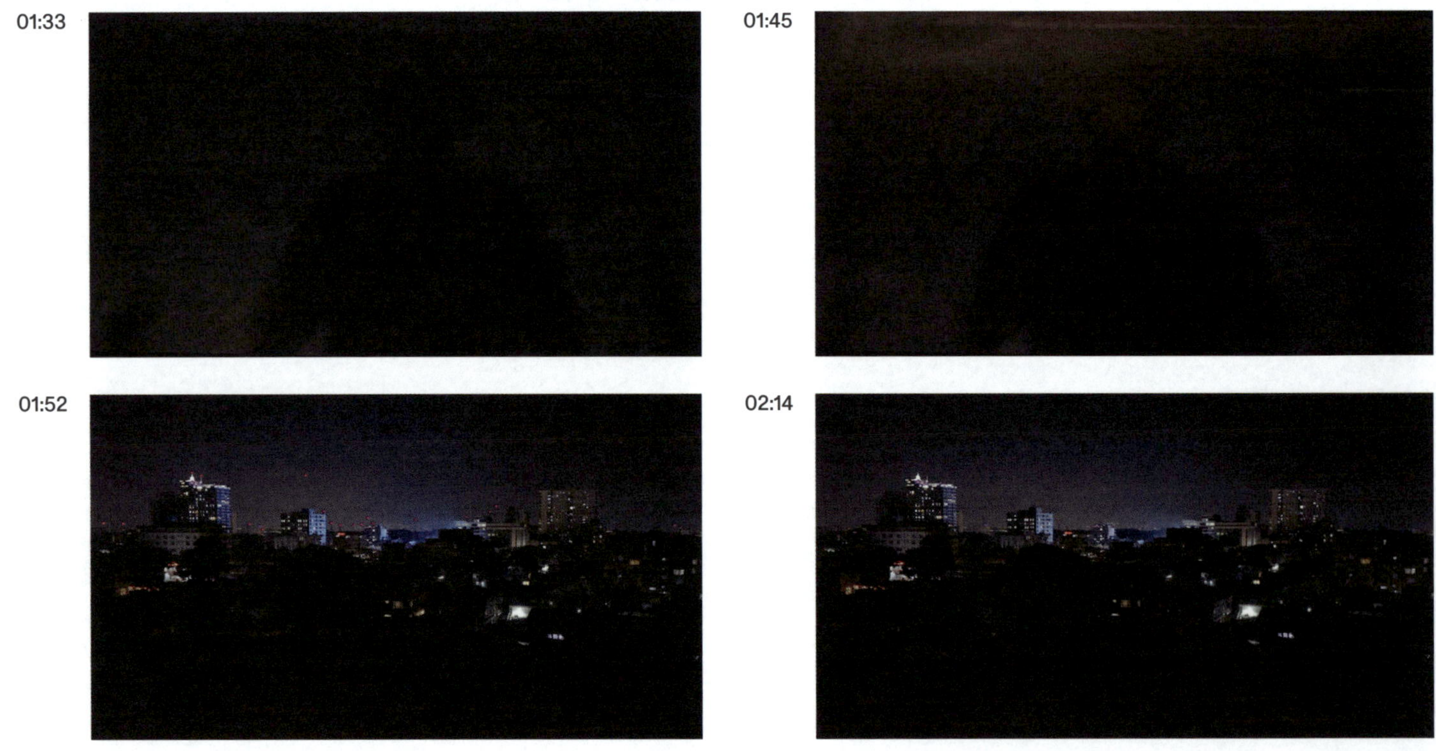

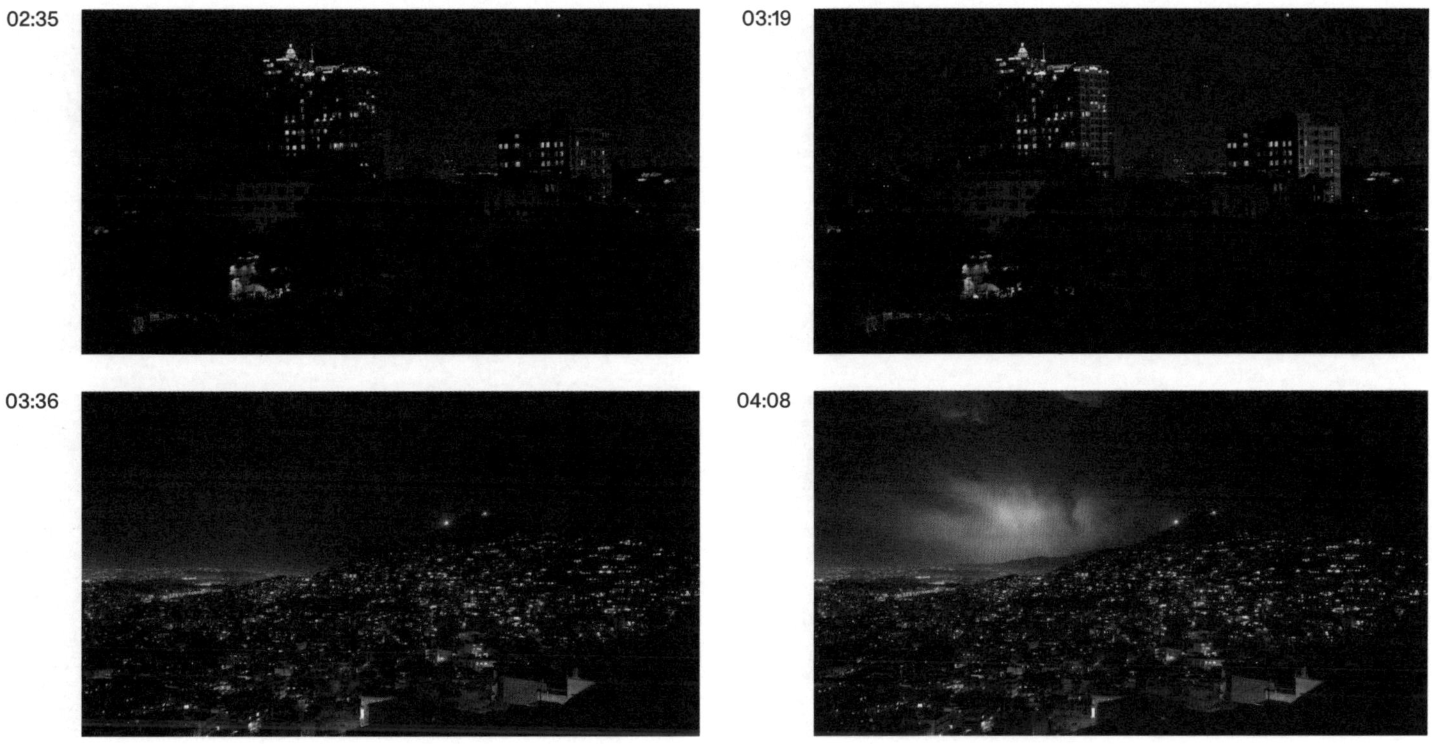

and cultural legacies of Afghanistan's foreign occupations, it is not easy to distinguish a firework from a military flare, a paper lantern from a surveillance balloon floating in the sky. The video has its metaphorical starting point in the 1980s, when the residents of Kabul used the darkness of the night as a space to protest against the ongoing Soviet occupation. As soon as the USSR withdrew from Afghanistan in 1989,

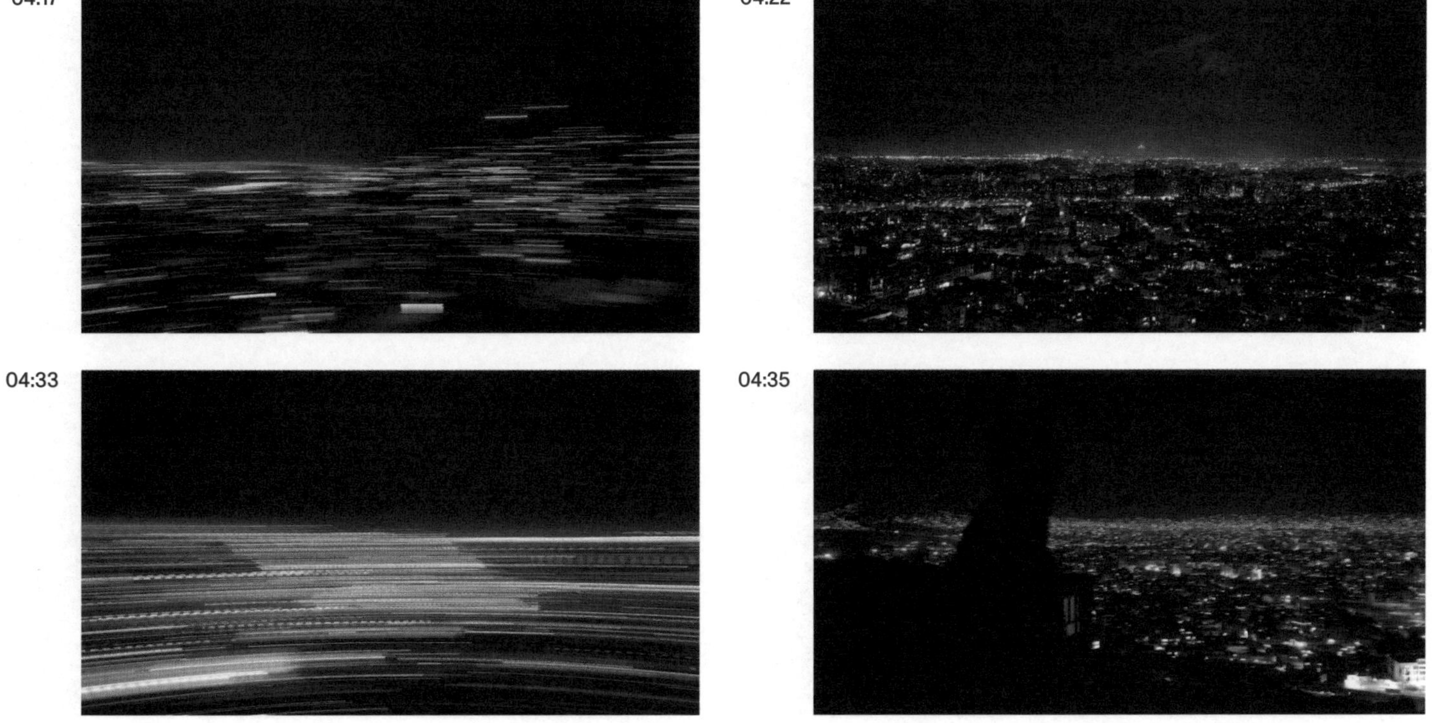

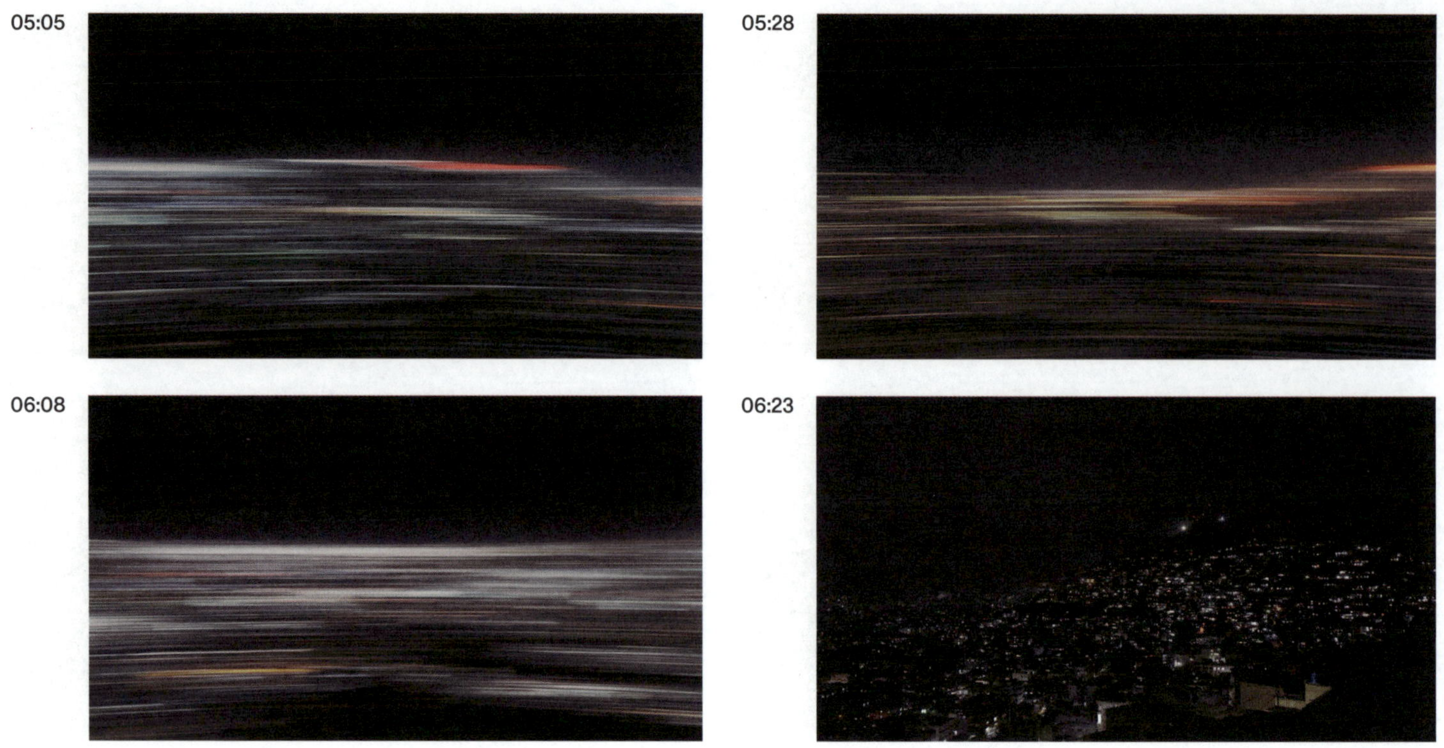

thirty-two years of guerrilla warfare began across the country. *Takbir* establishes a connection between that turbulent period in the history of Afghanistan with the end of the more recent US-led NATO invasion of the country in 2021, when the residents of Kabul once again went on their rooftops and shouted the Takbir: they chanted *Allah-u akbar* as a collective reclamation of space in the darkness. The artist brings

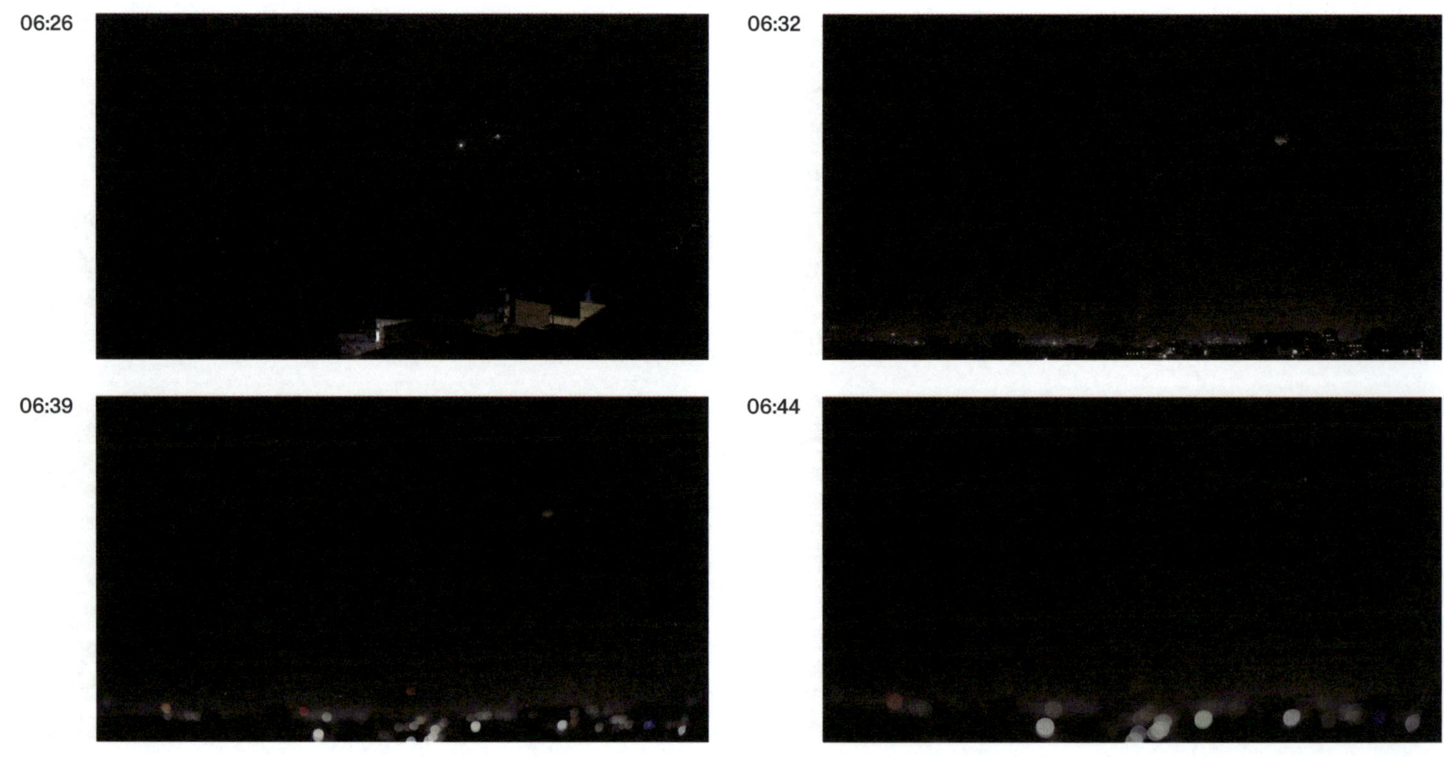

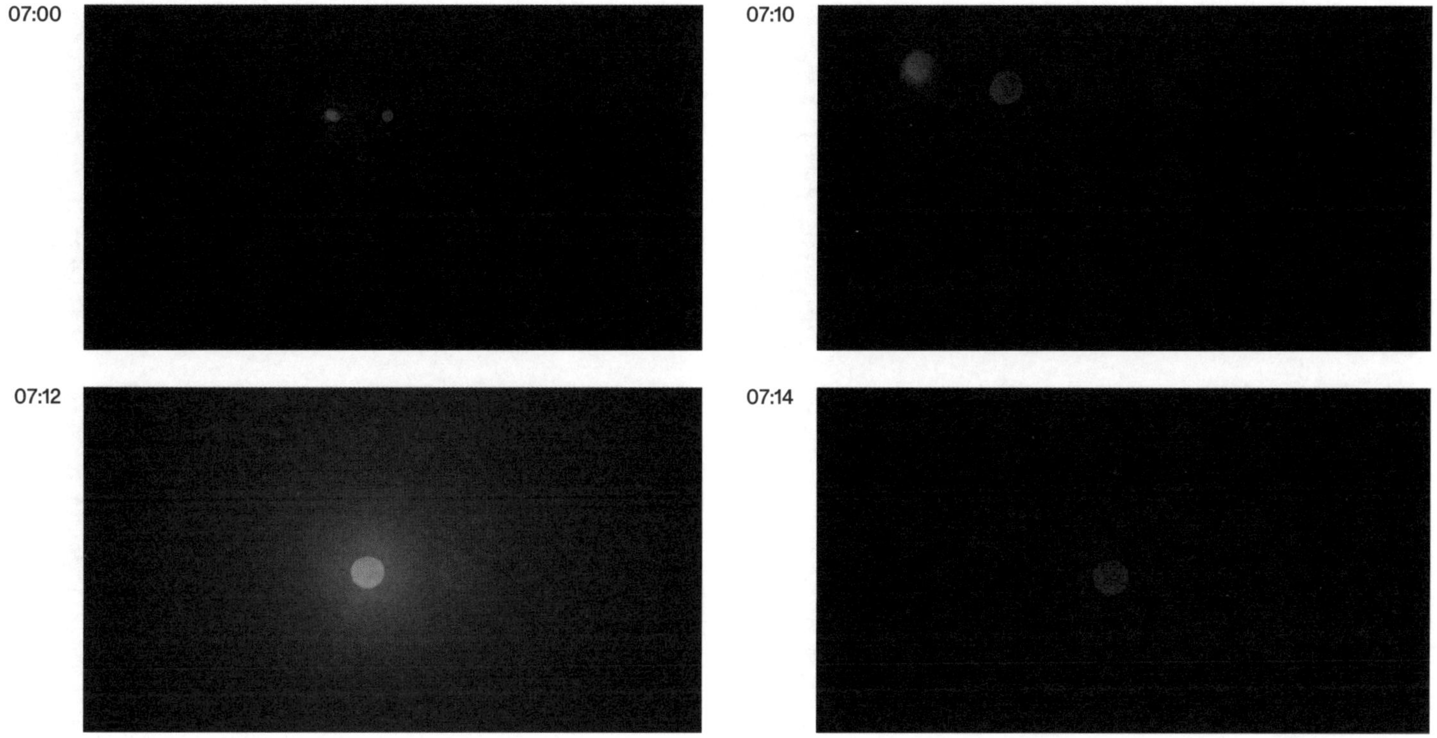

this sonic act of defiance into a powerfully disorienting scene where the lights of Kabul start spinning together with the voices of men, women and children around the viewer. Then the lights go out, the image gets blurry, and their voices are replaced by Haqani Naat songs that celebrate Jihad culture and praise those suicide bombers who committed bombings in Kabul. The video attends to the affective complexity

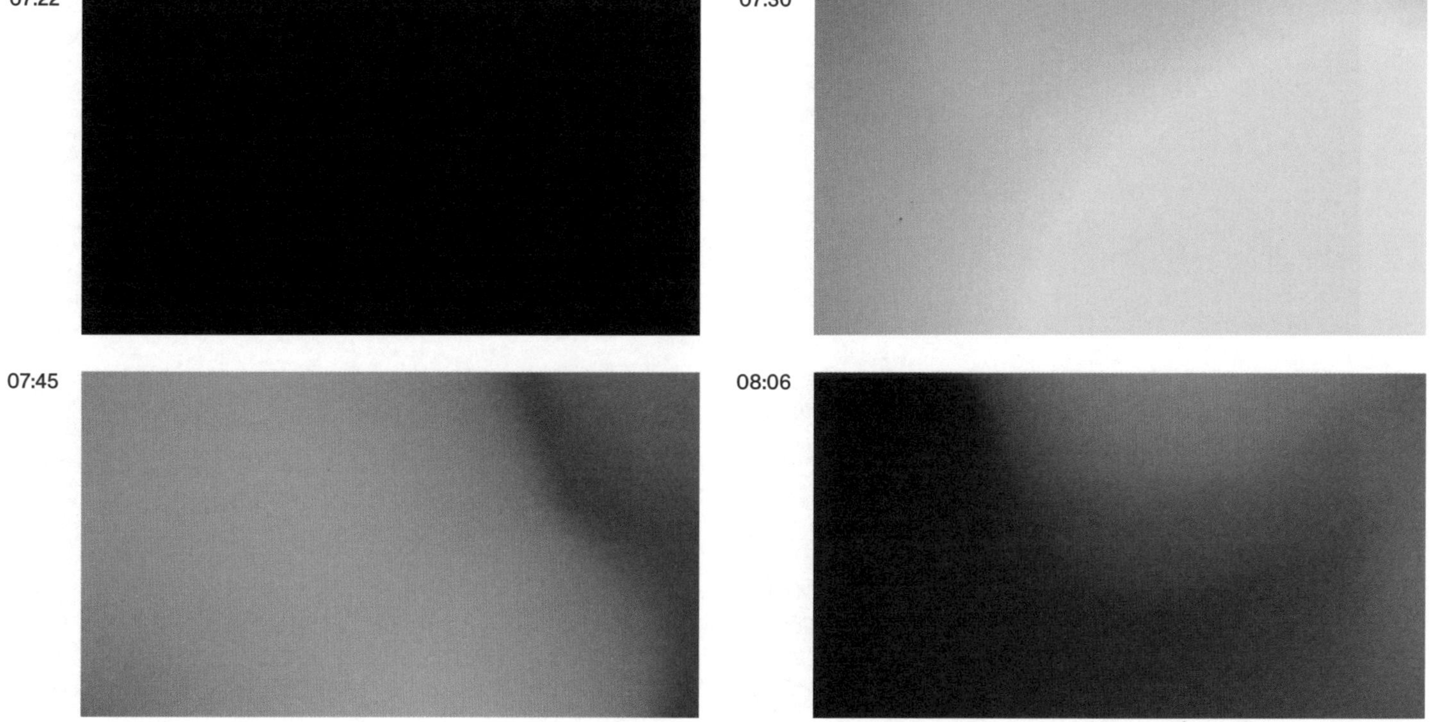

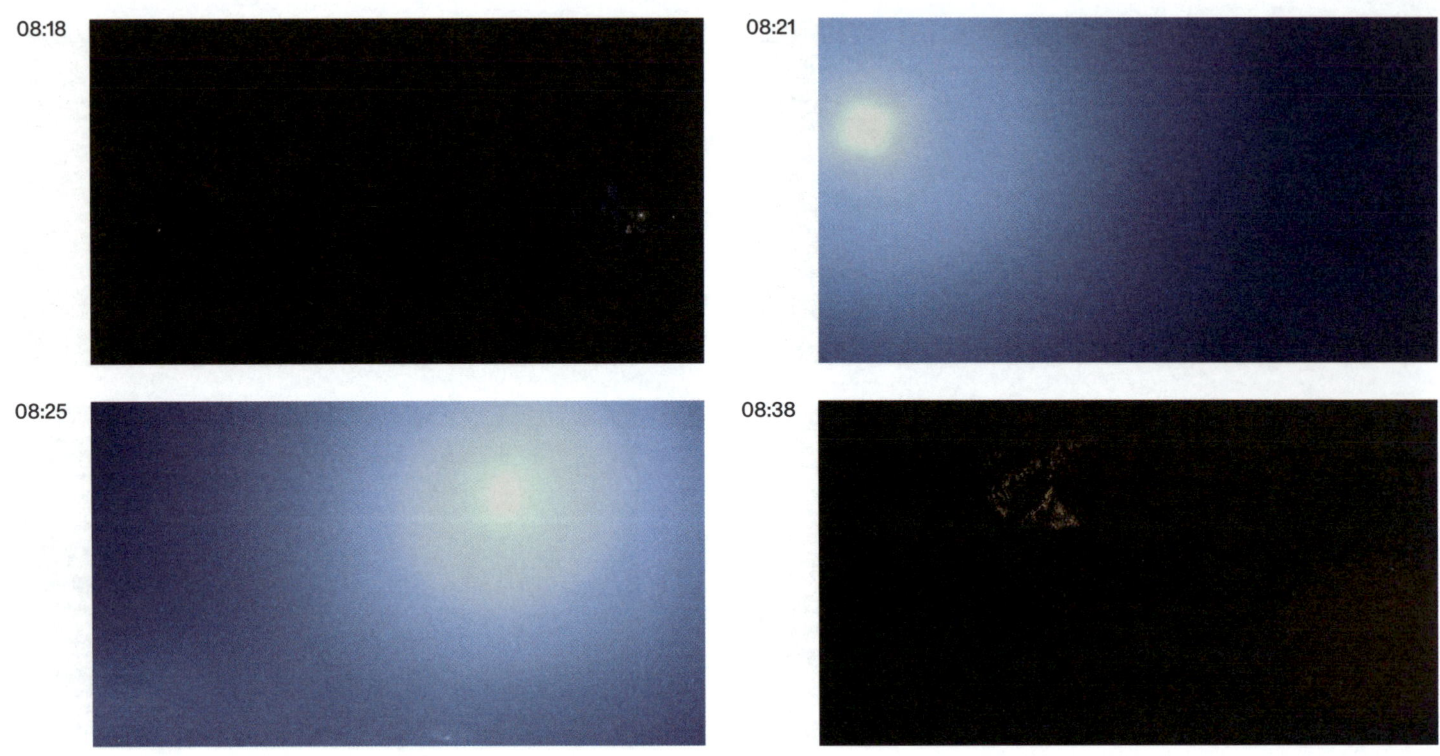

of truth, incorporating near and far geographies, memories, and identities to sidestep the attempts that both the incumbent US-backed Afghan government and the Taliban forces made to appropriate the aural demonstrations of the people of Kabul for their own propaganda.

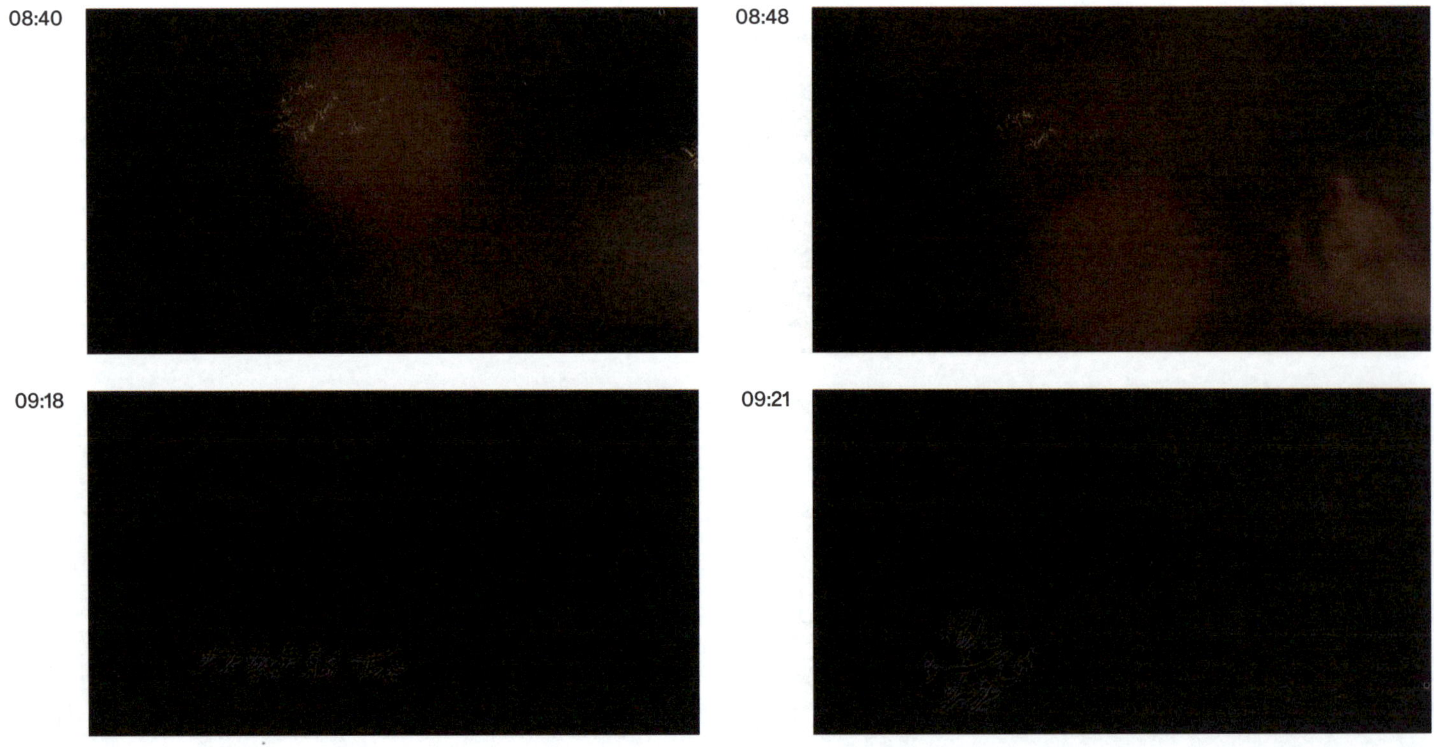

Aziz Hazara, *Takbir*, 2022

HD digital video, color, 5.1 surround sound, 9'58"

Produced and commissioned by
Fondazione Between Art Film

With generous support from
Colomboscope

Protagonist
Anwar Rahimi

JAFFNA

Videography
Yashoda Suriyapperuma

Field recording
Aziz Hazara

Location and logistics
Kälam and Colomboscope

KABUL

Videography
Zakir Mandegar and Mustafa Rsooli

Field recording
Aziz Hazara, Ghulam Reza Nazari, Hadi Rahnaward, Anwar Rahimi

Location and logistics
Rawzana Production

PARIS

Videography
Aziz Hazara

Field recording
Aziz Hazara

Color correction
Yanning Willmann

BERLIN

Studio Assistant
Leonie Hugendoubel

Sound design
Hayden Dean

Sound composition
Aziz Hazara

Edited by
Aziz Hazara

Naat (نعت) collected from Kabul to Pishawer (2017–20)

Produced by:
دالبـــدرخـــپرندويه اداري
لخواوړاندي كـــيږي
http://pushtutarany.wordpress.com/
دتوره بوره نشراتی ارگان
Http://toorabora.info
ادعام ولس.mp3
nahat (39).mp3
ترانه مظهری.mp3
دشتوكي قبرونه دي.mp3
¤بهار¤شرافت جمالي دغفلت خوب فري ده.mp3
دكور.mp3
دكشنی نات.mp3
دلتہ غولامے غواړ.mp3
دميخوارغوندی.mp3
اوس نه بريزدو ده.mp3
دهلمندشيهدان.mp3
دوطن ناوي زخمي.mp3
راجي.mp3
رباعي زينت الله.mp3
رنگين سفرلی سف رنگين.mp3
زخـــمي زخـــمي.mp3
زم زم.mp3
زه هم ورسره زمه.mp3
دين وكو جنكونه زوانانو فاسي جي فه.mp3
سه شكلي زيباشهيد.mp3
سي سنكركي يمه فروت.mp3
شاكر؟پدنياكی بہ جہادكوو.mp3
شاكر؟سپيسلی شهيدان150.mp3
شاكر؟سردی رسيدلي كناروتہ.mp3
منگ مينان يو.mp3
كري مورمي خبره.mp3
SalisUmerDa.mp3

Special thanks
Alessandro Rabottini, Leonardo Bigazzi, Natasha Ginwala, Francesca Reechia, Künstlerhaus Behtanien, KfW Stiftung, and Experimenter Kolkata

Courtesy of the artist, Experimenter, and Fondazione In Between Art Film

The Eye of God
Francesca Recchia

The truth itself is made.
—Giambattista Vico

ENTRANT

Don't blink
Do not blink.
Keep your eyes open.
Stare.

Stare at the light until the light becomes darkness
Stare at the light until there will be light out of that darkness.

Why is so much evil perpetrated in the name of God?
Why so much cruelty?

Why do men of god so often assume that they know better and impose a single, narrow, shortsighted vision of the world as supposedly demanded by their god?
Why is it that fundamentalists cannot see otherwise?
Why are they terrified of the unbridled visionary potentials of the imagination?

FIAT LUX
γενηθήτω φῶς
Let there be light

Don't blink
Do not blink.
Keep your eyes open.
Stare.

In an endless cycle of courses and recourses, history will teach us. Or maybe not. But the future will know.

EXEUNT

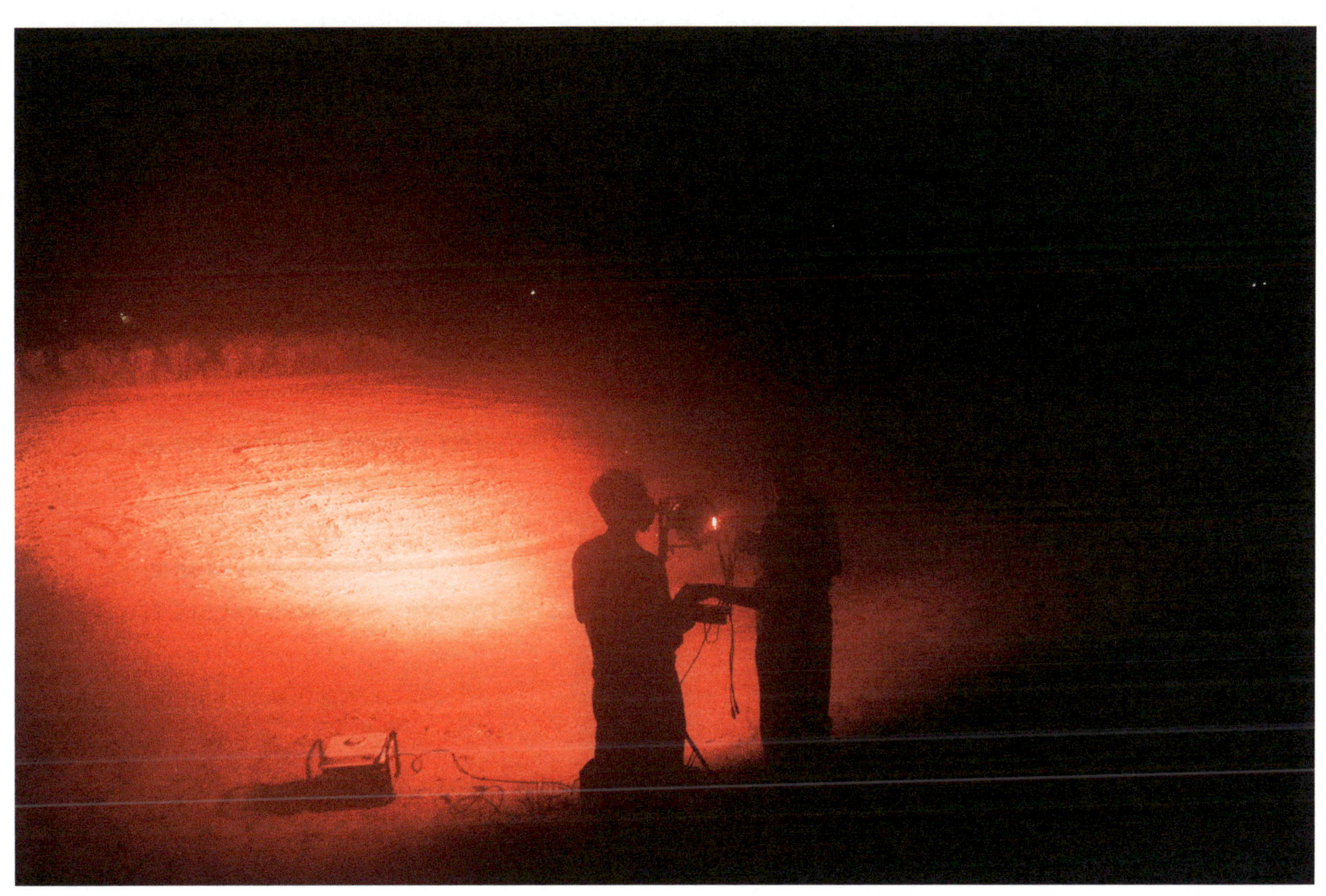

Ca. 7th Century CE—Third Kalima: Tamjeed (Glorification)

سُبْحَانَ اللهِ وَ الْحَمْدُ لِلّٰهِ وَ لَآ اِلٰهَ اِلَّا اللّٰهُ وَ اللّٰهُ اَكْبَرُ وَلا حَوْلَ
وَلاَ قُوَّةَ اِلَّا بِاللّٰهِ الْعَلِىِّ الْعَظِيْم

Subhanallah-e wal hamdulillah-e wa laa ilaha illal laho wallahooakbar. wala haola wala quwwata illa bilahil aliyil azeem

Glory be to Allah and all praise be to Allah, there is none worthy of worship except Allah, and Allah is the Greatest. There is no might or power except from Allah, the Exalted, the Great One.

December 16, 2007—*Raining Stones*, Aman Afridi

Is it raining stones or not?
Do you feel my weakness or not?
From every place there is a voice saying
"Do you imagine martyrdom or not?"
The destination to which only one step remains;
Do you remember it or not?
How can I illustrate the present picture just with dots?
Has the good life stopped breathing or not?
People's look communicated this to me:
"Do you receive my regards or not?"
He is able to make deserts green and habitable;
Aman! Beg and pray that you may be accepted.[1]

July 25, 2013—Kabul from above

Earlier this morning I sent him a photo I took last night: three dots—two yellow and one orange against a black background. This is all my phone could record of the stunning view of Kabul I was surprised with. "Maybe you should delete it.

1 *Poetry of the Taliban*, ed. Alex Strick van Linschoten and Felix Kuehn, trans. Mirwais Rahmani and Hamid Stanikzai (London: Hurst and Co., 2012), 103.

The one in your mind will always be brighter," he said. It is one of our usual early morning email exchanges. We generally talk about writing and the small, cherished details that life in Kabul offers us. Like the little bird that the guards keep at the entrance of the compound, or the policeman who stops the taxi driver to offer him dates to break the fast during Ramadan. The last email of this morning's thread ends with these words and no salutation: "Everything in Kabul is caged . . . the women, the birds, the bookstore, the city itself."

As I read his words, my eye fill with last night's breathtaking view of Kabul. We climbed up a spiral staircase and an immense sky opened over our heads. We were on the seventh floor of a building in the very heart of the city; Kabul surrounded us in all her beauty. I stood in the wind and turned on my feet, three hundred and sixty degrees, the city was all around me. I felt happy and free and blessed with the opportunity to experience a moment like that.

A gigantic orange moon was rising above the hills. I was surprised by the amount of little, dim lights; I was not expecting the hills to be so densely populated. The hills embrace that side of the city as a crescent, they look like a necklace full of sparkling precious stones—an unintended homage to the wealth of this country.

There was something peaceful and liberating about the view. Kabul is not a city in a cage, this is a city that secretly hatches hope and the possibility of change. It is a city that is growing, aggressive and resilient, powerful in all the potentials that are yet to be revealed.

August 3, 2021—9:08 p.m.

Allah-u akbar echoes from streets to hills to rooftops.
Allah-u akbar in the voices of women, men, and children resonates across the night.

Allah-u akbar is a cry of defiance, a quest for belonging as the Taliban swiftly advance and take over the country.

Allah-u akbar is a cry of protest that passed on through generations, elders tell youth that it was a collective invocation they used against the Soviet occupation in the 1980s.

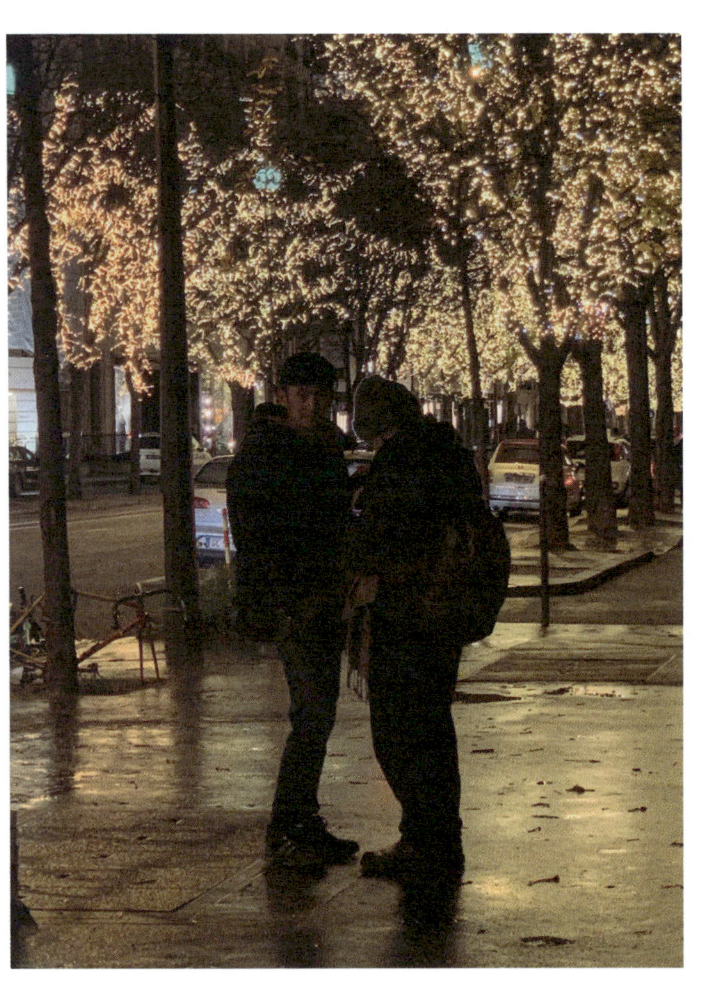

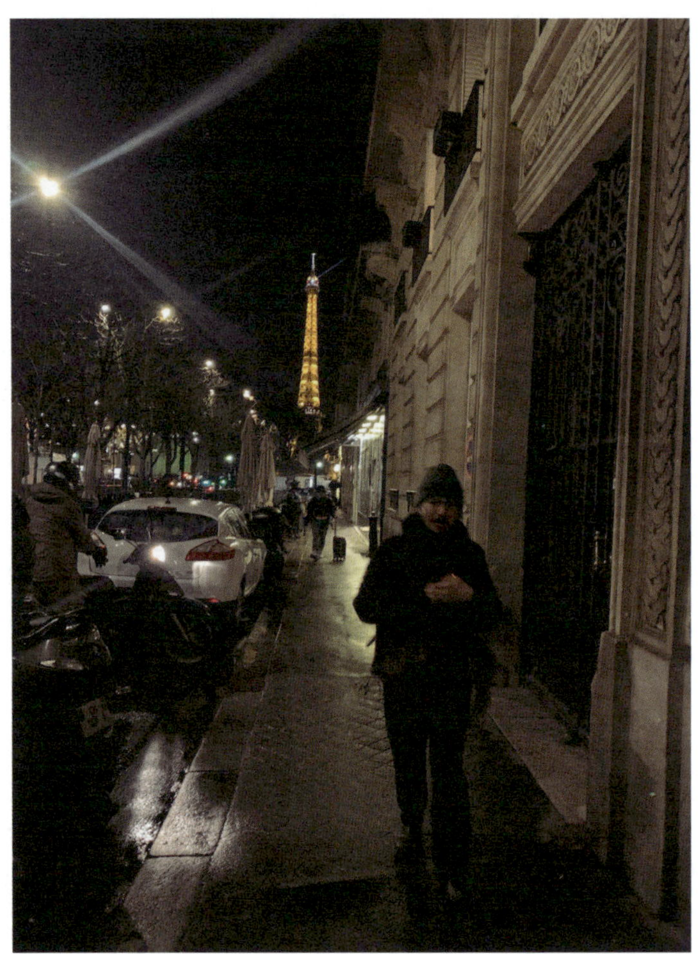

In an interview to Al Jazeera, Professor Ali A. Olomi thus described this collective echo: "It is a declaration that God, no matter the circumstances whether in victory, or defeat, is greater than any and all. It is a cry of defiance when facing an overwhelming oppressor, or experiencing the vicissitudes of persecution."

There is no God but God. Both sides worship the same God. Were those shouting their despair into the night also trying to reclaim a merciful God beyond the vengeful avatar that inspires the Taliban?

As the name of God reverberated across the city, Hadi Rahnaward and Mohammad Anwar Rahimi, from a rooftop in West Kabul, recorded the sound of this collective invocation.

August 15, 2021, 1—Caught by surprise?

That's the day when history changed.
Kabul fell peacefully to the Taliban and the transition took everyone by surprise—including the Taliban themselves.

Yet, everyone knew.
But what did they know?

Pockmarked by the scars of the bullet holes from the time of the Civil War in the 1990s, Kabul did not want to see more carnage. For a city known for its feisty spirit, this was a choice, not a defeat. As the former president made his undignified exit from the country, sneaking out like a thief amid allegations of embezzling millions of dollars, wide-eyed mountain boys entered the city on pickup trucks and motorbikes waiving their white flags. People in the meantime locked themselves at home and waited. Nobody was really sure what they were waiting for. For the dust to settle? And then what?

INTERLUDE I

In the 1980s, the American government gave the University of Nebraska Omaha a grant of $60 million to compile an abecedary for the children of Afghan refugees in Pakistan. It spelled *te* for *topak* (weapon) and *jim* for *jihad*.

August 15, 2021, 2—Erasures

Toward the end of the first day of the confused and confusing fall of Kabul, an image circulated on social media. A man in a white *pirhan tumban* holds a long paint roller to paint over the photographs of women in bridal dresses and makeup decorating the shop windows of the beauty parlors in central Kabul. It is a work in progress of several layers of white paint that leave a trace of what is underneath: a phantasmatic presence, a ghost, a testament of what has been and is yet to come.

According to Islamic art historian Oleg Grabar, Islam is aniconic rather than iconoclastic. If throughout history there have been phases of resistance toward the pictorial representations of beings that are part of the divine creation, the violent destruction of images is nevertheless episodic and not intrinsic to a religious credo or ideology.

Nowhere in the Quran is mentioned that Islam forbids the use of images; iconoclasm is therefore a fetish that accompanies certain coloration of religious extremism.

A coloration that aspires to homogeneity.

The brides on shop windows have been turned into ethereal monochromes and their otherworldly gaze remains fixed—and accusatory—on the passersby.

August 16, 2021—Icarus

What does it mean to fall off the sky?
What thoughts cross one's mind? What poisonous blend of hope and despair?

The myth of Icarus never dies.

On a bright morning, the pilots of the US Air Force C-17 Globemaster departed as quickly as they could from a runway dangerously full of people. Could this ever be considered a legitimate escape? Does panic make people blind and oblivious to the desperate quest of other human beings?

Twenty-one men sat *on* that plane—not inside the plane, but on it—perched on the wheels or hanging on to the retracting landing gear. Were they aware of the destiny they would face? Did terror and exhilaration make them run toward the future or toward the certainty of an immediate death?

Fada Mohammed, a young dentist, fell from the sky and so did Zaki Anwari, a seventeen-year-old footballer with the Afghan national youth team.

A final jump.

And their bodies, along with their dreams, crashed and shattered into a million pieces, with a loud bang, against someone's rooftop.

August 20, 2021, 1—Ya Hussein

The fifth day of Taliban rule marked the tenth day of the month of Muharram, the holy day of Ashura. On this day, Shi'as remember the killing of Imam Hussein, the grandson of Prophet Muhammed, in the battle at Karbala in 680 CE.

For ten days people gather on the street and commemorate Imam Hussein's sacrifice through processions, mournful singing, and self-flagellation.

In the first Ashura of the new Taliban era, fear overpowered grief. The demon of sectarianism cloaked over the congregation; the black and red Ashura banners in stark contrast with the white Taliban flag.

In the first Ashura of the new Taliban era, the old tears for the death of Imam Hussein mixed with the new tears for the possible death of the imagination.

August 20, 2021, 2—The wait

Mohammad Anwar Rahimi spent two days waiting outside Kabul Airport when he finally managed to board a French military aircraft. He first landed in Abu Dhabi and then arrived in Paris on August 23, 2021, maybe prepared for a new beginning.

What does it mean to wait outside the gates of an airport for an indefinite amount of time and with no certainty that the wait will lead anywhere?
What does it mean to wait for hour after blurred hour with your body pressed against the bodies of a thousand nameless others?

Where does your mind wander? How do you make sense of time? How do you make sense of destiny? How do you make sense of you?

August 24, 2021—After five days and three times

Hadi Rahnaward, like many others—urban legend numbers them by the thousands—reached the French Embassy in central Kabul. Someone started printing and copying bootleg visas and fake documents that were then distributed in piles as the rumor was that whoever made it to the gate with the blessed paper would be taken in by the French. Hadi was kept or maybe willingly stayed in the Embassy for five days and, after three attempts to reach the airport, he was finally able to board a French military aircraft on August 23 and landed to Abu Dhabi. From Abu Dhabi he boarded a flight to Paris where he arrived a day later. There he spent two weeks in quarantine and a further week sitting for his interviews and processing all the papers necessary to acquire refugee status. He was then sent to Lille.

I don't know if he was able to choose the location or whether he even knew where Lille was before it was made the destination of such a life-changing journey.

INTERLUDE II

On the verge of winter, in a country on the brink of starvation, baby girls are sold for five hundred dollars. To give them a future? To feed the rest of the family? To have one less stomach to fill?

The stench of desperation will haunt for generations to come.

October 7, 2021—Islamic Imperative for Women's Education in Afghanistan

"The Universal Islamic Declaration of Human Rights (UIDHR), adopted by the Islamic Council of Europe on 19 September 1981/21 Dhul Qaidah 1401 H states:

> XII. Right to Freedom of Belief, Thought and Speech
> [. . .] b) Pursuit of knowledge and search after truth is not only a right but a duty of every Muslim.

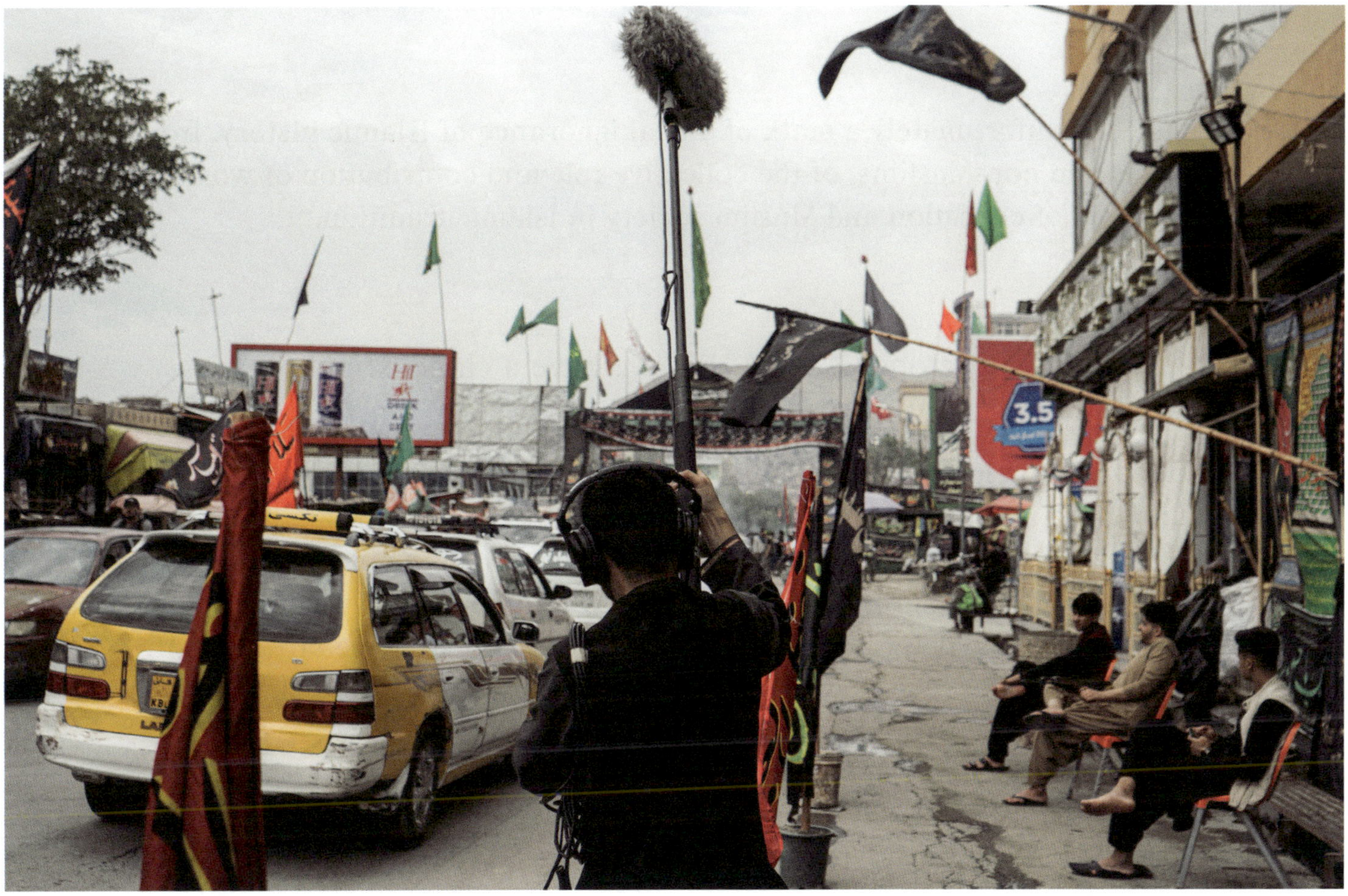

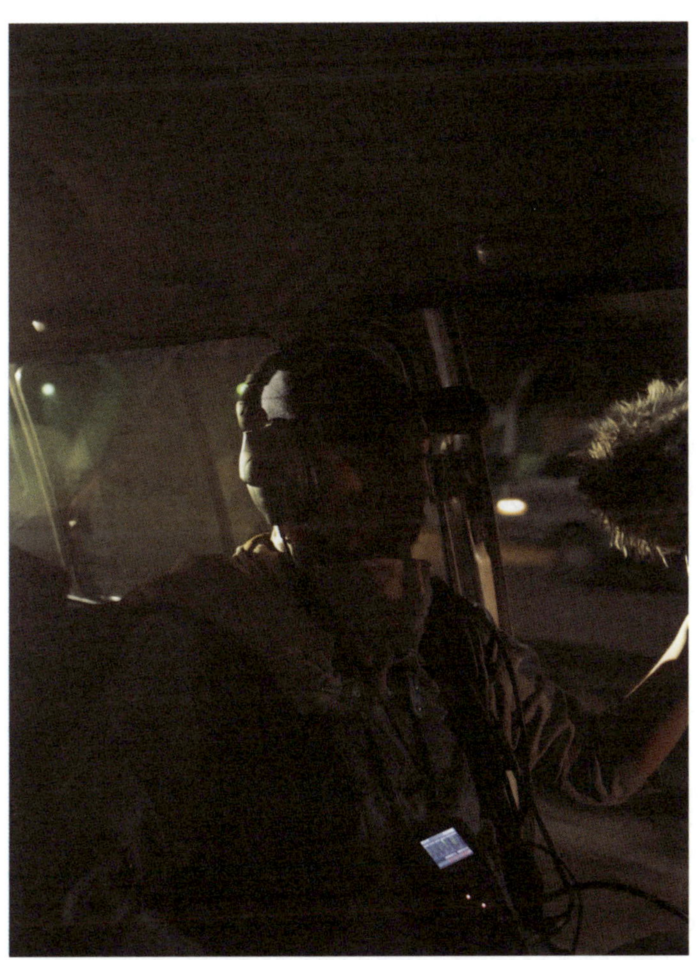

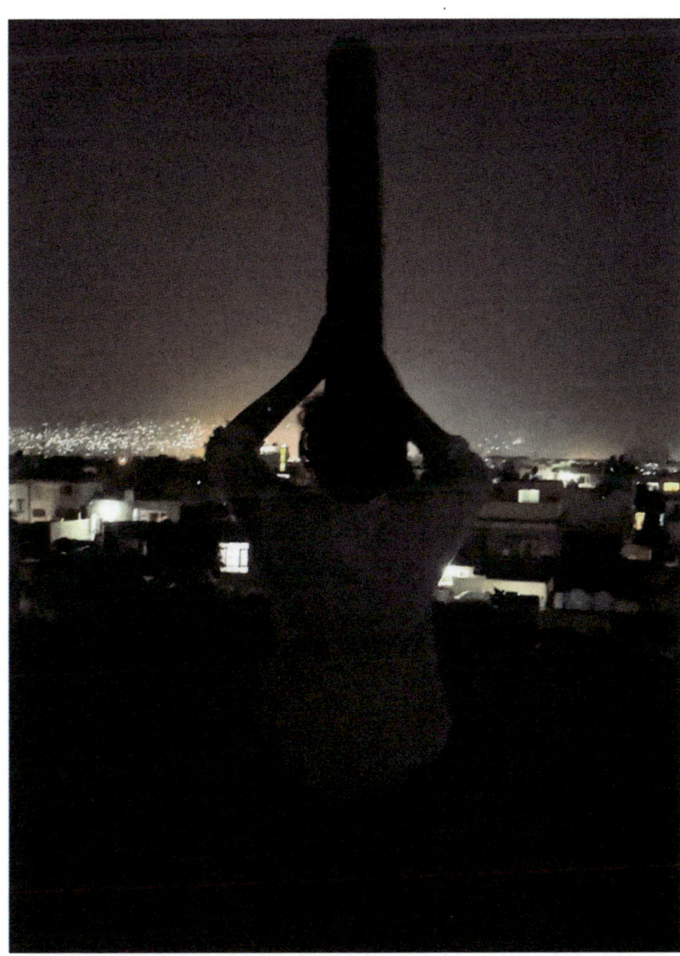

It has been unfortunately a mark of global ignorance of Islamic history, from both Muslims and non-Muslims, of the collective role and contribution of women in every facet of education and Muslim society in Islamic tradition."[2]

October 7, 2021—Sir, we have a clandestine.

The Washington Post reported that Xavier Chatel, the French ambassador to the United Arab Emirates, adopted Juji, the myna that an Afghan girl managed to smuggle into Abu Dhabi in a cardboard box all the way from Kabul. The girl was very upset that she could not continue her journey with the pet bird, as sanitary regulations to enter Europe did not allow it. The ambassador was moved by the girl's affection and determination and decided to look after the bird himself. "The fierce little fellow showed me that if he survived the Kabul airport, I was no match," he said on Twitter.

We all need a feelgood story in times like these.

A rescue bird that traveled in a cardboard box from a cage in one country to a cage in another country has become a symbol of hope.

What do we hope for? And is the measure of what we hope for ourselves the same as what we hope for others? Or are there hierarchies of worth and, consequently, of hope? Are there lesser people who deserve lesser hope?

Who defines the measures of rightful hope?

INTERLUDE III

How do we remember? How do we recall the past? Is it images, sounds, smells, scents? Is it like reliving a grainy old movie where details that we no longer retain appear like burnt celluloid?

2 Joint Statement on Afghanistan, "Islamic Imperative for Women's Education in Afghanistan," *Medium*, 6 October, 2021. Available online.

October 19, 2021—The Blurred Photo

Sirajuddin Haqqani, the Minister of Interior of Afghanistan for the Taliban, is on the FBI's Most Wanted list. Also known as Siraj, Khalifa, Mohammad Siraj, Sarajadin, Cirodjiddin, Seraj, Arkani, Khalifa (Boss) Shahib, Halifa, Ahmed Zia, Sirajuddin Jallaloudine Haqqani, Siraj Haqqani, Serajuddin Haqani, Siraj Haqani, and Saraj Haqani, the minister has a huge bounty on his head. The FBI website says: "The Rewards For Justice Program, United States Department of State, is offering a reward of up to $10 million for information leading directly to the arrest of Sirajuddin Haqqani."

On October 19, Haqqani spoke at an event at Kabul's Intercontinental Hotel where he lauded suicide bombers and promised money and land to their surviving families. He was there, he spoke, but his face was never visible in any of the photographs documenting the event. He was either hidden behind a bouquet of flowers or in the folds of someone's embrace. The only image where he would have been fully visible was published with a hazy halo blurring his face. Regarding the unusual appearance, social media speculations and conspiracy theories did not miss a beat.

Was it to protect him from a possible hit job? Or from those who may fall to the temptation of cashing the $10 million reward? Some invoked the known hostility toward images of the previous Taliban regime, others thought it was a way to surround him with an aura of sanctity.

October 20, 2021—The great hatch

I read what I wrote on July 25, 2013, in Kabul—another world, another life.

It all feels so naive, yet it was so real.

The gate of the cage has now closed—it was already there back then, it was just ajar. But the gate is now shut—and the hope of the city trapped and suffocated by despair. Can the city still secretly hatch the possibility of change?

EPILOGUE

In lesson number seventeen of his book *On Tyranny: Twenty Lessons from the Twentieth Century,* Timothy Snyder warns us: "Listen for dangerous words. Be alert to the use of the words *extremism* and *terrorism.* Be alive to the fatal notions of *emergency* and *exception.* Be angry about the treacherous use of patriotic vocabulary."[3]

EX POST

Reality plays out not unlike a shadow puppet show.
Dark silhouettes dance against the bright light.
Ephemeral, transient shapes—they come, play their part, and leave.
They are born, live their lives as an act, die and exit the scene.
Blurry, there is no stark transition between what is past and what is future.

Everything must change
for everything to remain the same.
—Giuseppe Tomasi di Lampedusa

References

Kadri Sadakat, *Heaven on Earth: A Journey through Shari'a Law* (London: Vintage Books, 2012).

Messages to the World: The Statements of Osama Bin Laden. ed. Lawrence Bruce, trans. by James Howarth (London and New York: Verso, 2005).

Images from the backstage of *Takbir* by Aziz Hazara. Courtesy of the artist.

3 Timothy Snyder, *On Tyranny: Twenty Lessons from the Twentieth Century,* graphic edition (New York: Ten Speed Press, 2021), 91.

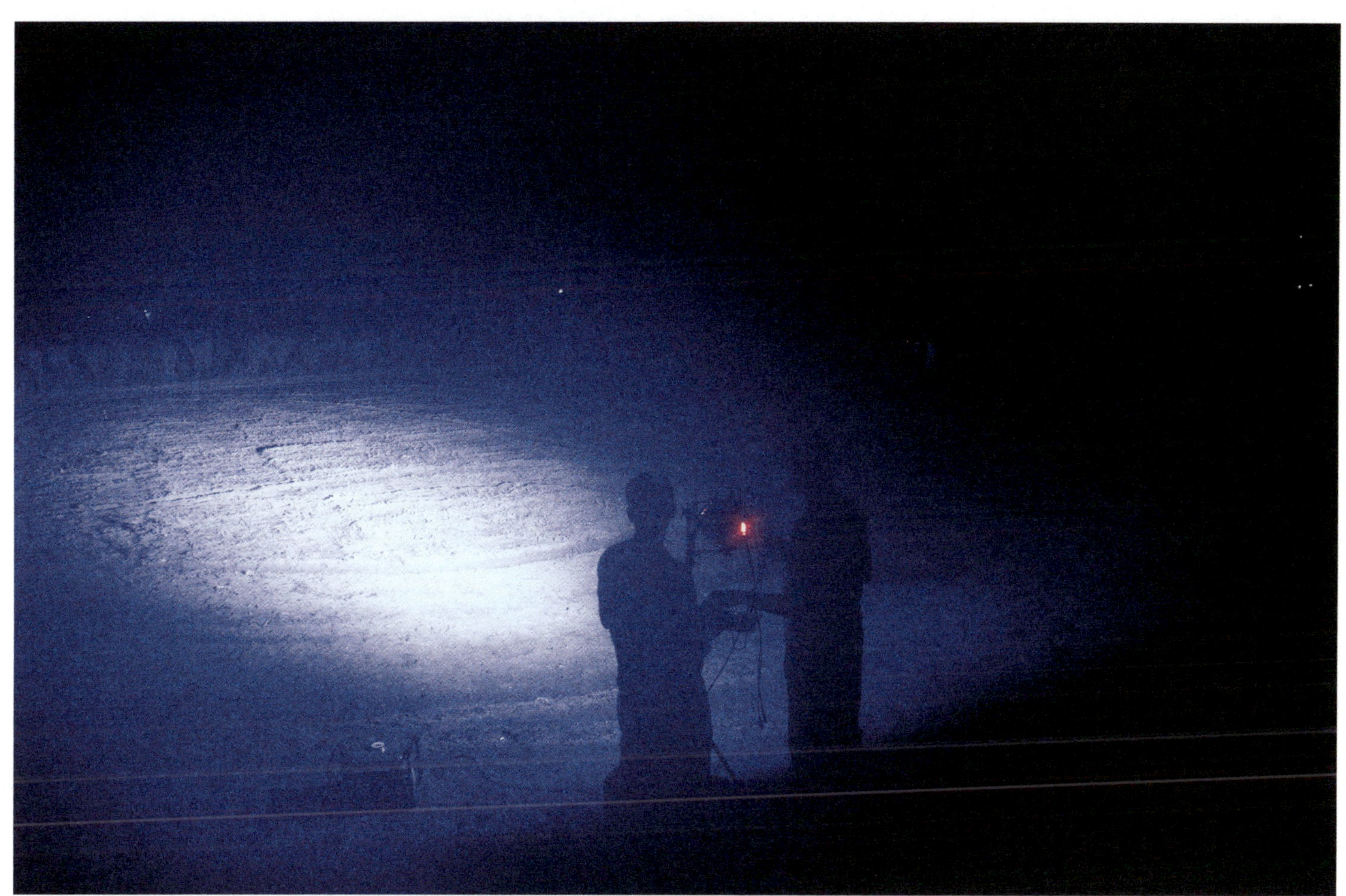

Sensing Films: The Spatial Concept for *Penumbra* 2050+

Ippolito Pestellini Laparelli

Through the past years our lives have progressively migrated online. For many the digital has taken over, turning into a pervasive virtual public sphere where our social, political, and cultural interactions are consumed and reiterated at the speed of light. If each and every experience can potentially be replicated in the realm of the digital, what is left within the spheres of the physical, of the tactile, of the spatial? Has video art—a medium that, due to its intangibility, scalability, and replicability seems supremely suitable for online engagement—any life left outside the digital metaverses?

Our work for *Penumbra* stemmed from a different assumption: that the precise topography ensured by a space is lost online and that the experience of a video is first and foremost a corporeal one, able to unlock a journey into other bodies, spaces, and times ... leading back to us, the viewers.

Since the very early stages of the project, we worked organically with Alessandro Rabottini and Leonardo Bigazzi, toward connecting the spaces of the Complesso dell'Ospedaletto in Venice and the films on view with the role of our installation. Rather than looking at the exhibition design as merely a support or a simple backdrop, the process of dissecting the spaces of the former hospital and of designing the scenography for the show has served to expand, reflect upon, and spatialize the curatorial concept. It is no coincidence that early communications regarding the exhibition centered around some enigmatic pictures by Giacomo Bianco, depicting details of the baroque church of Santa Maria dei Derelitti—a visual statement on the pivotal role that that space played as a central signifier for *Penumbra*.

According to the curators, "penumbra" is both a physical condition—literally the moment of transition between light and shadow, but also the absence of light that characterizes the experience of moving images—and a metaphorical notion, widely referring to the threshold between reality and fiction, object and subject, the individual and the collective, et cetera. It is the nebulous area where distinctions are lost and potentials are unlocked, beyond a Cartesian and binary understanding of the world.

Interpretations of the word "penumbra" are various and can be found across many disciplines: from science to technology, law, anthropology, art, theater, scenography, and so on. The question for us, as spatial practitioners, was how to manifest this notion in connection to the heterogeneous spatial character of the Complesso dell'Ospedaletto, the films on display, and the experience of the audience. Rather than focusing on the orchestration of a rigid sequence of screens, we looked at those spaces "in between," at the intangible qualities of light and air, at the atmosphere filling the space-time between one film and another. As professor Andreas Rauh writes in "In the Clouds: On the Vagueness of Atmospheres:"

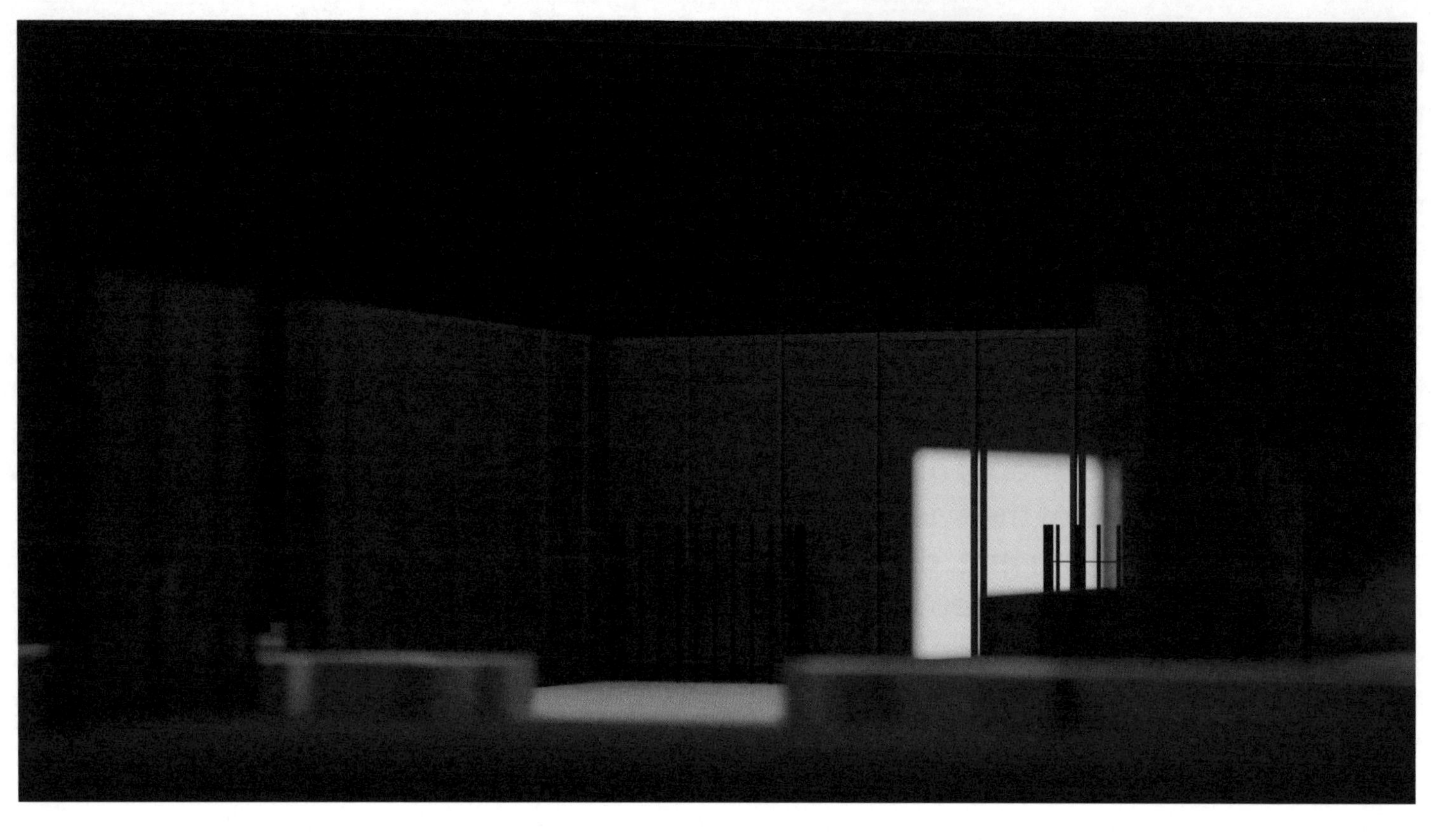

"Atmosphere is [...] to be situated in this penumbra, in a conceptual or maybe ontological half-shadow, as an 'and' mediating between a subjective state and the qualities of one's surroundings. There are atmospheres that, in line with the classical concept of Vagueness, are 'fickle,' that appear 'restless' and unstable, that are 'vagabond.'"[1]

It is in these in-between spaces that the experience becomes theatrical, that visitors move away from being passive viewers to become wanderers of a deconstructed play. Similar to the work of scenographer Anna Viebrock, in these moments of transition the device of the exhibition disappears (and with that the subject-object relationship). The visitors become active participants, drawing personal connections between each film. The making of a narrative does not emerge from the exhibition as a whole, but from the visitors' spontaneous associations, memories, and participation. It is in this plurality of meanings and interpretations, emerging from blurred boundaries between film, set, architecture, and audience, that *Penumbra* manifests in space.

Through a series of repetitive structures, the exhibition design colonizes and reacts to the heterogeneous assemblage of spaces that make up the Complesso dell'Ospedaletto: wooden modular stretchers covered with dark fabric—a system developed with our production partners, Altofragile, which is able to adapt to different geometries and layouts and can be dismantled and repurposed for future uses. This system unfolds across the monumental sixteenth-century church of Santa Maria dei Derelitti—the seventeenth-century spiral staircase, the illusionistic frescoes of the eighteenth-century music room, and more modern adaptations from the 1950s and 1960s, which connect the historical rooms. Specifically framing and staging each film on display and reflecting on the interconnected notions of human and architectural anatomy, the setup is conceived as a collection of pieces from a dismembered body, at times enhancing, and others concealing the existing rooms. The space-time between one film and another is occupied by darkness, glimpses of light, and fragments of structures. Visitors are thus immersed in a cinematic journey through a dormant building—floating across past, present, and future, without fully grasping the distinction between moving images, set, and architecture. The stage becomes an added piece of the exhibition by unifying it while establishing a specific dialogue with each of the films.

The videos become part of the space—and vice versa—and they are transformed into a visual and aural kaleidoscope. In dialogue with both the curators and the artists involved, the installation design turned into an integral part of each work, intensifying the audiences' physical and empathic connection with the stories and conditions narrated on-screen.

1 Andreas Rauh, "In the Clouds: On the Vagueness of Atmospheres," *Ambiances* 3 (2017), available online.

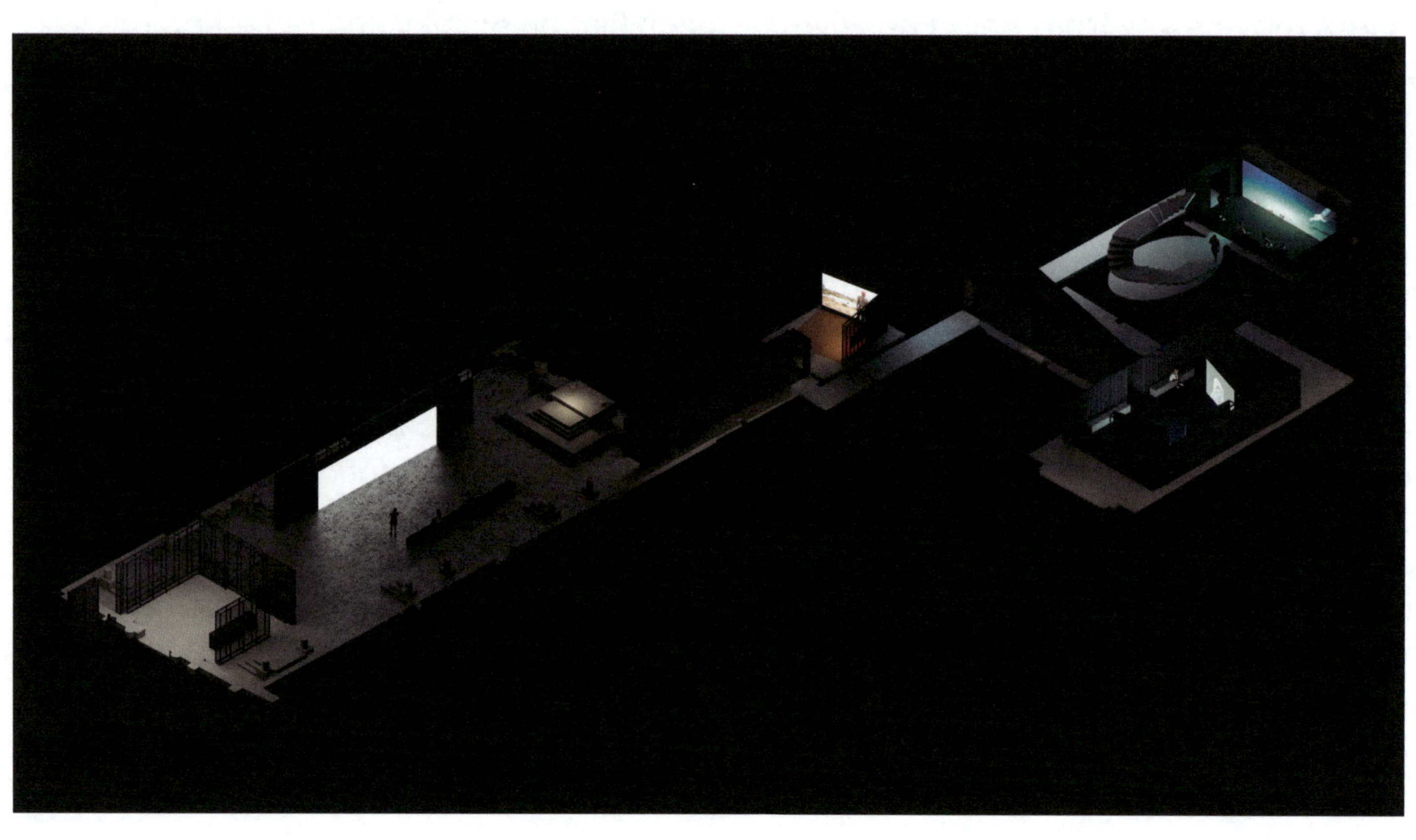

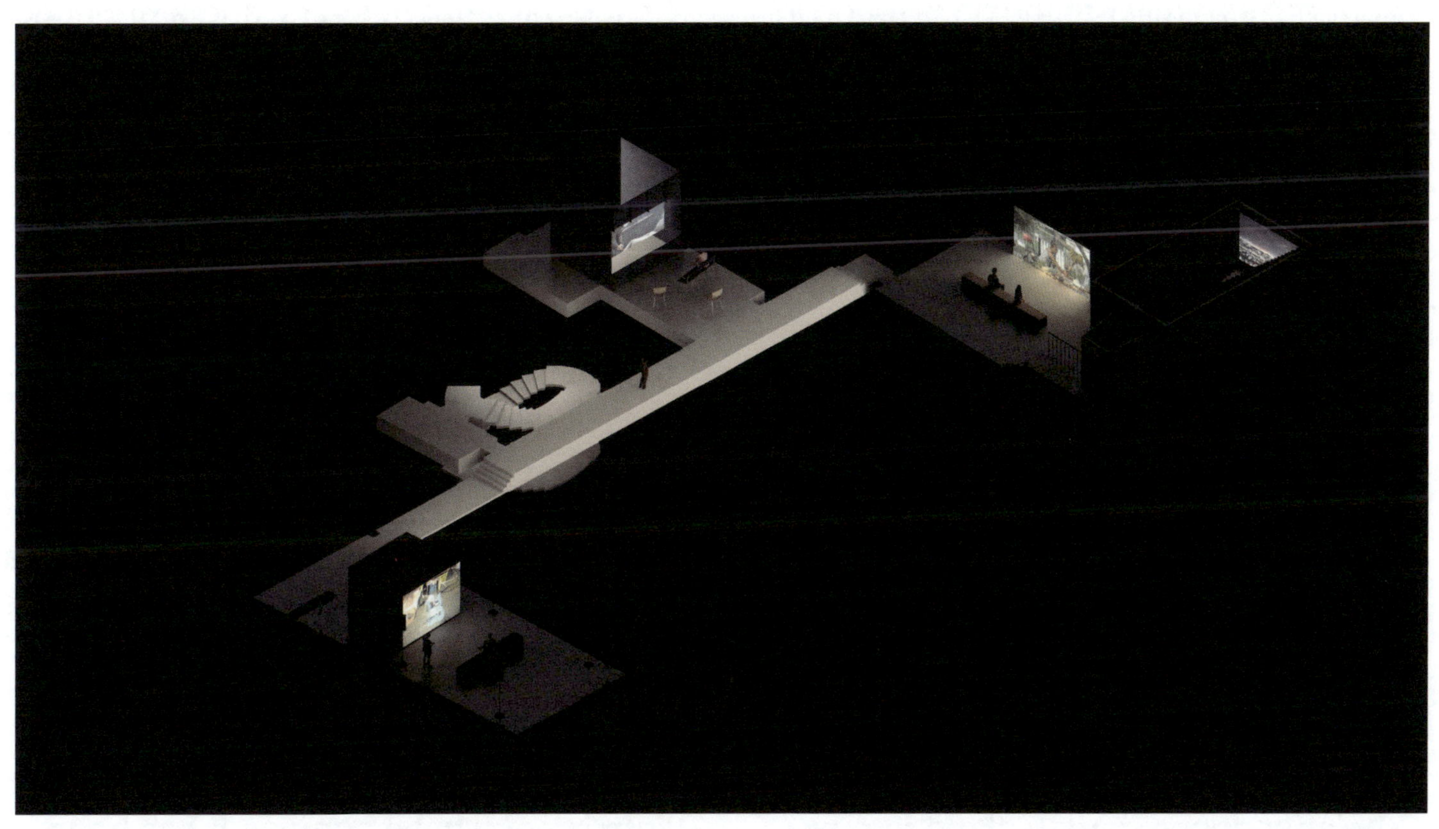

Films in *Penumbra* are *sensed*, rather than just watched.

As audiences walk into the church, they are confronted with the monumental screen showing *Pantelleria* (2022) by Masbedo. Placed on one side of the nave, the video engages in a tridimensional dialogue with the baroque interiors, while its soundscape fills the volumes of the architecture. Proceeding through darkness, following a pathway system of light boxes similar to the ones found in old movie theaters, visitors are suddenly projected into a small modern room cladded in clinical white ceramics, which was once the crematorium of the former hospital. Here they encounter *Plateau* (2021) by Karimah Ashadu. Compressed within the walls of this tight chamber, they are intimately exposed to the exploitation of bodies and the brutal labor conditions of the Nigerian miners portrayed on two screens, one of which takes over an entire side of the room. Moving along a partially dilapidated corridor, visitors enter another dark space to approach from afar the three-channel video *É Noite na América* [It is Night in America] (2021) by Ana Vaz. The work is in a modern room overlooking the abandoned garden of the former hospital, in a symbolic connection with the urban gardens of Brasília—where the wild animals documented in the films seek refuge—and between the architecture of the hospital and the ones of the Brazilian capital. As visitors attune themselves to the multiplicity of perspectives shown in the video—human as well as other-than-human—the room lingers in between a space of rescue and captivity.

The exhibition path continues across a brighter corridor facing the inner courtyard on the ground floor, before plunging back into the dark marine abyss of *Aphotic Zones* (2022) by Emilija Škarnulytė. Consistent with her practice, Škarnulytė's work is fully spatialized, allowing the audience to inhabit it—instead of watching it—across a room turned into a virtual techno-aquarium using a reflective ceiling, moving lights colonizing the seventeenth-century helicoidal flight of stairs, and a projection on its roof—a reference to the typical trompe l'oeil of baroque cupolas.

A black cube faces the entrance to the eighteenth-century music room on the first floor. Visitors are forced to walk around it, getting glimpses of the frescoes by Jacopo Guarana adorning the room, before turning and facing *Qualities of Life: Living in the Radiant Cold* (2022) by James Richards. The dissolving images, objects, and bodies in Richards's film animate the other bodies painted in the space, in a dialogue between times and anatomies, the virtual and the physical. The audience continues onto a luminous loggia, where light is not what it seems—it has been tuned gray, and shadows are almost entirely dissolved through an invisible film applied on the windows, in an attempt to fictionalize the intangible, to raise doubts about the materiality of space itself. Here, a black curtain leads into the entrance of a wing of the abandoned hospital and to *House of Nations* (2021) by He Xiangyu. Traces of the former hospital—locked doors,

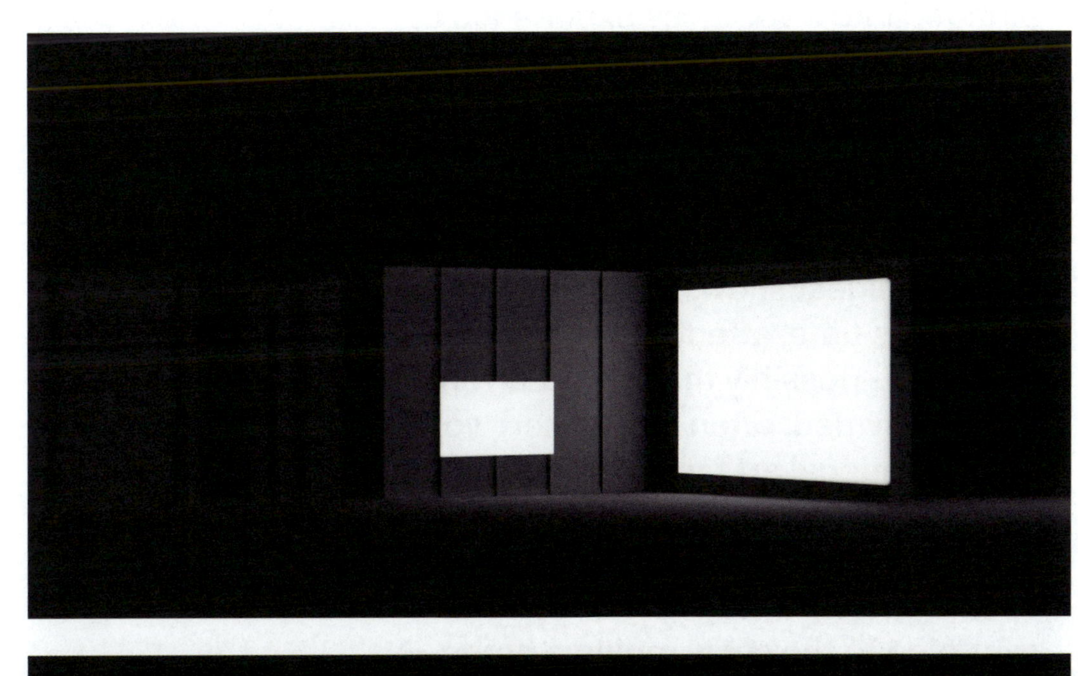

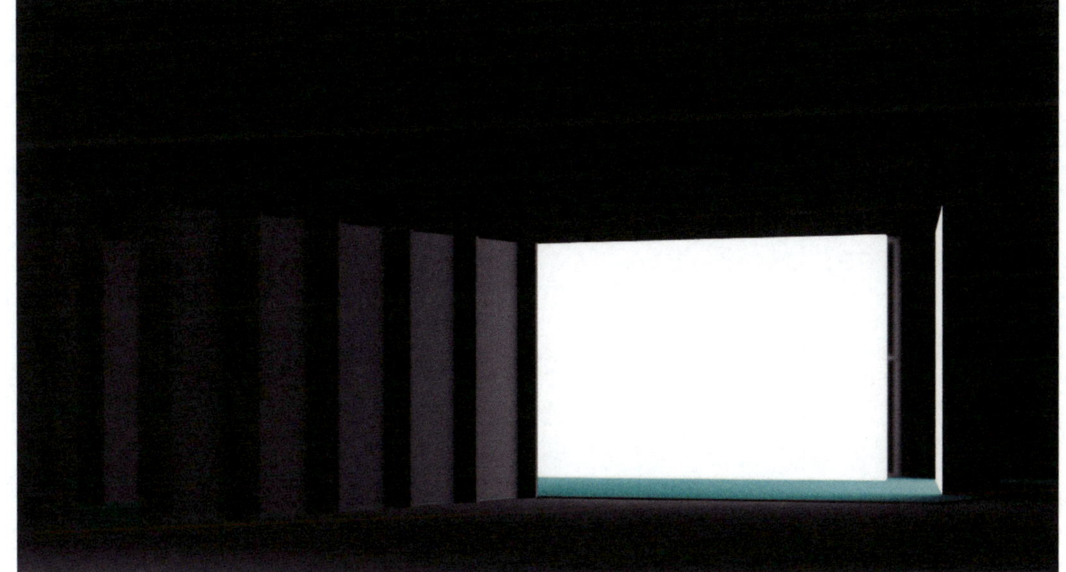

a guardian window, venetian blinds, generic floors—resonate with and expand the Berlin modernist social housing through which the character of the film moves, in a quasi-tautological relationship. A room treated like a public square—or an open stage—hosts *Olho da Rua* [Out Loud] (2022) by Jonathas de Andrade, allowing the queer collectivity portrayed in the film to address and engage in a direct conversation with the community of viewers on the other side of the screen. Finally, entering the suspended atmosphere of a small pitch-black chamber, visitors are confronted with *Takbir* (2022) by Aziz Hazara, and plunged into a vorticose experience of images and sounds shot at night in Kabul, where darkness is reclaimed as a space of invisibility, freedom, and resistance.

Penumbra is not necessarily a feel-good, easy-to-digest show. To be appreciated, it requires time, attention, dedication, and care—possibly the rarest currencies in the crowded, often fast-paced world of international art festivals and biennials. Yet, throughout the past months, we heard from visitors that they enjoyed spending hours at *Penumbra* and returning to the show multiple times. It might seem paradoxical, but maybe the experience of moving images is really one of the rare brackets of stillness—a locus of pause and reflection—in the totalizing vortex of our digital feeds and frantic lives.

Images: concept view, ground floor axo, first floor axo.
Courtesy of 2050+.

GROUND FLOOR

ONE, MASBEDO
TWO, KARIMAH ASHADU

THREE, ANA VAZ
FOUR, EMILIJA ŠKARNULYTĖ

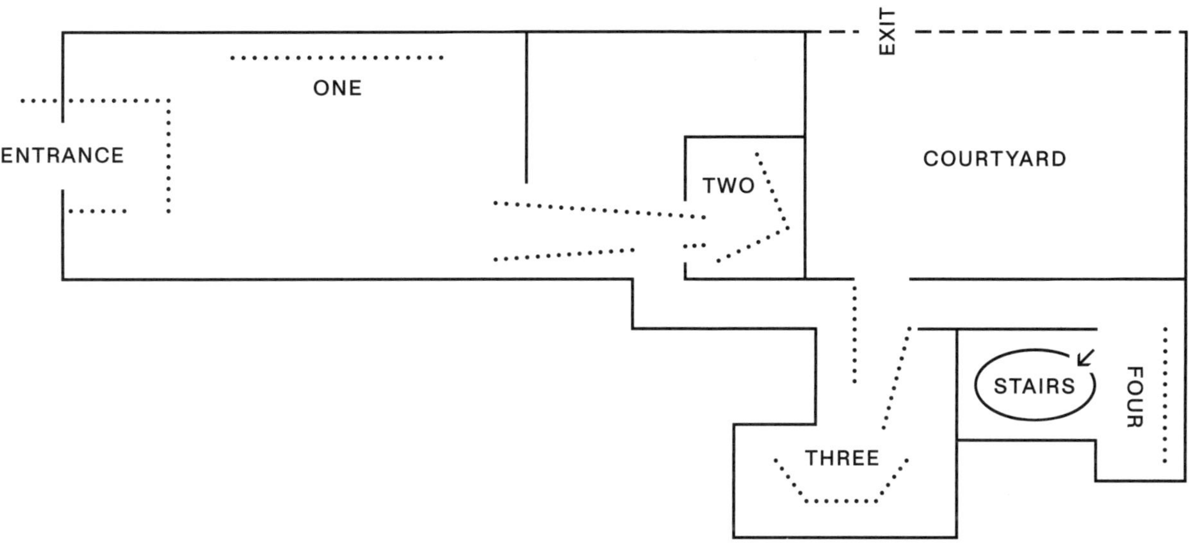

FIRST FLOOR

FIVE, JAMES RICHARDS
SIX, HE XIANGYU

SEVEN, JONATHAS DE ANDRADE
EIGHT, AZIZ HAZARA

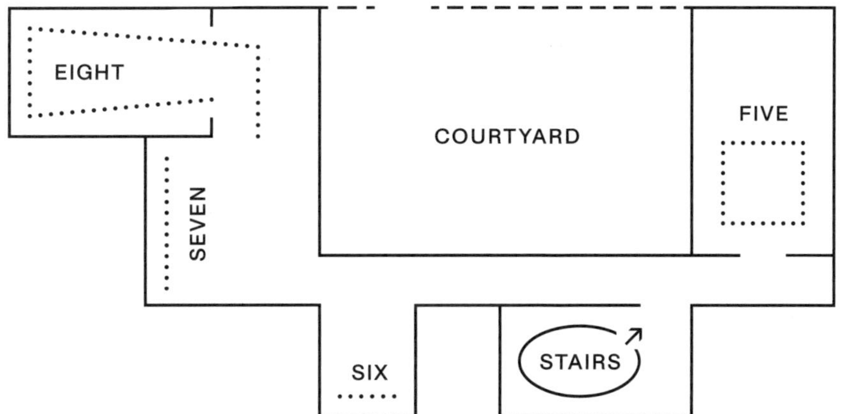

Vanishing Points: The Public Program of *Penumbra*

Bianca Stoppani
and Paola Ugolini

"Now there's another crucial fact I must explain – so mark / My words – that there are images of things – a skin, or *bark*, / As we can call it, shed from objects, since it bears the same / Form and likeness of whatever thing from which it came." —Lucretius[1]

For the Epicurean philosopher and poet Lucretius, the image is a volatile substance that appears on the surface of things, and there has never been a more precise definition of the immaterial, almost magical nature of moving images. According to theorist Giuliana Bruno, it is there that the visual is materially manifested, "where time becomes material space" and in this transfer the surface becomes the space in which substantial transformations happen.[2]

Penumbra was an exhibition of individual visions through which to narrate our uncertain and porous time. The title refers not only to the scientific definition of penumbra, the lack of full light that makes the contours of things shady and vague, but also to an indefinite state of mind that reflects the unpredictability of the present and the future. Inside the Complesso dell'Ospedaletto, a place poised between the splendor of Baroque architecture and the anonymity of a hospital, the curators Alessandro Rabottini and Leonardo Bigazzi, with architect Ippolito Pestellini Laparelli and his agency, 2050+, created an exhibition journey as much as a visual device with which to analyze the present world, through the works of Karimah Ashadu, Jonathas de Andrade, Aziz Hazara, He Xiangyu, Masbedo, James Richards, Emilija Škarnulytė, and Ana Vaz.

Troubling topics such as the massive exploitation and contamination of the planet, war in the past and present with its social, economic, and political implications, propaganda that overwhelms truth. Wildlife put at risk of extinction due to the spread of big cities, hunger, celebration and suffering, the alienation of those who leave their homeland and their life behind. And then, real and fictional nights, joy and despair, images that enchant us with their beauty and are striking at the same time for their crude force. All this was *Penumbra*, and an essay could not suffice to narrate the experience of an immersive journey into the utopias and dystopias of the contemporary; it was necessary to invent a sort of navigation manual, a compass, a written atlas of emotions to trace a conceptual route through the stories told by the eight video installations.

In the desire to make *Vanishing Points* capable of generating new mental constellations based on the works in the show, we constructed a critical-conceptual framework around the weak point of linear perspective, arguably the most significant technique of representation not only for the European history of art but also for

1 Lucretius, *The Nature of Things* (*De rerum natura*), (London: Penguin Classics, 2007).
2 Giuliana Bruno, *Surface: Matters of Aesthetics, Materiality, and Media* (Chicago, IL: The University of Chicago Press, 2014).

Western thinking as a whole. According to this theory, a vanishing point is the location—both real and virtual—where the elements of an image converge on the horizon line. It is that particular and universal point on which the construction of an image depends, which the eye is invited to observe; nevertheless, it is also the place where the observation of that image is paradoxically depleted. It is the mythical and ideological point of origin and end of *a* world in its plane of space-time possibility.

For a long time in the West, the vanishing point established by linear perspective was considered the origin and end of *the* world. The writings of the Renaissance humanist and architect Leon Battista Alberti had built a bridge between medieval optical geometry and the visual arts, raising the practice of painting to the status of the natural sciences and endowing it with the capacity to study and comprehend physical reality. Within this mathematical-conceptual framework, the image was conceived as a window overlooking reality, but one from which what characterized its experience had been removed, such as the unexpected, the imperfection, the invisible, and the unfolding in time. Later, Renaissance visuality was utilized by René Descartes to construct a theory of knowledge that on a philosophical plane eliminated—in the separation of subject, object, and vision—the presence and the responsibility of the subject in the act of looking.

The artists in *Penumbra* have taken a visual posture that is in contrast with the traditional use of the camera, which enacts a similar separation. Instead, they have situated their gaze and relationship with the world in a political and critical way to experiment with methods of representation that are not hegemonic, but transverse and personal. For this reason, with *Vanishing Points* we wanted to create spaces of sharing and discussion precisely in those points where the sight blurs, becoming ambiguous, and where sound emerges as an autonomous language that complicates vision. It was crucial for us that the invited speakers could come to terms with the complexity and variety of the narrations of *Penumbra*, thus engaging with the relationship between visual culture and eco-social critique, geopolitical factors, post-colonialism, sociology, history, science, technology, and media archaeology, from the perspective of moving images.

Vanishing Points was also an opportunity to involve artist Janis Rafa, whose video *Lacerate*, which Fondazione In Between Art Film commissioned and produced in 2020 for *Mascarilla 19 – Codes of Domestic Violence*, was presented by Cecilia Alemani in the group show *The Milk of Dreams* for the Biennale Arte 2022. Likewise, we extended the discussion on moving images to historical positions, with the involvement of the academics Lara Conte and Francesca Gallo, authors of the publication *Artiste italiane e immagini in movimento. Identità, sguardi, sperimentazioni* [Italian women artists and moving images. Identities, gazes, experiments] (2021), acknowledging the importance of the

KARIMAH ASHADU IN CONVERSATION WITH
OSEI BONSU

09.06.2022

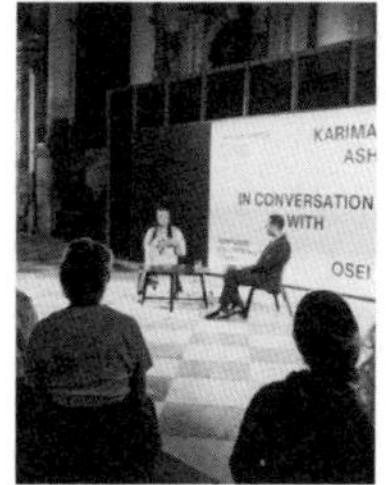

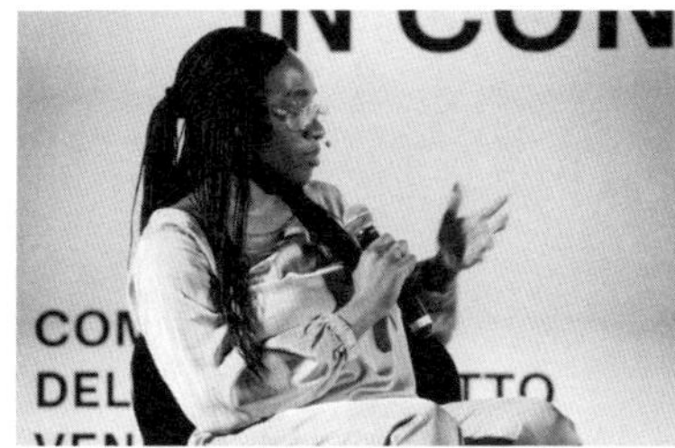

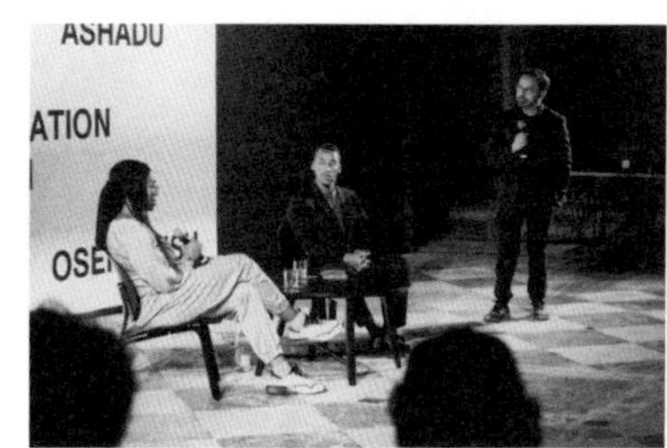

JONATHAS DE ANDRADE IN CONVERSATION WITH
JACOPO CRIVELLI VISCONTI

23.06.2022

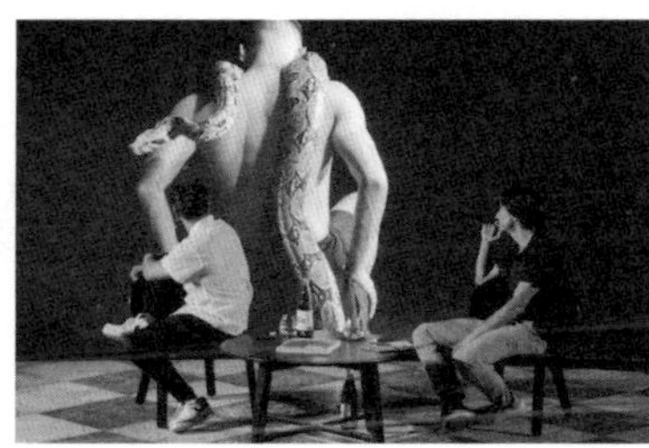

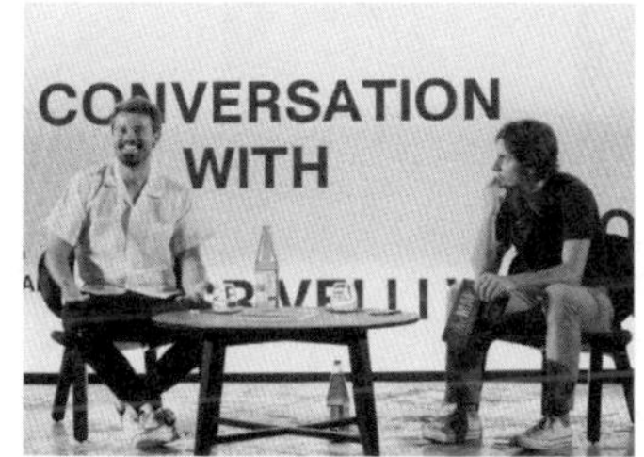

ANA VAZ IN CONVERSATION WITH
FILIPA RAMOS AND PATRICIA SARAGÜETA

02.07.2022

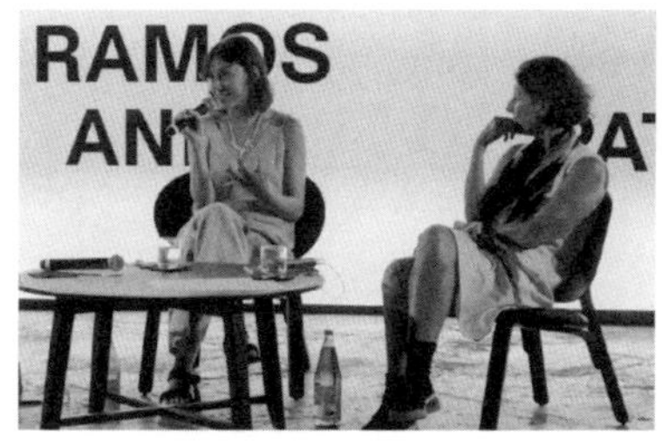

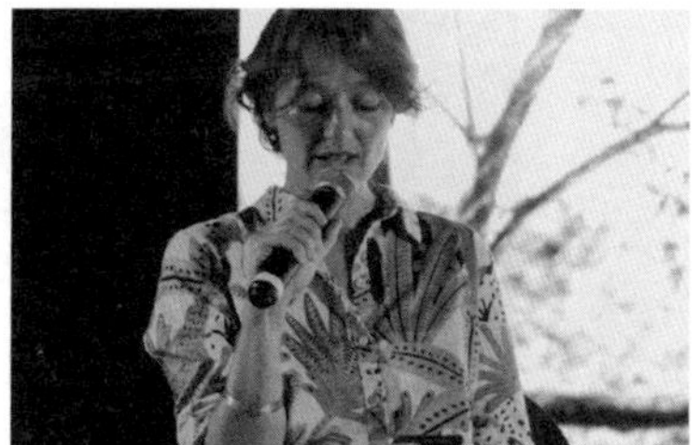

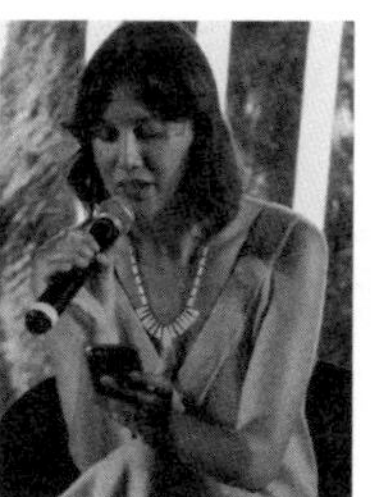

AZIZ HAZARA IN CONVERSATION WITH
NATASHA GINWALA AND SUSAN SCHUPPLI

22.09.2022

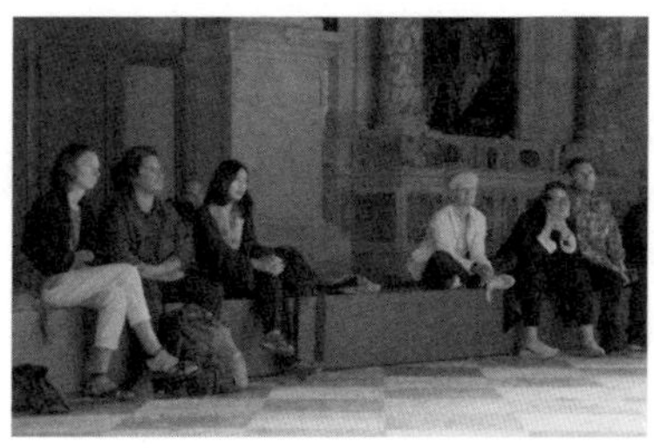

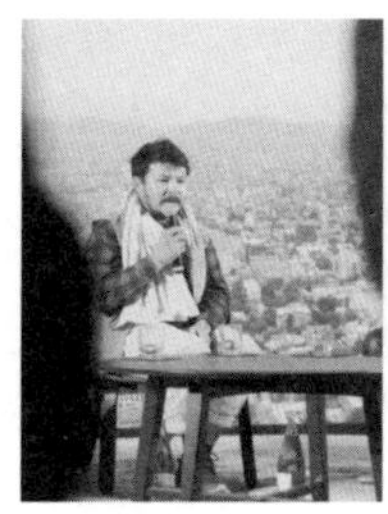

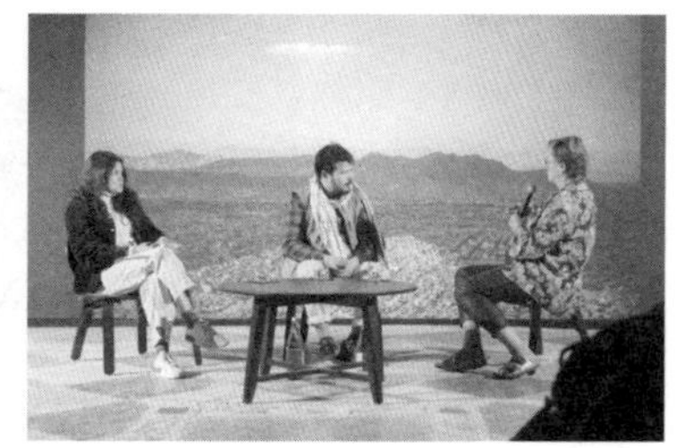

HE XIANGYU IN CONVERSATION WITH
HOU HANRU AND KATHRYN WEIR

23.09.2022

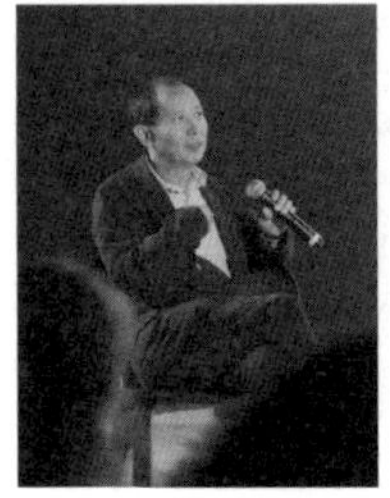
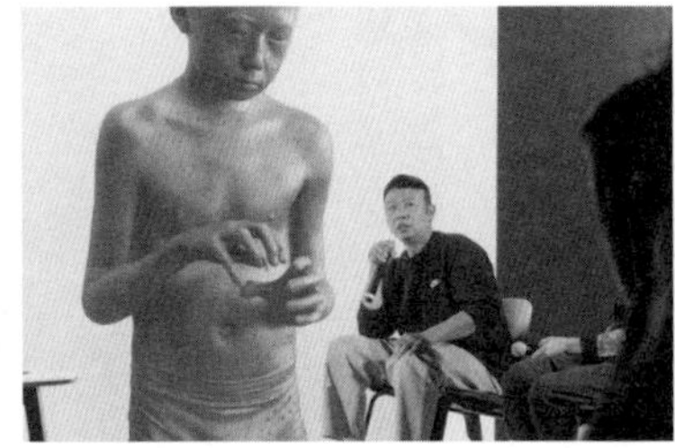
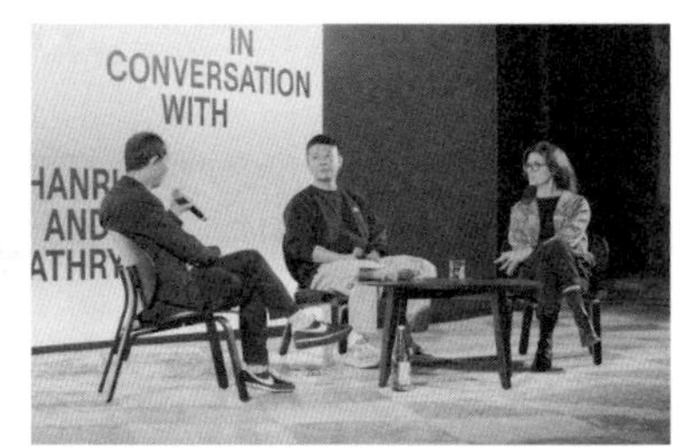

LARA CONTE AND FRANCESCA GALLO
IN CONVERSATION WITH MALVINA BORGHERINI

27.09.2022

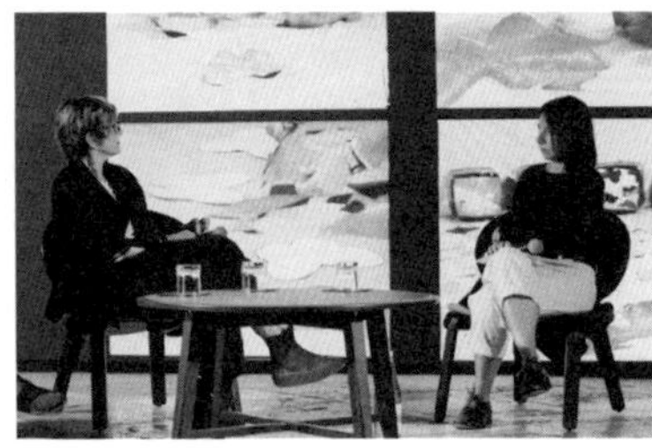
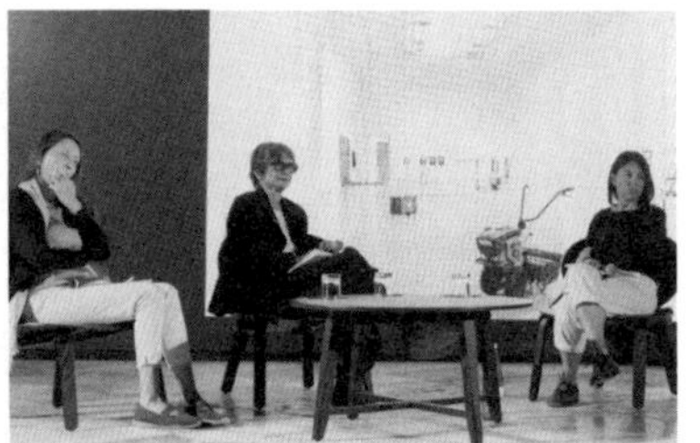

JAMES RICHARDS IN CONVERSATION WITH
EDWIN CARELS

28.09.2022

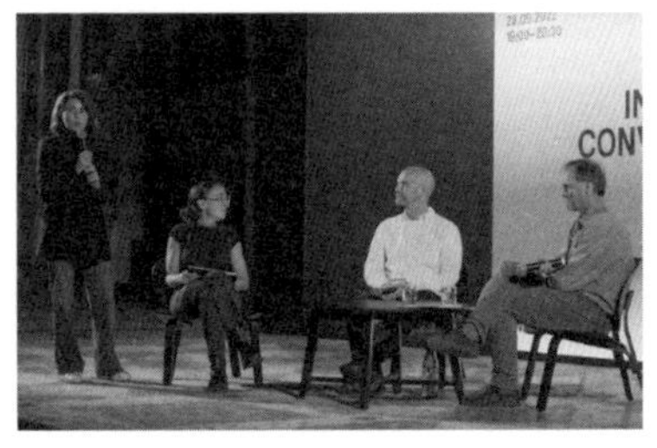
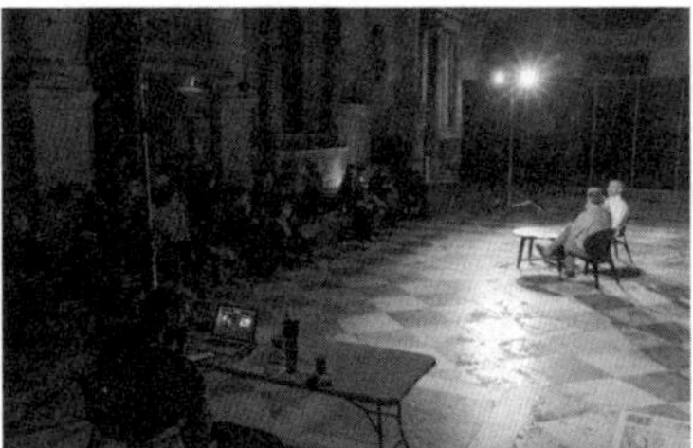
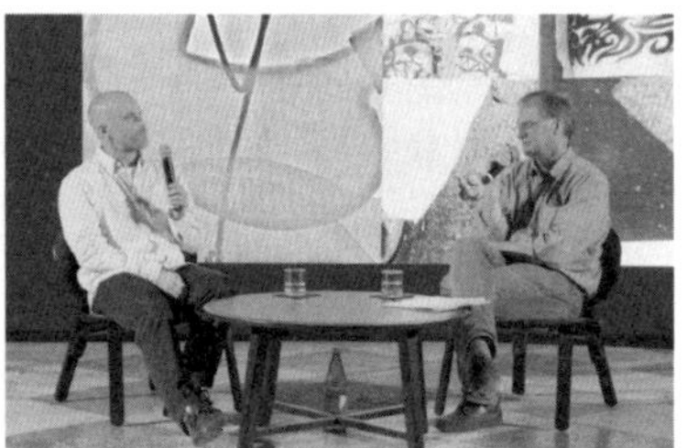

EMILIJA ŠKARNULYTĖ IN CONVERSATION WITH
MARINA OTERO VERZIER

06.10.2022

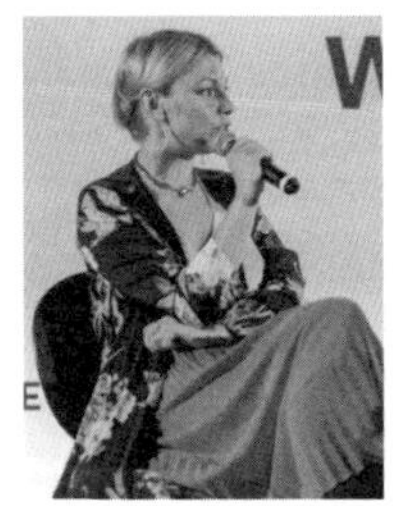
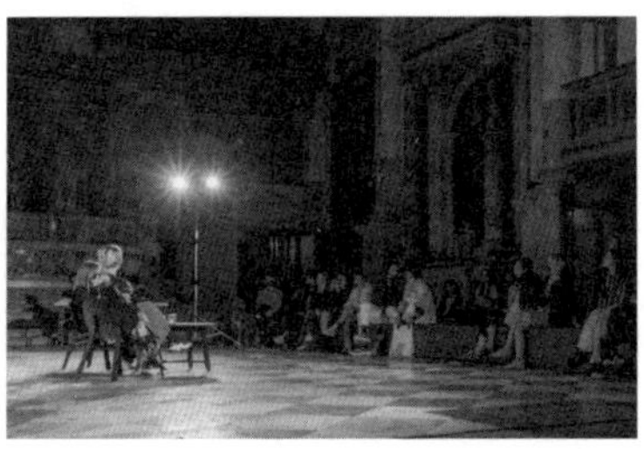
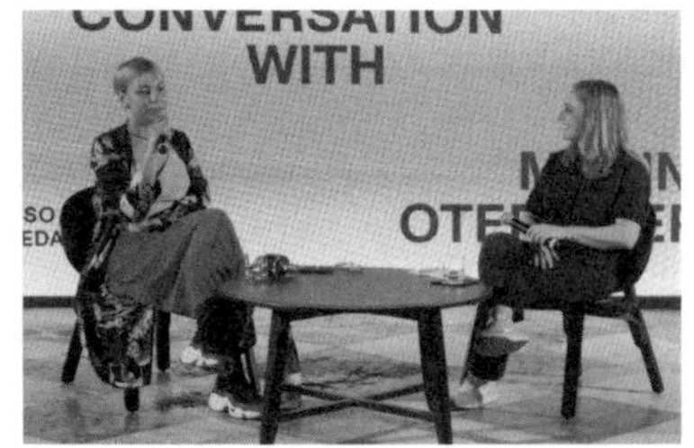

first experiments with video in Italy, a medium that in the 1960s and 1970s was mostly approached by women artists. Finally, we invited Pestellini Laparelli of 2050+ to share the reasoning behind the design of the scenography for *Penumbra*.

From June to October 2022, in the monumental spaces of the church of Santa Maria dei Derelitti, we called on curators, researchers, scientists, architects, designers, historians, and philosophers to take part in interdisciplinary conversations, with the aim of encouraging original strategies of interpretation in discursive fields that differ from those of the exhibition. The eleven gatherings examined the artists' methodology as well as focused on the themes around which their researches pivot, generating different readings of the works at the center of the discussion. *Vanishing Points* was a coring experiment through which to connect the surface of the moving images to their deeper meaning, and each session indeed raised questions and opened up unexpected scenarios.

The reflection upon various approaches to the conceptualization and formalization of moving images was discussed through a poetic examination of dominant and emerging points of observation, narratives and counter-narratives, homogeneous and heterogeneous epistemologies. Rafa spoke with Federica Timeto about image making at the time of the Anthropocene from a feminist and anti-speciesist viewpoint, asking if it is possible to establish a relationship with an other-than-self that encompasses difference and relies precisely on that diversity in the care devoted to sharing space and safeguarding the planet. Vaz, in the encounter with Filipa Ramos and Patricia Saragueta, shared her hypothesis on the use of the camera to interact with other lives, even if cinema is a language based on observation from a distance. Inside that paradox, it is possible to imagine forms of circularity between the one who looks and the one who is looked at, forms of visibility and invisibility, that go beyond the traditional idea of the camera as an objective, disembodied witness. The idea that the camera has an objective gaze was also challenged by Hazara during the conversation with Natasha Ginwala and Susan Schuppli, because images are often the result of the atmosphere of the moment, of the dominant way of seeing. Recognizing this, it becomes possible to recover the independence of the gaze, to produce counter-images and to resist, as in *Takbir* (2022), regimes of political and military visibility. Masbedo (the art duo composed of Nicolò Massazza and Iacopo Bedogni), with Cristina Baldacci and Andrea Pinotti, approached the complex relationship between image and document. When the image is asked to certify an event, the possibility opens up of producing the event to be certified, and thus to make reality depend on the image that represents it. Between these two conditions of documentation of reality and production of the plausible, there is a threshold on which *Pantelleria* (2022) is positioned.

The manipulation of images was the focus of the conversation between Richards and Edwin Carels, who talked about technology and its changes, and how they can reach the point of altering the way we see.

During the making of the works, the personal stories of the artists and of communities more or less close to them intertwined in the sharing of a moment of their life. This is particularly noteworthy if we consider that the current historical phase is marked by political and social fragmentation, digital hyper-connection and resulting physical distancing, which have produced polarized thinking and have challenged the cohesion of democracies. De Andrade told Jacopo Crivelli Visconti that to make *Olho da Rua* [Out Loud] (2022) he involved a group of people residing in his city who live in conditions of marginalization and poverty also due to the fascist politics of Jair Bolsonaro. Together they formed a temporary community, inventing ways to express their own identity, speaking their own language, and asserting their right to have political representation. In the conversation with Hou Hanru and Kathryn Weir, Xiangyu described the making of *House of Nations* (2021) in collaboration with its protagonist, starting with a shared feeling of hanging in the balance between cultures and languages, then leading to friendship and the sharing of spaces, seeking the gray areas of mutual non-verbal comprehension. Ashadu reflected with Osei Bonsu about the fact that in *Plateau* (2021) she has inserted language for the first time, specifically the voices of the community of miners, who are invisible to the eyes of formal economy. For her, this was a way to grant importance to the experience they permitted her to have, allowing her to enter a world that would otherwise be difficult to access.

There was also a discussion on the failures of a certain idea of science that searches for universal knowledge and has a teleological faith in progress. Škarnulytė and Marina Otero Verzier, in an intense conversation, explored the possibilities of knowing what surrounds us in a different way, like immersing ourselves in the ocean to understand what is not immediately comprehensible on the surface, from the depth of history to the passing of time. Pestellini Laparelli of 2050+, with Formafantasma (Andrea Trimarchi and Simone Farresin) and Beatrice Leanza, spoke not only about making exhibitions as an experience of mediation from which to understand the transformations of the public and society, but also about urgent issues of climate and contemporary policies, which were also addressed in many of the works of the artists in the show.

The video experiments of Giosetta Fioroni, Ida Gerosa, Maud Ceriotti Giaccari, Laura Grisi, Federica Marangoni, and Marisa Merz were at the center of the conversation between Lara Conte, Francesca Gallo and Malvina Borgherini, to fill a gap that still exists in traditional art history, which is prevalently androcentric and thus incomplete.

Vanishing Points brought together a series of sensibilities that speak to us of our time, in our limited part of the world, such as the need to support an interdisciplinary, interspecies future, within the healing and transformation of the present. It is our hope that this albeit partial overview can be useful to suggest further connections and leaps of the imagination.

2050+ IN CONVERSATION WITH
FORMAFANTASMA AND BEATRICE LEANZA

07.10.2022

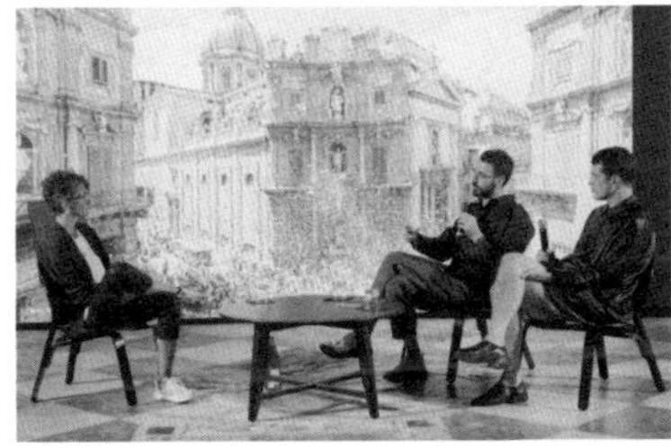

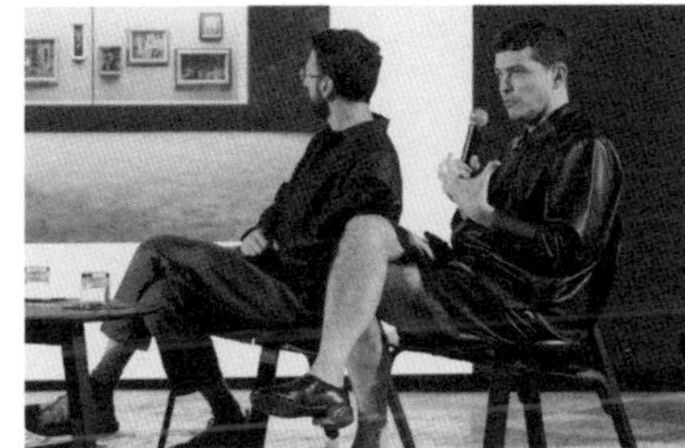

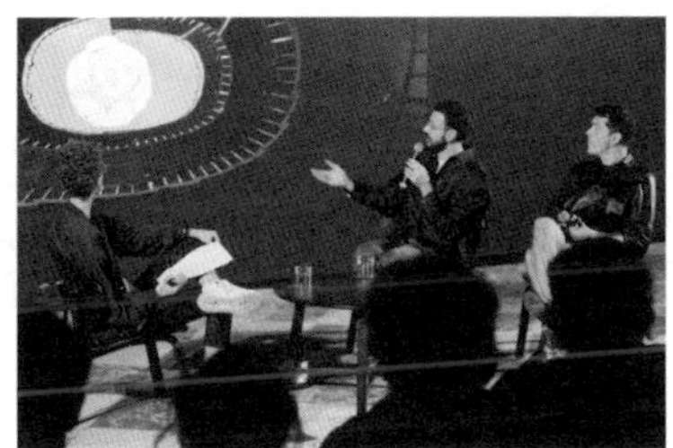

JANIS RAFA IN CONVERSATION WITH
FEDERICA TIMETO

13.10.2022

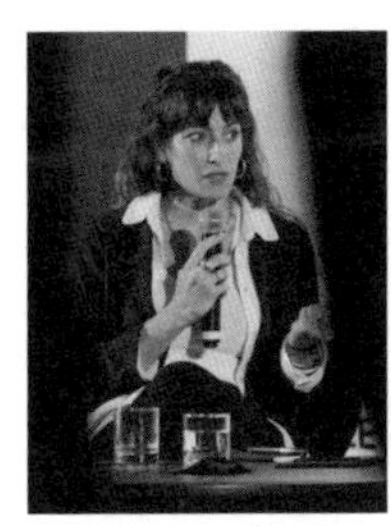

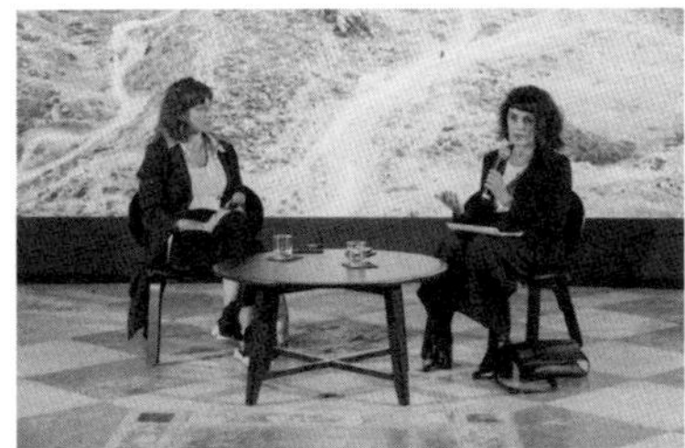

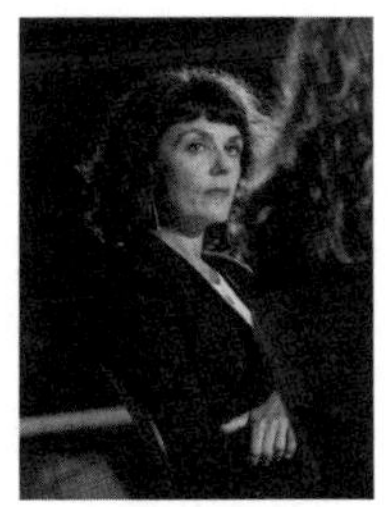

MASBEDO IN CONVERSATION WITH
CRISTINA BALDACCI AND ANDREA PINOTTI

20.10.2022

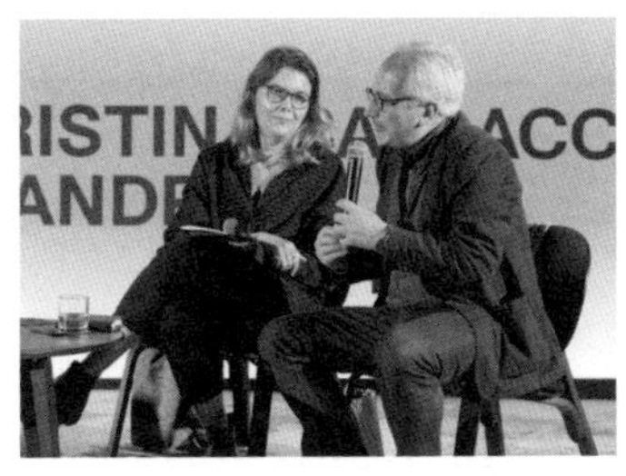

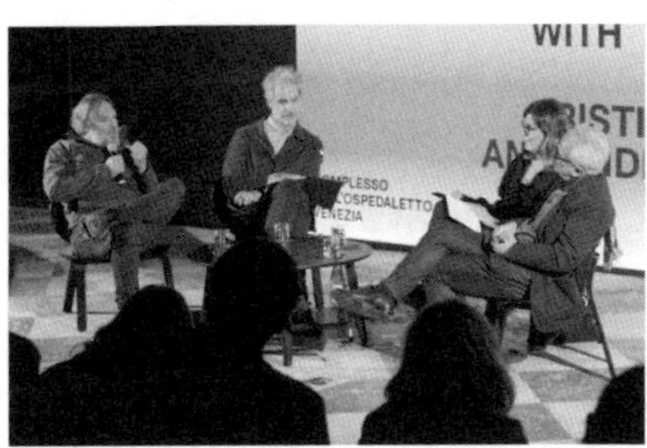

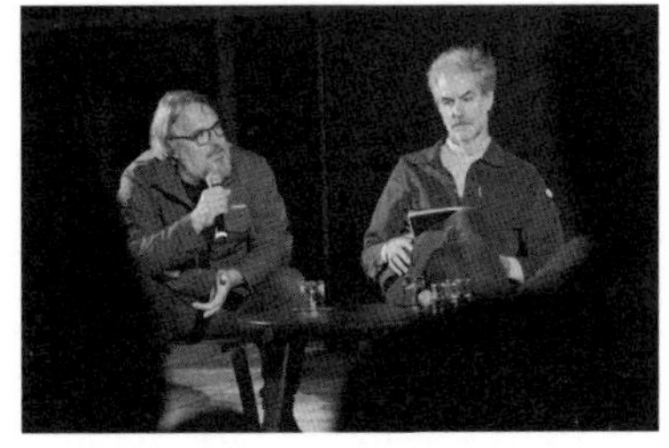

BIOGRAPHIES

TAYLOR RENEE ALDRIDGE

is a writer and curator based in Los Angeles. Currently she is the Visual Arts Curator and Program Manager at the California African American Museum (CAAM), Los Angeles. In 2015, she co-founded the online journal, *ARTS.BLACK*, with critic Jessica Lynne. Aldridge is from Detroit, Michigan.

KARIMAH ASHADU

is a British-Nigerian artist who lives and works between Hamburg and Lagos. Her work has been exhibited and screened in institutions such as Schirn Kunsthalle, Frankfurt; South London Gallery; Tate, London; Secession, Vienna; Kunstverein, Hamburg; Galerie für Zeitgenössische Kunst, Leipzig; MoMA, New York; and Centre d'Art Contemporain Geneva. Her work is part of the public collections of MoMA, New York; and FMAC – Fonds d'art contemporain, Ville de Genève. In 2020, Ashadu founded her film production company Golddust by Ashadu, which specializes in artists' films on black culture and African discourses. She was named Abigail R. Cohen Fellow 2021 at the Columbia Institute for Ideas and Imagination, Paris. Ashadu received the 2020 ars viva prize, and the 2022 Kunstpreis der Böttcherstraße, Bremen, 2022.

GIACOMO BIANCO

is a photographer who lives between Venice and Berlin. After receiving his BA in Industrial and Multimedia Design from IUAV in Venice, he graduated from ISIA U in Urbino with a MA in Photography. His works have been shown at institutions such as Triennale di Milano; Istituzione Fondazione Bevilacqua La Masa, Venice; Kommunale Galerie Berlin; Paratissima, Turin; Rotterdam Photobook Market; Focus. Artphilen gallery, Centrale festival; among others, and in several magazines such as *GUP Magazine*, *L'Essenziale Studio Journal*, *Discarded Magazine*, *C41*, and *Arts Life*. He was included in the Fresh Eyes Talents 2021 by *GUP Magazine*, and the NEW TALENTS 2021 by PEP Photography. He participated in residency programs at Lunigiana Land Art (2022), and Bevilacqua La Masa, Venice (2021–22). Currently, he works as an assistant photographer to Giovanna Silva, with whom he teaches at ISIA U, Urbino. Previously, he worked as an assistant photographer to Matteo De Mayda.

LEONARDO BIGAZZI

is a curator and artist's film producer based in Florence. At Fondazione In Between Art Film, he is Curator and part of the editorial team of STILL – Studies on moving images. He is also the Curator of Lo schermo dell'arte – Contemporary Art and Cinema Festival since 2008, Founder and Curator of VISIO – European Programme on Artists' Moving Images since 2012, and was Founder and Co-director of Feature Expanded (2015–18). For the Festival he was also responsible for projects with artists Hito Steyerl, Rosa Barba, Hassan Khan, Omer Fast, Hiroshi Sugimoto, and Melik Ohanian. He curated exhibitions and film programs at Fondazione Merz, Turin; Paul Klee Zentrum, Bern; Fundació Antoni Tàpies, Barcelona; CAC-Passerelle, Brest; Palazzo Grassi-Pinault Collection, Venice; MAXXI Museum, Rome; Palazzo Strozzi, Florence; and Marino Marini Museum, Florence. He commissioned and/or produced over twenty artist's films which were presented at Tate, London; MoMA, New York; Centre Pompidou, Paris; Biennale Arte, Venice; Manifesta 14, among others.

BEATRICE BULGARI

lives and works between Rome and New York. She is Founder and President of Fondazione In Between Art Film, which aims to support artists, institutions, and researchers that work with moving images. From 2012–19, she founded and directed the film production company In Between Art Film, dedicated to providing artists and directors with the opportunity to freely explore an interdisciplinary creative approach between the language of cinema and contemporary art. In 2007, she created CortoArteCircuito, a multifaceted platform that produced documentaries by international directors on the work of contemporary artists. Beatrice Bulgari also collaborated as a set and costume designer in many films, including Giuseppe Tornatore's *Nuovo Cinema Paradiso*.

BRUNO CARVALHO

works on cities as lived and imagined spaces. Often, he investigates how socio-cultural processes of the past converge in and with the present. Carvalho is writing *The Invention of the Future: A Transatlantic History of Urbanization*. He is the author of the award-winning *Porous City: A Cultural History of Rio de Janeiro* (2013). He has published numerous articles and essays. His interdisciplinary approaches tend to focus on relationships between cities and culture, bridging history, politics, literary analysis, visual media, and urban studies. He co-edited books like *Occupy All Streets: Olympic Urbanism and Contested Futures in Rio de Janeiro* (2016), and the book series "Lateral Exchanges" devoted to historical and contemporary issues in design and the built environment. At Harvard University, he is Professor of Romance Languages and Literatures; Affiliated Professor in Urban Planning and Design, Harvard Graduate School of Design; and Co-Director, Harvard Mellon Urban Initiative.

BARBARA CASAVECCHIA

is a writer, independent curator, and educator based in Venice and Milan, where she teaches in the Department of Visual Cultures and Curatorial Practices of the Brera Academy. She is Contributing editor of *frieze*, and her articles and essays have been published in magazines such as *art-agenda*, *ArtReview*, *D/La Repubblica*, *Flash Art*, *Mousse*, *Nero*, *South*, and *Spike*, among others, as well as in artist books and catalogues. In 2021–23, she leads the cycle "The Current III" promoted by TBA21–Academy at Ocean Space, Venice. With the title "Mediterraneans: 'Thus waves come in pairs' (after Etel Adnan)," it acts as a transdisciplinary and transregional exercise in sensing and learning with, by supporting situated projects, collective pedagogies, and voices along the Mediterranean shores across art, culture, science, conservation, and activism. In 2018, she curated the solo exhibition *Susan Hiller, Social Facts* at OGR, Turin.

JONATHAS DE ANDRADE

is an artist who lives and works in Recife. His works have been shown in solo exhibitions at the MAAT—Museum of Art, Architecture and Technology, Lisbon; Estação Pinacoteca, São Paulo; CRAC Alsace, Altkirch; Kunsthal ExtraCity, Antwerp; FOAM, Amdsterdam; MCA, Chicago; New Museum, New York; The Power Plant, Toronto; MASP – Museu de Arte de São Paulo; MAR – Museu de Arte do Rio; MAC – Musée d'art contemporain de Montréal; Kunsthalle Lissabon; Centro Cultural São Paulo; among others. De Andrade's works were also presented at the Bienal de Arte Contemporanea Sesc. Videobrasil (2020), MOMENTA Biennale de l'image, Montreal (2019); Istanbul Biennial (2019); SITE Santa Fe (2016); Bienal de São Paulo (2016); Performa, New York (2015); La Biennial de Lyon (2013); New Museum Triennial, New York (2011); and Mercosul Biennial (2009); among others. De Andrade represented Brazil at the Biennale Arte 2022.

AZIZ HAZARA

is an artist who lives and works between Berlin and Kabul. He has shown his works at institutions such as Smack Mellon, Brooklyn; Wanås Konst, Knislinge; PinchukArtCentre, Kyiv; Hessel Museum of Art, CCS Bard College, New York; Netwerk Aalst; Busan Biennale (2020); Biennale of Sydney (2020); and IKOB, Eupen; among others. He has also participated in residential programs at Colomboscope, Colombo; Embassy of Foreign Artists (EoFA), Geneva; Camargo Foundation, Cassis; and KHOJ – International Artists' Association, New Delhi. He is currently artist-in-residence at Künstlerhaus Bethanien, and a grantee of Kf W Stiftung. In 2021, Hazara was awarded with the Future Generation Art Prize.

HE XIANGYU

is an artist and film director who lives and works in Berlin. His works have been shown at institutions such as CCA, Berlin; UCCA Center for Contemporary Art, Beijing; OCAT Institute, Shanghai; Para Site, Hong Kong; The Drawing Center, New York; Solomon R. Guggenheim Museum, New York; Smart Museum of Art, Chicago; Kadist Foundation, San Francisco; LACMA, Los Angeles; KW Institute for Contemporary Art, Berlin; Centre Pompidou, Paris; and Castello di

Rivoli, Turin, among others. His works have also been presented at the Biennale Arte 2019 – China Pavilion, La Biennale de Lyon (2016), Shanghai Biennale and Yokohama Triennale (both 2014), and Busan Biennale (2013). Xiangyu was shortlisted for the Mario Merz Prize (2021) and the Future Generation Art Prize (2014).

MARTIN HERBERT

is a writer based in Berlin. He is Associate Editor of *ArtReview*, a frequent contributor to international art journals, and the author of books including *Unfold This Moment* (2019), *Tell Them I Said No* (2016), and *The Uncertainty Principle* (2014).

MATT KEEGAN

is an interdisciplinary artist based in New York. His work has been widely exhibited at institutions such as SculptureCenter, New York; the Carpenter Center for the Visual Arts, Cambridge, MA; CAMH – Contemporary Arts Museum Houston; Grazer Kunstverein, Graz; The Art Institute of Chicago, and the New Museum, New York. Keegan's work is represented in public collections, including MoMA, Solomon R. Guggenheim Museum, and The Metropolitan Museum of Art, all in New York, among others. His book *1996* was published in 2020 by New York Consolidated. Keegan is a Senior Critic in the Painting and Printmaking Department at Yale University, New Haven.

ANA LAURA MALMACEDA

is a writer and filmmaker. A PhD. candidate in Romance Languages and Literatures at Harvard University, she is interested in ecological thinking, postcolonial thought, and practices of regeneration in the Anthropocene through the perspectives of Indigenous and Afro-Brazilian epistemologies. Her research currently focuses on the Thayer Expedition (1865–66) and its repercussions in Brazil. She holds a Master's degree in Brazilian Studies from the University of Lisbon (2017) with a passage at Paris 3 – Sorbonne Nouvelle. As a filmmaker, she is working on a project about Ver-o-Peso, Latin America's biggest market hall.

MASBEDO

is an artist duo composed of Nicolò Massazza and Iacopo Bedogni. They live in Milan and have been working together since 1999. Their works have been exhibited in museums, biennials, and institutions including ICA, Milan; MAMM – Multimedia Art Museum, Moscow; Manifesta 12, Palermo; Centre Pompidou / Forum des Images, Paris; Haus der Kulturen der Welt, Berlin; Museum of Contemporary Art, Zagreb; MART, Rovereto; Fondazione Merz, Turin; Leopold Museum, Vienna; MAMBA – Museum of Modern Art of Buenos Aires; Castello di Rivoli, Turin; MAXXI, Rome; Museo Nacional Centro de Arte Reina Sofía, Madrid; and Biennale Arte 2009, among others.

IPPOLITO PESTELLINI LAPARELLI

is an architect and curator whose work encompasses technology, politics, design, and environmental practices. Formerly a partner at OMA, he founded the interdisciplinary agency 2050+ in Milan to deploy space as a medium rather than a goal. Ippolito teaches Data Matter, a research and design studio exploring the entangled relationship between data and the material world, at the Royal College of Arts, London. His work has been shown internationally in various institutions, festivals, and exhibitions.

ALESSANDRO RABOTTINI

is an art critic and curator who lives in London. He is Artistic Director of Fondazione In Between Art Film and initiator of STILL – Studies on moving images, a research platform promoted by the Fondazione to support theoretical studies on time-based media practices. Rabottini has curated exhibitions in museums and institutions including MAXXI L'Aquila; Center d'Art Contemporain, Geneva; GAMeC, Bergamo; Bergen Kunsthall; Le Consortium, Dijon; Triennale di Milano; PAC, Milan; Villa Medici, Rome; MADRE Museum, Naples, and GAM, Torino. Rabottini contributed to museum catalogues on the practices of artists such as Uri Aran, Cecily Brown, Victor Man, Dana Schutz, Piotr Uklański, and Paloma Varga Weisz. He edited books and catalogues upon the work of Giovanni Kronenberg, Michael Anastassiades, Gianfranco Baruchello, Robert Overby, Ettore Spalletti, David Maljkovic, Adrian Paci, Giuseppe Gabellone, Andrea Branzi, Elad Lassry, Massimo Grimaldi, Tim Rollins and K.O.S., Latifa Echakhch, Tris Vonna-Michell, Sterling Ruby, and Victor Man, among others.

FILIPA RAMOS

is a writer and curator based in Basel. She is Director of the Master in Fine Arts of the Institut Art, Gender Nature of the Academy of Art and Design (HGK) at the University of Applied Sciences and Arts Northwestern Switzerland (FHNW).

FRANCESCA RECCHIA

is an independent researcher and writer. She is Founding Member and Creative Director of The Polis Project, Inc. She is interested in the geopolitical dimension of cultural processes and in recent years has focused her research on the spatial relation between (tangible and intangible) heritage, politics and creative practices in countries in conflict. Her practice-based work is grounded on an interdisciplinary approach that combines heritage, design, visual and cultural studies. She is the author of *The Little Book of Kabul* (2014, with Lorenzo Tugnoli), and *Picnic in a Minefield and Devices for Political Action* (2014, with a photo-essay by Leo Novel).

JAMES RICHARDS

is an artist who lives and works between Berlin and London. His works have been presented in personal exhibitions at Castello di Rivoli, Turin; Malmö Konsthall; Künstlerhaus Stuttgart; Chapter Arts Center, Cardiff; ICA, London; Bergen Kunsthall; Kunstverein München; Chisenhale Gallery, London, among others. Richards' works have also been featured in group shows at the Camden Art Centre, London; Whitney Museum of American Art, New York; Walker Arts Center, Minneapolis; MoMA, New York; Artists Space, New York; and the Biennale Arte 2013. Richards represented Wales at the Biennale Arte 2017, and was shortlisted for the Turner Prize 2014.

EMILIJA ŠKARNULYTĖ

is an artist and film director. Škarnulytė won the Future Generation Art Prize 2019, represented Lithuania at the XXII Triennale di Milano, and was included in the Baltic Pavilion at the Biennale Architettura 2018. Her work has been featured in solo exhibitions at Tate, London; Kunsthaus Pasquart, Biel; Den Frie, Copenhagen; National Gallery of Art, Vilnius; CAC, Vilnius; Kunstlerhaus Bethanien, Berlin; as well as in group exhibitions at Ballroom Marfa, SeMA – Seoul Museum of Art, Kadist Foundation, and Riga Biennial. Her films are included in the collections of IFA, Kadist Foundation, and Centre Pompidou, and have been screened at Serpentine Galleries, London; Centre Pompidou, Paris; as well as at film festivals in Rotterdam, Busan, and Oberhausen. Škarnulytė is Founder and Co-director of Polar Film Lab; and a member of the artistic duo New Mineral Collective.

BIANCA STOPPANI

is a researcher who lives between London and Turin. At Fondazione In Between Art Film, they are Editor of the research and publishing initiatives, including STILL – Studies on moving images. Previously, they were part of the curatorial team of Almanac Projects, London/Turin (2020–22). They have curated exhibitions, edited publications, organized reading groups, participated in talks and seminars, and co-founded the artist-run space Armada, Milan. They have written for catalogs and magazines such as *Flash Art*, *Il Foglio*, *Kaleidoscope*, and *Mousse*, among others.

PAOLA UGOLINI

is an art critic and independent curator who lives in Rome. At Fondazione In Between Art Film, she is Curator and part of the editorial staff of STILL – Studies on moving images. Since 2015, she has been Guest Curator at Richard Saltoun Gallery, London, where she curated group exhibitions with Greta Shödl, Tomaso Binga, Silvia Giambrone, and Marinella Senatore. Recently, she co-curated the group exhibitions *Io dico Io / I say I* (2021), *Corpo a Corpo* (2017) at Galleria Nazionale di Arte Moderna di Roma, and *Oltre limiti e confini* at MAXXI Museum, Rome (2014).

Since the end of 1980s, she has curated exhibitions focusing on the work of female artists, video-art, body art, performance art, and on the relationship between art and feminism. She worked as Assistant Curator for the group exhibitions *Machine for Peace* for the former Yugoslav Pavilion at the Biennale Arte 1993, and *Ubi Motus Ubi Fluxus* at the Biennale Arte 1990.

GIORGIO VASTA

is a writer who published *Tre orfani* (Casagrande, 2021), *Presente* (Einaudi, 2012, with Andrea Bajani, Michela Murgia, and Paolo Nori), *Spaesamento* (Laterza, 2010), and *Il tempo materiale* (minimum fax, 2008). With Emma Dante and Elena Stancanelli, he co-authored the scripts for *Misericordia* (forthcoming in 2023) and *Le sorelle Macaluso* (2020), and with Dante the script for *Via Castellana Bandiera* (2013). With photographer Ramak Fazel, he co-authored *Palermo. Un'autobiografia nella luce* (Humboldt Books, 2022) and *Absolutely Nothing. Storie e sparizioni nei deserti americani* (Humboldt Books with Quodlibet, 2016).

ANA VAZ

is an artist and film director. Her works have been presented, screened, and discussed at film festivals, seminars, and institutions such as Tate, London; Palais de Tokyo, Paris; Jeu de Paume, Paris; LUX Moving Images, London; New York Film Festival – Projections; TIFF Wavelengths, Toronto; BFI, London; Cinéma du Réel, Paris; TABAKALERA, San Sebastián; Whitechapel Gallery, London; MAM – Museu de Arte Moderna de São Paulo; Sesc-Belenzinho, São Paulo; Matadero, Madrid; Jameel Arts Center, Dubai; Confort Moderne, Poitiers; Savvy Contemporary, Berlin; Sonic Acts, Amsterdam; among others. Her film *É Noite na América* [It Is Night in America] (2022) was awarded by Entrevues Belfort IFF; FIDOCS – Festival Internacional de Documentales de Santiago; Festival dei Popoli, Florence; and Locarno Film Festival. Vaz is also a founding member of the COYOTE collective along with Tristan Bera, Nuno da Luz, Elida Hoëg, and Clémence Seurat, an interdisciplinary group working between ecology and political science through conceptual and experimental formats.

This book is published on the occasion of *Penumbra*, an exhibition conceived, commissioned, and produced by Fondazione In Between Art Film

with
Karimah Ashadu
Jonathas de Andrade
Aziz Hazara
He Xiangyu
Masbedo
James Richards
Emilija Škarnulytė
Ana Vaz

EXHIBITION

Penumbra
20.04 – 27.11.2022
Complesso dell'Ospedaletto, Venice

Curators
Alessandro Rabottini, Leonardo Bigazzi

Project Manager
Alessia Carlino

Research
Bianca Stoppani

Set Design
2050+ – Guglielmo Campeggi, Francesca Lantieri, Ippolito Pestellini Laparelli, Massimo Tenan

Exhibition Set-up
Altofragile – Sara Bernasconi, Lapo Gavioli, Giulia Mainetti, Francesco Rovaldi

Design
Lorenzo Mason Studio – Lorenzo Mason, Dafne Pagura, Simone Spinazzè

Technology
Giochi di Luce

Display
Definizioni

Lighting
Riato

Graphic Lab
Colorzenith, Graphic Report

Organizational Office
Venews C563 Arts – Massimo Bran, Paola Marchetti
Ospedaletto Con/temporaneo – Mariachiara Marzari
Fondazione In Between Art Film – Simona Iandoli, Chiara Nicolini

Legal Advisor
Chiomenti Studio Legale – Giovanni Cristofaro, Angela Saltarelli

Fiscal Advisor
Benigni&K

Institutional relationships with Soprintenedenza and Comune di Venezia
Oblò Architetti – Piero Vespignani

Location Advisor
Pia Capelli

Press relations and Communications
Lara Facco P&C – Lara Facco, Claudia Santrolli
Sam Talbot – Matthew Brown, Jennifer Kibazo, Sam Talbot

Visual Story-telling
Giacomo Bianco

Gallery Invigilators
Davide Borrella, Giulia Gasparini, Marica Petkovic, Mohammed Salhi, Michela Seren, Sepideh Yeganehdoost

Thanks to
Gianmatteo Caputo
Delegato Patriarcale Beni Culturali Ecclesiastici per il Patriarcato di Venezia
I.P.A.V. (ex I.R.E.)
Luigi Polesel, Presidente; Agata Brusegan
Fondazione Venezia Servizi alla Persona
Claudio Beltrame, Presidente Laura De Rossi, Laura Marcomin, Edoardo Rizzi, Elisa Torri

Further thanks to
Beatrice Galluzzo, Paola Mirashi, David J Sheldon, Camilla Toschi

PUBLIC PROGRAM

Penumbra was accompanied by the public program *Vanishing Points*

Curators
Bianca Stoppani, Paola Ugolini

Coordination
Giovanni Paolin with Emma Terlizzese

Audio-Visual Service
Giulio Polloniato

Documentation
Nicolò Rampazzo

09.06.2022

Karimah Ashadu, artist
with Osei Bonsu, Curator of International Art at Tate Modern, London

23.06.2022

Jonathas de Andrade, artist
with Jacopo Crivelli Visconti, freelance art critic and curator, São Paulo

02.07.2022

Ana Vaz, artist
with Filipa Ramos, writer and curator, Basel
and Patricia Saragüeta, IBYME-CONICET Researcher and Professor at the Department of Physiology, Molecular and Cellular Biology, School of Exact and Natural Sciences, University of Buenos Aires

22.09.2022

Aziz Hazara, artist
with Natasha Ginwala, Associate Curator at Large at Gropius Bau, Berlin, and Artistic Director at Colomboscope, Colombo
and Susan Schuppli, Reader and Director at Centre for Research Architecture, Goldsmiths, University of London

23.09.2022

He Xiangyu, artist
with Hou Hanru, Artistic Director at MAXXI, Rome
and Kathryn Weir, Artistic Director at Madre, Naples

27.09.2022

Lara Conte, Associate Professor, Università degli Studi Roma Tre
and Francesca Gallo, Associate Professor, and Chair of the Graduate Program in Art History, Sapienza University of Rome
with Maria Malvina Borgherini, Associate Professor at IUAV, University of Venice, and Scientific Head of MeLa Media Lab

28.09.2022

James Richards, artist
with Edwin Carels, curator, film programmer, and Teacher at KASK & Conservatorium, Ghent

06.10.2022

Emilija Škarnulytė, artist
with Marina Otero Verzier, Head of MA Social Design, Design Academy Eindhoven

07.10.2022

2050+, interdisciplinary agency, Milan
with Formafantasma, design studio, Milan/Rotterdam
and Beatrice Leanza, Director at mudac, Lausanne

13.10.2022

Janis Rafa, artist
with Federica Timeto, Associate Professor at Ca' Foscari University, Venice

20.10.2022

Masbedo, artists
with Cristina Baldacci, Associate Professor at Ca' Foscari University, Venice
and Andrea Pinotti, Full Professor at University of Milan

PUBLICATION

Editors
Alessandro Rabottini and Leonardo Bigazzi with Bianca Stoppani

Texts
2050+ / Ippolito Pestellini Laparelli, Taylor Renee Aldridge, Leonardo Bigazzi, Beatrice Bulgari, Bruno Carvalho and Ana Laura Malmaceda, Barbara Casavecchia, Martin Herbert, Matt Keegan, Alessandro Rabottini, Filipa Ramos, Francesca Recchia, Bianca Stoppani and Paola Ugolini, Giorgio Vasta

Synopses
Bianca Stoppani except the synopsis for *É Noite na América* by Ana Vaz

Design
Lorenzo Mason Studio
Lorenzo Mason, Simone Spinazzè

Visual essay
Giacomo Bianco (pp. 1–16)

Installation views
Andrea Rossetti (pp. 113–191), Anna Lott Donadel (pp. 148, 150, 154, 157)

Project Manager
Alessia Carlino

Copy-editing and proofreading
Rachel Walther, Agnese Cantelmi

Translations
Sarah Elizabeth Cree for the text by Leonardo Bigazzi
Stephen Piccolo for the texts by Alessandro Rabottini, Giorgio Vasta, Bianca Stoppani and Paola Ugolini

Published and distributed by
Mousse Publishing
Contrappunto s.r.l.
via Pier Candido Decembrio 28
20137, Milan–Italy

Available through

Mousse Publishing, Milan
moussemagazine.it

DAP | Distributed Art Publishers, New York
artbook.com

Les presses du réel, Dijon
lespressesdureel.com

Ideabooks, Amsterdam
Ideabooks.nl

Antenne Books, London
antennebooks.com

First edition
2023

Printed in Italy by
Grafiche Veneziane, Venice

ISBN
978-88-6749-574-0

€ 35 / $ 40

© 2022 Fondazione In Between Art Film, Mousse Publishing, the artists, the authors of the texts

All rights reserved. No part of this publication may be reproduced in any form or by any electronic means without prior written permission from the copyright holders.

The publisher would like to thank all those who have kindly given their permission for the reproduction of material for this book. Every effort has been made to obtain permission to reproduce the images and texts in this catalogue. However, as is standard editorial policy, the publisher is at the disposal of copyright holders and undertakes to correct any omissions or errors in future editions.

FONDAZIONE
IN BETWEEN ART FILM

President
Beatrice Bulgari

Artistic Director
Alessandro Rabottini

Curators
Leonardo Bigazzi, Paola Ugolini

Project Manager
Alessia Carlino

Editor
Bianca Stoppani

Administrative Office
Simona Iandoli

Archive
Chiara Nicolini